MILTON AND THE ENGLISH REVOLUTION

Also by Christopher Hill

MILTON

and the

ENGLISH REVOLUTION

by Christopher Hill

THE VIKING PRESS   New York

Copyright © Christopher Hill, 1977

Published in 1978 by The Viking Press
625 Madison Avenue, New York, N. Y. 10022

LIBRARY OF CONGRESS CATALOGING IN PUBLICATION DATA
Hill, John Edward Christopher, 1912–
  Milton and the English Revolution.
  Bibliography: p.
  Includes index.
  1. Milton, John, 1608–1674—Political and social views.
2. Milton, John, 1608–1674—Religion and ethics.
I. Title
PR3592.P64H5   821'.4   77-21548
ISBN 0-670-47612-9

Printed in the United States of America

Set in Monotype Garamond

This book is dedicated in gratitude to the memory of

DON M. WOLFE,

who devoted a lifetime to the study of Milton, but never forgot Richard Overton and Gerrard Winstanley.

Contents

Part VI—THE GREAT POEMS

Part VII—TOWARDS A CONCLUSION

Preface

In this book I have modernized seventeenth-century spelling and punctuation, and have used the new style in dating. I have quoted Milton's prose writings mostly from the Yale edition of his *Complete Prose Works*. Since Volumes VII and VIII are not yet to hand, I have cited items in these volumes from the Columbia edition. I was, however, able to see Professor Woolrych's Introduction to Vol. VII. In order to help readers to identify any work cited, I have listed Milton's major writings on pp. xvii–xviii, with the volume number and pages which each pamphlet occupies in the edition which I have used. Latin works are listed separately, so that readers can ascertain when they are reading a translation rather than Milton's own words. I have had to mention many of Milton's contemporaries in my text: some of these are briefly described in the Index.

In writing this book I have incurred many debts. The first is to my parents, who brought me up to revere Milton, for reasons which I would not now altogether share. Mrs. Isabel Rivers, Professor Michael Fixler, Thomas Hodgkin and Edward Thompson helped me to clarify my ideas at an early stage. Peter Clark, Andrew Foster, Margot Heinemann, Leo Miller, Professor K. W. Stavely and Mr. P. A. Trout all very kindly allowed me to read unpublished work. Professors John Carey and Christopher Ricks, Margot Heinemann and Dr. Brian Manning all read the lengthy typescript, and laboured enormously to help me to say what I meant: so did Mrs. Elizabeth Renwick. I am also grateful for various kindnesses to Dr. David Aers, Ms. Barbara Breasted, Professors N. T. Burns, Harriett Hawkins, Stella Revard, Alice-Lyle Scoufos, Mrs. Elisabeth Sifton, Mr. Keith Thomas, Ms. Jill Tweedie, Dr. Nicholas Tyacke, and to the many groups with whom I had the pleasure of discussing Milton. The dedication acknowledges a debt which goes back at least to Don Wolfe's pioneering *Milton in the Puritan Revolution* of 1941. Paul Hamilton and Andrew Hill undertook the laborious task of reading the proofs, and Mrs. Marion Cross gave me skilful assistance with the typing. Balliol College generously allowed me a sabbatical term in 1973, during which some of the necessary reading was done, and another in 1976, which I was invited to spend at the Folger Shakespeare Library in Washington discussing Milton with a most stimulating group of scholars. By that date the typescript was in the publishers' hands, so I was not able to incorporate as much from these exciting exchanges as I would have wished; but I owe a great debt of gratitude to the Folger Library for the invitation, to its unfailingly kind and helpful staff, and to all who attended the seminar, especially perhaps Professors Stanley Fish, Gary Hamilton, Fredrica Lehrman, Joseph Martin, Jean-Kathleen Moss, Florence Sandler, Edward Weismiller and Dr. Brenda Szittya. My greatest debt is to my family for their forbearance, and especially to Bridget for her sympathetic understanding, unfailing encouragement and judicious goading.

Abbreviations

The following abbreviations have been used in the text and notes:

C. and C.   C. Hill, *Change and Continuity in 17th-Century England* (1974)

C. and F.   *The Poems of John Milton* (ed. J. Carey and A. Fowler, 1968)

C.M.   ed. F. A. Patterson and others, *The Works of John Milton* (Columbia U.P., 1931–40, 20 vols.)

C.P.W.   ed. D. M. Wolfe, *Complete Prose Works of John Milton* (Yale U.P., 1953. 6 vols. so far published)

C.S.P.   *Calendar of State Papers*

French   ed. J. M. French, *Life Records of John Milton* (Rutgers U.P., 1949–58, 5 vols.)

Masson   David Masson, *Life of Milton* (1859–80, 7 vols.)

O.U.P.   Oxford University Press

P.L.   *Paradise Lost*

P.R.   *Paradise Regained*

Parker   W. R. Parker, *Milton: A Biography* (O.U.P., 1968, 2 vols.)

S.A.   *Samson Agonistes*

S. and P.   C. Hill, *Society and Puritanism in Pre-Revolutionary England* (Panther edn., 1969). First published 1964

U.P.   University Press

W.T.U.D.   C. Hill, *The World Turned Upside Down* (Penguin edn., 1975). First published 1972

Milton's Principal Writings

I—VERSE

On the Morning of Christ's Nativity (1629)
L'Allegro and *Il Penseroso* (c. 1631?)
Comus, A Masque (1634, published 1637)
Ad Patrem (1630s)
Lycidas (1638)
Epitaphium Damonis (1640)
Poems (1645)
Paradise Lost (1667)
Paradise Regained (1671)
Samson Agonistes (1671)
Poems (second edn., 1673)

II—ENGLISH PROSE

Commonplace Book (1630s onwards). *C.P.W.*, I, pp. 362–508
Of Reformation (May 1641). *C.P.W.*, I, pp. 519–617
Of Prelatical Episcopacy (June or July 1641). *C.P.W.*, I, pp. 624–52
Animadversions upon The Remonstrants Defence against Smectymnuus (July 1641). *C.P.W.*, I, pp. 662–735
The Reason of Church Government (January or February 1642). *C.P.W.*, I, pp. 746–861
An Apology against a Pamphlet (April 1642). *C.P.W.*, I, pp. 868–953
The Doctrine and Discipline of Divorce (August 1643). *C.P.W.*, II, pp. 222–356
Of Education (June 1644). *C.P.W.*, II, pp. 362–415
The Judgment of Martin Bucer (July 1644). *C.P.W.*, II, pp. 422–79
Areopagitica (November 1644). *C.P.W.*, II, pp. 486–570
Tetrachordon (March 1645). *C.P.W.*, II, pp. 578–718
Colasterion (March 1645). *C.P.W.*, II, pp. 722–58

III—LATIN PROSE

MILTON AND THE ENGLISH REVOLUTION

Chapter 1

Introduction

> The civil war of the seventeenth century, in which Milton is a symbolic figure, has never been concluded. ... Of no other poet is it so difficult to consider the poetry simply as poetry, without our theological and political dispositions, conscious and unconscious, inherited or acquired, making an unlawful entry.
>
> T. S. Eliot, *Milton* (1947)

Milton is a more controversial figure than any other English poet. Many of the controversies relate to Milton's participation in the seventeenth-century English Revolution, yet Milton is more controversial even than that Revolution itself. Those who dislike Milton dislike him very much indeed, on personal as well as political grounds. How could the American who proclaimed himself Royalist, Anglo-Catholic and classicist have any use for England's greatest republican anti-Catholic? Blake, Shelley and Herzen were more attuned to Milton: so were Jefferson, Mirabeau and the Chartists.

Yet the controversies around Milton are not simple. He was, for instance, a propagandist of revolution, a defender of regicide and of the English republic. Dr. Johnson and many since have found it hard to forgive him for this, or to be fair to him. Yet Milton frequently expressed great contempt for the common people, and so cannot be whole-heartedly admired by modern democrats. He was a passionate anti-clerical, and in theology a very radical heretic. Since he was also a great Christian poet, 'orthodox' critics have frequently tried to explain away, or to deny, his heresies. We may feel that these attempts tell us more about the commentators than about Milton, but they have not been uninfluential. On the other hand, Milton's radical theology is far from conforming to the sensibility of twentieth-century liberal Christians.

The popular image of Milton is of a sour Puritan, an arrogant and hypocritical male chauvinist who ill-treated his own wife and daughters.

I

But his contemporaries denounced him as a libertine who encouraged the insubordination of women, as an advocate of 'divorce at pleasure' and polygamy. Milton has been criticized for approaching serious political and social problems from a totally personal angle – for writing about divorce only after his own marriage had broken down, about liberty of printing only after he had himself run into trouble with would-be censors; for attacking in an unbalanced way the leaders of the Long Parliament (in the 'digression' to his *History of Britain*) because he himself had had difficulties with some of that Parliament's committees. A similar accusation of making political issues out of personal problems was made against the Leveller leader John Lilburne. Even if the charge is true, the ideas still remain to be judged on their merits.

Although Milton was a considerable scholar, and classicist enough to satisfy T. S. Eliot, he offends many readers by his apparent rejection of all human learning in *Paradise Regained* and the *De Doctrina Christiana*. Stylistically, he is accused of writing an old-fashioned prose, lacking in simplicity and directness; and verse in a style which (because of its alleged Latinisms and grandiloquence)[1] proved a deplorable model and is to blame for the artificial eighteenth-century 'poetic diction'. His great reputation was thus a disaster for English literature. Milton has been regarded as playing a big part in the 'dissociation of sensibility' which is said to have taken place in seventeenth-century England; critics have wagged fingers at him for not being Shakespeare or for not being a metaphysical poet.

For all these reasons – and no doubt for many more – a determined attempt was made not so long ago to demote Milton, to remove him from the canon. We forget to-day how near it came to success. 'Milton's dislodgment, in the past decade, after his two centuries of predominance, was effected with remarkably little fuss.' So F. R. Leavis wrote, triumphantly if prematurely, in 1936.[2] In 1956 the volume of the *Penguin Guide to English Literature* which succeeded *The Age of Chaucer* and *The Age of Shakespeare* was not called *The Age of Milton* but *From Donne to Marvell*. The chapter devoted to 'Milton's religious verse' was not enthusiastic.

As late as 1968 W. R. Parker wrote 'after having disliked Milton's ideas for three centuries, while admiring his poetry, the English have finally decided . . . that the poetry too is bad'[3] – a statement even more astonishing for what it says about the countrymen of Blake and Shelley,

---

[1] Cf. pp. 403–4 below.
[2] Leavis (1967), p. 42; (1976), p. 12.
[3] Parker, p. 1204.

Wordsworth and the Chartists, than for its finality about the present. It is historically quite untrue, but indicative of the success of the propaganda of those whom William Empson calls the 'neo-Christians'. Fortunately these were not united in their strategy. Over against those who tried to dismiss Milton were others, less politically shrewd perhaps, who with C. S. Lewis at their head believed that they could annex Milton for 'orthodoxy'. In Lewis's *Preface to Paradise Lost* (1942) the poet is represented as a traditional authoritarian who can be used to rebuke the sinful modern world. Eliot himself on second thoughts joined in the game of salvaging as much of Milton as possible for 'orthodoxy'. It was part of a movement, now one hopes defunct, which saw Shakespeare as a propagandist of something called 'Christian humanism', defender of a hierarchical society, and Milton as the product of 'the Christian tradition'.

It is, in my view, quite wrong to see Milton in relation to anything so vague and generalized as 'the Christian tradition'. He was a radical Protestant heretic. He rejected Catholicism as anti-Christian: the papist was the only heretic excluded from his wide tolerance. Milton shed far more of mediaeval Catholicism than did the Church of England. His great theological system, the *De Doctrina Christiana*, arose by a divorcing command from the ambiguous chaos of traditional Christianity.[1] Milton rejected the Trinity, infant baptism and most of the traditional ceremonies, including church marriage; he queried monogamy and believed that the soul died with the body. He cannot reasonably be claimed as 'orthodox'.

Demotion is now impossible. Since Christopher Ricks's *Milton's Grand Style* (1963) routed the Leavisites, Milton's poetical reputation stands to-day as high as ever. Yet Milton needs to be defended from his defenders almost more than from the declining band of his enemies. There is the immensely productive Milton industry, largely in the United States of America, a great part of whose vast output appears to be concerned less with what Milton wrote (still less with enjoyment of what Milton wrote) than with the views of Professor Blank on the views of Professor Schrank on the views of Professor Rank on what Milton may or may not have written. Milton has been described as 'the poet of scholars and academic critics' – no longer either a people's poet or a poet's poet.[2] What a fate for the arch-enemy of academic pedantry: better dead than buried alive, surely!

---

[1] See pp. 152–8, 218–21, 306–8 below.
[2] Barker (1969), p. 50. If in the preceding sentence I have inadvertently named a real scholar, I apologize for my unintended rudeness.

Yet how far is Milton read with enjoyment by ordinary people? On the one hand there are those who would persuade us that we must swallow Milton's theology whole if we are to appreciate his poetry; on the other are those who, in the hope of getting the young to read him, tell us that we must forget that he was a 'Puritan' and a classical scholar, things which no one can take seriously in the late twentieth century. We must somehow let the poetry speak to us directly, and then all will be well.[1] I applaud the intention, but I doubt whether it will succeed, at any rate with the major poems. Milton was not just a fine writer. He is the greatest English revolutionary who is also a poet, the greatest English poet who is also a revolutionary. The poems will not speak for themselves unless we understand his ideas in their context. But the context is historical, and it is very difficult to grasp Milton's ideas without placing them in relation to those of his contemporaries. That is what I try to do in this book.

It is not then a straightforward biography of Milton. I am arguing a case, and attempting to refute traditional interpretations and assumptions where they appear to conflict with this case. So I must begin by declaring my hand. I believe that Milton's ideas were more directly influenced than is usually recognized by the events of the English Revolution in which he was an active participant: and that the influences brought to bear on him were much more radical than has been accepted. Some minimum understanding of the world in which Milton acted and wrote is, I think, necessary if we are to appreciate what his poetry is doing.

A long time ago Milton used to be the great 'Puritan' poet, with iron-grey homespun clothes and iron-grey homespun character. Critics nagged away at the problem of how a 'Puritan' could also be a humanist. Modern studies of Puritanism have abolished this problem by abolishing the killjoy concept of Puritanism: there was nothing abnormal in a seventeenth-century Puritan loving music, song, wine and plays, or defending, as Milton did, elegance, fine clothes, dancing, theatres, bagpipes and fiddles, ale-houses. Passions and pleasures, he declared in *Areopagitica*, if 'rightly tempered, are the very ingredients of virtue'.[2] Sexual austerity was at least as likely to be associated with Catholicism in seventeenth-century opinion: radical Protestants were thought to be more sexually indulgent.[3] Milton was a 'roundhead' whose portraits show him with long hair. It was Archbishop Laud who insisted on undergraduates cutting their hair short: long hair luxuriated in Oxford after the

---

[1] See E. S. Sirignano, 'To be a true poem', in Broadbent (1973).
[2] *C.P.W.*, II, pp. 523–7. Cf. p. 58 below.
[3] Miner (1974), p. 342.

victory of the 'roundheads'. Milton was not unique in choosing as a symbol of strength and virtue the long flowing locks of Samson.[1] The stereotype of the dour Puritan seemed applicable to Milton so long as it was believed that he wrote his first divorce pamphlet within a month of marrying Mary Powell. But historical research long ago disproved that myth.

I believe that other problems can be dissolved by a historical approach. Take the question of the sources of Milton's ideas. Critics obsessed with the poet's great reputation and great scholarship tend to look exclusively to literary sources for his ideas – to the Greek and Roman classics, to the early Christian Fathers. There are useful works on Milton and Plato, Milton and Origen, Milton and Lactantius. More to my point, there have been studies of Milton and Servetus, Milton and Ochino, Milton and Du Bartas, Milton and Boehme. My not very daring suggestion is that Milton got his ideas not only from books but also by talking to his contemporaries. As Saurat put it, 'to take up a thread at the beginning of human culture and follow it up till it reaches Milton is a pure illusion, a mere abstract fabrication of the academic mind.'[2] It is a prevalent donnish assumption that ideas are transmitted principally by books. But 'Marxist' and 'Freudian' ideas are held to-day by people who never opened a book by Marx or Freud. How many of those whom we call 'Arminian' in seventeenth-century England had read Arminius? Milton had; but his learning was exceptional. Ideas which scholars solemnly trace back to the fifth century B.C. or the third century A.D. were commonplaces to seventeenth-century Baptists, Levellers, Diggers, Seekers, Behmenists, Socinians, Ranters, Muggletonians, early Quakers and other radical groupings which took part in the free-for-all discussions of the English Revolution. The ideas had previously circulated only in the heretical underground: now they could suddenly be freely discussed. Milton celebrated this ferment in *Areopagitica*. I see him in permanent dialogue with the plebeian radical thinkers of the English Revolution, and I see him drawing on the same traditions as they drew on – traditions which include Servetus, Ochino and Boehme, but which also include Hermeticism, whose rediscovery in the fifteenth century gave new life to many ideas from classical antiquity.[3]

Milton's relation to this underworld of thought has not yet been properly investigated. Fifty years ago M. Saurat seized on Milton's radical heresies but put us on the wrong track by attributing them to

---

[1] For Samson see chapter 31 below.
[2] Saurat, p. 205.
[3] See pp. 110–11 below.

Jewish sources. We need more specific studies of Milton and his links with this radical background. The best to date is N. T. Burns's *Christian Mortalism from Tyndale to Milton*, which sets the poet against a century and more of underground heretical thought in England. There is also Leo Miller's *Milton among the Polygamophiles*, which relates some of Milton's views on marriage to previous history; but a wider study of Milton and preceding ideas about the relation of the sexes is needed. There are general histories of Unitarianism and of Socinianism in which Milton's name occurs; but no study of his ideas in the light of this tradition, also strong in the English underground. There is no work on Milton and contemporary millenarianism, antinomianism, materialism or Hermeticism. Despite Saurat's pioneer work, quite recently very respectable scholars could assume that the Milton who read Cicero and Virgil could not possibly 'have given his serious attention to the naive and superstitious Robert Fludd', or to 'the vulgar astrological flimflam of Dr. John Dee'.[1] But John Selden was a great admirer of Fludd, and Sir Isaac Newton took very seriously thinkers who seem by twentieth-century standards to be no less irrational than Dee and Fludd. Our understanding of the seventeenth century has been greatly enriched of late by scholarly work which has restored Dee and Fludd to the predominance which contemporaries gave them.[2] There is a book to be written on 'Milton and Fludd' which will be far more important than any studies of Milton's classical or patristic sources. But whoever writes it will need both more courage and more Latin than I possess.

I believe that the historian's approach can help by trying to explain how Milton came to hold the views he did at the time he held them; and perhaps to explain changes in his views over time. Milton was not an original thinker, in politics or theology. Almost every one of his ideas can be paralleled among his radical contemporaries. He is unique only in the way he combined their ideas and related them to the Bible If we restore him to the seventeenth-century context we shall no longer see originality where none exists. For instance, Milton's notorious 'He for God only, she for God in him' is one of the few of his statements which would have been totally acceptable to the orthodox among his contemporaries. Similarly, there is no need to make a pother about Milton's climatic theories once we appreciate that the belief that northerners were stronger than but intellectually inferior to southerners was the stalest of chestnuts in the

---

[1] Adams, pp. 132–3; cf. Conklin, pp. 83–5, who speaks of Fludd's 'mumbo-jumbo'.
[2] Yates (1964, 1972); K. V. Thomas (1971); P. J. French. For Selden see p. 151 below.

seventeenth century.[1] Where commentators have supposed that Milton was strikingly original he is often only fusing with the orthodox Puritan tradition ideas from the Familist/Hermeticist tradition which I shall be investigating.[2]

Milton, wrote J. H. Hanford, 'contemplated no activity as a poet which did not involve an intimate relation with the currents of life and thought in which he lived'.[3] By replacing Milton in history we shall be able to catch in his writings echoes of discussions and controversies which meant much to him and to those for whom he wrote, but which lose this resonance when they are treated in isolation. Milton, like many of us, combined traditional ideas unquestioningly accepted with others which were, by the standards of his day, highly unorthodox. That is why each critic can create his own Milton. C. S. Lewis, an old-fashioned authoritarian Christian surviving into the twentieth century, found some of the more traditional aspects of Milton's thought congenial and expounded them very effectively for his time. Empson, a dashing modern atheist, has more sympathy for those aspects of Milton's thought which were wildly heretical in the seventeenth century, though they were perhaps not quite so positively anti-Christian as Empson wished to think.

But Milton was neither a twentieth-century authoritarian Christian nor a twentieth-century atheist. He has more in common with a Ranter like Laurence Clarkson than with Lewis and the neo-Christians; but he also has more in common with Lodowick Muggleton, who believed he was one of the two Last Witnesses, than with Empson.[4] Whilst keeping Milton in the seventeenth century we must recognize that in the sixteen-forties and -fifties there was an outburst of radical thinking in England which transcended the orthodoxies of the day, and with which in some respects we still have not caught up.

When the orthodox in the seventeenth century heard the ideas of the radical underground they called for the whip and the branding iron. When Milton heard them he said they reminded him of the early Christians, and that the way to truth was through fearless discussion. It was only the strength of the radical movement, and its vigorous defence by brave men like Milton, which gave the ideas a dozen or so years of uniquely free discussion before orthodoxy got the lid back on again. If a twentieth-

---

[1] Cf. Ley, p. 59, a sermon preached before the House of Commons. Ley was quoting Vossius, who was no doubt equally unoriginal. Cf. Cowley (1905), p. 7, and p. 347 below.
[2] See pp. 75–6, chapter 6 below.
[3] Hanford (1966), p. 108.
[4] For Clarkson and Muggleton, see chapter 8 below.

century neo-Christian had met John Milton in the flesh he would not have liked him. The dislike, I suspect, would have been mutual.[1]

Milton scholarship, in my view, has been put on a wrong track by W. R. Parker's *Milton's Contemporary Reputation* of 1940. Parker argued that little notice was taken of Milton's pamphlets of the sixteen-forties, and that he was virtually unknown until he was invited to undertake the defence of the English republic (in Latin for a continental audience) in 1649. Parker looked in the wrong places for Milton's reputation. The orthodox, the good and the great, either ignored Milton's ideas of the sixteen-forties, or dismissed them with a snide comment. But the radicals, I suspect, read them avidly, and commented on them more than Parker recognized. In the course of casual reading I have come across many references to Milton, and echoes of him among the radicals, that Parker missed; I am confident that a systematic search would produce many more. Thanks to the work of W. K. Jordan, D. W. Petegorsky, G. H. Sabine, H. J. McLachlan, C. Webster, B. S. Capp and above all A. L. Morton and K. V. Thomas, a great deal more is known about the radicals of the revolutionary decades than when Parker wrote.

In a pioneering essay a generation ago Edgell Rickword said that 'each successive book about him [Milton] tends to turn into a polemic with its predecessors.'[2] I do not expect in this book to put everybody right. Nor do I think everybody wrong whom I have mentioned above. C. S. Lewis, for instance, made invaluable contributions to our understanding of Milton; Empson's insights are worthy to set beside those of the great Miltonists – Masson, Saurat, Tillyard, Hanford, Barker, Wolfe, Kelley. I want to look at Milton from a rather different angle, from the angle of his radical contemporaries. It was in the process of writing a book about these radicals – way-out characters like Diggers, Ranters and early Quakers – that it struck me that some of their ideas bore a curious relation to those of Milton.[3] Yet many of them were politically well to the left of the Levellers, themselves to the left of Milton. I do not intend to suggest that Milton *belonged* to any of these groups, that he was a Leveller, a Ranter, a Muggletonian or an early Quaker. But he lived in the same world with them, they took the same side in a civil war which Milton believed to be a conflict of good versus evil; and Milton insisted on their

---

[1] I have cribbed this remark from Empson, who, however, applies it to Milton's Samson. See p. 443 below.
[2] Rickword, p. 131. Rickword's explanation of this fact is relevant: 'the principles he [Milton] evolved demand a re-ordering of society for their realization.'
[3] See *W.T.U.D.*, appendix 2.

right to be heard. Their ideas illuminate his and may well have influenced him, both positively and negatively.

Milton himself is the worst enemy of Milton's biographers. He prepared the record for posterity as carefully as to-day's civil servant pruning his files with the thirty-year rule in mind. Most of us have been brought up to accept Milton's own image of himself as an aloof, austere intellectual, an image all the more plausible because it fits the stereotype of the gloomy Puritan from which historians have with difficulty liberated themselves. I shall suggest later detailed arguments against accepting this picture of Milton, and reasons why everything he writes about himself should be checked carefully against the circumstances in which he wrote, and against everything else that we know about him.[1] None of us would accept one of our own acquaintances at his own propagandist valuation.

That is what this book is about. In Part I I have high-lighted possible radical influences on the young Milton; I have argued that he was more sociable and clubbable than is often thought, less aloof and austere. In Parts II–IV I re-examine Milton's political career and pamphleteering, proposing some revisions in our estimate of his standing among his contemporaries, indicating parallels between his ideas and those of the radicals, and suggesting points at which he disagreed with them. This prepares for a more thorough-going reconsideration of Milton's heresies in Part V, in which I again try to relate his views to those of his contemporaries. This finally leads me in Part VI to suggest a greater 'political' content in *Paradise Lost, Paradise Regained* and *Samson Agonistes* than is normally recognized.

I should like to see the vast energy at present devoted to Milton studies redirected – away from the classics and the Christian Fathers to Milton's contemporaries and immediate predecessors. If this book helps to redirect this energy, it will have served its purpose – and will soon be superseded by more learned and better books. One of the very real pleasures of writing it has been to make the acquaintance, personally or through the printed word, of many younger Milton scholars in England and elsewhere who are impatient of the traditional stereotypes and who do not limit their seventeenth-century reading to Milton and other 'classics'.[2] I have drawn gratefully on their work.

I have tried to make acknowledgments when I am conscious of taking

---

[1] See chapter 32 below.
[2] Boyd M. Berry's *Process of Speech: Puritan Religious Writing and and Paradise Lost* (Johns Hopkins U.P., 1976) and Loretta Mannucci's *Ideali e Classi nella Poesia di Milton* (Milan, 1976) unfortunately appeared too late for me to draw upon their stimulating ideas.

over other people's ideas, but so many people have written well about Milton that this is impossible. Among those whom I have listed as the great Miltonists, David Masson must come first. For many years I have known that, whenever I think I have had an original idea about seventeenth-century England, I am apt to find it tucked away in one of S. R. Gardiner's footnotes. So it is with Masson on Milton. Saurat had remarkable insights, and Don Wolfe's *Milton in the Puritan Revolution* placed Milton in relation to his radical contemporaries.[1] I must also pay tribute to Douglas Bush, Northrop Frye, Earl Miner, Christopher Ricks, John Carey and Alastair Fowler, with whom I do not always agree but from whom I have learnt much; and to J. M. French, whose monumental *Life Records of John Milton* is indispensable to anyone who writes about Milton. Finally there is W. R. Parker. In some respects this book is a polemic against his *Milton's Contemporary Reputation*, and I reject his dating of *Samson Agonistes*. Yet I am well aware of my debt to his massive biography, which not only gives almost every known fact about Milton's life but also, on the many occasions when Parker was not mounted on one of his hobby-horses, contains a great deal of shrewd reflection. His index, as Thomas Hobbes might have said, is rare. The next generation will I trust come to see further than Parker; but it will do so by standing on his shoulders.[2]

---

[1] See also Wolfe's Introduction to *C.P.W.*, IV; Rickword, *passim*, and Visick, pp. 178–91.

[2] In what follows I have not normally given references for facts which can be found in French or Parker.

PART I

SHIPWRECK EVERYWHERE

Si recte calculum ponas, ubique naufragium est.
                Petronius Arbiter
(If you estimate it correctly, there is shipwreck everywhere.)
                Title-page of the memorial volume to Edward King
                in which Milton's *Lycidas* first appeared (1638)

Chapter 2

Pre-revolutionary England

> God may leave a nation that is but in outward covenant with him, and why not England? ... Our God is going, and do you sit still on your beds?
>
> Thomas Hooker, *The Danger of Desertion* (1641): a farewell sermon 'preached immediately before his departure out of old England' in the early sixteen-thirties

I Political background

Milton was born in December 1608, and was self-consciously slow in maturing. The years before 1640 we can regard as the period of his apprenticeship. The world in which he grew up was changing rapidly. Under the pressures of expanding population, economic crisis and ideological rivalry, the consensus which had held Elizabethan society together was breaking down. All thought about economics and politics at this time took religious forms; men saw the national crisis primarily as a religious crisis, though Milton (I shall suggest) came to see it also as a cultural crisis.

National sentiment in England had been intimately associated with Protestantism ever since Henry VIII declared England's independence of the papacy. Under Elizabeth, when the great Catholic power of Spain emerged as the national enemy, the connection of Protestantism and nationalism was sedulously emphasized. Foxe's *Book of Martyrs* was used as government propaganda. A legend was carefully built up, of Catholic cruelty and treachery. Evidence in plenty could be found to support it: Alva's Council of Blood in the Netherlands, the Massacre of St. Bartholomew in 1572, innumerable Roman Catholic plots in England culminating in that of Guy Fawkes in 1605, on which Milton in his teens wrote five Latin poems. England's victory in 1588 over the Spanish Armada – allegedly full of whips and instruments of torture for use on Protestant Englishmen – was attributed to direct divine intervention, and played a

13

big part in building up the conception, which Milton adopted, of Protestant England as a chosen nation.

James VI of Scotland succeeded Elizabeth in 1603, five years before Milton's birth. James had many disadvantages. He was a foreigner, married to a papist, and son of Mary Queen of Scots who had been the Spanish and papal candidate to replace Elizabeth on the throne. But Gunpowder Plot gave James a good start, and he might have continued to exploit the patriotic anti-Catholic legend, since he was certainly a more convinced Protestant than Elizabeth. For a variety of reasons, however, good, bad and indifferent, James hankered after the role of peace-maker in Europe, of mediator between Protestant and Catholic extremists. But he was short of cash, for which he depended on the vote of M.Ps. most of whom accepted the full Protestant legend and had no use for James's pacific schemes. He suffered the normal fate of the would-be mediator who lacks the wherewithal to intervene effectively. Spain was interested only in preventing Parliament from driving James into the Protestant camp as Europe lined up for the Thirty Years War.

When war started in 1618 James failed – despite prodding from Parliament whenever it met – to give effective military aid to his son-in-law the Elector Palatine, who had been ignominiously ejected not only from the Bohemian throne to which he had aspired but also from his hereditary dominions in the Palatinate. Instead, James sent his favourite the Duke of Buckingham with Prince Charles to Madrid to woo the daughter of the King of Spain. It looked in the early twenties as though all continental Europe was going to fall before the Catholic sword. Church lands were being resumed in Germany, and it seemed only a matter of time before England's national independence and the property of the inheritors of monastic lands fell too. When John Rushworth began to publish his documented history of the English Revolution in 1659, he found it necessary to go back to the outbreak of the Thirty Years War in 1618, though he had originally intended to start in November 1640.[1]

Charles I, who succeeded in 1625, did not share his father's illusions of European grandeur; but he too suffered from lack of money. He abandoned the unpopular scheme for a Spanish marriage alliance: instead he married the daughter of the King of France. In terms of *Realpolitik* this was sound: France was as hostile to Spain as could be wished. But Queen Henrietta Maria was no less Catholic than the Infanta of Spain; the marriage involved concessions to English Catholics, seen by many as a

---

[1] Rushworth, I, Sig. b 3v.

potential fifth column in England. Buckingham continued to be influential under Charles as under James, and many of his relations were Catholics. After Buckingham's assassination in 1628 the influence of Henrietta Maria over her husband grew; conversions to Catholicism became fashionable; and in 1637 a papal agent was admitted to England, for the first time since the reign of Bloody Mary. Contemporary fears of an international Catholic plot against English independence appeared to be confirmed when eight years later a papal nuncio arrived in Ireland to head a full-scale Catholic revolt against English rule. Two generations earlier Nicholas Sander had been papal legate to the Irish rebels who rose in 1579.

The French alliance involved Charles in what Milton was to call a 'treacherous and antichristian war against the poor protestants of La Rochelle'.[1] The Protestant cause in Europe was finally saved not by England but by Gustavus Adolphus of Sweden, who in 1630 marched into Germany to win spectacular victories. Court sentiment was expressed by Carew:

> What though the German drum
> Bellow for freedom and revenge, the noise
> Concerns not us, nor should divert our joys.[2]

That was written in 1632, the year of the death of Gustavus Adolphus. On that occasion John Bradshaw, later President of the court that tried Charles I, perhaps Milton's kinsman, wrote that 'more sad or heavy tidings hath not in this age been brought since Prince Harry's death to the true-hearted English.'[3] At the time of Gustavus's intervention the English government was actually negotiating with Spain for an alliance against Sweden and the Netherlands. Those patriotic Englishmen who were bitterly ashamed that Sweden and not England had saved the day for Protestantism did not know of these negotiations. But plainly the English court was less than enthusiastic about the Protestant cause. In 1632 a financial deal with Spain helped the latter to pay her armies in the Netherlands; in 1639 Dutch and Spanish fleets fought a battle in English territorial waters, with the English fleet passively looking on.

Nor was it only a question of foreign policy. There were alarming developments in England itself. William Laud, in effect head of the church from 1628 onwards, introduced innovations which to many Englishmen seemed steps in the direction of popery. Transference of the communion table from the centre of the church to the east end, where it

---

[1] *C.P.W.*, III, p. 436.
[2] Carew, p. 125.
[3] Newton, p. 135. For Prince Henry, James I's eldest son, see pp. 30–31 below.

was railed off, seemed to imply the Catholic doctrine of the real presence.
'A table of separation', Milton was to call it. It elevated the priest above
the congregation, thus undoing what for many had been one of the
Reformation's most important achievements. There was a deliberate re-
introduction of Catholic motifs into ecclesiastical architecture and
sculpture. Laud was also effective Prime Minister of England. He made the
Bishop of London Lord Treasurer – the first cleric to hold that office since
the Reformation, Laud proudly noted in his Diary. Laud attempted to
increase tithe payments from the laity to the clergy; to recover for the
church tithes which had passed to laymen at the dissolution of the monas-
teries. His partisans dominated the two universities, and got the best
preferments in the church; their opponents were silenced or driven into
exile. In the eleven years without Parliament, 1629–40, Laud and his
dependants ruled through the prerogative courts, Star Chamber and High
Commission, which fiercely enforced government policy, regardless of the
social rank of those who opposed it. 'Lordly prelates raised from the
dunghill', 'equal commonly in birth to the meanest peasants' as their
opponents elegantly called them, inflicted corporal punishments on
gentlemen with the same ferocity as the latter flogged and branded the
lower orders;[1] as soon as a Parliament met they were certain to be called
to account.

Parliament ultimately had to meet because of Scotland. The English
government had imposed bishops on the Scottish Kirk, and under Laud
their power was enhanced. There had been dangerous talk of a resumption
of Scottish church lands. When a new prayer book was brought in, with
changes which weakened Protestant doctrine, the Scottish gentry and
aristocracy encouraged a resistance which soon reached national propor-
tions. Most patriotic Englishmen sympathized with the old but now
Protestant enemy against their own government. When Charles sent an
army north, the rank and file were more hostile to their papist officers than
to the Scots, better at pulling down altar rails than at fighting. National
disaster and bankruptcy could be avoided only by calling a Parliament.

By now the idea had taken root in England that the government, under
the baleful influence of Henrietta Maria and Laud, was involved in a
vast international Catholic plot against the liberties of Protestant Englishmen. Laud of course was no papist. We know, as contemporaries did not,
that he refused the offer of a cardinal's hat. But if they had known, the fact
that the Pope thought the offer worth making might have seemed more

---

[1] C. Hill (Sphere, 1969), p. 67. Cf. chapter 7 below.

significant than Laud's refusal. Events in Scotland seemed to fit into this international conspiracy. So did events in Ireland.

There, in natural resentment at the oppressions of English colonizers, Catholicism had become equated with nationalism just as Protestantism had in England, and as Presbyterianism had in Scotland. In 1598 a Spanish landing in Ireland had been beaten off with difficulty: the possibility of its recurrence was a perpetual nightmare. The appointment of Sir Thomas Wentworth as Lord Deputy of Ireland in 1632 increased anxiety. Wentworth was a Protestant, but he was also a renegade leader of the opposition in the English Parliament. He made what many Englishmen thought excessive concessions to the Catholic majority in Ireland, and started building up an army there composed largely of papists. What for? Wentworth himself suggested using it against the Scottish Covenanters; for most Protestant Englishmen this was equivalent to using it against England, for the subversion of their liberties, religion and property.

II Court versus country

This is the background against which we must set court/country rivalries in the early seventeenth century. Under Elizabeth, the danger from Spain and from the Pope, and perhaps from the English lower classes, had forced unity on the ruling class. Every man, as Fulke Greville put it, believed that 'his private fish-ponds could not be safe whilst the public state of the kingdom stood in danger of present or expectant extremities'.[1] But after the defeat of the Armada in 1588, political attitudes, especially attitudes to foreign affairs, began to diverge. Gradually what had been healthy tensions between different groupings on Elizabeth's Privy Council became ruthless faction feuds. Ultimately two sides lined up to fight a civil war. A deep breach opened up between the early Stuart court and the main body of respectable opinion in the country. In so far as this opinion was expressed in any organized way, 'Puritanism' in a very wide and loose definition of that over-worked word can serve to describe it. But the roots of hostility to the court were not merely theological but political, moral and cultural as well.

The divergences showed up more clearly under James I. Neither Elizabeth's own behaviour nor the conduct of her courtiers had always been impeccable. Yet certain standards of decorum had been maintained, not least because of the prudent parsimony of the Virgin Queen. But

---

[1] Greville, p. 188.

there were many things about James I which shocked country squires and London merchants – the drunken orgies which marked the visit of the King of Denmark in 1606 for instance. James's public fondling and slobbering over his male favourites might have been forgiven, but not the fact that he allowed them to influence policy. This was utterly foreign to the Elizabethan tradition. When the Earl of Somerset, a Scottish favourite, wanted the Earl of Essex's wife, James egged on a bevy of bishops to declare the marriage annulled on the grounds of Essex's impotence and his Countess's intact virginity. Some were prepared to believe the former, none the latter. When civil war came, Essex was Lord General of the Parliamentary army.

An even greater scandal broke in 1615, when Somerset and his new Countess were convicted of poisoning Sir Thomas Overbury because he knew too much about their affairs. The only way in which the anti-Spanish party at court could think of ending James's subservience to the Spanish Ambassador was by getting the Archbishop of Canterbury to introduce him to a new boy-friend. The ruse was successful; but as the new minion was the future Duke of Buckingham, the remedy proved worse than the disease. There were scandals of a more conventional sort: two Lord Treasurers and a Lord Chancellor were convicted of taking bribes. With more money about, corruption either increased or was believed to have increased. The price of a peerage, of a baronetcy, and of most court offices was publicly known. Sir Simonds D'Ewes, writing in cipher for his own eye only, accused James of 'the sin of sodomy', and added 'all his actions did tend to an absolute monarchy.'[1]

Lucy Hutchinson sums up the Puritan view, though she has her own heightened and telling way of putting things. 'The court of this king [James I] was a nursery of lust and intemperance. . . . The generality of the gentry of the land soon learnt the court fashion, and every great house in the country became a stew of uncleanness.' When James died, 'the face of the court', Mrs. Hutchinson admits, 'was much changed . . . for King Charles was temperate and chaste and serious.'[2] Gross errors of taste and probity were eliminated. Charles was a better judge of men than his father, and his personal fastidiousness offered a more acceptable public image. But the charge of lack of Protestant patriotism ultimately proved fatal. Charles was too devoted to his French wife, too dependent on unpopular bishops. Nor did it do the Church of England any good that the Bishop

---

[1] Bourcier, pp. 92–3, 59.
[2] Hutchinson, pp. 42, 46. Selden, however, thought Charles's court worse than his father's (p. 101).

of Waterford and Lismore had the misfortune to be convicted of whoredom and sodomy in the autumn of 1640.[1]

The growing court/country rivalries came to include attitudes towards patronage of the arts. Under Elizabeth, the Earl of Leicester, the first great English art-collector, led the party which favoured an active pro-Protestant foreign policy. Leicester's nephew, Sir Philip Sidney, was a leader of international Protestantism as well as a great English literary figure. The mantle of Leicester and Sidney fell upon the Russells, Earls of Bedford and upon Shakespeare's Earl of Southampton, but especially upon the Herberts, Earls of Pembroke. The wife of the second Earl was Sidney's sister: the fourth Earl was christened Philip after Sidney. The third Earl of Pembroke and the Earl of Arundel were brothers-in-law; but in 1616 Arundel was described as 'head of the Catholics' and Pembroke as 'head of the Puritans'; Southampton was 'head of the malcontents'.[2] Arundel and the fourth Earl of Pembroke were to be on opposite sides in the Civil War.

In literature we can trace a line of descent from Spenser (patronized by Leicester) through a group of poets patronized by Southampton, Bedford and Pembroke, ranging from Shakespeare, Drayton, the two Fletchers, William Browne and Samuel Daniel to George Wither. While drama was decaying under court influence, the third Earl of Pembroke encouraged Thomas Middleton's attempt to produce an opposition drama in the anti-Spanish *A Game at Chess*.[3] George Herbert, Pembroke's kinsman and protégé, withdrew from court to write his great poetry in a country parsonage. In such an atmosphere 'no free and splendid wit can flourish', Milton was soon to say. For the concomitant of Charles I's patronage of the arts was a savage censorship which, in George Wither's words, brought 'authors, yea, the whole commonwealth and all the liberal sciences into bondage'.[4]

The court culture, like court religion, came to be isolated from the mass of the population, and – a new feature – from many of the propertied class. The censorship and government pressures prevented many of the intelligentsia from expressing their point of view, or frightened them out of doing so. Art, like everything else at Charles's court, was smeared with the trail of finance. The King's most ambitious projects were paid for by abuses which contributed to bring about the Civil War. Thus the

---

[1] Shuckburgh, pp. 149–50. For the case of Lord Castlehaven see pp. 43–5 below.
[2] *C.S.P. Venetian, 1615–17*, p. 245.
[3] Heinemann, pp. 232–50.
[4] See pp. 64–6, 217–18, 405–9 below.

unrealized plan for reconstructing Whitehall as a single great palace, comparable with the Escorial or the Louvre, was a magnificent design which 'reflects clearly enough the absolutist ideals of the King'. But it was also a megalomaniac idea. As Sir John Summerson says, it 'would have been a grave and fitting backcloth for the bloodier revolution which it would most certainly have helped to precipitate'. There was 'a close association between the arts of the court and those elements in Stuart policy which precipitated the constitutional upheavals of the seventeenth century.'[1]

As the narrow ruling circle became more and more isolated from public opinion, so it needed the flattery of artists and poets to buttress its morale. How different things had been under Elizabeth! When the monarchy was really popular, it did not need to be so repeatedly reassured that it enjoyed divine approval. All the masques allegorizing peace and concord imposed by royal authority, the apotheoses and descending goddesses, betray a deep insecurity and longing for help from outside.

There was then an abnormal cultural situation in the England in which Milton reached maturity. P. W. Thomas speaks of 'two warring cultures'. With 'the growing isolation, exclusiveness and repression of the Court' he contrasts the earlier 'literature that had been the authentic voice of patriotic high seriousness and protestant nationalism'. The Caroline court, 'however refined, seemed to speak for narrow snobbery and effete indulgence'. 'Royal patronage had failed to sustain . . . a culture . . . of unequivocal moral and intellectual vigour. It mistook . . . a governing clique for the nation. . . . It managed to create a mythology of itself that was deeply divisive.' This was seen by the Puritan opposition as 'the pollution of the high seriousness and moral earnestness of the mainstream of English humanism'. Ben Jonson represents the last attempt to infuse moral commitment into court art; and he was first absorbed into the court and then ultimately squeezed out. Milton was aware of 'a decadent Court, its art an index to a deep malaise'. Thomas rejects the view which sees Cavalier humanism as 'life-affirming', by contrast with Puritan prudery. We shall find ample reason, at least so far as Milton is concerned, to confirm his opinion that 'far from suppressing the sensual and sentimental element in sexual relationships, English Puritanism exposed it to the full force of its habit of scrupulous analysis.'[2] As the unity of Elizabeth's reign slowly dissolved, the Laudian innovations isolated bishops from the mass of the population. One may suspect that popular hostility extended

---

[1] Whinney and Millar, pp. 39, 6–7; Summerson, pp. 127, 134.
[2] P. W. Thomas, pp. 174–5, 184–90.

to the new taste for Counter-Reformation absolutist art favoured by the court clique.

There is an inevitable danger in history of falling for 'the illusion of the epoch', of accepting a ruling group at its own valuation whilst ignoring evidence from other sources. It is the criticism which Paine made of Burke on the French Revolution: he pitied the plumage but forgot the dying bird. We must not go to the opposite extreme and say that the aesthetic taste of Charles and his circle was a significant cause of the Civil War; that would be as absurd as to argue that the Civil War destroyed English art. What we can say is that the years in which Milton grew up were years of increasing national disillusionment, of a widening gap between the court and the more Protestant elements in the country. The golden age of the drama and of English literature generally was over; so was the golden age of English music, and of English miniature painting. The religion of court and universities was diverging from the Elizabethan consensus; the new scientific ideas were popular in London, and had won some advocates in both universities, but no official recognition. The censorship grew increasingly severe.[1] The young gentlemen who went to the Inns of Court continued to be consumers and patrons of literature, but after the first decade of the seventeenth century 'the energies which had previously been devoted to literature and scholarship were channelled instead towards political and theological concerns.'[2]

I quote Thomas again: 'There were two warring cultures. But it is more accurate to talk of a breakdown of the national culture, an erosion through the sixteen-thirties of a middle ground that men of moderation and good will had once occupied.' 'The civil war was about the whole condition of a society threatened by a failure of the ruling caste to uphold traditional national aims and values, and to adapt itself to a rapidly changing world.'[3] It is important to remember this cultural component in what we call 'Puritanism', as well as the political and religious tensions between court and country on which the books normally dwell. It was felt especially strongly by John Milton. It has been suggested, on the evidence of the Nativity Ode and *Lycidas*, that Milton's 'imagination of revolution as the supersession of one ground of values by another' antedates the historical revolution in which the poet was to play a leading part.[4]

---

[1] Cf. C. Hill (1965), pp. 7–13; cf. pp. 221, 291.
[2] Prest, pp. 153–7.
[3] P. W. Thomas, p. 184.
[4] Grossman, p. 294.

Chapter 3

Milton's Apprenticeship

> It is commonly seen that historians are suspected rather to make their hero what they would have him be than such as he really was.
>
> John Toland, *The Life of John Milton* (1698)

I Early influences

The family into which John Milton was born in December 1608 was Protestant, bourgeois and cultured. His father, John Milton the elder, had been turned out of his Oxfordshire home by his yeoman father, who adhered to the old religion whilst his son became a Bible-reading Protestant. John the elder came to London some twenty-five years before the poet was born, and pursued a very successful career as a scrivener. Scriveners performed functions for which to-day one would go to a solicitor or an investment adviser; but their main business, and certainly their most lucrative business, was money-lending. It was a time of rapidly rising prices, and of ostentatious expenditure among an aristocracy slow to adapt itself to new economic realities; it was also a time when merchants and business men often needed the sort of bridging loan for which they would to-day turn to a bank. The scrivener might be the go-between linking borrower and lender, as well as lending on his own account. Interest rates were high; by close attention to detail, good timing and firm use of legal processes, there were handsome profits to be made. John Milton senior did well. By 1632, when he was nearly seventy years old, he had made enough money to retire. After setting up his younger son, Christopher, as a lawyer, and providing a good marriage portion for his daughter, he was still able to maintain his elder son in a leisure which included an expensive fifteen months' continental tour.

So successful a career in such a profession suggests considerable toughness, not to say ruthlessness. In the last resort legal processes had to be used; the scrivener could not afford to be too squeamish when faced with

22

the protestations of a garrulous widow who claimed that she had not understood what she had committed herself to. In 1625 the elder John Milton made an apprentice his partner, perhaps to look after the less agreeable aspects of the business. His retirement may even have been connected with the increasingly brash behaviour of this partner. We do not know. But even when John Milton senior had retired to rural Horton, he continued to assert himself. He built a pew in the parish church which exceeded the authorized height, and he was ordered to cut it down to size.[1] The poet, growing up in London, in a street 'wholly inhabited by rich merchants',[2] must have absorbed the 'protestant ethic' with the air he breathed. It would be taken for granted that hard work was a religious duty, that bargains were made to be kept, and enforced by law against those who could not or would not keep them, that the weakest went to the wall, that God helped those who helped themselves. A tough tenacity was one of the younger Milton's lasting characteristics. He inherited some of his father's property and – as we shall see – some problems of debt-collection. The poet frequently expressed dislike of the legal profession; but he never hesitated to use legal process to enforce what he believed to be his rights, and he had a remarkably extensive knowledge of the law. Unlike the elder John, the poet remained on excellent terms with both his parents until their death. He worried from time to time about the ethics of usury, but decided on balance that it was lawful.

But though it was a business-like bourgeois household, it was also a civilized household. The Mermaid Tavern was just round the corner. The scrivener loved music, and was himself no mean composer. In 1601 he participated in *The Triumphs of Oriana*, a tribute to Queen Elizabeth from the best composers in the country. In 1614 (twice), 1616 and 1621 he contributed to other collections, again in excellent company. He is said to have composed a 40-(or 80-)part song for a Polish (or German) prince in 1583 (and/or 1611).[3] The elder Milton was also capable of turning a sonnet himself. So though he had hoped originally that his eldest son would go into the church, he was amenable to discussion when John decided otherwise. Father-like, the scrivener would have preferred his son to have entered some recognized profession – the law if not the church – rather than dedicating himself to poetry, which was even less likely to bring in a regular income in the seventeenth century than to-day. (Only after the publishing outburst of 1640–60 did the literary market develop

[1] Brinkworth, p. 46.
[2] Stow, p. 309.
[3] Brennecke, pp. 34, 54, 64–8, 71–2, 82, 98.

sufficiently for the career even of hack-writer to become possible. Milton's nephews, John and Edward Phillips, seem to have made a living of sorts this way. But aristocratic patronage was still desirable.) The discussions in the Milton family seem to have been fairly amicable, and the elder John financed his son's expedition to Italy (with serving man) at a time when the future career of the thirty-year-old poet was still uncertain. John senior was clearly a patient, sensitive man, who remembered his difficulties with his own father. Posterity as well as his son should be grateful to the scrivener for his discernment. His biographer comments on the paradoxical combination in the elder Milton of Puritanism with a respect for the complex traditions of mediaeval church music; he set vernacular texts from the Geneva Bible to polyphonic music. His son was to experience similar fruitful tensions between the old and the new.[1]

The poet's mother was the daughter of a London merchant taylor, and may have been a widow when she married the scrivener; perhaps she brought him a useful dowry. But we know very little about her. Mrs. Milton appears to have been related to the Bradshaws, though if there was any connection with the John Bradshaw who presided over the trial of Charles I in 1649, it was very distant. She had weak eyes, which John inherited; his father read without spectacles at the age of eighty-four. Otherwise all that history records is her son's remark that she was very charitable. John's later attitudes would suggest that Mrs. Milton accepted with docility the position of subordination expected of seventeenth-century wives. Yet the poet had an exceptionally high ideal of married love, and he believed that a sexual union was a true marriage only if mutual compatibility created a genuine oneness. It is difficult not to suppose that these views are somehow related to the music-loving sociable home in which he grew up, and to the mother whose generosity was the characteristic which he most remembered.

Among early influences on the young Milton we must notice the rector of his parish, Richard Stock (1569?–1626). All Hallows was one of those rare parishes where the congregation had the right to elect their own minister; another was St. Stephen's, Coleman Street, whose minister in the sixteen-forties was John Goodwin. We shall often encounter his name in association with Milton. Stock was naturally a Puritan. He was one of the Feoffees for buying in impropriations – a Puritan attempt to reconstruct the church from within.[2] Three of the five ministers involved in this

---

[1] *Ibid.*, p. 89. Cf. chapter 27 below.
[2] C. Hill (1956), chapter XI; Pearl, p. 162.

scheme were incumbents of parishes where the minister was elected. As befitted the rector of a parish of rich business men, Stock was a well-known sabbatarian, with strong views about the duties of servants. Milton was to repudiate many of Stock's ideas – his firm defence of tithes, his decisive rejection of polygamy and of divorce for any reason other than adultery, his insistence that the principal object of marriage was the propagation of children, his surprisingly sharp condemnation of usury and his frequent citation of the early Fathers of the church.[1] But Stock's preaching may have started Milton thinking on some of these topics; so may his anti-papal sermons on November 5. Milton's poems on Gunpowder Plot were all written in Stock's lifetime. Others of Stock's views proved more acceptable to the poet – for instance that a man should be charitable to himself and his family as well as to others.[2]

Stock had a strong sense of social justice. He denounced usurers whose ostentatious charity restored only a fraction of their ill-gotten gains; and the landlord or employer who oppressed his inferiors, confident that 'there is no civil law against him, or if there be, either his greatness or purse will carry it out well enough'. In 1606 Stock had been rebuked as a 'greenhead' for criticizing the system of assessing rates by which they fell especially heavily on the poor. Stock repeated his charge when he could describe himself as a 'greyhead'. This is testimony to his consistency and social sympathy, but does not suggest great influence on the financial conduct of citizens. One wonders whether Milton's phrase in *The Reason of Church Government*, 'now while green years are upon my head', was consciously echoing Stock; an author should be judged by the validity of his arguments, not by his age, Milton added. Stock gave much thought to justifying the ways of God to men. 'The Lord ofttimes destroys the wicked, enemies of God and his church, by the hands of his church and by their means' was his enigmatical gloss on Malachi 4: 3. Among his flock was Captain John Venn of the City militia, future M.P. in the Long Parliament and regicide, as well as John Milton, future defender of regicide.[3]

Other important early influences on Milton were teachers and friends at St. Paul's School. None of his Cambridge tutors or contemporaries seems to have won anything like the confidence which he gave to Thomas Young, the younger Alexander Gil and Charles Diodati. Young was a Scottish minister who came south some time before 1612, when episcopacy

---

[1] Stock, pp. 44–51, 77–80, 172–88, 223–31.
[2] See p. 264 below.
[3] *C.P.W.*, I, p. 806; Stock, pp. 23–35, 113, 165, 196–7, 254. Stock's *Commentary* was dedicated to Venn among others.

was being imposed on Scotland. We cannot say definitely that Young decided to emigrate because of Presbyterian convictions, but in 1606 his father had protested against the introduction of episcopacy, and the rest of Young's career makes it a likely assumption. As a refugee in London Young assisted the Puritan Thomas Gataker in his 'private seminary for divers young gentlemen'. He presumably got the job of tutor to Milton through Richard Stock, a friend of Gataker's.[1] We do not know exactly when Young taught Milton. It may have been before he went to St. Paul's. (We do not know the date of that either.) Or Young may have given him extra tuition whilst at school. What we do know is that he won John's affection and respect, in a way that few of the poet's seniors were to do. We know too little about Young's personality to account for his hold over his pupil: but we may guess that Milton was impressed by Young's austere courage in refusing to 'subscribe slave', preferring the hazards of an exile's life in a foreign land.

Young's subsequent career fits the pattern. By 1620, Milton tells us, England was becoming too hot to hold Young, and he accepted a post in Hamburg as chaplain to a company of English merchants. He returned in 1628, to a living in Stowmarket worth £300 a year, where for ten years he managed to avoid wearing the surplice. During this period Milton went to visit him, sent him letters and poems from time to time, and clearly valued both his friendship and his literary judgment. In 1639 Young published (anonymously) a sabbatarian tract, *Dies Dominica*, which was not translated into English until 1672. If Milton read it – as is probable – he may have noticed a statement of the progressive evolution of truth: 'Men of every age, studiously following after the known truth, . . . are blessed with a new light of knowledge not observed by their predecessors. It sometimes also falleth out that some things may be revealed to men of inferior condition, which are hid to others of greater name and authority.'[2] In the long run Milton was to reject the Presbyterianism and sabbatarianism which meant so much to Young. But the poet's attitudes in the early forties owe a good deal to the previous influence of his tutor, who almost certainly instigated Milton's participation in the attack on episcopacy in 1641–2. Milton's emphasis on the Bible as the source of all truth may also derive from Young. But after the mid-forties the two drifted apart, as Young became two things Milton now heartily disliked – a Presbyterian pluralist and the head of a Cambridge college.[3]

---

[1] Haller (1955), p. 37.
[2] Young, p. 15.
[3] Cf. *C.P.W.*, V, pp. 447, 455; see also pp. 80–81 below.

The two Alexander Gils were successively High Masters of St. Paul's School, the father during Milton's years there. The elder Gil's literary tastes, and particularly his devotion to Spenser and the Spenserians, may well have influenced Milton. He perhaps also imbibed at St. Paul's Gil's disparaging attitude towards 'ploughmen, working-girls and river-men' as contrasted with 'learned and refined men'.[1] Gil's treatise on the Trinity, originally published in 1601, was reprinted in 1635. Milton may have been interested enough to read it, though there is no evidence of any connection between this and his own anti-Trinitarian speculations. The elder Gil's *Sacred Philosophie of the Holy Scripture* (1635, reprinted 1651) was an attempt to make reason, 'that especial and principal gift of God to mankind', serviceable to 'the principal and especial end for which man himself is created, that is his drawing near unto God by faith in him'.[2] In this work Gil argued that there could be no clash between faith and reason, a view which Milton later found attractive.

The younger Gil's influence was very different. He was an usher during Milton's time at the school, ten or a dozen years older than the poet. Their friendship continued for many years after Milton left. Alexander was a brash, swaggering intellectual, who never seems quite to have recovered from being a very clever young man. He was 'accounted one of the best Latin poets in the nation'. Milton admired his poems, and Gil succeeded Young as literary mentor to the young poet. Milton thought him 'the keenest judge of poetry in general and the most honest judge of mine'. He never talked to him 'without a visible increase and growth of knowledge'. But Gil also had political opinions. Ben Jonson, attacking the elder Gil in 1623, spoke of 'licentious persons' who 'censured the Council' of the King. 'We do it in Paul's, . . . yea and in all the taverns.'[3] In October of that year, when Prince Charles delighted the nation by returning from Spain without the popish Infanta whom he had gone to woo, the 114th Psalm was sung in St. Paul's Cathedral – 'when Israel came out of Egypt and the house of Jacob from among the barbarous people'. It was a political gesture. So was Milton's paraphrase on this Psalm, 'done by the author at fifteen years old' – i.e. in 1623-4:

> When the blest seed of Terah's faithful son
> After long toil their liberty had won.

If Milton was not incited to translate this Psalm by the younger Gil, he must certainly have shown it to the usher. Ten years later he sent Gil a

---

[1] Gil (1972), I, p. xiii; II, p. 87.
[2] Gil (1635), Sig. ¶ 5.
[3] A. Wood, III, pp. 42-3; *C.P.W.*, I, pp. 313-14; Demaray, p. 47.

Greek translation of the same Psalm. In Psalm 136, which Milton also translated about 1623–4, the neutral phrase 'the Lord of Lords' is expanded to (him) 'who doth the wrathful tyrants quell'.[1]

In 1628, when the hated favourite, the Duke of Buckingham, was assassinated by John Felton, the younger Gil was foolish enough to propose the assassin's health. He had recently become a Bachelor of Divinity, and was visiting his old college, Trinity College, Oxford, where he no doubt thought he was among friends. Most of those present cheerfully joined in the toast. But one of them denounced him to the all-powerful Bishop Laud – almost certainly the famous William Chilling-worth, Laud's protégé. Not only did Gil speak slightingly of Buckingham, and place him in hell; he also wrote of James and Charles as 'the old fool and the young one', in papers which were seized. Charles, Gil added, was 'fitter to stand in a Cheapside shop with an apron before him and say "What lack ye?" than to govern a kingdom'. Under examination he did not improve matters by adding that drinking Felton's health was common in London and elsewhere. He admitted saying that 'he had oftentimes had in mind to do the same deed upon the Duke, but for fear of hanging'. He was explicit about Buckingham's homosexual tendencies. A poem was found in which Gil called on God to save

> My sovereign from a Ganymede
> Whose whorish breath hath power to lead
> His Majesty which way it list.

The song continued in denunciation of flatterers, court corruption, illegal taxes, papists and especially Jesuits.[2]

It was decided to make an example of Gil, who was certainly right in saying that he had only expressed what many felt.[3] He was had up before Star Chamber, degraded from the ministry and from his degrees, fined £2,000, sentenced to the pillory and to lose both his ears. Under great pressure from his friends – his father no doubt had useful connections – the physical mutilation was remitted. But he stayed in prison for over two years before being pardoned, and the sentence was not just *in terrorem*. In the same year Alexander Leighton suffered the tortures which had been designed for Gil, and then languished in prison for ten years, for publishing *Sions Plea against the Prelacie*. This was the first of many savage sentences, including those on Prynne, Burton, Bastwick and Lilburne, for which Laud

---

[1] Le Comte, p. 54. Parker seems to have missed this article.
[2] Laud, VII, p. 18; D. L. Clark, pp. 138–141, 146–7.
[3] Cf. Davenant (1972), pp. 273–4.

was usually held responsible.[1] Milton's revulsion against episcopacy and clerical interference in politics must have been intensified by the Gil case. The line in his sonnet on the new forcers of conscience, 'Clip your phylacteries but baulk your ears', may refer to Gil as well as to Prynne and the others.[2]

We can assume that Milton knew the political views of the loquacious and extrovert Gil: they had 'almost constant conversations' together. Two months before Gil's attack on Buckingham and Charles, Milton confided to him his own fear lest 'the priestly ignorance of a former age may gradually attack our clergy'. Two years later – probably writing to Gil in prison – Milton chose for special praise the latter's poem celebrating a Dutch victory over the Spaniards, and hoped that Gil might have the opportunity of writing something even greater 'if by chance our own affairs [become] at last more fortunate'. Already in his Sixth Prolusion Milton had sneered at Buckingham's foreign policy. There is never the slightest suggestion in his letters to Gil of political disagreement or disapproval: whether or not he supported Gil's seditious sentiments in 1628, he certainly did so later. In 1631–2 Gil published verses and pamphlets on behalf of the Protestant cause and Gustavus Adolphus. In 1639 a poem by him was prefixed to Henry Glapthorne's *The Tragedy of Albertus Wallenstein*. This poem was dated 1634, but the date could refer to Wallenstein's death rather than to Gil's poem. Both in Glapthorne's play and in Gil's poem Wallenstein is referred to as 'the Duke', 'traitor Duke'.[3] Margot Heinemann suggests that Gil may have seen an analogy between Wallenstein, whose assassins claimed to be executing God's sentence, and the Duke of Buckingham.[4] Ultimately Gil turned round and won the favour of Laud and the King sufficiently to succeed his father as High Master of St. Paul's in 1635. His friendship with Milton does not seem to have survived this *volte face*. Gil lived to tell Charles in 1641 that the sentence on Strafford was tragic but just.[5] He was dismissed from St. Paul's in 1640, and died soon after. He may have failed to trim his sails to the new political winds in time.

So two of the people who most impinged on the young Milton were

---

[1] Cf. p. 65 below.
[2] Dorian, p. 260.
[3] *Op. cit.,* Act V, Scene iii.
[4] See her forthcoming book, *Puritanism and the Theatre: Middleton and Opposition Drama.* Glapthorne is an obscure character. He tried at first to win courtly patronage, but by 1642 he was writing elegies on the deaths of the Earls of Bedford and Manchester, more popular with middle-of-the-road Parliamentarians. Some time before 1639 he had been in prison, but we do not know for what (Glapthorne, 1643, Sig. B 4v, C 2; 1639, p. 15).
[5] A. Gil, *Decollato Comite Straffordio, in Gratulatoria Dicata . . . Carolo Regi* (1641). Gil's *Parerga* (1632) has introductory poems by Tom May and others.

relatively radical. Gil was perhaps not very stable, but eloquent, witty and outrageous in his political views: Young a dour, solid martyr for convictions which Milton would leave behind in the forties but which represented in the twenties and thirties a fundamental critique of the existing order. The third influence, the greatest of the three, is similar – Charles Diodati. Their friendship probably dates from Milton's schooldays at St. Paul's. The Diodatis were an immensely talented family, originally from Lucca. They found the religious and political atmosphere of Counter-Reformation Italy stifling, and in various exciting ways they escaped into exile. The main branch settled in Geneva, where Giovanni Diodati was Professor of Hebrew and an internationally famous theologian – liberal by Genevan standards. He translated the Bible into Italian and attended the Synod of Dort in 1618–19 as Genevan representative. He was an important figure in international Protestant circles, secretly revisiting Italy several times and travelling to Holland and England. He collaborated closely with the English Ambassador to Venice, Sir Henry Wotton, in attempts to win the republic for the Protestant cause in 1608. He was a patron of John Dury's attempts at Protestant reunion.[1] Diodati's *Annotations* on the Bible were translated into English in 1643, and were selling excellently in London by the following year. In 1645 Milton referred to Diodati as a theologian 'of best note', although by that time Diodati had expressed Royalist sympathies.[2]

Another branch of the Diodatis settled in Paris: we shall meet them later.[3] Charles Diodati's father, Theodore, came to England about 1598, and for a refugee prospered remarkably. He became tutor to Sir John, second Lord Harington, an intimate friend of the heir to the throne, Prince Henry. When Harington died in 1612 Richard Stock preached his funeral sermon. Theodore then became physician to Henry's sister Elizabeth, until she left England on marrying the Elector Palatine in 1613. With this flying start Diodati went on to a very successful medical career, claiming in 1621 to be as good a man as the President of the College of Physicians. His will was witnessed in 1649 by (probably) Major-General Skippon, a member of the Council of State which had just appointed Milton Secretary for Foreign Tongues.[4]

---

[1] Dorian, pp. 99, 169–70, 248–50, 264; Turnbull, p. 149. For Wotton and Dury see pp. 53–4 and 146–8 below.

[2] Baillie (1775), II, p. 22; cf. p. 70; *C.P.W.*, II, p. 615.

[3] See p. 54 below.

[4] Dorian, pp. 236, 297; G. N. Clark, I, p. 190. The other witness was Colonel William Rolf, Skippon's son-in-law. He was an ex-Agitator, 'a fellow of low extraction', who had been one of Charles I's jailers in the Isle of Wight in 1648 and was accused of plotting to assassinate him. 'Murderous Rolf, as lieger-hangman feed', Bishop Henry King called him (Clarendon, V, pp. 457–60; Saintsbury, III, p. 264).

The circle around Prince Henry included many internationally minded radical Protestants, who were critical of James I's pacific foreign policy. After Henry's premature and much lamented death in 1612, the husband of his sister Elizabeth became the key figure in this international grouping. His acceptance of the throne of Bohemia in 1619 precipitated the Thirty Years War: throughout the sixteen-twenties and -thirties the Queen of Bohemia was the toast of the Parliamentarian and patriotic opposition, her exile and the defeat of her cause standing evidence of the ineffectiveness of the government. It is inconceivable that Milton did not discuss these matters with Charles Diodati as well as with Alexander Gil. Diodati's family was almost a symbol of international Protestantism, and knowing them must have contributed to Milton's bitter criticisms of the Stuarts' failure to live up to the ideals of Protestant patriotism and internationalism. These ideals were accepted not only by the Parliamentary opposition but also by devotees of the Winter Queen of Bohemia like Sir Henry Wotton, a friend of Lord Harington. The international connections of the Diodatis must have been of great use to Milton in his careful preparations for his Italian journey.[1]

We can only speculate on Charles Diodati's influence over Milton before his premature death in 1638. Milton clearly adored him more than he ever adored any human being except possibly his second wife. Diodati was slightly younger than the poet, but he went up to the university earlier and started a career earlier. He had all the ebullient charm of Alexander Gil and much more sense. Clearly he took the lead and Milton followed: the latter developed slowly as long as Diodati lived. His death during Milton's absence in Italy was a terrible blow. The *Epitaphium Damonis* was the first poem Milton took the trouble to get separately printed. In Latin because of the continental connections of the Diodatis, it marks some sort of a turning point and re-dedication of Milton. One of the most extraordinary passages which Milton ever wrote is the conclusion of *Epitaphium Damonis* in which he envisaged the dead Charles enjoying Bacchic orgies in heaven.[2] Earlier lines suggest that he may have seen himself as married to Diodati (65 – 'innube'). Psychologists may speculate on the significance for Milton of what looks like a platonic homosexual passion (cf. Milton's sexual confidences to Diodati in Elegy I).[3] What is its

---

[1] Dorian, pp. 47–8. It may have been through the Diodatis that Milton received his invitation to write *Arcades* and *Comus* – though there are many other possibilities (*ibid.*, pp. 145–50, 268). See pp. 43–44 below.

[2] C. and F., p. 283. Cf. pp. 58, 121 below.

[3] John Carey reminds me, however, that in the Sixth Elegy Milton encouraged Diodati to dance and mix with girls.

relation to the ideal of chastity in *Comus*? Is there any connection between Diodati's death and Milton's decision to marry at the age of thirty-three? What is the relation between Milton's high standards of matrimonial compatibility and this earlier quasi-sexual relationship? Did the first Mrs. Milton suffer for her inability to fill Diodati's place? We can neither answer these questions nor refrain from asking them. What we do know is that, unlike Young and Gil, Diodati did not live to get left behind as Milton grew more and more radical in the sixteen-forties: his memory remained sweet and pure.

II Cambridge

Milton went up to Christ's College, Cambridge, in 1625. It was an unhappy period in the university's history. On the one hand government and bishops were trying to bring both universities and their colleges under tighter control. Since the universities trained parsons – the opinion-formers – and were also attended by many gentlemen – the ruling class – control seemed more and more necessary as tensions increased in church and state. On the other hand, the universities were failing to keep pace with intellectual developments in the country, and greater control from on top tended to make for conformity, playing safe, careerism, idleness. But among some younger dons and undergraduates hostility to traditional scholasticism was accompanied by receptivity to new ideas. Milton, as was to be expected, soon aligned himself with the reformers.

Milton's allusions to Cambridge and its teaching are uniformly critical, in sharp contrast to his respectful references to Young and Gil. Not that Christ's was an obscurantist college, as colleges went. It had a solid Puritan tradition. William Perkins (Fellow 1584–94), who died six years before Milton was born, was by general consent the leading English Puritan theologian, one of the few Englishmen with a continental reputation. Other distinguished theologians were William and Laurence Chaderton and Edward Dering in the early years of Elizabeth's reign; Hugh Broughton (Fellow 1572–8), Andrew Willett, the hammer of the papists (Fellow 1583–8), Arthur Hildersham (M.A. 1584), Francis Johnson the separatist (Fellow 1584 till his expulsion in 1589), George Downham the Ramist (Fellow 1585–1616), Samuel Ward (Scholar 1592–5), John Smyth the Se-Baptist, Francis Johnson's pupil (Fellow – probably – 1594–8), Thomas Taylor (Fellow 1599–1604), Paul Baynes (Fellow 1600–4). This was a very radical collection of Puritans. Greatest of all Perkins's successors was William Ames, undergraduate and Fellow of Christ's

(1602–10), who was suspended by the Vice-Chancellor for preaching against 'licence' in Cambridge colleges during the ten days' Christmas saturnalia. His theology, acclaimed by Thomas Young in *Dies Dominica*, was to be one of the starting points for Milton's *De Doctrina Christiana*.

Puritanism and poetry went together at Christ's. Sir Philip Sidney was followed by Sir John Harington, translator of Ariosto, both favourites of Milton's headmaster, and by Francis Quarles, cup-bearer to Elizabeth of Bohemia (John Dively, Secretary to the Queen of Bohemia, was also a Christ's man) and John Cleveland, 1627–32. Among Milton's contemporaries were Humphrey Otway, father of the dramatist, Charles Hotham, translator of Boehme, and Luke Robinson, both of whom we shall meet again, and Samuel Torshell, Puritan divine, a friend of Stock's who published and amplified his posthumous works. Torshell was the author of *The Womans Glorie* (1645), which Milton no doubt read. Of the Fellows in Milton's time the most distinguished was Joseph Mede (Fellow 1614–38), who was thought at one time 'to look too much to Geneva'.[1] Mede studied mathematics as a preparation for divinity, and was a great chronological scholar of the school which extends from John Napier through Thomas Brightman to Isaac Newton. Mede's *Key of the Revelation* (published in Latin in 1627) could not be translated into English under the Laudian censorship. But in 1643 a committee of the House of Commons ordered it to be printed in a translation made by a Member of Parliament, with Preface by William Twisse, Prolocutor of the Assembly of Divines. Mede believed that the Pope was Antichrist, and had a carefully worked-out chronological scheme of his decline and fall, from the Waldensians to the seventeenth century. Mede was cautious about giving precise dates for the end of the world, but he expected it between 1625 and 1716, with 1654 and 1670 as possibilities.[2] His timetable was influential among Presbyterian and Independent divines, and almost certainly contributed to Milton's belief that Christ's coming was 'shortly expected', as well as to his interest in the Waldenses.[3]

We do not know that Milton was ever taught by Mede. We do know that Mede's pupils were introduced to authors like the mathematicians Recorde, Digges and Hariot, to Sidney, to Sir Thomas Smith (whose *Commonwealth of England* was a favourite of Milton's), to Ramus (whose *Logic* – dominant at Cambridge in his day – Milton adapted and amplified in his own *Art of Logic*), to Purchas (briefly rector of All Hallows in 1626,

---

[1] *C. and C.*, p. 270.
[2] Cooper, XVIII, p. 360; XIX, p. 30.
[3] C. Hill (1971), pp. 27–8, 39; cf. chapter 22 below.

whose writings form the basis of Milton's *Brief History of Moscovia*), to Bacon and Alsted; and that Mede put a special emphasis on cosmography. We also know from Mede's correspondence that in the sixteen-twenties he warmly supported Parliament against the Duke of Buckingham. In the next decade he was wary about committing himself to any views of which the government and in particular Laud were likely to disapprove.[1]

Another Fellow of Christ's in Milton's time was Robert Gell (1623–39), who probably married Milton to his third wife in 1663. Like Mede, like Milton, Gell anticipated the Second Coming in the near future. He was well known later as a patron of astrology, a Familist who was critical of Ranters, a defender of liberty of the press who in the dangerous year 1661 petitioned the House of Lords in favour of toleration.[2] Gell's name reminds us of another tradition at Christ's: it was a great centre of Cabbalistic studies. Henry Broughton, Joseph Mede and Henry More (one of the Fellows of Christ's College who accepted Parliamentary rule in 1644) were experts in the Kabbalah. Milton may already have become acquainted with such studies at St. Paul's, since the elder Alexander Gill was interested. So were Du Bartas and Robert Fludd, both of whom Milton almost certainly read at one stage or another; so was Samuel Hartlib, later Milton's friend, who was a correspondent of Mede's.[3]

Early in his Cambridge career Milton had some trouble with the college authorities, the exact nature of which has never been explained. It apparently led to his being rusticated for a short period, and when he came back he changed tutors. He was taken over by Nathaniel Tovey, Ramist son of a friend of the Diodatis.[4] The man with whom Milton had been unable to get on was William Chappell, later made an Irish bishop by Laud's favour. We do not know whether this was an ideological or a personal quarrel. By 1628 Milton had taken a firm stand as a Baconian, a supporter of George Hakewill's defence of the Moderns against the Ancients, a critic of scholasticism and an advocate of more science and more history in the university. 'This unseemly battle of words tends neither to the general good nor to the honour and profit of our country.'[5] Milton was defending

---

[1] H. F. Fletcher, II, pp. 119, 140, 148, 315, 319, 325, 334, 337–50, 557–8, 563–4, 610, 614–15.

[2] C. Hill (1971), pp. 112, 187; K. V. Thomas (1971), p. 377; Turnbull p. 429; C. E. Whiting, p. 319. Gell conformed however and became chaplain to Archbishop Sheldon.

[3] Hirst, pp. 144–54. For Fludd see pp. 110–11, 324–8 below. His step-father, the poet William Alabaster, was also a great Cabbalist.

[4] Dorian, pp. 78, 114–15.

[5] *C.P.W.*, I, p. 246; Third and Seventh Prolusions. A lecturer at All Hallows before Milton's time, Anthony Wootton, had been in trouble with ecclesiastical officialdom in 1604 for defending the Moderns against antiquity. He was a Ramist, a friend of Thomas Gataker, and was accused of being a Socinian.

the thesis of George Hakewill's book within a year of its first publication in 1627. If for no other reason he is likely to have read Hakewill because the latter cited Charles Diodati's father as a physician who had put the Ancients to shame. Some of Milton's earliest Latin poems adopt a political stance, following that of his schoolboy translations of the Psalms. No less than five poems are about Gunpowder Plot, one of them denouncing the papal Antichrist. Although at the age of seventeen Milton wrote conventional Latin elegies on two bishops, the Vice-Chancellor and the university bedel, he never composed poems to royalty. Edward King, his junior contemporary, between 1631 and 1637 contributed to six collections of Latin verse celebrating royal births, marriages, etc.[1]

Some of Milton's undergraduate orations which he printed many years later are difficult to interpret, full of inside jokes and allusions which cannot now be fully understood. Scholars have made very heavy weather of some of Milton's remarks which they take to imply that he was, or had been, unpopular with his contemporaries. I think they are better interpreted as audience-baiting of a kind that fitted the rather rough humour of the occasion.[2] If Milton was called 'the Lady of Christ's', this was not necessarily an unfriendly nickname for a slight, 'fair' and handsome young man: he seems to have remembered it with some satisfaction. More to the point is that Milton's contemporaries called on him to speak at their more riotous functions and that he rose to the occasion with a freedom of vocabulary that shocked nineteenth-century editors.

The scrivener's son sneered at rank, and especially at lords, referred gratuitously to 'Junius Brutus, that second founder of Rome and great avenger of the lusts of kings', and criticized Charles I's foreign policy.[3] In Prolusion V, whose unpromising subject was 'There are no partial Forms in an Animal in addition to the Whole', Milton introduced a totally irrelevant passage about Roman history. This may have been intended to remind his audience of Isaac Dorislaus, the history lecturer recently silenced for using Roman history 'to speak too much for the defence of the liberties of the people', as Joseph Mede's friend Samuel Ward put it on 16 May 1628.[4] For Milton's apparent irrelevance leads up to the conclusion: 'You have been wondering long enough, my hearers, what can be my reason for enlarging on all this: I will tell you. Whenever I consider and reflect

---

[1] Masson, I, pp. 69, 183, 511–12.
[2] C.P.W., I, pp. 268, 290; cf. pp. 218–20, 251, 267–8 – academic jokes. Parker is sensible on this subject (p. 775).
[3] C.P.W., I, pp. 282, 284, 267, 285, 317. 'Lusts' may well refer to Buckingham. See p. 28 above.
[4] Parr, II, p. 393.

upon these events, I am reminded afresh of the mighty struggle which has been waged to save Truth, and of the universal eagerness and watchfulness with which men are striving to rescue Truth, already tottering and almost overthrown, from the outrages of her foes. Yet we are powerless to check the inroads which the vile horde of errors daily makes upon every branch of learning.'[1]

So he leads in to his subject, the scholastic nature of which he admitted to finding distasteful. In the Seventh Prolusion, references to Roman history and Turkish tyranny are followed by a complaint of 'our bad methods of teaching the arts'. It was after he had gone down from Cambridge that Milton sought 'to learn what was new in mathematics and music, then the objects of my special studies'. Like John Wallis at about the same time, he rightly expected to find better mathematics teaching in London than in Cambridge. Both Gils had been proficient mathematicians: the younger published on the subject. In the early sixteen-forties Milton taught his own pupils arithmetic, geometry, trigonometry, and mathematics played a prominent part in the scheme offered in *Of Education*.[2]

From 'our Bacon',[3] whom he regarded as one of 'the greatest and sublimest wits in sundry ages', and perhaps from Hakewill, Milton acquired a belief in the possibility of an almost unlimited improvement in the conditions of material life – so great that it might undo the intellectual consequences of the Fall of Man. This should be the object of education, Milton declared in 1644; though full truth would not be known until Christ's Second Coming. At Cambridge Milton foresaw a time when 'the spirit of man, no longer confined within this dark prison house, will reach out till it fills the whole world and the space far beyond with the expansion of its divine greatness. Then at last most of the chances and changes of the world will be so quickly perceived that to him who holds this stronghold of wisdom hardly anything can happen in his life which is unforeseen or fortuitous. Earth, sea and stars, Mother Nature herself, will obey him.'[4]

Milton's reaction against scholasticism and the Cambridge curriculum helps to explain his later attitude towards the universities. As a Baconian undergraduate he wanted to see less disputation, more science – just as a present-day student might call for fewer written examinations, more

---

[1] *C.P.W.*, I, p. 258.
[2] See chapter 10 below. For Gil see H. F. Fletcher, I, p. 367.
[3] *C.M.*, XI, pp. 24–5.
[4] *C.P.W.*, I, p. 296. For Milton's consciousness of space, see pp. 398-402 below.

sociology, more psychology.[1] After going down from Cambridge Milton undertook a strenuous course in world history as well as pursuing his mathematical interests. By 1641–2 (and no doubt earlier) he had decided that the universities were unsuitable places for training the clergy, and thought that any gifted craftsman could preach better than ungifted academics.[2]

Milton did not escape from his Cambridge training: he had become superlatively good at what he regarded as a tedious game. The structure of an academic disputation underlies *L'Allegro* and *Il Penseroso, Comus* and *Paradise Regained*. And though Milton jeered at the atmosphere in which refusal to accept the authority of Aristotle was tantamount to heresy,[3] his own thought – especially on politics – remained very Aristotelian. Probably at Cambridge he acquired an interest in astronomy and astrology. The natural concomitant of an interest in science for Milton's generation was the Hermetic philosophy, to which he seems also to have been attracted at Cambridge. He may have read Robert Fludd at this time, the fashionable synthesizer of Hermeticism and modern science; he almost certainly did so later.[4]

In December 1631 Milton wrote

> How soon hath time the subtle thief of youth
> > Stolen on his wing my three and twentieth year!
> > My hasting days fly on with full career,
> But my late spring no bud or blossom sheweth.

The complaint anticipates Schiller's

> Drei und zwanzig Jahre
> Und nichts für die Unsterblichkeit getan![5]

But Milton's conclusion, unlike the romantic poet's, was that time and the will of heaven were leading him to a significant future:

> > If I have grace to use it so,
> As ever in my great task-master's eye.

III Hammersmith and Horton, 1632–8

The years from 1632 to 1638 are in one sense well documented, in another sense rather mysterious. From about 1635 we know in considerable detail

---

[1] For Bacon's influence on Milton as historian, see Bryant, pp. 27–9.
[2] *C.P.W.*, I, pp. 247, 718–20, 854–6, 923, 934; cf. Darbishire, p. 169. See chapter 8 below.
[3] *C.P.W.*, I, p. 252.
[4] See pp. 110-11 below.
[5] Schiller, *Don Carlos*, Act I, Scene ii.

what Milton was reading. In *Comus* (1634) and *Lycidas* (1638) and in his poem to his father we have indications of Milton's intention to dedicate himself to poetry. A carefully planned programme of reading would fill the gaps which, he well knew, had been left by Cambridge. He aimed at something like universal knowledge. But at his internal development during this six-year period biographers have to guess.

This used to be spoken of as 'the Horton period', but we now know that the first three years were spent in the elder Milton's country house in the suburban village of Hammersmith. Nor was Horton itself, in the Buckinghamshire woodlands, quite the escapist rural retreat which some romantics have depicted, on the false assumption that *L'Allegro* and *Il Penseroso* were written there.[1] As early as 1614 Michael Drayton noted that 'the Chiltern country' was 'beginning . . . to want wood' – deforested by James I despite the growing fuel famine. It was not in Horton that

> the rude axe with heaved stroke
> Was never heard the nymphs to daunt
> Or fright them from their hallowed haunt.
> (*Il Penseroso*)

Horton was an industrial village. In the year the Miltons moved to Horton the owner of a paper-mill there was presented to the ecclesiastical court for working his mill on the Sabbath throughout the year. He paid wages so low that they had to be supplemented by poor relief to the extent of £7 5s 0d a week. Paper-making was an unpopular industry: it depended on rags, which were alleged to import the plague. In 1626 there had been 34 plague deaths at Horton; in 1637, the year in which Milton's mother died, 14 out of 31 deaths there were ascribed to the plague.[2]

Horton was a large parish, which included the chapelry of Colnbrook a mile away from the village. Robert Fludd the Hermetic philosopher seems to have been living there in the sixteen-thirties or earlier.[3] Colnbrook was something of a radical centre. In 1634 Joan Hoby was in trouble there for saying 'that she did not care a pin nor a fart for my Lord's Grace of Canterbury'; she hoped that she would live to see the Archbishop hanged. In the following year the town received a new charter – which meant that it was brought under closer government control. The first mayor died of a surfeit of drink. In 1646 Thomas Edwards described the heretic John Hall of Henley as 'sometime of Colnbrook'.

---

[1] 'Procul urbano strepitu' in *Ad Patrem* must refer to Hammersmith rather than Horton, if the critics are right to date it before 1635.
[2] *Victoria County History of Buckinghamshire*, II, pp. 106, 111; III, p. 282; Summers, pp. 208–9.
[3] Fludd, p. 117.

Colnbrook was one of the places visited by the Digger emissaries in 1650 in quest of financial and moral support for their communist colony on St. George's Hill.[1] The class divisions which the Lady in Milton's *Comus* denounced so fiercely in 1634 would have been found in the parish of Horton as well as in the City of London.

The vast amount of reading, especially in history, that Milton got through at Hammersmith and Horton stood him in good stead for the rest of his life; he drew on it both for his prose pamphlets and for the great poems. His father observed, in a not entirely complimentary spirit, that he had kept John till the age of thirty. The poet admitted the justice of the charge; he referred later to the obligations incurred by living so long off the sweat of other men's labours. Milton's later rejection (in *Areopagitica*) of a fugitive and cloistered virtue may sound like a condemnation of the Hammersmith-Horton period. But we should not see these years, even in retrospect, as an escapist interlude. In 1629 Milton had been prepared to sign the three Articles of the Church of England, in order to take his degree. By so doing he accepted the royal supremacy, agreed that the Book of Common Prayer contained nothing contrary to the Word of God and declared that the Thirty-nine Articles were agreeable to the Word of God. But within three or four years he had decided that he could not take up a career as parson of the Church of England. It was no doubt out of pride as well as moral revulsion that he refused to 'subscribe slave and take an oath withal'.[2] In these years he was consciously and deliberately preparing himself to be the poet who would speak to and for the English nation.

So various influences combined to push Milton in a radical direction. From his father he learnt that authority – even parental authority – could be disobeyed. From his parents (probably), from Richard Stock and Thomas Young certainly, he learnt to be critical of the episcopal state church. In Young he admired the courage which led an opponent of the bishops to prefer exile and poverty to submission. From the younger Gil Milton heard a great deal of criticism of court and government. Milton was expressing hostility towards monarchy while still a schoolboy. From the elder Gil he learnt that reason had a place in religious discussion; he also acquired from him a keen linguistic patriotism and a respect for the 'Puritan' line of poets from Spenser to Wither. At Cambridge he came to feel a modern-style contempt for the old-fashioned curriculum and

---

[1] *W.T.U.D.*, pp. 24, 101–2; Gyll, pp. 250, 283; T. Edwards, III, p. 171.
[2] *C.P.W.*, I, p. 823; C. Hill (1956), p. 215; *S. and P.* p. 45.

teaching methods: we may assume that he was already familiar with
Bacon, Hakewill and Dorislaus as well as with Fludd and the Hermetic
tradition. Milton was aware of a crisis in the universities, one form of
which was the conflict between the Ancients and the Moderns. He was
also aware of a crisis in literature and the arts, of a religious crisis caused
by the Laudian régime. During the sixteen-thirties he may have come to
see all these as one crisis.

Chapter 4

Comus and *Lycidas*

> I find it impossible for a prince to preserve the state in quiet unless he hath such an influence upon churchmen, and they such a dependence on him, as may best restrain the seditious exorbitances of ministers' tongues.
>
> J. Gauden, *Eikon Basilike* (1649). Believed by contemporaries to be by Charles I

I New values

The conflict of cultures in England sprang from the appearance of new value systems. The rank and file of European Protestantism came from great cities – Strasbourg, Geneva, Amsterdam, La Rochelle, London – and from rural industrial areas like Essex, Somerset or the West Riding of Yorkshire. Great aristocrats used the movement; many gentlemen adhered to it from conviction or self-interest; but its mass support came from merchants and artisans, the middling sort. Economic developments – greater prosperity, better housing, more privacy – led to the household, the home emerging as the centre of a new middle-class culture. The recently invented craft of printing and Protestant translations of the Bible catered for the needs of this new culture: literacy, education and Protestantism expanded together. In England, Puritans especially concerned themselves with spreading London's ways of thinking into the dark corners of the north, Wales and the south-west, the Catholic areas which were also to be Royalist areas during the Civil War. W. K. Jordan has studied the charitable foundations through which rich merchants tried to extend the civilization of London into the outlying areas – by providing schools and scholarships, preaching, apprenticeships for godly youths, marriage portions for virtuous spinsters, etc., etc. And William Haller has convincingly demonstrated the build-up by Puritan preachers over the fifty years before 1640 of a middle-class public convinced that God spoke

41

directly to their consciences.[1] Truth is in the inward parts: externals in religion were rejected, whether they took the form of sacred church buildings or of a mediating priesthood: all such things were forms of idolatry. Men brought up on Bible-reading reacted vehemently from anything that savoured of idol-worship, which distracts men and women from communion with God.[2]

The preachers were consciously organizing middle-class men and women against the concept of hierarchy, itself an import into Christianity that reflected the social realities of mediaeval agrarian society. For the middle-class Puritan God seemed a better lord than any peer of the realm; he spoke directly and familiarly to his dependants: the duty to obey God was greater than any traditional social obligation. The vehemence with which Elizabethan exponents of orthodoxy defend hierarchy shows that it is already under attack: as the vehemence with which gold is denounced shows that money is beginning to talk a newly authoritative language.

The young Milton was a sturdy Protestant, but we find him writing epitaphs on the high-flying Bishop Lancelot Andrewes and praising the sage and serious doctrine of virginity. Perhaps we should think of him at this stage not in association with a 'Puritan' opposition but with those like George Herbert, who left the court for a country living, or Nicholas Ferrar, who withdrew from the City to his Anglican nunnery at Little Gidding. Ferrar believed the Pope to be Antichrist no less than did Milton: George Herbert spoke of religion under Archbishop Laud as

> on tiptoe in our land
> Ready to pass to the American strand.

A man like Peter Sterry, later associated with Milton, resigned his Cambridge fellowship some time in the sixteen-thirties in order to take refuge in a private chaplainship to Robert Greville, Lord Brooke, soon to emerge as one of the leaders of the Parliamentarian radicals, much admired by Milton.[3] Others emigrated to the Netherlands or to New England. At least one of the latter did so only after 'having preached much'; but 'seeing the danger of the times he changed his profession of divinity into physic'.[4] Milton in retrospect spoke of himself as 'church-outed by the prelates', and biographers have recognized that he could never have 'subscribed slave' to the Laudian régime.[5] But the depth of his revulsion

---

[1] Jordan (1959), and related works, *passim*; Haller (1938), *passim*.
[2] See chapter 12 below.
[3] Pinto (1934), p. 11.
[4] *Winthrop Papers*, p. 397.
[5] *C.P.W.*, I, p. 823.

calls for emphasis. It perhaps needed the crisis of the sixteen-forties to convince Milton that directly political solutions were both necessary and possible. Yet in the later thirties his Commonplace Book shows him aware of a religious, political and cultural crisis. It was already, its editor tells us, 'pointedly anticipating' the 'revolutionary ideas of *Areopagitica*, the divorce pamphlets and *The Tenure of Kings and Magistrates*'.[1]

II *Comus*

The court for Milton from the late sixteen-twenties suggested 'the lusts of Kings', the homosexual relationship of James I to Buckingham, to which the younger Gil had openly referred in the poem which got him into trouble.[2] Buckingham continued to be a favourite of Charles I, although his family had papist associations. A major scandal of the early thirties concerned Lord Castlehaven, who was executed for buggery, for conniving at the rape of his wife by a servant who was also his lover, and for the prostitution of his daughter-in-law to another servant. Castlehaven was reputed to be a papist. Milton would certainly be aware of this *cause célèbre*; but it was brought forcibly to his notice when he was asked to write a masque for the Earl of Bridgwater, whose wife was Lady Castlehaven's sister.

Milton's *Masque at Ludlow Castle*, his most ambitious work so far, was produced in 1634, published in 1637. The occasion celebrated the reunion of the Egerton family at Ludlow, whither the head of the family, the Earl of Bridgwater, had in 1633 proceeded as President of the Council in the Marches of Wales. Lady Alice Egerton and her two brothers were already enthusiastic masquers. Why Milton was asked to write the script for the masque we do not know. He was an unknown young man of twenty-five, with no experience of writing in the genre. The occasion would seem to call for someone better known. But the Egertons had Puritan leanings, and were patrons of the Spenserian line of poets. Relations of the family borrowed money from the elder Milton, who seems to have known the Earl. In 1613 the scrivener had signed a presentation epistle to Bridgwater, prefixed to Sir William Leighton's *The Teares or Lamentations of a Sorrowfull Soule*, and twenty-two years later he may have rented his house in Horton from the Earl.[3] Other clients of the elder Milton's were related to the Countess of Derby, who married the Earl of Bridgwater's father. She too

---

[1] *Ibid.*, I, p. 10. See p. 166 below.
[2] See pp. 28–9 above.
[3] Gyll, p. 235.

patronized the Spenserians. It was for her that the younger John wrote *Arcades*, performed (perhaps in 1633) at Harefield, only ten miles from Horton. The Egertons resided at Ashridge, Hertfordshire, a further fifteen miles north of Harefield. Alternatively, Milton may have received his invitation through Henry Lawes, who composed the music for the masque. Lawes was music teacher to Lady Alice Egerton, and would certainly have been known to the elder John Milton. Or the connection may have been made through the Diodatis.[1]

The masque is a simple fairy story. The Lady Alice gets separated from her two brothers in a 'drear wood' on the way to Ludlow. She is vainly tempted by the magician Comus, rescued, and the family is reunited. It is likely that the theme of the masque would either be given to Milton, or would be worked out by him in consultation with the family and Lawes. Even Ben Jonson did not have it all his own way when he wrote a masque: the young Milton certainly would not. In a fascinating article Barbara Breasted has suggested some reasons why the theme of resistance to temptation by a lady might have been chosen. The Castlehaven scandal of 1631–2 was still fresh in everyone's memory. Lady Alice, who acted the Lady in Milton's masque, was the niece of the raped Lady Castlehaven and cousin of the prostituted daughter. The theme of chastity, of virtue resisting temptation, may well have been suggested to Milton: one object of the masque would be to proclaim the spotless virtue of the Egerton ladies, unlike their too notorious relatives.[2]

But how much more than the general theme was suggested, how free a hand Milton was given, how far the Lady in *Comus* speaks for him, we do not know. In his Sixth Elegy he recommended chastity for a young epic poet. But at Cambridge he was on one occasion assigned the task of defending learning against ignorance when he would have preferred the other side: a scholar could argue either way.

One ingenious suggestion is that Milton was drawing on the imagery of Revelation 12, of the lady wandering in the wilderness, who figured in many mediaeval and early Protestant plays down to John Foxe.[3] In these plays the Lady, who regularly has two attendants, personifies the true church, a virgin but a virgin destined for marriage to Christ.[4] On this interpretation Comus represents Antichrist, who in Foxe's *Christus*

---

[1] See pp. 30–32 above.
[2] Breasted, pp. 201–24.
[3] Scoufos, pp. 113–42.
[4] For analogous images of a reformed church represented by a chaste woman, cf. Yates (*Shakespeare*, 1975), pp. 5, 55, 75.

Triumphans seduces the whole world with his 'Circean cups of luxury'.[1] Circe, 'daughter of the sun', was Comus's mother.[2] Her chalice turned men into beasts: Antichrist put the mark of the Beast on the foreheads of his followers. The brothers, A.-L. Scoufos suggests, personify the clergy, who have neglected their duty of protecting the church. When mobilized by the good daemon their militant action secures a partial victory, but Comus escapes and the Lady remains immobilized (though her mind is free) until Sabrina releases her. Sabrina, who was deified after committing suicide in order to avoid rape, is a final rejection of the Castlehaven connection. She may, if we wish to stress the specifically Christian content of the masque, represent divine grace or the water of baptism, though the later Milton would not have wished to attach too much significance to the outward ceremony of baptism. Sabrina is also a necessary piece of machinery to bring the masque to a close by reuniting the children with their parents in the precise geographical location of Ludlow Castle by the Severn.

A masque appears at first sight rather a surprising thing for a Puritan to write – if we can properly call Milton a Puritan at this time. Masques were associated with the court, where they were costly and extravagant spectacles, the machinery often as important as the verse. And the expenditure was for one or very few performances: conspicuous waste was essential to a masque. So was social snobbery: the object of a masque was to flatter the great personages who deigned to participate. Ben Jonson tried to write masques with significant content, but he failed to educate his courtly audience.[3] We recall his onslaught on Inigo Jones for killing poetry in the interests of spectacle:

> Painting and carpentry are the soul of masque!
> Pack with your piddling poetry to the stage!
> This is the money-get mechanic age![4]

We can guess where Milton would stand in that controversy. He may have intended in *Comus* to succeed where Johnson had failed. He never wrote another masque, and the genre itself did not survive the court which had brought it into existence.

---

[1] Archbishop Parker and Ascham made the equation Circe-Antichrist-Rome as well as Foxe (Scoufos, pp. 131, 142). Circe was also associated with atheism in renaissance mythology (D. P. Walker, 1972, p. 149). In *Eikonoklastes* and *The Defence of the People of England* Milton linked her with political servitude (*C.P.W.*, III, p. 688; IV, p. 518).

[2] William Browne also made Circe daughter of the sun, though apparently only Milton made her Comus's mother (C. and F., pp. 178–9).

[3] Orgel, *passim*.

[4] Jonson, *Poems*, p. 304.

There is another mystery about the poem. The masque was performed in 1634. In 1637 it was published by Henry Lawes, with no mention of Milton, though with some additions to his text, clearly made by him. Milton did not own the poem until 1645. He was not usually backward in such matters. Why was his name not given in 1637? Parker has speculated that John Milton senior objected to his son writing anything so courtly as a masque, and that *Ad Patrem* is the poet's self-defence and attempt to convince his father of the propriety of this kind of poetry.[1] If we had any real evidence of paternal hostility, this would be plausible: but we have none. Another suggestion is that between 1634 and 1637 some breach had occurred between Milton and the Egertons. It has even been argued from the passages added in 1637 that Milton had perhaps fallen in love with the Lady Alice and got a little above his station.[2] Again this is not impossible: but a great many bricks have to be made with very little straw. Certainly the Egertons never again patronized Milton,[3] though the fact that the masque was published suggests that it had not dissatisfied them. John Egerton, the younger brother in *Comus*, subsequently wrote on his copy of Milton's *Defensio* 'the book should be burnt, the author hanged.' But that was after a civil war, in which the Egertons had been Royalists, and after the execution of their King, which Milton's book was defending. It looks as though some disagreement occurred: perhaps Milton was snubbed, though not necessarily for raising his eyes to the Lady Alice. He would not be likely to take kindly to the role of hired hack writer, which is no doubt how his patrons saw him. But Milton would not have published the masque with his other poems in 1645 if he had changed his mind about the genre.

Comus is in one respect like Satan in the earlier books of *Paradise Lost*: his character is so well drawn that he steals the show from the Lady in a way that Milton may not have intended. The Lady is almost as unexciting as God in *Paradise Lost*. But we must not break butterflies on wheels. Whoever played Comus was almost certainly the best actor in the masque: the Lady and her brothers were amateurs, and children at that. *Comus* is a dramatic dialogue, recalling the debates in which Milton was accustomed to take part at Cambridge. In such a debate, as in *L'Allegro* and *Il Penseroso*, one gave the best arguments one could find to both protagonists – as the prim Samuel Richardson was to make out a surprisingly good case for his Lovelace. Certainly Milton had conversed with libertines. 'What hath

---

[1] Parker, pp. 125–8.
[2] Saillens (1964), pp. 51–5; (1959), pp. 100–11.
[3] Unless, as John Carey points out to me, *Arcades* should be dated later than *Comus*.

night to do with sleep?' ''Tis only daylight that makes sin' (lines 122, 126) are as accurately epigrammatic as anything Bunyan put into the mouth of his Mr. Badman, a recollection of the days when he moved in Ranter circles.

It may be right to hear some political overtones, provided we do not assert them too confidently. The suggestion that there is a covert attack on the courtly cult of Platonic love[1] may be reinforced by the Castlehaven connection; Milton and his patrons would be anxious to differentiate their position from papist worship of the Virgin Mary or of Henrietta Maria, as well as from the practices of the papist Castlehaven. There is indeed a certain class-consciousness in *Comus*. The Lady's aristocratic assumptions about the morals and manners of the 'loose unlettered hinds' (173) are rebuked by the subsequent action. Courtesy 'oft is sooner found in lowly sheds ... than ... courts of princes' (321–4). She ultimately goes out of her way to plead for greater economic equality:

> If every just man that now pines with want
> Had but a moderate and beseeming share
> Of that which lewdly-pampered Luxury
> Now heaps upon some few with vast excess ...
> The giver would be better thanked.
>
> (767–74)

A masque is a light-hearted entertainment. Critics who warn us against over-reading the text, against worrying about pseudo-problems, may well be right.[2] We should accept the magic as magic, and not try to press too deep allegorical meanings. We may be encouraged in this by the divergences among those scholars who think they have a key to the details of the allegory.[3] But some things may be said about the spirit which informs the poem. It is, in James Maxwell's words, about virtue rather than specifically about virginity.

> Virtue may be assailed but never lost,
> Surprised by unjust force but not enthralled.

That was the Elder Brother. The Lady herself tells Comus:

> Fool, do not boast,
> Thou canst not touch the freedom of my mind.

---

[1] See pp. 63, 179–80 below.
[2] Maxwell ('Comus'), pp. 376–81; Adams, pp. 28, and *passim*.
[3] Demaray, pp. 88–91. Moly has been variously interpreted as grace, temperance, human philosophy; haemony as Christian revelation or conscience (Adams, p. 14; Klein, pp. 43–5).

'Love virtue, she alone is free' is the conclusion. When the poem was published in 1637, Milton drew special attention (line 996) to the addition glorifying marriage. This new passage (999–1011) celebrates both the earthly love of Venus and Adonis and the heavenly love of Christ for his eternal bride, who is both the church and the individual soul, Psyche. Together she and Cupid beget Youth and Joy. Pleasure is illusory without this freedom, is self-enthralled. The Lady's apparently negative attitude was essential to the preservation of her freedom. In the eternal conflict of good and evil good must win.

> If this fail
> The pillared firmament is rottenness,
> And earth's base built on stubble.
>
> (592–7)[1]

The true church cannot fail, and God will come to the help of men and women when they have done all they can to resist evil. This is a recurrent Miltonic theme. Christ on the pinnacle of the temple, Samson clutching the pillars, both receive a miraculous accession of power. They illustrate the conclusion of *Comus*:

> Or if virtue feeble were
> Heaven itself would stoop to her.[2]

In the masque there is no problem of moral choice, only confidence and exultation in being on the right side. Haller rightly links the theme of the Masque with the preachers' exhortation to spiritual wayfaring and warfaring.[3] The Lady in *Comus* never seems in the least likely to succumb to the wiles of the tempter; very different from Eve in *Paradise Lost*.[4] Milton was not ready to write *Paradise Lost* in 1634. He too had been called 'the Lady' at Christ's; and his mind was still filled with ideas of romantic chivalry, of knightly gallantry: his epic aspirations long circled round King Arthur. And yet there is continuity, for all the greater sadness of Milton's later poetry: *Paradise Regained* lacks the gorgeous plenitude of *Comus*, the sense of the pulsing richness of nature; but its theme is analogous, the serene rejection of temptation, not a negative attitude but a sense of the irrelevance, the emptiness, of pleasure that is separated from virtue.[5]

---

[1] See pp. 352–3 below.
[2] Frye (1970), p. 151. Cf. p. 364 below.
[3] Haller (1938), pp. 318–19.
[4] Wedgwood, p. 113.
[5] Maxwell, 'Comus'.

In *Comus* Milton creates what I have called the Robinson Crusoe situation. The hero – or heroine – is isolated from society, to face an ordeal alone.[1] This is characteristic of the Puritan-individualist tradition, from Milton to *Clarissa Harlowe*. Adam and Eve in Paradise, Jesus in the wilderness, Samson isolated by blindness and finally alone in the temple, Bunyan's Christian deserting wife and children: all face their destiny alone with God. They are as solitary as Hobbist man before Leviathan set up a law-abiding community.

Milton used the occasion of *Comus* to try to bring order into what he saw as the moral chaos that court and papists were bringing upon England. As against the Inns of Court wits, who combined acceptance of sexual promiscuity with social sneers against the bourgeoisie, Milton aligned himself with the Puritan middle class, on aesthetic as well as moral grounds. It is this, rather than mere controversial opportunism, that made Milton in 1642 criticize Joseph Hall's *Mundus Alter et Idem* because it offered no vision of a better world in which evil would be eradicated: Milton specifically contrasted *Utopia* and *New Atlantis* with Hall's book. Milton's anti-episcopal tracts contain elements of his own Utopian ideals, which Haller has described as 'a society ruled by public opinion, enlightened not only by preachers but by intellectual and moral leaders of all sorts, lay and cleric, above all by poet-prophets like himself'.[2]

III *Lycidas*

Social concern is even more apparent in *Lycidas*. Its occasion was the death by drowning of Edward King on his way to Ireland in 1637. There is no reason to suppose that Milton was particularly fond of King, who had been made a Fellow of Christ's in 1630 – the Fellowship which Milton might have hoped for. But Milton was by this time well known in Cambridge, and especially in his own college, as a poet: whilst still in residence he had turned his hand to elegies on ecclesiastical and university dignitaries. What more natural than that he should be invited to contribute to the memorial volume for his contemporary?

He did not perhaps produce quite what was expected. *Lycidas* is ostensibly a poem about the tragedy of youthful death. Why should Edward King be cut off in his prime whilst others live? The poem calls God's justice in question, not for the last time in Milton's career. But this leads

---

[1] C. Hill (Panther, 1969), pp. 364–5; *W.T.U.D.*, pp. 253, 331–2. Cf. Marx, p. 83; MacCaffrey, pp. 188–94.
[2] *C.P.W.*, I, pp. 880–1; Haller (1938), pp. 339–58, 362–3.

the poet on to ask how important worldly success is, and to assess his own life in the light of King's death. *Lycidas* turns into a tremendous denunciation of the dominant clique in the Church of England, the Laudians.

Here the pastoral tradition stood Milton in good stead. Fulke Greville made it clear that the allegorical form of works like *Arcadia*, 'this representing of virtues, vices, humours, counsels and actions of men in feigned and unscandalous images, is an enabling of freeborn spirits to the greatest affairs of state.'[1] Sidney himself in *The Defence of Poesie* had said 'sometimes under the pretty tales of wolves and sheep [pastoral poetry] can include the whole considerations of wrongdoings and patience.'[2] Spenser did just that in *The Shepheardes Calendar* and *Colin Clouts come home again*. Of *The Faerie Queene* Spenser admitted almost in so many words that 'I chose the history of King Arthur as . . . furthest from the danger of envy and suspicion of present times.' The Spenserians Browne and Wither made a similar use of pastoral. Browne directly anticipates *Lycidas* by his reference to 'The prelate in pluralities asleep / Whilst that the wolf lies preying on his sheep.'[3]

The advantage of the pastoral mode, then, was that sharp criticisms could be made, and the key supplied to those in the know. The innocent would miss the point. The essence of pastoral was ambiguity, something perhaps forgotten by those who continue to labour at the mysteries of *Lycidas*. Thus everybody would know *in general* what Milton meant by 'the grim wolf with privy paw': it meant Rome, popery. But just because this is pastoral, is allegory, it need not mean only Rome. Archbishop Laud too perhaps has some wolfish characteristics? Similarly 'the pilot of the Galilean lake' sounds like St. Peter, the good bishop; but again we can read other things into it. If you object to bishops, the pilot can be the good pastor, the preacher, Jesus Christ even:[4] there is only one identification – the Pope – that we are clearly not intended to make.

We have then to pick up clues as we read. In 1638 *Lycidas* lacked the full introductory note which alerts modern readers. The words 'and by occasion foretells the ruin of our corrupted clergy, then in their height' could not be added until *Lycidas* was reprinted in 1645, after the fall of the bishops. The geographical references

> Where the great vision of the guarded Mount [St. Michael's Mount]
> Looks towards Namancos and Bayonna's hold

---

[1] Greville, pp. 2–3. This work was too hot to publish in Greville's lifetime, and did not appear until 1652.
[2] Sidney, p. 27. Cf. Berkeley, pp. 208–10.
[3] W. Browne I, p. 220.
[4] Berkeley, pp. 75–6.

have a patriotic and anti-Spanish connotation which would not be missed by readers in 1638, when the government was on friendlier terms with Spain than with the Protestant Netherlands. The line

> Look homeward Angel now and melt with ruth,

has been described as 'a cry to St. Michael to look at the state of England'.[1] It has even been suggested that the famous close of the poem,

> At last he rose and twitched his mantle blue:
> To-morrow to fresh woods and pastures new,

may refer to the fact that blue was the colour of the Scottish Covenanters, already in revolt against Charles I by November 1637 when Milton wrote.[2]

And then there is that 'two-handed engine at the door', which 'stands ready to smite once and smite no more'. Critics who complain of Milton's obscurity here forget the censorship. He could hardly say in plain terms either that Laud should be impeached (if the engine equals the two Houses of Parliament); or executed (if it is an axe, or Michael's two-handed sword (*P.L.* VI. 250–1), or a two-handed sceptre, or the 'twa-handed sweard' given to John Knox by the martyr George Wishart (the Scottish emphasis again); or called to account by the two kingdoms of England and Scotland. The two-handed weapon might also be the Old and New Testaments, or the law and the gospel, or 'the sword of his mouth' (Revelation 1:16 2:10) or a shepherd's rod and crook – all various ways of describing the Protestant preaching which Laud was thought to be trying to suppress.[3] (But then why 'smite once and smite no more'? Preaching is surely a cumulative activity?) The whole beauty of the pastoral mode, under a strict censorship, was that meanings could be multiple, slippery, conveying an attitude rather than a precise statement. It was an art of which Milton was to become a master.

Two things about this memorial poem to a clergyman are especially remarkable. First, its fierce anti-clericalism and its covert hostility to the state church.

> That fatal and perfidious bark
> Built in th'eclipse and rigged with curses dark

has plausibly been identified with the Laudian church.[4] In *Comus* the true

---

[1] Woodhouse and Bush, II, pp. 733, 578–81.
[2] But see Berkeley, pp. 34–5, for some more plausible suggestions.
[3] Woodhouse and Bush, II, p. 695; Reesing (1968), pp. 31–49; Berkeley, pp. 78–9.
[4] Berkeley, chapter IV, *passim*, pp. 184, 198, 201. Professor Berkeley is one of the few commentators to stress how much allowance must be made for the fact that Milton was writing under strict censorship (see esp. pp. 148, 184, 205–10).

church of the faithful, though tempted in the wilderness, had the inner resources which enabled it to survive. But in *Lycidas* there is no hope for the visible church in England. Individual souls, like Lycidas, may be saved when the ship founders; but the institution is doomed. This might be the attitude of a radical sectary rather than that of the relatively moderate Puritan that Milton is assumed to have been until the mid-forties. So indeed might Comus's reference to 'the canon laws of our foundation', added to the text in 1637 (line 807). Milton's later virulent hatred for the clergy is anticipated in his passionate denunciation of 'hirelings' who are in the ministry for what they can get out of it, as contrasted with the true pastor:

> such as for their bellies' sake
> Creep and intrude and climb into the fold.
> Of other care they little reckoning make
> Than how to scramble at the shearers' feast,
> And shove away the worthy bidden guest,
> Blind mouths!
> (*Lycidas*. 114–19)[1]

A second point to note is the rather perfunctory part that the consolations of immortality play in the poem (lines 165–81). The forthcoming vengeance on the Church of England and its unworthy pastors interests Milton far more. The poem ends, as so many of Milton's greatest poems will, by reminding us that life on earth goes on. He was always more concerned with this world than the next.[2] *Lycidas* was published in 1638 only over the initials J.M.; Milton owned it for the first time in 1645. By then times had changed.

---

[1] C. Hill (1956) attempts to analyse some of the abuses which Milton expects to be in the minds of his readers.
[2] See pp. 322–3 below.

Chapter 5

Revolution Approaches

> Although I desired also to cross [from Italy, in 1639] to Sicily and Greece, the said tidings of civil war from England summoned me back. For I thought it base that I should travel abroad at my ease for the cultivation of my mind while my fellow-citizens at home were fighting for liberty.
>
> Milton, *Second Defence of the English People* (1654)

1 The Italian journey

The fifteen months of Milton's Italian journey are of crucial importance in his intellectual development. But again we have to guess at their precise significance. Milton's route was wholly conventional: the only unusual thing about his tour was his enthusiastic and flattering reception by intellectuals of the academies in the Italian towns which he visited.[1] We have no certain answer to the perplexing question of why this thirty-year-old middle-class Englishman, with virtually no publication to his credit in English or Latin, was received so ecstatically. Milton prepared very carefully for his tour. He obtained an introduction to Sir Henry Wotton doyen of British diplomats, either through Henry Lawes, with whom Milton had collaborated in *Comus*, or through the Diodatis.[2] Wotton gave him introductions to the English embassy in Paris, and doubtless others.

Wotton had been thrice Ambassador to Venice. In the course of his efforts to win Paolo Sarpi's republic for the Protestant cause he must have worked with Giovanni Diodati, and have made contacts with other liberal elements in Italy, as well as earning the hostility of Spain. Wotton was a keen Baconian. He knew and admired Galileo, whom Sarpi protected and whom Milton visited in Florence. Wotton's liberalism extended to friendship with Isaac Dorislaus, the history lecturer who to Milton's indignation

---

[1] Stoye, pp. 223–5.
[2] See pp. 30–2 above.

had been hounded out of Cambridge by the Laudians for his radical political attitudes. Dorislaus subsequently helped to prepare and manage the trial of Charles I, and was assassinated by Royalists when he was Ambassador of the English republic in the Netherlands.[1]

In Paris Lord Scudamore gave Milton recommendations to English merchants in Italy. But the poet's most important introductions probably came through the Diodatis. Thanks to Charles he must have known the English branch of the family well. In Paris he made contact with Charles's cousin Élie, who was a translator and regular correspondent of Galileo, to whom he may well have given Milton an introduction. Élie moved in intellectual circles in Paris, acting as go-between to Lord Herbert of Cherbury and Gassendi, whose close friend Élie was; he also knew Samuel de Sorbière, Gabriel Naudé and Guy Patin, and was friendly with Peiresc and Campanella. But Milton could have been introduced to Galileo by the friend he made in Florence, Carlo Dati, a former pupil of Galileo's. The great astronomer is the only contemporary to be mentioned in *Paradise Lost*, where he occurs three times.[2] Milton may also have had introductions from London booksellers – one of whom might have been George Thomason, to whom Milton presented copies of his pamphlets in the early sixteen-forties.[3]

In Paris Milton managed to meet Grotius, another correspondent of Galileo's, who had been a contemporary of Charles Diodati's father for several years at Leiden University, and may have maintained contact with him. Milton was to quote Grotius later, and almost certainly read and was influenced by his *Adamus Exul*.[4] He would be aware of his reputation as a suspect Socinian. During his Italian journey Milton paused at Siena, where Faustus Socinus was born, and may have discussed him with his Florentine friends. He spent several days at Lucca, the town from which the Diodatis originated and in whose academic life they were deeply involved.[5]

It has been suggested that the Italian academies, or some of them, acted as secret societies, preserving vestiges of the spirit of intellectual inquiry which had led men like the Diodatis to emigrate. The spirit of Galileo still ruled over Florence, where Milton felt most at home; and Naples, where

---

[1] Arthos, p. 120. In 1629 Wotton had assured Samuel Ward of his love for the person of Dorislaus, though he would not 'espouse his cause' (L. P. Smith, II, pp. 315, 486). See p. 35 above.
[2] Dorian, pp. 340–1; Saillens (1964), pp. 66, 71–3.
[3] Hanford (1964), pp. 59–60.
[4] See pp. 117, 288, 395n. below; J. M. Evans, pp. 213–16.
[5] Dorian, pp. xii, 171–3, 280–1; Arthos, p. 207; MacCallum, p. 95.

Campanella was not forgotten, had a reputation greater than that of any other Italian city for propagating Galileo's views.[1] The academies preserved something of the neoplatonist/humanist tradition: J. V. Andreae received a new sense of mission from his Italian journey of 1612 no less than did Milton a quarter of a century later.[2] Some such suggestion would help to account for the enthusiasm with which a young liberal Englishman with the right introductions was received. It would also explain Milton's favourable reaction to Italy, unexpected since for over a dozen years he had expressed the strong anti-papal sentiments which he was never to abandon. He clearly felt a close intellectual and spiritual kinship with some at least of those whom he met. He must indeed have been especially at home among the Apatisti and Svogliati in Florence – recently founded small private academies, pietistic yet liberal and humanist.

Consider the analogous Italian journey of another English intellectual, John Cook. Cook, like Milton, made the Italian tour 'in his younger years'. Like Milton, he spoke at Rome with so much 'liberty and ability against the corruptions of that court and church' that he had to beat a speedy retreat. Cook then 'resided some months in the house of signior Gio. Diodati' at Geneva.[3] He returned to England to become a leading Independent and legal reformer, prosecutor at Charles I's trial.

Milton recorded later how his learned Italian friends counted him 'happy to be born in such a place of philosophic freedom as they supposed England was, while themselves did nothing but bemoan the servile condition into which learning amongst them was brought'. Such conversations must have started up many lines of thought. In *The Reason of Church Government* Milton announced that if England missed her chance of winning freedom, at least it would not be for lack of his speaking out: he had no intention of merely 'bemoaning' a servile condition, but of fighting against it.[4] When he came to write *Areopagitica* he remembered that he had been greeted in Italy as a citizen of a country of greater intellectual freedom, who had something to give Italian intellectuals as well as to take from them. His contempt for the 'prelatical duncery under which no free and splendid wit can flourish' would be reinforced by contact with men who chafed under an even stricter censorship, and under the corruption of youth and good learning which was attributed by 'many

---

[1] Bailey, pp. 20–2; Arthos, pp. 12, 98, 120; Ginzburg, *passim*; R. J. W. Evans, p. 284. Galileo, the only modern named in *Paradise Lost*, is referred to three times – as well as in *Areopagitica*.
[2] Montgomery, I, p. 87.
[3] Ludlow, II, p. 309. For Cook see pp. 101, 196, 282 below.
[4] *C.P.W.*, I, p. 804.

wise and learned men in Italy' to the Jesuits.[1] Milton already knew of the
two worlds from the Diodatis, who had kept their faith so pure of old in
the Italian fields where popery still ruled.[2] Milton's visit to Lucca followed
by the news of Charles's death must have brought the contrast much more
directly home to him. He would feel the same sort of obligation to his
Italian friends as a West European socialist to-day feels towards dissident
socialist intellectuals in Czechoslovakia. It strengthened his sense of
England's international responsibilities to radicals of other nations,
Catholic as well as Protestant.

Critics have expressed scepticism about the motives which Milton
attributed to himself in the passage cited as epigraph to this chapter. So far
from hurrying back to England in 1639, Milton spent several months on
the return journey. But for our purposes what Milton believed in 1654 is
no less important than his unascertainable motives in 1639. The Bishops'
War of that year brought Charles I's first defeat, and opened up the
possibility of fundamental changes in England too.

The Italian visit must have intensified Milton's *cultural* hatred of popery
and absolutism, which had reduced Italian writing to 'flattery and fustian',
and stiffened his hatred of the Laudian régime, which seemed to him to be
dragging England down to the Italian level. He thought that his Italian
friends had illusions about English liberty; but his interest and pride in
English history seem to have been excited, and he set about writing a full-
dress History of Britain from the earliest times.[3] When freedom really was
established after 1640, Milton was equipped and eager to play his part in
politics. In 1641 he wanted to see Parliament stimulating 'the learned and
affable meeting of frequent academies', in order to 'civilize, adorn and
make decent our minds'.[4] One of the eight authors most frequently cited
in Milton's Commonplace Book was Paolo Sarpi, whose *History of the
Council of Trent* he seems to have been reading in 1643. He quotes and
echoes him regularly, especially in *Areopagitica* and *Eikonoklastes*.[5]

Milton's Italian journey, combined with his historical reading, no doubt
helped him to get English affairs into perspective. His studies of the early
church had fortified all his prejudices against popery, acquired at home
and at school; but Italian intellectuals still had much to offer – the new
astronomy of Galileo, the neo-Hermeticism of Bruno and Campanella, the

[1] *Ibid.*, II, pp. 537–9; I, p. 586.
[2] Cf. p. 86 below.
[3] *C.P.W.*, V, pp. xxvi-xxxvi.
[4] *Ibid.*, I, p. 819.
[5] *Ibid.*, II, pp. 492, 500–3; III, pp. 511, 589; Parker, pp. 802, 883.

mortalism of Padua, the libertinism of Vanini, who denied the divinity of Christ and affirmed the eternity of nature, and of Malatesti. Malatesti was a friend and possibly pupil of Galileo. He dedicated to Milton a series of mildly indecent sonnets, *La Tina*. Biographers have shaken their heads over Malatesti's stupidity in not knowing his Milton better, but perhaps the laugh is on them. Certainly in 1647 Milton sent good wishes to Malatesti via Carlo Dati, which he need not have done if he disapproved of him. He may even have studied Malatesti's sonnets carefully enough to adopt some of his tricks of word-play in the *Second Defence of the People of England*.[1]

II Milton's personality

It still seems to be necessary to combat the view that Milton was a gloomy Puritan. This is part of a general misunderstanding, arising from reading back into the seventeenth century the characteristics, or alleged characteristics, of nineteenth-century nonconformity, and adding the idea that Milton was a 'misogynist', though in fact, as we shall see, his views were on the whole more favourable to women than those of most of his articulate contemporaries. The 'nonconformist' interpretation is quite inappropriate to Milton, the poet and musician who regarded elegance as one of the virtues.[2] All who knew him stressed his 'very cheerful humour', his 'sweet and affable nature', his 'unaffected cheerfulness and civility'; he was 'delightful company, the life of the conversation' and 'very merry'.[3]

Milton was no shy recluse, no sexless scholar. F. W. Bateson, speaking of the poet's letters to Alexander Gil in 1628, rightly describes their tone as 'humorous and self-assured, ... exactly that of "L'Allegro" and "Il Penseroso".'[4] Milton's First Cambridge Elegy celebrates the attractions of British girls. His Fifth Elegy is, in Tillyard's words, 'full of sex', of lustful satyrs ('a god half-goat, a goat half-god'), of beds and bared breasts, of nymphs as anxious for rape as the earth is ready for the embrace of the sun.[5] When he published these elegies in 1645 Milton felt obliged to apologize for them, for reasons which we shall discuss later.[6] The Seventh Elegy describes a hopeless passion, the Italian sonnets probably record an experience with a real but unidentified Italian girl – Emilia – which, however, came to nothing. Even in the Nativity Ode, Parker points out,

---

[1] Singer, pp. 146–7; Kliger, pp. 208–12; Gilbert (1953), pp. 59–60; *C.P.W.*, II, p. 765.
[2] See p. 260 below.
[3] Aubrey, II, p. 67; Parker, pp. 472, 638.
[4] Bateson, p. 160.
[5] Tillyard (1949), p. 32.
[6] See chapter 32 below.

Milton is 'conspicuously and unnecessarily concerned about guilty passion'.[1]

We should not make too much of Milton's erotic imagery. But we should not make too little of it either. It is in part neo-Platonic common form; in part it derives from the Song of Songs and from Revelation. 'To be with Christ is to have the marriage consummated', Sibbes had written.[2] Nevertheless, Milton exploited to the full the sexual imagery which the Christian tradition had read into the Bible. Its recurrence, especially in his early writings, is remarkable, from the Muses in Prolusion VII who granted him 'the supreme favour' to the conclusion of *Epitaphium Damonis* which envisaged Diodati taking part 'for ever in the immortal marriage rite, . . . where the festal orgies rave in Bacchic frenzy'.[3] In his divorce tracts and in the *De Doctrina Christiana* Milton was to speak of 'the accident of adultery' as a relatively venial sin. Love, Milton thought, was 'not in Paradise to be resisted'.[4] 'Without love no happiness', as Raphael blushingly put it (*P.L.* VIII.621; cf. 365, 633). In *Paradise Lost* Milton suggested that 'fierce desire' which could not be satisfied was 'not the least' of the torments which Satan suffered (IV. 505–11).[5] Even after his blindness Milton could still flirt with a girl whose singing voice impressed him so much that he swore she must be beautiful.[6]

Milton quotes God's own example to justify man's need of woman. 'God himself conceals not his own recreations before the world was built. "I was", said the Eternal Wisdom, "daily his delight, playing always before him."' Solomon 'sings of a thousand raptures between those two lovely ones, far on the hither side of carnal enjoyment'. And in *Areopagitica* Milton asked 'wherefore did he [God] create passions within us, pleasures round about us, but that these rightly tempered are the very ingredients of virtue?'[7] As in so many other matters, Milton here appears far closer to the antinomian fringe than to the austerities of orthodox Puritanism, though his firm conception of self-discipline and personal dignity held him back from libertinism.[8] But it is not surprising that this distinction

---

[1] Parker, p. 67.

[2] Sibbes, I, p. 339.

[3] *C.P.W.*, I, p. 289; C. and F., pp. 279, 283. Cf. pp. 31–2 above.

[4] *C.P.W.*, II, p. 252; cf. *C.P.W.*, VI, p. 355. See chapter 32 below.

[5] Kermode (1960) p. 114.

[6] Darbishire, p. 204.

[7] *C.P.W.*, II, pp. 596–7, 527; cf. *P.L.* VII. 1–12. Orthodox commentators are very uneasy about these passages. The sexual element in God's relation to Sophia was well-known to the Gnostics; the word 'converse' in *P.L.* VII, 9–10 probably has a sexual connotation. Cf. *P.L.* IX, 909.

[8] See Chapter 24 below.

escaped those of his contemporaries who called him a libertine. On the surface they had a point.

In the Seventh Prolusion Milton assumed that human society and human friendship offer the greatest earthly happiness. To Diodati in 1637 he spoke of taking chambers in one of the Inns of Court, 'both for companionship, if I wish to remain at home, and as a more suitable headquarters if I choose to venture forth'.[1] Milton's nephew Edward Phillips tells us of the 'gaudy day' which in the early forties Milton used regularly to keep with 'some young sparks of his acquaintance, the chief whereof were Mr. Alphry and Mr. Miller, two gentlemen of Gray's Inn, the beaux of those times'. When in 1642 Milton was accused of haunting brothels and playhouses, he indignantly and at length refuted the first allegation: he did not deny the second, and three years later he published evidence of its truth in his First Elegy. He smoked, wore a sword whilst he retained his sight, and was skilled in using it. He seems to have been a betting man.[2] Music and exercise always played an important part in his life: both are emphasized in *Of Education*. The sonnet to Harry Lawes springs from friendship as well as professional respect.

At Cambridge Milton had been invited to make bawdy speeches, and he accepted. Prolusion VI is a rumbustious playing to the gallery, a piece of knockabout undergraduate humour. Yet it was not just a lapse. Milton clearly enjoyed the bawdry in this speech; he printed it in 1674, and in the fifties he equally enjoyed the firework display of obscene puns in his *Defences* – to the considerable embarrassment of commentators ever since who cling to the 'aloof Puritan scholar'.

About Milton's literary tastes we have to guess. He told Dryden much later that Spenser was 'his original'. The publisher of Milton's *Poems* introduced them in 1645 as imitations of Spenser; and Milton himself referred to Spenser as 'a better teacher than Scotus or Aquinas'.[3] Spenser, like Milton, was the son of a London citizen. Neither was a court poet. But in Spenser's time national unity survived in face of the threat from Spain and Catholicism: Spenser was associated with the radical Protestant wing in government circles, with Leicester, Walsingham, Ralegh. Spenser, like Milton after him, saw the poet's as a high calling, reserved for the elect. He was God's chosen agent, responsible to God for his country: in return

---

[1] *C.P.W.*, I, p. 327. For Milton and Gray's Inn, see Parker, p. 837.

[2] Darbishire, pp. 62, 32, 164, 203; *C.P.W.*, I, pp. 886, 892; C. and F., pp. 20, 23, 124. I owe Milton 'calling the odds' to a review by Robert Nye in *The Times* of 25 November 1976. Cf. p. 131 below.

[3] Cory, pp. 311–73; Greenlaw (1917) and (1920), *passim*; Sirluck (1950–1), pp. 90–6; Hanford (1966), pp. 49–54; A. Williams, pp. 62, 71.

God would send him inspiration. Spenser too was anxious to justify God's
ways to men. In the cave of despair belief that God was the author of evil
could lead men to suicide or murder.

Spenser had affinities with the Puritans. Virtue is perfected by trial, in
The Faerie Queene as in *Areopagitica*. False truth offers herself; real truth
(Una) has to be won. The destruction of the Bower of Bliss has been
regarded as an act of iconoclasm,[1] to which Spenser certainly had no
aesthetic objection. But his *Epithalamion* is not in the later sense of the
word a 'Puritan' poem.

> Pour out the wine without restraint or stay
> Pour not by cups but by the bellyful.

Spenser cultivated some bourgeois virtues – Idleness, Gluttony and
Lechery are the first three vices encountered in the House of Pride: waste
is what they have in common. Sloth is the height of wickedness, parent of
poverty and dissipation.[2] Spenser's is a philosophy of hard work, verging
on a morality of success. Like Milton, he stresses the victory of small
things over great, and denounces over-spending, waste which leads to
stagnation and decay.[3] 'The general end . . . of all the book is to fashion a
gentleman or noble person in virtuous and gentle *discipline*' – note the
profoundly Miltonic word (cf. 'This wild man being undisciplined' – VI.
v. 1.). In *The Shepheardes Calendar* Spenser was almost Brownist in his
praise of a primitive unpaid priesthood.

Milton's headmaster at St. Paul's used to praise Spenser especially ('our
Homer'), together with Sidney ('our Anacreon'), Harington ('our Martial'),
Wither ('our Juvenal'), Daniel ('our Lucan') as well as Edward Dyer,
John Davies and Ben Jonson.[4] (Similarly Quarles called Phineas Fletcher
'the Spenser of this age'. For Abraham Holland Browne and Drayton
recalled Spenser.)[5] That good Parliamentarian Anne Bradstreet's political
heroine was Queen Elizabeth: her literary heroes Spenser, Sidney, Ralegh
and Du Bartas.[6] The Spenserians, it has been said, could equally well be
called Bartasians.[7] There is no need to revive the question of Du Bartas's
influence on Milton; but Milton was reading him as early as 1625, he

---

[1] P. W. Thomas, p. 172.
[2] *The Faerie Queene*, I. iv; III. vii. 12.
[3] *Ibid.*, I. vi. 33; 'Visions of Bellay', 'Visions of the Worlds Vanitie'; *The Faerie Queene*, II. xii.
18–20, 80. For 'small things' see pp. 388–90 below.
[4] Gil (1972), I, pp. 151–2, 160, 171, 181.
[5] Quarles (1880), I, p. lxviii; Grundy, p. 18.
[6] Bradstreet, pp. xxvi, 78, 118; cf. pp. 57, 182–8, 304–5; P. W. Thomas, p. 184.
[7] Grundy, pp. 43–4, 64.

breathed the same intellectual atmosphere, and some of Milton's less
orthodox points are anticipated by Du Bartas/Sylvester.[1]

Greatest of the Spenserians is Walter Ralegh, whom I shall mention
from time to time because of his association with the unorthodox ideas of
Hariot and his circle. Milton, like most English radicals, greatly admired
Ralegh. Toland says that Milton published Ralegh's *Maxims of State* in 1642;
in 1658 he printed *The Cabinet Council*, attributing it to Ralegh, from a manuscript which had long been in his possession. 'Methought I saw my late
espoused saint' echoes Ralegh's 'Methought I saw the grave where Laura
lay.' Ralegh's biographer suggested that Ralegh's influence on Milton's style
would repay further investigation. It 'is greater . . . than that of any other
English prose writer'. We might go further and speculate on the attraction
of Ralegh's whole mode of thought for the young man who copied him so
copiously into his Commonplace Book. Ralegh's openness to the magical
tradition as well as to Calvinist orthodoxy, the daring speculations current
in his circle, his tolerance, the wide embrace of the *History of the World*, whose
object was to justify the ways of God to men – all these must have
reinforced the political attraction of Ralegh's anti-Spanish stance to which
he died a martyr when Milton was ten years old.[2]

Another Spenserian, William Browne, was a protégé of the Pembrokes.
Browne's Inner Temple Masque of 1614 has its affinities with *Comus* – the
Circe myth, moly, freedom and the Fall. Milton's 'Epitaph on the
Marchioness of Winchester' appears to echo Browne's 'Epitaph on the
Countess Dowager of Pembroke'.[3] Browne was very consciously in the
Protestant patriotic tradition. He praised Ralegh, Essex and Drake, and
was very anti-Spanish. Browne never had a good word for James I, still
less for his favourites and courtiers; but he lavished praise on both
Elizabeth and Prince Henry. The latter's death in 1612 cut England off from
the Continent.[4] Browne's 'freeborn Muse' scorned patronage. One of his
characters 'had as quickly all things past forgotten / As men do monarchs
that in earth lie rotten'.[5] Browne praised Spenser and Sidney, Drayton, John
Davies and Wither; he was a friend and political ally of Selden and Sir
Benjamin Rudyerd.[6] Browne was a fierce critic of 'the clergy's crimes'.[7]

---

[1] See pp. 318, 325, 332 below. Cf. G. C. Taylor, pp. 7–10, 13.
[2] Darbishire, p. 188; E. Thompson, pp. 236–9. See C. Hill (1965), chapter IV, *passim*. There are
many echoes of the *History* in *Paradise Lost* – e.g. p. 362 below.
[3] W. Browne, I, p. 175; II, pp. 169–70, 177, 184, 248, 294; *C.P.W.*, I, p. 472; Hanford (1966),
pp. 37, 51.
[4] W. Browne, I, pp. 119–23, 129–30, 142–8; II, pp. 51–61, 208, 253, 276–7.   [5] *Ibid.*, I, pp. 317, 58.
[6] *Ibid.*, I, pp. xxi, xxv, xxxi, 9, 87–90, 170–1, 180, 184–5, 225–7, 240; II, pp. 5, 87, 211, 213, 219,
237, 313, 321.
[7] Cf. p. 50 above; W. Browne, I, p. 220; II, p. 251.

Another poet who saw himself in the Spenserian succession was George Wither, friend of William Browne and John Selden, protégé of the third Earl of Pembroke and Elizabeth of Bohemia. He has many striking affinities with Milton. He criticizes dumb dogs and the scholastic curriculum of the universities, the effete luxury of the court and its unpatriotic foreign policy.[1] Wither believed in liberty of private judgment on individualistic grounds, though not for papists. We shall encounter Wither later as one who shared some of Milton's positions.[2] They part company only in their poetry, though even here it may be that Wither's early poems are under-rated.

More than half of Milton's lesser poems are addressed to individuals – relations, friends, girl-friends – and they reveal 'a writer with a distinctly social tone'.[3] The sonnets to young Lawrence and one of those to Cyriack Skinner are invitations to a convivial evening. Much of Milton's Cambridge poetry had been social too, written for a group. The Latin elegies, the poems about Guy Fawkes Day, and perhaps the English *Epitaph on the Marchioness of Winchester* were also written with a university public primarily in mind. It may be that *On the Morning of Christ's Nativity*, *L'Allegro* and *Il Penseroso* and others were circulating in manuscript before Milton went down from the university. Otherwise it is hard to understand how he came to be asked to contribute a poem to the second folio of Shakespeare, edited by Ben Jonson. In 1632 Milton's poem was anonymous: when it was reprinted in 1640 it was signed I.M. His light verses, like those of his nephew John Phillips, appeared in anthologies with titles like *A Banquet of Jests*, *Wits Recreations* and *Wit Restor'd*.[4] That the only time Wordsworth got drunk should have been in Milton's room at Christ's may not have been as totally unfitting as the later poet thought.

It is right to emphasize the jovial and sociable side of Milton because it has been overlooked, at least in the popular legend. But he was more than a mere cheerful extrovert. Nobody any longer equates him with his own Il Penseroso, but there are hints in *The Doctrine and Discipline of Divorce* that Milton thought of himself as 'inclined to melancholy', 'of a pensive nature and course of life.'[5] His aspirations were already polemical and outward-looking as well as literary and personal. In 1633 he told a friend that 'to defend and be useful to his friends, or to offend his enemies' was 'that which all mortals most aspire to'.[6]

---

[1] Grundy, p. 210.
[2] See pp. 64, 275, 283, 309, 346.
[3] Parker, p. 632; cf. pp. 782, 804.
[4] See p. 228 below.
[5] *C.P.W.*, I, pp. 247, 254, 273.
[6] *Ibid.*, I, p. 319.

In many ways Milton developed slowly, but by the time he returned to England in 1639 to face the Revolution, he had been jolted out of the traditional orthodoxies of his class and generation. He had abandoned a clerical career: he had strong if unspecific liberal Puritan predilections; he believed that he might become a major poet in the English language. He already had a mind, I suspect, more open than most of his peers to change, to novelty, to improvement, to heresy. At all events, that is the way he went.

III   A cultural crisis

I suggested that we should read *Comus* and *Lycidas* in the light of the growing alienation from Charles I's court of large numbers of English intellectuals (though not only intellectuals). It is in this light too that we should regard Milton's elevated conception of the poet's role in society. He, no less than the preacher, could 'imbreed and cherish in a great people the seeds of virtue and public civility'. So Milton believed that, though church-outed, he still had a message for the people of England.

'Ease and leisure were given thee', he told himself, 'for thy retired thoughts out of the sweat of other men.' It was therefore his duty to society, to the church of God, especially in this time of national crisis, to use his talent and 'the honest liberty of free speech' to contribute what he could to the betterment of society, by way of repayment for what he had received. He was prepared to undertake 'the meanest under-service if God by his secretary Conscience enjoin it'.[1] It was one approach to an advocacy of lay preaching, different from that of the 'mechanic preachers' with whom Milton's enemies were soon to associate him.

Milton's idea of poetry was firmly opposed to that of Charles I and his courtiers, just as his idea of chastity was poles apart from Henrietta Maria's 'Platonic love'. The epic poet, Milton had told Diodati in Elegy VI, must be as pure as the priest who rises to face the angry gods – an anger which our sins have provoked. Listen by contrast, to Charles I rebuking Sir John Denham for writing poetry: 'When men are young and have little else to do, they might vent the overflowings of their fancy that way; but when they were thought fit for more serious employments, if they still persisted in that course, it would look as if they minded not the way to any better.'[2] The difference between that point of view and

---

[1] *Ibid.*, I, pp. 627, 804–5, 816–17, 822–3.
[2] Denham, Dedication.

Milton's could hardly be more complete, though Charles's is the attitude more usually associated with the vulgar idea of Puritanism. Milton's attitude is not of course unique. George Wither, that good Spenserian, saw himself as no less a dedicated poet than Milton.[1] Ben Jonson spoke of 'the impossibility of any man's being a good poet without first being a good man', words that Milton was to echo in 1642.[2]

What we have then is a reaction of disgust from the flippancies, obscenities and trivial wit of the court and Inns of Court poets, the Randolphs, Carews, Sucklings, combined nevertheless with a conviction of the power of true poetry. A healthy patriotism depends on having a healthy country which one can love, Milton told an Italian friend in September 1638.[3] As poet and scholar no less than as Puritan, Milton felt a deep need for liberation from Laudianism. Idolatry is a short summary of what he detested: regarding places as holier than people; interfering with the strongly-held convictions of Christians about how they should and should not worship God; use of financial and corporal punishments in spiritual matters; all the sordidness of church courts progging and pandering for fees. No free and splendid wit could stand it. Milton's brief period of support for Presbyterianism sprang perhaps from the idea that because Presbyterians opposed Laud they also shared Milton's hatred for ecclesiastical interference with freedom of expression, whether religious or literary. He even urged Parliament to open a state theatre for public 'recreation and instruction'.[4]

The point at which religion and culture met was the censorship. It is difficult for us to grasp to-day how severe this censorship was in the early seventeenth century, and it is even more difficult to establish its consequences for literature. But something can be conveyed. Glynne Wickham suggested that 'the decadence in Jacobean and Caroline dramatic writing' was 'due in far greater measure to the censorship ... than to any particular failing in the writers themselves'.[5] Among those who suffered from censorship were Chapman, John Davies of Hereford, Donne, Drayton, John Fletcher, Fulke Greville, Ben Jonson, Massinger, Middleton, Wither; Francis Bacon, Robert Burton, Camden, Sir Edward Coke, Nicholas Ferrar, Joseph Hall, Thomas Hariot, Sir Walter Ralegh, John Selden, Archbishop Ussher, Peter Heylyn. Laud was said to have refused

---

[1] Wither (1628), I, pp. 199–201; II, pp. 564–9, 572. Cf. Hensley, pp. 63, 65.
[2] Jonson, dedicatory epistle to *Volpone* (1607); *C.P.W.*, I, p. 874; see p. 88 below.
[3] *C.P.W.*, I, pp. 328–32.
[4] *Ibid.*, I, pp. 819–20; cf. pp. 91–2 below.
[5] Wickham, p. 94.

licences to print Luther's *Table Talk*, Bishop Jewell's *Works*, Foxe's *Book of Martyrs*, Bishop Bayley's *Practice of Piety*. He blue-pencilled even writers like William Chillingworth and Joseph Hall. We know of many who deliberately refrained from publication before 1640 – Sir Henry Spelman, Sir Simonds D'Ewes, Joseph Mede: there must have been hundreds more. Censorship was tightened as the Revolution approached, enforced by savage corporal penalties against Bastwick, Lilburne and others who evaded it. The number of pamphlets published after the press was liberated from what Elias Ashmole called 'the malice of the clergy' shot up from 22 in 1640 to 1,966 in 1642; the number of newspapers, ballads and almanacs increased in like proportion.[1] Many works were published after 1640 which could not have appeared earlier because of 'the iniquity of the times' – I quote from the title-page to Thomas Taylor's *Works* (1653). Examples are Fulke Greville's *Life of Sidney*, Sir Robert Naunton's *Fragmenta Regalia*, the later volumes of Coke's *Institutes*, the memoirs of Arthur Wilson and Bishop Goodman, the millenarian writings of Joseph Mede, and translations of Brightman, Alsted and many others, William Gilbert's *Physiologia Nova*, many of Bacon's works, translations of Harvey.[2]

Those rather tedious but too often forgotten points may perhaps be summed up by recording the *Advice* which the Duke of Newcastle, a survivor from the old régime, gave to Charles II after the Restoration. Bishops, he said, are 'the most effective guards against dissemination of wrong opinions among the people', and so must be selected with great care. Too much preaching is a bad thing, and should be replaced by the reading of homilies, which will instruct the people in 'their obedience to their superiors and governors, with all the respect that may be'. There should be less education, and books on controversial subjects should be printed in Latin only, 'for controversy is a civil war with the pen which pulls out the sword soon afterwards'.[3]

The reader may from time to time think that I am reading too much between the lines, that I treat what Milton and others wrote as cryptograms to be decoded. But I believe this is the right way to read rebellious writers in the decades before 1640. 'These times are dangerous for men to write,' said a Kentishman in the fifteen-nineties, 'much more to write opinions.'[4] 'Things with us are in such a condition', the great mathematician Hariot wrote to Kepler in 1608, 'that I still cannot philosophize

---

[1] Josten (1966), II, p. 501; Siebert, pp. 145, 157, 191, 203; cf. C. Hill (1965), p. 50.
[2] C. Hill (1965), p. 32; (1971), p. 28; *W.T.U.D.*, p. 96.
[3] Turberville, pp. 173–6.
[4] P. Clark, p. 266.

freely. We are still stuck in the mud.'[1] 'The times are dangerous', John Chamberlain told Sir Dudley Carleton in 1622, 'and the world grows tender and jealous of free speech.'[2] 'I dare go no further,' wrote Joseph Mede, Fellow of Milton's college, in a private letter of July 1635, after referring to the Thirty Years War; 'it may be I have said too much already.'[3] Under the Laudian régime Mede dared not even publish the results of his researches into the date of Christ's Second Coming. Yet if there was an acknowledged scholarly expert in England on this important topic, he was the man.

Aesopian writing is familiar to anyone in the twentieth century who has had to live and write under a censorship. We must be on the alert all the time when reading what Milton published before 1640 and after 1660, for he then had truths to convey which he felt to be vitally important, and which authority felt to be wickedly seditious.[4]

---

[1] C. Hill (1965), pp. 32–3.
[2] Bourcier, p. 53.
[3] Mede, p. 829.
[4] For more about the censorship, see pp. 217–18, 405–9 below.

PART II

TEEMING FREEDOM

The minds of men are the great wheels of things; thence come changes and alterations in the world; teeming freedom exerts and puts forth itself.

John Warr, *The Corruption and Deficiency of the Laws of England* (1649)

It was not a mere reform in the government but a social revolution which this [third] party worked to bring about. . . . The party was followed by a large number of inferior free-thinkers and fantastical dreamers, the one set in hope of licence, the other of equality of property and universal suffrage.

F. Guizot, *History of Civilization in England,* lectures delivered 1828–30

Chapter 6

The Radical Underground

Nothing can be more contemptible than to suppose public records to be true.

William Blake

Historians have long recognized the existence of two conflicting bodies of ideas in the seventeenth century. But increasingly of late they have become aware of a third body of ideas, the popular heretical culture, which rejected the ideas both of court and established church, and of orthodox Puritanism. This third culture is difficult to identify, because its records are normally unwritten: our evidence comes from hostile accounts of church courts prosecuting heretics, of orthodox spokesmen denouncing them. What I say about it in this chapter is necessarily tentative.

Because there was no freedom for unorthodox men and women of the lower classes to print their views before 1640, still less to submit them to rational discussion, such views were often expressed crudely, jumbled up with magical and prophetical ideas: in attempting rational analysis we no doubt flatter the ideas actually held. Nevertheless, from the fifteenth to the seventeenth centuries certain themes recur in lower-class heresy. Whether they have a continuous underground existence, or whether they crop up spontaneously from time to time, the evidence does not permit us to decide. My hunch is the former, but I could not prove it.

Readers of Foxe's *Book of Martyrs* believed that they were heirs to a great popular tradition. To the sneering question, 'Where was your church before Luther?' they answered (as John Aylmer had done): Wyclif begat Hus, Hus begat Luther, Luther begat truth.[1] Perhaps the continuities which certainly existed in some areas between fifteenth-century heresy and seventeenth-century radicalism (e.g. in Kent, Essex, Buckinghamshire, the West Riding of Yorkshire) relate to the traditional

---

[1] J. Aylmer, Sig. P 4v, Rv.

association of weaving with heresy. Domestic work in the clothing industry was spreading in these two centuries. In the revolutionary decades the radical elements in the Lollard tradition were emphasized by men like Lilburne, Overton, Walwyn and Dell. The point was regularly made from the other side – for example by Charles I,[1] by Bishop Joseph Hall, by John Cleveland ('Presbyter Wyclif', 'Tyler's toleration'), and by John Collop.[2] Cowley in 1643 repudiated not only 'Wyclifians, Hussites and the Zwinglian crew' but Luther and Calvin as well, preferring Rome to Calvinism.[3]

We should not with historical hindsight impose too much organizational coherence upon those who transmitted these ideas. In the fifteenth and early sixteenth centuries the orthodox spoke of 'Lollards'; under Elizabeth of 'Anabaptists' or 'Familists'. There were indeed Lollard and Anabaptist groups, and the Family of Love also had some sort of organization. We do not know much about any of them: more research is needed. But I suspect that clerical inquisitors imposed classifications, '-isms', for their own convenience. They started with some idea of what 'Lollards', 'Anabaptists' or 'Familists' ought to believe, just as they started with assumptions about what 'witches' believed. Leading questions would no doubt encourage suspects to conform to the expected type.

So though there were 'Lollard', 'Anabaptist' and 'Familist' trends in popular thought, we should not postulate the existence of an organized underground. There are tantalizing hints. Elizabethan Familists are said to have been linked by itinerant weavers, basket-makers, musicians, bottle-makers, joiners. In 1555 servants and husbandmen came long distances for a secret meeting in Colchester. Sixty-seven years later, also in Essex, Thomas Shepard heard of the Grindletonian Familists, lurking in the obscurity of a Yorkshire Pennine valley.[4] The clothing industry linked Essex and the West Riding. The Grindletonians were to be associated retrospectively with Coppinger and the Yorkshire gentleman Arthington, disciples of William Hacket who in the fifteen-nineties believed he was the Messiah.[5]

Familists – like Lollards before them – tended when challenged to recant, but to remain of the same opinion still. This unheroic attitude was related to their dislike of all established churches, whether Protestant or

---

[1] See p. 89 below.
[2] Manning, p. 43; Cleveland, p. 506; Collop, p. 48; K. V. Thomas (1971), p. 663.
[3] Cowley (1973), pp. 112, 89, 109. Cf. *Semper idem: Or, a Parallel betwixt the Ancient and Modern Fanaticks* (1661), in *Harleian Miscellany*, VII, pp. 376–85.
[4] Spufford, p. 247; *W.T.U.D.*, pp. 26–7, 45, 83–4.
[5] K. V. Thomas (1971), pp. 134–6.

Catholic. Their refusal of martyrdom no doubt helped their beliefs to survive, but it increases the difficulty of identifying heretical groups with confidence. Only after the excitement of the reign of Edward VI were lower-class heretics for a brief period prepared to court martyrdom: after 1660 one suspects that many former Ranters and Baptists reverted to the ways of their Familist predecessors and returned formally and unbelievingly to the national church. The Ranters 'would have said as we said and done as we commanded, and yet have kept their own principle still', said Durant Hotham, stressing this Lollard and Familist reaction as the main difference between Ranters and Quakers.[1]

With all these reservations, let me suggest some continuing ideas of the lower-class heretical culture which burst into the open in the sixteen-forties. First comes anti-clericalism, the view that a layman is as good as a parson. It may extend to seeing the whole ecclesiastical hierarchy as anti-christian, to rejection of tithes and a state church, to hostility towards universities as training centres for the clergy, to advocacy of 'mechanic preachers' who enjoy the spirit of God, so much more important than academic education. All these views are familiar, from Wyclif and the Lollards through Anabaptists and Familists to Levellers and sectaries in the sixteen-forties and -fifties; full documentation would be superfluous. The Familists' ministers were itinerant craftsmen, and indeed the conditions of underground sectarianism forced the emergence of mechanic preachers. Anti-sacerdotalism was a necessity as well as an ideology. Some Lollards, and a reformer like William Tyndale, even thought that women might preach.[2]

Secondly comes strong emphasis on study of the Bible, and use of its texts – as interpreted by the individual conscience – to criticize the ceremonies and sacraments of the church. Worship of images, for instance, was denounced as idolatry. Sacredness was denied to church buildings: worship and prayer could take place anywhere.[3] Such criticism could be extended to secular institutions. Wyclif thought that the exercise of civil jurisdiction by the church, and in particular the use of force, was anti-christian. The rhyme 'When Adam delved and Eve span / Who was then the gentleman?', which played its part among the 'pure Levellers' (the

[1] *W.T.U.D.*, p. 257. For Durant Hotham see p. 329 below. Cf. G. Alexander, p. 383.
[2] Dickens, pp. 9, 19, 28, 45, 48, 59, 77, and *passim*; M. Aston, pp. 9–12, 38–9; Leff (1967), II, pp. 520, 526, 558, 576, 581–3, 589; Thomson, pp. 27, 31, 47, 77–81, 129, 246–8, and *passim*; Coulton (1945), p. 624; Harriss, pp. 166, 221; Fuller (1842), I, p. 442; Emmison, p. 110; K. V. Thomas (1971), pp. 70–5; Horst, pp. 122–3.
[3] Leff (1967), II, pp. 576–7; Thomson, pp. 40, 44, 50, 63–70, 76–83, 91, 104, 122, 126–30, 160, 245–7, and *passim*; Dickens, p. 9; Coulton (1918), p. 463; K. V. Thomas (1971), pp. 57–9; J. Phillips, p. 31; cf. Leff (1966), pp. 22–3.

words are Fuller's) of 1381, was repeated under Edward VI; this 'Levelling lewd text' (Cleveland's words) was often quoted in the sixteen-forties.[1] Sir Thomas Aston in 1641 referred to 'the old seditious argument, that we are all the sons of Adam, born free; some of them say, the Gospel hath made them free. . . . They will plead Scripture for it, that we should all live by the sweat of our brows.'[2] John Ball and later Lollards said that property should be held in common; the idea reappeared from time to time, culminating in the Diggers of 1649–50.[3]

Some specific heretical doctrines have an uncanny persistence. Here I am not attempting to be inclusive: I have picked out those only which have some relevance to Milton. From the later Lollards onwards they include the millenarianism frequently met with in lower-class underground movements; it reappeared in England in the fifteen-nineties and sixteen-forties.[4] Many English popular heretics rejected predestination, attached greater value to works than to faith, and emphasized human freedom and effort – a sort of pre-Arminianism. This can be found among Lollards and Familists, as well as among continental Anabaptists, from whom it was taken over by the English General Baptists. A Kentish heretic, Henry Hart, 'a froward freewill man', wrote a treatise against predestination in Edward VI's reign. He anticipated Milton in saying that human freedom to choose between good and evil was essential if God was to be absolved of responsibility for evil. Groups of 'free-willers' were to be found in Essex as well as in Kent under Edward and Mary.[5] An Essex heretic in 1592 thought that 'all the world shall be saved'; Thomas Edwards in 1646 attributed the idea of universal salvation to believers in the Everlasting Gospel, who included Familists, Behmenists and other radicals.[6] Thomas Shepard's interest in the Yorkshire Grindletonians led him to ask 'whether that glorious state of perfection might not be the truth?' The belief that perfection could be attained in this life had been held by London tradesmen in 1549 and 1631 and by many Familists in between. Under Elizabeth men claimed to be Christ.[7]

Another recurrent doctrine is anti-Trinitarianism, heretical emphasis on the humanity of Christ. Some Lollards denied the divinity of Christ and

---

[1] Leff (1967), II, pp. 519, 522–3; Pilkington, p. 125; Crowley, pp. 163–4; Cleveland, p. 402; Fuller (1842), I, p. 451; cf. *W.T.U.D.*, p. 35.
[2] T. Aston, Sig. I 4v. Milton had read Aston's pamphlet.
[3] M. Aston, pp. 23–4; Fuller (1842), II, p. 71; Petegorsky, p. 68; *W.T.U.D.*, pp. 115–16, 119–20.
[4] Thomson, pp. 240–1; K. V. Thomas (1971), p. 144; C. Hill (1971), p. 51; cf. chapter 22 below.
[5] Horst, pp. 122–3, 130, 139–40; cf. p. 153.
[6] Thomson, pp. 45, 106; Dickens, p. 9; Emmison, p. 101; *W.T.U.D.*, pp. 147–8, 184.
[7] K. V. Thomas (1971), pp. 133–4; *W.T.U.D.*, pp. 83–4, 162, 166, 184.

of the Holy Ghost.[1] The rapid spread of anti-Trinitarianism both in the liberty of Edward VI's reign and in prisons under Mary gave rise to great alarm among the orthodox. In 1555 the divinity of Christ was the subject of discussions in an underground meeting in a Colchester tavern.[2] Between 1548 and 1612 at least eight persons were burnt in England for heresies concerning the Trinity, including Marlowe's friend Francis Kett, grandson of the leader of the Norfolk rebels of 1549.[3] Bishop Jewell at the beginning of Elizabeth's reign spoke of a 'large and inauspicious crop of Arians and Anabaptists' in England.[4] One of the few avowed disciples of Servetus was minister of the Spanish Protestant congregation in London for the first five years of Elizabeth's reign, and there were anti-Trinitarians in other foreign churches in England.[5]

The heresy was especially associated with Familists. H.N. (Henry Niklaes, the Familist leader), Samuel Rutherford assured his readers, denied Christ to be God. Christopher Vittels, the itinerant joiner who linked Familist groups in Elizabethan England, had to recant anti-Trinitarian views.[6] The defence of the Trinity written by the elder Alexander Gil was directed against an Anabaptist who said Christ 'was but man only'. Written in 1597, published in 1601, it was still worth reprinting in 1635.[7] In his *Apology for the Thirty-nine Articles of the Church of England* in 1607 Thomas Rogers defended the Trinity against Servetus and H.N.[8] Legate and Wightman, the last two heretics to be burnt in England, were both anti-Trinitarians. In 1614 a Latin edition of the Socinian *Racovian Catechism* was also burnt in London.[9] Familists rejected the theology of the Atonement, the sacrifice of the cross, and some abandoned the idea of the existence of Christ. For them the word 'Christ' was a metaphor for the divine spark which exists in every man.[10]

Another heresy which recurs among underground groups was mortalism, the doctrine that the soul either sleeps from death until the general resurrection or dies with the body. N. T. Burns has so thoroughly demonstrated the continuous existence of *Christian Mortalism from*

---

[1] Thomson, pp. 36, 82, 106, 196, 248; cf. Wilbur, p. 168; Emmison, p. 110.

[2] Spufford, p. 247.

[3] G. H. Williams, pp. 778–81; McLachlan (1951), pp. 31–2; Fuller (1842), III, pp. 67, 75.

[4] Jewell, II, p. 1241.

[5] Gordon, p. 15; G. H. Williams, pp. 781–4; Horst, p. 136. See pp. 287–8 below.

[6] Rutherford (1648), Part I, p. 55; Gordon, pp. 15–16; Wilbur, p. 176.

[7] See p. 27 above.

[8] Rogers, pp. 13–24. See also pp. 287–9 below. For other examples of early anti-Trinitarianism see K. V. Thomas (1971), p. 169.

[9] L. A. Wood, p. 28. For Milton and the Racovian Catechism, see p. 184 below.

[10] Burns, pp. 66–7; cf. Perkins, III, p. 392, for Familists allegorizing the Bible. I have benefited by discussing Familism in England with Joseph Martin and Jean Moss.

Tyndale to Milton that readers may be referred to him for evidence, though
with a caution that mortalism existed in England well before the Reformation, among 'Lollards'.[1] It was a native heresy.

Tyndale as well as Luther was a mortalist, not least because the doctrine
disproved the existence of Purgatory. Calvin opposed the doctrine, and it
came to be associated with Anabaptists, radicals beyond the pale. For
them it was a commonplace. Servetus was accused of mortalism, and the
doctrine was taken up by Socinians. Joseph Mede, attributing mortalism
to Socinians in 1638, admitted to Hartlib that it was a powerful argument
against Purgatory. In England the Forty-two Articles of 1552 condemned
mortalism, though the condemnation was omitted in the Thirty-nine
Articles of 1562. Under Elizabeth mortalism was proclaimed by heretics
who thought the resurrection occurred in this life: some believed that the
soul was annihilated at death. The anti-Trinitarians Francis Kett and
Edward Wightman, burnt respectively in 1589 and 1612, believed that the
soul was mortal.[2]

Mortalism then, like anti-Trinitarianism, was a subject of popular
controversy in England at least from Edward VI's reign onwards. A
theologically unsophisticated musician like Thomas Whythorne had heard
of the doctrine.[3] Spenser and his friend Lodowick Bryskett were both
deeply interested in the mortalist controversy.[4] In 1599 Sir John Davies
wrote a poem against the heresy, *Nosce Teipsum*; *Microcosmos* (1603), by
John Davies of Hereford, also attacked it. The elder Alexander Gil, in his
Sacred Philosophie of the Holy Scripture (1635), denounced the heresy, which
suggests that it was widespread. It travelled to New England, where Mrs.
Anne Hutchinson and Samuel Gorton were accused in the sixteen-thirties
of being mortalists as well as Familists.[5]

Mortalism could be accompanied by, or lead to, a species of materialism.
The Lollard Margery Backster in 1428 anticipated Milton in a crude
reference to the ultimate physical fate of bread eaten in the Eucharist, in
order to show that it could hardly be the body of Christ. William Senes in
1537 declared that 'God is here upon my hand, in my body, in this stulpe
[pillar] and everywhere' – a doctrine which Familists and Ranters were to

---

[1] Burns, chapters 1 and 2, *passim*; Thomson, pp. 36, 41, 76, 82, 160–1, 185–6, 190, 248;
Dickens, p. 19; K. V. Thomas (1971), pp. 168–9. See pp. 317–18 below. 'A fully elaborated
defence of the specifically Christian doctrine' of the immortality of the soul, as the *Oxford
Dictionary of the Christian Church* innocently puts it, did not appear until the thirteenth century.
[2] Mede, p. 883; Burrage, I, pp. 215, 219.
[3] Whythorne, p. 73.
[4] Bryskett, pp. 271–8.
[5] Ziff (1962), p. 143; Burns, pp. 69–72.

echo.[1] Some early heretics also believed – again like the later Ranters – that 'all comes by nature', that matter is good in itself. Such doctrines by a natural progression can lead to anti-asceticism, glorification of the body, a belief that life is to be enjoyed here and now. This may be expressed as an antinomian libertinism: the elect are exempt from the moral law since God is in them, they partake of Christ's nature. Such doctrines were denounced by Thomas Rogers in 1607.[2]

If at death the body returns into its elements, as a drop of water taken out of the ocean returns to it again, mortalism can also lead to scepticism about the physical existence of heaven and hell. Some Lollards denied their existence, and placed Purgatory in this world. The devil, too, was internalized. This could combine with allegorical interpretations of the Bible to make the whole Christian myth describe conflicts which take place only within the believer. Familists were said to believe that Christ and Antichrist were not real persons, heaven and hell not real places: all were states of mind. The Grindletonians, like Thomas Münzer before them and Gerrard Winstanley after them, emphasized the spirit as against the letter of the Bible, a doctrine not unknown to Milton.[3] Lollards objected to church marriage, thinking that it should be a civil ceremony. 'Marriage is superfluous', the Venetian Ambassador reported heretics as saying in 1499.[4] Familists married and divorced by simple declaration before the congregation. Through them the attitude passed to Ranters and Quakers. Some Lollards may have advocated polygamy, though the evidence is doubtful. It was defended by Kentish heretics in 1572.[5]

Another complex of ideas that interwove with the Lollard-Familist tradition was Hermeticism. The rediscovery and translation of the Hermetic texts in the fifteenth century was of great intellectual significance all over Europe. These writings almost certainly date from the third century A.D., but they were widely believed to be of much greater antiquity. The original Hermetic philosophers appear to have fused Platonic and Stoic ideas, adding some Jewish and Egyptian concepts.[6] Through them many tenets of the ancient world were given fresh life in renaissance Europe. The belief that there was a primitive theology which antedated but anticipated Christianity was attractive to many intellectuals, including

[1] Foxe, III, pp. 594–5; Dickens, p. 41. Cf. p. 331 below, and for Milton, p. 457.
[2] Rogers, p. 39. See chapter 24 below.
[3] C. Hill (1971), pp. 142–3; *W.T.U.D.*, p. 83; Thomson, pp. 36, 184, 248; K. V. Thomas (1971), p. 169; cf. *C. and C.*, p. 15.
[4] Thomson, pp. 66, 78, 127, 159; Dickens, p. 19; Harriss, p. 221.
[5] *W.T.U.D.*, pp. 310–12; Thomson, pp. 64, 130, 177. I owe Kent to Peter Clark.
[6] W. Scott, I, pp. 8–10, 474; II and III, *passim*; *C. and C.*, p. 256.

Francis Bacon, as was the idea of a secret, esoteric wisdom known only to initiates. Hermetic doctrine stressed the original unity of all mankind. But at a lower level Hermeticist ideas fitted in with the magical practices of the peasantry, and were taken up by 'cunning men' who catered for the needs of ordinary people, especially in Protestant countries where Catholic magic was frowned on, and also by astrologers.[1]

The fact that Hermeticist ideas could appeal both to élitist intellectuals keeping their secret wisdom from the vulgar and to lower-class magicians makes their place in the great melting-pot of ideas in the sixteen-forties and -fifties difficult to assess. They contributed to the thinking of medical radicals like Culpeper, of political and social radicals like Winstanley and the Ranters – and of Milton. Not all Hermeticists were radicals, by a long way; but most radicals were Hermeticists.

There were other sixteenth-century influences from the Continent – not only German and Dutch Anabaptism, which historians have stressed perhaps too much, but also the more elusive influence of anti-Trinitarians like Servetus and Ochino, and of the Dutch Familist Henry Niklaes.[2] In this book I deal principally with Milton's relation to the English underground tradition: I say little about continental influences, such as that of Jacob Boehme (1575–1624), many of whose works were translated into English in the liberty of the sixteen-forties and -fifties. They had probably circulated in manuscript earlier: they were certainly widely influential among the radicals.[3] There are problems in this area with which I am not competent to deal. What is the relationship of plebeian English Familism to the intellectual Familism of the Netherlands and Spain?[4] And to 'libertine' trends among advanced intellectuals from Elizabeth's reign onwards? Frances Yates has postulated the existence of a European intellectual underground extending from Bruno to the Rosicrucians, with important English links.[5] This hypothesis might explain, for example, how Milton so easily gained his entry into Italian academies, and how he obtained his early knowledge of Familism.[6] There is room for detailed research in this area.

Before 1640 the traditions I have been describing circulated verbally. Historians, themselves the products of a literary culture, relying so much

---

[1] K. V. Thomas (1971), chapters 9–12, pp. 270–1, 375.
[2] See chapter 23 below.
[3] Nuttall (1946), p. 16; cf. appendix 3 below.
[4] Rekers, *passim*; van Dorsten, pp. 21–39, 75–85.
[5] Yates (1964) and (1972), *passim*.
[6] See pp. 53–5 above.

on written or printed evidence, are always likely to under-estimate verbal transmission of ideas. Men did not need to read books to become acquainted with heresy: indeed censored books were the last place in which they would expect to find it. Again and again the great heresiarchs deny being influenced by their predecessors. Luther was astonished to find that he was reproducing Hus's heresies; Milton was astonished and delighted to find that many Protestant divines had anticipated his views on divorce.

I see Milton as a man who moved uneasily between the second and third cultures. In this he is not unique. John Foxe had claimed Lollards and Marian martyrs as predecessors of the Elizabethan church, though many of them would have been persecuted only slightly less ferociously by the authorities of that church. The preaching brethren whom Haller studied hoped in the first four decades of the seventeenth century by Bible-teaching and by discipline to control and organize the powerful forces of the third culture: Oliver Cromwell and others like him decided that toleration of spokesmen for this culture was necessary if popular energies were to be harnessed to defeat the Royalists. Milton's belief that God reveals truths 'first to his Englishmen' drew on this popular heretical tradition.[1]

In speaking of two cultures, I refer to two bodies of ideas, not to groups of individuals. When we analyse the ultimate logic of these blocks of ideas we can see that they are antagonistic. Some men in the seventeenth century consistently adhered to the full logic of one or other ideological position: some were aware of political consequences. Others pursued a course of action which led steadily in one direction – Lilburne, Wither, Milton. Ideas are not, however, a reflex of economics. Once a body of ideas is in existence, individuals can take up some or all of it for the most diverse and personal reasons. But the fact that individuals hedge, fudge, are inconsistent, seek a quiet life, does not preclude the possibility of differentiating between the bodies of ideas which they muddle. On the whole, Puritans supported Parliament in the Civil War; but some whose ideas at least contain elements of Puritanism supported the King. Richard Baxter moved one way, Francis Quarles and Richard Holdsworth the other. Many like George Herbert and Nicholas Ferrar straddle the gap untidily. Such exceptions prove nothing. In our day some millionaires subscribe to Labour Party funds, and there are Tory working men. This does not invalidate the generalization that on the whole the Labour Party is a working-class party, the Conservative Party the party of men of property.

---

[1] See p. 280 below.

This consideration applies especially to what I have called the third culture. Ideas tend to be expressed by intellectuals: that is what intellectuals are for. Before 1640 authentic expressions of well-thought-out ideas of the third culture are hard to come by. Intellectuals of lower-class origin, if they were to get on in the world, had to adopt (and mostly no doubt conscientiously did adopt) ruling-class ideas, or at least the 'respectable' alternative ideas of Puritanism. Those intellectuals who played with the third culture were often arrogant and irresponsible aristocrats and their hangers-on – like Sir Walter Ralegh and his dependants who were accused of atheism in the fifteen-nineties. Ralegh patronized a group which runs across classes, from intellectuals of plebeian origin like Marlowe and Hariot down to the shoemaker in Sherborne who said that men in his locality believed that hell was poverty in this world.[1] Hariot had doubts about the existence of heaven and hell, but he insisted on the social necessity of maintaining popular belief in them, since 'this opinion worketh so much in many of the common and simple sort of people that it maketh them have great respect to their governors, and also great care what they do to avoid torment after death and to enjoy bliss.'[2]

Such men drew on the European libertine tradition as well as on the body of ideas which I have called Familist. The two are strangely intermingled.[3] Upper-class intellectuals who played about with libertine or Familist ideas were perhaps not always wholly serious. Often a desire to shock, to *épater*, entered in – as with Inns of Court poets who glorified the supposed promiscuity and communism of the Golden Age. Conversely, we should not look for a coherent body of ideas among lower-class Familists. Rather there was a confused remembrance of ideas floating down from various systems of thought, some obsolete;[4] a great deal of popular magic and naive belief in direct divine intervention were mixed up with what in the free discussion of the sixteen-forties were to emerge as serious and coherent rational ideas. But so far as the evidence goes, it suggests much more frequent recurrence of the heretical ideas in one form or another among the lower classes than among their betters. In nineteenth-century Russia it was the intellectuals of Narodnaya Volya and Marxism who imposed order and coherence on ideas that had long circulated among the peasantry and working class.

---

[1] *W.T.U.D.*, pp. 144, 162–3, 175–6; K. V. Thomas (1971), pp. 20, 167. See pp. 318–22 below.
[2] Rosen, pp. 13, 24, 27. Nicholas Hill of this group accepted the same view (Shirley, p. 113).
[3] See pp. 310, 318, 325, 328 below.
[4] Cf. K. V. Thomas (1975), pp. 91–109.

My attempt to survey in this chapter the underground traditions which existed before 1640 is, I am well aware, incomplete; when more work has been done on the subject it may also turn out to be unsatisfactory. But I am sure that the ideas which surfaced in the forties had a long pre-history, and are important for our understanding of Milton's thinking (and not only of his). The rest of this book will try to demonstrate the latter point.[1]

---

[1] If I had come across it earlier I would have made more use of Sir Edmund Leach's 1972 Presidential Address to the Royal Anthropological Institute. Leach links millenarianism (both in the early Christian church and in the seventeenth century) with anti-Trinitarianism, Jesus 'as a kind of super-prophet rather than a God', and with social revolt ('Melchisedec and the Emperor: Icons of Subversion and Orthodoxy', *Proceedings of the Royal Anthropological Institute for 1972*, pp. 8–9. I am grateful to Ioan Lewis for drawing my attention to this address.) At least in the sixteenth and seventeenth centuries the list of linked heresies could be extended, as I shall suggest later.

Chapter 7

Ecrasez l'infâme!

> As if the womb of teeming truth were to be closed up, if she presume
> to bring forth aught that sorts not with their unchewed notions and
> suppositions.
>
> Milton, *The Doctrine and Discipline of Divorce* (1643)

I tried to suggest in Chapter 4 some reasons for Milton's violent reaction
against the Laudian régime. It outraged him as poet and intellectual no less
than as Puritan and led him, once his pen was liberated, to say things
about bishops which seem exaggerated to those who are acquainted only
with their harmless twentieth-century successors. Take Charles I's Book of
Sports, for instance, which encouraged the traditional rural games on
Sundays. Sentimentalists have deplored Puritan vehemence against this;
but the frolics which occurred at wakes and church ales could end in
murder, and more often did end in illegitimate conception.[1] The attempt
to suppress these pagan survivals should be seen as part of a move to
spread a new ethos to the dark corners of the countryside. In Milton's
Nativity Ode Christ drives out demons just as Protestants were striving
to drive out saints and fertility gods. The Book of Sports symbolizes the
difference between the two cultures.[2]

It is in this context that we should see Milton's participation in the attack
on episcopacy which followed the meeting of the Long Parliament in
November 1640. The old régime collapsed at once: Strafford was tried
and executed, Laud was imprisoned, episcopacy itself was challenged. The
manifesto of the anti-episcopal party was *An Answer to An Humble
Remonstrance by Joseph Hall* (March 1641). The name on the title-page was
Smectymnuus, composed from the initials of the authors (Stephen
Marshall, Edmund Calamy, Thomas Young, Matthew Newcomen and

---

[1] Cf. *S. and P.*, pp. 184–5.
[2] Ziff (1973), pp. 20–1; cf. C. Hill (Penguin, 1969), p. 116.

William Spurstowe), the clerical leaders of the Presbyterian party. The Smectymnuan controversy led to Milton's five anti-episcopal pamphlets. *Of Reformation* appeared in the month of Strafford's execution, May 1641, *Of Prelatical Episcopacy* and *Animadversions upon The Remonstrants Defence against Smectymnuus* within the next two months, the longer *The Reason of Church Government* at the beginning of 1642 and *An Apology Against a Pamphlet call'd A Modest Confutation of the Animadversions* in April.

Parker plausibly suggested that Milton was invited to intervene in the controversy because he was known from his Cambridge days as the master of a boisterous and flippant manner which sober divines like the Smectymnuans could hardly use themselves. Spurstowe and Newcomen had been undergraduates when Milton delivered his Speech at a Vacation Exercise. There are interesting parallels between the Sixth Prolusion and some passages in *Animadversions*.[1] Milton no doubt learnt some tricks from the Marprelate Tracts of 1589, which were reprinted in the early sixteen-forties and whose slashing irreverence would appeal to him.

In the anti-episcopal pamphlets, alongside much routine propaganda, we can trace Milton's special interest in the cultural and moral consequences, as he saw them, of episcopacy. He believed, or said he believed, that the bishops' intention in plucking men 'from their soberest and saddest thoughts, and instigating them by public edict to gaming, jigging, wassailling and mixed dancing' on Sundays was to 'prepare and supple us either for a foreign invasion or domestic oppression'. 'To make men governable', the prelates' 'precepts mainly tend to break a national spirit and courage by countenancing upon riot, luxury and ignorance.' The 'tympany of Spaniolized bishops' have 'hamstrung the valour of the subject by seeking to effeminate us all at home'. The communion table 'stands like an exalted platform upon the brow of the choir, fortified with bulwark and barricado, to keep off the profane touch of the laics, whilst the obscene and surfeited priest scruples not to paw and mammock the sacramental bread as familiarly as his tavern biscuit. And thus the people, vilified and rejected by them, give over the earnest study of virtue', and commit 'the whole managing of our salvation' to the priests. A 'servile and thrall-like fear' has replaced 'the adoptive and cheerful boldness which our new alliance with God requires'.[2]

The bishops have become the praetorian guard of tyranny; 'faithful and freeborn Englishmen' emigrate to New England. Instead of imposing the

---

[1] W. R. Parker (1940), p. 269.
[2] *C.P.W.*, I, pp. 572, 587–8, 522, 547–8; cf. pp. 838, 843.

sort of discipline which would make men industrious and conscientious, bishops use church courts for exploitation. 'Their ceremonies and their courts' are 'two leeches . . . that still suck and suck the kingdom.' It was not only that the lowest classes liked 'the corrupt and venal discipline of clergy courts' and hated true discipline; the courts were undertaking functions which were not their business. Excommunication was prostituted 'to prog and pander for fees, or to display their pride and sharpen their revenge, debarring men the protection of the law'. Antichrist, as Milton put it, was Mammon's son. 'Jurisdictive power in the church,' he concluded, 'there ought to be none at all'. John Selden agreed with him. So does the modern world.[1]

In his Commonplace Book Milton had already been noting the dangers 'to both King and country' of clerical flatterers, and the desirability of separating church and state. He noted the uses of religion to rebels: and that their enemies unjustly charged reformers with sedition, 'as happens to-day'. What he found quite intolerable was the contempt with which the bishops treated the common people whom they had endeavoured to keep in ignorance. 'While none think the people so void of knowledge as the prelates think them, none are so backward and malignant as they to bestow knowledge upon them', as witness their suppression of sermons and of marginally annotated Bibles. Pluralism left many 'waste places' in darkness. If 'the poor mechanic' had difficulty in distinguishing 'between faithful teachers and false', it was because 'his ear was unaccustomed to good teaching.' And 'now with a most inhuman cruelty they who have put out the people's eyes reproach them of their blindness.'[2]

The Laudian ceremonies infuriated Milton, and many others, to an extent with which it is difficult to sympathize emotionally in our Laodicean age, so much less passionate about symbolism. The crucial phrase for understanding is Milton's reference to the Laudian altar as a 'table of separation'. For the radicals Holy Communion was not a sacrifice mediated by a priest whose magic alone could turn bread and wine into body and blood; it was the shared celebration of a congregation of equal believers, symbolized by their sitting around a table. If the minister (the word means servant) had any role at all, it was to serve bread and wine to the congregation. The Laudian insistence on railing off the altar was thought to imply

---

[1] *Ibid.*, I, pp. 852, 585, 589–93, 608, 613, 831; II, p. 279. Cf. I, pp. 849, 854–6; Selden, p. 95. Milton's 'venial discipline of church courts' is probably a misprint rather than a pun.

[2] *C.P.W.*, I, pp. 439, 420–1, 499–505, 932–3; cf. p. 446. William Sedgwick may have recalled this passage two months later in a sermon before the House of Commons. Darkness, he said, causes divisions: it was still but half day in England, the mist was not quite dispelled (1642, p. 50). Cf. p. 102n. below.

the Catholic doctrine of the real presence, and (like the surplice and other vestments) to mark the priest as a being superior to the congregation. Thus under apparently trivial disputes over communion rails and the 'piebald frippery and ostentation of ceremonies' there lurked disputes about human (or Christian) equality. Milton was criticizing the withdrawal of the church from the people.[1]

Milton and those who felt like him feared that Laudian rule was taking England back to Catholicism. This seemed to be true in ceremonies. It seemed also to be true in Laud's determined attempt to elevate the status of the clergy, bringing bishops into the government, making clergymen J.P.s, trying to recover alienated church property and to increase the emoluments, political influence and prestige of the clergy as a whole.[2] Censorship and the prerogative courts were used to silence radical Protestant criticism. Meanwhile Laud was trying to extend the authority of bishops over Presbyterian Scotland, and was severing long-standing connections with continental Protestants, in the Palatinate, the Netherlands and France, regarding them as 'no better than a sort of sacrilegious and puritanical rebels, preferring the Spaniard our deadly enemy before them'. This threatened 'to leave us naked of our firmest and faithfullest neighbours abroad'.[3]

To think well of the reformed religion is cause enough to make Laud one's enemy, the Earl of Northumberland told the Earl of Leicester in December 1639.[4] Government policy seemed to make sense only on the analysis put before the House of Commons in September 1642 by John Pym. It was the consequence of the undue influence of the 'Jesuitical and prelatical faction' which 'threatened ruin ... to all ... the reformed churches'.[5] In what seemed to many men to be a universal struggle between international popery and international Protestantism, Laud's little Englandism looked hopelessly provincial: a step on the way to surrender to the Counter-Reformation culture which attracted the courtiers of Charles I and Henrietta Maria. 'You and your prelatical party are more truly schismatics and sectaries', Milton was to remind them in 1660, 'than those whom you revile by those names.'[6]

It is worth emphasizing how very radical were some of the positions which Milton adopted in his earliest pamphlets. For reasons of political

---

[1] *C.P.W.*, I, p. 522. See *S. and P.*, p. 476 and *passim*.
[2] See C. Hill (1956), *passim*.
[3] *C.P.W.*, I, p. 586.
[4] Mathew, p. 127.
[5] Pym, p. 2.
[6] *C.M.*, VI, pp. 162–3.

discretion, perhaps, he aligned himself with the Smectymnuans. But he must already have been aware of wide discrepancies between himself and them. I shall mention later his not unfriendly reference to Familists.[1] His contemptuous dismissal of 'the ignoble hucksterage of piddling tithes' was more than resentment at financial extortion: it was part of a total rejection of any state church – not only of ecclesiastical jurisdiction but of the very existence of a separate clerical caste paid to preach. Ministers should be elected by their congregations, by plain artisans whom the defenders of prelacy call 'the mutinous rabble'.[2] Milton may not yet have fully worked out the implications of this attitude: soon it was to unite him with all true radicals in the English Revolution. The issue of tithes – a state church or none – came to be the crucial issue dividing right from left.

Or take an apparently more remote and theoretical point. The opening paragraphs of Milton's first pamphlet, *Of Reformation*, discuss the Emperor Constantine. The official English Protestant tradition – the tradition of Jewell and Foxe – looked back to Constantine's reign as the epoch in which Christianity triumphed, when the state became Christian. The really radical tradition, however, saw Constantine's reign as the beginning of the apostasy. Several criticisms are involved – the close union of church and state, the rise of prelatical episcopacy, and the endowment of the church with great wealth. Erbery dated the rise of Antichrist from the time 'when kingdoms came to be Christian'. John Reeve thought the apostasy began towards the end of the third century A.D.[3]

So when Milton speaks in *Of Reformation* of the 'most virgin times between Christ and Constantine' he is aligning himself with this tradition, as against middle-of-the-road men who followed Foxe. 'I am not of opinion to think the church . . . cannot subsist without clasping about the elm of worldly strength and felicity.' Bishops 'extol Constantine because he extolled them'. Through 'Constantine's lavish superstition' the bishops set up 'Mammon and their belly' as their two gods.[4] Milton returned to the same theme in 1659.[5] The point was social as well as religious. Against the 'large immunities' and 'great riches' which Constantine had given to the clergy, against the 'deluge of ceremonies', Milton set 'the homely and yeomanly' religion of earlier Christians.[6]

---

[1] See pp. 95–7 below.
[2] *C.P.W.*, I, pp. 600, 838, 840, 933–4. See pp. 103–4 below.
[3] See pp. 112–13 below. *W.T.U.D.*, pp. 194–5; Reeve (1711), p. 56; cf. Saltmarsh (1648), pp. 215–217; Yates (*Astraea*, 1975), pp. 41–5 for Elizabethan use of Constantine.
[4] *C.P.W.*, I, pp. 551–60, 576–9.
[5] *C.M.*, VI, pp. 48–9, 81, 97.
[6] *C.P.W.*, I, p. 556.

In the *De Doctrina* Milton adopted the radical view that religion had been 'defiled with impurities for more than thirteen hundred years'.[1] If the apostacy dates from the union of church and state, then the English Reformation cannot be seen as a great turning point. The overthrow of papal power marked an advance. But the royal supremacy was a reversion to the least desirable aspects of Caesaro-papalism, and under it the prelatical authority of bishops flourished. The real reformation, a return to the practices of the primitive church, the reformation of ordinary believers, remained to be achieved. Foxe's *Book of Martyrs* depicted the common people as the main enemy of Antichrist who is also the Pope. But 'the people' were expected to operate under the control of their betters: the example of Constantine justified 'tarrying for the magistrate'. In the fifteen-eighties the Brownists and Field had called for reformation without tarrying for any. Since Christ is the only king, why tarry for an earthly magistrate? Now in 1641 the learned Milton gave this popular cause a historico-philosophical case. He was followed by William Prynne, in his brief radical phase, and by the Levellers.[2]

Milton later tells us that it was because he had from his youth studied the distinctions between religious and civil rights that he felt he must intervene in the Smectymnuan controversy.[3] *Lycidas* seems to confirm that these studies date at least from the late thirties. He may have arrived at his conclusions in his study at Horton. But nothing in the Commonplace Book suggests this: all references to Constantine that Milton copied out of books before 1641 are favourable or neutral.[4] Wherever they came from, Milton's conclusions reinforced those of the radical underground, and put their demands within a scheme of history. Not without reason did one of his early critics accuse Milton of associating with the 'mutinous rabble', and bringing 'the very beasts of the people within the borders of the Mount'.[5]

Milton, then, like the radicals, attached less significance to the Reformation than did either party to the Smectymnuan controversy. For him the true reformers were the Waldenses and in England Wyclif and his Lollard successors, the humble Marian martyrs and the persecuted sectaries. 'The divine and admirable spirit of Wyclif' anticipated Luther and Calvin, whose names might never have been known if the English reformer had

---

[1] *Ibid.*, VI, p. 117; cf. pp. 112–13.
[2] *Ibid.*, I, pp. 110, 525–40.
[3] *Ibid.*, IV, pp. 621–2; I, pp. 822–3.
[4] *Ibid.*, I, pp. 380, 430–3.
[5] *A Modest Confutation* (1642), quoted in *C.P.W.*, I, p. 204.

not been silenced.[1] Milton knew that the Protestant Reformation had always been sullied by the material interests of 'princes and cities'. In his perspective the Reformation was only an incident, part of a rising curve which extended from Wyclif to the English Revolution.

Milton looked back with especial sympathy to 'our first reformers', the Waldenses, on whose behalf he wrote his glowing sonnet in 1655. He links Charles Diodati with the Waldenses by echoing the *Epitaphium Damonis* in the sonnet. 'Priscamque fidem coluisse piumque' (line 33) leads on to 'Even them who kept thy truth so pure of old'.[2] From the sixteen-forties Milton was studying the history of the Waldenses. He thought that their religion might have continued 'pure since the Apostles'; they endowed no churches and paid no tithes, maintaining their ministers 'by alms only'. Their preachers 'bred up themselves in trades, and especially in physic and surgery ... that they might be no burden to the church'. Milton also – like John Goodwin – cited the Waldenses against pacifists, to argue that civil and religious liberty might be defended by force of arms. We shall see later the significance of these emphases. In 1649 Milton praised the Waldenses because 'they have held the same doctrine and government since the time that Constantine with his mischievous donations poisoned ... the whole church.'[3]

We should not, then, be too surprised that the Reformation is not mentioned in *Paradise Lost*: the scamper over human history in the last two books is going very fast when we get to this date. In the early sixteen-forties 'the bright and blissful Reformation' had seemed one stage in a movement which started with Wyclif and culminated in the English Revolution. From the perspective of post-Restoration England the Reformation seemed just another false start under the rule of Antichrist, its permanent outcome the episcopal Church of England. The Restoration had put paid to the idea of 'continuous reformation', and this may have lessened the tactical desirability of looking back to Protestant predecessors. Psychologically, too, it meant that the sense of a continued upward movement was lost. But the Reformation for Milton had never played a unique part in human advance. Wyclif, perhaps because he was an Englishman, was almost equally important.[4]

Lycidas, then, seems to me to lead directly on to the anti-episcopal pamphlets. Whatever consolations immortality might bring for the death

---

[1] *C.P.W.*, II, pp. 231–2, 552–3, 707.
[2] Cf. p. 56 above.
[3] *C.P.W.*, I, p. 379; III, pp. 222n, 227, 514; IV, p. 658; *C.M.*, VI, pp. 64, 80–1, 87.
[4] *C.P.W.*, I, pp. 524–6, 704; Saurat, pp. 28, 164, 64. See pp. 69–71 above.

of an individual, only divine intervention, the two-handed engine at the door, could remedy the apostacy of a church. 'Of all those blessed souls which you have persecuted', Milton told the bishops five years later, 'and those miserable ones which you have lost, the just vengeance does not sleep.'[1] The strength of *Lycidas* comes from its fusion of the cultural and the personal. Until the land has 'enfranchised herself from this impertinent yoke of prelaty, under whose inquisitorious and tyrannical duncery no free and splendid wit can flourish', Milton could find no outlet for the creative powers which he felt within him. Neither liberty nor a voluntary self-discipline was possible: Milton lived under chaos tempered by arbitrary suppression – of a kind with which he had become familiar in the Italy which had silenced Galileo. A break-through to a different political order was needed if the frustrations of the poet and his country were to be remedied. He wanted to live in a society in which 'adoptive and cheerful boldness' would replace 'servile crouchings',[2] in which human dignity was possible, in which gifted laymen might preach if they wished and poets had inspiring subjects and a welcoming audience.[3]

But 'adoptive and cheerful boldness' was the consequence of 'our *new* alliance with God'.[4] The political upsurge of the sixteen-forties gave Milton his vision of Christ as 'shortly-expected King', of a just society to be produced by political reformation, a society in which God's Englishmen will at last realize their destiny and the poet will find his fit audience for celebrating God's 'divine mercies and marvellous judgments in this land throughout all ages'. The forties gave Milton a new vision, but he had long held an exalted view of the poet's role, 'to imbreed and cherish in a great people the seeds of virtue and public civility'. This he contrasted with 'the corruption and bane which [our youth and gentry] suck in daily from the writings and interludes of libidinous and ignorant poetasters'.[5]

Here we come back to the cultural crisis. Milton's problem was to break through to his public. Spenser had written for a relatively unified audience, in which court and country were not widely separated. But since his time things had changed. 'Drayton's difficulty was that he tried to find a public not centred on the court. Ben Jonson, whose view of poetry was as public [as] and perhaps more professional than that of Spenser, created a form of poetry which was more courtly and aristocratic, less national,

---

[1] *C.P.W.*, I, p. 793; cf. Fixler, pp. 59–61.
[2] 'I ever protested against their altars and their cringes', wrote Samuel Torshell, Milton's contemporary at Christ's, perhaps echoing Milton's phrase (Torshell, 1644, Epistle Dedicatory).
[3] Tillyard (1949), pp. 84–5, 135; Barker (1942), pp. 6, 14–19, 35, 47.
[4] My italics.
[5] *C.P.W.*, I, pp. 616, 816–18.

but which was socially and ethically directed none the less.' Milton's early poems revealed him as a son of Ben; but by the sixteen-thirties national unity no longer existed. 'Social and ethical' considerations necessitated parting company with Henrietta Maria and the court poets.[1]

Ben Jonson had spoken of his dead son as 'Ben Jonson his best piece of poetry'. Milton went one better by claiming that the true poet 'ought himself to be a true poem; . . . not presuming to sing high praises of heroic men or famous cities unless he have in himself the experience and practice of all that which is praiseworthy'. None but good men can either be truly eloquent or love freedom.[2] Poetry and liberty are always closely linked in Milton's thinking: so are poetry and God.

But there is another aspect of Milton's thought which impelled him towards the radicals. The cultural crisis was also a social crisis. Historians are becoming increasingly aware of the threat of popular revolt which underlay the apparent stability of Charles I's reign. The Tudor consensus among the ruling class had long been breaking up. All over England class bitterness was fierce. Many thought that the lower orders were ripe for revolt. The moderate Simonds D'Ewes in 1622 spoke of 'a hoped-for rebellion'. Such hopes or anxieties were outspoken in the depression of the early sixteen-twenties.[3] In the south-western counties between 1628 and 1631 there were sporadic uprisings against enclosure, and revolt was endemic there throughout the thirties. The temptation to members of the propertied class to give a lead – with all the risks that this would involve – increased with the shame of England's non-intervention in the Thirty Years War.

In 1628 Sir Robert Cotton circulated a paper entitled *The Danger wherein the Kingdome now standeth,* whose object was to warn that if Parliament pushed its case against the Duke of Buckingham too hard it might unleash a revolt by 'the loose and needy multitude, . . . with a glorious pretence of religion and public safety, when their true end will be only rapine of the rich'. This could be used as an argument to persuade Buckingham to come to terms with Parliament; but the bluff must not be carried too far.[4] Such considerations may explain the collapse of the opposition when its bluff was in fact called in 1628–9. Wentworth and Noy joined the government; Eliot and Chambers were left in jail. In 1628 the London populace did indeed get out of hand, lynching the Duke of Buckingham's astrologer,

---

[1] Broadbent (1973), pp. 90, 102, 278; cf. Rivers, pp. 82–3.
[2] *C.P.W.*, I, pp. 804–5, 822, 890, 874; Jonson, 'On my First Sonne'.
[3] Bourcier, p. 64.
[4] *Op. cit.*, p. 19.

Dr. Lambe. No one was ever called to account for his death, though a heavy fine was levied on the City. Later in the year Buckingham himself was assassinated, to the joy of many more than the younger Alexander Gil. In 1630, in a funeral sermon on the Earl of Pembroke, T. Chaffinge warned of the danger of civil war between country and City, from which Spain alone would benefit.[1] This is the background to those flattering court masques in which all the problems of a divided nation are solved by the descent of a royal deity in the last scene. Twenty years later some despairing radicals turned to Fifth Monarchism in a similar spirit; the direct intervention of Jesus Christ was necessary because there seemed to be no other way of winning the reforms which they desired.

There was intense class feeling then – not only a hatred of gentry and aristocracy on the part of the lower classes, but a reciprocal contempt. Abraham Cowley, himself a merchant's son, saw the Civil War in historical perspective as an uprising of 'the base rout', of 'Kets and Cades and Tylers'.[2] He was quoting Charles I, who in his answer of 18 June 1642 to Parliament's Nineteen Propositions warned that, if opposition to him continued, 'at last the common people . . . [will] set up for themselves, call parity and independence liberty, . . . destroy all rights and properties, all distinctions of families and merit', so that eventually government would 'end in a dark, equal chaos of confusion, and the long line of our many noble ancestors in a Jack Cade or a Wat Tyler'.[3] A later Royalist song contrasted 'the loyal gentry' with 'the perfidious clown', and said of the latter

> Let them, like treacherous slaves, be always bound
> To pay rack rents, and only till the ground.

Another song depicted the people saying to one another

> We'll teach the nobles how to stoop
> And keep the gentry down.[4]

The scrivener's son aligned himself with the poor and middling sort against wealthy courtiers. The Lady in *Comus* observed that

> courtesy
> . . . oft is sooner found in lowly sheds
> With smoky rafters, than in tapestry halls
> And courts of princes, where it first was named
> And yet is most pretended.
> (321–4)

---

[1] Heinemann, p. 244.
[2] Cowley (1973), pp. 88, 103; cf. pp. 109, 115, 117.
[3] Rushworth, V, p. 732.
[4] *Rump* (1662), I, pp. 110, 16.

From his Cambridge days Milton had shown a good deal of contempt for
mere hereditary aristocracy. High social rank was a hindrance to virtue,
he thought, 'in respect of the wealth, ease and flattery which accompanies
a nice and tender education'.[1] The Lady's socially conscious retort to
Comus's magnificent invocation of the plenitude of nature,[2] and the
virulent attack on the established church in *Lycidas*, suggest that Milton,
well before the Civil War, was prepared to look for allies outside his own
social milieu. Like Oliver Cromwell, like Bulstrode Whitelocke, he saw
'plain men' who had 'the root of the matter in them' where his adversaries
saw 'the very beasts of the people'.[3] 'The old Puritans observed hierarchy
and rank', John Bastwick complained in 1646; not so the upstart new
sectaries.[4]

In the sixteen-twenties and early -thirties many of Charles I's most
passionately sincere opponents chose emigration because they despaired
of change – though no doubt most of them hoped, like the Marian exiles
eighty years earlier, to return to a reformed England. Oliver Cromwell and
Lord Brooke contemplated emigration: Sir Henry Vane went to New
England. Opposition was carried on from the Netherlands by extreme
democrats like Lilburne, at home by fanatics like Prynne, and by passive
refusal to pay Ship Money. Only those led by Captain Poverty were likely
to resist more actively.[5] What made revolution possible in 1640 was the
Scottish army. The terms of the Treaty of Ripon, by which Charles had to
promise to pay the Scottish army in occupation of northern England,
forced him to summon a Parliament. So the Scottish presence was not
only a check on the King; it also enabled the Parliamentary leaders to
unleash popular demonstrations in confidence that our brethren of
Scotland would in the last resort co-operate to prevent the lower classes
going too far. Hence the extraordinary scenes of 1640–2 when some
leaders of Parliament almost encouraged London mobs and anti-Catholic
mobs, turned a blind eye to anti-enclosure riots and the meetings of
seditious sectaries in London. The preachers called on the lower classes to
fight against Antichrist, confident that they would remain under the
control of their betters. 'I am far from the monster of a democracy,' said
Edward Bowles, chaplain successively to the Earl of Manchester and Sir

---

[1] *C.P.W.*, I, pp. 471–3, 923. Cf. p. 35 above.
[2] See p. 47 above.
[3] For Cromwell see C. Hill (Penguin, 1972), p.64; for Whitelocke see Spalding, pp. 69–72. See
    also p. 84 above.
[4] Bastwick, Sig. Ev.; Manning, esp. chapters 6 and 7.
[5] *C.P.W.*, I, p. 487 – Commonplace Book; cf. pp. 480–2, 485.

Thomas Fairfax; 'that which I call to the people for is but a quick and regular motion in their own sphere.'[1]

Milton was never a democrat. But in the years between his return from Italy and the outbreak of civil war he was thinking a great deal about government and the subjects' right of rebellion, and at least considering anti-monarchical sentiments which he did not find it expedient to express openly until 1649.[2] At the time of writing *Areopagitica* he had perhaps more confidence in God's Englishmen than in the Scottish army or the Presbyterian clergy. Yet in 1640 things had seemed very different. The brotherly assistance of Scottish Presbyterians appeared to have revived the Protestant international which Laud had laboured to disrupt, and which the Thirty Years War had weakened, since German and Dutch Protestants could survive only under the protection of Catholic France; French Huguenots had to resign themselves to a position of permanent subordination. Perhaps for the Scots too acceptance of the English alliance was an attempt to escape from French patronage – the auld alliance – and to achieve the century-old dream of a single Protestant church uniting the whole island – a project which, Milton thought, had always hitherto been sabotaged by the papacy.[3]

So when Milton joined in the campaign against bishops in 1641–2, he was attacking on a very broad cultural front. He was expressing deeply felt and long-pondered opinions, which potentially went well beyond the clerical Presbyterianism that he initially defended. He really believed, as he put it later, that 'those who were esteemed religious ... asserted liberty', just as tyranny was inevitably linked with 'false religion'.[4] He was already aware of distinctions between his own position and that of the Presbyterians. There was nothing naive in his support for Smectymnuan opposition to episcopacy. If he was too optimistic in supposing that the Presbyterian programme in any way corresponded to his own political, religious and cultural ideals, that is the sort of mistake that arises at the beginning of any revolution, when opponents of the ruling group are united in hostility and have had no opportunity (because they have been denied freedom of discussion and of the press) to clarify and sort out their own views. Richard Baxter had never asked himself what Presbyterianism and Independency were until 1641. John Owen, another professional

---

[1] *W.T.U.D.*, p. 60.
[2] *C.P.W.*, I, pp. 420–1, 431–2, 439, 446, 454–5, 460, 474, 484, 487, 499–501, 505; cf. the covert warning to a would-be tyrant in *The Reason of Church Government*, *ibid.*, I, pp. 851–2.
[3] *Ibid.*, I, pp. 502, 527, 586–7, 791.
[4] *Ibid.*, III, pp. 448, 509.

theologian, did not get beyond 'opposition to episcopacy and ceremonies' until 1643, when he began to study the congregational way.[1] Sir Edward Dering, an experienced politician, had never heard either Presbyterianism or Independency defended in the House of Commons before November 1641.[2] Men's ignorance and uncertainty were glossed over by respect for the Scots whose opposition had brought Charles's government crashing down, and for the courage of Laud's victims – Leighton, Prynne, Bastwick, Burton and Lilburne – who included Presbyterians as well as men who would become Independents and Baptists.

It is probable that Milton, in rejecting Constantine and defending Familists, knew exactly what he was doing. By the sixteen-forties he was already questioning the institution of monarchy. So we need not take too seriously his adoption of the argument that bishops must be opposed because they threatened kingship.[3] There were sound political reasons at that stage for submerging differences between the opponents of bishops. We need not reject Milton's later claim that his concern was already 'the liberation of all human life from slavery'.[4] When he scented danger that slavery might be reimposed, *Areopagitica* made clear his priorities. His dialogue with the radicals had begun.

[1] J. Owen, XIII, p. 223.
[2] Nalson, II, p. 665.
[3] *C.P.W.*, I, p. 79, 114, 120; cf. pp. 150–1 below.
[4] *Ibid.*, IV, p. 622.

Chapter 8

Milton and the Radicals

> I never knew the time in England when men of truest religion were
> not counted sectaries.
>
> Milton, *Eikonoklastes* [1]

1 'Much arguing, much writing, many opinions'

The early sixteen-forties were a formative period for English radical thinking, and for Milton. We do not ask ourselves often enough what Milton's life would have been like if the Long Parliament had not met in 1640. He would presumably have lived in obscurity in London, taking in a few pupils and trying out his educational theories; he might ultimately have written a poem on early British or English history, which would have been very different from *Paradise Lost*.

The unique fact about the years after 1640 was that the censorship broke down, church courts collapsed, and with them upper-class control over the third culture. What was revealed was fierce popular hostility to gentry and aristocracy, and to the monarchy which protected them. Evidence for this is overwhelming.[2] For the first time in English history the ideas of the radical underground could be freely preached, discussed and criticized: they could even be printed. A printing press in the seventeenth century was a relatively inexpensive piece of machinery, and most printers were themselves small men open to radical ideas. It took a year or two for men and women to realize what was happening, but some time before September 1643 Abraham Cowley listed antinomians, Arians and libertines among the most enthusiastic London supporters of Parliament.[3] In December Robert Baillie told his Scottish friends that the Independents

---

[1] *C.P.W.*, III, p. 348. Cf. *C.P.W.*, IV, p. 644; VI, pp. 123, 698–700.
[2] Petegorsky, pp. 28, 42; C. Hill (1971), p. 82; *W.T.U.D.*, pp. 19–25, 223–4; *C. and C.*, chapter 8, *passim*. See pp. 88–90 above.
[3] Cowley (1973), pp. 110–11.

were growing, the Anabaptists more, the antinomians most of all. By
April 1644 he was reporting even more deplorable ideas – the mortality of
the soul, denial of the existence of angels and devils, rejection of all
sacraments. Two months later Socinianism had been added to his list, and
Roger Williams was said to be advocating no church at all. 'Very many are
for a total liberty of all religions', Baillie reported in July. A year later
there were 'Libertines', and by April 1646 'divers, from whom I least
expected it, are for putting away the whole royal race.'[1]

If I were writing a Miltonic epic, this would be the place for an invocation of the Muse, as we enter the new world of liberty, fecundity and
plenitude which opened up in the forties. Instead, let us consider Thomas
Edwards's *Gangraena* (1646), which, despite his horror and fury, gives a
marvellous picture, still insufficiently analysed, of the heresies now being
freely discussed by the lower classes. In the same year the respectable
inhabitants of Great Burstead, Essex, petitioned against 'a dangerous sect'
which had arisen in their parish, admitting and re-baptizing all comers,
'setting up mechanics for their preachers, denouncing the order and
ministry of the Church of England as antichristian', disturbing public
worship. They taught 'unsound opinions' like universal grace, the
abrogation of the law, the sinfulness of repentance.[2] Thomas Edwards
and the worthies of Great Burstead had a different angle of vision, but the
scene they describe is the same as that triumphantly celebrated by Milton in
Areopagitica: 'A nation not slow and dull, but of a quick, ingenious and
piercing spirit, acute to invent, subtle and sinewy to discourse, not
beneath the reach of any point the highest that human capacity can soar
to. . . . Behold now this vast City, a city of refuge, the mansion house of
liberty. . . . The shop of war hath not there more anvils and hammers
waking, to fashion out the plates and instruments of armed Justice in
defence of beleaguered Truth than there be pens and heads there, . . .
trying all things, assenting to the force of reason and convincement. . . .
The people, or the greater part, more than at other times, wholly taken up
with the study of highest and most important matters to be reformed, . . .
disputing, reasoning, reading, inventing, discovering . . . things not before discovered or written of. . . . All the Lord's people are become
prophets.' To re-impose a censorship on such a society would be 'an
undervaluing and vilifying of the whole nation', a reproach to the common
people.[3]

---

[1] Baillie (1775), I, p. 408; II, pp. 3, 24, 34, 43, 109, 142, 149, 170-1, 205, 216.
[2] A. C. Edwards, pp. 77-8.
[3] *C.P.W.*, II, pp. 551-7, 535.

In this flux new syntheses developed rapidly. We may distinguish political groupings like the republicans (Henry Marten, Edmund Ludlow, Henry Neville), Levellers (democratic republicans, whose leaders include John Lilburne, Richard Overton, William Walwyn), later the Fifth Monarchists (who not only shared the widely held belief that Christ's second advent was imminent but felt it to be their duty to expedite it by political action). Among radical religious groups (if the distinction between religion and politics has any meaning) were Congregationalists like John Goodwin, General (Arminian) Baptists, Seekers (hardly an organized sect, but including men like Milton's friend Roger Williams, Giles Randall, John Saltmarsh, William Walwyn, William Erbery), Behmenists, Socinians, Ranters. Ranters were hardly a sect, but Fuller and many others saw them as descendants of the Familists.[1] The name must serve to cover radical antinomians like Laurence Clarkson and Abiezer Coppe. From the Ranters, partly by reaction, were to derive the Muggletonians (led by John Reeve and Lodowick Muggleton, the two Last Witnesses of Revelation 11) and the early Quakers (not yet pacifist in the sixteen-fifties, politically and socially very radical) led by George Fox and James Nayler. Ranters, Quakers and Muggletonians inherited much of the Familist tradition, and many radicals took over some Hermeticist ideas.[2]

The Introductions to Volumes II and IV of the Yale edition of Milton's *Complete Prose Works* show how closely the evolution of the poet's ideas was linked to the general development of radical Parliamentary thinking. The traditional orthodoxy of Calvinism was rejected: so was belief in the Trinity. New-old heresies were preached – Arminianism, millenarianism, antinomianism, mortalism, materialism. In these heresies Milton shared an interest with Levellers, Diggers, Ranters, Seekers, Behmenists, Muggletonians, Socinians, some Baptists, some Quakers. Milton's reaction to the confusing flux of the mid-forties was to return to the Bible, to evolve his own Bible-based theology; the ultimate outcome was the *De Doctrina Christiana*.

Milton drew his ideas both from the Puritan and from the popular radical traditions. Recall once more the savage anti-clericalism of *Lycidas* and Milton's repudiation of Constantine in his first pamphlet: both smack more of radical sectarianism than of orthodox Puritanism.[3] As early as 1641 Milton was sneering at conservatives' fear lest 'we shall be all Brownists, Familists, Anabaptists. For the word "Puritan" seems to be

---

[1] Fuller (1842), III, p. 211. For Behmenists see pp. 328–30 below.
[2] See chapter 6 above.
[3] See pp. 51–2, 84–5 above.

quashed, and all that heretofore were counted such are now Brownists.'[1] In 1642 he declared that 'the primitive Christians, in their times, were accounted such as are now called Familists and Adamites, or worse.'[2] This was an astonishingly liberal attitude for Milton to have taken. It is comparable with Gerard Manley Hopkins writing (in 1871, of all years) 'horrible to say, in a manner I am a communist.' But that was in a private letter.[3] Milton mentioned Familists in the same breath with the early – and truest – Christians, in print, at a time when even Lord Brooke was carefully dissociating himself from Familism so as not to prejudice his plea for toleration. In *The Reason of Church Government* Milton spoke up for Arians as well as Anabaptists and Familists. By 1643 he had added anti-nomians to those on whose behalf he called for liberty. In the first edition of *The Doctrine and Discipline of Divorce* Milton referred to the 'fanatic dreams' of these sectaries; in the 1644 edition he added '(if we understand them not amiss)',[4] as though to make it clear that he was not necessarily condemning them.

Familists and Anabaptists were the bogeymen of orthodoxy, accused of all sorts of heresies and anti-social beliefs: they were irredeemably lower-class and unrespectable. Spenser had damned them in the conventional way; Milton suggested that prelates used the unsavoury reputation of the radicals to smear all Puritans – a point often repeated without acknow-ledgement to Milton.[5] Only one pamphlet spoke in defence of Familists before Milton wrote, and it may have been a papist *reductio ad absurdum*.[6] Not until September 1643 did the future Leveller William Walwyn, in *The Power of Love*, join Milton's courageous stand.[7] As late as 1648 Samuel Rutherford thought it worth devoting a hundred pages of *A Survey of the Spirituall Antichrist* to 'A Discovery of Familism in Mr. Saltmarsh'.[8] Milton's was an audacious position to take up so early, and it was not one that he found in the reading recorded in his Commonplace Book. As with his rejection of Constantine, the stimulus to his thinking is likely to have come from discussions after his return from Italy. It

---

[1] Milton's reference is to the Canons of 1640, which denounced 'Anabaptists, Brownists, Separatists, Familists' (*C.P.W.*, I, p. 989).
[2] *C.P.W.*, I, pp. 783–5, 788; II, p. 178; cf. *W.T.U.D.*, p. 395. Milton also spoke not unfavourably of the Traskites, whom Cowley listed among zealous London Parliamentarians (1973, p. 111).
[3] Hopkins, p. 27; see p. 337 below.
[4] *C.P.W.*, II, p. 278. Cf. Lord Brooke's 'if they are not much belied' in a similar context (Haller, 1933, II, p. 134).
[5] *W.T.U.D.*, pp. 100–1.
[6] *C.P.W.*, I, p. 144.
[7] Haller (1933), II, pp. 134, 273.
[8] Rutherford (1648), pp. 194–297.

suggests once more that we should not dismiss Milton as an intellectual unaware of what humbler men and women were thinking. Was there perhaps a Familist group in Horton/Colnbrook?[1] In *The Reason of Church Government* Milton may have been consciously quoting the petition which English Familists presented to James I in 1604, claiming that they were misrepresented 'much like as it was practised in the primitive church against the Christians'.[2] Saurat pointed out that Milton's diatribe in *Areopagitica* against Church Fathers who 'discover more heresies than they well confute, and that oft for heresy which is the true opinion', included Irenaeus and Epiphanius, who wrote mostly against the Gnostics – comparable in many ways with the Familists.[3]

The context in which Milton related Familists to early Christians is his criticism of those who smear and slander good men. There are two possible explanations of Milton's attitude. One – the less likely – is that he was a Familist sympathizer himself, who made the comparison with early Christians as explicitly as he thought prudent. The other explanation is that Milton's remark was (consciously or unconsciously) deliberately ambiguous: conservative slander of Familists reminded him of attacks on the early Christians, but he did not need to commit himself on whether the similarity extended any further: perhaps he himself did not know. We shall meet again with equivocations which may be tactical or may be genuinely revealing of Milton's ambiguous relationship to the third culture.[4]

There is a good book to be written one day on the subject of taverns and ale-houses as centres of political information and organization during the English Revolution. Henrician Anabaptists, Marian and Elizabethan Familists used ale-houses as bases for proselitization.[5] James I allowed the traditional village sports on Sundays because he feared that otherwise men would go to ale-houses and there talk sedition.[6] In 1641 religion was 'the common discourse and table-talk in every tavern and ale-house'. News-sheets were read aloud in taverns, so that the illiterate could know what was going on: taverns were distribution centres for pamphlets and news-books. In the early forties information was disseminated to supporters

---

[1] See p. 39 above.
[2] Fuller (1842), II, p. 208.
[3] Saurat, p. 220.
[4] See chapter 27 below. I am greatly indebted to discussions with Christopher Ricks on this point.
[5] Horst, p. 86; Spufford, pp. 232, 247, 255–6, 261, 348; *W.T.U.D.*, pp. 26–8, 209–10, 236–7, 257; K. V. Thomas (1971), p. 19.
[6] C. Hill (Sphere, 1969), p. 81.

of Parliament in London through 'daily tavern clubs in each ward'. It was convenient that Isaac Penington, leader of the London Puritans and father of Milton's friend, ran an ordinary. Baptists, Levellers, Ranters, Muggletonians, Quakers and the precursors of the Royal Society all met in taverns. The Rota Club in 1659–60 alternated between a coffee-house and a tavern. Men competed to 'make themselves famous' in the society of taverns and ale-houses, as they no doubt did in Charles II's reign in the coffee-houses and 'twopenny clubs' for mechanics. In the revolutionary decades smoking was still rather a naughty new habit: for Ranters and others it was a means of heightening consciousness akin to drug-taking in our own society.[1] We should not read anything of this into the evening pipe which Milton enjoyed, but we may assume that the author of *Areopagitica* would be familiar with the tavern society of 'the mansion house of liberty' in which these exciting discussions were going on. 'Where there is much desire to learn,' Milton wrote, 'there of necessity will be much arguing, much writing, many opinions; for opinion in good men is but knowledge in the making. ... What some lament of, we should rather rejoice at. ... Yet these are the men cried out against for schismatics and sectaries.'[2]

For the Scots Samuel Rutherford and Robert Baillie, for Daniel Featley, former rector of Milton's church, All Hallows, Bread St., for Thomas Edwards, Herbert Palmer, Alexander Ross, William Prynne, Ephraim Pagitt, and for countless other conservative Parliamentarians the heresies which were appearing in print seemed blasphemous and intolerable. Milton was named by Edwards, Baillie and Pagitt in their lists of dangerous heretics; he was unmistakably referred to by others. He was associated in the minds of enemies of the radicals with their heresies. Milton did not reject the association. In *The Doctrine and Discipline of Divorce* he suggested that the 'fanatic dreams (if we understand them not amiss)' of Anabaptists, Familists and antinomians derived 'partly if not chiefly from the restraint of some lawful liberty'.[3] In his sonnet 'On the new forcers of conscience' he aligned himself with

> Men whose life, learning, faith and pure intent
> Would have been held in high esteem with Paul

---

[1] Chestlin, p. 30; Pearl, pp. 233–4; *W.T.U.D.*, pp. 198–201; Hayden, pp. 19, 97–8; Aubrey, I, pp. 289–90; II, p. 322; Peacham, p. 286. For the Rota Club see p. 202 below.
[2] *C.P.W.*, II, pp. 553–5.
[3] *Ibid.*, II, pp. 278–9. Milton seems to be suggesting, in a surprisingly modern way, that religious fanaticism and libertinism might be produced by sexual frustration. Walwyn and Winstanley had similar thoughts (*W.T.U.D.*, p. 181).

but who

> Must now be named and printed heretics.
> By shallow Edwards and Scotch what d'ye call.[1]

This sonnet was written two years later than *Areopagitica*, but it suggests that the passage which I quoted at the beginning of this chapter is the positive to which Edwards's *Gangraena* is the negative.

Masson and nineteenth-century biographers perhaps too easily assumed that Milton was recognized in his own day as a great poet and a great man, too easily assumed that everybody read *Areopagitica*. But Parker carried reaction against this much too far when he suggested in *Milton's Contemporary Reputation* that no one really read or knew about Milton until one day in February 1649 he was suddenly invited to become the republican Council of State's Secretary for Foreign Tongues and polemicist-in-chief. (On Parker's thesis one wonders why Milton received the invitation.) I believe that Milton had a very considerable reputation before 1649, among the radical wing of the Parliamentarians. I fear that one reason why Parker missed this was that he had a strong dislike for radicals and 'rabble-rousers'. So he looked in the wrong places.[2] Milton himself tells us that he was 'loaded . . . with entreaties and persuasions' to write *Areopagitica*, by 'many who honour ye' (Parliament). He was expressing 'the general murmur', 'the common grievance of all those who had prepared their minds and studies above the vulgar pitch to advance truth in others'.[3] His divorce pamphlets and *Areopagitica* were received with hostility or – even more damning – by a conspiracy of silence among conservative Puritans and Parliamentarians. But among radical reformers – Baptists, Socinians, Levellers, Ranters and many others – there is evidence, if we look for it, that Milton was read and appreciated.

Milton himself was not an extreme radical, Leveller, Digger or Ranter.[4] He agreed with these groups on some issues, but only on some. What I suggest is that this is the milieu in which we should set Milton. He very soon parted company with Young and the Presbyterians, and he never aligned himself with any other group. He remained the great eclectic, the asserter of Christian doctine who was a member of no church. But if we look for analogies with Milton's ideas among the radicals we shall easily find them.

---

1 'Scotch what d'ye call' is one of Milton's endearing jokes, a piece of sheer cheek at the expense of one of the best-known political figures in London, Robert Baillie.
2 See p. 226 below.
3 *C.P.W.*, II, p. 539.
4 See pp. 113–14 below.

II   The radical milieu

In *Gangraena* Thomas Edwards denounced Further Errors Nos. 47–9 –
that all officers ought to be elected by the people, that the House of
Commons had the supreme power, that the people were sovereign, that
all men were born equal and had natural rights to liberty and property, and
that precedents were not binding.[1] Views like these were soon to be proclaimed by the 'civil heretics they call the Levellers'.[2] Milton was closer to
them than to that reluctant republican Oliver Cromwell. Milton's political
theories were expressed with force and eloquence, but they were for the
most part not original. He pointed out to the Presbyterians in 1649 that
the ideas they cried out upon as subversive in fact derived from sixteenth-
century Calvinists. Both *Areopagitica* and *The Tenure of Kings and Magistrates*
drew on traditions of radical thinking that were common to Independents,
Levellers and others. William Sedgwick, for instance, described kings as
'deputies and commissioners' just as Milton did.[3] Milton's statement,
first made in 1641 and repeated in *The Tenure*, that all men since Adam are
born free, had been – as we have seen – a traditional lower-class reading of
the Bible ever since the Peasants' Revolt of 1381, and no doubt earlier.[4]

   Milton agreed with the Leveller leaders in rejecting the communist
theories which Diggers, some Ranters and the author of *Tyranipocrit
Discovered* (1649) preached. He agreed with Levellers (and Diggers) in
their opposition to tithes, their rejection of monarchy and the House of
Lords, their belief that magistrates should be elected, and that resistance
to tyranny was not only a right but a duty.[5] Like them he thought too
much government a greater danger than too little, and like them he
accepted the desirability of legal decentralization; like them he adopted a
radical version of the Norman Yoke theory.[6] In his Commonplace Book he
collected many favourable references to Alfred and Edward the Confessor :
he longed for an Alfred 'to rid us of this Norman gibberish'. In *Of
Reformation* he associated prelates with the Norman Yoke. *The Tenure of
Kings and Magistrates* picked up his earlier reference to 'their gibberish
laws, . . . the badge of their ancient slavery'. In *Eikonoklastes* he bewailed
men's readiness 'with the fair words and promises of an old exasperated
foe . . . to be stroked and tamed again into the wonted and well-pleasing

---

[1] T. Edwards, III, pp. 15–16.
[2] *C.P.W.*, VI, pp. 795–6; Lawrence, Sig. A 2.
[3] *C.P.W.*, III, p. 199; W. Sedgwick, *Some Flashes,* pp. 275–6.
[4] *C.P.W.*, I, p. 624; cf. pp. 71–2 above.
[5] *C.P.W.*, IV, p. 94; VI, pp. 795–801.
[6] For this see C. Hill (Panther, 1969), pp. 58–125; Manning, pp. 301–6.

state of their true Norman villeinage'.[1] This looks forward to lines in
Samson Agonistes:

> My nation was subjected to your lords.
> It was the force of conquest; force with force
> Is well ejected when the conquered can.

Edwards's Further Error No. 50 was Richard Overton's famous phrase
'Whatever our forefathers were, or whatever they did or suffered or were
enforced to yield unto, we are the men of the present age, and ought to be
absolutely free from all kinds of exorbitances, molestations or arbitrary
power.'[2] Filmer quoted an echo of this from Milton: 'If at any time our
forefathers, out of baseness, have lost anything of their right, that ought
not [to ?] hurt us, they might if they would promise slavery for themselves,
for us certainly they could not, who have always the same right to free
ourselves that they had to give themselves to any man in slavery.'[3]
Similarly Milton's suggestion that 'to take away from the people the right
of choosing government takes away all liberty' is virtually identical with
Rainborough's famous words in the Putney Debates: 'Every man that is
to live under a government ought first by his own consent to put himself
under that government.'[4]

Milton was sarcastic about lawyers whilst still at Cambridge – in the
First Elegy and the Seventh Prolusion as well as in his Commonplace
Book; he repeated his jibes in *Of Education*. He noted Savanarola's
preference for 'the spirit rather than the letter of the law', and consistently
rejected arguments from precedents, authorities and any similar 'crochet
of the law'.[5] Against mere legalism he appealed to the law of nature and
the Law of God: like John Cook he argued that Charles I was condemned
by 'the unanimous consent of all rational men in the world, written on
every man's heart with the pen of a diamond in capital letters'.[6] This took
the Levellers' argument in a direction which they did not wish to travel;
but it was a Leveller argument.

Overton appears to refer to *The Doctrine and Discipline of Divorce* in
Mans Mortalitie.[7] There is much similarity between the arguments of
Walwyn's *The Compassionate Samaritane* and *Areopagitica*. In their turn
Lilburne and Overton seem to have been influenced by Milton's tract.

---

[1] *C.P.W.*, I, pp. 378, 382, 386–7, 424–30, 447, 592; III, pp. 193, 581; cf. *C.M.*, VI, p. 132;
XVIII, pp. 4–5.
[2] Wolfe (1944), p. 114; T. Edwards, III, p. 16.
[3] Filmer, pp. 259–60.
[4] *C.P.W.*, VI, pp. 795–6; Woodhouse (1938), p. 53.
[5] *C.P.W.*, I, pp. 301, 423–4, 468–9; II, pp. 265, 383, 572; III, p. 193; IV, p. 319; cf. p. 678.
[6] *Ibid.*, IV, pp. 466–7; J. Cook (1649), p. 22.
[7] Saurat, p. 269.

The Yale editors show how close Milton was to Leveller sentiments in the *Digression* to his *History of Britain*, probably written in 1647-8 though not published until 1681.[1] In 1649 he parted company with the Levellers, but he still used many Leveller arguments in *The Tenure, Eikonoklastes* and *A Defence of the People of England*. He never attacked them, even though invited to do so by the Council of State.[2] He was not slow to accept an invitation, issued on the same day, to attack Irish Royalists. Lilburne in 1652, Sexby in 1657, quoted Milton with approval still. His break with the Levellers came partly on tactical grounds: there was no basis of support in the country for the Leveller democratic programme.[3]

It has been said that under the 1648 Blasphemy Ordinance Milton would have been liable to five capital charges and eight involving life imprisonment.[4] Like so many people who make telling points, M. A. Larson has been accused of exaggeration. Let us halve his estimate, and have Milton liable to only two and a half executions, imprisonment for only four lives; it still gives us an idea of the dangers that beset him. That Parliament's Blasphemy Ordinance was not fully enforced is quite another matter: the reason for this was the popular reaction to it which Milton himself and brave men like him helped to create. Against this background of orthodox Puritanism's fears and suspicions let us consider some of Milton's heresies.

First, religious toleration, the greatest of all evils, Thomas Edwards thought. This included the right of assembly, the right of free discussion, and by extension liberty of printing, with which Milton was especially concerned. This was common ground to sectaries, Levellers and others leftwards. Milton's point in *An Apology against a Pamphlet*, that heresies were a consequence of the darkness in which the bishops had kept the people, was echoed by William Sedgwick in a sermon preached in 1643 'before sundry of the House of Commons'. 'When we have more light', the preacher said, 'we shall consent [i.e. agree] quickly.'[5] *Areopagitica* is the most eloquent pamphlet on this subject, but its arguments had been anticipated by Walwyn and Henry Robinson, and were to be repeated by many others. This position led some (though not Milton) to reject the very idea of heresy and blasphemy as punishable offences. Milton has been described, justly, as the first great English writer to urge his readers not to

---

[1] *C.P.W.*, II, pp. 84-7, 91-2, 490, 542-3, 551, 566; V, pp. 421-2, 445, 454-5.
[2] *Ibid.*, III, pp. 36-8, 232, 486-7; IV, p. 425.
[3] *Ibid.*, IV, p. 3; see p. 225 below.
[4] Larson, p. 891.
[5] W. Seigwick [i.e. Sedgwick] (1643), pp. 37-8. This was the second time Sedgwick had echoed Milton: see p. 82n. above.

react automatically to smear and bogey words like 'sect', 'schism', 'heretic' or 'blasphemer'.[1] But he had been preceded by John Goodwin's *Imputatio Fidei* (1642); Selden, Agricola Carpenter and many others were to repeat the point.

Toleration of the tender consciences of university-educated divines was one thing: in the early forties Presbyterians and Independents might have agreed on that. But when unlettered laymen began to usurp the pulpit that was something quite different. The acid test of radicalism came to be anti-clericalism, rejection of any distinction between clergy and laity, of any special clerical caste. The separatists Barrow and Greenwood had repudiated the word 'layman' as popish. A true church, they thought, could exist without ministers; any layman might preach.[2] 'New Presbyter is but old priest writ large', Milton told the Presbyterian clergy. As so often he was putting into epigrammatic form a radical commonplace. 'So antichristian and dividing a term as clergy and laity,' said no less a person than Oliver Cromwell; 'a term unknown to any save the antichristian church', William Dell echoed him.[3]

From this attitude followed the doctrine denounced by Thomas Edwards, not only that laymen might preach but that 'a poor plain countryman' with the spirit of God was better than 'the greatest philosopher, scholar or doctor' without it.[4] This was the religious equivalent of Cromwell's russet-coated captain, who knew what he fought for and loved what he knew, and was therefore preferable to a gentleman who had rank and nothing more. From his first pamphlet Milton insisted that the essentials of Christianity were simple and easy to understand. 'A plain unlearned man that lives well by that light which he has is better and wiser and edifies others more' than 'a learned hypocrite'. Any congregation might elect its own minister, any believer might preach. This looks forward to Christ's attitude towards learning in *Paradise Regained*, and to Milton's 'We are all equally priests in Christ' in the *De Doctrina Christiana*, where 'philosophizing academics' are attacked. A religious service should be a discussion, in which 'the weakest of the brethren should have an opportunity' to take part.[5] In 1644 Milton envisaged higher education for lawyers and medical doctors, but not for the clergy.[6]

---

[1] Frye (1966), p. 123; *C.P.W.*, II, p. 554; VI, pp. 123, 699–700.
[2] White (1973), pp. 76–9.
[3] Cromwell, II, p. 197; Dell, pp. 264–5. Cf. *C.P.W.*, I, p. 838; II, p. 109. Cf. p. 228n. below.
[4] T. Edwards, I, pp. 29–30; Dell, pp. 273–4.
[5] *C.P.W.*, I, pp. 379, 566, 600, 690, 720, 838–40, 932–5; II, pp. 531, 537; VI, pp. 127, 558, 568–73, 593–601, 608; cf. p. 805.
[6] *Ibid.*, II, p. 380.

The logic of all this was rejection of a state church, and in particular of 'the ignoble hucksterage of piddling tithes', 'wrung out of men's purses to maintain a disapproved ministry against their consciences'.[1] From the 'blind mouths' of *Lycidas*, through *Areopagitica*'s rejection of the legend that 'the tenth part of learning stood or fell with the clergy', down to *The Likeliest Means to Remove Hirelings* (1659), Milton's attitude was consistent. Abolition of tithes was necessary to guarantee real religious liberty. If no clerical caste with legally fixed maintenance, then no training of such a caste at the universities. In 1659 Milton echoed Dell to write: 'It is a fond error, though too much believed among us, to think that the university makes a minister of the Gospel.'[2] Oxford and Cambridge colleges were largely financed by impropriated tithes, and university divines by pluralism. As early as *Areopagitica* Milton had mocked 'the complaint and lamentation of prelates' that learning would be 'for ever dasht and discouraged' if pluralism were abolished, and he repeated the point in relation to tithes in *The Likeliest Means* of 1659.[3] The wail was often heard in between.

Tithes proved to be a dividing sword among the radicals, symbolized by the claim that Oliver Cromwell had promised to abolish them but failed to carry out this promise when he had the power to do so: instead he came down in favour of a state church. No Parliament ever voted down tithes, not even the Barebones Assembly, not even the restored Rump in 1659, of which Milton hoped so much. Far too many vested interests were involved. Nor were even the sectaries unanimous. Some Baptist ministers were prepared to accept livings in the Cromwellian church. Those who opposed 'hirelings' with the same passion as Milton were Levellers, Diggers, Quakers, most Baptists, Fifth Monarchists, the extreme radicals.

Instead of a regular beneficed clergy, Milton came to advocate itinerant preachers, maintained by voluntary contributions.[4] This nostrum of the radicals was tried out by the Commissions for Propagating the Gospel in Wales and in the North Parts in the early fifties. The experiment was unpopular with conservatives; quarrels over it had something to do with the fall of the Rump in 1653. Milton's sonnet to Oliver Cromwell in 1652 aimed at persuading him to resist conservative pressure for preservation of a state church, as another sonnet praised Vane for supporting a freer system. In 1659 Milton hoped to see the itinerant system backed up by

---

[1] *Ibid.*, I, pp. 613, 719–20.
[2] *Ibid.*, VI, pp. 568–73; *C.M.*, VI, p. 93; *C. and C.*, pp. 136–43. In the *Second Defence* Milton went out of his way to praise Pickering, who had been zealous against tithes in the Barebones Parliament.
[3] *C.P.W.*, II, pp. 530–1; *C.M.*, VI, pp. 65–6.
[4] *C.M.*, VI, pp. 75–7.

local lay preachers. His proposals recall the organization of the Baptists and the Society of Friends: even more perhaps they look forward to the Methodists (just as *Of Education* looks forward to the Dissenting Academies).[1]

Milton rejected not only 'the corrupt and venal discipline of clergy courts', but all 'coercive jurisdiction in the church'. He thought not only that the Pope was Antichrist, but that bishops were more antichristian than the Pope. Like John Saltmarsh, he thought that any state church was necessarily antichristian. When he made Antichrist Mammon's son Milton may even have hinted at social interpretations akin to those of Gerrard Winstanley.[2] Milton pointed out that Christ used force only once – to drive money-changers out of the Temple. The coercive power of the secular magistrate in religious matters Milton similarly denied.[3] 'Since God became flesh', John Reeve told the Lord Mayor of London in 1653, 'no civil magistrate hath any authority from above to be judge of any man's faith, because it is a spiritual invisible gift from God.'[4] Milton would have agreed with the conclusion. Repudiation of a state church divided sectaries from Episcopalians and Presbyterians; denial of the authority of the magistrate brought about a division somewhere farther to the left. In each case Milton came to be with the more radical party.

If there is no distinction between clergy and laity, ordinary people have the right to interpret the Bible for themselves. This led to what Edwards called anti-Scripturism – criticism of the contradictions of the Bible, denial that it was the Word of God.[5] Milton did not go so far as Clement Writer, Walwyn, some Ranters and the Quaker Samuel Fisher.[6] But – unlike Edwards – he would have insisted on the principle that the individual had a right and indeed a duty to study the Bible for himself, not taking his religion at second hand from Pope, church or priest. He likewise insisted that 'the spirit of God, promised alike and given / To all believers' was the test for interpreting the letter of the Bible. Such 'spiritual illumination . . . is common to all men.'[7] The distinction is a narrow one between this position and the Ranter and Quaker view that the spirit within believers was *superior* to the letter of Scripture, overriding it.

---

[1] See p. 149 below.
[2] C. Hill (1971), pp. 94, 116–19.
[3] *Ibid.*, pp. 92–3; *C.P.W.*, VI, pp. 797–8; *C.M.*, VI, pp. 44–5; T. Edwards, I, pp. 26, 32–3.
[4] Reeve and Muggleton, p. 4; Muggleton (1764), pp. 71–2, 106.
[5] T. Edwards, I, pp. 18–19, 104–5, 113–16; cf. p. 248 below.
[6] *W.T.U.D.*, chapter XI.
[7] *P.L.* XII. 519–20; *C.P.W.*, VI, p. 204.

Milton's belief that worship is discussion, that the spirit in man is more important than any ecclesiastical authority, that each of us must interpret the Bible for himself, thus aligns him with Ranters, Quakers, anti-nomians: so does his conviction that men and women should strive to attain perfection on earth, even though Milton did not think they could ever succeed. His ultimate belief in the necessity of good works for salvation, the consequence of his emphasis on human freedom, aligns him with Arminians of the left like John Goodwin, General Baptists and Quakers, whilst his total rejection of sacramentalism and a state church puts him at the opposite pole to the Laudian 'Arminians' of the right. Milton accepted the heresy of adult baptism, at a time when the medical reformer William Rand thought that Henry Lawrence's publication of his *Treatise of Baptism* was a more courageous act than risking his life on the field of battle.[1] This links Milton with Socinians and Anabaptists, though he seems to have joined no Baptist congregation. His decisive rejection of sabbatarianism also puts him beyond the pale of 'respectable' Puritanism.[2]

Milton was a radical millenarian long before Fifth Monarchism was thought of: he equated monarchy with Antichrist. In 1641 he associated his belief that Christ's kingdom 'is now at hand' with his confidence in the potentialities of free and democratic discussion.[3] He had a vision of England as leader of an international revolution, which links him both with the Fifth Monarchists and with the pre-pacifist George Fox, who in 1657 rebuked the English army for not yet having sacked Rome.

Milton agreed with Servetus, Socinians and Ranters in many of his views on the Trinity, with Servetus, Socinians, some Levellers, Diggers, Ranters and Muggletonians in his mortalism. Milton's heresies on divorce linked him in the minds of contemporaries with Ranters and libertines. His emphasis on the absolute authority of conscience meant that believers were redeemed from the curse, freed from the law. This led him to the very verge of antinomianism which the Ranters overstepped. Milton's emphasis throughout his writings on the light/darkness antithesis links him with Clarkson, Bauthumley and other Ranters, and with the Quakers; it looks back to Hermeticist and alchemical writers culminating in Robert Fludd. Milton's insistence that Adam and Eve made love before the Fall links up with Ranter attitudes to sex; the fact that they laboured before the Fall associates him with popular traditions drawn on by the Diggers. That hell was an internal state (whether or not it was a geographical

---

[1] Riolanus, Sig. B – dedication by Rand to Lawrence.
[2] *C.P.W.*, VI, pp. 353–4, 639, 708–14.
[3] *Ibid.*, I, pp. 706–7. See chapter 22 below.

location as well) goes back to Marlowe and beyond, and is found in
Boehme, Wither, Overton.[1] To many of the radicals Milton must have
seemed one of them, as he did to Edwards, Baillie, Pagitt, Ross, Fuller.

Once this point has been established, as I think it can be, it appears
superfluous and rather foolish to hunt for the sources of Milton's ideas
only in the writings of classical philosophers or early Christian theologians.
It is possible that Milton, a very learned man, might have got from Plato,
Seneca, Origen, Lactantius or the Cabbalists ideas that were current
among his radical contemporaries. But this assumes an isolated Milton:
it is at least worth reminding ourselves what ideas were current in London
taverns at this time. Milton would certainly have read *Gangraena* before
associating himself so firmly with Edwards's victims.[2] No doubt the
poet's exceptionally wide reading gave an extra dimension to his theology,
and this often led him to conclusions different from those of his radical
contemporaries. But all around him men and women were eagerly and
freely debating these matters, verbally and in print. Milton acclaimed the
debate in *Areopagitica*; he took part in it, both in his published tracts and
in his dialogue with himself in *De Doctrina Christiana*.

Such an approach enables us to side-step many scholarly, not to say
scholastic, discussions – such as whether Milton is or is not properly
described as an Arian.[3] Milton claimed to base all his views on Scripture
only. Although his strong prepossessions enabled him to argue away
certain crucial Biblical texts which he did not like, he would never have
followed any thinker, orthodox or heretical, against his own reading of
the Bible. That would have signified being a heretic in the truth, adopting
an implicit faith.[4]

III Overlapping circles

Few of Milton's views were original. But the vigour and eloquence with
which he expressed them, and the circumstances in which he expressed
them, call for comment. To say that 'language is but the instrument conveying to us things useful to be known' is in one sense the conventional
Baconian doctrine that things are more important than words. Yet Milton
extends the point to argue that 'any yeoman or tradesman competently

---

[1] R.O., pp. 38–42, 68, 96; West (1955) pp. 104, 199–200. Milton had echoed Marlowe in *Arcades*.
[2] MacCallum, pp. 88–104.
[3] See p. 285 below.
[4] See chapter 19 below.

wise in his mother dialect only' is as estimable as a university pedant. So even the 'élitist' *Of Education* unexpectedly echoes Milton's defence of mechanic preachers, his preference for 'a homely and yeomanly religion'.[1]

In *The Doctrine and Discipline of Divorce* Milton had insisted that men must be liberated from the tyranny of custom, of accepted ideas. 'Error supports custom, custom countenances error.' Custom's defenders decried free reasoning 'under the terms of humour and innovation'. This line of argument had often been repeated since the authoress or author of *Haec Vir* in 1620 had said 'Custom is an idiot.'[2] But to defend innovation and liberty of speculation in 1643 was to defend the right of the lower classes to challenge the assumptions of their betters. It led Milton within six years to the ultimate revolutionary position, defence of regicide. *The Tenure of Kings and Magistrates* also starts with an attack on the 'tyranny of custom'.[3] The traditional humanist emphasis on the superiority of reason and virtue to mere birth is used in *Eikonoklastes* to justify regicide: 'it were a mad law that would subject reason to superiority of place.'[4] Milton went well beyond orthodox Puritanism in his belief that the whole Mosaic law was abolished, moral as well as ceremonial; that Christians are emancipated from Sabbath observance, and that the words 'blasphemy and heresy' are mere bugbears.[5]

In the late forties a whole range of certainties had broken down. King Charles had gone: was King Jesus coming? Church courts, 'the bawdy courts', had disappeared: what restraints on moral behaviour were henceforth legitimate? The press was free, assembly was free: what limits, if any, should there be to liberty of speculation? Was Christianity itself open to question? Such problems worried or attracted large numbers of ordinary men and women in London, the Home Counties, East Anglia and the army. We may call them Seekers so long as we do not thereby imply any unity of outlook among the large numbers who were dissatisfied with traditional forms and beliefs. Their discussions, unrestrained by the presence of social superiors or by the discipline of a traditional education, led to a proliferation of wild heresies. 'The new upstart wantons that deny God's ordinance, or new notionists,' said a pamphleteer of 1649, were 'full of whimsies'.[6]

---

[1] *C.P.W.*, II, pp. 369–76. Cf. p. 84 above.
[2] *C.P.W.*, II, pp. 222–4, 343; *Haec Vir*, Sig. B 2v.
[3] *C.P.W.*, III, p. 190.
[4] *Ibid.*, III, p. 462.
[5] *Ibid.*, VI, pp. 708–14; *C.M.*, VI, pp. 10–14; cf. chapter 24 below.
[6] Purnell, *A Word*, p. 62.

We know something of what went on from the autobiographies of Ranters, Quakers, Muggletonians, Bunyan and many others. Such men, in the words of a Cromwellian ordinance of March 1654, 'contended against magistracy, against ministry, against Scriptures and against ordinances, . . . running after fancies and notions'. They justified themselves 'under the notion of liberty', saying that 'the magistrate hath nothing to do . . . in . . . these things.'[1] Milton operated at a more sophisticated level than Fox or Bunyan, Reeve or Clarkson. But he knew of the discussions and speculations which went on in London congregations and taverns, and I would guess that he participated in them.[2] He certainly disapproved of the ordinance from which I have just quoted, since it confirmed the existence of a state church and set up Triers to judge the doctrines of ministers.

In 1649 Clement Walker described Milton as 'a libertine', who 'will be tied to no obligation to God or man'. In 1660 he was called a 'Christian libertine'; seventeen years later, 'a great agent for libertinism'.[3] As the word was used in the sixteenth and seventeenth centuries, this was accurate enough. Calvin attacked the Libertines of his Geneva for saying that they had found the way back to the state of Adam before the Fall – a Paradise within them, happier far.[4] Samuel Rutherford, denounced in Milton's sonnet, in 1648 criticized Familists for saying that God is 'the being of things'; Henry Niklaes, the founder of Familism, he described as 'a blasphemous libertine' because he said that 'God hath godded us with him' – a phrase frequently used by Ranters in the sixteen-fifties, as well as by 'the Maids of Aldgate' whom Milton defended in *Colasterion*. Many thought mortalism a mere excuse for libertinism. William Lilly, on the other hand, used the word as a synonym for 'free men': English help to the Dutch had 'wholly made them libertines and weakened ourselves'. For Rutherford libertines included those who condemned the condemnation of heretics, and who made 'conscience, not the Word of God, their rule'. He described William Dell as a libertine, and no doubt would have added Milton if he had read the *De Doctrina Christiana* – or even *Areopagitica*.[5]

We recall Milton's possession from the late fifties (and we do not know for how long earlier) of a manuscript of Jean Bodin's *Heptaplomeres*, so

---

[1] Cromwell, III, pp. 226–8.
[2] Cf. Empson (1961), pp. 142, 275.
[3] C. Walker, II, p. 199; Wolfe (*Milton in the* P.R., 1941), p. 455; G. S., p. viii; John Warley, *The Reasoning Apostate*, quoted by Sensabaugh, p. 51.
[4] Cohn, p. 19.
[5] Lilly, *Annus* (1652), p. 19; Rutherford (1647), pp. 358, 465; (?1648), pp. 115, 262, 402; (1648), I, pp. 193–4, 238–9; *C.P.W.*, II, p. 750; cf., p. 355. Cf. p. 316 below.

subversive and critical of Christianity that it was not published, even in
Latin, until the nineteenth century. It circulated in manuscript and copies
were very difficult to come by. (Did Milton obtain his copy on his Italian
journey, as his friend Nathan Paget appears to have acquired Familist
and Behmenist manuscripts during his stay in the Netherlands?[1]) From
Heptaplomeres – a disputation between spokesmen for all religions and
none – Milton could have found confirmation of many of his ideas – the
desirability of religious toleration, rejection of the decalogue and the
Trinity, climatic theories. He would not have gone so far as some of the
Biblical criticisms in Bodin's work, but he might have been interested in
the idea that 'each of us is his own Adam'. The suggestion that the Genesis
story is 'a pretty allegory' would be more likely to appeal to Gerrard
Winstanley than to Milton.[2]

Milton's ideas also have many links with the Hermetic tradition, and
especially with his Buckinghamshire neighbour Robert Fludd, the great
synthesizer of this tradition.[3] Milton seems to have possessed a copy of
the Hermetic writings. He refers several times to 'thrice-great Hermes' –
in the undergraduate *De Idea Platonica*, and in *Il Penseroso*. Hermetic
influences have been found in *At a Vacation Exercise*, and in the Third
and Seventh Prolusions. Frances Yates suggests that the Hermetic trance
is described at length in *Il Penseroso*.[4] Milton twice refers to John Dee, and
in *Areopagitica* there may be an echo of Giordano Bruno.[5] More important
perhaps is the parallelism of Milton's thought with that of the Hermeticists.
Though this body of ideas embraces magic, alchemy and astrology, it is
completely devoid of ritualism or sacramentalism.[6]

Milton's daemons in *Il Penseroso* and the Seventh Prolusion, and the
Attendant Spirit in *Comus* (called Daemon in the manuscript – like Comus
himself),[7] may or may not be Hermetic: likewise the 'millions of spiritual
creatures' who 'walk the earth unseen' in *Paradise Lost* (IV. 677–8) and
the 'demonian spirits' of *Paradise Regained*.[8] But the corporeality of angels

---

[1] See appendix 3 below.
[2] Bodin, pp. 205, 77, 31, 164, 181–94, 141–61, and *passim*. Grotius apparently possessed a copy
of this work (*ibid.*, pp. 4–5). For Winstanley see *W.T.U.D.* pp. 111–20. For a suggestion that
Heptaplomeres may 'reflect some encounter' between Bodin and the Family of Love, see
Kirsop, pp. 114–18. D. P. Walker suggests that Bodin was no longer a Christian at the time of
writing *Heptaplomeres* (1958, p. 171).
[3] See p. 38 above.
[4] Yates (1964), p. 280; Hanford (1966), pp. 61, 106; cf. Woodhouse and Bush, I, pp. 143,
179, 324–6 for other suggestions of early Hermeticist influences; Allen (1970), pp. 14–15.
[5] Jacobus, p. 387; Yates (1964), p. 256.
[6] W. Scott, I, p. 8.
[7] Scoufos, pp. 129, 132.
[8] Cf. W. Scott, I, pp. 268–71, 344–5; II, p. 430. Cf. chapter 26 below.

links with this tradition, as Fludd himself tells us. The names of some of Milton's angels come from Fludd, who, like Milton, gave Satan's name before the Fall as Lucifer. Milton's phrases in *Paradise Lost*, 'potable gold' and 'vegetable gold' may refer to Fludd's experiments. Messiah was armed in 'radiant urim', the stone that in Fludd's philosophy mediates between God and the material world.[1] Like Milton, Fludd used mathematical arguments against the Trinity, and speculated on whether light was created or eternal.[2] Fludd has something very like Milton's theory of creation. He referred directly to Hermes Trismegistus, and also drew on the related Paracelsan tradition.[3] Milton later championed the Paracelsan view that like cures like, as against the Galenic theory, which he had earlier espoused, that contraries cure.[4]

I shall have many occasions in the following pages to cite parallels between Milton's thought and that of Hermeticism, particularly as mediated by Fludd.[5] Milton's anti-Trinitarianism, mortalism and materialism, for instance, may be linked with this tradition, as well as with the ideas of radicals like the Leveller Richard Overton, or John Goodwin, a fellow defender of regicide, or the Socinians Paul Best and John Bidle. Maurice Kelley is right to emphasize that Milton was not a lone seeker in theology but rather 'part of a small, unorganized but vigorous movement that manifested itself openly in the second half of the sixteen-forties'. He is equally right to argue that scholars should be looking for Milton's sources among post-Reformation radicals rather than among Greek Fathers;[6] though we may note that Milton's favourite early Christian writer, Lactantius, was influenced by Hermes.[7]

I tried once to list those sects and radical groups which shared any of Milton's radical views: anti-clericalism, millenarianism, antinomianism, anti-Trinitarianism, mortalism, materialism, hell internal. I was a little startled by the result: the group closest to Milton was the Muggletonians, followers of John Reeve and Lodowick Muggleton, who in 1652 were commissioned by God as the Two Last Witnesses foretold in Revelation 11. This was very salutary. I have in my time criticized other historians for

---

[1] See Fowler's notes to *P.L.*, I. 533–4; III. 596–601, 608; IV. 217–21; V. 658–9; VI. 761; cf. *P.R.*, III. 14–15.

[2] See p. 240 below; West (1955), p. 74; (1950), pp. 211–23.

[3] Fludd, pp. 42–5, 48–9, 52, 133–4, 138, and *passim*; Saurat, pp. 252, 261–7, and *passim*; Woodhouse (1945), pp. 221–33; Werblowsky, pp. 90–113.

[4] Foreword to *Samson Agonistes*; contrast *C.P.W.*, II, p. 668. Cf. Debus (1972), pp. 185–99; (1975) pp. 22–4.

[5] See esp. chapter 26 below.

[6] *C.P.W.*, VI, pp. 68, 85–6, 108–9.

[7] Hartwell, pp. 115–21.

treating the radicals of the English Revolution as a 'lunatic fringe'. Yet I had always placed the Muggletonians outside my pale of sanity. I was wrong. A religious group which survived for three hundred years among solid London artisans cannot be dismissed as mad. Reeve and Muggleton moved in London radical circles, the circles from which Ranters, Quakers and such emerged: early London Quakers saw the Muggletonians as perhaps their most serious rivals. Muggletonians preserved, fossilized, many of the ideas of this Seeker milieu of the fifties, the milieu from which many of Milton's ideas seem to derive.

The curve of Milton's political career quite surprisingly follows that of the Quakers: his support for Cromwell in 1649 and 1653, his growing disillusion under the Protectorate, his rejection of all organized churches, the traumatic effect on him of the Restoration, leading to apparent political quietism and withdrawal from politics whilst still hoping for ultimate divine revenge. Many others followed a similar course. Milton's friend Roger Williams early denied 'any true church in the world'. He 'will have every man to serve God by himself alone, without any church at all'.[1] In 1648 the near-Socinian John Bidle asked 'whether any public worship was justified, or a papal usurpation?' Walwyn could not 'associate in a church way, . . . not knowing any persons to be so qualified as ministers of the Gospel ought to be', though in 1649 he still had hopes for the future.[2] Winstanley found rest 'in no outward form of worship'. Ranters thought that men no longer needed 'such lower helps from outward administrations' once Christ had come into their hearts. Giles Randall and other Seekers, Clarkson and many Ranters, John Gratton in his pre-Quaker days, refused to go to any church.[3]

'Better no ministry than a pretended ministry', was the view attributed to William Erbery by John Webster. 'In this darkness' of the apostacy 'he had rather sit down and wait in silence than be beholding to the pretended light and direction of deceivable guides.' Erbery moves parallel to Milton in many respects. He was 'ever entire to the interest of this Commonwealth'; he was accused of being a Socinian; he was a passionate foe to any state church, any intolerance. He expected to see God and his saints ruling on earth and judging the world. Like Milton, he rejected Fifth Monarchism; his attitude to the Ranters was – and was thought by contemporaries to be – ambiguous.[4]

---

[1] Baillie (1775), II, p. 24.
[2] Bidle (1648), p. 34; Haller and Davies, pp. 337, 392.
[3] *W.T.U.D.*, pp. 206–7; Clarkson (1660), pp. 9–10; Sabine, pp. 46–8, 230; Gratton, p. 16.
[4] Erbery, pp. 22–3, 40–2, 263–5, 338; Cheynell (1646), p. 38; cf. *W.T.U.D.*, pp. 192–7.

John Reeve was another who believed that all visible worship was done away with by Christ, 'that the invisible worship of the invisible God may take place in the hearts of his people for ever.' There had been no true worship since Constantine's day. 'Inward, spiritual silent praying and praising' should now replace 'outward praying, preaching, fasting . . . to be seen of men'.[1] When Lodowick Muggleton after the Restoration advised his followers to 'keep all at home . . . as long as the powers of the nation doth forbid you to go to any meetings', rather than attend the parish church, he added that there was no 'necessity for any public meetings at all'.[2] Perhaps closest of all to Milton was Colonel Hutchinson, who when he was asked after the Restoration where he went to church replied, 'Nowhere.' To the question 'How he then did for his soul's comfort?' he replied, 'Sir, I hope you leave me that to account between God and my own soul.'[3]

If Milton was known to and trusted by London radicals, this would help to explain Edward Phillips's story that at one time his uncle was proposed as Adjutant-General to Sir William Waller's army. Biographers since Masson have tended to dismiss this, perhaps because they related it to 1645, when Waller indeed had a vacancy for an Adjutant-General, but when he was an extinct volcano: there is no reason why Milton should want to be employed by him then. Masson suggested 1643, when London radicals were running Waller as a win-the-war leader against the conservative and dilatory Essex. Some of them may have approached Milton as a possible civilian aide, or commissar, for Waller's army, which they were hoping completely to remodel. The fact that Waller's star sank rapidly and that he later revealed himself as little less conservative than Essex himself would explain why the project fizzled out. If I am right, Milton was not interested in a military career as such; he might have been persuaded to undertake this particular job at this particular time. It was presumably City radicals who urged Milton to write *Areopagitica*. Hartlib for one knew Waller well.[4]

Lest I be misunderstood, I repeat that I do not think Milton was a Leveller, a Ranter, a Muggletonian or a Behmenist. Rather I suggest that we should see him living in a state of permanent dialogue with radical views which he could not wholly accept, yet some of which greatly

---

[1] Reeve (*Joyfull News*, 1706), pp. 39–42; cf. Muggleton (1764), pp. 19, 147.
[2] Reeve and Muggleton, p. 23; cf. pp. 186–7, 447, 466–7.
[3] Hutchinson, p. 250; cf. Carroll (1971), pp. 78–9. There is much evidence for failure to attend at the parish church after 1660 – e.g. M. Robinson, p. 61 – Richmondshire; Capp, p. 195 – Hertfordshire; Chalklin, p, 224 – Kent; G. Holmes, p. 25 – Worcestershire. Cf. p. 238 below.
[4] For Hartlib see pp. 146–7 below.

attracted him.[1] In the *De Doctrina Christiana* Milton criticized those (Fludd, Richard Overton, Ranters, Diggers) who equate God and nature;[2] and those (Ranters, Behmenists) who attribute sin to God.[3] He was prepared to allow the magistrate some restrictive power in religion which sectaries denied him.[4] Unlike most radicals (except the Muggletonians) Milton had no objection to judicial oaths;[5] unlike Lilburne and the Quakers he could see nothing wrong with hat honour.[6] Bowing 'to superior spirits is wont in heaven', we are told in *Paradise Lost* (III. 737) – though, with typical ambiguity, the example Milton gives is Satan. Milton praised equality, but opposed 'the absurdity of equalling the unequal'; 'each person should be cared for according to his rank and eminence.' He no more shared the Leveller confidence in democracy than he shared the Digger distrust of private property. He denied the equality of the Irish, proclaimed by some Levellers, and the equality of women, proclaimed by very few indeed.[7]

In his ultimate lack of respect for Parliament Milton was closer to the Fifth Monarchists than to republicans or Levellers: yet he was no Fifth Monarchist.[8] The Levellers had carried the myth of Anglo-Saxon freedom, which Sir Edward Coke had used to idolize the common law, to conclude 'our very laws were made by our conquerors' and should be rejected: Milton went even further and argued that Parliament was 'a Norman or French word, a monument of our ancient servitude': the name should be abolished, and perhaps the thing too.[9] Milton never accepted Ranter antinomianism, nor the early Quaker doctrine of the self-sufficiency of the inner light. He referred to the Blasphemy Act of 1650, directed mainly against Ranters, as 'that prudent and well-deliberated act'.[10] He never abandoned his belief that the Bible contained truths necessary for salvation. He parted company with Socinians in attributing divinity to Christ. On some of these questions Milton drew fine distinctions which we shall be examining later.[11]

In this chapter I have been advancing a thesis. My object was to emphasize the intellectual milieu from which Milton's ideas arose, to

---

[1] *W.T.U.D.*, pp. 401–2.
[2] *C.P.W.*, VI, pp. 130–1.
[3] *Ibid.*, pp. 144–5.
[4] *C.M.*, VI, pp. 4–5.
[5] *Ibid.*, VI, p. 103; *C.P.W.*, VI, pp. 684–6.
[6] *C.P.W.*, VI, p. 673.
[7] *Ibid.*, VI, pp. 673, 686, 790.
[8] Fixler, esp. chapters IV and V.
[9] *C.M.*, XVIII, pp. 4–5.
[10] *Ibid.*, VI, p. 11. Contrast the Blasphemy Ordinance of 1654 (p. 109 above).
[11] See esp. chapter 27 below.

suggest affinities between his ideas and those of his radical contemporaries, not to claim identity. Often his views developed in conscious disagreement with those of Levellers or Ranters or Socinians. If we think of two eccentric circles, one representing the ideas of traditional Puritanism, the other those of the radical milieu, Milton's ideas form a third circle, concentric to neither of these but overlapping both.[1] But the bubbling ferment of discussion and speculation going on in the sixteen-forties should not be left out of any attempt to understand Milton's own thinking. Perhaps the London radicals were, if not better teachers than Origen, Lactantius and Arius – to none of whom Milton subscribed slave – at least a more immediate influence and stimulus.

Down to 1642 Milton's career had been an almost consistent success story. He developed slowly, but at Cambridge he won the affection and respect of undergraduates and dons alike. He was dissatisfied with the education he received there, but thanks to his father's generosity he was able to spend many years educating himself more satisfactorily, culminating in his journey to Italy – a privilege usually restricted to sons of the aristocracy. In Italy his reception had bolstered his self-confidence as well as directing his thoughts towards politics. He slowly came to realize that he might become a great poet, and to believe that in this role he could serve his church and his country even better than in the pulpit. Finally, in 1641-2 he had the satisfaction of seeing the hated Laudian régime overthrown. This promised to open up a new era of liberation for England and perhaps for the world, to prepare for a society in which the poet would be listened to and honoured as God's spokesman to his people. His dedicated life seemed to be justifying itself: he could look back on thirty-four years of what might not unreasonably be called true poetry.

Then, in the moment of apparent triumph, things started to go wrong. In 1642 he married Mary Powell. This marriage, contracted with poetic ideals and expectations, was a disastrous failure. A similar disappointment awaited his political hopes. In the New Jerusalem 'ignorance and ecclesiastical thraldom . . . under new shapes and disguises begins apace to grow upon us.' (Those were Milton's last published words before *Areopagitica*, in which he declared that 'bishops and presbyters are the same to us both name and thing.')[2] The pamphlets in which Milton had tried to salvage his high ideal of matrimony by associating it with divorce for incompatibility of temperament were attacked as incitements to promiscuity and

---

[1] I owe this image to Joseph Martin.
[2] *C.P.W.*, II, pp. 479, 539.

libertinism by clergymen who clearly had not read them.[1] His name was dragged through the mud. He was denounced to Parliament. The poet came down to earth with a bump. This is our next subject.

---

[1] See pp. 126, 130–3 below.

Chapter 9

Marriage, Divorce and Polygamy

> Mother Eve, by her vice of curiosity or levity, or admirable facility
> rather than fatuity, was deceived by the serpent in desiring to know
> future things, which folly descends naturally to women.
>
> Sir John Milton, *The Figure Caster*
>
> Thy mate, who sees when thou art seen least wise.
>
> Raphael to Adam, *Paradise Lost*, VIII. 577

I Seventeenth-century attitudes

It is ironical that the popular image of Milton to-day is of an austere
Puritan who advocated the subordination of women. For his contemporaries it was chiefly Milton's sexual libertinism which made them link him
with the radicals. Posterity has remembered 'He for God only, she for
God in him.' On the basis of this line, taken out of context, the poet has
been blamed for failing to rise above his age in this one respect, despite all
the others in which he did rise above it. Posterity has forgotten too that
this line is only a poetical version of St. Paul's 'wives submit yourselves
unto your own husbands as unto the Lord'; 'the husband is the head of
the wife even as Christ is the head of the church.'[1] Given Milton's
assumptions, it is difficult to see how he could have rejected St. Paul's
clear and explicit statements. What Milton says about the subordination
of women is strictly Biblical, backed up in the *De Doctrina Christiana* by an
impressive array of texts.[2]

Feminists were few in the seventeenth century. The liberal Grotius,
whom Milton quoted in favour of divorce, and who in *Adamus Exul*, like
Milton, made Adam's love for Eve a major reason for the Fall, nevertheless in the same drama put words very similar to Milton's into Eve's
mouth, and more specifically than Milton emphasized that Adam sinned

---

[1] Ephesians 5: 22-3.
[2] *C.P.W.*, VI, pp. 609, 782; cf. II, p. 589; Bunyan, II, pp. 429, 438, 560-2, 658-74.

through subservience to his wife.[1] Historians rightly see the Baptists as a
sect which helped the liberation of women. Yet in 1658 the messengers of
the Abingdon Association of Particular Baptist churches discussed the
question: 'How far women may speak in the church?' Their agreed
answer was that 'they may not so speak as that their speaking shall show a
not acknowledging of the inferiority of their sex and so be an usurping
authority over the man.'[2] The only people in the seventeenth century who
came anywhere near making women equal with men were Diggers, Ranters
and Quakers, who believed that men and women were perfectible on
earth, could get back behind the Fall. Milton was more orthodox in this
respect, and thought that the subordination antedated the Fall of Man.
In 1680 Fox said 'Neither did God set the man over the woman whilst they
kept the image of God and obeyed his voice' in Paradise. Nevertheless,
twenty-four years earlier, in Milton's lifetime, Fox had spoken rather
differently, more like the Abingdon Baptists: 'I suffer not a woman to
teach, nor to usurp authority over the man, but to be silent. . . . If they
will learn anything, let them ask their husbands at home.'[3] Between the
two statements I have quoted Fox had himself married.

So to criticize Milton because he stated a theory of male superiority is
like criticizing him because he did not advocate votes or equal pay for
women. No one, to my knowledge, in the seventeenth century claimed
that women were wholly equal to men, just as no one, not even Levellers,
seriously proposed to give them the vote. Edwards asked, as the height of
irony, whether women should have political power, together with servants
and paupers. Milton's enemy Richard Leigh was not untypical when he
wrote in 1675

> The wife no office seems to have
> But of the husband's prime she-slave.[4]

The courtly Marquis of Halifax put it more agreeably in his *Advice to a
Daughter* (1688), but what he said was not so very different.[5] Consider
the Puritan Lucy Hutchinson. She was clearly a stronger character than
her husband. Yet she fully accepted the subordination of her sex,
praising Queen Elizabeth for 'her submission to her masculine and wise

---

[1] *C.P.W.*, II, p. 418; Grotius, *Adamus Exul*, in Kirkconnell, pp. 199–202, 206, 214.
[2] White, *Records*, p. 185.
[3] G. Fox, pp. 77–8, 724; cf. p. 991. Muggleton's attitude towards women was similar, despite
his numerous female correspondents (Reeve and Muggleton, p. 422).
[4] T. Edwards, III, Sig. c. 4v (after p. 16); cf. Filmer, p. 287; Leigh (1947), p. 49. For Leigh see
pp. 142, 214 below.
[5] Halifax, p. 277; cf. Miner (1974), pp. 187–96, on Hobbes and Samuel Butler.

councillors' (!). If we could date her *Memoirs* with more precision we might think she had been reading *Paradise Lost* just before she wrote.[1]

Let us try to put Milton back into history. The sixteenth and seventeenth centuries saw the emergence of new marriage patterns – a rejection of papal doctrines of the superiority of celibacy as well as of the traditional feudal concept which saw marriage as a property transaction, with love as something normally to be found outside marriage. The Puritan attitude towards women assumes the world of small household production, in which the wife had a position of authority over servants, apprentices and children, though in subordination to her husband. The state of matrimony was glorified, and heavy emphasis was laid on love in marriage (and therefore on monogamy), on freedom of choice in marriage (as against what Milton called the 'savage inhumanity' of direction of children by parents),[2] on the wife as 'help-meet', as the junior partner in the household which contemporaries saw as a little church, a little state, a little school.[3] These ideas are to be found in the Puritan guides to godliness, in the writings of William Perkins and William Gouge; they are also in Spenser and Shakespeare, in Roger Williams and Harrington.[4] 'He for God only, she for God in him' expresses Spenser's view of the relation of the sexes; and let us not forget *The Taming of the Shrew*. It was only after the family ceased to be the real productive unit in society that wives of more successful householders began to ape the habits and attitudes of their social betters, to cultivate white hands and vapours: their menfolk meanwhile gave them a sentimentalized elevation to compensate for their effective demotion from the productive process.[5] The inequality was more apparent than real so long as the wife was the helpmeet of her husband in the family firm: deference to the middle-class lady only conceals her powerlessness once she has been cut off from production. Eve was a gardener.

Milton, an intellectual who wished to give reasons for what he believed, theorized about the male supremacy which no one denied. In the course of theorizing he shocked his contemporaries by being prepared to contemplate a situation in which the wife may 'exceed her husband in prudence and dexterity, and he contentedly yield'. Then 'a superior and more

---

[1] Hutchinson, pp. xviii, 32, 48–9. She probably wrote between 1664 and 1671.

[2] *C.P.W.*, II, p. 275; cf. Geneva Bible, marginal note on Genesis 24: 57: 'Parents have not authority to marry their children without consent of the parties.'

[3] Lewis (1936), W. and M. Haller, *passim*; *S. and P.*, chapter XIII; *W.T.U.D.*, chapter 15.

[4] 'Persons may with less sin be forced to marry whom they cannot love than to worship where they cannot believe' (R. Williams, p. 223; Harrington, pp. 109–10).

[5] I owe this point to conversations with the late Alick West; cf. the first two essays in his *The Mountain in the Sunlight* (1958), and *S. and P.*, esp. chapter XIII.

natural law comes in, that the wiser should govern the less wise, whether male or female.' This, however, he regarded as an exceptional case, though taking care to note examples of outstanding women in his Commonplace Book.[1] He gave his youngest daughter, born in May 1652, the name of Deborah, the inspired poetess and judge of Israel who stirred the Israelites up to take arms against their oppressors.

Milton was also attacked because 'all his arguments . . . prove as effectually that the wife may sue a divorce from her husband upon the same grounds.'[2] In *An Apology* he argued that unchastity was worse in men than in women. We must see these attitudes in the light of the Protestant concept of the priesthood of all believers, which helped to enhance the status of women, for 'the soul knows no difference of sex';[3] women too had consciences to which God might speak direct. Protestantism did a great deal for the education of girls. They must learn to read and write, if only to be able to read the Bible. Being able to read, they read other things as well. It was the Cavalier poets who in the seventeenth century had a low view of women, and who looked back to the golden age as a time of sexual promiscuity.[4] As an example of an orthodox attitude towards marriage less elevated than Milton's, consider the discussions between the Earl of Rochester and Gilbert Burnet in 1679. Rochester objected to Christian prohibitions on extra-marital sex, and to Anglican refusal of divorce. Burnet's reply started from the sanctity of property. 'Men have a property in their wives and daughters, so that to defile the one or corrupt the other is an unjust and injurious thing.'[5]

Milton, then, was far from unique in holding that women were inferior to men. The importance of keeping them in their place was confirmed for him, as for Lucy Hutchinson, by the shocking example of Charles I and Henrietta Maria. 'How great mischief and dishonour', Milton reflected in *Eikonoklastes*, 'hath befallen to nations under the government of effeminate and uxorious magistrates, who being themselves governed at home under a feminine usurpation' were incompetent to rule others. In the *History of Britain* Boadicea was chastised for usurping a masculine role, though other women were praised: Milton presumably approved of Deborah. Salmasius's alleged deference to his wife was used against him: 'In vain does he prattle about liberty in assembly and market place who at home

---

[1] *C.P.W.*, II, p. 589; I, pp. 385, 389, 400, 459, 481, 484, 487, 492.
[2] [Anon.], *An Answer to a Book Intituled The Doctrine and Discipline of Divorce* (1644), p. 13.
[3] Torshell (1645), pp. 2, 10–11.
[4] Cf. p. 78 above.
[5] Burnet, *Rochester*, p. 51.

endures the slavery most unworthy of man, slavery to an inferior.' The
criticism follows logically from Milton's Biblical position – as does his
ecstatic praise of the exception who proved his rule – Queen Christina of
Sweden.[1] She fortunately had no husband.

II Milton's first marriage

We know little about Milton's reasons for marrying. At what Charles
Diodati's death meant for him we can only guess.[2] In the *Epitaphium
Damonis* Milton reflected on the hardness and loneliness of man's life, on
the instability of human affection (lines 106–11). The loss of Diodati may
help to explain Milton's brief flirtation with celibacy as an ideal. The
idealization of chastity in *Comus*, however we interpret it, taken together
with Comus's paean in praise of fecundity, seems to hint at unresolved
tensions. The additions to the version printed in 1637 may be intended to
suggest a way out: chastity is far from precluding true marriage. At the
end of the *Epitaphium Damonis* Diodati was admitted to the heavenly
Bacchic orgies because he had been chaste. Virginity as an ideal was
explicitly disavowed in the divorce tracts, where Milton went out of his
way to correct St. Paul: marriage was not a defilement, 'the Apostle . . .
pronounces quite contrary to [the] Word of God.'[3] The joke in *Animadversions* about nunneries providing 'convenient stowage for their withered
daughters' hardly suggests an elevated view of chastity.[4] The thirty-three-
year-old bachelor may have decided that it was time for him to take a wife.
In April 1642, when he was twitted with aspiring to marriage with a rich
widow, he announced that he would prefer 'a virgin of mean fortune
honestly bred'. Perhaps the gay and lively Mary Powell was the next one
he met. The angry gods had their revenge.[5]

Milton's father had lent £300, secured by a bond of £500, to the feckless
Richard Powell, who lived in an Oxfordshire village a mile or two from
the one in which John Milton senior had been born. There may have been
a long-standing acquaintance between the two families. In June 1642 the
poet went down to Oxfordshire, perhaps to collect this debt, perhaps
combining the trip with a visit to relatives, perhaps with a few days
working in the Bodleian Library. He returned married to the seventeen-

---

[1] *C.P.W.*, III, p. 421; cf. p. 538; IV, pp. 603–9, 625; cf. pp. 534, 556; Parker, pp. 283, 339.
[2] See pp. 31–2 above.
[3] *C.P.W.*, I, pp. 892–3; II, p. 596. For *Comus* see pp. 46–8 above.
[4] *C.P.W.*, II, p. 718.
[5] *Ibid.*, I, p. 929. Cf. pp. 57–8, 63 above.

year-old Mary, one of Richard Powell's eleven children, and with the promise of a dowry of £1,000 (never received). We know nothing of how this happened. We may imagine the Powells as a scheming family, anxious to evade their financial obligations. We may think that Milton was anxious for marriage in the abstract. 'He who wilfully abstains from marriage, not being supernaturally gifted', Milton wrote in 1645, is 'in a diabolical sin.'[1]

Milton had recently taken a big house in Barbican for himself and a number of boys whom he was teaching. Perhaps he already had marriage in mind. There has been much speculation about what happened, or did not happen, in the matrimonial chamber of this house. Mary may or may not have refused to consummate the marriage; certainly she found the surroundings oppressively quiet and lonely after the crowded household she had come from. The silence was punctuated by occasional cries from pupils undergoing a beating. Within 'a month or thereabout' of marriage Mary, who was only a child herself, had gone back home, ostensibly on a brief visit. She did not return, and the emissary whom Milton sent was rudely repulsed.

Meanwhile civil war had broken out. The Powells were Royalists, living in a Royalist area; Milton an ardent Parliamentarian. Oxford became the King's headquarters, so communications were difficult. If the Powells were cunning schemers, they may have calculated that now they had a chance of bilking altogether on their debt. Or they may suddenly have found their son-in-law's political views, tolerable six months earlier, insupportable now that fighting had actually broken out. Or Mary may just have said No. We do not know.

We can likewise only guess at the effect on the poet of the breakdown of his marriage; it must have been traumatic. No man enjoys that sort of blow to his pride. We may suspect that Milton was aware of an element of incompetence on his side which did not please him. But equally important were the consequences for his way of thinking. Marriage had proved no more satisfactory than chastity as a solution to his sexual problems. The anonymous biographer tells us that Milton had already reflected a good deal about marriage before his own personal problem arose, and had adopted his own version of the Puritan and Shakespearean ideal – that marriage should be a union of two minds, that mutual solace and delight was as important an object of marriage as the procreation of children. And Milton had already speculated, in the abstract, on the desirability of

---

[1] *C.P.W.*, II, p. 595.

divorce where a couple proved mutually incompatible: it was the natural corollary of the new emphasis on marriage as a voluntary union of like-minded people, though not all who cherished the ideal pushed this logic as far as Milton did.[1] For a century and more the relation of the sexes had been the subject of eager discussion, as the vernacular printed Bible was studied, and as attempts were being made to impose the monogamous family on to populations many of which had never hitherto really accepted it; and this at a time when the opening up of Asia, Africa and America to European trade revealed whole civilizations in which monogamy was not the rule.[2]

Against this background of speculation Milton suddenly had to face the failure of his own marriage. The life which was to have been a true poem was jarred by a piece of cacophonous prose. Milton's ideas about divorce were not suddenly adopted because of his own predicament; but his predicament certainly sharpened his thinking on the subject, and the urgency of his writing.

III Divorce

Milton's ideas on divorce, as on much else, go back to the thinking of the early Protestant reformers. They were not his sources, but he was to find to his delight that they (and Wyclif too) had anticipated some of his conclusions. Not to mention More's *Utopia*, an impressive list could be drawn up of early Protestant divines who sanctioned divorce – Tyndale, Calvin, Melanchthon, Bucer, Osiander, Paraeus. Advocacy of divorce was one of the charges against the Marian martyr Bishop Hooper in 1555. Cranmer's *The Reformation of the Ecclesiastical Laws* insisted that the grounds for divorce should be the same for both sexes.[3] Milton also noted in his Commonplace Book that Bodin was in favour of divorce – for incompatibility. This position was, however, more characteristic of radical Protestants, especially Anabaptists.[4]

The Anglican church remained more conservative on the subject of divorce than other reformed churches. Judicial separation *a thoro et mensa* could be obtained, sometimes for reasons other than adultery; but not divorce permitting remarriage. Things were tightening up from the end

---

[1] *Ibid.*, VI, p. 374; Darbishire, p. 23. The point is confirmed by Milton's Commonplace Book – *C.P.W.*, I, pp. 393–414, esp. pp. 406–10.
[2] See pp. 137–9 below.
[3] *C.P.W.*, II, pp. 716–18; Cardwell (1850), pp. 49–58.
[4] *C.P.W.*, I, p. 409; G. H. Williams, pp. 504–17; cf. pp. 287–9, 357.

of Elizabeth's reign. Some Puritans had advocated divorce – Perkins (for desertion, and where one of the spouses was an unbeliever, as well as for adultery), Rainolds, Silver-tongued Smith (who thought it was 'the physic of marriage' – but for adultery only), Stock and Joseph Hall (both for adultery only). A radical like Robert Browne was more liberal, allowing divorce 'for religion and conscience', and in 1605 it was claimed that members of Francis Johnson's congregation in Amsterdam 'accused themselves of adultery so that they might be rid of their wives', so easy was it to obtain a divorce.[1] Divorce was also easier in New England. The Socinian *Racovian Catechism* authorized believers to desert an obstinately unbelieving spouse.[2] In 1576 there had been agitation in Parliament for matrimonial cases to be taken away from the church courts and transferred to the common law. That would be the logical consequence of ceasing to regard marriage as a sacrament and treating it as a civil contract. This seemed obvious common sense to Milton: it was recommended again by Hugh Peter in 1651, and finally carried into effect by the Barebones Parliament in 1653.[3] Under their act Milton was married to his second wife by a J.P. In August 1653 an attempt had been made to insert a divorce clause in the marriage bill before Parliament.

Milton decided in 1643 to write on the subject of divorce, in the general interest, not merely with respect to his own case. He did so with fantastic, reckless courage, flying in the face of received respectable opinion in England. He displayed the same sort of courage in isolation later in *The Tenure of Kings and Magistrates* and *The Ready and Easy Way*, though it is difficult to be absolutely certain in any of these cases just how far Milton was aware of his isolation.

The opening passage of his first divorce pamphlet, *The Doctrine and Discipline of Divorce*, suggests that others as well as Milton had expected that after the defeat of episcopacy 'man's nature would find immediate rest and releasement from all evils. But ... such as have a mind large enough to take into their thoughts a general survey of human things would soon prove themselves in that opinion far deceived.'[4]

Milton had learnt from his own experience that 'the strongest Christian' who found himself 'bound fast ... to an image of earth and phlegm ... will be ready to despair in virtue, and mutiny against divine Providence.' The 'pain of loss' in such cases was 'in some degree like that which

---

[1] White (1973), pp. 107–10. See p. 32 above for Perkins and Johnson.
[2] *The Racovian Catechism* (English translation, 1652), pp. 96–7.
[3] *C.M.*, VI, p. 71; *C.P.W.*, VI, p. 561 and n.; *W.T.U.D.*, p. 310.
[4] *C.P.W.*, II, p. 234.

reprobates feel'. It might lead to 'thoughts of atheism'.[1] Already the ways of God to men had to be considered and explained before they could be justified. *The Doctrine and Discipline of Divorce* was published in August 1643. A second edition followed within six months, and two more in 1645. *The Judgment of Martin Bucer*,[2] in July 1644, together with *Tetrachordon* and *Colasterion* (March 1645) completed the series.

Milton's problem was to explain away Christ's apparent flat prohibition of divorce on any grounds other than adultery. To do this he went back to first principles. Whereas previously he had claimed that the Bible was easy for simple men to understand, now he argued that 'there is scarce any one saying in the Gospel but must be read with limitations and distinctions to be rightly understood'; interpreting the Bible calls for 'a skillful and laborious gatherer'.[3] Above all, we must not 'enslave the dignity of man' by setting 'straiter limits to obedience than God had set'. 'The ways of God . . . are equal, easy and not burdensome: nor do they ever cross the just and reasonable desires of men.'[4] Milton was consistent in expecting greater freedom, more Christian liberty, under the Gospel than under the Mosaic law. If therefore Christ's words seem stricter than God's law in the Old Testament, we must approach them very carefully and with an assumption that they do not mean what they appear to. Perhaps 'fornication' means something less precise than we would think: perhaps something more like 'a wife's constant contrariness, faithlessness and disobedience', 'a constant alienation and disaffection of mind'. 'Uncleanness' may mean 'any defect, annoyance, or ill quality in nature, which to be joined with makes life tedious'. So Milton doubted not 'with one gentle stroking to wipe away ten thousand tears out of the life of man'.[5] Since marriage is a union of minds, not merely of bodies, it must be freely entered into and freely dissoluble: the marriage contract is analogous to the church covenant, or the contract between king and people. The liberty of Christian men (and women) to live moral lives according to conscience depends on their being freed from external encumbrances. Milton's emphasis on Christian freedom in divorce may have been the first step in his advance to Arminianism.[6]

---

[1] *Ibid.*, II, pp. 247, 254, 260, 269, 339; cf. Satan in *Paradise Lost*, p. 58 above.
[2] Milton's title, no doubt intentionally, repeats that given to a tract contained in a pro-episcopalian pamphlet, *Certain Briefe Treatises Written by Divers Learned Men* (1641) (*C.P.W.*, I, pp. 193-4).
[3] See p. 103 above, and p. 233 below. Do we detect here the origins of the *De Doctrine*?
[4] *C.P.W.*, II, pp. 338-9, 228; cf. I, pp. 247, 249, 587; II, p. 342. See also p. 247 below.
[5] *C.P.W.*, II, pp. 244, 335-6, 620, 672-4; VI, p. 381.
[6] *Ibid.*, I, p. 245; cf. II, pp. 527, 595.

Milton restored to his own satisfaction 'that power which Christ never took from the master of the family'. The right of divorce 'cannot belong to any civil or earthly power against the will and consent of both parties, or of the husband alone'. It was an essential part of Milton's high conception of the dignity of man. This right of divorce applies in cases of permanent incompatibility of temperament – 'indisposition, unfitness, or contrariety of mind arising from a cause in nature unchangeable', since loss of mutual solace and peace is a more important reason for divorce than 'the accident of adultery'. 'Marriage must give way to . . . any really irresistible antipathy', Milton concluded in the *De Doctrina*. He never paid detailed attention to the question of women's rights in divorce, though on the title-page of *The Doctrine and Discipline of Divorce* he announced that the pamphlet was 'to the good of both sexes'. He threw in phrases like 'mutual consent', and said that the law must 'take care that the conditions of divorce be not injurious'. Nor did he consider the problem of children very deeply, though aware that they were likely to suffer from matrimonial discord. In the *De Doctrina* he argued that the possibility of divorce is advantageous to a woman, even if it is at the discretion of her husband.[1]

Milton certainly did not intend to provide 'divorce at pleasure', as his enemies suggested; but he laid himself open to the charge by his failure to think out the mechanics of divorce. He never determined how selfish men could be prevented from taking advantage of the freedom which Milton felt to be necessary for the elect. His main interest was to establish – re-establish, Milton would say – the rights of masters of families 'to dispose and economize', which in *The Tenure of Kings and Magistrates* he saw as 'the root and source of all liberty'.[2] Subjection of wives to husbands was conventionally accepted in the seventeenth century as an image of the political subjection of peoples to rulers.[3] Milton's view that the institution of marriage can be idolized is parallel to his view that monarchy can be idolized. Both must be subordinate to the liberty of Christian men.

A curious and possibly revealing point – Milton more than once associated usury and divorce. Usury, 'so much as is permitted by the magistrate and demanded with common equity, is neither against the Word of God nor the rule of charity': it is right if it is entered into with the right motives of conscience. So with divorce. In the *De Doctrina*

---

[1] *Ibid.*, II, pp. 242, 318, 332, 343–4, 350, 587, 630–2; cf. pp. 324–5, 347, 353, 589–90, 604–5, 625–8; VI, pp. 375–6.

[2] *Ibid.*, III, p. 237; cf. p. 168 above.

[3] Cf. pp. 375–6 below.

Christiana Milton gave 'usury, divorce, polygamy and the like' as matters in which the regenerate must be left free to decide for themselves according to conscience.[1] The scrivener's son approached all these matters from the point of view of the head of a business household.

In Milton's final divorce pamphlet he advanced a more general argument. The Fall had social consequences: private property and inequality replaced universal equality, political power protected social inequality. 'In the same manner and for the same cause . . . our imperfect and degenerate condition of necessity required this law [of divorce] among the rest.' 'In the beginning, had man continued perfect, it had been just that all things should have remained as they began to Adam and Eve', including community of property and indissoluble marriage. 'But who will be the man shall introduce this kind of commonwealth, as Christianity now goes?' The marriage of true minds is an attempt to get back behind the Fall: the marriage of incompatible minds must therefore be dissoluble because it had never been a true marriage. Forcing incompatible partners to remain together negates marriage's potential realization of divine harmony, its recapturing of Eden. It is 'an act of blasphemy'. 'The world first rose out of chaos' by God's 'divorcing command': it is not for the church or the magistrate to bring chaos back again, but to renew the world 'by the separating of unmeet consorts'.[2]

Milton's ideas were not startlingly original. His emphasis on mutual solace as the sole or principal end of marriage had been anticipated by Thomas Gataker among others. To say that he was 'the first great protagonist in Christendom' of divorce by mutual consent[3] ignores Bucer, and may seriously underestimate the unpublished tradition which Ranters, Muggletonians and Quakers inherited from the Familists, of marriage and divorce by mutual declaration before the congregation.[4] Milton was putting together ideas which were under discussion among his radical contemporaries. What was new was the courage with which he faced the logical consequences of these ideas. Since marriage is not a sacrament but a civil contract, it could in Milton's view be terminated by notification to the magistrate, though the husband should first state his case before his minister and some elders of the church in order to establish his good

---

[1] *C.P.W.*, II, p. 322; cf. pp. 656, 661; VI, p. 651. See also pp. 306–8 below.
[2] *C.P.W.*, II, pp. 273, 661–2, 665–6; cf. VI, pp. 371–9, 355; Halkett, pp. 92–3, 53–4. For the suggestion that Milton took this line of thought over from Parliamentarian political propagandists, see *C.P.W.*, II, pp. 131–3, 156–7.
[3] Halkett, p. 30; Olsen, pp. 136, 140. For Gataker see p. 26 above.
[4] *C.P.W.*, II, pp. 455, 464, 472; Clarkson (1660), pp. 15–16; Reeve and Muggleton, pp. 249–52; *W.T.U.D.*, chapter 15.

faith. Milton attacked both the common law's exclusive stress on adultery
as the sole ground for divorce, and the 'cold restrictiveness of the Puritan
ethic as it appeared in its extreme form among the Presbyterians'.[1] A right
to divorce is necessary to preserve love. 'Places of prostitution will be less
haunted, the neighbour's bed less attempted.'[2]

Women may divorce their husbands for adultery or heresy, though
Milton appears to think women much more likely to have the incurable
temperamental defects which render marriage null. But if the divorce
tracts dwell on women's alleged defects, and on the inferiority of their
position, let us recall how devastating Mary's desertion must have seemed
to the poet. *Paradise Lost* does something to redress the balance. Milton
corrects the commentators in giving Adam's wife the name Eve ('mother
of all living') *before* the Fall, perhaps to enhance the status of sexuality and
motherhood.[3] The lines

> Emparadised in one another's arms,
> The happier Eden,
>   (*P.L.* IV. 506–7)

go a little beyond Genesis, even if the words are Satan's.

It is obvious to the most casual reader of *Paradise Lost* that there are
tensions between the authoritarian male dominance proclaimed in many
of the narrator's and Raphael's comments on the one hand, and some
of Adam's words and actions on the other. Unfallen Adam expresses
'vehement desire', 'transport', 'passion' in Eve's presence (VIII. 525–31),
and appears to recognize her as in some respects his superior. He
describes himself as torn between his theoretical awareness of male
superiority ('For well I understand in the prime end / Of nature her the
inferior' – VIII. 540–1) and his 'awe' before Eve's beauty and her 'greatness of mind' (VIII. 557). This is strengthened by the give-away line 'thy
mate, who sees when thou art seen least wise', spoken by Raphael (VIII.
577). Milton insists that Eve is capable of intellectual conversation
(VII. 48–58). And – going beyond anything in the Biblical text or the
commentaries – Adam is prepared to back his judgment by preferring
death with Eve not only to loneliness without her but to the society of
any other woman.

> How can I live without thee, how forgo
> Thy sweet converse and love so dearly joined,

---

[1] Barker (1942), p. 68.
[2] *C.P.W.*, II, p. 230. These points were repeated by Godwin and Shelley 150 years later.
[3] As suggested by Fowler, C. and F., p. 640.

> To live again in these wild woods forlorn?
> Should God create another Eve, and I
> Another rib afford, yet loss of thee
> Would never from my heart; no no, I feel
> The link of nature draw me: flesh of flesh,
> Bone of my bone thou art, and from thy state
> Mine never shall be parted, bliss or woe
>   (IX. 908–16)

– with that cry still ringing in our ears, how can we take seriously Milton's attempt to restore traditional male superiority by blandly observing that Adam was 'fondly overcome by female charm'? Milton's heart here has reasons that his reason does not know:[1] as Empson realized, the emotion underlying the poem is far more subversive than the ostensible argument. Milton went beyond Genesis when he made Adam ask for a helpmeet, and proclaim the equality of the sexes to the Creator himself:

> Among unequals what society
> Can sort, what harmony or true delight?
> Which must be mutual, in proportion due
> Given and received
>   (VIII. 383–6)

After the Fall, it was Eve who first repented and through her love saved Adam (X. 909–46). The contradiction between the traditional sexual morality to which Milton pays lip-service and the morality of Adam's heart has its analogies with the division in Milton himself between the second and third cultures. Both in the divorce tracts and in the *De Doctrina* he is extraordinarily 'un-Puritan' and broad-minded about 'casual adultery'. He is contrasting mere physical adultery with the graver offence of spiritual adultery. But few Puritans would have dismissed the former as 'but a transient injury', 'soon repented, soon amended', which can be forgiven 'once and again'.[2] (Did Mary have something to forgive which took place during her absence?) Edwards would have seen here confirmation that Milton was a libertine. When Raphael blushingly admitted that angels interpenetrate, he said nothing about monogamy. Milton is defending natural sexuality *against* traditional Puritanism.

> Our maker bids increase: who bids abstain
> But our destroyer?
>   (P.L. IV. 748–9)

---

[1] Pascal made this psychological discovery at almost exactly the time Milton was writing *Paradise Lost*.

[2] *C.P.W.*, II, pp. 331–3, 591, 674; VI, p. 381.

Abstinence as such is no virtue. Milton in this one point is with the Ranters. After describing Eve's nakedness, Milton attacked 'dishonest shame, ... sin-bred, ... mere show of seeming pure' (*P.L.* IV. 313–16). Telling us that Adam and Eve made love before the Fall, he added:

> Whatever hypocrites austerely talk
> Of purity and place and innocence,
> Defaming as impure what God declares
> Pure, and commands to some, leaves free to all.
>
> (P.L. IV. 744–7)

This was unacceptable to many orthodox theologians; Milton seems to be deliberately blurring the distinction between fallen and unfallen sexuality.[1]

It is, when we come to think of it, remarkable that Milton could still write 'unpuritanically' about sex in *Paradise Lost*, after the fiasco of his first marriage and the scandal over the divorce pamphlets. Modern commentators have compared his attitude to Blake, to Hardy; *Paradise Lost* is 'probably the last piece of imaginative literature before *Jude the Obscure* to treat sexuality in serious practical detail'. The *De Doctrina*'s reference to 'the human seed, the noblest and most intimate part of the body', looks forward to D. H. Lawrence.[2] 'The frank eroticism of some of the descriptions of the naked Eve' has been seen as a recovery of Spenser's vision of human love and perfectibility without Spenser's elusive allegory. The Adam and Eve who walk out of *Paradise Lost* hand in hand are human, practical, down-to-earthy, in a way that might not have been conceivable before Milton's experience in the English Revolution.[3]

IV   The reaction

However little attention Milton's tracts on episcopacy had attracted, he could not complain that his divorce pamphlets were ignored. Royalists naturally took advantage of what they saw as confirmation of their view that heresy led inevitably to social licence and chaos. Cowley may have referred to *The Doctrine and Discipline of Divorce* in *The Civil War*, a piece of Royalist propaganda written in the summer and autumn of 1643:

> The number of their wives their lusts decree;
> The Turkish law's their Christian liberty.

If he does refer to Milton, it is the earliest known hostile reaction (though

---

[1] See pp. 260, 456 below.
[2] *C.P.W.*, II, pp. 331–3, 591, 674; VI, p. 381; Broadbent (1960), pp. 89, 245.
[3] P. W. Thomas, pp. 189–90.

unpublished).[1] Respectable Puritan divines, far from sharing the libertarian outlook of the early reformers, were acutely embarrassed by Milton's arguments. They met them either with silence or with unargued denunciation.

Milton's old friend Thomas Young referred cautiously to his pupil in a sermon preached before the House of Commons in February 1644, warning against advocates of 'digamy'. Milton was denounced as a licentious libertine by Herbert Palmer to the same august congregation six months later: Palmer called for action against Milton and his book. There followed attacks by William Prynne,[2] by the Stationers' Company (who denounced him to the House of Lords), by Daniel Featley, Ephraim Pagitt, Robert Baillie, Joseph Caryl (a conservative licenser who attacked Milton whilst licensing a book against him), John Bachiler (one of the most liberal of the Parliamentarian licensers, who also thought he must dissociate himself from Milton),[3] Thomas Edwards and many others. Milton's ideas were caricatured in *Little Non-Such* (1646),[4] glanced at by Thomas Case in a sermon to the House of Commons in 1647, noticed by Edward Hyde in the same year. The ministers of Sion College denounced them; so did T.C., the anonymous *A Glasse for the Times* (1648), Joseph Hall, Clement Walker, Henry Hammond, James Howell, Alexander Ross, the Royalist newspaper *Mercurius Pragmaticus*, and many others.[5]

After the Stationers' attack Milton was summoned before the House of Lords, but nothing seems to have happened. Edwards tells us that Milton's views were well received by the sectarian preacher Mrs. Attaway. She took the initiative in discussing them with two gentlemen of the Inns of Court who attended her meeting. I should like to be able to prove that they were the two young sparks with whom Milton shared his 'gaudy days'.[6] Mrs. Attaway subsequently acted on what she took to be Milton's principles by eloping with William Jenny, who like her suffered from an uncongenial spouse.[7] Mrs. Attaway is an interesting figure, who has been treated rather flippantly by male historians. She encouraged free discussion after her sermons. Like Milton she was a mortalist. She believed that there was no hell save in the conscience, and that it could not stand with the

---

[1] Cowley (1973), pp. 109, 166.
[2] Prynne links advocates of 'divorce at pleasure' with mortalists (Parker, 1940, p. 73).
[3] Featley associates Milton with Roger Williams and Richard Overton, Pagitt and Bachiler with Roger Williams (*ibid.*, pp. 74-5).
[4] *C.P.W.*, II, pp. 810-17.
[5] *Ibid.*, II, pp. 800-7; Barker (1942), p. 142.
[6] See p. 59 above.
[7] *C.P.W.*, II, p. 144; T. Edwards, I, p. 34; II, pp. 10-11; III, pp. 26-7.

goodness of God to damn his own creatures eternally. She held herself to
be as free from sin as Christ was when in the flesh.[1]

We may suspect that Mrs. Attaway was not the only one in radical
circles who read Milton with approval. John Robins the Ranter 'gave
authority unto some of his disciples, both unto men and women, to change
their wives and husbands', setting an example by changing his own.
William Franklin rejected his wife and lived with Mary Gadbury, who had
been deserted by her own husband.[2] Hugh Peter and Laurence Clarkson
were among those who spoke up in favour of divorce, and many Ranters
simply rejected the tie of monogamous marriage altogether, as a fruit of
the curse.[3]

Milton was defended by Henry Robinson and Henry Burton in 1646, and
there were several later laudatory references. In 1660 'G.S.' suggested that
'the vulgar' agreed with Milton.[4] (Not only the vulgar, of course. The
Earl of Rochester thought 'denying the remedy of divorce' was 'an
unreasonable imposition on the freedom of mankind'.[5] Shadwell in
Epsom Wells (1672), Farquhar in *The Beaux Stratagem* (1707) and Halifax in
his *Advice to a Daughter* (1688) all contemplate divorce for incompatibility:
Farquhar at least based his arguments on Milton.)

Milton was not entirely delighted by the approbation of such as Mrs.
Attaway. In the second edition of *The Doctrine and Discipline of Divorce* he
claimed rather defensively that he had published it in English out of 'the
esteem I have of my country's judgment, and the love I bear to my native
language'. But in the *Second Defence* he expressed regret that he had not
kept his divorce pamphlets in the decent obscurity of Latin. In 1655 he
told a Dutch admirer that if these tracts were to be translated in the
Netherlands he would prefer Latin to Dutch; but he did not reject the idea
of translation into the vernacular.[6]

The 'clamour of so much envy and impertinence' with which *The
Doctrine and Discipline of Divorce* was received, and still more the failure to
answer it, surprised and upset Milton. In the second edition (1644) he
supported his arguments from reason and Scripture by the authority of
orthodox Protestant divines: his schoolboy delight in finding that Bucer
had anticipated his arguments shows how shaken he had been – despite his
professed contempt for arguments from authority. He felt, or claimed to

---

[1] *W.T.U.D.*, pp. 105, 175, 188.
[2] Reeve (1711), p. 12; *W.T.U.D.*, pp. 316–17.
[3] *W.T.U.D.*, pp. 227, 313–17, 395–6; Cohn, p. 323.
[4] *C.P.W.*, II, pp. 142–3; G.S. p. 70.
[5] Burnet, *Rochester*, p. 47.
[6] *C.P.W.*, II, p. 233; IV, pp. 610, 872.

feel, that perhaps he had been divinely inspired to recover this lost truth –
a claim which he took seriously enough to repeat in his *Defence of the
People of England*.[1] The Presbyterians remained unimpressed, however,
despite the fuller Scriptural exegesis of *Tetrachordon* and the invective of
Colasterion.

So the cruel blow of the breakdown of his marriage was followed by a
no less cruel outburst of reprobation and denunciation as a libertine, an
advocate of sexual promiscuity. It must have been exceptionally galling
for a man whose views on the sanctity of marriage were in fact far more
austere than those of most Puritans and whose sensibility – already made
raw by Mary's desertion – now had salt rubbed into it. The sonnet, 'I did
but prompt the age to quit their clogs', shows how much he was affected
not only by the vituperation of the orthodox but also by his unexpected
allies. 'Licence they mean when they cry liberty.'

Again we have to guess how Milton faced life in the years between
1642 and 1645. He found consolation in agreeable feminine society – that
of Boyle's sister, the talented Lady Ranelagh, of Lady Margaret Ley, of
Mrs. Katharine Thomason, wife of the Presbyterian collector of pamphlets,
of Mrs. Hester Blackborough, Milton's cousin, married to a leather-seller.
Margaret Ley was 'daughter to that good Earl' of Marlborough, whom
'the sad breaking of that Parliament' of 1628–9 'broke'. Now wife of
Captain John Hobson, she was 'a woman of great wit and ingenuity', and
seems to have taken special care of Milton after his wife left him, as Lady
Ranelagh was to be his stand-by in his blindness and widowerhood. Lady
Ranelagh was an old friend and patron of Hartlib and Dury. Her house
may have been the meeting-place of the Invisible College in the later
sixteen-forties.[2] She perhaps introduced Henry Oldenburg to Milton. In
the fifties she was Milton's near neighbour, and was 'like a near relative'
to him. Parker even hints at a more intimate relationship, but without
evidence. Milton taught her nephew and her son. She almost certainly
used her considerable influence on the poet's behalf in 1660.[3]

During Mary's absence there was also a mysterious Miss Davis, so far
unidentified, whom Milton was said to have thought of marrying. This
would presumably have been after divorcing Mary for desertion, unless
the poet was already a serious advocate of second marriages without
divorce.[4] The Powells got to know of this plan, and 'set all engines on

---

[1] *Ibid.*, II, p. 224; IV, p. 536; cf. Featley, pp. 32–6, and p. 409 below.
[2] C. Webster (1975), p. 62.
[3] *C.M.*, XII, p. 81; Turnbull, pp. 28, 247, 258; Parker, p. 478; see pp. 146–7 below.
[4] See pp. 137–9 below.

work' to restore Mary. The Civil War was over; the Royalists were defeated; travel between Oxfordshire and London was again easy. The Powells secured the collusion of the Blackboroughs, whom Milton was in the habit of visiting. On one of these occasions Mary reappeared, and in a theatrical scene flung herself on her knees before her husband, begging him to take her back. The Blackboroughs are more likely than the Powells to have thought of this approach to the young poet who had absorbed high chivalrous ideals from his early reading.[1] Reluctant though he no doubt was, Milton succumbed to this well-calculated attack: Mary resumed her position as Mrs. Milton. Within less than a year Milton was saddled with her whole family, now apparently ruined – Mr. Powell, Mrs. Powell, and at least five children.

Biographers have not sufficiently contemplated the possibility of Milton saying No to Mary. He had decided that the marriage was irretrievably broken; the economic motivation of Mary's return was transparently obvious; and Milton may still have had hopes of Miss Davis. His chivalrous gesture was, he may soon have realized, an error of judgment. Samson did not make the same mistake when Dalila tried a similar appeal; and Milton seems to have lost interest in the chivalric ethos.

We can only guess at the horrors of this transformation of the house which Mary had found too quiet in 1642. Milton did his best to help the Powells financially, assisting his father-in-law to compound for his delinquency, and trying to sort out the worst of his money tangles. But guarded letters referring to the noise which surrounded him hint at something of what he suffered. We can only guess too at his relations with Mary, who bore him a son and three daughters before she died in 1652. Parker sentimentally imagined that the marriage, against all the odds, proved successful: argued even that Mary was 'my late espoused saint' about whom Milton wrote one of the most moving sonnets in the English language. One wonders. The description in the *De Doctrina Christiana* of the sordid bickerings in a marriage of incompatibles may look all the way back to 1642; or it may recall more recent experiences.[2] Christopher Arnold, who knew Milton in 1651, spoke later of his 'unhappy marriage'.[3] Milton did not remember the date of Mary's death. His relation with Mary's daughters was never easy; and when he came to make his will, the unpaid dowry still rankled. Surely he would have forgiven and forgotten if his life with Mary had been happy? Finally, there is the fact of his long

---

[1] *C.P.W.*, I, p. 891; Darbishire, p. 66.

[2] *C.P.W.*, VI, pp. 369–81.

[3] L. Miller (1974), p. 304.

silence in the years of readjustment to Mary. The first interruption in his pamphleteering, between May 1642 and August 1643, can be precisely related to the breakdown of his marriage. The second and longer interruption, from March 1645 to February 1649, may equally be related to the disaster of its resumption. Though the Powells were financially completely dependent on Milton, one doubts whether they had the tact to repress their very different political views. *The Tenure of Kings and Magistrates* may well have been the product, among other things, of discussions in the family circle. Never again was Milton to be silent for so long, even in his blindness, until the years after the Restoration when he was working on *Paradise Lost* and was precluded from pamphleteering by the censorship.

V   Martha Simmonds

The case of Mrs. Attaway reminds us of the importance of women among the radical sects, and of the new opportunities which freedom of organization and discussion made possible. In New England in the sixteen-thirties Mrs. Hutchinson usurped the role of teacher and political leader hitherto confined to men. In England in the forties and fifties women took part in church government, preached, prayed, prophesied, wrote. In the Quaker movement especially they played a leading role as missionaries; two went off to convert the Grand Turk, others – who were less tolerantly received – to convert New England. Women played a prominent part in the tragedy of James Nayler, the Quaker who in 1656 made a symbolic entry into Bristol, riding on a donkey, accompanied by women singing Hosanna and strewing palms in his path. Nayler's subsequent trial and punishment for 'horrid blasphemy' proved a great divide in the early history of Quakerism, leading to the ascendancy of George Fox over the 'Ranter' wing – the anarchic individualism which surrendered completely to the motions of the spirit. The anti-political and pacifist tendency in the movement was strengthened. Nayler might have been saved from the terrible penalties inflicted on him if more M.P.s had shared Milton's scepticism about blasphemy as an offence.

One of the women involved with Nayler may have been known to Milton – Martha Simmonds. Her brother and publisher was Giles Calvert, the printer who acted as link between radical groups in the sixteen-forties and -fifties. She herself married Thomas Simmonds, possibly related to Milton's publishers, Thomas, Mary and Sarah Simmonds. In the mid-fifties Martha Simmonds attached herself to Nayler, and must bear some responsibility for his entry into Bristol. Friends felt it necessary to claim that Nayler had been 'bewitched'.[1] Nayler's condemnation was a great blow against the cause of religious toleration, so dear to Milton, and a setback to women's participation in religious or political action. Milton preserved a letter about Nayler among his papers, and must have taken cognizance of all this. Martha Simmonds was the Eve who led Nayler astray, the Dalila (Nayler had long hair) who took political decisions upon herself.[2] In depicting Eve's fall, or in describing Dalila, Milton was not merely getting his own back on Mary Powell or either of his other wives. He may have been – not necessarily consciously – reflecting on the role of women in politics, and on the defeat of toleration and the Good Old Cause. This is not a total explanation, nor do I see Dalila as a figure in an allegory to which this is the key. Interregnum experiments in the equality of the sexes had not been uniformly successful, as Winstanley found, though he remained unshaken in his belief in equality. Such failures confirmed Milton in his acceptance of traditional male superiority. In thinking of Dalila, and to a lesser extent of Eve, we might bear in mind the political world in which Milton lived, in which he so eagerly participated, as well as his private life. Taken in conjunction, the passage in the *De Doctrina Christiana* which comments approvingly on Christ taking advantage 'of the service and liberality of the women who accompanied him wherever he went', and the later words 'women however are instructed to keep silence in church', give us Milton's reflections on Nayler, Martha Simmonds and the political activities of women.[3]

VI Polygamy

Although Milton may have regretted his marriage to Mary Powell, and although he wished he had not written about divorce in the vernacular, nothing suggests that he ever changed his mind on these subjects. In *Paradise Lost* acceptance of male superiority is less secure than in the divorce pamphlets: perhaps his second wife, Katherine Woodcock, had something to do with that. The poignancy of the passages on wedded love is all the greater if, as is probable, they were written after her death and before his third marriage. But in the *De Doctrina* he reiterated the position he had adopted in 1643–5: 'Marriage is, by definition, a union of the most intimate kind, but it is not indissoluble or indivisible.' 'When God originally gave man a wife he intended her to be his help, solace and

---

[1] Carroll (1972), pp. 31–52; Brink, pp. 99–112.
[2] Nickolls, pp. 143–4.
[3] *C.P.W.*, VI, pp. 541, 609; cf. p. 782. See pp. 443–4 below.

delight. So if, as often happens, she is found to be a source of grief, shame, deception, ruin and calamity instead, why should we think it displeasing to God if we divorce her?' Marriage without love is 'a crushing slavery'. Milton clearly still felt that this right belonged particularly to the husband. 'Marriage gives way to religion and it gives way to the right of a master.' It had been 'an act of papal encroachment ... to pluck the power and arbitrament of divorce from the master of the family, into whose hands God and the law of all nations had put it'. The restricting of divorce was the first loosening of Antichrist, and England's divorce laws still conform to Antichrist's unrighteousness. Milton hoped to restore to the father of the family the power which mediaeval canonists had taken away from him. To the traditionally quoted texts, 'They will be one flesh', Milton, perhaps following Ochino, pointed out that St. Paul had said that 'he who couples with a prostitute is one body with her.'[1]

The Bible also authorized polygamy – more clearly than it authorized divorce. If polygamy was totally wrong, then many of the patriarchs had been very sinful men indeed. The orthodox seem to have worried about this less than Milton did, but there is a continuing radical and Protestant tradition which defends polygamy – not only Münster Anabaptists but also Paracelsus, David Joris, Castellio, Ochino, various German and Swiss Anabaptist groups. Luther, Melanchthon and Bucer were not opposed, in principle at least, to bigamy. Giordano Bruno discussed polygamy seriously.[2] Montaigne noted in his essay 'Of the Cannibals' that American Indians had polygamous customs which recalled those of the patriarchs of the Old Testament.[3] Milton was aware of this tradition of thought long before his first marriage, noting many favourable references to polygamy in the Commonplace Book. He cited with special approval Ralegh's remark that 'the kingdom of Congo was unhappily diverted from the Christian religion' because of Europeans' rejection of polygamy, '"I know not", saith he, "how necessarily, but more contentiously than seasonably."' In The History of Britain Milton referred to 'the liberty, not unnatural, to have many wives'.[4]

Milton's explicit defence of polygamy was not published until 1825, in the De Doctrina; but he appears to have talked freely about it in the

[1] Ibid., VI, pp. 371, 374–6, 356–8; cf. p. 379; II, p. 431. See Genesis 2: 24; Matthew 19: 5; 2 Corinthians 6: 16.
[2] C.P.W., VI, pp. 96–9, 356–81; G. H. Williams, pp. 372, 378, 414n., 484, 493, 511–13, 633; Bullough, p. 100; Cairncross, pp. 27, 49–50, 73, 97–8. L. Miller, passim, gives evidence of Milton's reputation as a defender of polygamy before publication of the De Doctrina.
[3] See p. 139 below.
[4] C.P.W., I, pp. 393–414, esp. p. 411. Cf. p. 129 above – Raphael on angelic intercourse.

sixteen-fifties. Jan Van Vliet, Private Secretary to the Dutch Ambassador, had a conversation with the poet on the subject in 1652, and from him Milton's reputation as a defender of polygamy spread on the Continent.[1] It has been plausibly argued that the phrase 'as saints and patriarchs use' in Milton's 'hymn to wedded love' (*P.L.* IV. 758–62) must be intended to hint at polygamy; what other reason could there be for dragging the patriarchs in? The lines come just after Milton's denunciation of 'Puritan' hypocrisy (744–7).[2]

In 1657 Bernardino Ochino's *Dialogue of Polygamy* appeared in English translation. This version is sometimes attributed to Francis Osborn, to whom it was dedicated. Osborn expressed approval of polygamy both in his very popular *Advice to a Son* (1656–8) and in his *Political Reflections upon the Government of the Turks* (1656).[3] Ochino, like Milton, combined advocacy of polygamy and divorce with anti-Trinitarianism. Interestingly enough, Ochino married a girl from the Diodatis' Lucca.

Commentators usually shy away from Milton's explicit defence of polygamy: 'the law itself, then, and even the authority of God's own voice, wholly approve of this practice.' Milton's case is in part Biblical, in part an expression of a wish to see the population expanded. 'Our maker bids increase.' Emphasis on the need for increased population recurs in *Proposalls of Certaine Expedients* (1659) and in the *De Doctrina*.[4] Ochino made this need a principal justification for polygamy. Monogamy, like celibacy of the priesthood, like the indissolubility of marriage, had been introduced under the Roman Antichrist. If the one could be thrown off, why not the others? Petty spoke of 'Popish countries where polygamy is forbidden'.[5] In Bacon's *New Atlantis* polygamy might be permitted in order to increase the population: More's *Utopia* had recognized that polygamy was normal in the New World. The republican Henry Neville set his *Isle of Pines* (1668) in the New World; he depicted both the happiness and the remarkable procreative possibilities in polygamy.

The demographer John Graunt, who became a Catholic, crossed swords with Petty by referring to 'irreligious proposals to multiply people by polygamy'. Petty noted that polygamy depressed the status of women;

---

[1] *C.P.W.*, VI, pp. 356–81; L. Miller, pp. 56, 78; cf. p. 283. See also pp. 121–35, 150, 157, 336, for other examples of Milton's reputation as a defender of polygamy before 1825.

[2] Rudrum, pp. 19–23. Mrs. Sadleir, Cyriack Skinner's aunt, spoke of Milton having two or three wives.

[3] Osborn, I, pp. 34, 138, 177; II, pp. 236, 256. In 1655 Osborn expressed cautious approval of Socinianism (I, pp. 91–2). Cf. L. Miller, pp. 27–34, 218. For the authorship of Ochino's *Dialogues*, see McNair, p. 365.

[4] *C.P.W.*, VI, pp. 356–68; see pp. 201–2 above, 287–8 below.

[5] Petty, II, pp. 377–8; Lansdowne, I, p. 267; II, pp. 49–58; Cairncross, p. 70.

but 'antitrinitarianism, polygamy and communism were never far below the surface of the Anabaptist movements.'[1] We must try to make sense of this. Radical acceptance of polygamy may have had something to do with the preponderance of women among the sects.[2] What has been called 'Puritan polygamy' was designed among other things to protect unmarried women. The new insistence on the sanctity of the marriage bond in an increasingly commercial society had perhaps, paradoxically, led to an increase in prostitution. Certainly the position of the unmarried woman, when patriarchialism was replacing the bonds of kinship, was less secure than it had been. Puritan polygamy was intended to be combined with severe laws against extra-marital sex: there would have been no unmarried mothers in a Puritan polygamous society. Before adequate contraceptive devices were available polygamy might have been less exclusively favourable to men than it would be in our very different world. Polygamy seems not to have been unpopular with the women of Münster in 1535. The experience of Islam suggests that polygamous families where the senior wife chooses her junior partners can be cosy communities.[3] In nineteenth-century America the polygamous Mormons were very advanced in the education of women, and were the first to give women the vote.[4]

The Leveller William Walwyn and the Behmenist John Pordage were both accused of defending polygamy. No doubt they used some of Milton's Biblical arguments, though Walwyn also read Montaigne. In 1647 congregational societies and Anabaptists in and around London were defending themselves against charges of polygamy. Thomas Washbourne in 1654 observed, with heavy irony, that 'polygamy's no sin / In a free state.'[5] Gilbert (later Bishop) Burnet defended polygamy about 1670, though he lived to regret this indiscretion. Sir Isaac Newton, who shared so many of Milton's heresies, is a possible advocate of polygamy. In 1737, we are told, 'polygamy is daily defended' in England, 'and often in print.' Samuel Richardson hankered after polygamy. So did that good Miltonist William Blake.[6]

---

[1] McNair, p. 369; see pp. 287–9 below.
[2] R. Thompson, pp. 22, 50, 91.
[3] I am grateful to Dorothy Hodgkin for this point. See Marmaduke Pickthall, *Veiled Women* (1913) and other novels by him.
[4] Cairncross, pp. 138, 216. Jill Tweedie recently suggested that an extension of the family by polygamy might be more satisfactory than divorce with all its problems in breaking up families (*The Guardian*, 8 September 1975).
[5] *W.T.U.D.*, p. 319; Washbourne, p. 227; cf. Cowley, quoted on p. 130 above.
[6] Burnet (1897), I, p. 471; Cairncross, pp. 139, 141; L. Miller, pp. 112–13; C. Hill (Panther, 1969), p. 372.

VII Milton and *Jane Eyre*

I have written elsewhere of the importance of the Puritan conception of
marriage in *Clarissa Harlowe*. Richardson goes a step further forward than
Milton in *Comus*, by allowing his heroine to be raped under the influence
of drugs. The conflict between her inner purity, chastity of mind, and the
conventional attitudes of society is thus laid bare.[1] A later novelist who
deals with Milton's problems is Charlotte Brontë. If Milton's doctrine of
divorce had prevailed, there would have been no plot for *Jane Eyre*.
Whether Charlotte Brontë intended it or not, there is a close analogy
between Rochester's marriage and Milton's own. Rochester first met his
wife when he 'was sent out to Jamaica to espouse a bride already courted
for me', daughter of a business acquaintance of his father's. He felt that he
was swindled by her parents into marriage without realizing that his wife
could never be a compatible helpmeet. He did not feel truly married, but
the world condemned him to her in perpetuity. Jane Eyre was in exactly
the position Miss Davis would have been in if she had been in love with
Milton. By the time Jane could marry Rochester he – like Milton at the
time of his happy second marriage – was blind. Jane Eyre invoked *Samson
Agonistes* in describing the blind Rochester, who had defied God and
almost cursed divine providence. The disasters which came thick upon
him, including blindness, were the ultimate means of his regeneration.
Was Charlotte Brontë consciously thinking of Milton when she wrote
Jane Eyre? When she advised Emily to read only the best poets, she put
Milton first – before Shakespeare.[2] But there is no evidence that she was
well informed about Milton's private life or his prose writings. The name
Rochester, like Richardson's Lovelace, seems designed to suggest a
rakehelly Cavalier.

Charlotte Brontë was not making an impassioned plea for reform of the
divorce laws: she takes them as given, and her attitude is quite unfeminist.
She was less than fair to the first Mrs. Rochester (as Jean Rhys saw),[3] side-
stepping the whole problem by depicting her as someone who could hardly
have exercised rights even if she had had any. It is remarkable evidence of
the fluidity of accepted certainties in the sixteen-forties, and of Milton's
radical approach, that he could envisage what still seemed impossible two
centuries later. Milton pushed too fast and too far for his own time,
making compatibility the principal justification for marriage centuries

---

[1] C. Hill (Panther, 1969), chapter 14, esp. pp. 366–70.
[2] Gaskell, p. 113.
[3] See her novel, *The Wide Sargasso Sea*.

before the social equality of women had been proclaimed. Half a century after *Jane Eyre* Jude Fawley and Sue Bridehead encountered social disaster by acting on Milton's principles. (A passage from Milton forms the epigraph to Part 4 of *Jude the Obscure*.)

Two hundred years before Charlotte Brontë wrote, many Jane Eyres would happily have accepted the position of mistress to Rochester; twentieth-century society would not have demanded so insistently that they got married. In the seventeenth century Henry Marten had the courage to live openly with a woman who was not his wife, but it wrecked his reputation in Puritan England. Milton knew Marten, but we do not know what their relations were: he was on good terms with Sir Thomas Wentworth, the other M.P. denounced by Cromwell as a 'whore-master'.[1] What made Marten's solution impossible for Jane Eyre, and perhaps for Miss Davis too, was the victory of the Protestant ethic. This helped women to stand on their own feet; it also proclaimed the sanctity of monogamy. Jane Eyre accepted exactly Milton's ideal of independence in subordination: the tirade in which she claimed spiritual equality with the socially superior Rochester is one of the crucial – and most Protestant – passages in the novel. But Jane could see no solution except in marriage. Moll Flanders had made the same point from rather a different angle when she said 'a woman should never be kept for a mistress that had the money to make herself a wife'.[2]

VIII   Milton and his daughters

Milton had bad luck in the surviving record of his relations with women. We have the scandal of Mary Powell, the grudging scene of reunion, and then silence on six and a half years of married life. We know virtually nothing of Katharine Woodcock unless, as I believe, 'Methought I saw' is about her.[3] That sonnet and *Paradise Lost* establish Milton's capacity for equal and two-sided love. Yet of his third wife, with whom he seems to have been happy, we know only that Milton praised her for cooking his favourite dishes. Of his daughters we hear only complaints and grudges – possibly deliberately exaggerated.[4]

---

[1] Samuel Pepys seems to have been more successful in winning acceptance for Mary Skinner, niece of Milton's great friend Cyriack. See p. 216 below.

[2] D. Defoe, *Moll Flanders*, I, p. 60.

[3] Katharine was the daughter of Captain William Woodcock, who appears to have been dead by 1644. Could she have been related to the Quaker William Woodcock who in 1659 was invited to serve in the militia? (Brink, p. 101).

[4] See p. 145 below.

The story of how Milton made his daughters read to him in languages they did not understand is heart-rending. Conflict between parents and teenagers no doubt existed in the seventeenth century, but evidence for it from the children's point of view is scanty. (Curiously enough, Milton's friend Thomas Ellwood provides a rare example.)[1] Recalling the remark of the old bachelor John Aubrey, that before the Revolution 'the child perfectly loathed the sight of his parents as the slave his torturer',[2] we may suspect that tension was not unknown, though normally recorded only by grown-ups who assumed the rightness of absolute parental authority.

> In arbitrary families,
> Which seem domestic tyrannies,
> Parents with Turkish rigour sway

sang Richard Leigh.[3] It was Milton's bad luck that Deborah's story appears to make her a unique victim rather than the daughter of a typical seventeenth-century English father placed in abnormally difficult circumstances.

The clue to an understanding of the relationship between Milton and his daughters, it seems to me, is contained in Milton's nuncupative will, where he left to his daughters the £1,000 which he was still owed by the Powell family – and which he knew they were very unlikely to get. But the pettiness, and the refusal to forget, is revealing. Thirty-two years earlier, Milton thought, he had been swindled into marriage to the daughter of a man who owed money to his father. When he had resigned himself to the breakdown of his marriage, and perhaps to look elsewhere for a helpmeet, he had been fooled into taking Mary back, and with her had followed the whole rowdy, Royalist, bankrupt, intolerable family. They had made his life a misery – and Mary did not even bear him a live son, but first of all a retarded daughter.

Biographers have given Milton too little credit for the fortitude with which he endured all this. He is eloquently silent about the years with Mary after her return – and he is rarely silent about himself. His letter of April 1647 to Carlo Dati may refer only to his in-laws: 'those whom perhaps proximity or some unprofitable tie has bound to me, whether by accident or by law, commendable in no other way, daily sit beside me, weary me – even exhaust me, in fact – as often as they please.' Parker thinks it 'incredible' that this should refer to Mary; but the other Powells

---

[1] Ellwood, pp. 46–54.
[2] Powell, p. 278.
[3] Leigh (1947), p. 50.

were bound to Milton 'by accident', only Mary 'by law'. Mr. Powell had died four months before this letter; the rest of the family left Milton's house soon after. Milton was still for many years involved in trying to sort out the tangled indebtedness of the Powell property. In August or September 1647 the Miltons left the Barbican house for a smaller house in High Holborn, in which there would be no room for the Powells.[1] There was also no room for pupils. Milton was left alone with Mary and the crippled Anne.

Milton had not been silent about Mary in the divorce pamphlets. We need not refer to her all the abusive epithets which Masson collected on four pages;[2] but it is difficult to think that none of them applied. It is hardly likely that her submission – clearly dictated, like the marriage, by economic considerations – led to a complete change in her nature, such as Milton deemed impossible in certain cases of incompatibility. Milton was later to date his first awareness of eye trouble to about 1644. In the later forties he suffered from headaches and dizziness; by 1649 his left eye was useless. When Mary died in May 1652 he was totally blind. His daughters were then nearly six, three and a half and a few days old. This was a time when Milton had committed himself to exacting responsibilities in government service, so that his family must have been looked after by someone hired for the purpose. In November 1656 he married again, but in 1658 the children, now aged twelve, ten and six, were once more left motherless.

Aubrey dated Milton's resumption of work on *Paradise Lost* to two years before the King came in – that is, shortly after the death of his second wife. Prostration by grief might lead Milton to write out his problems: it would be difficult for a middle-aged blind man, probably never very domesticated, to keep the welfare of his young daughters at the front of his mind. On top of desolate grief and blindness he had to face the collapse of the English Revolution. Simultaneously he was struggling to write what he must have known was to be one of the greatest poems in any language. 'A good book', he had written in *Areopagitica*, 'is the precious life-blood of a master-spirit.'[3] He is not the only man of genius who has exploited others in order to create what he had to create.

Milton himself felt that much of the blame for the deterioration of relations lay on the daughters' side, as witness his account of their

---

[1] *C.P.W.*, II, p. 762; Parker, pp. 309–12.
[2] Masson, III, pp. 50–1, 305–6.
[3] *C.P.W.*, II, p. 493.

conspiring with his servants to deceive their blind father and sell his books. This is confirmed by the independent story that Mary, aged fifteen, said that her father's death would be better news than his third marriage. If we enter imaginatively into the situation, the escalation of ill feeling is not altogether surprising, especially if we bear in mind Milton's initial, probably unconscious, resentment of the three daughters who were the only return for his father's loan to Richard Powell. Milton's third marriage to Elizabeth Minshull in February 1663 was presumably entered into in order that she should cope with the children as much as for any other reason. But her brisk step-motherly way seems to have alienated the daughters and worried him. The daughters, or rather Deborah, had the last word with posterity. Mrs. Powell also left a message for us, when she spoke in 1651 of her son-in-law as a harsh and choleric man, who would take it out of his wife if Mrs. Powell entered on legal action against him. This at a time when Milton was allowing her considerably more from her husband's estate than the law required him to.

Anne, the eldest daughter, was deformed, possibly a spastic: she had a speech defect. All the daughters were taught by a governess and all except Anne could certainly write. Deborah became a schoolmistress. Milton's education of his daughters compares unfavourably with the lavish expenditure on his own and his brother Christopher's education. But we do not know how it compares with that of his sister; and apprenticing his daughters in the sixteen-sixties may have cost Milton relatively more than his own education had cost his father. Christopher's daughters never learnt to write, though Sir Christopher was better off than his brother.

Milton's *Of Education*, unlike most writings of the educational reformers of the Revolution, is silent on the education of women. Milton lagged behind the most advanced thought of his day here. His oft-quoted remark, 'one tongue is enough for any woman' is another piece of bad luck. It was a proverbial phrase, used by John Taylor the Water-Poet long before Milton, and by Ray and Swift long after.[1] I suspect that, in context, the remark was intended as a joke – one of Milton's grisly jokes, Empson might say.

There we must leave it. Some of Deborah's much later stories can be discounted: she was not more than seventeen when she left home. Others can be explained, if not explained away. Shakespeare left his wife his second-best bed; Henry Vaughan had to be sued before he would contribute to the support of his daughter; the kindly Samuel Pepys beat his wife.

---

[1] John Taylor, quoted in *C.P.W.*, I, p. 137; Tilley, p. 675.

Parker ingeniously speculated that the harsh words of the nuncupative will were 'a drastic way to force the hand of the oddly behaving Powells', evolved by the legal mind of Christopher Milton in order to extract from them what they had owed the family for thirty years – as they could now very well afford to do.[1] Elizabeth Milton's relatively generous settlement with the daughters suggests that this is indeed a possible explanation: but she may have settled only because she and Christopher saw that the nuncupative will was going to fail.

This chapter has tried to correct the image of Milton as a harsh and loveless Puritan. His contemporaries saw him rather as a libertine, the founder of a sect of divorcers. Both are caricatures, and I do not wish to replace the later caricature by the earlier one. Somewhere between the two we must set the bold if unlucky thinker of whom Blake wrote that he 'descended to redeem the female shade / From death eternal'.[2]

---

[1] Parker, p. 649; Masson, VI, p. 743.
[2] W. Blake, p. 530.

Chapter 10

1644

Why should I not confess that earth was then
To me, what an inheritance, new-fallen,
Seems, when the first time visited, to one
Who thither comes to find in it his home?
He walks about and looks upon the spot
With cordial transport, moulds it and remoulds,
And is half pleased with things that are amiss,
'Twill be such joy to see them disappear.
                              Wordsworth, *The Prelude*

I   *Of Education*

Of Education appeared in June 1644, before the two final divorce tracts. It was written in response to a request from Samuel Hartlib, who has been described as the middleman of reform in the English Revolution. He knew everybody, and brought into contact all those whom he could interest in reforming schemes. He first mentioned Milton in 1643 as a 'great traveller, . . . full of projects and inventions' – a further hint of the importance of the Italian journey in the formation of Milton's personality, a further hint that he was no aloof recluse. Hartlib had been in Cambridge whilst Milton was an undergraduate, in 1625–6; there is no evidence that they met, but they had mutual friends. Hartlib knew Thomas Young and Joseph Mede, and so did his collaborator, John Dury. Milton and Hartlib both knew Lady Ranelagh, whose aunt (the sister of Edward King, Milton's Lycidas) Dury married with Lady Ranelagh's assistance.[1] Milton remained in touch with this Comenian group of reformers. When Hartlib listed proposed 'Commissioners for the Act of the Council for Schooling', he included Milton together with Dury, Pell, William Rand,

---

[1] Turnbull, pp. 13, 28–9, 34, 40, 149, 244, 247; C. Webster (1975), *passim*.

Marchamont Nedham, Moses Wall, Israel Tonge and others. Hartlib knew
Milton well enough to be aware that he owned a manuscript of Bodin's
dangerous *Heptaplomeres*.[1]

Dury, who had long known Giovanni Diodati, Charles's relative, was
also on friendly terms with Milton. The poet presented him with a copy of
Eikonoklastes in 1649, and Dury translated it into French. Other members
of the Comenian group who may be counted among Milton's admirers are
John Hall and Sir Cheney Culpeper, each of whom approached Milton
through Hartlib, Robert Boyle (Lady Ranelagh's brother),[2] John Pell,
Benjamin Worsley, John Sadler, Theodore Haak, Henry Oldenburg.[3]
The educational reformer Samuel Gott, whose *Nova Solyma* was once
attributed to Milton, may have belonged to this circle.

Of Education has been criticized as 'élitist' and out of step with the
forward-looking schemes of the Comenian group. But this is perhaps to
misconceive its purpose. Milton was describing an academy for the
education of a select few, who are expected to become national leaders: it
was a scheme of a familiar renaissance type, but with quite a new programme. Milton was not drafting a total educational plan for society,
though he hoped that schools of the type he recommended would be set
up 'in every city throughout the land'.[4] He later showed his agreement
with many aspects of the plans of the Hartlib group. In *A Second Defence
of the People of England* (1654) Milton urged Cromwell to pay greater
attention to popular education of both sexes, which should be 'at the
public cost'. In *The Likeliest Means* (1659) he spelt this out, proposing 'to
erect in great number all over the land schools and competent libraries to
those schools, where languages and arts may be taught free together'. In
these the youth 'may be at once brought up to a competence of learning
and to an honest trade', with 'the hours of teaching so ordered as their
study may be no hindrance to their labour or other calling'.[5] Theory and
practice had been similarly combined in Milton's own teaching, and in
Of Education.

The main duty of governments is to leave the governed alone, Milton
thought, but he gives them a positive role in education. In *The Ready and
Easy Way* he called for the setting up of schools and academies for the
gentry in every county, 'at their own choice, wherein their children may

---

[1] C. Webster (1970), pp. 42–3; French, II, pp. 168–9, 214–15, 235–6, 245, 371–4. For Nedham
see p. 184 below, and for Wall, pp. 191–3, 201–2, 214 below.
[2] See pp. 223–4 below for Hall; for Boyle see Jacob, *passim*.
[3] For Haak see pp. 214, 391–2 below, and for Oldenburg, pp. 182, 215.
[4] *C.P.W.*, II, pp. 380–1.
[5] *Ibid.*, IV, p. 679; cf. pp. 142, 262; *C.M.*, VI, p. 80.

be bred up . . . to all learning'. This was possible only in a commonwealth, and was there especially necessary. For if the people are to be fitted to elect their governors, and if the elected are themselves to be fit to rule, then we must 'mend our corrupt and faulty education', and replace it by a system which will 'teach the people faith, not without virtue, temperance, modesty, sobriety, parsimony, justice', and to subordinate selfish interests to 'the public peace, liberty and safety'.[1]

No doubt by 1659–60 Milton had learnt from the mass of educational writing published since 1644. Yet it would be wrong to think of him as ever antagonistic to the ideas of the reformers.[2] In 1641 he was demanding bishops' lands to finance schools. John Hall referred in 1644 to Milton's 'excellent discourse of education', and repeatedly asked Hartlib to introduce him to Milton. Dury too referred favourably to Milton, and was himself 'obviously directly influenced by Milton' in writing his *Reformed School*. Though Milton allowed himself what seems to be a disparaging remark about Comenius in *Of Education*, nevertheless his Baconian vision that learning will 'repair the ruins of our first parents' agrees exactly with Comenius's definition of 'the general aim of the entire education of man' as being 'to restore man to the lost image of God – i.e. to the lost perfection of the free will'.[3] In the *De Doctrina* Milton argued that in believers 'the intellect is to a very large extent restored to its former [i.e. prelapsarian] state of enlightenment.'[4] So if the proffer of redemption for all is to mean anything, all men and women should be educated – even though education by itself will not make them virtuous. Censorship can only be a hindrance.

Nicholas Culpeper thought that the English educational system was devised to maintain the privileges of the ruling class. 'They have imposed such multiplicity of needless rules in the learning of the Latin tongue that unless a man have gotten a very large estate he is not able to bring up his son to understand Latin, a dozen years expense of time will hardly do it as they have ordered the matter, in which time, by whipping and cruel usage, the brains of many are made so stupid that they are unfit for study, but are fain to pin their faith upon the sleeve of that monster, Tradition. . . . The poor commonalty of England is deprived of their birthright by this

---

[1] *C.M.*, VI, pp. 131–2.
[2] This point is most clearly stated in C. Webster (1970), pp. 42–3, which corrects the editorial comment in *C.P.W.*, II, p. 209.
[3] *C.P.W.*, I, p. 703; II, pp. 366–7; Comenius, pp. 98–9—from the posthumous *Pampaedia*. John Wilkins in 1661 also expected science to help mankind to reverse the Fall (Manuel, 1968, p. 128).
[4] *C.P.W.*, VI, pp. 478–83, 502–13.

means.'[1] Whether or not Culpeper had read Milton's *Of Education*, and whether or not Milton would have agreed with Culpeper's ideological slant, Milton's teaching methods were aimed at remedying the defects of which Culpeper complained. Latin was to be learnt in a year, and used as a tool, not an end in itself. Milton's textbook, *Accidence commenced Grammar*, was written in English and made as concise as possible.[2] 'Basically rebellious and revolutionary', Parker calls Milton's educational ideas, not least in 'ignoring the conventional division of secondary and higher education' and in proposing to abolish universities – Milton's last revenge on Cambridge. The replacement of Oxford and Cambridge by improved colleges ('one at least in every great town or city') was an idea later taken up by William Dell, who may well have read Milton.[3]

We should then consider *Of Education* in the light of Milton's own educational practice, as he had intended to carry it out in the great house in the Barbican which had so unfortunate a history. If we recall Milton's exceptional emphasis on arithmetic, geometry and trigonometry, on agriculture, modern languages and natural science, astronomy, geography and medicine, at a time when Pepys was unable to divide or multiply, we may see Milton as a forerunner of the dissenting academies, which after 1660 were to play so important a role in English education. They were 'at once both school and university', since dissenters were excluded from Oxford and Cambridge.[4] Dissenting academies gave an all-round education, classically based, like Milton's, but including science, mathematics and modern languages. Remembering Milton's contempt for the Cambridge syllabus, and his rejection of the idea of a separate clerical caste educated at universities, this might have pleased him. He would certainly have been gratified that in the early sixteen-eighties, when his political writings were being condemned to the flames by the University of Oxford, they were eagerly read in the dissenting academies of Hackney, Newington Green, Homerton, Northampton and no doubt others.[5]

II *Areopagitica*

Areopagitica was published on 28 November 1644, selling at 4d a copy.[6] It was Milton's reply to Herbert Palmer's attack on him in a sermon before

---

[1] Culpeper (1650), Sig. B-Bv.
[2] J. M. French, pp. 644–50.
[3] Parker, pp. 258–9, 295; Masson, III, p. 239; Dell, pp. 642–8.
[4] *C.P.W.*, II, pp. 380, 386–7; cf. p. 195.
[5] French, V, pp. 67, 420; Parker, pp. 1185–6. Cf. p. 230 below.
[6] L. Miller (1975), p. 309.

the House of Commons. Many of its ideas were commonplaces among the
radicals. We may quote Servetus, for instance. 'It would be easy to judge if
it were permitted to all to speak in peace in the church, that all might vie
in prophesying.' So far from his *Restitutio Christianismi* disturbing Christendom, Servetus argued at his trial, Christendom would profit by it and
the truth would be worked out little by little: things are often at first
repressed which are afterwards received.[1] In England radical sectaries had
worked out a theory of toleration long before Milton wrote. John
Stoughton had said in a sermon preached at Paul's Cross 'take heed thou
strike not a schismatic, and a saint be found to lie a-bleeding and thou to
answer it.' But Stoughton quoted Pico della Mirandola for the sentiment, so Milton may have got it direct. Compare 'If I . . . should meet a
poor soul wandering from parish to parish, from sermon to sermon, to
find her well-beloved, I durst not wound her.' But some shepherds,
Stoughton added, are wolves.[2] Stoughton was a friend of Dury and
Hartlib. The latter published his millenarian *Felicitas ultimi saeculi* after
Stoughton's death – a work in which he linked Bacon, Comenius and Dury.

Many passages in Milton's *Of Prelatical Episcopacy* echo or are echoed by
(scholars are not quite sure) passages on toleration in Lord Brooke's
Discourse on Episcopacie. In the year or so before *Areopagitica* appeared, its
arguments had been anticipated by William Walwyn, later the Leveller, by
Henry Robinson and by Henry Burton.[3] Walwyn in June or July 1644
recognized the necessity of restricting Royalist propaganda in wartime,
but pointed out that 'by reason of the qualifications of the licensers' this
had 'wrought a wrong way, and stopped the mouths of good men'.[4]

Areopagitica starts from the assumption that, given freedom of debate,
the reason which is common to all men is likely to lead them to recognize
the same truths. Such a view would appeal to those whose economic life
demanded freedom of trade from monopoly: it did not seem self-evident
to the big City merchants who read *Gangraena*. We can see *Areopagitica* as
Milton's attempt to focus the tolerationist case on one point, liberty of
printing, using arguments from the attack on monopolies; or we can see
him trying to unite the Protestant nation against priests, the Westminster
Assembly and the censorship, as he had earlier tried to unite the nation
against bishops. His immediate object was to appeal to Parliament against

---

[1] Bainton, pp. 67, 192.

[2] G. W. Whiting, pp. 301–10; Stoughton, pp. 124, 87.

[3] Walwyn (1643) and (1644) – which Milton had almost certainly read; H. Robinson (1644);
    H. Burton. For all these see *C.P.W.*, II, pp. 82–7, 114, 490, 542–3, 551.

[4] Walwyn (1644), Sig. A4–A5.

the Assembly of Divines, and especially to Erastians in and out of Parliament, who came nearest to sharing his views at this time. Thomas Coleman, one of the few Erastian ministers to preach before Parliament, cited Milton with approval in August 1643.[1] Coleman's most famous Erastian sermon was preached eight months after *Areopagitica* appeared.

The leading figure among the Erastians was John Selden, whose books Milton had been reading and annotating since at least 1638. In 1642-5 he studied Selden's *De Jure Naturali* in connection with his divorce pamphlets, quoting it and praising its author in *The Doctrine and Discipline of Divorce*.[2] In *Areopagitica* he again cited 'the chief of learned men reputed in this land', this time in support of the view that 'all opinions, yea errors, can help us to attain truth.'[3] Selden's *Uxor Hebraica* of 1646 seemed to confirm some of Milton's positions on divorce, and was quoted triumphantly in *The Second Defence* and in the *De Doctrina*.[4] In *The Likeliest Means* Milton again quoted Selden against the necessity for marriage to be administered by a priest.[5] Selden was a favourite of the Spenserian poets, a friend of William Browne. It was to Selden that in 1636 George Wither dedicated his translation of Nemesius's *The Nature of Man*, used by R. O. in *Mans Mortalitie*.[6] Selden was said by some to have been Oliver Cromwell's first choice when a reply to *Eikon Basilike* was needed.[7] There are many convergences between Selden's ideas and Milton's. Selden, for instance, thought that 'there's no such thing as spiritual jurisdiction', and that ''tis a vain thing to talk of a heretic'.[8]

So long as Milton retained confidence in the ability and willingness of the Erastians in Parliament to curb Presbyterian intolerance, he did not insist on the necessity for separating church and state, notwithstanding his attack on Constantine.[9] Anxious to enlist the support of 'anyone' who would 'bring his helpful hand to the slow-moving Reformation which we labour under', he felt that 'those neighbouring differences, or rather indifferences, ... in some point of doctrine or discipline, ... need not interrupt the unity of spirit, if we could but find among us the bond of peace.'[10] We shall often find Milton exhibiting this sort of tactical moderation in the interests of strategic extremism.

---

[1] Fixler, p. 119.
[2] *C.P.W.*, II, p. 350.
[3] *Ibid.*, p. 513.
[4] *Ibid.*, IV., p. 625; VI, p. 378; cf. I, p. 402 – Commonplace Book.
[5] *C.M.*, VI, p. 72; cf. *C.P.W.*, VI, p. 561.
[6] R.O., p. xxii.
[7] Parker, p. 360.
[8] Selden, pp. 95, 140; *C.P.W.*, I, p. 204. Selden spoke up for liberty of printing.
[9] See Sirluck's Introduction to *C.P.W.*, II, *passim*; cf. pp. 84-5 above.
[10] *C.P.W.*, II, p. 565.

What must also be emphasized, however, is the apocalyptic atmosphere of the early sixteen-forties, in which men could believe in progressive revelation, in the evolution of truth, and could hope for a state of permanent reformation. Here writers as diverse as the Smectymnuans, the Five Dissenting Brethren of the Westminster Assembly, Lord Brooke, Thomas and John Goodwin, Henry Robinson, Roger Williams, Walter Cradock and John Saltmarsh can be linked.[1] Hence the necessity of toleration, said the anonymous author of *The Ancient Bounds* (1645), without which truth 'cannot be so easily brought forth'. 'Better many errors of some kind suffered than one useful truth be obstructed or destroyed.'[2] Similarly Cromwell would rather tolerate Mohammedanism than persecute one of the elect. Truth, said Milton, 'may have more shapes than one'. Fifteen years later, in a phrase that suggests a reference to Hobbes, he argued that 'no man or body of men in these times can be the infallible judges or determiners in matters of religion to any other men's consciences but their own.'[3]

We may recall some long-standing radical Protestant traditions: Foxe's paean in praise of the printing press, Peter Wentworth's demand for liberty of speech, John Penry's for liberty of printing, the contempt for expurgatory indexes shown by Thomas James, Bodley's first Librarian, who used the Papal Index to help him to decide what books to order for his Library.[4] Or we may compare the *Homily on Reading of Holy Scripture*: 'If you will not know the truth of God . . . lest you fall into error; by the same reason you may then lie still and never go [i.e. walk] lest, if you go, you fall into the mire.' Even more important in the history of toleration was the stand of radical sectaries – Baptists like Leonard Busher and John Murton, Socinians like Crell – who said that truth would always prevail in fair argument.[5]

Milton himself had argued in *Animadversions* for the right of 'the free-born people of England' at long last to speak their minds, and in *The Reason of Church Government* against using the existence of sects and errors as an excuse for delaying reform. There was tactical wiliness in Milton's determination to prove that censorship should be rejected because it was popish. Protestantism – and here Milton echoes Walwyn and Robinson – is opposed to implicit faith, because all believers are priests. If he takes it

[1] Smectymnuus, p. 20; Haller (1933), II, pp. 160, 202; *W.T.U.D.*, pp. 366–7; Haller (1927), pp. 875–900.
[2] Woodhouse (1938), p. 247.
[3] *C.P.W.*, II, p. 563; *C.M.*, VI, p. 6.
[4] Penry, pp. 165–6; James, pp. 233–68.
[5] Crell, pp. 28–35.

at second hand, 'a man may be a heretic in the truth.'[1] Toleration, Milton argued, followed necessarily from that reliance on the Bible which was common to all Protestants, and only to them. This made persecution of Protestants by Protestants even more inexcusable than by papists. In 1659, echoing Hobbes, Milton was to argue that popery was 'but a Roman principality . . ., endeavouring to keep up her old universal dominion under a new name and mere shadow of a catholic religion'. The only heretic is he who maintains opinions which cannot be proved by Scripture – the papist.[2] Nearly thirty years after *Areopagitica* Milton was still saying that 'no true protestant can persecute, or not tolerate, his fellow-protestant' without rejecting the principles on which his own religion was founded. 'What is freedom but choice?' he had asked; but the literal meaning of the word heresy *is* choice.[3]

Censorship, Milton argued, favours a dull conformity; the censor's 'commission enjoins him to let pass nothing but what is vulgarly received already'. In a revolutionary age, when ideas were developing as rapidly as they were in the England of 1644, this was intolerable. It was also unsuccessful: suppressing sects only helped them to spread. Unanimity was neither possible nor desirable. Here Milton abandoned age-old assumptions, expressed by Hooker and more recently by Hobbes, that anarchy was the only possible consequence if religious diversity, liberty of expression and publication, were permitted. Milton consequently abandons the attempt at (or pretence of) a one-minded community. It is a very big step towards the modern world, though Milton is only one of many who took it in the sixteen-forties.[4]

One of the earliest entries in Milton's Commonplace Book, made before his Italian journey, noted that 'in moral evil much good can be mixed': evil exists to exercise the good. 'If there were no opposition', he asked in *The Reason of Church Government*, 'where were the trial of an unfeigned goodness? . . . Virtue that wavers is not virtue, but vice revolted from itself.' The line of thought runs from *Comus* to *Areopagitica*.[5] It runs through *Paradise Lost*, where the evil angels and Adam fall of their own free will, and the Son freely offers to die in order to redeem man's sin. Christian liberty is triumphantly asserted in the *De Doctrina*, whose Preface proclaims 'how much it is in the interests of the Christian religion that men

---

[1] *C.P.W.*, II, pp. 259, 537, 543–5.   [2] *C.M.*, VI, pp. 19, 26–7.
[3] *Ibid.*, VI, pp. 11–12, 166.
[4] C. Hill (Panther, 1969), p. 175; Hanson, pp. 345–6.
[5] *C.P.W.*, I, pp. 362–3. Cf. W. Sedgwick (*Justice*, 1649): 'there is and always hath been in all things in the world some good, some evil, some light, some darkness'(p.1). Cf. chapter 28, *passim*, pp. 444, 472–3 below.

should be free not only to sift and winnow any doctrine, but also openly to give their opinions of it, and even to write about it, according to what each believes. . . . Without this freedom . . . there is no religion and no gospel. Violence alone prevails, and it is disgraceful and disgusting that the Christian religion should be supported by violence.' Here the idea that truth evolves, that revelation is progressive, seems to link up with the Protestant stance of which Oliver Cromwell is a prominent exemplar, of waiting on God, of watching for providences, signs, before acting: truth may appear in unexpected places, but it is none the less divine for that. And truth once known must lead to action, as Michael told Adam to 'add/Deeds to thy knowledge answerable'.[1]

Although in *Areopagitica* Milton says that Arminius was 'perverted', he describes him as 'acute and distinct'; Milton's definition of freedom as choice is already leading him on the road from Calvin to Arminius in theory, at the same time as his revulsion from 'new Presbyter' is leading him further away from Presbyterianism in practice.[2] The argument of *Areopagitica* – 'that which purifies us is trial, and trial is by things contrary' – assumes that men are free to choose good or evil.[3] So the cultural crisis which became a political crisis becomes a theological crisis as well. Milton had to rethink his position not only on discipline but also on doctrine. It is not so much a change in fundamental outlook – for virtue was purified by trial in *Comus* – as a realization of the full significance, in political, social and theological terms, of a conception of Christian liberty which started from the absolute integrity of the individual conscience.

The idea of being a heretic in the truth can be found in Giordano Bruno, in Paolo Sarpi and among the Socinians, as well as in Bishop Carleton, William Chillingworth, John Fry, John Knowles, Robert Boyle, James Nayler, Thomas Hobbes and Robert Barclay.[4] It too is a logical conclusion of the radical Protestant doctrine that revelation may be progressive. When Agricola Carpenter, a mortalist, called in 1652 for 'some wiser Columbus' to reveal 'an America of knowledge yet unfound out', he may have been echoing Milton, but more probably he was

---

[1] *C.P.W.*, VI, pp. 122–3, 521–41; cf. pp. 496, 652; *P.L.* XII. 581 seq. John Robinson taught that 'the Lord hath more truth and light yet to break forth out of his holy word' (I, p. 44).

[2] *C.P.W.*, II, pp. 519–20, 514–15. See chapter 21 below.

[3] *C.P.W.*, II, pp. 164–5; VI, pp. 82–6.

[4] 'Some men', wrote Bruno, 'are like those birds of night which, because of the weakness of their eyes, retreat into their shadowy haunts as soon as they see in the brightening east those bars of crimson which are the sun's ambassadors' (Yates, 1964, p. 256; cf. *C.P.W.*, II, pp. 543, 565). Cf. also Bruno, p. 9; F. Chabod, p. 115; G. Carleton, p. 20; McLachlan, 1951, pp. 83, 244–6, 265–70; Nayler, p. 625; Hobbes, 1928, p. 72: Barclay, p. 13).

repeating ideas that were current in radical circles.[1] John Bunyan in 1657 thought that truth profited from heresy.[2]

We recall the importance in sixteenth- and seventeenth-century Protestant thinking of the linked themes of spiritual struggle and spiritual pilgrimage, warfaring and wayfaring.[3] Lemot in Chapman's *An Humerous Dayes Mirth* (1599) asked 'how can you conquer that against which you never strive, or strive against that which never encounters you?' This is 'to make virtue an idle huswife, and to hide herself [in] slothful cobwebs that still should be adorned with actions of victory'.[4] The intention here is ironical, but the sentiment recurs. John Warr, like William Sedgwick, Milton (and Bruno) recognized that liberty in its full appearance would darken the eye newly recovered from blindness, and therefore approved of gradual methods of reform.[5]

It is difficult to be patient with those critics, innocent of historical knowledge, who tut-tut at Milton's refusal of toleration for Roman Catholics, suggesting that he failed to understand the logic of his own *Areopagitica*. Milton knew very well what he was doing, and it is evidence of the complete change in the politico-religious atmosphere since his day that this still has to be explained. Milton, like Marvell, regarded popery not primarily as a religion – that might have been tolerated – but as 'a priestly despotism under the cloak of religion', which 'extirpates all religious and civil supremacies'. He saw it as 'a Roman principality', the outward arm of the Italian potentate whom he regarded as Antichrist, leader of a potential Spanish or French fifth column in England.[6] Milton early wrote Latin poems to celebrate England's escape on Guy Fawkes Day; and what he saw in Italy did not change his belief in the existence of an international Catholic plot aiming at total suppression of free discussion. Milton swallowed whole the stories of Irish massacres of English Protestants, and himself subscribed to the suppression of the Irish revolt. He would not be at all surprised when a papal nuncio headed the Irish rebels. The Irish were 'an accursed race', Royalist support for whom was 'criminal madness'.[7]

Milton further regarded Roman Catholic worship as idolatry, and therefore as one of the most grievous sins described in the Bible, the main

---

[1] Carpenter, p. 24.

[2] Bunyan, II, p. 181.

[3] Haller (1938), pp. 150–3; cf. Foxe, VI, Appendix 10; Dod and Clever (1611), chapter XX, p. 114; D'Ewes (1693), pp. 328–9; Sprunger, p. 147.

[4] Chapman, I, pp. 62–3.

[5] *W.T.U.D.*, p. 276. See p. 102 above.

[6] *C.P.W.*, II, p. 565; IV, pp. 321–2; *C.M.*, VI, p. 19. Cf. pp. 218–21 below.

[7] *C.P.W.*, IV, p. 323; cf. p. 15 above.

offence of the chosen people, against which they had to be warned again and again. Popish (and Laudian) idolatry subordinated the dignity of man to the sanctity of material things, whether they were the bread and wine of the sacrament or consecrated churches. 'When all our fathers worshipped stocks and stones' was his summary dismissal of the Catholic Middle Ages. Milton knew that idolatry was a sin to which too many of the common people were addicted. He also believed that popery, even more than prelacy, encouraged laxness and corruption, since through 'easy confession, easy absolution, pardons, indulgences, masses' a man could 'buy out his peace with money which he cannot with repentance'. It was the negation of that strenuous self-discipline which Milton thought fundamental to Christian liberty. In view of popish idolatry, freedom of worship for papists, if allowed, would pander to all that was worst, least rational, most backward-looking, most lax, in natural man. Popery, because of its refusal to accept the fundamental status of the Bible and conscience, could not be met on equal terms. By insistence on implicit faith, Rome 'forfeits her Christian liberty'. For these reasons, political and cultural as well as religious, Milton in common with many other Englishmen felt that although Roman Catholics might be allowed liberty of conscience in secret, 'for just reason of state' they must not be permitted 'the public and scandalous use' of worship.[1]

Here Milton represented the normal English Protestant attitude, shared by liberals from Hooker through Selden to Locke.[2] More in need of explanation than Milton's position is that of those eccentric tolerationists who would have been prepared to extend liberty of worship to Catholics – Roger Williams, Richard Overton, William Walwyn, Colonel John Jubbes. None of them was a practical politician in the sense that Milton was, nor was ever associated with any government. Their views would have made this impossible. Sir Henry Vane, who may privately have favoured toleration for Catholics, did nothing in his public capacity to achieve this end. We may admire the consistency in charity of Williams, Walwyn, Overton and Jubbes; to contemporaries they must have seemed, in this respect, totally unrealistic. (I speak only of tolerationists on the radical wing of the Parliamentarians: no explanation is needed for those Laudians who favoured liberty of conscience for papists for exactly the same political reasons as led Milton and his like to oppose it.) Nor did

---

[1] *C.M.*, VI, pp. 19–20, 34–6. In *Of True Religion* (1673) Milton even opposed private worship for Catholics: this was a tactical move to win the support of M.P.s who agreed with him in disliking Charles II's Declaration of Indulgence.

[2] See pp. 220–1 below.

Milton urge the extension of toleration to Jews, as Roger Williams and
Oliver Cromwell were prepared to do.[1] A radical like William Erbery was
prepared for toleration to Jews and Turks, but not to papists.[2]

In *Areopagitica* Milton advocated limitations on publishing: the
Commonwealth should 'have a vigilant eye how books demean themselves
as well as men; and thereafter to confine, imprison and do sharpest justice
on them as malefactors'. He recommended abolition of licensing in
advance of publication, not the abolition of laws preventing publication
of that 'which is impious or evil absolutely, either against faith or
manners'.[3] It is possible – though I could not prove this – that Milton is
here making tactical concessions to those whose views were more conservative than his own. This seems to me more plausible than the suggestion that *Areopagitica* is a party-line document, 'a rationale of revolutionary
censorship', 'a militant and exclusivist revolutionary pamphlet', which
scholars have misinterpreted. We should be grateful to John Illo for
reminding us that Milton was indeed a revolutionary, not a nineteenth-
century liberal.[4] He did not 'misunderstand' the logic of his own argument, as liberal scholars have plaintively suggested. On the contrary:
Milton was facing not only the tactical problem of how to preserve the
greatest possible unity among the opponents of intolerance, but also the
difficulties resulting from the shock of new light breaking on 'eyes bleared
and dimmed with prejudice and custom':[5] the problem of how to establish
liberty before all men were educated up to it. His tolerance, like Cromwell's, was limited to those with 'the root of the matter' in them. Milton
and Cromwell would have thought it was necessarily so limited, since to
extend toleration to the intolerant would have defeated its fundamental
object – the establishment of a better society.

The proponents of unfreedom – Rome, Charles I, the Presbyterians –
were prepared to use violence to prevent the establishment of what Milton,
and posterity, regarded as necessary freedoms. Milton's policy of toleration
to the left, toleration of nearly all Protestants, could have been a very wide
toleration; if it excluded the advocates of intolerance ('to suppress the
suppressors'[6]), it would have excluded only those whose views had in the
past been widely propagated. New ideas came from the radical Protestant
left, and could do so only given the liberty of printing which Milton

---

[1] Wolfe (1961), pp. 834–8.
[2] Cheynell (1646), p. 35.
[3] *C.P.W.*, II, pp. 492, 565; cf. pp. 163–4, 178–81, 569.
[4] Illo, pp. 38–42.
[5] *C.P.W.*, II, p. 565.
[6] *Ibid.*, II, p. 568.

advocated so warmly. Milton's tolerance had its limits. but it is not quite fair to sneer at him as if he were a twentieth-century fellow traveller who had learnt nothing from the career of Joseph Stalin.

Milton had been drawn towards Baconianism at Cambridge.[1] In his anti-episcopal tracts he made especially good use of Bacon's *Certain Considerations touching the Church* and *Advertisement concerning the Controversies of the Church of England*, which the liberation of the press had allowed to be printed in 1640 and 1641 respectively. Even earlier Milton had noted Bacon's remarks on the unwisdom of prohibiting books.[2] The extent of Bacon's influence over Milton at this period has perhaps not been sufficiently noted. The remark in *Of Education* that 'the end . . . of learning' was 'to repair the ruins of our first parents' is pure Baconianism.[3] The denunciation in *Areopagitica* of the rich man who resolves 'to find himself out some factor, to whose care and credit he may commit the whole managing of his religious affairs' and resign 'the whole warehouse of his religion' also echoes Bacon's 'when men have once made over their judgment to others' keeping'. Milton had in fact quoted Bacon a page or two earlier. 'It is reserved only for God and angels to be lookers-on', Bacon had written, refusing to praise a fugitive and cloistered virtue;[4] and he attacked 'men of a devout policy' who discourage 'stirring in philosophy, lest it may lead to an innovation in divinity'. I am not necessarily suggesting direct Baconian influence here. More relevant perhaps is the common Puritan background. 'Not to try is a greater risk than to fail', wrote Bacon in the true vein of *Areopagitica*.[5] If we look forward to *Paradise Lost*, there too we can trace echoes of Bacon's view that the Fall was caused not by curiosity about the secrets of nature but by a desire for moral omniscience which would make man self-sufficient. In the *Defence of the People of England* Milton declared in Baconian style that things were more important than the names given to them.[6] Towards the end of his life Milton still insisted that 'the habit of learned vapouring should rather be ejected from the schools than retained.'[7]

So Milton, who in the pamphlets on episcopacy had gone out of his way to defend Anabaptists and Familists, by 1644 was sought after by the

---

[1] See pp. 36–7 above.
[2] *C.P.W.*, I, p. 450; cf. C. Hill (1965), pp. 116–17.
[3] *Ibid.*, pp. 89–91; Bacon, I, pp. 538–9; IV, pp. 21, 247–8; VIII, pp. 349–50.
[4] Bacon, IV, p. 14; V, p. 8; cf. *C.P.W.*, II, p. 544; C. Hill (1965), p. 115. Winstanley appears also to echo Bacon (Sabine, p. 523).
[5] Bacon, III, pp. 499–503, 617; cf. III, p. 219.
[6] *C.P.W.*, IV, pp. 454–5, 484; cf. p. 425 below. For other influences of Bacon on *Paradise Lost*, see C. Webster (1975), pp. 17, 22.
[7] *C.M.*, XI, pp. 430–1.

Hartlib group of reformers. His divorce pamphlets had outraged conservative Parliamentarians, who savagely attacked him as a subverter of morals; this brought him perhaps embarrassing allies on the libertine wing of the supporters of Parliament. In the *Apology* he had defended the right of smiths, carpenters, weavers, to a voice in the election of ministers, and attacked those who condemned 'the Christian congregation' as 'rabble'.[1] In *Areopagitica* he summed up with superb eloquence the radical demand for freedom of speech, and especially of printing. Experience taught him that new Presbyter was but old priest writ large. As divisions grew between radical and conservative Parliamentarians, Milton moved naturally and inevitably towards the radicals – to those like Oliver Cromwell who demanded religious toleration and a career open to the talents; to those like Walwyn who called for wider religious and political liberty.

The important transformation was in Milton's conception of the poet's role. In the sixteen-thirties, church-outed, he had seen himself as the dedicated poet, isolated in his purity from a corrupt society. The long preparatory period of study and travel was related to the fact that the world of affairs was closed to him. But now, in the Utopian enthusiasm of the early forties, Milton began to envisage the possibility of a reconstructed society in which the true poet could step forward as the acknowledged legislator of mankind. That is the point of the prayer at the end of *Of Reformation,* and of the autobiographical passage in *The Reason of Church Government.*

Poetry and politics thus got inextricably mingled. The 'impertinent yoke of prelaty' first cast off, the press must next be set free from the attempts of new presbyters to re-establish the old control, if the life of the spirit is to flourish. Then a mighty and puissant nation can emerge, a nation chosen by and dedicated to God, a nation of creative searchers for truth, among whom the poet will have an honoured and supremely important function.[2] At this stage Milton's romantic belief in the chosen English nation was explicit.[3] Censorship is 'an undervaluing and vilifying of the whole nation', a reproach to the common people. 'Now the time has come, wherein . . . all the Lord's people are become prophets.' This last sentence no doubt refers to the elect members of the nation; but other passages appear to think of the nation itself as elect. Such distinctions were

---

[1] *C.P.W.*, I, pp. 932–4.
[2] Rivers, pp. 81–3.
[3] See chapter 22 below.

forced on Milton only later, when he began to doubt whether the English people was in fact chosen.[1]

III Milton and the people

In 1641–5, then, as Milton moved towards Arminianism and anti-Trinitarianism, he envisaged the English people as the chosen nation, and the radicals as heirs of the Lollards and the Marian martyrs. The reception of his divorce pamphlets by ordinary people, as well as by Presbyterian divines, must therefore have upset him seriously. It may be that his middle-class and academic upbringing and outlook, together with his temperamental emphasis on discipline rather than love, always held him back from a real belief in the democracy of grace such as led Fox and the Quakers to proclaim human equality. Perhaps the violence of Milton's onslaught on episcopacy betrays an essential uncertainty in his own position.[2]

It is paradoxical that the élitist Puritan scholar found his most favourable audience among those whom he came to regard as 'the rabble' – those whose mode of life made them reluctant to accept the Protestant ethic at all, those whose spokesmen the Ranters were to become. Some at least of these were itinerant craftsmen, footloose, not tied to the household economy which was the basis for the Puritan ethic. Laurence Clarkson, for instance, had a legitimate wife, to whom he sent money whilst giving his body to other women on his preaching rounds. Others no doubt engaged in *de facto* marriages and *de facto* divorces. Some sectaries, Mrs. Attaway, for instance, found Milton's doctrine of divorce a convenient excuse for getting rid of a tiresome spouse.

That is why Milton's Sonnet XII, 'I did but prompt the age to quit their clogs' differs in its target from the one he printed immediately before it, 'A book was writ of late called Tetrachordon'. Sonnet XI attacks his Presbyterian opponents, the rabble-rousing critics of his views. Sonnet XII was double-edged; its target includes the vulgar who 'bawl for freedom in their senseless mood'. These are not conservative opponents; they are apparent allies, but allies whose theology, or lack of it, Milton found embarrassing. He had neither deserved nor wanted the reputation which he won among libertine and sectarian circles. Yet clearly he was not unaffected. Many heresies which Milton came to accept were prevalent among Anabaptists, Ranters and Quakers. The rest of his life, it

---

[1] *C.P.W.*, I, pp. 703–7; II, pp. 553–6, 535–6; cf. Lutaud pp. 58, 78.
[2] Jordan (1940), p. 205.

might be argued, was spent in assimilating, chewing over, selecting and rejecting from this new world of radical theory, which at once attracted and repelled him.

Hence perhaps the hate/love relationship between Milton and the common people, who failed to come up to his hopes for them. The fluctuations extend from the optimism of *Areopagitica* to the brutal rejections by Jesus in *Paradise Regained*. The people chose the right thing for the wrong reason, cried liberty when they meant licence. They welcomed divorce for libertine reasons, they abolished sin in order to be allowed to sin the more freely. They accepted materialism not because they respected the presence of God in all matter but in order to say 'Let us eat, drink and be merry'; their mortalism sprang from the hope of avoiding judgment. Gerrard Winstanley experienced a similar if less traumatic let-down at the hands of Ranters who came to his Digger commune in 1649–50 and disrupted it by their sexual libertinism. By 1652 Winstanley too had realized that his ideal society would need defending against 'the rudeness of the people'.[1] In *The History of Britain* Milton observed that love of the public good was rarer in England than love of money or vain honour: he was already prepared for the time when men would prostitute liberty to the illusion that kingship would restore trade.[2]

So Milton's enthusiasm for the chosen English people did not last long. Four factors, we may suppose, combined to disillusion him. First, the resumption of his marriage and the Powell invasion of his home. The poem that his own life ought to be was irreparably smirched. Though Milton was later to marry for love and happily, now in his late thirties and early forties he was tied to Mary Powell and her ghastly family. Secondly, his pride and sense of decorum must have been deeply shaken by the accusations of immorality, of advocacy of licence, which were showered upon him by Puritan preachers and conservative Parliamentarians – those on whose behalf he had first entered the lists of controversy. His error had been not libertinism but too high an ideal of purity, too high an ideal of matrimony. He could not with – say – Henry Marten cheerfully dump a wife and live with a woman whom he loved. Milton was trapped. Thirdly, there was the approach of blindness, of which he seems to have become acutely aware by 1648, when his translation of Psalms 80–88 seems to reflect a deep personal despair. Fourthly, the political situation in these years depressed him. The millenarian vision faded. The united nation of

---

[1] *W.T.U.D.*, pp. 134, 230, 319.
[2] *C.P.W.*, V, pp. 450–1.

earnest seekers after truth envisaged in *Areopagitica* was replaced by the reality of fierce faction fights between the Presbyterian majority in Parliament and the Independent-dominated army. It is a long time before we hear again of Milton's epic plans. His early adulation of Parliament gave place to the disappointed diatribe of *The Character of the Long Parliament*, probably written in 1647–8. With its sweeping criticisms of individual M.P.s (rather than of the institution) it breathes the same sort of despair for the nation as did the translation of the Psalms in Milton's personal life. It may also reflect Milton's unfortunate experiences in trying to help Richard Powell to compound for his delinquency, and the poet's failure even to get his own debt from his father-in-law recognized by the Parliamentary authorities. After 1648 Milton thinks less of God's special favour towards England: he worries more about whether his countrymen *deserve* to be free.

PART III

MILTON AND THE COMMONWEALTH

> The field
> To labour calls us now with sweat imposed,
> Though after sleepless night.
>
> Milton, *Paradise Lost*, XI, 171–3

Chapter 11

Defending the Republic, I

Let us never forget Milton, the first defender of regicide.
Friedrich Engels in *The Northern Star*, 18 December 1847

The Character of the Long Parliament shows how disillusioned Milton now felt with the men he had greeted so ecstatically only a few years earlier. The London radicals, with whom he might have felt more kinship, were a small group, not united, weak except in the army; their attempts to wrest control of the army from the generals had split the reformers. In so far as we can guess at Milton's political position between 1645 and 1655 it seems to have been close to Oliver Cromwell's; the army must remain united, since only it could enforce religious toleration and political liberty. The alternatives were surrender to the Presbyterian persecutors, and so to restoration of the King; or anarchy, disintegration and ultimate Royalist restoration by a different route. Milton never attacked the Levellers, but he never associated himself with their political position.

1645 to 1649 were years of pregnant silence, in which we must assume that the poet was nursing his wounds, personal and political, and waiting. *The History of Britain* reflects the gloom that Milton felt at this period. He had fewer pupils; he was alone with Mary; politically he already saw the avarice and ambition of the Parliamentary leaders frustrating the hopes of the revolutionaries. William Sedgwick was making similar points in the same year 1648.[1]

Milton probably started work on the *De Doctrina Christiana* at this time, when he was interested in the ideas of the radicals yet anxious to differentiate himself from them politically.[2] But seizure of power by the army in the winter of 1648–9 seemed to hold out new hopes for God's cause in England. When Milton published his next pamphlet, the situation – or his

---

[1] *C.P.W.*, V, pp. 432–5, 443–51; cf. W. Sedgwick (*Leaves*, 1648), pp. 20–31.
[2] See p. 233 below.

vision of it – was curiously analogous to that of 1641. Then the enemy had been episcopacy: a supreme national effort to overthrow bishops would set God's Englishmen on the path of liberty and truth. Now the enemy was monarchy; its overthrow would have the same cathartic effect: if not to unite the English people, at least to reunite the virtuous among them. So *The Tenure of Kings and Magistrates* was another pre-emptive bid from the poet–prophet, emerging once more from his inglorious cave.

The Tenure was as little a work of the moment as Milton's anti-episcopal or divorce tracts had been. In 1628 he had referred to the 'almost godlike mind' of Junius Brutus, 'that . . . great avenger of the lusts of kings'.[1] From 1637 at least Milton had been noting in his Commonplace Book remarks critical of monarchy and favourable to a popular right of resistance. In the anti-episcopal pamphlets he had avoided attacking Charles I, and had claimed to be anxious only to rescue the monarchy from the domination of bishops.[2] This may have been genuine, or it may have been a sensible tactic to avoid alienating support: it is as difficult to be sure as to know how far Pym and the Parliamentary leaders had their tongues in their cheeks when they claimed to be fighting the Civil War to liberate the King from 'evil counsellors' who had kidnapped him, and sent the more outspoken Henry Marten to the Tower.[3] But even at Cambridge Milton never produced the formal poetical tributes for royalty that he did for bishops and university officials; he sympathized with Dorislaus and the younger Gil. We note the detestation of the social snobbery and flummery of monarchy shown in *Eikonoklastes*, the *Ready and Easy Way* and *Paradise Lost*; we recall the grim remark in *The History of Britain*, that regicide was 'the only effectual cure of ambition that I have read'.[4]

If we look back from 1649 to 1641–2, however, it is clear that a great change had come over Milton's world outlook. At the opening of the Long Parliament he and thousands more hoped to reunite the Protestant international which Buckingham and Laud had disrupted – first in close unity with our brethren of Scotland, then linking up with the Dutch republic and French Huguenots. But in 1649 English and Scottish Presbyterians, Dutch Calvinists and French Huguenots, all denounced the execution of Charles I. Milton and others might claim that regicide was the logical consequence of Calvinist principles; but it completed the disruption of the Calvinist international just when hopes for its revival had reached their

---

[1] *C.P.W.*, I, pp. 265, 267.
[2] *Ibid.*, I, pp. 420–1, 431–2, 440, 446, 452–62, 474–5, 499–501.
[3] *Ibid.*, I, pp. 6–7, 1007.
[4] *Ibid.*, V, p. 255. See pp. 35–6 above, p. 264 below.

peak. Milton and the English revolutionary leaders remained Protestant internationalists: but now their emphasis was more apocalyptic. It was the job of the saints in England 'first to overcome those European kings which receive their power not from God but from the Beast'. The English had 'the honour to precede other nations who are now labouring to be our followers'.[1] Whether Scots Presbyterians, Dutch Calvinists and French Huguenots liked it or not, the people of Europe must be liberated. Perhaps one of the reasons for the intensity of Milton's (and other Englishmen's) feelings about the massacre of the Vaudois was that here was a Protestant people who had *not* rejected the regicide republic, who could still be claimed as one in the faith.

The situation in 1649 enabled Milton to recapture some of his first fine careless rapture, some of his millenarian hopes. In the *Tenure* he prayed that Christ's kingdom 'may come soon, and in so praying' he wished 'hasty ruin and a destruction to all tyrants'. That was one reason for identifying Charles I with Antichrist, and for claiming that the English people have chosen God as their King.[2] In other ways the analogy of 1641 and 1649 is not exact. Against bishops Milton might hope to unite King and people; against monarchy he must have known that it was impossible to unite the whole people, though he was taken aback by the strength of monarchy's magical appeal. What he hoped, I think, was to unite 'the middle class, which produces the greatest number of men of good sense and knowledge of affairs' against kingship. He said later that he was in favour of a republic because it was a cheap form of government, and this may well have been typical of his bourgeois-moralist approach.[3]

The strength and originality of *The Tenure* come from its frank acceptance of revolution as a force in history. Milton was one of the first Englishmen publicly to defend the right of the people to call their kings to account, just as in 1660 he was to be the last Englishman to nail his colours to the republican mast. Milton in 1649 rammed home against the Presbyterians the oft-repeated charge that regicide was only the logical consequence of the principles which had justified waging war against Charles I, principles deriving from Calvin, Knox, Paraeus, Buchanan and Rutherford.[4] Both *The Tenure* and *Eikonoklastes* are weaker in defence than in counter-attack: Milton never managed adequately to laugh off the

[1] *C.P.W.*, III, pp. 598–9, 236–7.
[2] *Ibid.*, III, pp. 256, 210, 316, 536, 598–9; cf. chapter 12 and p. 282 below.
[3] *C.P.W.*, IV, p. 471; Darbishire, p. 186. See p. 265 below.
[4] *C.P.W.*, III, pp. 223–6, 246–8; cf. IV, p. 592, and Frye (1966), p. 98.

Solemn League and Covenant's pledge to preserve and defend the King's person.[1]

Milton's rhetoric in *The Tenure* is admirable if sometimes imprecise. 'No man who knows aught can be so stupid to deny that all men naturally were born free' – a statement first made in *Of Prelatical Episcopacy* (1641). Kings and magistrates are 'deputies and commissioners of the people'. Government is a trust, and the people cannot give up their ultimate rights. To assert anything else were 'a kind of treason against the dignity of mankind'.[2] Yet when we look below the surface rhetoric, there are ambiguities. Who are the people? We are reminded of the divorce pamphlets when Milton speaks of the power of 'masters of families' to remove or abolish any governor as 'the root and source of all liberty'.[3] There were problems in this line of approach, of which Milton was not fully aware – or which he simply failed to solve. It was a splendid retort to Royalists and Presbyterians to say that even if the punishment of tyrants was God's business, God might nevertheless use the people as his agents: especially when Samuel Rutherford could be quoted in support.[4] But it remained difficult to equate the purged Rump of the Long Parliament with the people of England. Milton was really trying to have it both ways. If God can use the people to achieve his ends, no doubt he can also use a minority of the people. But, Filmer argued against Milton, even if we accept that 'the sounder, the better and the uprighter part have the power of the people . . . how shall we know, or who shall judge, who they be?'[5]

We are facing here the problem of any revolutionary minority which claims to act on behalf of the people, whether this is expressed by Jean-Jacques Rousseau as forcing to be free or by the Bolsheviks as the dictatorship of the proletariat. In the twentieth century we are suspicious of the notion of dictatorship on behalf of democracy; but the fact that the problem has proved insoluble does not mean that we should dismiss it. Experience has taught us that the substitution of a group for the people is apt to lead rapidly to the degeneration of the former. But Milton's age was facing for the first time in human history the problem of educating an electorate. Milton's advocacy of revolutionary dictatorship together with freedom among a wide ruling élite should not with the wisdom of hindsight be equated with Stalinism. The rule of the Rump, and later that of

---

[1] Cf. *C.P.W.*, III, pp. 593–4.

[2] *Ibid.*, I, p. 624; III, pp. 198–9, 202, 204.

[3] *Ibid.*, III, pp. 236–7, 254; cf. IV, p. 383 – the King can do no wrong.

[4] *Ibid.*, III, p. 211. Cf. Rutherford: 'God only by the action of the people as his instruments can dethrone a king' (1644, p. 406).

[5] Filmer, p. 252.

Cromwell, were far milder than those of Robespierre and Napoleon, of
Lenin and Stalin. Milton repeatedly warned those who held power in
England of the danger that they would be corrupted, as well as insisting
on their duty to educate those whom they were called upon to rule. The
Levellers were as little able to solve this problem as Milton was. It was
restated 150 years later, in an address of the Corresponding Society: 'How
is the peasant, the mechanic, the manufacturer, to obtain the necessary
knowledge? His time is fully employed in labouring hard to provide a
scanty meal for his family.'[1]

There were, however, many who during the English Revolution faced
the problem squarely. Hugh Peter spoke of using the army to teach
peasants to understand liberty. 'What's for their good, not what pleases
them', said Oliver Cromwell and Colonel John Jones.[2] 'It's unlikely, nay
impossible, that multitudes should make any good choice at this time',
declared the City radical Daniel Taylor in November 1651. Thomas Scott
envisaged a long period of cautious reform until the people were
'proselytized'.[3] Milton perhaps envisaged Cromwell as a transitional
dictator, who would ultimately hand power over to the people, rather as
Olphaeus Megalator did in Harrington's *Oceana*, or as Winstanley suggested
Cromwell should when he dedicated *The Law of Freedom* to him in 1652. Yet
in 1659, when Milton made a similar appeal first to Monck, then to a
perpetual oligarchy, he must have realized that it would be a very long
time before 'the people' could take over.

In *An Apology against a Pamphlet* Milton had pointed out how unfair it
was for defenders of episcopacy to jeer at the blindness of the people
when it was the bishops who had put out their eyes. In *Of Reformation* he
had defended 'the mob' and 'the people vilified and rejected' by the
bishops. In *The Reason of Church Government* he reminded his readers that
Christ took the form of a servant, 'choosing the meaner things of this
world that he might put under the high'. In *An Apology* he praised the
House of Commons for listening to 'the meanest artisans and labourers,
women and often the younger sort of servants', and had a good word for
'the mutinous rabble'. Even in *Eikonoklastes*, whilst denouncing the 'inconstant, irrational and image-doting rabble', he still defended 'popular
tumults' and 'this iron flail, the people'.[4] But in 1647–8 the Presbyterians
had shown that mobs could be used by either side, and something of

---

[1] *The London Corresponding Society's Addresses* (1792), pp. 13–14.
[2] Peter, p. 6; C. Hill (1972), pp. 199–200, 285.
[3] Worden, p. 289.
[4] *C.P.W.*, I, pp. 926, 932–3, 548, 825–6, 933–4; III, pp. 388–91, 397, 564–6, 601. See p. 177
below.

this is reflected in the strictures on the fickleness of the people in *The History of Britain*. In 1654 Milton asked what if the mob 'had demanded that Charles should be restored to the kingdom?'[1] It was a searching question.

Unlike Winstanley or Hobbes or Harrington, Milton was not an original political theorist. He took nearly all his ideas at second hand from his radical contemporaries. Thus he accepted many of the Levellers' arguments against monarchy – so much so that Professor Wolfe supposed that *Regall Tyrannie* and perhaps *The Peoples Right* 'lay on his desk as he wrote *The Tenure* and *A Defence of the People of England*'.[2] Yet Milton rejected the Leveller plea for a wider franchise, on the realistic ground that it would *increase* the power of the men of property, by bribery and corruption, to return their own nominees. Given the influence of landlords and parsons, in the absence of a secret ballot, a free vote of the electorate proposed by the Levellers would probably have established a Royalist government, and would certainly not have established a democracy. As early as 1644 Henry Burton had observed that 'if the whole world might vote this day, the generality would vote against Christ.'[3] Since then ordinary people had gained little from the Revolution except increased taxation. Milton's realistic approach was close to that of John Goodwin and John Canne (both of whom quote *The Tenure* with approval).[4]

So far as Milton's personal dignity was concerned, *The Tenure* was a complete success. There followed recognition at last, in an invitation from the Council of State to accept the post of Secretary for Foreign Tongues. We do not know who was responsible for inviting Milton – perhaps Luke Robinson, fellow-undergraduate at Christ's; perhaps John Bradshaw, to whom a copy of *The Tenure* was presented in February 1649; perhaps Bulstrode Whitelocke, whose family lived at Horton; perhaps Fairfax, to whom Milton had addressed a sonnet in 1648. The Council of State soon asked him to reply to Salmasius's attack on the regicide republic, and to *Eikon Basilike*. John Milton, Englishman, found himself defending his country in the face of Europe: the decision to forgo a European reputation by concentrating on writing poetry in the vernacular was thus reversed. And in *Eikonoklastes* he had an opportunity to defend a rational cultural revolution against the Royalist appeal to the primitive magic of kingship.

---

[1] *C.P.W.*, IV, p. 635; cf. *Salus Populi Solus Rex* (October 1648): 'Everywhere the greater party are for the King' (Brailsford, p. 345).
[2] Wolfe (*Milton in the P.R.,* 1941), pp. 184, 213, 458; cf. p. 200, and Zagorin, p. 106.
[3] Fixler, p. 138.
[4] See p. 224 below.

Chapter 12

Eikonoklastes and Idolatry

> Idolatry is not to be permitted a moment. . . . All that have power
> have right to destroy it, by that grand charter of religion whereby
> every one is bound to advance God's glory.
>   Thomas Fuller, *Church History*
> Every King is an image of God. . . . Thou shalt not make unto thee
> any graven image. . . . Revolutionary republicanism seeks to abolish
> effigy and show. . . . An end to idolatry is not so easy.
>   N. O. Brown, *Love's Body*

It was Milton's habit to intervene in controversy only against adversaries
worthy of his pen. As his pupil Thomas Ellwood put it in *An Epitaph*
on Milton,

> Mean adversaries he declined,
> And battle with the chiefest joined.[1]

Scorning the riff-raff among the defenders of episcopacy, he took as his
target 'two bishops of particularly high repute'. These were Joseph Hall
and Archbishop Ussher, 'the chief and most nominated opposers on the
other side, whom no one else undertook'.[2] In Salmasius Milton overcame
a scholar of European renown. In the *De Doctrina* he took on La Place, the
most eminent enemy of Socinianism. In *Paradise Lost*, whether we think of
his adversary as Satan or God, he was again going for the highest target;
he was consciously attempting to outdo Homer and Virgil, perhaps
Moses as well.[3] In *Eikonoklastes* he engaged not with Charles I's defenders
but with the royal martyr himself. 'No man ever gained much honour by
writing against a King', Milton disclaimed, since 'such courtly antagonists'
could not muster up much 'force of argument'.[4] Yet just because Charles's

---

[1] Webb, p. 241.
[2] *C.P.W.*, IV, pp. 622–3; I, p. 869. Later he left Bishop Parker to Andrew Marvell.
[3] Daiches, p. 63.
[4] *C.P.W.*, III, p. 337.

case did not rest on rational argument, he alone of Milton's antagonists won the day, at least in the short run.

Eikon Basilike, The Pourtraicture of His Sacred Majestie in His Solitude and Sufferings, was published at the beginning of February 1649, within a week of Charles's execution. It enjoyed an instantaneous and lasting success – thirty-five editions in London within a year, twenty-five more in Ireland and abroad.[1] Historians have perhaps not sufficiently emphasized the political importance of *Eikon Basilike* – partly because its intellectual content is nil, partly because they have been too occupied with sterile disputes about its authorship. These have now been finally settled; the author of *Eikon Basilike* was not King Charles himself but the Rev. John Gauden, a Presbyterian divine and supporter of Parliament during the Civil War, who defended tithes in 1653,[2] and became Bishop of Worcester after the Restoration – largely on the strength of his authorship of *Eikon Basilike*, though the secret still had to be kept. It is probable that Charles drafted most of the earlier chapters himself, but they were polished for the press by Gauden, who added three chapters. Almost all contemporaries were taken in, and believed that in *Eikon Basilike* they had the *ipsissima verba* of the royal martyr. The book enjoyed phenomenal success with the seventeenth-century equivalent of the *Daily Mirror* public. Even the young Isaac Newton copied out a poem from *Eikon Basilike* for his girl friend.[3]

It is difficult to-day to conceive of the aura which still clung around kingship. The King was a semi-divine figure, whose touch cured scrofula, the King's Evil. Not even the touch was always necessary. A napkin dipped in the blood of the royal martyr was said to have cured a Deptford girl.[4] The King's person had long been regarded as sacrosanct, and throughout the Civil War the Parliamentarian leaders had claimed to be fighting on the King's behalf against his evil councillors. High treason was a personal offence, a breach of personal loyalty to the King: the idea that the King himself might be a traitor to the realm was novel. For a king to be tried and executed in the name of his subjects was unheard of. Mary Queen of Scots was executed in 1587, after she had been deposed by her subjects and had fled to England where she had been a prisoner for nineteen years. Whether or not she was guilty of treason to Elizabeth,

---

[1] *Ibid.*, III, p. 150.
[2] Cf. pp. 104–5 above.
[3] *C. and C.*, p. 261.
[4] [Anon.], *A Miracle of Miracles wrought by the Blood of King Charles the First* (1649), pp. 1–5. I owe this reference to Mr. John Gifford.

whom she hoped to succeed on the English throne, at least the accusation of treason against her was not a revolutionary act – though Elizabeth very much disliked having Mary publicly tried and executed and would much have preferred her to be quietly murdered. Kings and queens had often been assassinated; but bringing even an ex-queen to trial, for treason against the sovereign under whose protection she lived – Elizabeth foresaw that this established an undesirable precedent.

Men were said to have died of heart failure when they heard of the execution of Charles I. It came at the height of an economic and political crisis, when men were starving in the streets of London. If, as some enthusiasts hoped, the reign of King Charles had been followed by the reign of King Jesus, if indeed a period of peace and prosperity had ensued, Charles might have been forgotten. But the military minority who outraged both Royalists and conservative Parliamentarians by executing the King were very busy in the next year or two suppressing those who had hitherto been the left-wing supporters of Parliament – Levellers, Diggers, Ranters. Some Leveller leaders indeed – Lilburne, Wildman, Sexby – decided that kingship was a lesser evil than the rule of the Rump of the Long Parliament, and made overtures to Charles II for his restoration on their terms – evidence both of the glamour that attached to the King's name and to a feeling that he was somehow above politics. Milton, like Gerrard Winstanley, never weakened in his opposition to monarchy.

Milton's attack on *Eikon Basilike* united for him three strands which were intertwined throughout his career – his political, religious and cultural interests. It was politically important to be able to expose *Eikon Basilike* as a fraud. Milton did not know about Gauden's authorship; we do not even know whether he suspected it. The secret was kept till the end of the century. But Milton was justified in holding Charles morally responsible for the content of the book.[1]

For Milton his title *Eikonoklastes*, the Iconoclast, perhaps had wider implications. He had already considered writing a tragedy to be called 'Gideon Iconoclastes', based on the story of Gideon, who at one time thought the Lord had forsaken him, but nevertheless overthrew the altars of Baal, blew his trumpet and smote the Midianites and Amalekites, and then refused to rule over Israel, preferring that the Lord should rule.[2] ('The matchless Gideon' reappeared in *Samson Agonistes*, 'a great deliverer' like Samson, unappreciated by the people – *S.A.* 279–80.) An ikon was an

---

[1] Hughes (1952), p. 139.
[2] Judges 6–8. Cf. Marvell, *The First Anniversary*, lines 249–56.

image. Images of saints and martyrs had been cleared out of English churches at the Reformation, on the ground that the common people had worshipped them. Protestantism, and especially Calvinism, was austerely monotheistic, and encouraged lay believers to reject any form of idolatry. This 'desacralization of the universe' in the long run was its main contribution to the rise of modern science.[1]

Iconoclasm covers various kinds of activity. It might be inspired by ideological hatred of image-worship, of idolatry, as when in the Parliamentary elections of early 1640 the crowd at Canterbury cried out 'No images, no papists,' and voted down the Archbishop's secretary.[2] In this spirit Milton referred to 'church masquers', who hide Christ's 'righteous verity with the polluted clothing of your ceremonies to make it seem more decent in your own eyes. . . . Ye think by these gaudy glistenings to stir up the devotion of the rude multitude. Ye think so, because ye forsake the heavenly teaching of St. Paul for the hellish sophistry of papism.'[3] Alternatively, iconoclasm could be directed against social ostentation shown by the construction of elaborate tombs, or by depicting family or royal arms in prominent places in church, 'churches . . . glazed with scutcheons like a herald's hall', as George Wither put it.[4] The greatest authority on sepulchral monuments, John Weever, said in 1631 that they should 'vary according to the quality and degree of the person deceased, that by the tomb might be discerned of what rank he was living'.[5] This posthumous continuation of the privileges of the well-to-do was not appreciated by poorer men and women who would leave no memorial after death, often not even a stone in the churchyard. They were apt, when they got the chance, to destroy such monuments, for social rather than for theological reasons. Bishop Gardiner had warned Henry VIII that destruction of religious images would weaken respect for the coats of arms of the nobility and even for the royal arms.[6]

Popular iconoclasm occurred in the sixteenth-century Revolt of the Netherlands, and again in the French Revolution. In England there was an outburst of iconoclasm in the popular relief which followed the end of Mary's reign. A proclamation of 1560 deplored the practice, by which 'the honourable and good memory of sundry virtuous and noble persons'

---

[1] Labrousse, pp. 80–7.
[2] Culmer, p. 19. Among those who condemned image-worship as idolatry was Sir John Milton in 1620 (Rowland, pp. 196–217).
[3] *C.P.W.*, I, p. 828.
[4] Wither (1628), I, p. 268.
[5] Weever, Preface. Weever was a staunch conservative and anti-Puritan (*ibid.*, pp. 54–6).
[6] L. B. Smith, p. 148.

was extinguished, for this might affect the descent of property.[1] Such iconoclasm recalls the destruction in mediaeval peasant revolts of documents establishing legal title to property: the two occurred together in the French Revolution.[2] After the breakdown of Stuart government in 1640, gangs smashed stained glass windows not because of their religious significance but because they were the 'monuments . . . of the nobility and gentry'.[3] This popular iconoclasm was almost encouraged by John Pym and the Parliamentarian leaders in 1643, when their position seemed desperate and they were appealing for lower-class support. As soon as the fortunes of war swung in their favour they hastened to clamp down against iconoclasm.[4] This did not stop Parliamentary soldiers destroying crucifixes, breaking windows, fonts, organs. In Somerset in April 1643 they cut up surplices from the church of Tintinghull and distributed them to the poor. But Royalist soldiers too could use iconoclasm to show class feeling, as when Sir William Waller's memorial in Bath Abbey was defaced.[5] In 1646 it was a Royalist farmer from Dorset who was 'moved by an angel' to destroy the image of the deceased Parliamentarian general, the Earl of Essex, set up in Westminster Abbey.[6]

In the *Second Defence* Milton looked back to the time before 1640 when the common people, 'maddened by priestly machinations, sunk to a barbarism fouler than that which stains the Indians', who 'worship as gods malevolent demons whom they cannot exorcise. But this mob of ours . . . set up as gods over it the most impotent of mortals.' Against the mob Milton set 'the English people', who had to contend with these long-held superstitions, and finally 'put slavery to flight'.[7]

Image-worship, then, was opposed by radical Protestants from the middle and lower middle class: the *locus classicus* is in the memoirs of the London turner, Nehemiah Wallington. It was defended by the very lowest classes, as Richard Baxter and Adam Martindale tell us.[8] It was also defended by the Laudians, who had been accused of trying to restore

---

[1] Cardwell (1839), I, p. 257; cf. 3 and 4 Edw.VI c.10 – 'images of any king, prince, nobleman or other dead person which hath not been commonly reputed and taken for a saint to be spared'.
[2] Cobb, pp. 648–54, 661–71, 684, 687–93. See esp. p. 664.
[3] D'Ewes (1923), p. 356; cf. Harleian MS. 165 f. 257.
[4] Trevor-Roper, pp. 311–14. 1643 saw Dowsing's campaign against monuments in East Anglia – though it has been argued that he was only carrying out a Parliamentary ordinance, which itself merely repeated Edwardian and Elizabethan legislation, against Laudian innovations (Varley, pp. 35–45).
[5] Underdown (1973), pp. 44, 62.
[6] Snow, p. 494. Cf. *C. and C.*, p. 193.
[7] *C.P.W.*, IV, pp. 551–2. I have altered the translation, which seems to me to have got the tenses wrong.
[8] *S. and P.*, pp. 178–80.

image worship, and by Royalist poets like Cleveland. Milton thought
Laudianism especially dangerous just because of this dual appeal. 'Idols,
they say, are laymen's books', he snorted.[1] He saw here an appeal to the
animism, the magic, the irrationalism inherited from the Middle Ages,
from the agrarian society which had existed for so many undisturbed
centuries before the invention of printing. Abstract ideas like those of the
Levellers, of Henry Parker, of Hobbes, of the Royal Society, would in due
course replace this peasant devotion to the concrete image on which the
ritualists played. What Milton regarded as the idolatry of the Laudians
came just at this dangerous point of junction between the ideas of the
lowest and highest classes – on which the royal Books of Sports had
played – the traditional culture of cakes and ale, of ceremonies and
sacerdotalism, of magic and monarchy. 'Natural man' could hardly avoid
being an idolator.[2]

The intention of *Eikon Basilike* was to depict Charles as a martyr,
analogies between the King and Jesus Christ being heavily stressed. If
Charles wrote it, these comparisons were at least immodest, not to say
blasphemous; if he did not, it was all fraudulent. Milton's denunciation of
'the Pamela prayer' – and indeed 'the whole rosary of his prayers' – must
be seen in the light of these claims for the King. His treatment appears
heavy-handed, but its object was political exposure. The 'Pamela prayer'
had been copied from Sir Philip Sidney's *Arcadia*. Milton we know was an
admirer of Sidney, so his shocked horror was no doubt overdone for
propaganda purposes. But *Arcadia* was not quite the simple pastoral
written for young ladies that it appears to innocent twentieth-century
readers. Milton's contemporaries would be more alert to the erotic double
entendres which abound at least in parts of the romance.[3] It was a good
debating point to stress that the church's martyr had used for his most
intimate devotions the prayer of a pagan girl in a bawdy romance; that he
was either so ignorant as not to know that it came from *Arcadia*, or so
unscrupulous (and so incompetent) as to hope to fool his readers into
believing it was his own.

In any case he used a set form of prayer, to which Milton could expect
Puritan readers to object strongly. The Smectymnuans had attacked set
forms, with Milton's support.[4] One at least of the heretics pilloried in

---

[1] *C.M.*, VI, p. 174.
[2] Sibbes, II, p. 386; see *W.T.U.D.*, pp. 357–8. I have benefited by discussing this matter with
Leonard Goldstein.
[3] Jones, pp. 32–47; cf. *C.P.W.*, III, p. 362.
[4] *C.P.W.*, I, p. 79, 685–92; cf. III, p. 505; VI, pp. 667–8.

Edwards's *Gangraena* thought the use of set forms of prayer was idolatry; 'that great gorbellied idol', the Westminster Assembly of Divines itself, spoke of the Book of Common Prayer as an idol.[1] In the year *Paradise Lost* was published, its licenser, Thomas Tomkins, wrote that conventiclers were still telling the people that the liturgy was 'a fearful idol'.[2] 'God every morning rains down new expressions into our hearts', Milton said, extending the principle of plenitude which meant so much to him; therefore prayer should not be limited to set forms.[3] All these were fair enough debating points, whose relevance can be assessed by comparing some words of John Cosin the Laudian divine. 'If men be left to themselves, whatsoever opinion in religion, whatsoever debate between neighbours, whatsoever public matter in church or kingdom a man pleases to make his interest, he may make the subject of prayer for the congregation.'[4] The issue of set prayers was political at least as much as religious.

So far from being a tragic drama, Milton suggested, Charles's execution was 'a ridiculous exit'; Marshall's engraving of the royal martyr was 'like a masking scene'. It was all a sham, 'devices begged from the old pageantry of some Twelfth-Night's entertainment at Whitehall'. Milton is fighting the battles of the thirties all over again.[5] *Eikon Basilike* lowered the tone of political debate, insulted the intelligence of the common people which he had so recently praised in *Areopagitica*. It side-stepped rational discussion of the arguments put forward by Milton and other defenders of regicide. The object of 'the factious and defeated party' in disseminating *Eikon Basilike* was 'to corrupt and disorder the minds of weaker men'. They aimed by policy to accomplish 'after death that revenge upon their enemies which in life they were not able'. This was 'a civil kind of idolatry'.[6] What Toland called 'the great revolution in civil and religious affairs . . . partly occasioned by the credit of that book' made Milton and many of his party despair of a rational reaction from the mass of the people.[7] Yet in *Eikonoklastes* Milton defended against Charles's attacks the popular 'tumults' which inaugurated the Revolution. 'This iron flail the people . . . drove the bishops out of their baronies, . . . threw down the High Commission and Star Chamber, gave us a Triennial Parliament.'[8] He never gave up his belief in human equality even in *Eikonoklastes*. 'It

---

[1] T. Edwards, I, p. 34; Baillie, II, p. 255; cf. Carruthers.

[2] Tomkins, p. 6. I owe this reference to Professor K. W. Stavely.

[3] *C.P.W.*, III, p. 505; cf. VI, p. 670.   [4] Cosin, V, p. 403.

[5] P. W. Thomas, pp. 186–7. For Milton's critique of the analogy between Charles and Christ see *C.P.W.*, III, pp. 417, 432, 447, 530, 567–8; cf. IV, pp. 599–600.

[6] *C.P.W.*, III, pp. 142, 68, 338, 342–3.

[7] Darbishire, p. 150; *C.P.W.*, III, p. 339.

[8] *C.P.W.*, III, pp. 388–91 – note the Spenserian allusion in 'iron flail'. Cf. III, pp. 397, 412, 564–6.

were a mad law that would subject reason to superiority of place.' Two
things have always been dreadful to the kings of this world – liberty and
equality.[1]

Liberty for Milton was always largely negative. It involved criticism,
destruction, iconoclasm: like Bacon, the free thinkers must knock down
idols.[2] The Protestant doctrine of the priesthood of all believers was
egalitarian in so far as it denied the superiority of clergy to laity. Mechanic
preachers asserted in practice the right of all men to proclaim the truth
that was in them. Rejection of Laudian ceremonies ('the idolatrous erection
of temples . . . to out-vie the papist, the costly and dear-bought scandals
and snares of images') had proclaimed the superiority of men and women –
temples of the Holy Spirit – over consecrated buildings and altars, 'faith
needing not the weak and fallible office of the senses'. This 'servile
crouching' is 'sometimes idolatrous', and the railed-off altar was treated
'like a dreadful idol'.[3]

A pamphlet of 1647 attributed to Wildman had accused the Army
Grandees of making an idol of the King.[4] The canonization of the
martyr King seemed to Milton to be creating a new barrier to human
equality, based on lies and shams. In the first edition of *The Ready and
Easy Way*, in a moving passage, he wrote 'thus much I should perhaps
have said though I were sure I should have spoken only to trees and stones,
and had none to cry to but with the prophet, O earth, earth, earth, to tell
the very soil itself what God hath determined of Coniah and his seed for
ever.' Milton's contemporaries would have recognized the allusion, and
its application to Charles II, still over the water. Coniah was 'a despised
and broken idol': 'to the land whereunto they desire to return, thither shall
they not return; . . . no man of his seed shall prosper.'[5]

Some of Milton's deepest feelings, about literature and sex as well as
about religion and politics, spring from horror of idolatry. Idolatry is
misuse of natural objects given by God for use. The objects worshipped
are not evil in themselves. What is wrong is to worship the creature – a
priest, a king, a queen, a woman, a parliament, a building, the Church
Fathers, the Prayer Book, classical learning. On the wickedness of 'the
idolizing of human learning' the Baptist Robert Purnell and the anti-

---

[1] *Ibid.*, III, pp. 462, 509; cf. p. 412; IV, pp. 303–4. Milton repeated this point in *Paradise Lost*:
see p. 382 below.
[2] Frye (1966), p. 104. See pp. 262–7 below.
[3] *C.P.W.*, I, pp. 590, 520–3; contrast, perhaps, Milton's attitude to stained glass in *Il Penseroso*.
[4] [Anon.], *A Call to All the Soldiers of the Army* (1647).
[5] *The Ready and Easy Way*, p. 18; Jeremiah 22; 24–30. Milton omitted the reference to Coniah in
the second edition, when Charles was already on his way back. Cf. Masson, V, pp. 654–5.

Trinitarian John Fry in 1649 were no less severe than Milton in *Paradise Regained*.[1] Covetousness is idolatry, Milton had said in *The Tenure*. Idolatry is the only heresy which may be prohibited by the magistrate, he added in 1659.[2]

We must be harsh against idolatry, because it is so very tempting, so seductive to natural man. Milton more than most men was susceptible to beauty, including the beauty of women and of pagan myths. Therefore the lines had to be kept rigidly drawn.[3] The one form of idolatry to which he was never tempted was king-worship, for that denied the dignity of man. We can be sure that Milton had no sympathy for the way in which the Protector's effigy was set up for the people to gape at after his death. 'Is this the end and final farewell of once noble Oliver?' asked the Quaker Edward Burrough. 'What, only the sight of an image carried and set up?'[4]

If either party in a marriage were guilty of idolatry, this was sufficient ground for divorce, Milton thought; it was worse than adultery. On the other hand, 'to enjoin the indissoluble keeping of a marriage found unfit against the good of man, both soul and body, . . . is to make an idol of marriage.'[5] There could be idols in marriage too. 'Never was there a passion more ardent and less idolatrous', wrote Lucy Hutchinson of her husband's love. She was referring obliquely to the court of the uxorious Charles I, as was Milton when he spoke of the 'idol Queen' in *The Ready and Easy Way*.[6] John Taylor the Water-Poet criticized in similar terms the drinking of healths, when the gallant

> Idolatrous, bare-headed on his knees,
> Bow[s] full down unto an absent whore.[7]

There may be implicit criticism of the idolatrous cult of courtly love in *Comus*; there certainly is in *Paradise Lost*. Satan's seduction of Eve recalls the cult ('sovereign mistress', 'heaven of mildness', 'thy awful brow', 'thee all things living gaze on', 'a goddess among gods' (*P.L.* IX. 532–4).[8]

---

[1] Purnell, *Good Tydings,* pp. 29–44; Fry (1649), *passim.* For Fry see pp. 290–5 below.

[2] *C.P.W.,* III, p. 241; VI, pp. 690–5; *C.M.,* VI, pp. 19–20.

[3] Cf. Tuve, pp. 63–9. See chapter 30 below.

[4] Burrough, pp. 458–60.

[5] *C.P.W.,* II, pp. 261, 268–9, 276.

[6] *C.M.,* VI, p. 147; Hutchinson, pp. 32, 48–9: see p. 47 above. For a late example see Nicholas Hookes:

> I am a Papist, zealous, strict, precise;
> Amanda is the saint I idolize. (p. 41)

[7] J. Taylor, II, p. 49.

[8] Ferry, p. 141.

These are attributes of divinity. Adam comes near to falling into the same sin. 'Was she thy God?' he was asked after the Fall. Eve herself commits symbolic idolatry, bowing to the tree whose fruit she had just eaten. 'Gay religions full of pomp and gold' seduced the sons of Eve to idolatry, a devil-worship highly reminiscent of popery (IX. 364–75).[1] Satan, 'exalted as a god', sat on 'his gorgeous throne', 'idol of majesty divine' (VI. 99–103). The temptation of the devil's table in Book II of *Paradise Regained* may have involved idolatry – and indeed the theme of the brief epic is Christ's refusal to commit in any form the sin of worshipping the God of this world.[2] In *Samson Agonistes* the Philistines were 'drunk with idolatry', as well as 'drunk with wine', 'with blindness internal struck' (1669–86). The climax came when Samson destroyed the temple of the idol Dagon.[3] It was the idolatry in popery which made Milton, like John Robinson, adamant against tolerating its worship. For Sir Isaac Newton, too, idolatry was worse than atheism.[4]

Milton, then, shared the radical Protestant horror of images, or worship of saints and martyrs. He was appalled by the popular success of *Eikon Basilike*, which showed how strong still was the popular appeal of saints, mediators, magic-makers – against which reason could not prevail. The iconoclasm of the early forties had been no mere outburst of hooliganism and destruction; it blended the social attitudes of the middling sort (opposition to noble escutcheons in churches) with the Protestant ideological disgust at idolatry. It appealed to the second and third cultures alike. Milton refused to justify the 'enormities the vulgar may commit in the rudeness of their zeal', but he was far more hostile to those who 'bemoaned' the pulling down of superstitious monuments.[5]

Eikon Alethine, an attack on *Eikon Basilike* published six weeks before *Eikonoklastes*, had referred to the 'lame and blind Jebusites' who were impressed by *Eikon Basilike* as 'idolators who make a king a God'. 'Magic' and 'conjuring' are *Eikon Basilike*'s weapons.[6] Milton began by complaining that 'the people . . . are prone ofttimes not to a religious only but to a civil kind of idolatry in idolizing their kings.' This 'idolized book' aimed to catch 'the worthless approbation of an inconstant, irrational and image-doting rabble', who were 'ready to be stroked and turned again into the

---

[1] Frye (1966), pp. 66–7, 79.
[2] Schultz (1955), p. 236; Fixler, p. 271.
[3] Bouchard, p. 156; cf. pp. 58–9, 82, 100.
[4] McLachlan (1950), pp. 49–51.
[5] *C.P.W.,* III, p. 535.
[6] *Op. cit.,* Sig. Av, quoted in *C.P.W.,* III, p. 149. Cf. Marchamont Nedham on superstitious reverence for kingship, quoted in *ibid.,* IV, p. 51.

wonted and well-pleasing state of their true Norman villeinage'. In the second edition, published in 1650, he recognized that understanding readers would be few.[1]

But the image prevailed over the rational critique, the imposture over the exposure. After the Restoration a pamphleteer said that astrologers had done more harm to the royal cause than all the writings of Milton and the regicides;[2] *Eikon Basilike* proved stronger than all the writings of Milton, Goodwin, Canne and Nedham against monarchy. What Lucy Hutchinson called the 'madness to restore this kingly idol' prevailed.[3] *Eikon Basilike* played no inconsiderable part in preparing public opinion for the restoration of monarchy. As the millennium failed to arrive and taxation was not reduced, as divisions and feuds rent the revolutionaries, so the image of his sacred majesty loomed larger over the quarrelsome, unsatisfactory scene. It was less perhaps a fear of freedom than a failure to embrace freedom with the athletic self-discipline that *Areopagitica* had recommended: but the mass of ordinary people came to long for a return to 'normality', to the known, the familiar, the traditional. Victims of scrofula who could afford it went abroad to be touched by the King over the water: after 1660 he was back, sacred and symbolic. *Eikonoklastes* was burnt by the common hangman together with *The Tenure of Kings and Magistrates*.

Only at the end of the century, after the fraud of *Eikon Basilike* had been exposed, did *Eikonoklastes* come into its own, playing a part in keeping James II out and William III in. Too late and too little, Milton might have thought. The men of property in 1659–60 had longed for 'a king with plenty of holy oil about him'. *Eikon Basilike* revealed the possibility of manipulating the magic of monarchy in the interests of the *status quo*, a lesson the rulers of England never forgot.[4]

---

[1] *C.P.W.*, III, pp. 339, 343–4, 601; IV, p. 364. 'Stroker' was the irreverent name given to Charles I because of the alleged healing power of his touch.
[2] K. V. Thomas (1971), p. 343.
[3] Hutchinson, p. 188; cf. *C.P.W.*, III, p. 596.
[4] *W.T.U.D.*, pp. 353–4.

Chapter 13

Defending the Republic, II

> You [Salmasius] offer an additional reason for your position: 'Things would seem turned upside down.' This would be a welcome change, for it would be the end of mankind if the worst situations were unalterable.
>
> Milton, *Defence of the People of England* (1651)

Milton's *Defence of the People of England* enjoyed a fantastic success. Salmasius was held to be Europe's greatest scholar; Milton was unknown outside his own country. Yet by general consent David beat Goliath.[1] Even those who disagreed listened and admired as Milton insisted on the right of any people to call their king legally to account rather than adopting the more traditional method, preferred by Salmasius, of assassination. Milton felt that his subject in the *Defence* was 'of paramount importance'; 'this cause, which is most noble and deserving of eternal remembrance', was God's cause: 'we followed him as our leader.' There had never been 'a greater or more outstanding instance' of a victory for civil freedom than in the English Revolution. 'The most heroic and exemplary achievements since the beginning of the world' was his phrase in the *Second Defence*. Milton had indeed performed his international duty in speaking for free England to the intellectuals of Europe – 'for the entire human race against the foes of liberty' – only a decade after his return from Italy.[2]

Milton was quite right too to see his victory over Salmasius as a triumph for his country and its revolution as well as for himself. 'I had expected nothing of such quality from an Englishman', wrote Vossius to Heinsius in April 1651, about the *Defensio*. No other Englishman had thus spoken to Europe on behalf of his country. Petrarch for Italy, Luther for Germany, Calvin for France, Grotius for the Netherlands: but who had spoken for

---

[1] The comparison is Marchamont Nedham's (*Mercurius Politicus*, No. 37, 13–20 February 1651, p. 604); it was repeated by Edward Phillips (Darbishire, p. 70).

[2] *C.P.W.*, IV, pp. 302, 305, 536, 529, 555–8; cf. pp. 495, 533, 548–51, 685–6. See pp. 55–6 above.

182

England? Bacon perhaps, but no one else. There were seventeen editions of the *Defensio*, five in the Netherlands; there were Dutch and French translations. Milton felt that he was not only listened to but approved by good men all over Europe in his call for a crusade against antichristian monarchy. The one victory of Salmasius which Milton recognized was detecting him in a false quantity in one of his Cambridge elegies. This was silently corrected in the 1673 reprint.[1]

In the *Second Defence* and the *Defence of Himself* Milton allowed himself to be too easily convinced that Alexander More had been the author of *Regii Sanguinis Clamor*, to which he was replying. We now know that it was written by Peter Du Moulin. Milton refused to admit his mistake; but since More certainly had a hand in publishing the *Clamor*, the distinction is not of great importance. One can understand Milton's reluctance to give up the extremely juicy scandals about More which he had unearthed, with the help of a bevy of foreign correspondents. Recent research has confirmed the accuracy of Milton's stories, outrageous though some of them are. The *Second Defence* may not be to the taste of every modern reader, but it is very learned in historical scholarship as well as hilarious in its bawdry.[2]

In 1654 Milton rejected a suggestion, made by Henry Oldenburg, that he was being distracted from more important pursuits. 'I am far from thinking that I have spent my toil, as you seem to hint, on matters of inferior consequence.' His writing in defence of the people of England had celebrated 'deeds that were illustrious, that were glorious, that were almost beyond any praise; and if I have done nothing else I have surely redeemed my pledge.'[3] At first he used his left hand, no doubt; but he conveyed a great deal of his message to the English people – and to all Europe – through these books. His English tracts probably reached a wider audience than did his poems, even if they were not read with the deferential attention which Milton thought due to a poet. His Latin writings were read from Greece to Sweden. At the end of the *Second Defence* Milton saw himself as an epic poet who had 'celebrated at least one heroic achievement of my countrymen'. It was not the theme from early British history which he had earlier contemplated; but he had written his long-promised patriotic epic.[4]

The author of *Areopagitica* has been criticized for acting as licenser to

[1] C. and F., p. 82.
[2] Svendsen (1961), p. 807; (1967), p. 118.
[3] *C.P.W.*, IV, pp. 536–7, 684–6, 866–7; Oldenburg, VIII, p. 253.
[4] *C.P.W.*, IV, p. 685; Grierson, pp. 72–3.

the government of the English Commonwealth, but this is an over-simplification. Milton may have had something to do with the Licensing Act passed in 1650, a few months after he had taken office. Although this act required strict censorship of all newsletters, Milton correctly told Hartlib that 'there are no licensers appointed by the last act, so that everybody may enter in his book, without license, provided the printer's or author's name be entered, that they may be forthcoming if required.' That had been one of the points on which Milton had insisted in *Areopagitica*.[1] In the pamphlet he had said nothing about newsbooks; he may have thought of them as being in a different category from creative literature.

Milton was the licenser nominally responsible under this act for Marchamont Nedham's *Mercurius Politicus* in the years 1651–2. Milton had acted as go-between to persuade Nedham, later and possibly already a friend of his, to put his considerable journalistic talent at the disposal of the republic. Since Nedham was an ex-Royalist propagandist, there were political reasons for supervising what he wrote. But there is no evidence that Milton was closely involved. He may have accepted the position of licenser out of friendship, as part of the bargain which persuaded Nedham to change sides. We do not know whether Milton contributed anything to *Mercurius*. It has been suggested that he may have influenced the paper's campaign against the Presbyterians in the summer of 1651, and its attack on Owen's 'fundamentals' in August 1652.[2] In an official letter to Hamburg dated 10 August 1649 Milton used the name 'Tarquins' for Royalists.[3] Nedham may have been following his example in calling Charles II 'Tarquin', but the usage was common.

In April 1652 Milton was questioned by Parliament for having given his approval to the translation of the Polish *Racovian Catechism* published in August 1650 and subsequently condemned by Parliament. According to the Dutch envoy Milton answered that 'in approving of that book he had done no more than what his opinion was', since 'he had published a tract on that subject, that men should refrain from forbidding books.'

Milton's role in the service of the republic, then, seems to have been selective. He was a committed defender of regicide and supporter of the Commonwealth; he accepted employment from the Council of State, but did not long retain illusions about its individual members, if indeed he ever had them. In a private conversation he spoke disparagingly of the Council of State as 'mechanics, soldiers, servants, strong and keen enough

---

[1] Turnbull, p. 41. Cf. p. 157 above.
[2] Worden, pp. 245, 308.
[3] *C.P.W.*, V, p. 495 and n.

but entirely ignorant of public political matters'. 'Not three or four of forty had been outside England.'[1] In his *Observations upon the Articles of Peace* in 1649 Milton vindicated Parliament and the middling sort of men against the Marquis of Ormonde's sneer that the ancient English constitution was 'trodden under impious and for the most part mechanic feet'; he asserted that Oliver Cromwell 'hath done in few years more eminent and remarkable deeds whereon to found nobility in his house' than Ormonde and all his ancestors put together.[2] But whilst thus ready to leap to the public defence of the republic against a Royalist aristocrat, Milton felt sufficiently detached and independent to issue repeated warnings, trading no doubt on his great reputation as conqueror of Salmasius and author of *Eikonoklastes*, and relying on his own conception of the role of the poet/prophet. The sonnet to Fairfax in 1648 had called the Lord General to a yet nobler task than fighting battles: the freeing of injured truth from violence, and rescuing public faith from public fraud. The sonnet to Oliver Cromwell, written soon after the 'crowning mercy' of his victory at Worcester, has the same theme ('yet much remains / To conquer still'), though now the enemy was 'hireling wolves, whose gospel is their maw' and who threaten 'to bind our souls in secular chains'. The reference appears to be to John Owen's proposals in 1652, which recommended the maintenance of tithes and of a state church, with a doctrinal test. The *Defence of the People of England* concluded with an appeal to Milton's countrymen to be as strong in peace as they had been in war.[3]

As the fifties moved on, Milton's confidence in 'the people' continued to wane. The popular reception of *Eikon Basilike* filled him with disgust, showing 'what a miserable, credulous, deluded thing that creature is, which is called the vulgar'. 'A besotted and degenerate baseness of spirit' was revealed, far removed from 'the old English fortitude and love of freedom'. For this the prelates' 'perpetual infusion of servility ... to all their hearers' was originally to blame, then 'the factious inclination' of Presbyterians and other supporters of monarchy on Parliament's side.[4]

Even in the *Defence of the People of England* Milton revealed his uneasiness by admitting that 'our form of government is such as our circumstances and schisms permit . . . , only as good as the stubborn struggles of the wicked citizens allow it to be.' 'Their sins were taught them under the monarchy.' Milton rejected Salmasius's jibes about power being in the

---

[1] French, II, p. 321; III, pp. 162–4, 206, 212–13.
[2] *C.P.W.*, III, pp. 312–15; Hughes (1949), p. 1066.
[3] *C.P.W.*, IV, pp. 535–6; cf. II, p. 505. For Milton's warnings, see also pp. 193–5 below.
[4] *C.P.W.*, III, pp. 426, 344–5, 601, 581.

hands of 'the wickedest rabble', 'the dregs of the people'. He argued that 'the act of the better, the sounder part of the Parliament, in which resides the real power of the people, was the act of the people.' Salmasius's accusations 'may be true of the dregs of the populace, but hardly of the middle class, which produces the greatest number of men of good sense and knowledge of affairs'.[1] Kings 'sheltered themselves behind the blind superstitions of the mob'.[2] Already we can hear the arguments with which Milton will defend a restricted franchise and a perpetual oligarchy in *The Ready and Easy Way*, because the majority is the 'worse' part.[3] Yet in the *Second Defence* he still praised the 'pre-eminent virtue' of the English people in the Revolution, who had shown 'a nobility and steadfastness surpassing all the glory of their ancestors'. 'Although they were indeed a multitude in numbers . . . the lofty exaltation of their minds . . . kept them from being a mob.' 'And so . . . they put slavery to flight.'[4]

It is difficult to make a final assessment of Milton's attitude towards 'the people', or even to be quite sure what he meant by the word. At one stage he appears to equate 'the people' with heads of households – those perhaps to whom the Levellers would have extended the franchise. Sturdy responsible citizens of independent means could be relied on more than either the uneducated or the corrupt and effeminate courtiers.[5] In *The Ready and Easy Way* those who thought kingship would restore trade, who put economics before ideals, appear to have been the middle class rather than the irresponsible rabble. The majority of the people were so far out-side politics that few remembered to include (or to exclude) them when they talked about 'the people'. Colonel Rich in the Putney Debates, and the Harringtonian Captain Baynes (who had been one of James Nayler's principal defenders in the Parliament of 1656), in 1659 contrasted 'the poor' with 'the people'. In 1651 Marchamont Nedham thought it necessary to explain that when he spoke of 'the people' he meant 'such as be duly chosen to represent the people successively in their supreme assemblies'. Were these 'the people' to whom the Son of God referred so scathingly in *Paradise Regained*?[6]

---

[1] *Ibid.*, IV, pp. 316–17, 386–7, 102–3, 457, 471; cf. p. 339.

[2] *Ibid.*, IV, pp. 551–2; cf. pp. 386, 634–6, 509–10.

[3] *Ibid.*, IV, pp. 457, 635–6, 680–6; *C.M.*, VI, pp. 114, 140; cf. *C.P.W.*, I, pp. 265, 156.

[4] *Ibid.*, IV, pp. 548–9, 552.

[5] Macpherson, chapter III.

[6] Woodhouse (1938), pp. 63–4; T. Burton, III, pp. 147–8; *Mercurius Politicus*, No. 78, 29 November – 4 December 1651, p. 1237. See pp. 246 below.

PART IV

DEFEAT AND AFTER

Chapter 14

Losing Hope

> What I have spoken is the language of that which is not called amiss
> 'The Good Old Cause'. . . . Thus much I should perhaps have said
> though I were sure I should have spoken only to trees and stones;
> and had none to cry to but with the Prophet, 'O earth, earth, earth!'
> to tell the very soil itself what her perverse inhabitants are deaf to.
> Nay, though what I have spoke should happen (which Thou suffer
> not, who didst create mankind free; nor Thou next, who didst
> redeem us from being servants of men!) to be the last words of our
> expiring liberty. But I trust I shall have spoken persuasion to abund-
> ance of sensible and ingenuous men; to some perhaps whom God may
> raise of these stones to become children of reviving liberty.
>
> Milton, *The Ready and Easy Way to establish a Free Commonwealth,*

1 Warnings

Milton had been very nearly the first to appear in print to justify the trial
of Charles I; he was the last significant figure to defend the Good Old
Cause in April 1660, a few weeks before Charles II returned. Some time
between 1649 and 1660 Milton must have realized that things had gone
badly wrong. In retrospect he probably thought the decisive year was
1653.

Long after the event Milton said that the Rump had been 'without
just authority dissolved';[1] but we do not know that this was his view at
the time. Like Oliver Cromwell, Milton had been unhappy about the
Dutch war of 1652-4. His sonnets to Vane and Cromwell show that he
was alarmed by schemes for re-establishing a state church. He may well
have sympathized with Cromwell when the latter dissolved the Rump in

---

[1] *C.M.*, VI, p. 102.

April 1653, though for Milton it meant a breach with friends like Vane, Bradshaw, Sir Peter Wentworth. It was still possible to believe in 1653 that Parliament had been dissolved in the interests of religious liberty. We may guess at Milton's attitude to the Barebones Parliament by the fact that in August 1653 he translated Psalms 1 to 8, which dwell on God's vindication of his cause and the enactment of righteousness – which the legal and ecclesiastical reforms then occupying the Parliament might seem to embody. The optimism revealed by this choice contrasts interestingly with the gloomy mood of 1648, when he chose to translate Psalms 80 to 88.[1]

What then did Milton feel when the Barebones Parliament was dissolved in December 1653 by its conservative members, one of the main issues being the preservation of tithes and a state church? As Masson put it, 'the Protectorate had come into existence, not only in a conservative interest generally, but very specially on the question of an established church'.[2] This must have faced Milton with agonizing decisions. Tithes and a state church seemed to him the negation of liberty. Yet – like William Dell and William Erbery, unlike Sir Henry Vane and Vavasor Powell – he decided to continue his support for the government. Since his disagreements concerned internal affairs, he may have felt, in the words of Robert Blake – presumably equally unhappy about the trend of events – that his job was to prevent foreigners fooling us.[3] The Protectorate preserved more of the Revolution's achievements than any possible alternative government. Milton respected Cromwell's tolerance, and may have tried to convince himself that reform was still possible. Yet the state church of the Protectorate was virtually that which Owen had proposed to the Rump in 1652, and Milton would have agreed with Vane's warning against 'antichristian tyranny' in 1656: 'since the fall of the bishops and persecuting presbyteries, the same spirit is apt to arise in the next sort of clergy that can get the ear of the magistrate.'[4] Change was more likely to be to the right than to the left.

The radicals were in retreat, at best holding on: further advance seemed for the moment impossible. Erbery felt that he was living in an age of universal apostasy, most evident among those who had the greatest reputation for godliness. Dell had similar thoughts.[5] From the fifties the sects began to organize themselves seriously: regular meeting books occur

---

[1] Woodhouse and Bush, III, p. 1000; II, p. 438.
[2] Masson, IV, pp. 566–8.
[3] *Ibid.*, V, p. 580; *C.P.W.*, IV, p. 671.
[4] Vane (1656), p. 307; cf. *C.P.W.*, VI, pp. 796–8.
[5] *W.T.U.D.*, pp. 195–6.

after the revolutionary wave had begun to ebb. They reveal a strong emphasis on defining the limits of the sect, on excommunicating those who did not come up to the expected standard: organization, defence, exclusion of the unfit, become increasingly the watchwords.[1] Milton joined no sect.

He continued to perform his duties as Secretary for Foreign Tongues, but they began to diminish with his blindness. At first he pressed to be allowed to stay on at his work, but his protests gradually ceased. Soon he stopped attending the Council of State except by special order, and from 1653 he was employed only on occasional translations. He had time to spend a week translating psalms. By 1654 he commented publicly on the fact that 'the chief men in the state . . . do not take . . . away' his public office.[2] In April 1655 it was proposed to reduce his salary and convert it into a pension, a polite form of retirement. The salary was reduced, but Milton did not wholly retire, mainly perhaps because his services were needed in connection with the government's protests and diplomatic action consequent on the massacre of the Vaudois, news of which reached England in May 1655. Milton was emotionally involved in this cause. In March 1656 the deputy who had replaced Milton in the preceding year, Philip Meadows, was despatched to Portugal, and some of his work was resumed by the blind poet. In September 1657 Andrew Marvell was appointed to the place Meadows had held, but Milton continued to be used for letters of the first importance.

After 1655, Edward Phillips tells us, Milton 'had leisure for his own studies and private designs'.[3] He did less work for the Protectorate than for the Commonwealth, and less for the second Protectorate than for the first, even though by then he must have adapted his style of work to his blindness. Milton was easing himself out of the government service. He 'was a stranger' to the 'private counsels' of the government, the anonymous biographer tells us, and not involved in their 'corrupt designs'. In 1657 he could still do a good turn for Spenser's grandson. But by December of that year he told Peter Heimbach 'my influential friends are very few since I stay nearly always at home – and willingly.' In October 1659 he assured Moses Wall that he had of late years ceased to have any direct personal share in government, 'not finding that either God or the public required more of me than my prayers for them that govern'.[4]

---

[1] Cf. White, *Records*, pp. 132–3.
[2] *C.P.W.*, IV, p. 591.
[3] Darbishire, p. 72.
[4] *C.M.*, VI, p. 101. For Wall see pp. 192, 201–2, 206, 214 below.

We can be certain that Milton disapproved of the increasing intolerance of the new constitution which the Protector accepted in May 1657, the Petition and Advice, as well as of the offer of the crown which Oliver refused. The tightening up of censorship in June 1658 must especially have tested Milton's loyalty. One not untypical Presbyterian was indifferent as to whether monarchy was established in the house of Cromwell or restored to the house of Stuart, so long as sectaries were kept out of power.[1] Milton was soon to be arguing strongly against any state interference in religious affairs, and in favour of a free commonwealth rather than the rule of any single person.

Cromwell, like Milton, had been with the radicals up to a point; had supported religious toleration, bringing the King to justice, abolition of the House of Lords; had been contemptuous of clerical pretensions. Both men were more interested in the liberty of God's people than in democracy. But Cromwell gradually moved away from his old allies in the sixteen-fifties, largely because of his socially conservative prejudices ('a nobleman, a gentleman, a yeoman; that is a good interest of the nation and a great one');[2] but also because of his realistic recognition that the country could not be governed indefinitely without the willing co-operation of the mass of the gentry and merchants. Milton shared some of Cromwell's social prejudices, though in his case perhaps intellectual fastidiousness did more to alienate him from the extreme radicals. But he never accepted Cromwell's conclusion that a state church must be maintained.

Cromwell and Milton appear to have been right to conclude that there was no social basis for Leveller democracy in the England of the sixteen-fifties. It must in practice have meant continued rule by the army. But there was no agreement about which godly should rule. Isaac Deutscher has used the phrase 'substitutism' to describe how the Soviet Communist Party in the nineteen-twenties usurped *de facto* the place which it gave to the proletariat *de jure*. Similarly the New Model Army substituted itself for the people of England, for whom in 1647–9 it might possibly have claimed to speak and act. By the mid-fifties the revolutionary army had been purged into a professional body, yet still 'by that force which we gave them to win us liberty hold us fast in chains'. 'You know who they were', Moses Wall continued in his letter to Milton of 25 May 1659, 'that watched our Saviour's sepulchre to keep him from rising.' They were soldiers. The army outraged radicals by its suppressions, by the ambitious

---

[1] H.M., *A Pair of Spectacles for this Purblinde Nation* (1659).
[2] Cromwell, III, p. 435.

self-seeking of the generals; it outraged gentry and merchants because it interfered with their rule in the localities. Wall in the same letter expressed his gratification to discover that Milton, whom he had given up as a courtier, still had his heart in the right place.

Servant of the Commonwealth though Milton was, he did not hestitate to admonish and warn, in public and private writings alike. In the *Defence of the People of England* in 1651 he told his compatriots that they must fight against 'faction, avarice, the temptations of wealth and the corruptions that wait upon prosperity'. 'The two greatest evils in human life, the most fatal to virtue', were 'tyranny and superstition'.[1] He had suggested the same causes for the frustration of the Revolution in his still unpublished *History of Britain* of 1647–8. In his sonnet of 1648 he had alerted Fairfax to 'avarice and rapine' and 'public fraud'. William Erbery in 1652 told Cromwell 'great things hath God done by you in war, and good things men expect from you in peace: to break in pieces the oppressor, to ease the oppressed of their bondage, to release the prisoners of their bonds and to relieve poor families with bread.'[2] Milton's sonnet to Cromwell stressed religious rather than political and social reform: otherwise it says in verse what Erbery says in prose.

In the *Second Defence* (May 1654), writing before the Lord Protector had had to face a Parliament, Milton interrupted a panegyric of Oliver to congratulate him on refusing the title of King, in words that conveyed a warning. To have done anything else would be 'as if, when you had subjugated some tribe of idolators with the help of the true God, you were to worship the gods you had conquered'. 'You yourself cannot be free without us.' Oliver must 'honour this great confidence reposed in you' by preserving liberty: 'he who attacks the liberty of others is himself the first of all to lose his own liberty, ... and he deserves his fate.' ('Thyself not free, but to thyself enthralled', Abdiel told Satan – *P.L.* VI. 181.) Cromwell had taken upon himself a burden 'that will put to the test your inmost capacities, ... whether there truly live in you that piety, faith, justice and moderation of soul' which alone could justify his elevation. 'A deeper wound' than the betrayal of liberty 'can never be inflicted on the human race.'[3]

Milton praised Fairfax for overcoming 'ambition ... and the thirst for glory which conquers all the most eminent men', and he went on to hint that Cromwell too might retire and '*restore* to us our liberty unharmed and

---

[1] *C.P.W.*, IV, p. 535. I have adopted some phrases from the Columbia translation.
[2] Nickolls, pp. 88–9.
[3] *C.P.W.*, IV, pp. 672–4.

even enhanced'.[1] Meanwhile he must cherish those who have been faithful
to the cause since early days – men of the middle rank in society. This
followed a two-page panegyric of Bradshaw – the man who had publicly
rebuked Cromwell for dissolving the Rump. Another of the twelve whom
Milton selected for warmest eulogy was Colonel Robert Overton, an
opponent of the Protectorate soon to be imprisoned for plotting against
the government, with whom Milton claimed special friendship and
similarity of tastes.[2] Among the rest, Pickering was an enemy of tithes,
Lawrence was a Baptist, Whitelocke and others favoured religious
toleration. Milton was anxious above all to retain unity with the radicals:
he scented the further shift to the right which was soon to come.[3]

Milton went on to urge Cromwell to 'remove all power from the
church' – and this he thought could be effective only if tithes were
abolished. It was more important to repeal bad old laws than to pass new
ones. Finally Cromwell was asked to take more thought for education and
to 'permit those who wish to engage in free inquiry to publish their
findings at their own peril, without the private inspection of any petty
magistrate'. He should 'listen least of all to those who do not believe
themselves free unless they deny freedom to others' and who wish to
'impose on the state and the church the worst of all tyrannies, that of their
own base customs and opinions'. 'May you always take the side of those
who think that not just their own party or faction, but all citizens equally,
have an equal right to freedom in the state.'[4]

In the *Second Defence* Milton reveals growing uneasiness about the role
of force in politics. Truth should be defended by reason, 'the only defence
truly appropriate to man', as well as by arms.[5] This uneasiness increased
from the middle fifties,[6] and it did not relate only to Cromwell. Milton's
final words of warning, in the *Second* as in first *Defence*, were addressed to
the English people; they were similar in tone though more urgent. Unless
they got rid of superstition, 'you will have those who will perch upon your
back and shoulders as if on beasts of burden. . . . Unless you repel avarice,
ambition and luxury from your minds, . . . you will find at home and
within that tyrant who, you believed, was to be sought abroad and in

---

[1] My italics.
[2] In December 1651 Overton was urged by his friends 'to be much in the mount with God'.
Could this be a reference to the Family of the Mount? (Nickolls, p. 161. For the date, see
Firth, 1895, p. xxxix).
[3] *C.P.W.*, IV, pp. 669–76, 637–9, 600–2. For Lawrence see p. 106 above.
[4] *C.P.W.*, IV, pp. 678–9.
[5] *C.P.W.*, IV, p. 553. The editorial note compares *P.L.* VI. 121–6; XII. 83–5.
[6] See pp. 209–10, 362–3, 415–18 below.

the field.'[1] The Parliamentarians themselves will become Royalists. If elections and offices are dominated by those with the longest purse, the fight for freedom will have been in vain. 'However loudly they shout and boast about liberty, slaves they are at home and abroad, although they know it not.' 'If to be a slave is hard, and you do not wish it, learn to obey right reason, to master yourselves.' Otherwise posterity will say 'the foundations were soundly laid, the beginnings, in fact more than the beginnings, were splendid; . . . but that to this opportunity men were wanting.' (More than twelve years earlier Milton had noted in his Commonplace Book that the Roman people, liberated before they were fit for freedom, 'became slaves to their own ambition and luxury'.[2])

Such warnings had often been heard before. But always they came from the radicals, from Leveller leaders, criticizing 'ambition and avarice', from the Socinian M.P. John Fry denouncing self-seekers 'who have raised handsome estates out of nothing . . . upon the ruin of many, as well friend as foe'.[3] Gerrard Winstanley in 1652 had warned Cromwell that there was no middle path between being 'a free and true Commonwealth's man, or a monarchical tyrannical royalist'. 'The enemy could not beat you in the field', he told the army, 'but they may be too hard for you by policy in counsel, if you do not stick close to see common freedom established. For if . . . kingly authority be set up in your laws again, King Charles hath conquered you and your posterity by policy, and won the field of you, though you seemingly have cut off his head.'[4]

The Fifth Monarchist John Spittlehouse denounced the avarice and ambition of M.P.s and army officers, who were 'carried up to the highest pinnacle of temptation' by 'vast treasures got by the sweat of other men's brows'. 'Are they choked with lands, parks and manors?' asked Vavasor Powell in 1653.[5] He was echoed by *The Humble Representation of many Thousands* on 21 April of that year: 'God . . . gave you large possessions. . . . Was all this that you only might . . . forget the vows you then made?'[6] William Dell in the same year spoke of 'men . . . I have known once

---

[1] Exactly the same point was made in *The Character of the Long Parliament* (*C.P.W.*, V, pp. 443–5, 451). Cf. the passages in *Paradise Lost* on the defeats of victory (II. 787–807; XII. 79–101). For an eloquent denunciation of the political disasters resulting from avarice and ambition, see Milton's favourite historian, Sallust (pp. 181–2).

[2] *C.P.W.*, IV, pp. 678–85; I, p. 420; cf. *C.M.*, VI, p. 118: 'The foundations indeed they laid gallantly . . .'.

[3] Fry (1649), p. 8. For Fry see pp. 290–5 below.

[4] Sabine, pp. 513, 573–4; cf. pp. 330, 336, 354–7, 527.

[5] Spittlehouse, p. 4; *C.S.P. Domestic, 1653–4*, p. 306; cf. A. Griffith, pp. 18–19.

[6] *Op. cit.*, pp. 1–2. For documentation of extensive land purchases by, e.g., Generals Lambert and Fleetwood, see Gentles, p. 625.

hopeful in the Army and elsewhere, ... now so full gorged with ... estates, manors, houses, parks, lands' that all they care about is 'to take their ease and to comply with the world', leaving 'the remainder to men that are as plain and mean as themselves were at first'.[1]

'As for spiritual graces', said William Erbery sadly, 'how soon have they withered in the wisest! Good men in Parliament, when come to power, how weak were they! When was the Self-Denying Ordinance kept? ... I could name godly men in the old and new-modelled Army, fallen from their first love, their lowliness of mind, meekness, mercy, tender-heartedness; their tears are all dried up as withered grass, and as the flower of the field, which fades in a month.'[2] George Wither in 1655 called on the Protector to perform his contract with God and the people by making them truly free. If not, God would exact vengeance.[3] John Cook the regicide refused high office in August 1655 because he dared not 'return with the dog to his vomit again', having once dedicated himself to reforming the law so as to guarantee 'cheap property'.[4] 'Was this what you fought for?' Hugh Peter cried. 'Where is the relief of the oppressed, the supply of the needy?'[5] Similar warnings came from William Sedgwick, Sir Henry Vane, John Goodwin, James Nayler and Henry Pinnell. Edward Burrough the Quaker, looking back from 1660, passed a similar verdict on 'some of the Army' who 'mocked God'; although 'raised up from a low estate' they 'became as great oppressors ... as ever they were that went before them'. 'Their hearts have yearned after self-honour and the treasures of the world.'[6]

Milton was no political innocent. Before the Civil War he had noted in his Commonplace Book 'with how much disturbance of conscience affairs of state are carried on', even in the case of 'upright men ... and zealous in religion'. But 'if he, the great defender of regicide, had openly attacked either the Rump or Oliver Cromwell, this would have played into the hands of royalist enemies of the régime.'[7] Warnings and innuendo, coupled with significant silences, were his weapons: the linked phrases

---

[1] Dell, p. 464.

[2] Erbery, pp. 175–6; cf. *P.L.* V. 567–8.

[3] Wither (1655), pp. 13–14; cf. (1659), pp. 2, 16, and (1653). Like Milton, 'that gallant man, Major George Wither' was praised by John Lilburne (Haller, 1933, III, pp. 291–3).

[4] MacLysaght, pp. 417–46.

[5] C. Hill (1972), p. 181.

[6] W. Sedgwick (1656), pp. 61–9, 82–3; *Clarke Papers*, III, p. 118; Pinnell, p. 38; Burrough, pp. 612–13; cf. *Thurloe State Papers*, I, p. 658; III, p. 294; Owen, VI, p. 112. For Pinnell and Boehme, see C. Webster (1975), p. 280.

[7] *C.P.W.*, I, pp. 464–5; Wolfe (*Milton in the P.R.*, 1941), p. 281; cf. Barker (1942), pp. 382–3.

'avarice and ambition', 'covetousness and ambition', 'superstition and tyranny' occur again and again.

So we can understand why Milton accepted the dissolution of the Rump and of the Barebones Parliament in 1653, and even condemned the Rump in 1654. Only with the hindsight of 1659 was he to praise it, and so by implication criticize Oliver Cromwell.[1] Milton never directly attacked the Protectorate. He did so in 1659, but in words so cautious and ambiguous that historians still disagree about their exact meaning.[2] Now if not earlier Milton took to heart the Italian phrase Wotton had commended to him in 1638: 'i pensieri stretti ed il viso sciolto', 'your thoughts close and your contenance loose'.[3] In private he denounced the generals, but henceforth Milton perhaps never fully spoke out in public. He poured his feelings, instead, into the *De Doctrina* and *Paradise Lost*. The Latin dictionary which he began to compile about 1655 may be seen as a distraction before he got down to the fundamental rethinking of his major works.

II Desperate remedies

Milton reached a pinnacle of personal fame and success in the years 1649–52, when he was a European figure of heroic magnitude, who seemed to shed lustre on the English Revolution and the Commonwealth rather than deriving his glory from them. His life must again have seemed a poem, an epic poem: the bitterness of matrimonial failure, the scandal of the divorce pamphlets, would be forgotten as praise poured in from all sides, and as distinguished foreign visitors flocked to see the great John Milton. He moved easily in the highest intellectual and ruling circles of the English republic. His friends in office included Lord President Bradshaw, who called him the excellent Mr. Milton and left £10 each in his will to Milton and Nedham; Sir Henry Vane, Robert Overton, Major-General Fleetwood, Sir Peter Wentworth and John Sadler, member of the Council of State and associate of Hartlib.[4] Milton was also on familiar terms with the son of the President of Cromwell's Council of State, with Lady Ranelagh, sister of the powerful Lord Broghill, with Sir Isaac Penington and his son Isaac, as well as with the grandson of England's most famous Lord Chief Justice, Cyriack Skinner, himself later chairman of Harrington's radical Rota Club.[5] Roger Williams taught Milton Dutch, and

---

[1] *C.M.*, VI, p. 102.
[2] See p. 217 below.
[3] *C.P.W.*, I, p. 342.
[4] *Ibid.*, IV, pp. 675–6.
[5] Darbishire, p. 7; Aubrey, I, p. 290. For the Rota see p. 202 below.

learnt 'many more' languages from him. Milton was acquainted with William Ryley, Norroy King of Arms and Keeper of the Records of the Tower. The sonnets of these years reveal a certain social suavity, an affability, a sense of elegance. This well-being must have been reinforced by his happy second marriage in 1656.

All the more terrible must have been the slow sapping of Milton's faith in the Revolution which he had made his own – as a state church was reconstructed, as the second Protectorate became a virtual monarchy. The cruel blow of his second wife's death in 1658 was followed by the false dawn of 1659, when he rushed back into pamphleteering. His revived optimism is demonstrated by the fact that his first concern, dealt with in two linked pamphlets, was to rescue the church from 'force on the one side restraining, and hire on the other side corrupting, the teachers thereof'. *A Treatise of Civil Power*, directed to Richard Cromwell's Parliament in February 1659, dealt with the former, calling in effect for a reversal of the Petition and Advice's religious settlement, and for resistance to pressure from the clergy to tighten it up further. Vane had been quite right to warn against clerical attempts to 'get the ear of the magistrate'; there was widespread agitation, which extended to the gentry as well as to clergymen like Richard Baxter and other promoters of local Presbyterian associations. Baxter was lobbying 'the magistrate' hard in the middle and late fifties on behalf of a more conservative and more authoritarian state church.[1] Since Milton knew that a majority of the M.P.s whom he was addressing were likely to wish to move in this direction, he had to express himself with care. He pretended that he was only putting forward demands common to all Protestants, whereas he was (as he revealed at the end of his treatise) very specifically arguing against 'magistrates who think it their work to settle religion'.[2]

'Hire ... corrupting the teachers' was the subject of *Considerations Touching the Likeliest Means to Remove Hirelings out of the Church*. This was published in August 1659, by which date the restoration of the Rump of the Long Parliament had made the political situation superficially more promising. Milton hoped, or persuaded himself that he hoped, or pretended that he hoped, that the Rump would resist the pressures for a persecuting and tithe-supported state church to which Oliver and Richard Cromwell had succumbed. But the tragedy of 1647–53 repeated itself as farce in 1659–60, and Milton's concern for liberty in the church soon gave

---

[1] *C.M.*, VI, pp. 4–5, 46–7; Schlatter, pp. 45–60. For Vane see p. 190 above.
[2] *C.M.*, VI, pp. 39–40.

way to anxiety for the Commonwealth itself. The negotiations between France and Spain which led to the Peace of the Pyrenees in November 1659 made him fear lest these 'two potent kingdoms', enemies of religion and liberty, intended 'a speedy invasion of this island' to restore Charles II.[1]

Milton's principal concern henceforth was to reunite the radicals, to bring to an end their self-righteous divisions, 'for the preventing of a civil war now feared'. 'Every faction hath the plea of God's cause', he noted, in a passage directed against the diversionary activities of the Fifth Monarchists.[2] For now the survival of the Revolution itself was at stake. Between October 1659 and April 1660 Milton put forward no less than six variants of his plan for averting a restoration of monarchy, and always the idea behind the changes was to make a commonwealth more widely acceptable. The tracts of this period are remarkably simpler in style than the elaborately orchestrated pamphlets of the forties. Milton was trying now to get across to the popular audience which the Levellers had so successfully reached.

Before attempting to assess these pamphlets, we might ask who else could have spoken out in 1659–60. Not Lilburne, who had died in 1657. But Walwyn and Coppe were practising as doctors, Overton and Wildman were still alive. So were Winstanley, Dell, John Goodwin. Vane and Hugh Peter were to be executed after the Restoration. Clarkson was busy denouncing his lurid past. Yet none of the survivors spoke. With some it may have been timidity, with others hopelessness; but one suspects that most no longer felt that they had anything to say which stood the slightest chance of being listened to. (Dell and Marvell, like Milton, tried to rally opposition by the cry of anti-popery as soon after the Restoration as they could get into print.[3]) Milton's pamphlets should therefore be judged not only as magnificently courageous gestures but also as attempts to reunite those who seemed fragmented beyond all hope. Few others, Harrington apart, had the persistence, the optimism, even to try. Milton probably knew it was hopeless too in his heart of hearts, at least by the time of the second edition of *The Ready and Easy Way*; but he still had to proclaim his faith, to argue, to plead: God *must* rally to his own cause. O earth, earth.... It had similarly been his duty to speak out in 1641, as it was to be his duty again in 1673–4. He remained to the end a profoundly *political* animal.

---

[1] *Ibid.*, XVIII, p. 3.
[2] *The Ready and Easy Way*, p. 15; passage omitted in the second edition.
[3] See pp. 219–20 below.

In *The Ready and Easy Way* Milton acknowledged that a majority of the nation shared 'the vain and groundless apprehension that nothing but kingship can restore trade'.[1] Their attitude filled Milton with contempt and indignation, but he still tried to produce alternatives which would vindicate 'our victory at once against two the most prevailing usurpers over mankind, superstition and tyranny', and ensure 'peace, justice, plentiful trade and all prosperity . . . even to the coming of our true and rightful and only to be expected King', Jesus Christ.[2] The perpetual oligarchy recommended in the tract was far from being Milton's ideal solution: it was the only remedy he could think of to check the Gadarene rush to monarchy.

On what basis could a stable government be established to carry out the radical programme? The Levellers had set out written fundamentals, which could not be violated by an elected Parliament. But they never determined who was to enforce their observance. A select senate was the shibboleth of the army generals in the years 1658–60, as a means of maintaining the veto on legislation which they had won in the Other House of the constitution of 1657; it was also adopted by republicans like Vane and Henry Stubbe who were beginning to despair of elected Parliaments. It recurs in Milton's Grand Council, though this was not merely a piece of balancing machinery: it was itself to be the government. Nor was it to last for ever: power would ultimately revert to the people. Milton pleads for time until people are better educated. But the people would regain power only when the Commonwealth was 'thoroughly settled in peace and safety'.[3]

There had been a real problem of continuity of government since the abolition of monarchy. Parliamentary government was a very recent experiment. Most M.P.s did not take kindly to establishing themselves permanently in London. How was stability to be ensured? How in particular was military intervention to be prevented? The Protectorate had attempted to restore some of the permanency of monarchy, but it had been accompanied by a social, political and religious conservatism which Milton abhorred. His perpetual Grand Council was intended to fill this gap. He rightly saw that what the 'natural rulers' of the countryside most objected to in military rule was interference in their running of local government. Hence his suggestion in *Proposalls of Certaine Expedients*, and

---

[1] Fuller's *An Alarm to the Countries of England and Wales* (1660) is an example of many tracts which argued along these lines.
[2] *C.M.*, VI, pp. 116, 132–3, 146. Note the recurrence of 'superstition and tyranny'.
[3] *Ibid.*, VI, p. 133.

more elaborately in *The Ready and Easy Way*, that 'every county in the land' should become 'a little commonwealth', with its own popular assembly to counterbalance the Grand Council. These county assemblies would make 'their own judicial laws, or use these that are, and execute them by their own elected judicatures and judges without appeal, in all things of civil government between man and man'. They would have the right to ratify – or reject – all laws 'of any great concernment to public liberty' passed by the Council. So 'the odious power and name of committees' dependent on the central government would be abolished. (In the *Letter to a Friend* of October 1659 Milton's local assemblies had been called committees!) What is more, there was to be a popular militia in each county, which would guard against the influence of the army at the centre.[1]

This scheme is a curious mixture of Leveller plans for decentralizing justice with the realities of social power in England. Milton assumed that authority in the elected county assemblies would be wielded by 'the nobility and chief gentry', as it was to be in England after 1688, when abolition of the traditional authority of the monarchy removed restraints on the natural rulers. We may compare Milton's scheme with the British constitution for India in 1935, by which considerable powers in local government were handed over to Indians as the price of maintaining English control of the central government.

New emphases in the pamphlets of 1659–60 show how Milton thought the tide was flowing. Free schools in every city and great town were an advance on the élitism of the earlier *Of Education*.[2] 'The just division of waste commons, whereby the nation would become much more industrious, rich and populous', in *Proposalls of Certaine Expedients*, was another novelty. The concern in the *De Doctrina* for population to labour the fields shows that it may not have been merely opportunistic. Also new was emphasis on 'the seizing of pots and pans from the poor . . ., from some the beds', by priests in pursuit of tithes, and Milton's desire to extend culture 'to all extreme parts', the dark corners of the land.[3] One wonders how far these new economic and social interests derive from the letter which the poet received from Moses Wall in May 1659: 'Whilst people are not free, but straitened in accommodations for life, their spirits will be dejected and servile.' To remedy this, 'there should be an improving of our native commodities, as our manufactures, our fishing, our fens, forests and commons and our trade at sea' as well as abolition of tithes and the

---

[1] *C.M.*, XVIII, pp. 5–6; VI, pp. 109, 126, 128, 132, 144–7.
[2] *Ibid.*, VI, p. 80; see pp. 146–9 above.
[3] *C.M.*, XVIII, pp. 6–7; VI, pp. 67–8, 145.

Norman Yoke of copyhold, 'whereby people care not to improve their land by cost upon it'.[1] It was a perceptive remark.

Alternatively, the interest may derive from the discussions on the relation of politics to economics which went on in the Harringtonian Rota Club in 1659–60.[2] This club made a last effort at constitution-mongering in order to defend 'the people' and their property against both the poor and reviving royalism. Harrington argued in *Oceana* (1656) and subsequent pamphlets that power must be based on property: the Rota Club brought together ex-Levellers (John Wildman, Maximilian Petty) and old republicans like Henry Neville, sometimes under the chairmanship of Cyriack Skinner – one of Milton's former pupils and closest friends, whom Aubrey called Milton's 'disciple'.[3] There is no evidence that Milton ever attended these debates; but *The Ready and Easy Way* makes concessions to Harringtonian ideas, though not to the perilous and injurious 'circumscription of men's lands and properties' by an agrarian law. The Royalist skit, *The Censure of the Rota Upon Mr. Miltons Book* (1660) takes as its starting-point the likelihood of the Rota Club discussing *The Ready and Easy Way*.[4]

In this pamphlet Milton's concern was to reject the 'bad men who have ill-managed and abused' what he still believed was 'a just and noble cause'. If our fathers had forsaken their good cause for such a reason, 'what had long ere this become of our Gospel and all protestant reformation, so much intermixed with the avarice and ambition of some reformers?'[5] Avarice and ambition, we note again: the cause, however, is greater than the men. But Milton knew he was writing for men who would prostitute religion and liberty to what they believed to be the interests of commercial prosperity, men who cared less for principles than for pocket. How was he to influence them? The task was of course impossible. But Milton threw in something for everybody – here a bit of 'partial rotation' for the Harring-tonians, there a select senate for the generals, decentralization for Levellers and Diggers. Milton praised the Dutch Republic especially for its de-centralized federal constitution, and yet opposed the 'cantonization' of

---

[1] Masson, V, p. 602; cf. pp. 191–3 above, and pp. 266, 465 below.

[2] See p. 197 above.

[3] Aubrey, I, pp. 290, 293; II, p. 72. Aubrey, who himself attended the Rota debates, lists Milton's (and Cyriack Skinner's) friend Andrew Marvell first among Harrington's friends, who also include John Pell, former member of the Hartlib circle. The Leveller John Jones probably supported the Harringtonians. An argument (not used by Parker) for Cyriack Skinner's authorship of the Anonymous Life of Milton is the appearance in it of the Harring-tonian phrase 'superstructure' (Darbishire, p. 24).

[4] *C.M.*, VI, pp. 133–4.

[5] *Ibid.*, VI, p. 117.

England of which the major-generals had been accused. Similarly he lauded Elizabeth, but recalled that she persecuted Presbyterians. In the second edition he eliminated a phrase critical of Fifth Monarchists: they too were now potential allies, dangerously diversionary though Milton thought their ideas had been.

Liberty of conscience seems almost incidental in *The Ready and Easy Way*, but Milton did not forget that 'the abandoning of all those they call sectaries, for the detected falsehood and ambition of some' would undermine 'their own chief strength and interest in the freedom of all protestant religion'. He ended by proclaiming his fidelity to the Good Old Cause, the blanket phrase used by all concerned for unity to defend 'our expiring liberty'.[1] There is no reason to doubt G.S.'s admission that *The Ready and Easy Way* 'was received by many with applause'.[2]

Even Milton's pitiful oligarchic proposals have their antecedents. In the earliest of his schemes, *Proposalls of Certaine Expedients*, he suggested making the Rump perpetual, and abolishing the name of Parliament – 'a Norman or French word, a monument of our ancient servitude'.[3] The word 'sifting' which Milton used about elections may recall that the radicals in 1643 had proposed a national protestation, an oath, as a means of 'sifting', distinguishing between true and fair-weather friends of the cause.[4] Milton's scheme may also owe something to Wither, who as early as 1653 had advocated rule by a perpetual Parliament, recruited from time to time by partial elections.[5] This idea was picked up by Harrington and Sir Arthur Haslerig. The latter in July 1659 was arguing for well-refining elections to a perpetual Parliament, from which one-third of the members would resign each year.[6] Milton may also have recalled Vane's innocent theory that sovereignty resides 'in the whole body of adherents to this cause', that only those who are 'freeborn in respect of their principles' should be free citizens. In 1659 Vane wondered 'how the depraved, corrupted and self-interested will of man, in the great body which we call the people, ... shall be prevailed with to espouse their true public interest?'[7] It was indeed a difficult question. Milton's solution was contorted: 'More just it is doubtless, if it come to force, that a lesser number compel a greater to retain, which can be no wrong to them, their

[1] *Ibid.*, VI, pp. 143, 148–9.
[2] See p. 225 below.
[3] *C.M.*, XVIII, p. 4.
[4] C. Holmes, p. 63.
[5] Wither (1653).
[6] Wariston, III, p. 125.
[7] Vane (1656), p. 311; (1659).

liberty, than that a greater number for the pleasure of their baseness, compel a less most injuriously to be their fellow-slaves.'[1]

The most astonishing thing about *The Ready and Easy Way* is the outspoken virulence of its anti-monarchism. In the second, enlarged, edition which Milton defiantly published, over his own name, and probably at his own expense, just before Charles II returned, many additions stress the moral objections to monarchy. This was so obviously foolhardy at that date that no bookseller's or printer's name was attached to this edition. A republic, Milton argued, is in conformity with the precepts of the gospels; monarchy is antichristian.[2] Avoidance of monarchy seems to Milton now more important even than liberty of conscience; or rather, we may be sure, he knew that monarchy restored by a free Parliament would mean the end of any hope of the kind of religious freedom he wished to see. The traditional electorate would never vote for that. By April 1660 he would even have settled for 'a reign or two' in the house of Monck if that would keep out the Stuarts.[3]

---

[1] *C.M.,* VI, p. 140–1. See p. 426 below.
[2] Cf. the *De Doctrina* on 'the immortality of royal courts'; persecuting kings are antichristian (*C.P.W.,* VI, pp. 796–8).
[3] *C.M.,* VI, p. 160.

Chapter 15

Back to Egypt

As good subjects we must maintain our liberties. . . . It was baseness and madness in Israel, that being free from Pharaoh's oppressions they would run back into Egypt in all haste. . . . Resolve never to come under the yoke and bondage of human traditions or yokes of Antichrist.

Thomas Taylor, *The Principles of Christian Practice*

In 1660 Milton foresaw a cultural as well as a political counter-revolution. After eulogizing, not utterly unhistorically, a free commonwealth, 'wherein they who are the greatest are perpetual servants and drudges to the public at their own cost and charges, . . . walk the street as other men, may be spoken to freely, familiarly, friendly, without adoration', Milton drew the contrast. 'A king must be adored like a demigod, with a dissolute and haughty court about him, of vast expense and luxury, masques and revels, to the debauching of our prime gentry, both male and female.' The nobility and gentry would be 'bred up then to the hopes not of public but of court offices, to be stewards, chamberlains, ushers, grooms even of the close-stool; and the lower their minds debased with court opinions, . . . the haughtier will be their pride and profaneness.'[1] If Milton did later say that his objection to monarchy was the expense involved, he was only quoting what he had already written.[2] Milton proved right. The latest authority speaks of Charles II's 'formidable extravagance', which 'tended to increase in proportion to his resources'.[3]

---

[1] *C.M.*, VI, p. 120.
[2] See p. 265 below. 'All stolen from the state', Milton added in the *Defensio* (*C.P.W.*, IV, pp. 520–1).
[3] Chandaman, pp. 208, 270–3. Cf. the estimate that in 1630 pensions and annuities cost the country nearly one-third more than they were to average in the sixty years between 1721 and 1780, despite the vast increase both in national wealth and in government expenditure since 1630 (M. V. C. Alexander, p. 161).

At the end of *The Ready and Easy Way* Milton saw the English people 'choosing them a captain back for Egypt'.[1] This theme was a Puritan cliché. A sermon preached in Oxford on Numbers 14:6 gave great offence to Laud in 1631, and Thomas Taylor's reference cited in the epigraph to this chapter assumes that his readers will be familiar with the story. Robert Norwood in 1653 fused the myth with that of Samson: 'We will not go down into Egypt, into the house of bondage from which the Lord our God hath set and kept us free. . . . We will not suffer our seven locks to be shaved off our heads by any Dalila whatsoever.'[2] John Saltmarsh, William Sedgwick and Abiezer Coppe used the theme: it was a favourite with the Muggletonians.[3] In 1654 'the clergy of this nation' were accused of 'a design . . . to bring us again into Egyptian bondage'.[4] Oliver Cromwell, addressing his first Parliament, referred to 'a people brought out of Egypt towards the land of Canaan', who 'through unbelief, murmuring, repining' lingered 'many years in the wilderness, before they came to the place of rest'.[5] In 1659 Moses Wall spoke of 'those who had made deep protestations of their zeal for our liberty' who now 'shall betray the good thing committed to them and lead us back to Egypt'.[6] An anonymous vindication of the army in the same year said 'We are upon our march from Egypt to Canaan, from a land of bondage and darkness to a land of liberty and rest.'[7]

The analogy was a favourite one with Milton. Psalm 114, which he paraphrased in 1623 and translated into Greek in 1634, began 'When Israel came out of Egypt'. In *Animadversions* Milton had been sure that God would not 'bring us thus far onward from Egypt to destroy us in this wilderness, though we deserve it'.[8] In *The Reason of Church Government* he referred to the bishops' 'Egyptian tyranny' over the church.[9] And in *A Defence of the People of England* he warned against any desire 'to resist your destiny and return to slavery after your freedom has been won with God's assistance and your own valour. . . . Your sin would equal the sin of those who were overcome with longing for their former captivity in

[1] *C.M.,* VI, p. 149.
[2] Robert Norwood, p. 57.
[3] Saltmarsh (1648), p. 22; W. Sedgwick, *Some Flashes* (1648), p. 211; (1661), p. 100; Coppe (1649) title-page and p. 52; Muggleton (1764), p. 24; *Divine Songs of the Muggletonians* (1829), p. 13 and *passim*.
[4] Ludlow, I, p. 546.
[5] Cromwell, III, p. 442; cf. Burnet (1897), I, pp. 77, 123.
[6] Masson, V, p. 602.
[7] *C.P.W.,* VII, p. 126.
[8] *Ibid.,* I. p. 706.
[9] *Ibid.,* I, p. 793.

Egypt and were at length destroyed by God in countless disasters.' In the *De Doctrina* he spoke of 'the slavery of a spiritual Egypt', and in *The Likeliest Means* Milton described Sir George Booth's rising as an attempt 'to call back again their Egyptian bondage'.[1] He summed up in *Paradise Lost*: 'Their delay/ In the wide wilderness' was to the advantage of the Israelites, not only because it gave them political experience of self-government but also because it obviated the danger that fear

> Return them back to Egypt, choosing rather
> Inglorious life with servitude.
>
> (P.L. XII. 218–24)

If we combine this passage with *Eikonoklastes*'s comparison of the revolutionary period to the Israelites' sojourn in the desert, the political point is clear.[2]

Another metaphor looks forward to *Samsom Agonistes*. The words 'O earth, earth . . .' quoted by Milton as though in ultimate despair – as no doubt he was – come from a passage in which the prophet Micah not only foretold the ruin of Jerusalem but also announced a Saviour. Already in the depths of his despondency Milton was looking for the miracle of destruction by which God would save his cause, despite the people's backsliding.

Just as the return of a 'free Parliament' brought a renewal of religious persecution, so the restoration of monarchy brought back the hideously barbaric cruelties of execution for treason. Many of Milton's friends were hanged, disembowelled and quartered. He had to go into hiding whilst a like fate was discussed for him. He was arrested and imprisoned, but escaped a traitor's sentence. Because it did not happen we tend to forget how likely it seemed in all human probability. Milton had publicly advocated the accountability of kings immediately after Charles I's trial, and had defended regicide in the face of all Europe. 'It was not a thing done in a corner' he, like Major-General Harrison, might have said. Short of actually signing the death warrant Milton could hardly have done more. In 1659–60, when so many of the King's former enemies lay low, Milton proclaimed his republicanism from the house-tops. Nor was he forgotten at the Restoration – how could he have been? The House of Commons called for three books to be burned. These were Milton's *Eikonoklastes* and the *Defence of the People of England*, and John Goodwin's *The Obstructours of Justice*. For some reason *The Tenure* was not included, though closely associated with Goodwin's book. *The Tenure* might have

---

[1] *Ibid.*, IV, p. 532; VI, p. 711; *C.M.*, VI, p. 102.
[2] *C.P.W.*, III, p. 580.

been even more damaging to Milton if recollected in 1660. His name was proposed for exemption from the Act of Indemnity, and this would have meant trial and execution.

How Milton escaped we do not know. 'How justly hath God struck Milton blind for writing against the King's book!', wrote Arise Evans in 1653.[1] The argument that his blindness was a divine punishment seems to have been turned round to suggest that the poet had already been punished sufficiently. A curious passage in *Samson Agonistes* tells us how some of the Philistines, 'more generous far and civil', confessed that 'they had enough revenged' upon Samson,

> having reduced
> Their foe to misery beneath their fears,
> The rest was magnanimity to remit.
>   (1467-70)

Milton's friends rallied to him – Marvell certainly, possibly the Earl of Anglesey, perhaps Monck's cronies, Sir Thomas Clarges and Secretary Morrice. Monck's physician, Dr. Samuel Barrow, was an admirer of Milton, though the evidence comes from 1674. The Boyle family were well placed to help. Lady Ranelagh was on friendly terms with the all-powerful Earl of Clarendon.[2] Her brother Roger, created Earl of Orrery in September 1660 for helping to bring about the restoration in Ireland, was also a friend of Sir William Davenant,[3] who is credited with intervening on Milton's behalf – repayment of assistance which the latter had rendered him under the Commonwealth. Milton's Royalist brother Christopher, made a serjeant at the Restoration, may have helped too. But we do not know how Milton managed to get off without even being incapacitated to hold political office, as Goodwin was. Somebody may have thought that he would be a useful servant to the restored government if he would turn his coat.

What we do know is that Milton had to go into hiding, first borrowing £400 from the faithful Cyriack Skinner. For sixteen long weeks in 1660 his fate was in the balance. Even after he knew he was not to be judicially sentenced, fear of assassination remained. There were many Royalist bravos about in London, and attempts were made to assassinate Algernon Sydney and John Lisle overseas, the latter being successful. In 1671 Sir John Coventry had his nose slit for an injudicious remark about Charles II and actresses: Milton's offence was considerably worse than that. The

---

[1] Evans (*Farley*, 1653), p. 31.
[2] Burnet (1897), I, p. 277; cf. pp. 283-4 for Burnet's surprise at Milton's escape.
[3] Boyle, I, p. 11.

thought of an attack of this sort must have been peculiarly repulsive to a man whose blindness made him incapable of using in his own defence the sword that all gentlemen still wore. What went on in Milton's mind during this terrible period we cannot even guess, but he must have had to push a good deal further with the rethinking that had begun in the fifties.

Did Milton feel uneasy about surviving whilst others perished? There are passages in the *De Doctrina* discussing Biblical authorization of flight from persecution which could have a personal application. Milton may indeed have had to sign some form of acceptance of the restored régime in order to obtain release from prison, but there is no evidence that he made any major concession; Colonel Hutchinson was afterwards bitterly ashamed of some such weakness on his part.[1] Milton's widow said that he was asked to use his pen on behalf of the court, to turn his coat in the way he had persuaded Nedham to turn his in 1649–50. Milton refused. This may be a garbled version of the story that he was consulted – as a great expert on divorce – much later, when some politicians were urging Charles II to divorce his popish Queen and beget a legitimate Protestant heir. Milton had indeed argued in *Tetrachordon* that where 'inheritance, crowns and dignities' were involved, divorce for barrenness might be considered, 'notwithstanding the waywardness of our school doctors'.[2]

Milton was left with the total ruin of his political hopes. The English had rejected the proffered role of chosen people: John Milton had sacrificed his eyes in vain. But the Restoration was not a sudden traumatic blow. The sonnet 'On the late massacre in Piedmont' is full of shocked horror at what the Almighty had allowed to happen to his people 'who kept thy truth so pure of old': the curt commands with which the sonnet opens – 'Avenge O Lord', 'Forget not' – form as it were a memo to God which should have been superfluous. Milton had contemplated the horrifying possibility that the Almighty might overlook what had occurred in the Alpine mountains cold. By writing the sonnet Milton may have restored his own confidence: the whole terrible episode had been a warning for papist Italians – or so it could be interpreted. His demand for revenge is a demand for reassurance that God is after all just. Note the ambiguity of 'where still doth sway / The triple tyrant'. 'Sway' is a word whose two meanings uniquely convey the impression of tyranny *and* instability (cf. 'Which way the wind / Sways them' – *P.L.* IV. 982–3). The sense of instability is reinforced by '*still* doth sway', '*Early* may fly the Babylonian woe', which is both inevitable and imminent. The fact that the vales and

---

[1] Hutchinson, pp. 229–45.
[2] *C.P.W.*, II, p. 594. Nedham turned again after 1660.

hills redoubled to heaven the moans of the slaughtered Piedmontese suggests a sympathy between man and nature such as existed before the Fall, and then ceased: its return would herald the last days. The concluding lines of the sonnet call on God to act through human beings:

> that from these may grow
> A hundredfold.

It was the Old Testament and Protestant principle of the remnant leavening the lump – an emphasis to which the poet was to return increasingly after 1660.[1]

In 1655, however, more positive help was brought to the Vaudois by Catholic France, for its own reasons of political self-interest, than by all the sound and fury emitted from Protestant England. The man who drafted Cromwell's diplomatic despatches began to lose confidence in solutions deriving from state action – an extension of the uneasiness he had revealed in 1654 about the use of force in politics.[2] Even Oliver, even the Protestant hero Charles Gustavus of Sweden, tended to use 'the protestant interest' as a mere instrument of a nationalist foreign policy (cf. the dismissive 'what the Swede intend and what the French' of the sonnet to Cyriack Skinner). Salvation must come from below, from the remnant of the people. To the second, enlarged, edition of *The Ready and Easy Way* Milton added an epigraph from Juvenal: 'I too have given advice to Sulla; now let me give it to the people.' ("'Tis for the people now' was Masson's translation.[3]) Whether we take Sulla as representing Cromwell or Monck, the point is the same.

Another way in which Milton was prepared for tragedy was in his personal life – by the failure of his first marriage, by the deaths of his second wife and his son; by his blindness. After 1660 he was at the mercy of Royalist sneers against the 'doubly blind bard'.[4] In *The Second Defence* and in *Samson Agonistes* Milton retorted on the *internal* blindness of his enemies. It was because the Philistines were 'drunk with idolatry, drunk with wine', that they fell victims to the blind Samson.[5] Milton must sometimes have wondered why God had not intervened to preserve his sight, which still might have been useful to the cause. Gradually from 1654 onwards he built up a conviction that the loss of his eyesight enhanced his

---

[1] See p. 388 below. Cf. Hyma, pp. 26–9.
[2] See pp. 190–1 above.
[3] C. and F., p. 416; Masson, V, pp. 678–9.
[4] [Anon.], *The Cloud opened: Or, the English Hero* (1670), *Harleian Miscellany*, IV, p. 143. Cf. pp. 374–5 below.
[5] *C.P.W.*, IV, p. 589.

unique status as the blind bard – like Homer, Tiresias, Thamyris, Phineus
(*P.L.* III. 35–6), as well as Zizka and other men of action – so increasing
his right to speak to and for his people. At an earlier stage he had thought
that chastity marked out the God-favoured poet: now it was blindness.[1]
Milton had to face the worst – in his personal life first, then in his political
hopes. But his remarkable escape in 1660 may have reinforced his belief
that God was preserving him for some purpose, to destroy some temple of
idol-worship.[2]

Deprivation of outer light no doubt confirmed and strengthened
Milton's reliance on the inner light. Physical blindness was much less to
be lamented than internal. To be classed with 'the blind, the afflicted, the
suffering and the weak' gave Milton the hope of approaching 'more closely
the mercy and the protection of the Father Almighty', of winning the
greatest strength through weakness. 'So in this darkness may I be clothed
in light'. His physical condition thus reinforced the conviction which he
shared with many radicals. Inner illumination was necessary.[3]

Satan and Samson speak for that part of Milton which still resented the
God who had willed the Restoration. Milton never accepted the com-
placent submission of the matchless Orinda, a former Presbyterian who
nevertheless sang

> And the same fate that seems to me reverse
> Is necessary to the universe.

Unlike Mrs. Phillips, Milton 'dare dispute with Providence divine'.[4] Nor
did Milton agree with the attitude summed up in his friend Marvell's
superbly ironical remark that 'the [Parliamentarian] Cause was too good to
have been fought for. . . . For men may spare their pains when Nature is
at work, and the world will not go the faster for our driving.'[5] Marvell had
accepted the Revolution after it had happened, and never experienced the
phase of romantic hope and illusion: so he could look at it with greater
detachment than Milton. Marvell's intention was not to disparage the
Cause for which he had not fought, but to stress that its success was
inevitable on Harringtonian grounds. 'The people' were too strong for the
King in politics because they were too strong in economics.[6] Marvell was

---

[1] Masson, IV, p. 594; cf. Sirluck (1961), p. 771. See also pp. 191, 208 above for Milton's blindness.

[2] If we are looking for a date for *Samson Agonistes*, it would fit very well here. See pp. 481–2
below.

[3] *C.P.W.*, IV, pp. 584–91. Cf. p. 438 below. Galileo had lost his sight when Milton saw him in
1638.

[4] Saintsbury, I, pp. 567–8; cf. pp. 564, 599. Katharine Phillips looks forward to Pope and deism
in many ways: 'the world's God's watch'; God is 'no tyrant'.

[5] Marvell (1971), p. 135.   [6] Cf. C. Hill (Panther, 1969), pp. 326–7.

right that in post-Restoration England most of the political, social and
economic demands of the Parliamentarians had been won. But for
Milton these were the least of the Revolution's objectives. Edward
Burrough's analysis of the Restoration would have been more congenial to
Milton. God had suffered it for reasons known only to himself: possibly to
punish the revolutionaries who had failed to honour their promises. But
Charles II should remember that 'the people . . . will not long bear any
degree of the yoke of slavery.'[1]

From at least 1641 Milton felt himself somehow responsible for the
English Revolution – or as he would say, for God's cause in England –
and possessive about it. Perhaps because of his historical studies, he
realized earlier than most that he was living through a great historical
epoch, which opened up limitless possibilities. His historical perspective,
like that of all his contemporaries who had one at all, was apocalyptic.
Christ's kingdom was at hand.

In these circumstances Milton as a privileged intellectual felt that he
had a duty to help. The anti-episcopal pamphlets are propaganda, of
course; but Milton I think saw them differently. He was trying to unite
the nation against the evil forces which had hamstrung it. Throughout his
career he makes this attempt. In 1644, and again in 1659, he is trying to
build unity against the privileged clergy and their censorship.[2] In 1649 he
tried to unite the nation against the King and his clerical idolaters. In
1655 the massacre of the Vaudois seemed to offer a chance of reuniting
Protestants.[3] Four years later Milton tried to reunite the radicals against
priests and tithes, and in 1660, with growing despair, the divided adherents
of the Good Old Cause against the threat of a return to monarchy.
Meanwhile the *De Doctrina* was inspired by the wider hope of a reunion of
Protestant Christendom in reason and tolerance. But England became so
unreasonable and intolerant that he could not publish his 'best and dearest
possession'. In *Paradise Lost, Paradise Regained* and *Samson Agonistes* he
wrote poems which were 'doctrinal and exemplary to a nation';[4] he was
wrestling with the problem of how God's servants should act in face of
national failure to take advantage of the glorious opportunities of the
English Revolution. Finally in 1673–4 Milton saw a new hope of uniting
Protestants against popery and absolutism – and acted at once.[5]

---

[1] *W.T.U.D.*, p. 351; cf. pp. 399, 404.
[2] See pp. 150–3, 198–204 above.
[3] Cf. *C.P.W.*, IV, p. 272.
[4] *Ibid.*, I, p. 815.
[5] See pp. 218–21 below.

Chapter 16

Last Years

So virtue given for lost
Depressed and overthrown, as seemed . . . ,
Revives, reflourishes, then vigorous most
When most unactive deemed.

Milton, *Samson Agonistes*

1 Milton and his friends

The procession for the funeral of Oliver Cromwell included a remarkable collection of literary figures. Milton walked with other members of the secretariat for Foreign Tongues – Hartlib, Marvell, Dryden, with Edward Phillips, Marchamont Nedham and Nathaniel Sterry, brother of Peter.[1] Marvell had long been Milton's protégé. In 1653 the older poet tried to get the younger employed as his assistant: Marvell was appointed to the job in 1657. He may have helped Milton with either *Eikonoklastes* or the *Defence of the People of England*. Marvell, James Harrington's friend, shared Milton's dislike of clericalism and monarchy, and perhaps his anti-Trinitarianism. Aubrey put Marvell first among Milton's 'familiar learned acquaintance'; one of Milton's companions, Wood called him. Marvell contributed a poem to the second edition of *Paradise Lost*. In *The Rehearsal Transpros'd* he defended Milton with great dignity against the slanders of Samuel Parker, and virtually quoted *Animadversions* when he wrote that God 'could not institute government to the prejudice of mankind, or exact obedience to laws that are destructive of human society'.[2] Samuel

---

[1] See pp. 42, 146–7, 184 above.
[2] *C.P.W.*, I, p. 699; Marvell (1971), pp. 236–43, 251; Darbishire, p. 7; cf. C. Hill (Panther, 1969), p. 326, and p. 191 above.

Parker's ally, Richard Leigh, saw Marvell and Milton as political 'fellow-journeymen'; 'there are many Miltons in this one man.'[1]

Nedham's friendship with Milton continued after 1660, and soon again had political overtones. Their names were linked in at least four pamphlets: 'a couple of curs of the same pack', Roger L'Estrange called them. A letter to Oldenburg of February 1671 refers to Milton, Nedham and 'their junto'.[2] Another friend of Milton's was Theodore Haak, of the Comenian group. He was ordered to translate into Dutch Parliament's declaration of the causes of the war with Scotland in June 1650, at the same time that Milton was to translate it into Latin – though later this task was transferred to Tom May. Milton would almost certainly know Haak's translation into English of the marginal notes to the Dutch Bible, which he had been asked to make by the Westminster Assembly and which was published in 1655. This book was in the library of Milton's friend, Nathan Paget. Haak became a Fellow of the Royal Society. He translated three books of *Paradise Lost* into German.[3] At some stage Milton was also friendly with Moses Wall, who had been chaplain to the Earl of Warwick during the Civil War and was one of those suggested by Hartlib to serve (together with Milton) on his projected council for schools. Wall appears not to have associated with Milton whilst the latter was in the service of the Protector; but he was reassured of Milton's radicalism by the *Treatise of Civil Power*. In 1659 he wrote Milton a remarkable letter, quoted above.[4]

Cyriack Skinner, friend also of Marvell's, remained close to Milton after the Restoration. The association with Marvell and Nedham continued, and Dryden remained on terms with the man who had been his senior in the Protector's entourage. Dryden seems to have acquired considerable respect for Milton, though the two were never intimate. Two other Royalist poets were Milton's friends – Sir William Davenant and Sir Robert Howard. Davenant played some part in saving Milton's life at the Restoration, in return for Milton's help to him a decade earlier when Davenant was imprisoned as a Royalist. He sent one of his sons to be taught by the blind poet. Milton perhaps quotes Davenant in *The Ready and Easy Way*.[5] Edward Phillips regarded Howard as a better poet than

---

[1] [Richard Leigh] (1673), pp. 131, 136, 147. Leigh deliberately emphasized the links between Marvell and Milton in the title of another pamphlet which he contributed to this controversy: *The Censure of the Rota On Mr. Driden's Conquest of Granada* (Oxford U.P., 1673). He referred to *The Censure of the Rota* on Milton in *The Transproser Rehears'd*, p. 146.

[2] Leigh (1673), p. 32; Oldenburg, VI, pp. 439–40.

[3] Barnett, p. 92, and *passim*. See also pp. 391–2 below.

[4] See pp. 191–3, 201–2, 206 above.

[5] *C.M.*, VI, p. 121; and see note on the passage in *C.P.W.*, VII.

Dryden, inferior only to Orrery among living English dramatists. Former Royalist though he was, Howard spoke in the Convention Parliament of 1689 of the divine right of the people.[1] He disliked priests who 'mislead the vulgar and profane (as they please to term them) into a blind implicit obedience to their inspired and divine authority. . . . They invented two great assistances, mystery and persecution.' Sir Robert pretends to be speaking of the pre-Christian era, but goes on to say that Christian priests began the worship of images. He was accused of Socinianism.[2] Another who contributed a poem to the second edition of *Paradise Lost* was Samuel Barrow, a doctor in Monck's army in Scotland, who played a significant part in bringing about the Restoration and became physician in ordinary to Charles II. He appears to have missed his knighthood because of his too close relations with Oliver Cromwell.[3] He later married Dorothy, widow of William Clarke, Secretary to the New Model Army. His poem, in Latin, is not insignificant.[4]

Milton's circle included several Fellows of the Royal Society – Henry Oldenburg, Abraham Hill, John Aubrey, John Winthrop Junior, in addition to Dryden and Haak.[5] Oldenburg, Secretary of the Society, friend of Lady Ranelagh and former tutor of her son, Richard Jones, Milton's pupil, was closely linked to Hartlib's group. He married Dury's daughter, and was arrested and imprisoned in 1667, the year of *Paradise Lost*'s publication.[6] Abraham Hill, merchant, another friend of Hartlib's who married Bulstrode Whitelocke's daughter, had been a friend of Milton's since the early fifties. He was reputed to retain republican senti-ments even after 1660.[7] The Earl of Anglesey, also a former friend of Hartlib's, was a 'constant visitor' to Milton.[8] Another friend was Milton's doctor Nathan Paget, whose library suggests radical leanings.[9]

Many of Milton's acquaintances suffered at the Restoration. Sir Henry Vane was executed. Robert Overton was arrested in 1663 and again in 1664. Fleetwood and Wentworth retired into obscurity. The former's step-daughter, Bridget, daughter of Henry Ireton and Bridget Cromwell, and her husband, Thomas Bendish, were 'in great intimacy' with Milton,

---

[1] I owe this information to Lois Schwoerer.
[2] Oliver, esp. pp. 148, 285–9.
[3] Routledge, p. 27; *Clarke Papers,* IV, pp. 274–6: Barrow's notes on Monck's problems, Decem-ber 1659 to April 1660.
[4] Wayman, pp. 336–42. For the poem see p. 401 below.
[5] Darbishire, pp. viii, xxxvi; Parker, pp. 1080, 1168.
[6] Oldenburg, III, pp. xxiii–xxviii.
[7] Darbishire, p. 14; Astle.
[8] Turnbull, pp. 28, 30; Darbishire, pp. 76, 186.
[9] See Appendix 3 below.

with whom they must often have discussed the past.[1] The regicide Isaac
Penington the elder died in prison in 1660. The younger Isaac was also in
prison from 1665 to 1668, a victim of the malice of the Earl of Bridgwater,
the Elder Brother in *Comus*.

Milton had often made friends of his pupils, and in his later years he
continued to draw young men around him – Andrew Marvell, Cyriack
Skinner, Edward Lawrence, Thomas Ellwood (when he was out of
prison), the egregious Samuel Parker, and Daniel Skinner, Cyriack's
nephew, to whom Milton apparently entrusted the manuscript of the
De Doctrina – unwisely, as it turned out. Daniel Skinner's sister Mary was
the unmarried second wife of Samuel Pepys for thirty years: it has been
conjectured that a principal reason for Pepys not regularizing his union
with her was the Skinner family's embarrassing connection with so
notorious a character as Milton – though Pepys owned a copy of Milton's
1645 *Poems* as well as of *Paradise Lost*.[2] George Thomason survived until
1666, but he and Milton diverged politically from the late forties. Other
printers and booksellers were friends including William Dugard, Edward
Millington.

II Politics regained

Throughout the whole of Milton's career we should be as aware as he was
of the existence of the censorship.[3] In the forties the press was freer than
under 'prelatical duncery', but Milton still thought *Areopagitica* necessary.
His reference in that pamphlet to 'the sad friends of truth, such as durst
appear' makes it clear that he appreciated the risks even then.[4] In 1652
he got into trouble over the *Racovian Catechism*. Many of his pamphlets
were unregistered. Always thought had to be taken. Milton's great
courage in seizing the moments of freedom – for example in the early
forties, in 1659–60 and in 1673–4 – makes us too easily forget that for more
than half his adult life a strict censorship prevailed; and that for half the
period in which censorship was non-existent (or was at least less strict) he
was in official employment and therefore not a totally free agent.

---

[1] Parker, pp. 1105, 1202.
[2] Ollard, pp. 212–13; cf. my review in the *New Statesman* for 27 September 1974. I owe Pepys's
possession of *Paradise Lost* to a letter from Mr. Ollard, who agrees that the Skinner connection
was probably the chief reason for the prudent Pepys not marrying Mary.
[3] See pp. 64–6 above, 405–9 below.
[4] *C.P.W.*, II, p. 549. Cf. Berkeley, p. 148, who fully recognizes the limitations under which
Milton wrote, and the need for constant vigilance on the reader's part. This adds greatly to the
value of his book.

To the censorship we must add Milton's political caution. Before 1649, for tactical reasons, he did not attack monarchy. In the fifties, anxious not to prejudice the cause in which he believed, he had to convey his doubts and anxieties about the trend of events indirectly. In 1659 and after, he wanted to avoid controversy among potential supporters of the Good Old Cause. Hence in *Of Civil Power* he discreetly addressed Richard's Parliament as 'Supreme Council', which could imply non-recognition of the Protectorate but did not proclaim it. (In *Hirelings* Milton's phrase for the restored Rump was 'Supreme Senate'.) In both tracts he reminded his readers of his credentials as the victor over Salmasius. Hence too Milton's choice of the phrase 'short but scandalous night of interruption' to greet the restored Rump.[1] This could refer to the whole period after April 1653; it could refer to Richard Cromwell's overthrow by the generals in May 1659; it could refer to Richard's succession to his father, which many at the time believed to be a put-up job. The ambiguity, I am sure, was intentional. As so often in the textual cruces of Milton, 'this very wily politician' was deliberately imprecise in the hope of offending as few enemies of monarchy as possible.[2]

Milton's sense of decorum is also relevant to considerations of the censorship. To have lost his ears rashly would have done neither him nor his cause any good. The ambiguities of *Comus* and *Lycidas* suggest caution, as did the very early stratagem of registering a political point by translating a Psalm in 1623. It is not surprising that in *Paradise Lost* the heresies of the *De Doctrina* are not flaunted: even to grasp its relevance to the English Revolution calls for very careful reading.

Archbishop Neile had wished to revive burning for anti-Trinitarians in 1639.[3] Thomas Hobbes was afraid after 1660 that the restored bishops might try to burn him. Some of them would no doubt have welcomed the chance. In 1676 Judge Rainsford expressed regret at being unable to sentence Lodowick Muggleton to death by burning.[4] Edmund Waller did not dare to praise Hobbes in print. Yet Hobbes was a friend and former tutor of the King, Waller a courtier and former Royalist. Milton by contrast was the most notorious defender of regicide to survive the holocaust of 1660–2, a marked man. Twenty-five years after his death a man was hanged for anti-Trinitarianism. Milton had demonstrated his

---

[1] *C.M.*, VI, p. 43; cf. p. 112.
[2] Wolfe makes this point (*Milton in the P.R.*, 1941, pp. 289–90, cf. p. 281); cf. p. 391 below; also Hunter (1965) pp. 252–9; Woolrych, pp. 209–11; *C.P.W.*, VII, pp. 86–7, 121. For other political concessions by Milton see above, pp. 83–4, 92, 150–1, 196–7, 201–3.
[3] See p. 288 below.
[4] Muggleton (1764), pp. 159, 165.

political courage: but after 1660 there was as little possibility of getting his heresies into print as his republicanism. Occasional hints are dropped in *Paradise Lost*, enough to make some early critics suspicious; but he deceived most of them. Milton's secret anti-Trinitarianism may be compared with that of Sir Isaac Newton (high priest of modern science, also secret Arian, alchemist, *magus*, busy calculating the date of the imminent end of the world on the basis of the Biblical prophetical books) and of John Locke (high priest of rational utilitarian ethics and politics, also secret anti-Trinitarian, mortalist, believer in sympathetic magic and the imminence of doomsday).[1]

In 1670, when Milton prepared his *History of Britain* for the press, he cut out the anti-Presbyterian references, 'out of tenderness to a party'.[2] Whatever his grudges against the Presbyterians, they too were now victims of the restored Royalists, and Milton was not going to give any comfort to that enemy. He still hoped to reunite the supporters of the revolutionary cause. Similar considerations may account for his admission in the *De Doctrina* that there are Biblical arguments for Calvinism. It need not imply reversion to the Calvinist beliefs of his earlier years: he went on making Arminian additions to the treatise.[3] Milton had considerable respect for Calvin's scholarship, even where he disagreed with him. But more important was a desire not to pick a quarrel with former enemies who were now potential allies. Milton very much preferred Presbyterians to Charles II's bishops. He was always a politician, and this influenced his tactical decisions again and again.[4]

After a long silence, in 1673 Milton thought it possible to resume prose pamphleteering. Charles II's Declaration of Indulgence of 1672 had opened up possibilities of toleration for Protestant dissenters, whilst at the same time it excited fears that its main aim was to secure toleration for Roman Catholics, for sinister political purposes. Until this date Milton had laid no special stress on hostility to popery: he took it for granted, and had more immediate enemies. Passages in *The History of Britain* 'wherein he exposed the superstition, pride and cunning of the popish monks in the Saxon times' were struck out by the censor in 1670 as a covert attack on Charles II's bishops.[5] By the sixteen-seventies it seemed quite possible that Charles might declare himself a papist – for political

---

[1] Cf. p. 295 below.
[2] *C.P.W.*, V, p. 440; cf. pp. 341, 407 below.
[3] See pp. 275–7 below.
[4] Cf. p. 461 below. My arguments in this paragraph seem to me probable, but they are hypotheses rather than proven conclusions.
[5] Darbishire, p. 185; *C.P.W.*, V, pp. 412–13.

reasons which Milton understood. Charles had close relations with Louis XIV, the personification of the union of popery with absolutism. Here was an international Catholic/absolutist menace, analogous to the régime of Laud and Henrietta Maria in the sixteen-thirties. Milton saw an issue on which it was possible for him to appear in print again.

In 1673 he published *Of True Religion, Heresy, Schism, Toleration*; *and what means may be used against the Growth of Popery*. 'The increase of popery is at this day no small trouble and offence to [the] greatest part of the nation', declared the opening sentence.[1] Milton's stated object was to unite all 'true protestants' against the national enemy. He even quoted the Thirty-nine Articles in an attempt to embrace Anglicans as well as dissenters in the alliance, and he seized the opportunity to plead for permission to publish freely 'in Latin, which the common people understand not: that what they hold may be discussed by the learned only'. He must have had in mind his *De Doctrina Christiana*. What is remarkable about *Of True Religion* is the daring breadth of its tolerance. Milton assumed that 'Anabaptists, Arians, Arminians and Socinians' are all Protestants, who should be tolerated equally with Lutherans and Calvinists. Rather surprisingly, Quakers are omitted from this list, in which Milton devoted more space to Arians and Socinians than to any other sect.[2]

Milton was not alone in using anti-popery for this purpose. William Dell had tried in 1667 to break his long silence by publishing a pamphlet entitled *The Increase of Popery in England*, but it was 'seized in the press', and did not appear until the greater liberty of 1681.[3] Meanwhile Marvell's much more substantial *Account of the Growth of Popery and Arbitrary Government in England* (1677) had elaborated (under cover of carefully preserved anonymity) on his friend Milton's theme of four years earlier. William Penn's *One Project for the Good of England* (1679) had the same aim of uniting English Protestants.[4]

Milton's last pamphlet purports to be a translation of *A Declaration or Letters-Patents for the Election* of John Sobieski as King of Poland in 1674. Milton's publication of this panegyric on a Roman Catholic king is less surprising than appears at first sight. Sobieski was an *elected* and patriotic monarch, who was to carry out a forceful foreign policy with great success. His military virtues and his respect for his coronation oath could

---

[1] *C.M.*, VI, p. 165. Cf. the opening sentence of Marvell's *Account of the Growth of Popery*.
[2] *C.M.*, VI, pp. 167–70, 178. For the *De Doctrina* see chapter 18 below.
[3] *C. and C.*, pp. 142–3. Cf. Peter Du Moulin's *England's Appeal* (1673).
[4] Cf. McKeon, chapter 4, for some sensible observations on the uses of anti-popery to reunite opponents of Charles II's government.

be agreeably contrasted with Charles II without actually naming the latter. The contrast was underlined, contemporary readers would know, by the fact that in 1672 a statue of Charles II had been erected in London which was said to be an adaptation of a statue of Sobieski. The King was represented on horse-back, trampling on a Turk. Poems attributed to Marvell (possibly) and Rochester (improbably) were witty at the expense of this statue:[1] it was left to Milton to make more serious political capital out of the event. For three centuries scholars could find no original of *Letters-Patents*; it seemed possible that Milton wrote it himself as an elaborate hoax. But I am told that the original has now turned up in the Ossolineum Library, Wroclaw, Poland.[2]

Neither Dell, Marvell, Penn nor Milton had seen the popish danger as a main issue during the Revolution; but the political advantages of attacking Stuart absolutist aspirations through traditional popular hostility to popery seemed clear to all of them. It was partly a political gambit: a way of breaking the silence which had been imposed on the revolutionaries since 1660. But it also expressed a genuine anxiety, based on the realities of the policies of Charles II and Louis XIV: the later revisions of the *De Doctrina* show 'a continued and increasing anti-Catholicism'.[3] We may perhaps gain some sense of the political atmosphere of this period from a story told by Daniel Defoe, son of a London tallow-chandler. In the early or mid-seventies he, 'then but a boy, worked like a horse' at copying the Bible into shorthand, 'lest when Popery came in we should be prohibited the use of it'. He 'wrote out the whole Pentateuch, and then was so tired I was willing to run the risk of the rest'.[4] That was written from the security of the early eighteenth century, but it gives us an inkling of what men must have felt. John Aubrey at the same time was wondering 'how strongly the Church of England stands' and asking 'what if the Roman religion should come in again' as 'the King of France grows stronger and stronger'.[5] Even the tragic farce of the Popish Plot did not destroy the appeal of anti-popery as a slogan: James II's folly kept it alive, and 1688 showed how strong a motivating force it was. We look at Catholic

---

[1] Marvell (1927), I, pp. 300–3; Rochester (1968), p. 225, where the poem is attributed to John Freke; cf. *W.T.U.D.*, pp. 399–400; Radzinowicz, *passim*. I labour this point a little, because neither French nor Parker could think of any reason for Milton's translating this tract except that he needed money. That may have been part of the explanation; I cannot accept it as the sole reason. Cf. Rochester (1953), p. 210. I am grateful to Professor L. R. Lewitter for help with this question, though he must not be held responsible for my conclusions.

[2] Information very kindly supplied by Professor Maurice Kelley.

[3] Kelley (1962), p. 70.

[4] Shinagal, p. 7.

[5] Powell, pp. 148, 167.

Emancipation from the perspective of the nineteenth century, when there was no longer any danger of Catholic absolutism in England or of the imposition of an alien régime through a French or Irish invasion supported by an internal fifth column. We associate anti-Catholicism with English repression in Ireland. But we should not read such attitudes back into the age of Milton and Locke.

In consequence of the Restoration Milton lost savings of £2,000. He is also, less certainly, said to have lost church lands worth £60 a year. Further losses came in 1666, when his only piece of real estate, the house in Bread St., was burnt down in the Great Fire. This came at a time when his needs as a blind man and the father of young daughters, whom he apprenticed and boarded out, must have been at their greatest. Although Milton and his earlier biographers cover up carefully, there seems little doubt that he was at least pinched, if not in real poverty. He sold his books, which now he could read only by proxy, and after *Paradise Lost* had revived his literary reputation he published every scrap of writing which he could hope to get past the censor. One way in which he refused to make money was by writing for the royal cause. Nevertheless he managed to keep out of political trouble. It is surprising that there is no record of his having been presented for non-attendance at church after 1660. Is this to be explained by his blindness, by friends in high places, by sympathetic church-wardens, or by a general breakdown of ecclesiastical discipline in London?

Poor he may have been, but all accounts of Milton in old age stress serenity, the blind man going for walks with Mr. Millington the book-seller, or courteously receiving distinguished visitors. His daughters had left him by now. His third marriage to the red-headed Betty seems to have brought him contentment. The last work he published was *Epistolae Familiares*. To this, as to *The Art of Logic* of the previous year, he proudly and audaciously put the name of Joannes Miltonus, Anglus – the name which had reverberated through Europe and terrified Salmasius less than a quarter of a century earlier, and which Milton hoped would be heard with even greater power when the *De Doctrina Christiana* was published. He was still fighting.

Ironically, for a man whose life is very fully documented, the exact date of Milton's death is uncertain. November 8, 1674 is generally accepted, but it may have occurred at any time during the week following that date. He died 'with so little pain or emotion that the time of his expiring was not perceived by those in the room'.[1]

---

[1] Darbishire, p. 33.

Chapter 17

Milton's Reputation

> Even they 'gainst whom he writ
> Could not but admire his wit. . . .
> More known his learning was not than admired.
> > Thomas Ellwood, *Epitaph on Milton*

A theme of this book has been that the nature of Milton's contemporary reputation has been misunderstood, and therefore that it has seemed less significant than in fact it was. The radicals thought as highly of his writings as conservatives deplored them. I listed above those who attacked Milton's views on divorce.[1] This roll-call of the orthodox and the respectable in the England of the sixteen-forties hardly confirms Milton's view that his pamphlets were greeted by a conspiracy of silence, even if he was right to believe that they were never confuted. We should also add those who attacked his earlier anti-prelatical tracts – 'Peloni Almoni' in 1642, Thomas Fuller and Bishop Bramhall in 1643, Bishop Hacket in the sixteen-fifties.

More interesting for our purposes are those who praised Milton or cited him. These were mainly radicals. As early as 1642 Lord Brooke was echoing him. The Erastian clergyman Thomas Coleman quoted *Of Reformation* with approval in the pulpit in 1643.[2] Henry Robinson alluded to the divorce pamphlets, and Mrs. Attaway, as we saw, was impressed by their argument.[3] There were other approving references, though few stuck their necks out by agreeing with Milton on this subject in print. But by 1644 his style, he claims, 'was known by most men'.[4] The *Doctrine and Discipline of Divorce* sold quickly, going through four editions in two years.

---

[1] See pp. 130–1 above.
[2] Fixler, p. 119.
[3] *C.P.W.*, II, p. 142; cf. p. 131–2 above.
[4] *C.P.W.*, II, p. 434.

In 1656 all the divorce tracts were reprinted again: the *Apology* and *Reason of Church Government* had been reissued in 1654, *Of Education* in 1653. In 1658 William London's list of 'the most vendible books', whose object was to bring culture to the north of England, contained *Of Reformation* and seven others of Milton's writings. John Wilkins mentioned Milton on divorce in his *Ecclesiastes* (1647). The reference is neutral: yet twenty years later, when the Puritan divine had become a bishop as well as having been Secretary of the Royal Society, Wilkins defied the hostility of most of his episcopal colleagues to speak in the House of Lords in favour of divorce.[1] Wilkins, Cromwell's brother-in-law, may well have met Milton; he might have come across him through the Hartlib circle or through Oldenburg. If it is true that Milton was consulted in 1670 about the possibility of a divorce for Charles II, it may well have been Wilkins – very influential at the time – who suggested him. It may be significant that *Tetrachordon* was on sale again in 1671.

In 1644 the Independent Henry Burton rejected 'divorce at pleasure', but argued against suppression of such views. Richard Overton seems to have read *The Doctrine and Discipline of Divorce*; *Areopagitica* influenced Lilburne, Walwyn and other Leveller leaders: Hezekiah Woodward alluded to it in 1644.[2] Gilbert Mabbott, editor of the Leveller newspaper, *The Moderate,* quoted its arguments when resigning his job as licenser in 1649. Echoes of *Areopagitica* are also to be heard in 1649 in the *Humble Motion* of the reformer John Hall (of Hartlib's group),[3] as well as in *The Vanity of the Craft of Physick* (1651) by the medical reformer Noah Biggs; possibly also in John Saltmarsh's *Dawnings of Light* (1645) and *Sparkles of Glory* (1647), in John Fry's *The Clergy in their Colours* (1650), in the mortalist Agricola Carpenter, in William Dell and John Goodwin.[4] Fuller, whether consciously or not, echoed *Areopagitica* on the indestructibility of truth. He can hardly have been unaware of his indebtedness to Milton when he stole one of his best jokes.[5] Walter Strickland may have recalled *Areopagitica* when during the Nayler debate in Parliament in 1656 he said 'where most power of the gospel, most prodigies of heresies and opinions'.[6] Clement Writer, whom Richard Baxter regarded as an infidel,

---

[1] Ludlow, II, p. 503.
[2] *C.P.W.*, II, pp. 143, 506.
[3] See pp. 147–8 above.
[4] Hall, *op. cit.*, pp. 28–9; Biggs, *op. cit.*, Sig. a 4; *C.P.W.*, II, pp. 87, 91–2, 209, 359, 506, 545–6; Wolfe (*Milton in the P.R.*, 1941), pp. 129–30; Carpenter, pp. i, 22, 24; Dell, pp. 212, 298. For Fry see pp. 290–5 below.
[5] Fuller (1842), I, p. 438, II, pp. 188–9; *C.P.W.*, I, p. 718 – *Animadversions*.
[6] T. Burton, I, p. 88.

repeated *Areopagitica*'s arguments against suppression of opinions.[1] Even
a foreigner like Christopher Arnold praised it in 1651.

One possible ground for the lack of specific criticisms of *Areopagitica* is
that its thesis was not original: Milton was only applying to books and
printing general arguments which had been put forward earlier, if less
eloquently, by Henry Robinson, John Goodwin, Roger Williams and
William Walwyn. There was thus no special incentive to single Milton out
for attack.[2] We happen to know that Elizabeth, Queen of Bohemia,
possessed a complete set of Milton's pamphlets published between 1641
and 1645; we do not know whether he presented them to her or not.[3]

From 1649 onwards there is less doubt about Milton's influence. John
Goodwin's *Obstructours of Justice* makes frequent acknowledgment to *The
Tenure*. Goodwin has many links with Milton – as an Arminian, a tolerationist, an exponent of the covenant of grace, an anti-Trinitarian. Contemporaries often associated them; and in 1660 *The Obstructours of Justice*
was called in for burning together with *Eikonoklastes* and the *Defence of the
People of England*. There are close parallels between *The Tenure* and John
Canne's *The Golden Rule*, published a few days after Milton's treatise,
which may suggest contact between the two men during writing.[4] Later in
the same year, *The Discoverer* (attributed to Canne or John Hall) echoed
and praised *The Tenure*. Clement Walker mentioned *The Tenure* less favourably, as did Claude Barthelemy Morisot (together with *Eikonoklastes*) in
1652. In the same year Sir Robert Filmer criticized it courteously and
respectfully. In 1650 George Wither had praised it.[5] It was quoted by
N.W., 'a friend to the Commonwealth' in his *Discourse concerning the
Engagement* of 1650. It may be echoed in another pamphlet resulting from
the *Engagement* controversy, T.B.'s *The Engagement Vindicated*.[6] Some time
in the sixteen-fifties the future Bishop Hacket attacked Milton's divorce
pamphlets, his defence of regicide and his disrespect for the Fathers of the
church. He hoped to see him 'fall into the hands of the avenger of blood'.[7]

Eikonoklastes was favourably noticed in *A Briefe Relation of Some Affairs*
(November 1649), and in other periodicals. Roger Williams recommended
it. Ephraim Elcock, Sir John Berkenhead and J. Drew in 1651, Thomas

[1] [Writer], pp. 80–4.
[2] Haller (1927), pp. 875–900.
[3] Cf. L. Miller (1974), pp. 100–1, 315. For Elizabeth see p. 33 above.
[4] *C.P.W.*, III, p. 56; G. W. Whiting, pp. 311–23. Cf. Baillie (1775), II, p. 442.
[5] *C.P.W.*, III, pp. 122, 125, 128. *Respublica Anglicana* is not attributed to Wither by French or
    Parker.
[6] N.W., *op. cit.*, p. 5; T.B., *op. cit.* (1650), p. 6.
[7] Hacket, III, pp. 161–2.

Manley and J.P. (just possibly John Phillips) in 1652, can be added to the list of those mentioning Milton. Nedham's *Mercurius Politicus* predictably praised the *Defence of the People of England*, in which David overthrew Goliath. Less predictably, William Lilly, the radicals' favourite astrologer, spoke well of Milton in *Monarchy or no Monarchy in England* (1651). Henry Stubbe, Sir Henry Vane's protégé, in 1657 cited 'the excellent Mr. Milton' as 'the glory of our English nation'.[1] Thomas Collier echoed him in 1659.[2] So possibly did Vane himself, and Henry Power. Harrington thought *The Likeliest Means* worth answering.[3] Even when attacking Milton in 1660, the Royalist G.S. admitted that *The Ready and Easy Way* was 'received by many with applause'. There are other scattered references in French and Parker. Walter Cradock may have possessed some of Milton's books, and appears to quote *Areopagitica*: Lazarus Seaman owned *Areopagitica, The Tenure* and two of the anti-episcopal tracts.[4]

The great majority of these names come from the left, left-centre and extreme left wing of the revolutionaries. John Bradshaw, President of the Court which sentenced Charles I, spoke of 'the excellent Mr. John Milton', when he left him £10 in his will; Milton in return praised him in the *Second Defence of the People of England*.[5] Sir Peter Wentworth, member of the Rump's Council of State, left him £100. Lilburne went out of his way to praise Milton (as well as George Wither and Marchamont Nedham) in 1652, noticing with approval Milton's 'excellent and faithful advice . . . to his masters' in the *Defence of the People of England*.[6] The ex-Agitator Edward Sexby also referred favourably to Milton in his *Killing No Murder* (1657).

Even more significant is the company Milton was believed by his enemies to keep. Daniel Featley and Ephraim Pagitt associated him with R.O., the author of *Mans Mortalitie*, and with Roger Williams, author of *The Bloudy Tenent* (1644), both regarded as wildly radical. The Presbyterian divines, in a concerted campaign in August 1644, preached to Parliament against Williams, John Goodwin, Clement Writer, Hanserd Knollys the Baptist, Giles Randall the Seeker, and Milton. In December the manifesto of Sion College linked Milton with R.O., Roger Williams, John Goodwin, Walwyn, Randall, Clarkson, John Bidle, Paul Best, Paul Hobson, William

---

[1] For further possible links between Stubbe and Milton, see *C.P.W.*, VII, pp. 55, 82, 128.
[2] *C.P.W.*, VII, p. 55. See also *W.T.U.D.*, pp. 363, 395.
[3] See *W.T.U.D.*, p. 363; *C.P.W.*, VII, Appendix.
[4] G.S., p. 5; Nuttall (1967), p. 127; *Catalogus . . . Librorum . . . Lazari Seaman* (1676), pp. 52, 63.
[5] *C.P.W.*, IV, pp. 637–9.
[6] Wolfe, (*M.L.N.*, 1941), pp. 360–3. Wolfe speaks of 'a closer ideological and perhaps personal bond with the Levellers than scholars have hitherto assumed'.

Erbery, John Saltmarsh, Thomas Webbe – a goodly collection of anti-Trinitarians, Levellers, Ranters. Cuthbert Sydenham in 1649 alluded to Milton in a pamphlet attacking the Levellers. Clement Walker, more simply, lumped Milton with John of Leyden, Familists and libertines. Richard Leigh associated him with Aretine and Martin Marprelate. An anonymous writer of 1660 attributed a tract to Milton on the grounds that 'it runs foul, tends to tumult'.[1]

Parker (for whom 'the word "radical" has an ugly sound') remarked with some distaste that Milton's reputation among his contemporaries was that of a rabble-rouser.[2] He was associated by one of his earliest opponents with the 'mutinous rabble', 'the very beasts of the people'. In *Of Reformation* the poet made the obvious retort: 'We must not run, they say, into sudden extremes': we must hold the balance equal between vice and virtue, truth and falsehood.[3] *The Censure of the Rota* in 1660 declared that Milton's tracts were 'written to the elevation of the rabble'. He was described as 'the diabolical rebel Milton' in the title of a pamphlet in the same year, and as a libertine in 1649, 1660 and 1677.[4] It was the Royalist poetaster Christopher Wasse who in 1649 coined the word 'Miltonist'; but Edwards and Pagitt had already claimed Milton as of the sect of the divorcers, and *The Censure of the Rota* called him the 'founder of a sect'. In a technical sense they were wrong, so far as we know. But they were right in stressing his influence over a group of 'Miltonists'. One wonders how many of his contemporaries received the honour of '-ist' after their names in their lifetimes. 'Vanist' appears in 1658, 'Muggletonian' in 1670.[5]

Interestingly enough, Milton's 'learning' was especially emphasized by the radicals: learning was not often to be found in the circles in which Milton was most admired. On this point William Burton, the astrologer William Lilly, the Leveller John Lilburne, the Agitator Edward Sexby, Sir Peter Wentworth, George Sikes (biographer of Sir Henry Vane), Thomas Ellwood, Andrew Marvell, the anonymous author of *The Life and Reigne of King Charls: or, The Pseudo-Martyr Discovered* (1651) ('a gent. of

---

[1] Masson, III, pp. 301, 165, 677–8; IV, p. 156; V, p. 665; Pagitt, Sig. B 3v; Haller (1955), p. 343; Wolfe (*Milton in the P.R.*, 1941), p. 444; Leigh (1673), pp. 55, 136–7.

[2] W. R. Parker (1937), p. xii; (1940), pp. 50, 58. In his biography Parker even added the epithet 'crackpot' (p. 559).   [3] *C.P.W.*, I, pp. 204, 601.

[4] See p. 109 above. For Milton's own attempts to suppress his radical reputation, see pp. 451–2 below.

[5] These are *Oxford English Dictionary* dates. As the earliest example of 'Miltonist' in the *O.E.D.* is 1806, 157 years too late, that great work is clearly not infallible. 'Vanist' in 1658 is from Richard Baxter: 'Baxterian' appears in 1680 (Baxter, Everyman, pp. xx, 73), though the *O.E.D.*'s earliest example is 1835. 'Foxian' from George Fox is dated 1823; the *O.E.D.* gives no example of 'Lambertonian', though I am fairly confident that I have seen the word used in the seventeenth century. See also W. R. Parker (1940), pp. 75–83.

such abilities as gives place to none for his integrity, learning and judgment') are at one with the Royalist G.S. and the German Peter Heimbach. The publisher of Milton's *Poems* in 1645 stressed the poet's learning. When *Milton's Republican Letters* were published in 1682 they were described as by 'the learned John Milton'. His earliest biographer used the same adjective.[1]

Milton's foreign public in the sixteen-fifties is less disputable than his English public in the forties. The seventeen editions of the *Defensio* speak for themselves.[2] We are told that *Eikonoklastes* was popular among French Protestants; that the *Defensio* was enthusiastically received in the Netherlands and in France.[3] Milton's own claims about the extent of his audience do not seem to have been exaggerated. In Sweden the Mayor of Köping told the English Ambassador in 1653 that 'he had read Milton's book and liked it, and had it at home'; Queen Christina 'highly commended' it.[4] By 1652 at least three German theses had been published attacking Milton's work; two of them were reprinted in 1657, with parts of a fourth thesis. The *Defensio* was condemned to be burnt at Toulouse and Paris in 1651; in 1653 the Diet of Ratisbon ordered 'all the books of Milton' to be confiscated. When in 1654 the prophet Arise Evans said that his books were 'translated into all languages, and are so famous that I am troubled to answer men that come from Turkey, from Italy, from Germany, yea from all parts of the world', I suspect that he was deliberately emulating Milton, whom he had attacked the year before.[5] In a well-known passage Aubrey tells us that Cromwell and Milton were the main sights which foreigners wished to see in England. There is plenty of evidence for such visits to Milton from 1651 onwards. They did not altogether stop even after 1660.[6] In 1663 the French Ambassador assured Louis XIV that the lead in the arts and sciences had now passed to France from England: Bacon, More, Buchanan and Milton were only a memory in England. So far as Milton was concerned, this anticipated slightly.

In 1644 *An Answer to the Doctrine and Discipline of Divorce* admitted that Milton's pamphlet was 'commended' for its 'fine language'. Joseph Hall reluctantly praised the 'too well-penned pages' of the divorce tracts. In his Introduction to Boehme's *The Teutonick Philosophie* (1650) Charles Hotham said: 'It's very hard to write good English, and few have attained it in this

---

[1] Darbishire, p. 18.
[2] *C.P.W.*, IV, p. 140.
[3] French, II, pp. 284, 340; III, pp. 15–16, 25, and *passim*.
[4] Whitelocke, I, pp. 203, 417, 439–40.
[5] *C. and C.*, pp. 71–2.
[6] Aubrey, II, p. 72; L. Miller (1974), pp. 70–9, 285. See this book *passim* for Milton's reputation outside England.

last fry of books but Mr. Milton.'[1] Hamon L'Estrange contributed in 1651 to the chorus of praise from the ranks of Tuscany. And G.S., whilst attacking the blind poet, was constrained to admit his awareness of 'the ability of Mr. Milton'. He praised the 'shrewd wit', 'ready invention', 'satirical pen', 'fluent and elegant style', which made him 'universally owned a learned man'; his language was 'smooth and tempting', apt 'to move the affections'. Milton lacked 'nothing on his side but truth'.[2] After the Restoration the younger Peter Du Moulin also commended Milton's 'fluent and florid style'. Peter Barwick, writing in the sixteen-seventies, called him 'a very good advocate for a very bad cause'. Charles Blount cited him as 'a late ingenious historian' against Milton's nephew Edward Phillips.[3]

Milton's poetic reputation was not negligible even before the publication of *Paradise Lost*. Francis Quarles may have expected his readers to recognize the echo of Milton when he asked 'But ah! what boots it to be wise or good?' in 1641. Milton was also echoed by George Daniel in 1645, by Benlowes (1646–52), by Marvell, perhaps by Henry Vaughan.[4] In 1647 and 1650 he was plagiarized by Robert Baron. We do not know whether John Chalkhill's *Thealma and Clearchus* (published 1683, but written earlier) echoes *Lycidas* or is echoed by it.[5] In 1657 Milton was extensively quoted by Joshua Poole in his posthumous *English Parnassus, or, a Help to English Poesie*, as an exemplar of English poetry. The Hobson poems were reprinted in *A Banquet of Jests* (1640, 1657), *Wits Recreations* (1640) and *Wit Restor'd* (1658). Peter Sterry, often associated with Milton in the affairs of the Protectorate, copied out the first seven lines of 'At a Solemn Musick' during his Cambridge days, perhaps in 1637; William Sancroft, the later Archbishop, copied out the whole of the *Nativity Ode* and Milton's paraphrase of Psalm 136, in or after 1646.

So I find it difficult to agree with Parker's conclusion that Milton was not well thought of by his contemporaries; still less that Milton's reputation has been magnified by looking through the wrong end of the telescope, because posterity happened to accept most of 'the brave futile words, the challenging ideas, that his own contemporaries had ignored'.[6] Parker

---

[1] See p. 33 above.
[2] G.S., Sig. a 2, pp. 2, 5.
[3] Barwick, p. 16on.; *C.P.W.*, V, p. xxxv.
[4] Quarles (1960), p. 36; Daniel, p. 75 (echoing *Il Penseroso*); Saintsbury, I, p. 372, etc. (Benlowes, 'an individual kiss'); Jenkins, pp. 163–4, 309–13; cf. Marvell (1927), *passim*.
[5] Saintsbury, II, p. 409; George Rust (Fellow of Christ's, 1649–59, later a bishop), quoted 'New presbyter is but old priest' in 1663 – *before* it had been published.
[6] W. R. Parker (1940), pp. 52–5.

looked in the wrong places for Milton's contemporary reputation. It was in Hartlib's circle, among reformers of the universities like John Hall, reformers of medicine like Noah Biggs, 'infidel' Biblical critics like Clement Writer, among Levellers and Behmenists, and radical political thinkers like John Goodwin, that Milton found his fame and influence. I am sure that an intensive search in sources of this kind will produce much more evidence. Fortunately French's *Life Records* corrected some of Parker's omissions, though even that voluminous source-book is far from complete. If we consider how many of Milton's early pamphlets were signed only by his initials – and there were many J.Ms. about – the speed with which he was acknowledged becomes the more remarkable. We recall that the censorship which influenced him not to sign his full name was 'a reproach' to the common people.

There is plenty of evidence for Milton's political reputation after the Restoration, over and above the burning of his books.[1] Now that the poet could not answer back, a multitude of hostile references to him appeared. His reputation as a ferocious polemicist may previously have deterred critics. His enemies clearly regarded him as one of the most dangerous spokesmen of the views they dreaded, and which they believed still had much popular support.[2] Yet there was some grudging admiration. George Bate attacked Milton's 'malicious wit'. Hobbes, Samuel Butler and John Eachard all praised Milton's latinity at the expense of his political views. Butler said that Milton had

> been admired by all the learned
> Of knaves concerned and pedants unconcerned.

Eachard admitted that the poet was 'a great wit and scholar' though 'a man of very vile principles'. Samuel Parker agreed that *Areopagitica* 'passed for stately wit and sense' in the revolutionary age. Another writer in 1675 believed that Milton had said more for toleration 'in two elegant sheets of *True Religion, Heresy and Schism* than all the prelates can refute in seven years'. Robert South thought him worth attacking.[3] The Catholic William Blundell complained in May 1673 that 'when the bloody deed was done, Milton and sundry others by writing (and others by the sword) defended it as just. Yet Milton and those are pardoned and live in security.'[4]

---

[1] See pp. 207–8 above.
[2] Sensabaugh, pp. 30–51.
[3] Parker, pp. 582, 628–31, 1144; Eachard, p. 104.
[4] Gibson, p. 33. Sir Peter Leicester referred to *Eikonoklastes* in 1670 as 'a base book'. He did not comment on *The History of Britain* which he also possessed (Leicester, pp. 120, 140).

After the official burning of *Eikonoklastes* and the *Defence of the People of England* in 1660, we are told that many private holocausts were perpetrated by 'high church priests, . . . well warmed with strong beer'. In 1683 the University of Oxford burnt books by Milton together with those of Knox, Buchanan, John Goodwin, John Owen, Baxter, Hobbes and (ironically) Samuel Rutherford – though the Bodleian Library did not sacrifice its presentation copy of *Eikonoklastes*.[1] In the same year James Parkinson was ejected from his fellowship at Lincoln College for recommending Milton's political writings to his pupils. It was at the dissenting academies that Milton's books were both popular and recommended.[2]

Milton's *Republican Letters* were printed in 1682 (probably overseas). *Letters of State* were placed on the papal Index in 1694. *Paradise Lost* was not so honoured until 1732. The *Defence of the People of England* – plagiarized in *Julian the Apostate* (1682) – contributed to the Rye House Plot. But it was especially after 1688 that his political writings came into their own with the radical Whigs.[3] Charles Blount in 1693 published two pamphlets largely composed of unacknowledged passages from *Areopagitica*. In 1694 James Quin, 'a melancholy gent., very learned and pious', told Evelyn (of all people) that Milton was 'the greatest man that ever rose in civil poetry, nor know I any greater in prose'.[4] At the beginning of George III's reign a Quaker even presented the King with Milton's tract against hirelings. Milton played a part in the American and French Revolutions, thanks in the latter case to Mirabeau's translation of *Areopagitica*. A Russian translation of *Paradise Lost* was one of the most popular books with the rank-and-file soldiers in the Russian army in 1905, and among the peasantry generally, although it was not allowed in school libraries.[5]

---

[1] Parker, pp. 661, 1086.
[2] See p. 149 above.
[3] Sensabaugh, *passim*.
[4] Quin to Evelyn, 28 March 1964 (Bray, III, p. 338); Evelyn, V, p. 170. In 1666 Evelyn named Milton as an advocate of tyrannicide and a defender of the English regicide (*ibid.*, III, p. 365).
[5] Baring, pp. 17–18, 253–5. See pp. 468–9 below.

PART V

MILTON'S CHRISTIAN DOCTRINE

> If I were to say that I had focused my studies principally upon Christian doctrine because nothing else can so effectually wipe away those two repulsive afflictions, tyranny and superstition, from human life and the human mind, I should show that I had been concerned not for religion but for life's well-being.[1]
>
> Milton, *Of Christian Doctrine*
>
> It is ... deplorable that literary students should be required to ... devote any large part of their time to solemn study of Milton's 'thought'.
>
> F. R. Leavis, 'Mr. Eliot and Milton'

---

[1] Cf. *C.P.W.*, IV, p. 535. Milton gave as an additional reason here the necessity for every man to work out his own beliefs for himself.

Chapter 18

Theology and Logic

> To guide nations in the way of truth
> By saving doctrine, and from error lead
> To know, and knowing worship God aright.
>
> Milton, *Paradise Regained*. II. 473–5

I   *Of Christian Doctrine*

We do not know exactly when Milton began to compile what became his 'dearest and best possession', the *De Doctrina Christiana*.[1] From at least the late sixteen-thirties he kept a commonplace book, and he seems to have started making a theological index at about the same time. It may have been the divorce controversy, and Milton's outrage at the reception of his views, that led him to contemplate a full-dress theological treatise – in the first instance perhaps for his own satisfaction only. Or it may have been the vicious attacks of Edwards and his like, lumping Milton together with extreme radical heretics, that made him want to sort out his own position. Or perhaps Milton – ever ambitious – was stimulated by the failure of the Westminster Assembly of Divines to produce an agreed theological system based on the Word of God. Every Protestant would accept that the Bible must be the exclusive source for such a system. The years 1645–9 were ones in which Milton published nothing. For all these reasons it seems a likely guess that in the second half of the forties he was beginning to construct his own theology.

Milton started with orthodox treatises as his groundwork – those of William Ames, formerly of Christ's College, and of Wollebius, a Professor of Theology at Basel who had died in 1629. But Milton steadily built up a tremendous array of proof texts – far more than any of his sources. This vast labour must have begun well before he lost his sight; but the blind

---

[1] *C.P.W.*, VI, p. 121. Cf. pp. 125, 165 above.

man went on checking and re-checking, adding and amending, as long as
he lived. Milton still hoped that it would be possible to publish his
treatise as an offering to the Protestant churches, which would place their
theology on a new, sounder and more inclusive basis. 'The citadel of
reformed religion', he thought, 'was adequately fortified against the
Papists.' But Protestant doctrine itself still needed reform.[1] By 1658
Milton could announce that he was 'hoping and planning still greater
things' than the *Defence of the People of England*, for 'all Christian men . . .
of every land'. No work other than the *De Doctrina* answers to that
description. Like the three *Defences*, it was signed John Milton, Englishman.[2] In February 1659 he suggested that he intended to write 'more some
other time' about the validity of the Mosaic law; by August he could hint
that 'somewhere or other . . . may be found some wholesome body of
divinity, as they call it, without school terms and metaphysical notions.'[3]

So long as Cromwell lived, schemes for Protestant reunion were still
being sponsored. Milton wrote his treatise in Latin, the language in
which he had attacked Salmasius before an international public. If *The
Ready and Easy Way* represented the dying words of liberty in England, the
De Doctrina was the legacy of free England to the Protestant world, all
that could be salvaged from the wreckage of God's cause in the chosen
nation. In the passage from *Paradise Regained* cited as epigraph to this
chapter, Milton made the Son of God say that educating peoples is much
more admirable than exercising political power (*P.R.* II. 473–80).

The sheer vastness and gravity of this enterprise, on top of everything
else Milton was doing, are staggering. He had to get his theology right
before he could write his epic. Once launched, the *De Doctrina* had to be
continually amended and improved as Milton's ideas developed. The
treatise had reached a relatively final form before *Paradise Lost* was
completed. Including the Preface, the whole was copied out fair and fully
prepared for the press, perhaps before the Restoration made publication
in England impossible, and publication abroad too dangerous for a man
who had just escaped a traitor's death. Milton waited for better days. He
may have thought they had come in the early seventies, when he had a
fresh transcript made.[4] Those who affect surprise at his failure to publish
the *De Doctrina*, and suggest that this shows he was dissatisfied with his

---

[1] *C.P.W.*, VI, pp. 120–1.
[2] *Ibid.*, IV, p. 537; VI, p. 117. Parker thought the *De Doctrina* was begun in 1656, completed
in 1658–60, before *Paradise Lost* (pp. 496, 1056–7).
[3] *C.M.*, VI, pp. 40, 78.
[4] Parker, p. 610; see p. 218 above.

'dearest and best possession', are either disingenuous, or very ill-informed, or both. The vigorous steps which Charles II's government took to prevent the treatise's publication in 1676–7[1] show how impossible it would have been in the sixteen-sixties for Milton – lucky not to be hanged, drawn and quartered – to have published anything so relevantly seditious.

This explanation of the apparent divergence between the *De Doctrina* and *Paradise Lost* is far more simple and satisfactory than elaborate theories about possible changes of Milton's mind which cannot be demonstrated and which ignore the fact that he was still working on his treatise in the sixteen-seventies.[2]

The *De Doctrina* is built up on the card-index system well-known to modern scholars. Collect as many references as you can; put them together in some sort of logical order, and try to make sense of them. If they appear to contradict one another, or not to point in the same direction, use normal scholarly techniques to decide which texts are of less authority than others, or may be interpreted to fit the rest. Since in this case the sources are by definition infallible, the task of accommodation becomes especially important but also especially delicate. Respect for the text must dominate even if it leads to unexpected or unpopular conclusions. Milton defends his heresies about creation and the death of the soul by close textual argument. No doubt his doctrine of the subordination of women was temperamentally congenial as well as generally accepted: but given his attitude to the Bible it would have been difficult to have avoided it. Those who did – Quakers, for instance – went a good deal further than Milton in asserting the superiority of the spirit in man over the letter of the Bible. They were on occasion contemptuous of the mere letter when it proved inconvenient. Milton never went further than to say that the Bible must be interpreted in the light of everything that we know about God's purposes.

The *De Doctrina* is the theological foundation on which *Paradise Lost* rests; but it is also Milton's testament to humanity. Since it was never published, we may assume that in it he made no concessions to the censor. But it must also be related to the time of its composition. The treatise is (among other things) about the problems of post-revolutionary England no less than is *Paradise Lost*. To illustrate: the Preface eloquently denounces 'those two repulsive afflictions, tyranny and superstition', and pleads for 'free discussion and enquiry', including the right to publish.[3] It proclaims the right and duty of resistance to tyranny: the Revolution is still justified.

---

[1] *C.P.W.*, VI, p. 37.
[2] See pp. 355–6 below.
[3] *C.P.W.*, VI, pp. 118, 121–2.

Its failure was the consequence of disobedience to God. 'A passage which politicians should read over and over again' is Deuteronomy 28, in which national prosperity and national power are described as dependent on diligent and joyful obedience to God. Otherwise 'the Lord shall bring thee into Egypt again . . . and there ye shall be sold unto your enemies for bondmen and bondwomen, and no man shall buy you.' 'God often hardens the hearts of powerful and arrogant world-leaders', through pride. As in *Paradise Lost*, pride is an essential cause of human failure to co-operate with God's purposes. The treatise also denounces false estimates of one's own wisdom.[1]

In the *De Doctrina* as in *Paradise Lost* Milton is determined to face the worst and make sense of it. He quotes God's words in Exodus 8:17: 'I have come down from that place to liberate them . . . and to lead them out into a good land.' 'In fact', Milton adds drily, 'they perished in the desert.' God's decrees are always conditional on man's freedom of action: he wills the good, but men may refuse to co-operate. The essential point is human responsibility. Men cannot blame God if they freely choose to fall. And if adversity comes – then they must analyse and learn from their mistakes. Milton applies this specifically to national failings. Quoting Jeremiah 18:9–10, he comments: 'in other words, I [God] shall reverse my decree because that nation did not keep the condition upon which the decree depended. Here we have a rule given by God himself!' Only so can we avoid concluding that God contradicts himself or is liable to arbitrary changes of intention. Men are free even to betray God.[2] In 1654 Milton had given warning: 'the nation which cannot rule and govern itself, but has delivered itself into slavery to its own lusts, is enslaved also to other masters whom it does not choose, and serves not only voluntarily but against its will.'[3] So human freedom, always so important for Milton, is necessary to exonerate God from responsibility for evil.

Milton cites many Biblical texts in favour of constancy in face of blighted hopes. 'In all this Job did not sin or attribute foolishness to God' (Job 1:22); 'the man who believes will not be in too much of a hurry' (Isaiah 28:16); 'he puts his mouth in the dust and says "Perhaps there is hope"' (Lamentations 3:29). Often punishment is the necessary cause of repentance. 'It is good for me, Jehovah, that you have humiliated me, so that I might know your ways' (Psalms 119:71). 'God sets a limit to his punishment, in case we should be overwhelmed by it. What is more, he

[1] *Ibid.*, pp. 800–4, 337, 649.
[2] *Ibid.*, pp. 155–6; cf. pp. 159, 506, and Traherne, quoted on p. 262 below.
[3] *C.P.W.*, IV, p. 684.

gives us strength to overcome even those afflictions which, as sometimes happens, seem to us to exceed that limit.'[1] Therefore, as Bunyan said, we dare not despair – only the reprobate do that – 'but will look for, wait for and hope for deliverance still'.[2]

Milton appeared to find some consolation in the reflection that it is a religious duty to hate the enemies of God or the church. Admonitions to subjects to live peacefully are linked with warnings to kings that to force consciences in the matter of religion is antichristian. Milton stresses the certainty of judgment, though 'only the Father knows the day and the hour' of the Second Coming. Doomsday and the Resurrection bring consolation for the evils of this earth, 'otherwise the righteous would be of all men the most wretched'.[3]

Milton's, then, is not the pacifism that Gerrard Winstanley sometimes, though not consistently, preached, nor the turning of the other cheek and abstention from politics that Reeve and Muggleton practised[4] and that the Quakers adopted after 1660. Milton's problems faced any sincere supporter of the Parliamentary cause in the years after the Restoration. William Sedgwick, for instance, had been a propagandist on behalf of the army in 1649, of Oliver Cromwell against Parliament in 1656; in 1660–1 he did his rethinking in public. The Parliamentarians, he declared, had learnt lordliness from the Cavaliers; self-seeking was 'at the root of all their religion'. Many 'are wholly taken off from war by the great experience we have had of the beastly deceit, the horrible cruelty and corruption that hath attended it'.[5] This was the atmosphere of heart-searching in which Milton wrote the *De Doctrina Christiana* and the three great poems: defeat, triumphant gloating by Royalists and – worst of all – an inner uncertainty, an awareness either that the cause had been totally misconstrued, or that the leaders had let it down and that it could not be rebuilt. The sneers of enemies were nothing compared with the doubts of former friends like Sedgwick. Had it all been a terrible mistake? All the suffering, bloodshed, expense? If not, what could be salvaged? These were not trivial questions, and after 1660 they must have been in the minds of all who had been seriously committed to the Cause.[6]

---

[1] *Ibid.*, VI, pp. 662–3, 469; cf. pp. 654–5. This is one of Milton's later additions (Kelley, 1962, p. 54). The point is relevant to the alleged pessimism of *Samson Agonistes*. See chapter 31 below.
[2] Bunyan, III, p. 353; cf. *C.P.W.*, VI, pp. 131–2, 159–65, 659.
[3] *Ibid.*, VI, pp. 743, 675, 797–8, 615–20. But cf. chapter 22, pp. 332–3, 336 below.
[4] Muggleton (1764), pp. 53, 91. See pp. 437–42 below.
[5] W. Sedgwick, *A Second View* (1649); (1660) and (1661), *passim*.
[6] See chapter 28 below.

Milton did not recant, as Sedgwick did. He wanted his chosen audience, fit though few, to know that he had not recanted. To them he was famous as the author of pamphlets defending divorce, regicide and republicanism rather than as a poet. They would know what he meant when in the invocation to the second half of *Paradise Lost* he wrote:

> I sing . . . unchanged
> To hoarse or mute, though fallen on evil days,
> On evil days though fallen, and evil tongues;
> In darkness, and with dangers compassed round,
> And solitude.
> (VII. 24–8)

Those lines, possibly written when Milton was expecting to be sentenced to a traitor's death, would not have been lost on his more discerning contemporaries.[1]

Milton's attitude indeed was close to that of the condemned but impenitent regicides, once they had had time to reflect on and adjust themselves to God's providences. The cause will have another resurrection, declared Colonel Okey at his execution. But meanwhile we must wait upon God, who will grant deliverance when it shall be most for his glory and the good of his people. Colonel Barkstead made an almost identical speech: God will in his own time carry out his own work – the answer which Jesus gives to the tempter in *Paradise Regained*.[2] Lucy Hutchinson tells us of her husband that 'when God afflicted him, he fell down at his feet; he cast away his crown before him, humbled himself in dust and ashes, and accepted punishment at his hands. But men . . . could never conquer him nor deject him.'[3] These responses are exactly Milton's.

We may note, finally, some attention to Milton's personal problems in the *De Doctrina*. Running away from persecution is justified unless there are strong reasons to the contrary – clearly a matter on which Milton was sensitive. 'In lawful matters it may be prudent to obey even a tyrant, or at any rate to be a time-server, in the interest of public peace and personal safety.'[4] Withdrawal from the state church was justified, and indeed total abstention from church attendance. Late additions to the treatise underline the illegitimacy of a state church or control of the church by the magistrate.[5] It is safer to decline or relinquish civic duties altogether if there is any

---

[1] See pp. 365, 404–5 below.
[2] Tibbutt, pp. 160–1, 163.
[3] Hutchinson, p. 13.
[4] *C.P.W.*, VI, pp. 605, 801.
[5] *Ibid.*, VI, p. 568; C. Hill (1971), p. 129; see p. 105 above.

danger that they would involve participation in idol-worship. We may lie
to deceive the enemies of God and anyone who has not earned the name
of neighbour – especially if this prevents them inflicting injury on others.
The Hebrew midwives who deceived Pharaoh did him no injury since
'they deprived him of an opportunity for committing a crime'. Rahab
'lied nobly ... because she deceived those whom God wished to be
deceived, though they were her fellow-countrymen and magistrates'.
There is no divine authority for obedience to magistrates 'when their
commands are wicked'. The relevance of all this to post-Restoration
England (or for that matter to pre-revolutionary England) is clear.[1]

The links between *Paradise Lost* and the *De Doctrina* are familiar. But
when Professor Low was writing *The Blaze of Noon* he was impressed by
'growing evidence of close compatibility between *Samson Agonistes* and the
Christian Doctrine'.[2] The *De Doctrina*, then, must be read carefully in conjunction with all the three last great poems. Its relation to them is rather
like that of Book I of Hobbes's *Leviathan* to the three books which follow.
It defines terms. Its arguments, including its heresies, must be assumed to
have been in Milton's mind as he wrote the poems. One object indeed of
compiling the *De Doctrina* was to clarify Milton's own position to himself.
It is a taking-off ground for the soaring flight that followed.

II *The Art of Logic*

Milton's ambition was boundless. In addition to being a great poet who
had written a world-famous defence of the English Revolution, he
aspired to write a definitive *summa theologica*, a definitive History of
England, perhaps a definitive English–Latin dictionary, and a definitive
Logic. The *Art of Logic* is a key text to set beside the *De Doctrina* and
Paradise Lost if we are to understand Milton. For him, as for Puritans
generally, logic was the essential handmaid of theology and of all right
learning. Sin, as Perry Miller put it, 'was most precisely defined as that
which prevents man from accurately employing logic'.[3]

In this secondary position logic is very important indeed. It can never
tell us what reason is, nor give us the kind of knowledge which leads to
action – the only true effective knowledge. But it teaches the art of reasoning within those limits. Logic is part of man's cultural inheritance which,

---

[1] *C.P.W.*, VI, pp. 694, 760–4, 800.
[2] Low, p. 222. This is an additional argument against an early date for *Samson Agonistes*: see
p. 485 below.
[3] P. Miller (1953), p. 428.

like the Bible, helps to curb the anarchical excesses of the uneducated. But logic itself must be purged from the scholasticism with which it had been overlaid, as religion had to be purged of popery. Ramus plays the same role in logic as the early Protestants in religion. 'Nothing is more alien from logic, or in fact from reason itself' than the grounds for the 'memorized canons' of the theologians.[1] Milton's sort of logic, he thought, helps us to reject transubstantiation. Logic looms large in his discussion of necessity and free will, and of the Creation.[2] It is also an important means by which he established his anti-Trinitarianism. His rather unusual mathematical arguments against the Trinity seem to accord with those used by Hermes Trismegistus and by Fludd in *Mosaicall Philosophy*, as well as by Ochino, Preston, the Racovian Catechism and William Penn.[3] Milton recognized 'no other type of necessity than the one which logic, that is reason, teaches'. Logic is also deeply involved in Milton's materialism.[4]

In *Tetrachordon* Milton wanted to sum up all his strength 'into one argumentative head, with that organic force that logic proffers us. All arts acknowledge that then only can we know certainly when we can define.' By defining Milton hoped to settle 'exactly what marriage is, . . . when there is a nullity thereof, and when a divorce'. In *The Tenure of Kings and Magistrates* he treated the questions 'What is a king?' and 'What is a tyrant?' as answerable by definitions in the same way as the question 'What is a wife?'[5] One of his arguments against tolerating Catholics in 1673 was the logical maxim that 'against them who deny principles we are not to dispute', though otherwise 'in logic they teach that contraries laid together more evidently appear'[6] and so logic favoured free publication.

'One reason for the great popularity of the Ramean logic among the Puritans', L. Howard suggests, 'was possibly the ease with which it permitted a superficial reconciliation between the doctrines of moral agency and prediction.' It postulated a set of converging causes rather than the chain of causation which the mechanical philosophy was to substitute in the second half of the seventeenth century. 'Trust in God and keep your

---

[1] *C.M.*, XI, pp. 5–7, 338–9.

[2] *C.P.W.*, VI, pp. 159, 307–11.

[3] *C.M.*, XI, pp. 58–9, 314–15; *C.P.W.*, VI, pp. 147–8, 212–18, 262–4; W. Scott, I, pp. 156–7; Fludd, pp. 131–8; L. A. Wood, pp. 59–60. For the Racovian Catechism and Penn see pp. 294–6 below. I cannot agree with Alastair Fowler that it was 'ridiculous' for Maurice Kelley to cite use of this argument in *Paradise Lost* as evidence of Milton's anti-Trinitarianism (VIII, 419–21), since it supports his anti-Trinitarian position in the *De Doctrina*. Cf. Preston, p. 40.

[4] Hoopes, p. 199; *C.P.W.*, VI, pp. 212–16, 302, 158–66; *C.M.*, XI, pp. 51–3. See also chapter 26 below.

[5] *C.P.W.*, II, p. 608; cf. p. 612; III, pp. 202, 212, 229–30.

[6] *C.M.*, VI, pp. 174, 178.

powder dry' is good Ramean logic. So is Milton's 'What is liberty but choice?'[1]

Milton learnt his Ramus as an undergraduate at Christ's, the most Ramist of colleges from Sidney's time onwards: Milton refers to Sidney in the Preface to his *Art of Logic*. William Ames's *Technometria* was the summation of Ramism – an attempted systematization and integration of all knowledge, an explanation of the nature and use of art in general and of all the individual liberal arts. All human knowledge should be practical, geared to action under the guidance of reason. When he has grasped this, man may imitate or make things as God does. So belief in the natural depravity of fallen man could be reconciled with the cosmic and rational optimism of revolutionary Puritanism.[2] Ames was one of the two theologians whom Milton followed most closely in the *De Doctrina*. The *Art of Logic* is presumed to have been written during or soon after Milton's Cambridge days. It was not published until 1672, when Milton seems to have needed money badly, and was printing everything he could find. Thus in logic, as in so much else, Milton found himself at the end of an intellectual tradition.[3] The movement of thought in the seventeenth century, to quote Perry Miller again, involved 'a lessening sense of the sinfulness of man' and 'a decreasing respect for formal logic. . . . One might say that these two changes were one and the same.'[4]

---

[1] Howard, pp. 168–72; Saillens (1964), p. 339; cf. Hill (1972), pp. 215–16, 226–9.
[2] Gibbs, pp. 615–24; Sprunger, pp. 105–26.
[3] Edward Phillips in 1658 republished a translation of Ramus's *Dialectics* in his *The Mysteries of Love and Eloquence* (Howell, p. 238). Cf. p. 490 below.
[4] P. Miller, *loc. cit.*

Chapter 19

Milton and the Bible

That book within whose sacred context all wisdom is enfolded.
Milton, *The Reason of Church Government* (1642)

William Empson's *Milton's God*, one of the few major books published about Milton in the last twenty years, was coolly received by the declining band of those whom he called 'neo-Christians'.[1] Empson was so sure that the Christian God is evil that he could not convince himself that Milton did not agree with him. There is a fine insight here into one part of Milton: but Empson does not do justice to the tension in the poet, his determination to justify God, warts and all; and so Empson does not probe deeply enough into the crucial question – why Milton could not let go his hold of God, even though some of his contemporaries could. This seems to me the starting point for an enquiry into Milton's beliefs which could perhaps be fruitful.

Empson's skilful analysis is the *reductio ad absurdum* of Lawrence's principle that we should trust the tale rather than the teller, ignoring evidence relating to the author's conscious intentions. In my view, if Milton's God seems to us wicked and his sense of humour grisly, whereas one part of Milton presumably intended him to be wholly admirable – or at least wholly acceptable – we must try to understand what the other half of Milton is up to. We should not assume that Milton did not have the intentions that he professed, any more than we should assume (with C. S. Lewis) that he succeeded in making God worthy of our admiration to-day. Here my stress on Milton's ambivalent relationship to the second and third cultures may help.

In the last paragraph I substituted 'acceptable' for 'admirable' as a description of how Milton saw God. There is no need to assume that Milton found God's ways in the Bible attractive. 'Theology was a science, not an

---

[1] See pp. 3, 7–8 above.

art, and he was out to find the truth about God, pleasant or otherwise.'
He himself realized that he needed divine help if he was to succeed in
justifying the ways of God to men.[1] It was not only in the Bible that
Milton found God's ways unattractive: it was especially God's treatment
of his people in England in the sixteen-forties and -fifties that presented
difficult problems.

Milton was appalled by what God had allowed to happen in England.
But whatever his subjective feelings, he could not allow himself consciously to accept the view of Winstanley, Erbery and some Ranters, that
the God whom most Christians worshipped was a wicked God.[2] If he had
done so, his life would have lost its structure, would have fallen in ruins
about his head like the temple of the Philistines. He had to justify the ways
of God to men in order to justify his own life; but he also had to justify the
ways of God to Milton. If we think of him as carrying on a continuous
dialogue with the extreme radicals it becomes easier to see him rejecting
with his intellect ideas which were familiar to him and which one half of his
being accepted. Empson is right to suggest that Milton was in some sense
aware of the terrible collapse that was always possible. He was not of the
devil's party without knowing it: part of him knew that part of him was.

The trouble with Empson's method is that it combines apparent
acceptance of Milton's myths, suspension of disbelief, with twentieth-
century critical attitudes. All this is implied in the phrase 'God's grisly
jokes'. Milton surely felt that what he made God say and do was forced on
him by Biblical evidence. God *did* mock people in the Bible, just as he had
mocked his servants in mid-seventeenth-century England. Milton's reply
to Empson (in twentieth-century terms) would be: 'The universe *is* grisly.
Injustice prevails. That is my problem. The Bible, the only key to its
interpretation, puts the responsibility on to God. What is the alternative?'
In the seventeenth century it was a very difficult question to answer.

Milton was aware of contemporary Biblical criticism, and sometimes
pushed his own interpretation of Scripture to the verge of explaining it
away.[3] Why could he not break loose altogether? At least to the extent of
denying that the Bible is the Word of God, as the anti-Trinitarian John
Hilton had done in 1585, and as John Goodwin, Clement Wrighter,
William Walwyn, Thomas Tany, Samuel Fisher and other Quakers did?[4]

---

[1] Carey, pp. 75–6; cf. pp. 79, 83–4, 97, 110–12, 135–6, chapter 7 *passim*. For an attempt to
defend Milton's God, see C. and F., pp. 453–4.
[2] The passage in *Of Reformation* against a God worshipped in servile fear is a rejection of
propitiation, not of God (*C.P.W.*, I, p. 522).
[3] *C.P.W.*, IV, p. 390n.; VI, pp. 353–4, 576, 588–9. Cf. p. 357 below.
[4] Fuller (1842), III, p. 75; *W.T.U.D.*, chapter 11. Cf. Hayden, pp. 106, 113, for Quakers.

It was, surely, the experience of the sixteen-fifties that confirmed Milton's earlier presuppositions. God is law, is truth, is historical fact. What had happened by 1660 was arbitrary, unjust, unfair, unpleasant – but true. It had to be lived with. The Fall is therefore the only way in which we can explain evil in the world; human sinfulness is the only way to explain (among many other things) the failure of the English Revolution. God's terrible words 'Die he or justice must' are to be accepted as a fact with which we have got to live. The Fall and sin are the traditional justification for the inequality of man, for class rule. In the last resort, perhaps, the reason why Milton never took the Ranter and Digger way out by totally allegorizing the Fall was exactly this. He was not prepared to trust the spirit in all men: that would be dangerous to things which he believed with the same sort of illogical conviction as he believed that evil cannot prevail over good, and that there is a distinction between right and wrong.

Those who 'think not God at all' – Ranters and such who 'walked obscure' (*S.A.* 295–6) – were those whose folly and indiscipline, Milton thought, had helped to make the Restoration possible. Milton believed in God because he believed in inequality, in social hierarchy, in heaven as on earth. He had to assert providence, law, justice, had to cling on to the Bible, in order to save himself from Ranterism, nihilism, chaos. He had to adhere, or appear to adhere, rigidly to the text of Scripture as the only framework. He not only accepted but in a sense rejoiced in the brutality of its scientific truth.

Milton was already escaping, in *Areopagitica* and earlier, from the Calvinist God who is arbitrary will, when he declared that all ordinances, human and divine, must be subordinated to the good of man, including his temporal good.[1] The Restoration of 1660 had brought back the spectre of the God of will, who does not care for man but whose omnipotence must be accepted. 'In short, God either is or is not really like he says he is [in the Bible]. If he really is like this, why should we think otherwise? If he is not really like this, on what authority do we contradict God?'[2]

The collapse of the Revolution must have put a tremendous strain on Milton's acceptance of God. In the forties he had confidently believed that he was serving a God who specially favoured England, who was about to use the English people to perform great deeds on his behalf. This was not an intellectually incomprehensible Calvinist God of absolute will: it was a rational being with whom free men could co-operate. The defeat of these

---

[1] See pp. 247–9 below.
[2] *C.P.W.*, VI, p. 136. Cf. p. 297 below.

hopes meant that Milton no longer felt tuned in to God, whose ways had become incomprehensible to human reason. God thus became more arbitrary than the deity whom Milton had known and served in the forties and fifties. Milton's subordinationism may have its roots here. He needed a second God if he was to escape from the Father of incomprehensible will: hence the Son as the acceptable face of deity. Milton had never been much interested in the Atonement, and even in the very early *Nativity Ode* the miracle of the Incarnation is avoided. But he needed someone through whom contact with God could be restored – the mediating Son of *Paradise Lost*, the perfect man of *Paradise Regained*.

We forget how central the God of arbitrary will had been in an age before men had learnt to control their environment, when 'acts of God' in their most unpleasant sense were daily occurrences. Throughout human history God had seemed an incomprehensible power who had to be propitiated. Luther had been terrified by this angry God who commands the impossible. John Whincop, preaching to members of Parliament in January 1645, warned them that God was angry with mortalists and divorcers: 'God has come nearer . . . with his bright sword brandishing in his hand, laying heaps upon heaps, heaps upon heaps, in most of our quarters, blood, ruin and destruction.' Amid the shrieks of ravished virgins, the preacher continued with obvious relish, amid the yells of poor infants stabbed, God is 'calling to and telling us that he is angry'.[1] God the avenger was a commonplace. In the forties Milton had hoped for a better God;[2] after 1660 it was more difficult to reject the vindictive God who demanded an eye for an eye, a tooth for a tooth, millions of lives for an apple: 'Die he or justice must.'[3]

For Milton as for most Protestants the Bible is the authoritative source of all wisdom.[4] Since it is the Word of God, everything in it must be respected. Nevertheless, the Bible is a large book, incorporating many different points of view: naturally different social groups selectively emphasized different parts of the Bible. Texts which were uncongenial could be ignored, or explained away. But any attempt at a *summa theologica* must endeavour to embrace the whole Bible, to make sense of its apparent contradictions, and not shirk its apparently unpleasant passages.

Some of what strike modern readers as the less attractive aspects of Milton's thought are due to his deliberate and dedicated faithfulness to the

---

[1] Whincop, pp. 10, 27.
[2] *C.P.W.*, I, p. 522.
[3] See p. 473 below.
[4] *C.P.W.*, I, p. 747.

text of the Bible. However we interpret the war in heaven, its basis is a dramatization of what Milton read in Revelation. God mocking his victims derives from the Psalms. Milton's attitude towards women is firmly based on St. Paul; God's visiting of the sins of the fathers upon innocent children is no less Biblical, though Milton was a little uneasy about this, pointing out that men are as bad.[1]

Seventeenth-century bourgeois man felt the existence of God the Creator written in his heart. The existence of injustice was a matter of daily observation. The rest follows, once given that the Bible is the Word of God. That too seemed self-evident to most seventeenth-century readers, as did its relevance to their problems. Before he came from Wales to London in 1629, Arise Evans tells us, 'I looked upon the Scriptures as a history of things that passed in other countries, pertaining to other persons; but now I looked upon it as a mystery to be opened at this time, belonging also to us.'[2] Many passages in George Fox's *Journal* read like the *Acts of the Apostles*; Bunyan's *Grace Abounding* shows how for him the Bible was self-validating.

The Bible was also important for what it did *not* say. If you assume that all necessary institutions, at least all necessary religious institutions, are to be found in the Bible, it is then very reassuring not to find prelatical bishops there, as Colonel Rainborough failed to find a propertied franchise there. As Milton put it, 'Let them chant what they will of prerogatives, we shall tell them of Scripture; of custom, we of Scripture; of acts and statutes, still of Scripture, till ... the mighty weakness of the Gospel throw down the weak mightiness of man's reasoning.' Christian doctrine, based on a study of the Bible, would put an end to 'tyranny and superstitition'.[3]

Yet Milton knew that the Bible had to be interpreted. He frankly admitted that, on a literal reading of the Scriptures, 'God would seem to contradict himself and be changeable.' One way out was – with Thomas Münzer, Familists and Grindletonians, Boehme, Winstanley, Bauthumley and many Ranters – to stress the spirit against the letter of the Bible.[4] Milton adopted this escape route only within very strict limits. Each reader must interpret the Scripture for himself according to his lights; but he may not give free reign to his fancies. 'God ... demands of us that each man who wishes to be saved should work out his beliefs for himself',

---

[1] *Ibid.*, VI, pp. 382–9.
[2] A. Evans, *An Eccho* (1653), p. 17.
[3] *C.P.W.*, I, pp. 700, 747, 827; VI, p. 118.
[4] *Ibid.*, VI, p. 156; *W.T.U.D.*, pp. 82–3, 176, 219–20, 264, 399.

from the Bible, taking nothing at second hand. As early as the *Apology* Milton had corrected St. Paul's praise of virginity by saying that 'marriage must not be called a defilement.'[1] Milton's rationalist approach is in fact remarkable. 'Every rule and instrument of necessary knowledge that God hath given us ought to be so in proportion as may be wielded and managed by the life of man without penning him up from the duties of human society; and such a rule and instrument of knowledge perfectly is the Holy Bible.'[2] 'The ways of God', Milton continued, can never 'cross the just and reasonable desires of men.' 'The great and almost the only commandment of the Gospel is to command nothing against the good of man.' 'No ordinance, human or from heaven, can bind against the good of man.' 'The general end of every ordinance ... is the good of man, yea his temporal good not excluded.' 'It is not the stubborn letter must govern us, but the divine and softening breath of charity, which turns and winds the dictate of every positive command and shapes it to the good of mankind.'[3] Henry Parker said something very similar at about the same time: 'We ought to be very tender how we seek to reconcile that to God's law, which we cannot reconcile to man's equity; or how we make God the author of that constitution which man reaps inconvenience from.'[4]

Milton tried to accommodate his Biblicism to the belief in progressive revelation which made change possible. His problem was to prevent this degenerating into subjective reliance on the inner spirit whenever it opposed the literal text. Here is the later Milton wrestling with this problem: 'The daily increase of light and truth fills the church much rather with brightness and strength than with confusion.' Yet 'in controversies, there is no arbitrator except Scripture, or rather each man is his own arbitrator, so long as he follows Scripture and the Spirit of God.' 'The pre-eminent and supreme authority however is the authority of the Spirit, which is internal and the individual possession of each man.' 'All things are eventually to be referred to the Spirit and the unwritten word.'[5] This attitude could easily slide over into the antinomianism of Ranters like Clarkson, Coppe and Bauthumley, or into quoting the Bible to confirm convictions already held – as Winstanley, Fox and Hobbes did.[6] Milton did not often make the allegorical use of the Bible which he could have

[1] *C.P.W.*, VI, pp. 583–5, 590, 118–24.
[2] *Ibid.*, I, p. 699; cf. pp. 125, 243 above.
[3] *C.P.W.*, II, pp. 342, 588, 604–5, 623–4, 638–9, 750; cf. pp. 263–5.
[4] H. Parker, p. 57. For similar views expressed by Robert Boyle, see Jacob, p. 18.
[5] *C.P.W.*, VI, pp. 121, 585–90; cf. pp. 640, 368. For Milton's methods in interpreting the Bible, see *ibid.*, VI, pp. 135–7, 170, 178, 568–90, 623, 638–40, 652, 711.
[6] *W.T.U.D.*, pp. 212–13. See pp. 308–11, 341–5 below.

found – for instance – in Bodin's *Heptaplomeres*, and that Winstanley and
some Ranters employed. But he does frequently treat its stories as myths,
which may be fused with those of classical Greece and Rome.[1] He indulges
in a good deal of Biblical criticism, though he does not dwell as strongly as
Clarkson, Writer or Samuel Fisher on the contradictions and inconsisten-
cies to be found in the Bible. Reeve and Muggleton used contemporary
scepticism about these contradictions to reinforce the authority of the
two last witnesses, who alone could interpret it. Reeve, for instance,
denied authority to the books attributed to Solomon, and Clarkson as well
as Muggleton followed him. Muggleton recognized that the text of the
Bible, especially the New Testament, was frequently corrupt: that is why
the spirit was superior to the letter.[2] Milton, like Mabillon and the
Bollandists after him, went as far in source criticism as one could go
without asking the fundamental question – Is this the Word of God? –
and answering it in the negative.[3] Milton would follow his own conscience
wherever it led him, but he lacked confidence in the inner light of other
men, more perhaps as time went on; he was always trying to find some
external, generally acceptable checks against a doctrine which, as Dr.
Johnson said, was 'utterly incompatible with social or civil security'.[4]

What explains this difference of emphasis between Milton on the one
hand and Quakers and Ranters on the other? In the first place, the Bible
was essential to the defence of a radical Protestant position against
Catholics. English Protestantism was dedicated to the proposition that the
Bible was the Word of God: Milton's life would have had little meaning if
the Bible lost its position of sacrosanct authority. But Milton also wanted
to preserve some restraints against the mere anarchy of individual interpretation. He was highly élitist, had little but contempt for the uneducated,
at least from the mid-forties. The *De Doctrina* was written in Latin, which
the common people could not understand. Milton respected scholarship,
and knew he was good at it. He *had* to have a certainty that was bolstered
by authority as well as by his own mere *ipse dixit*. His conscience found
the Protestant ethic in the Bible; those who rejected the Bible tended to be
those who also rejected the Protestant ethic.[5] Milton clung to the most

[1] C. and F., pp. 581, 589–90, 785; *P.L.* IX. 1060–1; XI. 581–92; *P.R.* II. 178–81. See chapter 28
below.
[2] *P.L.* V. 570–6; VI. 893–6; VII. 176–9; *W.T.U.D.*, chapter 11; Reeve (*Joyfull News*, 1706),
pp. 11–14; Muggleton (1668), p. 64; (1764), p. 62; Clarkson (1660), pp. 26, 32; cf. Tillyard
(1949), pp. 216, 223–8; Bodin, pp. 141–84.
[3] Cf. Plumb, p. 100.
[4] Boswell, I, pp. 392–3.
[5] *W.T.U.D.*, esp. chapters 11 and 16.

radical version of traditional Biblical Protestantism: he went back to the early reformers in preference to late Protestant scholasticism. But to throw the Bible away would mean abandoning certainty. The Bible proved the points of which 'it is absolutely requisite that those who wish to learn Christian doctrine should be convinced . . . from the outset' – namely that 'a God does exist, that he rules and governs all things, and that everyone must one day render to him an account of his actions, good and bad alike.'[1] Similarly Bidle felt that departure from the literal sense of Scripture would enable men to defend either the idolatries of the papists or the licentious opinions and practices of the Ranters.[2]

The Bible is subject to the overriding good of man in society: this means in effect that middle-class readers can assess it by their own standards. When Perkins tells us that what wealth we need for our family must be decided by 'the common judgment and practice of the most godly, frugal and wise men with whom we live',[3] this too is to let bourgeois society set its own standards. For Milton the Bible is not to be interpreted according to any individual conscience, however vulgar and ignorant. There must be objective definitions of man's good in society, definitions which are 'reasonable', written by nature on the hearts of educated men; and these can be used to test the Bible, and as a check on individual interpretation. Bunyan asked himself whether the Koran might not be as true, as authoritative, as the Bible, because it was equally widely accepted in the Moslem areas of the world.[4] Milton would have answered by appealing to the conscience of the educated élite whom he knew and respected.

In the Putney Debates of 1647 Colonel Rainborough was badly rattled by Ireton's argument that reliance on the law of nature could be used to justify communism: and who was to choose between the two interpretations of natural law? The Bible says 'Thou shalt not steal' was the Colonel's retort. It would seem a more satisfactory reply in the seventeenth century than it does to-day, when the Bible is less generally accepted as the Word of God. Milton too wanted to preserve the authority of the Bible, because (among other things) he wanted to preserve private property and class distinctions. This is what kept him with Oliver Cromwell for so long: their mutual respect for social hierarchy and recognized social classes. It helps to explain *The Ready and Easy Way*.

---

[1] *C.P.W.*, VI, p. 132.
[2] Bidle (1654), Sig. A 5v.
[3] Perkins, I, p. 769.
[4] Bunyan, I, pp. 17–18. The Quaker Samuel Fisher had similar doubts (*W.T.U.D.*, p. 266).

So Milton arrived at his eclectic conclusions, not based on anybody else's ideas but on his own scholarly study of the Bible, and his own prepossessions. He decided in favour of adult baptism, in running water, but unlike most Baptists he had no objection to oaths or fighting; and he disliked Anabaptist 'excesses'. He was in favour of marriage based on love, of freedom of divorce in case of incompatibility, but he insisted on the inferiority of women. He believed that soul and body could not be separated, that matter was good; but he was far from accepting all the materialist conclusions which Clement Writer, Diggers and Ranters drew from these premises. He rejected any form of state church, and was in favour of lay preaching by mechanic preachers elected by their congregations, earning their living by handicrafts: he had no use for universities as places where ministers should be trained; and yet he himself had the highest scholarly standards of Biblical interpretation and was no mean linguist and logician. He was in favour of liberty of conscience, of individual interpretation of the Scriptures according to the spirit within each individual; but he opposed social equality. He thought salvation was offered to all men, though he became increasingly pessimistic about their acceptance of the offer. He favoured the Protestant ethic, social subordination, charity to oneself, as well as 'elegance' and learning.[1] His ideas, in short, were as radical as is possible without endangering the essentials of propertied society. He could never cross the chasm which separated him from a man like Winstanley, whose position in society predisposed him against inequality and privilege.

What Milton felt most passionately was that freedom of individual development was absolutely necessary for himself and therefore for other men. By what objective standards could this liberty be defined? Milton had to recognize that others around him learnt different things from the spirit within, read different truths in their hearts. But there must be an objective criterion. Milton clung to his belief that the Bible tells us, clearly and simply, the truths essential to salvation. All we have to do is to find them. Although these necessary truths are few, simple and clear, nevertheless in the centuries of papal corruption many of them have been concealed and forgotten: customs which now seem second nature have obscured them. Labour and considerable scholarship are consequently necessary for a proper understanding of the Bible. This only confirms that we cannot – dare not – trust anyone else's conscience, anyone else's interpretation. We would no more hand our consciences over to someone

---

[1] *C.P.W.*, VI, p. 732; cf. pp. 728–31.

else than – if we were good business men – we would hand our business concerns over to some factor. Milton does not claim to be laying down theological truths in his 'dearest and best possession'. He hopes to help us to arrive at our own conclusions by showing us the way in which he had established and buttressed his.

With Milton we may compare Sir Isaac Newton – worrying away in secret at Biblical problems, collecting, sifting, rearranging. The solution must be there if one worked at it hard and long enough, in the right spirit. For Newton the problems were chronological, mathematical – almost cross-word; for Milton they were textual problems of congruence, logical problems. Both started from unspoken, unargued assumptions about society.

Many of Milton's heresies pick up where the early reformers had failed to go on. Luther and Tyndale were mortalists, not least because the doctrine finally annihilated Purgatory and the intercession of saints. To many theologians, as to Servetus and Isaac Newton, rejection of the Trinity seemed merely a natural consequence of rejection of the papal Antichrist. Acceptance of divorce and polygamy seemed to follow from rejection of papal doctrines of celibacy. 'By separating election from faith, and therefore from Christ, we become involved in perplexing and indeed in repulsive and unreasonable doctrines,' Milton declared.[1] This was to return to the Christology of the early reformers as against the scholasticism which had developed as a result of academic pondering over the eternal decrees. In appealing to Scripture against custom Milton might have been quoting Calvin; in rejecting the authority of the early Fathers he had Cartwright and Alexander Henderson on his side.[2] We remember the glee with which Milton discovered that Bucer and other early reformers shared his views on divorce. In *The Tenure* Milton reminded Presbyterians that Charles I's judges had only been putting into practice the principles that they had learnt from Calvin, Knox, Buchanan and Paraeus. 'Custom without truth is but agedness of error', was his epigrammatic rendering of an old saw. Against the lazy customs which had introduced themselves Milton wished to return to the early Protestant scholarly tradition. The reformers had made a revolution by pointing out that *'ecclesia'* meant 'congregation', not 'church'. Milton wished to initiate another revolution by suggesting that fornication meant general sexual incompatibility,[3] and by re-interpreting parts of the Bible away from accepted meanings by close

[1] *Ibid.*, VI, pp. 92, 180, cf. 175.
[2] Calvin, I, pp. 13–14; Strype, I, pp. 105–6, 135; Aiton, p. 647.
[3] Cf. p. 123 above.

textual scholarship, as in his argument that the world was not created *ex nihilo*. But from his Cambridge days Milton differentiated sharply between scholarship and scholasticism. Academic disputations contributed nothing to 'morality or purity of life', 'to the general good nor to the honour and profit of our country'.[1]

By stressing the liberating aspects of the priesthood of all believers Milton was returning to original Lutheranism, as against scholastic concern with predestination and the Eternal Decrees which had replaced the joyous liberation of Luther's original vision. Yet Milton would have felt, with Tyndale, that to follow one's own lusts was not freedom but bondage.[2] Freedom, which means action in conformity with God's will, derived from complete suffusion of the inner man with God. In *Of Prelatical Episcopacy* Milton recounted the long hold-up in completing the Reformation, which he believed was now at last approaching in England. He returned again at the beginning of the *De Doctrina* to the theme that philosophizing academics have subjected religion to a scholasticism not dissimilar to that from which the Reformation freed it.[3] He believed in continuous reformation.

---

[1] *C.P.W.*, I, pp. 561, 569, 246.
[2] Tyndale, pp. 182–5.
[3] *C.P.W.*, II, pp. 624–52; VI, pp. 117, 122, 127, 177, 180.

Chapter 20

The Dialectic of Discipline and Liberty

> If we look but on the nature of elemental and mixed things, we know they cannot suffer any change of one kind or quality into another, without the struggle of contrarieties.
>
> Milton, *The Reason of Church Government* (1642)
>
> That which purifies us is trial, and trial is by what is contrary. . . . Were I the chooser, a dram of well-doing should be preferred before as many times as much the forcible hindrance of evil doing.
>
> Milton, *Areopagitica* (1644)

I Discipline

The polarity between individual liberty (essential for the elect) and discipline (essential for society as a whole)[1] appears very early in Milton's published works. Everything that men normally attribute to fortune is more properly ascribed, Milton wrote in 1641, to 'the vigour or the slackness of discipline'. 'There is not that thing in the world of more grave and urgent importance throughout the whole life of man than is discipline.' 'The flourishing and decaying of all civil societies, all the moments and turnings of human occasions are moved to and fro as upon the axle of discipline. . . . Nor is there any sociable perfection in this life, civil or sacred, that can be above discipline; but she is that which with her musical cords preserves and holds all the parts thereof together. . . . Discipline is not only the removal of disorder, but if any visible shape can be given to divine things, the very visible shape and image of virtue.' Education and discipline have the same aim: to liberate us from the natural sinful state.[2] Discipline is social, national.

Yet for Milton freedom for the individual was no less essential to the life of virtue than discipline. 'God sure esteems the growth and completing

---

[1] *S. and P.*, chapter VI.
[2] *C.P.W.*, I, p. 751. Modern spelling obscures the pun in 'c(h)ords'.

of one virtuous person more than the restraint of ten vicious.'[1] Christ the liberator made possible 'our worthy struggle for freedom'. 'One cannot wish to dominate and remain a Christian.'[2] Milton's problem of combining liberty with discipline is similar to Rousseau's problem of justifying the chains which society imposes on the freedom of individuals. The free individual has to live in a society composed of other fallen individuals who may also claim an absolute liberty. Where we speak of society Milton would speak of the church, and here perhaps the ambiguity of the Calvinist concept of the church helped to confuse his thinking. For a Calvinist 'the church' meant both the whole community and the elect members of that community: when liberty was most heavily emphasized, it was natural to think most of the godly minority. A similar ambiguity, as we have seen, hung around the word 'people'. Discipline is 'the common consent of the church', not something imposed from above.[3]

The solution to Milton's paradox seemed to be self-discipline, internalized standards. It was thanks to self-discipline as well as to an externally imposed discipline that Cromwell's cavalry overcame Rupert's in the Civil War. But could this self-discipline be extended beyond the elect, those who by definition were serious and conscientious men anxious to please God? And how could one distinguish between the true elect and hypocrites?

The Protestant doctrine of the priesthood of all believers stressed the freedom, the dignity and self-respect of the elect. It was less clear in its attitude towards the unregenerate, those constitutionally incapable of self-discipline. Calvin's emphasis on predestination seemed to harden the lines of division: those who claimed freedom for themselves also felt it to be their duty to impose a rigorous discipline on the unregenerate majority. Yet there were always those more imaginative or more democratic spirits who fretted at this, who hoped that all men were saved, or savable: that it was their own fault if they were not. Pelagianism or Arminianism would keep breaking through, if only because Protestant preachers in a state church had to address themselves to congregations of all men, not just of the elect.[4] Boehme, for instance, believed that there could be no responsibility without absolute liberty.[5] But the facts continually defeated optimists like Luther, Boehme and Milton: the more optimistic the greater the defeat tended to be. Milton had enough his-

---

[1] *Ibid.*, II, p. 528.
[2] *Ibid.*, IV, pp. 374–5, 379, 534; cf. p. 387.
[3] *Ibid.*, VI, 607–9; cf. pp. 185–6 above.
[4] See chapter 21 below.
[5] See pp. 276, 329 below.

torical sense to blame the prelates for putting out the people's eyes: but he never solved the problem of restoring sight to the blind. Even if blindness was not their fault, still they must be led – like Samson, like Milton himself after 1652.

In this as in so many things, Milton's inner dialogue between liberty and discipline, liberty and licence, was never wholly resolved. Discipline is far from being merely negative, repressive: the head of the household's right to divorce is 'a most necessary part of discipline in every Christian government'.[1] *The Reason of Church Government* pictures the happiness of glorified saints, not 'confined and cloyed with repetition of that which is prescribed', but orbing itself 'into a thousand vagancies of glory and delight, . . . with a kind of eccentrical equation', becoming 'as it were, an invariable planet of joy and felicity',[2] as in *Paradise Lost*'s 'mazes intricate, / Eccentric, intervolved, yet regular / Then most when most irregular they seem' (*P.L.* V. 622–4). The order of heaven seems disordered to earthly eyes because it is based on total freedom. In both passages the paradox of linking liberty and discipline was resolved poetically. The greater difficulty of resolving it in real life accounts for some of Milton's fiercest resentments.

Milton started from an intense, an arrogant individualism, a self-confidence tempered by a strong internalized moral sense, the product almost certainly of his Puritan upbringing. The eagerness with which he supported the Presbyterians initially, and the venom with which he spat Presbyterianism out, both sprang from his own self-esteem. Discipline must be *self*-discipline: at least for those who *can* discipline themselves. And it must allow for self-development, for the flowering of those extraordinary capabilities which exist in greater numbers of ordinary men and women than was traditionally allowed for in seventeenth-century thinking. Here clearly the experience of the Revolution helped. *Areopagitica* suggests that Milton had been tremendously impressed by the libertarian thinking that had been released in London. Compared with Laudian England, still more with Italy, this was a new world, in which free and splendid wits could flourish.

So one of Milton's starting points was a determination that the fullest possible self-development and self-expression should be allowed to those who were capable of benefiting by it – even if this meant allowing liberty to those who were not. The only limitation was that there could be no liberty for papists, whom Milton associated with Italian-style repression.

---

[1] *C.P.W.*, II, p. 432, cf. p. 587.
[2] *Ibid.*, I, p. 752.

Theologically this libertarian insistence on self-realization came to be expressed in Milton's heresies on the Trinity.[1]

If the Presbyterian clergy failed to come up to Milton's exacting standards, so ultimately did the people of England: the confidence of *Areopagitica* contrasts sadly with Messiah's denunciation of the people in *Paradise Regained*. Initially the clergy were to blame for the failure of the laity to discipline themselves. 'The exclusion of Christ's people from the offices of holy discipline through the pride of an usurping clergy causes the rest to have an unworthy and abject opinion of themselves.' The original attractiveness for Milton of the disciplinary system recommended by Presbyterians and Independents alike was that it offered to bring laymen of the middling sort, heads of households, into the government of the church. Experience of governing the church would open the eyes of the man who exercised it 'to a wise and true valuation of himself'.[2] Milton's later change of heart suggests that others like him may have been thinking more of the Laudian system which they wished to get rid of than of a Presbyterian system as an end in itself.

Judging by his own high standards, it seemed to Milton wholly reasonable to ask all men to behave 'as ever in my great Taskmaster's eye'. Yet he soon discovered that the lower classes, even if they rejected 'the corrupt and venal discipline of clergy courts', hated true discipline even more. He found religious, political and moral sense strongest in the middling sort.[3] He soon came to see that Presbyterian discipline, imposed from outside by the clergy, was not the answer he was seeking. But what was? The assumption underlying *Areopagitica* was that in the new freedom being established God's Englishmen would internalize discipline, would acquire self-respect, self-control and temperance. Liberty was not to be absolute: profanity, popery and licentiousness were to be punished after publication. But Milton did insist on freedom for good men, for the self-disciplined. He never found a better solution to his dilemma than the rather barren conclusion that 'none can love freedom heartily but good men; the rest love not freedom but licence.'[4] 'To bad and dissolute men [liberty] becomes a mischief unwieldy in their own hands.'[5] This helplessness when faced with the need for precise definition tells us a lot about Milton. It perhaps helps to explain his later fierceness against hypocrisy.[6]

---

[1] See chapter 23 below.
[2] *C.P.W.*, I, pp. 841–4, 883.
[3] *Ibid.*, I, p. 982; *S. and P.*, pp. 236, 243, 301.
[4] *C.P.W.*, III, p. 190.
[5] *Ibid.*, V, p. 449.
[6] See pp. 387, 408, 463 below.

Without discipline, no achievement, certainly no political achievement. Self-discipline comes from awareness of what God wants. Yet politics, the art of the possible, necessarily contaminates the purity of those who act: Oliver Cromwell came to invoke 'necessity the tyrant's plea'. Milton's God demanded realization of the highest human potential, through disciplined liberty, through the education of an élite in self-knowledge. If there were no God there would be no alternative to Ranter antinomianism, undisciplined self-indulgence; and that was ineffective politically (in addition to the other objections).

How was liberty to be disciplined? Who should hold the ring? One can see how Cromwell's rule seemed at the time to men like Milton the only possibility, granted that manhood suffrage would almost certainly have brought back the King; that the Parliamentary electorate was certainly in favour of persecution and almost certainly for monarchy; that the rule of the godly might mean the rule of charlatans, cranks, crooks and hypocrites as well.

It may be that the problem of uniting the popular wing of the Parliamentarian revolutionaries for effective political action had always been hopeless because of the anarchic individualism which its doctrines fostered; and that this long-standing problem of the Familist underground was merely brought out into the open in the Revolution. After experiencing Ranter liberty in the early fifties, leading to licentiousness and a clerical revival (Baxter was prepared to pay even the price of episcopacy to get discipline restored), Milton's hopes sank steadily, until we reach the nadir of *The Ready and Easy Way*. After 1660, only disillusion remained; Milton would have withdrawn even if he had not been excluded from political life. But he still wanted to teach – to teach the necessity for self-discipline *and* liberty, humanism *and* the kingdom of God. He was prepared to stand and wait provided he could also serve, and was not without Samson's hope that one day still God would return to his people.

Liberty and self-discipline are both *individual* virtues, self-regarding. Neither are communal virtues of the type which Winstanley wished to encourage. Nevertheless discipline is based on the consent of the congregation, and self-discipline is needed to make community life possible. Without it we have anarchy – the pleasant anarchy of the Ranters or the unpleasant anarchy of the Hobbist state of nature. At the level of the church, the experience of the Quakers suggests that Milton may have been wise not to commit himself to any sect. For, in the fierce persecution which prevailed after 1660, the Quakers naturally and perhaps necessarily clung to certain points of principle – refusal of tithes, oaths and hat honour – to such an extent that these became shibboleths separating them from the national community. Quakers became a peculiar people, constantly involved in heart-searchings over what came to be trivia.

Milton's thought is dialectical: he prefers seeing unity rather than dualism. This underlies his anti-Trinitarianism and mortalism (soul and body are one as God is one). It also accounts for his rejection of the black/white, either/or categories of the Cambridge disputation and the syllogism. Debate, dialectic, is the law of the universe. 'Elemental and mixed things ... cannot suffer any change of one kind or quality into another, without the struggle of contrarieties. And in things artificial, seldom any elegance is wrought without a superfluous waste and refuse in the transaction. No marble statue can be politely carved, no fair edifice built, without almost as much rubbish and sweeping.' 'It was from out the rind of one apple tasted ....' 'How much we ... expel of sin, so much we expel of virtue.'[1] Mercy and justice are at strife even within the Father himself (*P.L.* III. 406–7; cf. 132–4).

Milton is always stressing the dialectical interrelation of apparent opposites – law and grace, faith and works, body and soul, heaven and earth, the just but remote Father and the merciful Creator-Son, God and man, life and death, mirth and melancholy, chaos and creation, freedom and necessity, liberty and licence, discipline and individualism.[2] Believers are freed from the whole Mosaic law, and yet divorce is sanctioned by the law and practice of the Old Testament. 'Inevitable cause' led the hero in *Samson Agonistes* freely to choose 'both to destroy and be destroyed' (lines 1586–7; cf. 1605–6). Samson is both active and passive, punished and rewarded, free and yet 'tangled in the fold of dire necessity' (1616).[3] Even the lesson which Adam learnt at the end of *Paradise Lost* – that we accomplish great things by attending to small detail – had been anticipated by Mammon, of all characters (*P.L.* XII. 566–9; II. 257–62).[4] Milton believed, throughout his life, that 'the standard of judgment will be the individual conscience itself, and so each man will be judged by the light which he has received', that no man can hand his conscience over to a factor. This is a fundamentally individualist doctrine. There is again Milton's defence of usury, which concerned him from his earliest Commonplace Book entries to his latest additions to the *De Doctrina*. Here he is in part defending his father, sometimes with a certain unease; but he is also drawing on

---

[1] *C.P.W.*, I, pp. 795–6; II, pp. 514, 527.
[2] *Ibid.*, VI, pp. 490, 159–66, 176; see the suggestive analysis of MacCaffrey, esp. p. 102.
[3] Low, pp. 82–9.
[4] See pp. 388–9 below.

a long-standing tradition among Protestants who had to take account of this commercial world in which they lived. His conclusion was not unorthodox by this date, but it is stated with unusual firmness: 'Usury . . . is no more reprehensible than any other kind of lawful commerce.'[1]

Some of Milton's verbal play reminds us irresistibly of Karl Marx, despite the frequent Biblical echoes. 'Lust is the friendship of ignorance or the ignorance of friendship'; 'to suppress the suppressors'; 'still watching to oppress / Israel's oppressors' (*S.A.* 232–3); 'defending the very defenders'; 'circumstances which are Judaical rather than judicial'; 'redeemed from the works of the law, or from the whole law of works'; 'in proportion as I am weak I shall be invincibly strong; and in proportion as I am blind I shall more clearly see.'[2]

The major Miltonic paradox is fundamental. He is a revolutionary, his dreams are forward-looking. Yet he wrote the last great epic, the last all-embracing synthesis of all knowledge; his was 'the last integration of a world-view that had already disintegrated'.[3] He was one of Europe's last great Latinists, who used the international language to defend the English Revolution. His was the last great voice of right reason, the last word of the old Puritanism before it split into libertinism or nonconformity. His ideas are always pressing tensely against the framework in which they are enclosed. If we took this approach more seriously, we might find out a lot about Milton. Self-discipline sounds appropriate to the austere Milton of the popular image. But we have I hope by now become somewhat sceptical of that image.[4]

II Fecundity and freedom

A sense of pleasure in the fecundity of the universe, in its divine plenitude, remained with Milton throughout. Scarcely less daring in its fusion of the sacred and profane than the end of *Epitaphium Damonis* is the opening line of 'At a Solemn Music': 'Blest pair of sirens', echoing the 'celestial sirens' of *Arcades* (1. 63). When we reflect that the sirens were the attendants of the sorceress Circe, Comus's mother, the enormity becomes apparent. In *Comus* praise of Nature's plenitude is given to the tempter:

---

[1] *C.P.W.*, I, pp. 418–19; II, p. 322; VI, pp. 31, 623, 775–8 and references there cited.
[2] *Ibid.*, I, p. 295; II, pp. 568, 332; IV, p. 554; VI, p. 531. In my last quotation I have used the Bohn translation of the *Second Defence* (I, p. 238). For this continuing idea of Milton's, see p. 211 above.
[3] Broadbent (1960), p. 56; cf. *W.T.U.D.*, pp. 297, 304–5.
[4] Cf. chapter 32 below.

> Wherefore did Nature pour her bounties forth
> With such a full and unwithdrawing hand,
> Covering the earth with odours, fruits and flocks,
> Thronging the seas with spawn innumerable . . .
> And set to work millions of spinning worms
> That in their green shops weave the smooth-haired silk
> To deck her sons?
>
> (ll. 709–16)

But in *Paradise Lost* the poet himself says something not dissimilar:

> Our maker bids increase, who bids abstain
> But our destroyer, foe to God and man?
>
> (IV. 748–9)

The account of Creation in Book VII is a hymn in praise of fecundity.

From the 'wanton wiles' of Mirth in *L'Allegro* (l. 27) to the 'wanton growth' of Paradise, where 'Nature . . . wantoned' in 'enormous bliss', there is a curious mingling of epithets.[1] Eve's hair was 'dishevelled', 'loose', long before the Fall (*P.L.* IV. 306, 629; V. 294–7). 'Love . . . here reigns and *revels*', Milton insists (IV. 763–5 – my italics). He seems determined to narrow the distinction between fallen and unfallen sex.[2] *Areopagitica* glorified the same 'teeming freedom' in human creativity: God 'gives us minds that can wander beyond all limit and satiety'.[3] Milton never lost his astonishment at the prodigality of Nature, even travestying it in the monstrous births resulting from Satan's incestuous intercourse with Sin (II. 778 seq.). Good or bad, there is plenitude, just as heaven is characterized by dance, song, play.[4]

Milton always had a certain fastidiousness, summed up by his emphasis on the virtue of 'elegance', which he defines as 'the discriminating enjoyment of food, clothing, and all the civilized refinements of life, purchased with our honest earnings' (this sentence in the *De Doctrina* is Milton's addition to his source, Wollebius).[5] Milton felt nothing but contempt for canary-sucking and swan-eating bishops, and for the drunkenness which characterized Philistines and restored Royalists. But he did not go to the opposite extreme of ascetic restraint traditionally attributed to 'Puritans'. The good things of life remain good even if discipline is required against licence. Gardening was necessary in Paradise even before the Fall, but

---

[1] See p. 128 above. But contrast the 'wanton dance' of Comus's rout in l. 175.
[2] See pp. 331–2 below. Cf. Watkins, pp. 132–47; Martz (1964), p. 128.
[3] *C.P.W.*, II, p. 528.
[4] Tillyard (1947), pp. 69–71; Bouchard, p. 105.
[5] *C.P.W.*, VI, pp. 728, 732; cf. *P.L.* V. 335; IX. 1018.

the creative luxuriance of Paradise was good in itself. Here again Milton holds his opposites in perpetual tension.[1]

If we follow up this clue through *Comus*, where the libertine gets the best lines; through *The History of Britain*, where Milton rebukes Etheldrith for 'thinking to live the purer life' by refusing to sleep with her husband;[2] through *Paradise Lost*, where Satan quotes *Areopagitica* when tempting Eve; to Milton's prosaic rebuke to Adam for abandoning all for Eve in some of the noblest lines in the poem, we discover a deeply divided Milton, divided between what he calls passion and what he calls reason, seeing reason as good and yet refusing to see passion as bad. What links the divorce tracts with *Paradise Lost* is the conviction that sexual appetite in itself is good; Milton's critique of university scholasticism is linked with *Paradise Regained* by the poet's conviction that action is superior to contemplation.

That is why Saurat saw Milton as the hero of *Paradise Lost*. He 'had Satan in him and wanted to drive him out'. It also explains the romantic view that Satan was the epic's hero, that Milton was of the devil's party without knowing it. He was in fact, as Saurat pointed out, of *both* parties: he wanted to master passion by reason, but he did not want to reject passion, without which he would not have been a poet. But in the dialectical conflict of freedom with necessity Milton was resolutely on the side of freedom.[3]

Without freedom we return to the traditional helplessness before the blind forces of nature and society which was characteristic of human thinking before those linked events, Renaissance and Reformation, and the economic possibilities of controlling nature which called forth modern science and Baconian optimism. For Descartes only animals were automata: the characteristic of human beings was their freedom.[4] Hegel expressed the point that Milton was trying to make: 'Consciousness occasions the separation of the Ego, in its boundless freedom as arbitrary choice, from the pure essence of the Will – i.e. from the Good. . . . If I hold to my abstract Freedom, in contraposition to the Good, I adopt the standpoint of Evil. The Fall is therefore the eternal Mythus of Man – in fact the very transition by which he becomes man.' Hence the interpretation of the Fall as fortunate has always appealed to radicals.[5]

---

[1] See pp. 253–9 above, 395–6 below.
[2] *C.P.W.*, V, p. 222. Cf. Muggleton (1764), pp. 109–10.
[3] Saurat, pp. 184–5.
[4] *W.T.U.D.*, pp. 152–3.
[5] Hegel, p. 333; cf. pp. 346–7 below.

Milton agreed with Traherne in glorifying human freedom: 'God made man a free agent for his own advantage, and left him in the hand of his own counsel, that he might be the more glorious.' But Traherne lacks Milton's consciousness of failure and defeat, for he goes on to apostrophize God: 'To give me a power to displease thee, or to set a sin before thy face which thou infinitely hatest, is more stupendous' than all God's other gifts.[1]

III Negative liberty

All Milton's most passionate feelings about politics and religion were negative – not in a merely restrictive, repressive, 'thou shalt not' sense, but in wishing to hinder hindrances to human freedom, especially intellectual freedom. He was *against* popery, bishops, persecution, against implicit faith in the church or its priests, against the constraints of marriage law, against censorship, against tyranny. All of these stood in the way of that liberty which Englishmen – or English heads of households – or godly Englishmen – ought to have. They were idols to be cast down: liberty is iconoclasm. 'This is not the liberty which we can hope, that no grievance should arise in the Commonwealth, that let no man in this world expect'; but that complaints should be 'freely heard, deeply considered and speedily reformed'.[2] Milton's advice to Cromwell in 1654 consisted mainly of negatives. Laws should be abolished rather than enacted: those only should be retained 'which, while they prevent the frauds of the wicked, do not prohibit the innocent freedoms of the good'. A passage about making laws in the digression in Milton's *History of Britain* was omitted in the 1681 edition which he may have prepared for the press. Milton shared the Levellers' and Adam Smith's view that the less government the better. 'So many laws argue so many sins', Adam observed in *Paradise Lost* (XII. 282–4).[3]

In *Comus* the Lady retained her freedom and her virtue by saying No. The virtues of Abdiel in *Paradise Lost*, of Jesus in *Paradise Regained* and of Samson consisted in rejecting offered temptation. Some have found here rather too negative an approach to virtue, but Milton clearly saw these refusals as the essence of freedom. Even in *Samson Agonistes*, though we are left with a sense of positive achievement, the hero has done nothing but destroy the Philistines: he has removed the obstacle to the freedom of

---

[1] Traherne, pp. 333–4; cf. p. 236 above.
[2] *C.P.W.*, II, p. 487.
[3] *Ibid.*, V, pp. 448–9; cf. Manning, pp. 301–6.

Israel. Just as the elect have no real need for the state and its laws on earth, so the final end of all things will see the withering away even of Christ's kingdom, when God shall be all in all.[1]

Another way of making the point would be to reflect on the social function of discipline. It helped to internalize the Protestant ethic. But this ethic of voluntary hard work, abstinence, accumulation, was naturally more attractive to the middle classes than to the working class. The former were more prepared to labour 'as ever in my great Taskmaster's eye' because they had never in fact known an earthly taskmaster.[2] Milton, the leisure-class intellectual, living on money inherited from his father, had no appreciation of or sympathy for what it was like to be a wage-labourer. His only comment on the class was that 'they are much better off than slaves', because they are not bought and sold: formal freedom was what mattered.[3] It perhaps seemed a less adequate liberty to those who enjoyed it. 'You cannot have liberty in this world', Blake was to admit, 'without what you call moral virtue; you cannot have moral virtue without the slavery of that half of the human race who hate what you call moral virtue.'[4]

Milton's is a bourgeois conception of liberty: the right to be left alone, to work, to make money, to trade freely. It assumes the possession of capital by those who hold it; their position in society needs no reinforcement if only they are given 'fair play', 'free trade', equal rights before the law. *Areopagitica* advocated free trade in 'our richest merchandise, truth', as Adam Smith was to do in more material commodities.[5]

At the risk of stressing the obvious, let me illustrate some of the bourgeois aspects of Milton's thinking. They were not of course peculiar to him: the trend of thought came with the rise of a class. The absolute right and duty of each individual to follow his own conscience in religious matters Milton expressed in terms of pure individualism, despite all the problems which had arisen since Luther proclaimed the principle of individual interpretation of the Bible.[6] Milton listed whole strings of bourgeois virtues – frugality or thrift, industry, selective rather than indiscriminate alms-giving, refusal to make provision for those who are idle, for 'vagrants and beggars from choice', rejection of vows of poverty,

---

[1] Frye (1966), pp. 2, 114; Saurat, pp. 2, 165. See pp. 302–5 below.
[2] *W.T.U.D.*, pp. 327–8, 400; *S. and P.*, chapter VI. This is of course a Protestant commonplace: see Dod and Clever (1662), p. 190. A servant should obey 'not principally because his master commandeth, but because God commandeth: not because his master's eye is upon him, but because God's pure eyes behold him'.
[3] *C.P.W.*, VI, p. 706.
[4] W. Blake, p. 843.
[5] *C.P.W.*, II, p. 548.
[6] *C.M.*, VI, pp. 6–7.

respect for 'the correct market price'.[1] Adam and Eve worked in Paradise
before the Fall, different though this pleasurable work was from post-
lapsarian labour.

There is the rather unattractive idea of charity being due to oneself,
which makes a man 'love himself next to God, and seek his own temporal
and eternal good'.[2] 'This self-pious regard', 'a wise and true valuation of
himself', was 'a requisite and high point of Christianity'; it was also part
of Milton's insistence on the dignity and self-respect of heads of households for which he argued so fiercely in *The Reason of Church Government*
against clerical claims to superiority. 'The scornful term of laic . . . causes
the rest to have an unworthy and abject opinion of themselves.' Milton's
object was to make such men stand up, to see themselves as 'more sacred
than any dedicated altar or element'.[3] It is worth recalling that the gentle
Traherne also believed that 'self love is the basis of all love'.[4]

'A man's righteousness towards himself means right reason in self-
government and self-control.' In addition to the master of a household's
right to divorce his wife, in the *De Doctrina* Milton gave him the right 'to
distribute the Lord's supper to his dependents': 'we are all equally priests
in Christ' – all except those who are dependent on an earthly master. If a
people had not power to remove any governor, superior or subordinate,
they lacked 'the natural and essential power of a free nation', 'that power,
which is the root and source of all liberty, to dispose and oeconomize . . .
as masters of family in their own house and free inheritance'. Servants are
in their masters' power; freedom is forfeited by insolvency. If Milton had
secured for masters of families the right to make each household a church,
with its head as priest,[5] he would have got his final revenge on the church
which 'outed' him in the sixteen-thirties. We should relate his failure to
attend any place of worship after 1660 to these considerations.

Milton's contempt for mere hereditary aristocracy, his emphasis on the
aristocracy of grace, of merit, was of course traditional in humanist circles.
Yet Milton carried it to the extent of applauding the abolition of the House
of Lords and the monarchy, whilst retaining his conviction of the sanctity
of the property even of evil persons.[6] The case against bishops and church

---

[1] *C.P.W.*, VI, pp. 719–20, 746, 790, 731, 735; I, pp. 417–18; cf. II, p. 750; VI, p. 681; cf. the
defence of market society by Walwyn and Culpeper cited in *C. and C.*, chapter 8.
[2] See *W.T.U.D.*, pp. 333–4 for a contemporary criticism of this idea by the Ranter Abiezer
Coppe.
[3] *C.P.W.*, I, pp. 842–4, 883.
[4] Traherne, pp. 339–41.
[5] *C.P.W.*, III, pp. 256–7; VI, pp. 719–20, 558, 602, 681, 787–91; cf. II, p. 750.
[6] *Ibid.*, I, p. 608. This latter was the orthodox view: cf. Sibbes, IV, pp. 15–17.

courts had been in part – though only in part – an economic case. 'Their trade being, by the same alchemy that the Pope uses, to extract heaps of gold and silver out of the drossy bullion of the people's sins.' They 'prog and pander for fees; . . . I remember not whether in some cases it bereave not men all right to their worldly goods and inheritances.'[1]

Part of the case against hireling ministers was their expense. Unless they had private incomes – as Milton, no doubt thinking of his own case, expected they would – ministers should live by their hands, like the Apostles.[2] Similarly Milton – presumably with his tongue partly in his cheek – told Sir Robert Howard that he was a republican 'among other reasons because theirs was the most frugal government; for that the trappings of a monarchy might set up an ordinary commonwealth'.[3] Milton often went out of his way to praise the middling sort; it was not right for 'the teachable and the unteachable, the diligent and the slothful, to be maintained side by side at the public expense'.[4] Milton seems to aim at an aristocracy of merit, an opportunity state. The very idea of 'equalizing the unequal' was absurd.[5]

Yet Milton's attitude to degree was far from traditional. His was a hierarchy of virtue; no social hierarchies must stand in the way of those capable of taking advantage of the free educational opportunities which he wished the state to offer. Under God men were relatively equal. In *Paradise Lost* the two archangels spoke of 'just equality' (VII. 487, Raphael), of 'fair equality, fraternal state' (XII. 26, Michael).[6] Milton's pragmatism, his lack of specific programmes, links him with Oliver Cromwell, who was 'not wedded and glued to forms of government', and with Marchamont Nedham, who wrote in *Mercurius Politicus* on the eve of the dissolution of the Rump, 'it matters not what the forms be, so we attain the ends of government.' Baillie in 1645 had attributed to the Independents in general a 'principle of mutability, whereby they profess their readiness to change any of their present tenets' – and he quoted a passage in favour of progressive revelation from the *Apologeticall Narration* of the five dissenting brethren. Members of Parliament, Milton wrote in the *Defence of the People of England*, 'ought never to be otherwise than entirely free and

---

[1] *Ibid.*, p. 592; cf. pp. 44–50, and p. 82 above.
[2] *C.P.W.*, II, p. 531.
[3] Darbishire, p. 186; cf. *C.P.W.*, VI, pp. 598–601; cf. pp. 167, 205 above.
[4] *C.P.W.*, IV, pp. 679, 457–8, 471, 533.
[5] *Ibid.*, VI, p. 790.
[6] Cf. *C.M.*, VI, p. 122, and p. 382 below. Cf. Miner (1974), pp. 253–6, who says that 'Milton really was more libertarian than . . . any major poet before the eighteenth or nineteenth century', and speaks of 'the possibility of rising above one's class' in relation to *Paradise Lost*.

uncommitted, . . . nor so bound to their former opinions as to scruple to change . . . to wiser ones thereafter for their own and the nation's good'. Milton, like Hugh Peter, thought good men were more important than good laws.[1]

There was always a tension in Milton between good government and self-government, aristocracy and liberty. Milton was a revolutionary, more interested in securing the revolution than in equality. The best must rule if a good society is to be constructed. The passion for virtue conflicts with the passion for liberty, just as the demand for liberty conflicts with the demand for discipline. By the time of Blake, Shelley and the French Revolution, the assault on the mediaeval theory of degree could be carried further: political consciousness now extended to larger sections of the population thanks to the greater commercialization of English society – as Moses Wall had predicted.[2] But their attitudes are implicit in Milton's faith in individuals when they are educated up to the knowledge and goodness necessary for freedom.

Saurat remarked that 'in our eyes Milton was each time in the right – against bishops, against presbyters, against censors, against royalists. . . . He did represent human nature.'[3] In view of the foregoing we might modify this a little. Gerrard Winstanley and Bunyan are surely the great seventeenth-century literary figures to whom we should turn as representatives of our common humanity. Bunyan tried to adapt the Christian myth to the needs and aspirations of the common man, of those who had supported Levellers and Diggers. Milton is an élitist intellectual. He does not define those for whom he speaks in economic terms, apart from his preference for the middling sort; but a certain level of education, of culture, of 'elegance' is assumed. Milton is not necessarily the worse for his class limitations; but he lacks the Digger emphasis on human love. (Recall the rather chilling trinity in *Comus* – faith, hope and chastity.[4])

Milton's God is a god of justice more obviously than of love. Against the *De Doctrina*'s passages on the duty of charity to oneself and on the religious duty of hating God's enemies, let us place Winstanley's 'Alas! you poor blind earth moles, you strive to take away my livelihood and the liberty of this poor weak frame my body of flesh which is my house

---

[1] *Mercurius Politicus,* No. 354, 19–26 March 1653; Woodhouse (1938), p. 36; Baillie (1645), p. 101. For analogous waverings between democracy and the rule of the virtuous in some Leveller leaders and their supporters, see Manning, pp. 314–17.
[2] Cf. pp. 201–2 above.
[3] Saurat, p. 67.
[4] Ross, p. 196. For Winstanley see p. 473 below.

I dwell in for a time; but I strive to cast down your kingdom of darkness, and to open hell gates and to break the devil's bonds asunder wherewith you are tied, that you my enemies may live in peace; and that is all the harm I would have you to have.'[1] Winstanley, unlike Milton, had worked for wages, for taskmasters.

The problem of the English Revolution (as of all middle-class revolutions) was to create a world in which bourgeois individuals could be free, without this freedom extending to self-destruction. Hobbes had seen that absolute freedom for equal and competing natural men would lead to anarchy: his solution was an ultimate supreme authority of the state over all individuals, which would rarely be used but whose presence would act as a permanent check on the autonomous individuals who composed the society. Milton wanted this check to be internalized. He rejected the Hobbist paradox of a freedom dependent on absolute sovereignty. For Milton liberty is licence, tending to anarchy, unless it is tempered by a recognition of God's purposes. But this is not merely Obedience with a capital O.[2] Obedience involves human reason, which is capable of understanding and appreciating God's intentions. Freedom is knowledge of necessity, said a later revolutionary theorist. So for Milton acceptance of the divine plan becomes the condition, the definition, of true liberty. Discipline must be internalized. The problem, however, remains of reaching agreement on what God's purposes are.

---

[1] Sabine, p. 333; cf. p. 473 below.
[2] 'The Fall is simply and solely Disobedience – doing what you have been told not to do: and it results from Pride – from being too big for your boots' (Lewis, 1942, p. 69). Cf. Fish (1967), pp. 259, 240, and pp. 389–90 below.

Chapter 21

Radical Arminianism

> This is flat to hang God's will upon man's will, to make every man an Emperor and God his underling, and to change the order of nature by subordinating God's will . . . to the will of man.
>
> William Perkins[1]

By the beginning of the seventeenth century the dominant mode of religious thought in England was Calvinist; it strongly emphasized God's eternal decrees and his initiative in man's salvation, playing down the efficacy of works. By the end of the century high Calvinism had lost its intellectual appeal. Bishops and many dissenters alike preached a theology of works, and – even more important – the dominant philosophy of John Locke was wholly Arminian as well as wholly secular. The predestinarian theology which had dominated Protestant Europe in the sixteenth century, and which shook England in the Revolution of 1640–60, disintegrated. It is an important turning point in human thought. It took place in other countries of Europe, but in England the transitions are especially clear-cut.

Around 1600 the official theology of the Church of England was no less firmly Calvinist than that of those whom we call Puritans. John Whitgift, Archbishop of Canterbury 1583–1604, and George Abbot, Archbishop of Canterbury 1610–33, were both Calvinists in this sense: Richard Bancroft, who came in between, is less easily placed because he was an administrator rather than a theologian. James I himself was a theological Calvinist. The Thirty-nine Articles combine predestinarian positions with articles capable of a different interpretation, but three theological commitments of the church between 1595 and 1619 seemed to confirm the Calvinist interpretation as the orthodox one. These were the five Lambeth Articles of 1595, the Irish Articles of 1615, and the fact that in 1619 the English representatives

---

[1] *Works*, I, p. 295. The study of Perkins, we are told, led Arminius to abandon Calvinism.

268

concurred in the condemnation of Arminianism at the Synod of Dort, and in the uncompromising reaffirmation of the Eternal Decrees.

The church left itself loopholes. Whitgift's Lambeth Articles were never officially adopted; neither the Irish Articles nor the decisions of the Synod of Dort were ever adopted in England, though Puritans pressed for full acceptance of the latter. But before the sixteen-twenties only a minority in the universities seriously questioned the Calvinist theology, which predominated among higher and lower clergy alike, and was preponderantly the religion of that sector of the laity which the House of Commons represented. In the great Elizabethan controversies between the Presbyterian Cartwright and Archbishop Whitgift, theology had not been an issue. The reluctance of the rulers of the Church of England, from the Elizabethan settlement onwards, to define its theology in exclusively Calvinist terms was, I suspect, due more to a desire not to provoke the continuing Catholicism of simpler members of the church than to any theological uncertainty – unless Elizabeth herself, apparently so coldly secular, cherished secret papist leanings.

The first rumblings of premature Arminianism were heard in Cambridge in the fifteen-nineties. The initiative, significantly, came from a continental convert from Catholicism to the Church of England, Peter Baro. His case was a nine-days' wonder, until he was thumped down by Whitgift's Lambeth Decrees. But circumstances soon became more propitious for a theological thaw. For most of Elizabeth's reign England had been a beleaguered garrison, with predestinarian Protestantism as the ideology uniting its most stalwart defenders. This was no time for exploring the openings to the right which some of the Thirty-nine Articles offered. But many things changed in the nineties. The great patrons of Puritanism, the Earl of Leicester and Sir Francis Walsingham, died in 1589 and 1590 respectively. After the defeat of the Spanish Armada in 1588 and continuing Dutch successes, it became clear that England's insular independence was secure: there was to be no restoration of Catholicism by Spanish or Irish arms. The peaceful succession of James, the crushing of rebellion in Ireland and the peace with Spain which followed, all pointed in the same direction. The grim ideological unity of the years of siege could be relaxed. Provoked by the ribald, bawdy and popular pamphlets of Martin Marprelate, the bishops went over to the offensive against radical Puritans, exploiting an unsuccessful revolt by three possibly deranged predestinarians in 1591 to accuse all Puritans of plotting or at least encouraging social subversion. The extremists were isolated and silenced, some accepting the logic of separatism and going into exile, others remaining in

England and accepting the rule of the Church of England by bishops. The bishops' policy of breaking up the alliance between Puritan ministers and a section of the gentry and town oligarchies had social consequences: the government came more and more to rely on Catholic or crypto-Catholic elements among the gentry and aristocracy. This is reflected in the foreign policy of James and Charles – in their desire to arrive at an understanding with Spain, their rejection of the leadership of Protestant Europe.[1]

We can see the first stirrings of proto-Arminianism in England as a reflection of these political developments: hitherto existing inhibitions were removed. Most notable was Richard Hooker's monumental *Of the Laws of Ecclesiastical Polity*, commissioned by the bishops as an anti-Puritan work and warmly welcomed in Rome. It was as ambiguous as the Thirty-nine Articles themselves on the predestinarian issue. Anti-Calvinist sentiment became modish in the universities, especially Oxford, culminating in the Laudian movement.[2] M.P.s were right to stress the affinities between the Arminianism of the Laudians and Roman Catholicism. There was a nostalgia in the clericalism and sacramentalism of this reaction from Calvinism. It was naturally associated with absolutist political theories. It was utterly different from the later radical Arminianism of men like John Goodwin and John Milton.

Calvinism's historical importance lies in the doctrine of the oligarchy of the elect. These favoured individuals, chosen from all eternity by God, are set apart from the sinful mass of mankind. The suitability of this theology for welding revolutionary minorities into tight groups is obvious enough. Nor was the usefulness of Calvinism restricted to revolt by urban groups. The doctrine that revolution could be justified if led by the magistrate made it appropriate for use by a dominant class in any society. But the effectiveness of Calvinism as a revolutionary doctrine is short-lived: it is at its most vigorous in the period of revolutionary crisis, of national siege, when a tautening of morale is required. Hence Calvinism too underwent a sea-change after the relaxation which the political victories of the nineties brought about. The high Calvinism of the universities became increasingly scholastic and arid: academics tended to brood over abstruse problems like assurance of salvation and the visibility of the elect, in a way which drove those who looked for a warmer, more emotional religion back to the sacramentalism of popery or Laudianism. Congregational preachers, on the other hand, faced with the problem of talking to mass audiences in

---

[1] Collinson, pp. 198–201; cf. pp. 14–15 above.
[2] Tyacke, pp. 119–43.

times which were no longer of crisis, had perforce to mitigate the rigours of high Calvinism. It served no useful pastoral purpose to reiterate that most of your congregation were probably damned and unable to do anything about it, though some parsons went on saying just that. Puritan divines, faced with the problem of talking to regular congregations in normal times, had to act as if most of their flocks were capable of salvation. Theologians like William Perkins and John Preston came slowly to liberalize their theology, to readmit good works by the back door. Perkins taught that God takes the will for the deed, that a strong desire for God's grace is presumptive proof that a man has received or is about to receive it. The covenant theology helped to bind the inscrutable God in chains comprehensible to mere humans: it also helped to ward off antinomianism and radical Arminianism.[1]

There was a difference between the moral approach, the emphasis on conduct, of the liberal Calvinists, and the sacramentalism of papists and Laudians. For the Calvinist the emphasis is always on the individual, his conscience, his personal relation to God: for the papist or Laudian the emphasis is on the church, the community led by its clergy, united by its sacraments. The Laudian emphasis on the holiness of church buildings which must be consecrated, on the sanctity of the altar, to which men must bow, on confession to a priest, on the absolute necessity of baptism; elevation of the liturgical side of worship and set forms of prayer as against preaching, the belief that salvation came only through the church and its sacraments – all these were reversions from the Protestant emphasis on the supremacy of the individual conscience and individual study of the Scriptures, from the Protestant critique of any mediators between man and God.

So before 1640 the choice for most educated Englishmen seemed to lie between a religion of ceremonies, whether papist or Arminian, and a religion of direct relation to God, whether the scholastic high Calvinism of the universities or the more liberal pastoral Calvinism of the Puritan divines and the émigré Presbyterian and Independent congregations. Both religions assumed a state church, though some of the émigrés wanted considerable modification of the disciplinary structure of the Church of England. Both assumed the necessity of a priesthood, though the tendency of Calvinism was to associate some laymen with the clergy in the government of the church. This could be done either structurally, as in the Presbyterian system of including lay elders among the rulers of the church,

---

[1] P. Miller (1939), chapter XII.

or in the more Erastian manner which appealed to members of Parliament – by subordinating the church centrally to the rule of Parliament, and local congregations to the natural rulers of the realm, the gentry and merchant oligarchies.

But there was a third force – the popular Pelagianism of the sectaries, whose significance grew rapidly during the revolutionary decades. This tradition, which appeared in Edward VI's reign, but then was driven underground, rejected the sacramentalism of papists and Laudian Arminians even more vehemently than did the Calvinists; but it also rejected the oligarchy of grace preached by Calvinists themselves, in favour of a universalism that was in no way associated with the sacraments of the church. Arminians of the right *assumed* that salvation was possible only through the church, through the mediation of the priesthood. Most Calvinists, whilst rejecting all mediators except Christ, wished to retain a state church, an established ministry. Those Calvinists who did not – Troeltsch's sect-type – still thought of the predestined elect as a corporate body of persons, however hard it was to know who they were. The elect, difficult to identify in practice, were in theory a clearly identifiable body of persons. Arminians of the left carried the individualist implications of Calvinism to their logical conclusion. Men and women were not saved through the church, and were not pre-ordained to salvation by an irreversible divine decree thanks to Christ's imputed righteousness. God foresaw that they would save themselves by their own efforts. But the works by which Arminians of the left expected to be saved were not the formal ceremonies of the old Catholicism, penance and absolution: they were acts of love and charity voluntarily done by free individuals.

It is therefore highly superficial to classify, for instance, William Laud and John Goodwin together as Arminians, or Richard Montague and John Milton. The formal similarity of their rejection of predestinarianism conceals the fact that they rejected it for totally different reasons. There is more in common between Laudianism and Presbyterianism than between Laudianism and Milton's Arminianism. Presbyterianism, like Laudianism, is a clerical creed, believes in salvation through the church. Both are far removed from Milton's apotheosis of the true wayfaring and warfaring Christian, who runs his race and fights his battle alone. The Reformation's onslaught on sacramentalism ultimately cleared the way for this new radical Arminianism, once Calvinism had served its destructive purpose. But the original reaction against predestinarianism was nostalgic, backward-looking, rightly associated by contemporaries with popery. The affiliations of the Arminianism of the left are forward-looking, to rationalism and deism. It took the second shock of the revolution of the sixteen-forties to undermine both the new sacramentalism of Laud and the scholastic predestinarianism of the Presbyterians, and to open the gates to radical Arminianism, which hitherto either had led a suspect, proscribed, underground existence as part of the third culture, or was the subject of abstract speculation in closed intellectual circles like that of Great Tew.[1]

When Catholics or Laudians spoke of 'the church' they meant both the whole community and in a more special sense the clerical hierarchy; Presbyterians and many other Protestants similarly thought of the elect as more specifically 'the church' than the community at large. Some really radical Arminians in the sixteen-forties thought of the church as all men, universalizing grace and salvation. Milton, in this as in so many matters, was poised between the second and third cultures.

It is difficult to be precise about the origins of this radical Arminianism in England. The later Lollards were fiercely, brutally, anti-clerical and anti-sacerdotal. But it is harder to trace positive elements of universalism in their theology, though it is present among Familists. The early Ana-baptists were predestinarian in theology: the courage with which they attacked all known certainties of their world needed the moral support of a belief in immediate divine backing, a conviction that they were indeed God's elect. The earliest continental ancestors of the General Baptists seem to have been pacifist, quietist, not to have needed the heaven-storming morale of the men of 1525 or of Münster. They rejected the existing state and church in the same anarchical way as their more bellicose co-religionists, but they did not postulate a dictatorship of the godly as an alternative government which it was their task to set up. Lacking this collectivist theory, this demand for discipline, which predestinarian Baptists shared with Calvinists, 'Arminian' Baptists gave free reign to the individualist and democratic logic of Protestantism: if all men could be saved, then the priesthood of all believers was an essentially democratic doctrine. For Lutherans, Calvinists and early Anabaptists it had meant at best democracy within the oligarchy of the elect: the great leap is from predestinarianism to universalism in theology. This leap, on a significant scale, came in the sixteen-forties, when Milton and Goodwin decided that they were not Presbyterians, whatever they had thought in their passionate rejection of Laudianism. The advent of the masses of the population into effective political action during and after the Civil War led to the downfall of the Calvinist theology.

---

[1] *W.T.U.D.*, pp. 35–6.

For what indeed had Calvinism to offer the lower orders except a critique of sacerdotalism and sacramentalism? Its positive content was discipline, which meant restrictions on the freedom of the lower classes. The discipline, the fighting morale, could hold a party together as long as there was an enemy to overcome; but after victory in England in the sixteen-forties, as after the success of the Revolt of the Netherlands, Calvinism tended to be strongest where clerical influence was greatest, weakest in the great centres of industrial and commercial civilization. For the individualist in opposition needs organization; when power has been won individualists demand freedom above all. Arminianism became popular among the victorious patrician class in the big cities of the Netherlands after the revolt; predestinarian theologies descended the social scale after the English Revolution. The respectable Presbyterian churches slid into Unitarianism; the Particular Baptists and the Calvinistic Methodists in the eighteenth century throve among the classes excluded from political power. Arminianism replaced millenarianism.

Servetus had rejected the doctrine of predestination on the ground that it denied human freedom.[1] This view was held, among others, by the General Baptists with whom Richard Overton the mortalist was associated. But there were many converging streams, including the Familist tradition. Once censorship and church courts collapsed, radical Arminians preached openly. Congregations of laymen took upon themselves the power of governing their church, including the right to excommunicate; and this, Robert Baillie darkly observed, 'driveth to universal grace'. A former weaver near Wisbech was writing in favour of universal grace in 1643. Mrs. Attaway, in addition to being a mortalist who favoured divorce for incompatibility, also believed that 'it could not stand with the goodness of God to damn his own creatures eternally.'[2] Preachers of Fast Sermons in 1646–7 denounced Arminianism and universal grace. In various parts of England, Edwards noted, men rejected the Calvinist doctrine of election, and believed that 'there shall be a general restoration wherein all men shall be reconciled to God and saved', even the heathen. He associated this view with the Everlasting Gospel.[3] In 1647 the Rev. Zephaniah Smyth preached a sermon in defence of absolute reprobation, 'because this is a doctrine not often insisted upon and at this time denied'. He believed that he was preaching to a crowd of 'Levellers'.[4] Winstanley,

---

[1] Bainton, p. 138.
[2] T. Edwards, I, p. 86; *W.T.U.D.*, pp. 175, 187.
[3] Arrowsmith, Newcomen; T. Edwards, I, pp. 20, 23.
[4] Schulz (1955), p. 128.

Walwyn, Coppin, John Robins, Erbery and the author of *Tyranipocrit Discovered* thought that all men shall be saved. John Reeve was at one time 'strongly deceived with an imagination of the eternal salvation of all mankind', through 'a lying doctrine of a pretended universal love to the whole creation', which he took from the Ranters.[1] The Blasphemy Ordinance of May 1648 included this belief among those to be penalized. By 1654 Paul Hobson thought that the 'opinion of free will' was increasing in the north parts. He and other Baptists denied the doctrine of eternal torment. Henry More and others rejected the wicked God of the Calvinists: John Goodwin dedicated his *Redemption Redeemed* to the Cambridge Platonist Benjamin Whichcote (among others) in 1651.[2] The Quakers' 'bottom is much tending to Arminianism', Lord President Lawrence noted in 1656.[3] George Wither followed the same course as Milton, towards an undenominational Arminianism.

We do not know how early Milton abandoned Calvinism. In 1641 he assumed that Pelagianism was a heresy, but refused to accept Calvin as an authority; in *Areopagitica* he referred to Arminius with respect but apparent disagreement. Yet his argument that trial can purify only those who have freedom of choice points irresistibly away from Calvinism.[4] The Arminianism which he certainly adopted in the fifties put Milton in the company of John Goodwin, General Baptists, Quakers, Ranters and other radicals. Milton's Arminianism sprang from his deep belief in human dignity, human freedom. Unless the will is free, worship and love towards God are vain and of no value, he thought: 'some measure of free will' must be allowed to men 'if the ways of God to men are to be justified'.[5]

Milton needed Arminianism to save God. He justified God's ways to men by substituting for the Calvinist God of arbitrary power an Arminian God of goodness, justice and reasonableness.[6] As with Servetus, Milton's rejection of the Eternal Decrees aimed to preserve human freedom. Spiritual illumination is 'common to all men'.[7] There is no freedom without responsibility, no responsibility without freedom. Predestination to damnation implies an unjust God, who cannot shake off his responsibility

---

[1] D. P. Walker (1964), pp. 104-5; Winstanley, *The Breaking*, p. 17; Sabine, p. 381; Reeve, *An Epistle to a Quaker*, pp. 1-2, in (1711); *W.T.U.D.*, pp. 166, 185-6, 192, 222-4.
[2] *W.T.U.D.*, p. 74; D. P. Walker (1964), pp. 147, 154.
[3] T. Burton, I, p. 63.
[4] *C.P.W.*, I, pp. 533, 553, 707; II, pp. 519-20; VI, p. 82. See p. 154 above.
[5] *C.P.W.*, VI, pp. 160-6, 175, 204, 343, 397.
[6] *Ibid.*, VI, p. 166; G. D. Hamilton, pp. 87-100.
[7] *C.P.W.*, VI, pp. 175, 204.

for the existence of sin and evil upon earth. Both *Paradise Lost* and
the *De Doctrina Christiana* emphasize very strongly the Arminian point,
stressed also by Boehme, that the angels stand by their own strength:
here as so often heaven is more like earth than men think.[1] So we come
back again to Milton's political concerns, for which the theology tries to
give universal solutions. The English revolutionaries fell freely, fell by
their own attachment to self-interest, their neglect of the divine purposes.
They can blame no one but themselves, certainly not divine providence.[2]
Milton, who knew Dutch Remonstrant theology but pressed a good deal
further, seems to have continued making 'Arminian' additions to the *De
Doctrina* until a very late date.[3]

'A true and living faith', Milton insisted, 'cannot exist without works.'
Predestination is to salvation, not to damnation; and it does not exclude
human freedom. (In Grotius's *Adamus Exul* Satan urged predestination
against Eve's fears about eating the apple.[4]) 'Those who persevere, not
those who are elect', Milton continued, 'are said to attain salvation' – a
remark relevant to the dogged holding-on which was his position when he
wrote the *De Doctrina*. The regenerate will persevere, he tells us, 'so long
as they do not prove wanting in themselves'. We can be restored on earth
to the pre-lapsarian freedom of the will. Milton's apparently Calvinist
lines in *Paradise Lost*:

> Some I have chosen of peculiar grace
> Elect above the rest
> (III. 183–4)

are sandwiched between two unequivocally 'Arminian' passages (lines
111–34, 185–202).[5]

Perfection is not fully attainable on earth, but we should strive towards
it 'as an ultimate goal'. 'That faith alone which acts is counted living.'
Both in *Paradise Lost* and in *Paradise Regained* Milton emphasized that
Christ is 'by merit more than birthright Son of God'. Unfallen men might

---

[1] *Ibid.*, VI, p. 343; J. Pordage (1776), pp. 54, 71–2; West (1955), pp. 162–74. See p. 329 below.
[2] See chapter 28 below.
[3] *C.P.W.*, VI, pp. 85, 108–9.
[4] *Ibid.*, VI, pp. 490, 168–73, 180; Kirkconnell, p. 160.
[5] The phrase 'peculiar grace' has given rise to some discussion. See G. D. Hamilton, pp. 97–8,
and a letter from Maurice Kelley in *The Times Literary Supplement*, 5 September 1975. 'Peculiar
grace' does not imply predestination, does not preclude freedom of the will. Cf. Vane: 'A
more peculiar condescension and effect of God's bounty and good will to some sinners beyond
others'. God gives recipients of this peculiar grace 'a better light . . . than in a way of mere
restoration they could attain unto' (Vane, 1662, p. 41). See also p. 393 below. I have benefited
from discussing this question with Stanley Fish and Gary Hamilton.

have been 'by degrees of merit raised' to Sonship, and 'all believers are called saints', however imperfect their holiness.[1] Although Milton accepted the concept of original sin, and argued that it was physically inherited – in accordance with his monistic materialism – he nevertheless shows uneasiness about the idea of visiting the sins of the fathers upon the children. He had rejected the hereditary principle in politics, and justified the inheritance of original sin by analogy with attainder.[2] Unlike, say, Bunyan, he seems more concerned to stress the possibility of escaping from the hereditary taint than to dwell on its mechanism or consequences. He may have been equally uneasy about the idea of 'satisfaction' contained in 'Die he or justice must' (P.L. III. 210). Yet I cannot agree with Empson that Milton in any conscious sense thought that God was wicked. The morality of an eye for an eye goes back to a very primitive society, a society comparable to that which in England produced the blood feud and the wergild. But (apart from Biblical authority for this morality) it had recently been reinforced in England by the morality of the capitalist market, the morality which The Merchant of Venice criticized. The scrivener's son was in no position to reject that morality.

Milton's abandonment of traditional Calvinist Puritanism did not lead him to the extremes of Diggers or Ranters.[3] Arminianism was a way of preserving standards of conduct, a respectable alternative. Many roads were thus leading simultaneously to the decline of Calvinism: the Cambridge Platonists, the General Baptists, the Quakers. Locke summed up a secularized Arminian Puritanism. Little more than a century after Milton's death, 'predestination' was for Blake simply a dirty word.[4] Paradise Lost appeared at exactly the time of Arminianism's victory. This perhaps helped to make the epic seem acceptably orthodox, helped readers to miss the heresies.[5]

But the Arminianism that triumphed in the later seventeenth century was not the sacramental Arminianism of the Laudians, despite the success of individual Laudians in winning positions of authority in the church after 1660, despite the cult of King Charles the Martyr. The Non-Jurors after 1688 were the loyal adherents of a defeated cause. In the eighteenth century individual parsons played harmlessly with ceremonial, but the Laudian ideology was dead. Fear of the consequences of the French

---

[1] C.P.W., VI, pp. 506–9, 478–83; cf. pp. 165, 183, 202, 513; W.T.U.D., p. 321; P.L. III. 309; VII. 157; P.R. I. 166. Cf. pp. 296–306 below.
[2] C.P.W., VI, pp. 385–7.
[3] See pp. 311–16 below.
[4] W. Blake, pp. 944–8.
[5] C.P.W., VI, pp. 157–8; cf. W.T.U.D., pp. 276–7; C. Hill (Sphere, 1969), p. 254.

Revolution and of liberalism led to a revival of something like it in the Oxford Movement.[1] But this proved as ineffective as Laudianism in the sixteen-thirties at holding back the popular tide: as after 1660, subtler ideological methods had to be adopted.[2]

---

[1] Newman makes this very clear in his *Apologia pro Vita Sua* (Everyman), p. 52.
[2] See p. 469 below.

Chapter 22

The Millennium and the Chosen Nation

Who would not be glad to see Jesus Christ?

John Cook (1647)

Millenarianism was hardly a heresy in the England of the sixteen-forties, but it had been earlier. 'Chiliastic sentiment had been endemic in English society since at least the 15th century', Keith Thomas remarks; 'and it was primarily the absence of the normal restraints which made the civil war period so remarkable for the extent and variety of its millenarian activity.'[1]

Several ideas coalesce in the radical millenarianism of the forties: (1) that the end of the world is imminent; (2) that the Pope is the Antichrist whose overthrow will immediately precede the millennium; (3) that God's Englishmen are the main opponents of Antichrist; (4) that the poor and humble have a special part to play in the battle against Antichrist, which (5) is being fought out in England now; (6) that in the millennium Christ and his saints will reign on earth for a thousand years.

Spenser's earliest published verse was written for a treatise whose main object was to denounce the Pope as Antichrist. The theme recurs in *The Faerie Queene,* and was taken up by Sylvester – not only in translating Du Bartas but also in his own additions – and by Spenserians like Phineas Fletcher and George Wither.[2] There are millenarian overtones in the writings of Francis Bacon, and the scientific optimism of the early experimental scientists and Comenians contributed to the Utopian hopes held by many as well as Milton in the sixteen-forties and -fifties. Walter Blyth, the agricultural reformer, thought that England 'might be made the Paradise of the world, if we can but bring ingenuity into fashion'. 'Reason and experience showeth how we may be restored to Paradise on earth', Lady Ranelagh was assured in 1657.[3] The concept of God's special

---

[1] K. V. Thomas (1971), p. 144.
[2] C. Hill (1971), pp. 19, 46, 185–6.
[3] C. Webster (1975), pp. 24, 86, 482–3. She expected the millennium soon (Jacob, p. 20).

favour to Englishmen recurred often after the Reformation had established England's national independence. 'See ye not to what honour God calleth our nation?' Morison asked in 1539. 'God is English', declared the future Bishop Aylmer. This tradition was especially emphasized by the radicals: Fitz's privy church of 1567-8 saw England as the Israel which God favoured. God 'hath yet ever had this island under the special indulgent eye of his providence', wrote Milton in 1641.[1] England was 'chosen before any other, that out of her as out of Sion should be proclaimed and sounded forth the first tidings and trumpet of reformation to all Europe'.[2] Even a relative conservative like Arise Evans thought that 'God hath a special regard to England'; 'the elect are nowhere else but here in England.'[3] This attitude helped to get Reeve and Muggleton accepted as the two Last Witnesses: who else but God's Englishmen could qualify for such a role?

The sudden upsurge of popular self-confidence in the revolutionary decades took the form of a radical millenarianism. For a long time chronologists like Napier, Brightman and Mede had been interpreting the Biblical prophecies to suggest that important events, and in particular the fall of Antichrist, would take place in the mid-seventeenth century. Astrologers had arrived at similar conclusions from studying the stars.[4] For a long time too English Protestants had been eagerly studying the writings of John Foxe, which showed the common people as the most determined opponents of Antichrist in the perennial struggle of right versus wrong. Given the intoxicating revolutionary atmosphere of the early forties, plus the fact that the Puritan preachers were calling for the widest support for Parliament's fight against the antichristian enemy – it is easy to see how popular millenarianism arose. 'God uses the common people and the multitude to proclaim that the Lord God Omnipotent reigneth', proclaimed a Puritan divine in 1641. 'The voice that will come of Christ's reigning is like to begin from those that are the multitude, that are so contemptible, especially in the eyes and account of Antichrist's spirits and prelacy.'[5] Men sensed that they stood on the verge of great historic transformations.

There are many echoes of Foxe and Brightman in Milton's writings, combined with acceptance of the fact that the present was 'an age of ages

---

[1] *C.P.W.*, I, pp. 526, 704; Zeeveld, pp. 232-3; White (1973), pp. 31-2.
[2] *C.P.W.*, II, p. 552.
[3] A. Evans (1652), pp. 19, 37.
[4] This point is made in Trout, pp. 130-8, 145, 156. Dr. Trout also emphasizes the contribution of magical ideas to millenarianism (pp. 48-52, 109, 120, 127-30). I am very grateful to him for sending me a copy of his thesis.
[5] [T. Goodwin] (1938), pp. 233-41.

wherein God is manifestly come down among us, to do some remarkable good to our church or state'. England must never 'forget her precedence of teaching nations how to live', Milton proclaimed, a precedence which goes back to 'our English Constantine that baptized the Roman Empire' and included Willibrode and Winifred, Alcuin and Wyclif.[1] In *Areopagitica* he depicted censorship as a device of the Roman Antichrist; when reformation itself is to be reformed, 'Britain's God' turns, 'as his manner is, first to his Englishmen'. It was 'our wonted prerogative' to be 'the first assertors in every great vindication'.[2] So the chosen nation became the chosen people – the common people, not the royal government.

Like many radicals, Milton fused Foxe's and Brightman's myths with the constitutional myth of the Norman Yoke – that Englishmen used to be free before the Norman Conquest, and thereafter 'wrested their liberties out of the Norman gripe with their dearest blood and highest prowess'. Milton wrote that at a time when he was still contemplating an epic on some 'king or knight before the Conquest' as 'the pattern of a Christian hero'.[3]

In *Animadversions* and in *Of Reformation* (1641), Christ was 'shortly expected king'. Prelaty, Milton wrote, was 'more anti-christian than Antichrist himself' – i.e. than Rome. He later declared that he focused his studies principally on Christian doctrine because 'nothing else can so effectively wipe away those two repulsive afflictions, tyranny and super-stition' – which he saw personified in Laudianism. It is a neat way of illustrating the inextricable links between religion, politics and culture in his opposition to prelatical episcopacy – links which meant that he expected his poetic powers both to be liberated by the overthrow of episcopacy, and to be made more acceptable to the English people.[4]

I have discussed elsewhere the millenarian spirit which in the exciting days of the sixteen-forties gripped many supporters of Parliament, especially among the lower classes.[5] Milton shared this widespread millenarianism, as was appropriate for a man educated at Joseph Mede's college. It was because Christ's kingdom 'is now at hand' that Milton expected him to 'vouchsafe to us (though unworthy) as large a portion of thy spirit as thou pleasest'. In the minds of the less sophisticated this turned into a belief that the common people 'are the men that must help

[1] *C.P.W.*, I, pp. 703–4; II, pp. 231–2, 707.
[2] *Ibid.*, II, pp. 551–9, 232; cf. p. 414; I, pp. 614–16; IV, p. 495.
[3] *Ibid.*, I, pp. 592–3, 813–14.
[4] *Ibid.*, II, pp. 520, 850; cf. pp. 614, 673, 939; I, pp. 616, 705–7, 924–8; VI, p. 118.
[5] C. Hill (1971), *passim*; *W.T.U.D.*, pp. 95–7.

to pull' Antichrist down, here and now. It was expressed by the author of
Macaria in 1641, who hoped that the Long Parliament would 'lay the
corner stone of the world's happiness'.[1] In *The Tenure* Milton stressed
Charles I's affinities with Antichrist; he prayed for Christ's coming to
bring 'hasty ruin and a destruction to all tyrants'.[2] In *Eikonoklastes* he
echoed John Cook's argument that the court which sentenced Charles
'was a resemblance and representation of the great day of judgment, when
the saints shall judge all worldly powers'.[3] Erbery too believed that
'God appearing in the saints shall punish kings of the earth upon the
earth.'[4]

For many of the revolutionaries millenarianism stimulated proposals for
international action to accelerate Antichrist's fall. Milton himself at the
age of seventeen, in a poem about Gunpowder Plot, made the devil
describe England as 'the only nation . . . which rebels against me'; and
God spoke of 'me and my Englishmen'. Satan foresaw a time when the
Protestant God 'will fill the Tyrrhenian Sea with his swarming battalions
and plant his glittering standards on the Aventine hill'.[5] A quarter of a
century later, in *The Tenure* and the two *Defences of the People of England*, in
which Milton spoke to the people of Europe, he still assumed that God had
a special interest in the English people.

If England was 'to be the first restorer of buried truth', as Milton and
many others hoped, this entailed obligations to the churches abroad, the
Huguenots, the Dutch, the Swiss and the Scots from whom Laud had
tried to isolate English Protestants. It was always the Pope, Milton
thought, who had tried to prevent the union of England and Scotland,
for which radical Protestants had worked since the middle of the sixteenth
century. In *Of Reformation* Milton urged a restoration of that 'unity with
our neighbour reformed sister churches' which Laud had broken.[6] But –
at least since his visit to Italy – he was more than a Protestant international-
ist. 'Who knows not', he asked in *The Tenure of Kings and Magistrates*, 'that
there is a mutual bond of amity and brotherhood between man and man
over all the world, neither is it the English Sea that can sever us from that
duty and relation?'[7] When in *Of Reformation* he declared his belief that

---

[1] *C.P.W.*, I, pp. 706–7; C. Hill (1971), pp. 79–80; *Macaria*, Preface.
[2] See p. 167 above.
[3] Cook (1649), p. 40. John Canne made the same point (p. 14). In his *Defence of the People of England* Milton defended Cook against Salmasius.
[4] Erbery, p. 40. Cf. pp. 299–300 below.
[5] C. and F., pp. 45–8.
[6] *C.P.W.*, I, pp. 502–3, 576–7, 586, 598; cf. pp. 680, 703–4, 791–3.
[7] *Ibid.*, III, p. 214.

Christ would come shortly it was 'to judge the several kingdoms of the world and . . . put an end to all earthly tyrannies'.[1] Milton reiterated this conviction in *The Tenure*, and in *Eikonoklastes* he declared it to be the duty of the English revolutionaries 'first to overcome those European kings which receive their power not from God but from the Beast', just as Salmasius was to urge the kings of Europe to unite against the English Revolution.[2] In 1652 Milton declared, with some hyperbole, that he would be glad to see the English army and navy liberate Greece from the Turks. He retained his sense of England's priority when he declared that the Fronde showed that the French had been stirred up 'to our imitation'.[3] In the *Defence of the People of England* Milton felt that he spoke 'not on behalf of one people . . . but rather for the entire human race against the foes of human liberties'; in the *Second Defence* he claimed that news of the English Revolution brought the idea of freedom to all the enslaved peoples of the Continent.[4] Even in the disillusion of April 1660 he still spoke of England as 'this extolled and magnified nation', and looked forward to the Second Coming.[5]

Others who share this revolutionary Protestant internationalism include William Sedgwick, Hugh Peter, John Spittlehouse, John Canne, Gerrard Winstanley, John Owen, John Rogers, Andrew Marvell, William Erbery, George Wither, George Fox, Roger Williams, perhaps Admiral Blake and Oliver Cromwell.[6] Peter Sterry, preaching before Parliament in November 1651, expected 1656 to be a decisive year, because the Flood had occurred in the year 1656 from the Creation.[7] Robert Gell made the same point in 1655.[8] Milton's sonnet 'On the Late Massacre in Piedmont' shows him clinging fiercely to his international allegiances.

Milton, then, had been a radical millenarian long before an organized Fifth Monarchist movement existed. (His favourite Lactantius was a millenarian.) The Fifth Monarchists shared many of Milton's views, including condemnation of tithes and a state church. But they were a plebeian semi-anarchist group, and as they saw Christ's cause foundering

---

[1] *Ibid.*, I, p. 616.
[2] *Ibid.*, III, pp. 256, 581; cf. pp. 654–5; IV, p. 103.
[3] *Ibid.*, IV, p. 853; C.M., VI, p. 112.
[4] *C.P.W.*, IV, pp. 554–8.
[5] *C.M.*, VI, pp. 117, 133. The words quoted were added in the second edition of *The Ready and Easy Way*. I cannot understand how Professor Patrides came to conclude that Milton's millenarianism is restricted to a 'brief moment of fanaticism' in 1641 (p. 272).
[6] Capp, p. 53; Sabine, p. 385; Winstanley (?1648), pp. 62–3; (*The Law of Freedom*, 1652), title-page; C. Hill (Panther, 1969), pp. 133–4, 144–6; (1971), pp. 102–5; K. V. Thomas (1971), p. 149.
[7] Sterry, p. 44; Nuttall (1946), p. 109.
[8] Gell, pp. 16–17; cf. Vane (1662), p. 64.

in the fifties, some of them were goaded into direct action by a combination of impatience and despair, both of which Milton repudiated. Milton's position is somewhere between that of traditional millenarian Puritanism and activist plebeian Fifth Monarchism. He came to share the latter's pessimism about the possibility of establishing Christ's kingdom without miraculous divine assistance, but not their immediate tactical optimism. Like Bunyan, Owen and many others, Milton gradually became less certain that the Second Coming was imminent: the radicals had been mistaken in their chronology. 'Only the Father knows the day and the hour of Christ's coming', wrote Milton – echoing Wollebius, but with a different emotional emphasis. But he remained certain that when that day came Christ and his saints would reign on earth for a thousand years.[1]

Meanwhile premature revolt could only do harm to the cause: in Erbery's words, 'to shake off the yoke before the season came was to rebel against the Lord.'[2] The lesson was reinforced by unsuccessful Fifth Monarchist revolts in 1657 and 1661. After the Restoration Milton found himself 'almost expatriated' in the land he had hailed as God's chosen nation. 'One's country is wherever it is well with one', he grimly concluded.[3]

---

[1] C.P.W., VI, pp. 615, 623–7. For Bunyan and Owen, see C. Hill (1971), p. 147. See also pp. 415–16 below.
[2] Erbery, pp. 209–10.
[3] C.M., XII, pp. 113–15.

Chapter 23

Sons and the Father

> The Son, O how unlike the Father! First God Almighty comes with a
> thump on the head. Then Jesus Christ comes with a balm to heal it.
> > William Blake

I Anti-Trinitarianism

A great pother is sometimes made about the exact ancient heresy with
which Milton is to be labelled. Was he an Arian? A Nestorian? A Mon-
archian? A Sabellian? A subordinationist? Or was he a Socinian? The
worried attempts of orthodox Trinitarian scholars to persuade themselves
that the poet agrees with them would bring a grim smile to his face if he
could read them. So would attempts to tie him down to the beliefs of some
early Christian theologian.[1] Milton was an eclectic, the disciple of no
individual thinker. He would claim that his only starting point was the
Bible, his only aid the spirit of God. Milton was by no means wholly
original, uninfluenced by the ideas which he encountered. But it is not
helpful to label him; he does not fit easily into the ready-made categories
of academics. I shall concentrate on the substance of his unorthodoxies,
not their names. His heresies point in two directions – towards individual
freedom for man, and towards the goodness of matter.

Milton's Son is not co-eternal with the Father, but created by him in
time.[2] Like Hermes Trismegistus, Arians, Servetus and Ochino (but not
the Socinians), Milton believed that the Son was begotten before all other
created things, and was the instrumental cause of the creation of the
world. For Milton the Father and the Son are one in will but not in
essence. The Son's equality, in so far as he is equal to the Father, is a gift.
He becomes omnipotent through the Father's proclamation. (This equal/
unequal relation between the Father and the Son is rather like that

---

[1] Though it is perhaps not totally a coincidence that Lactantius had Arian leanings (Hartwell,
pp. 97–9).
[2] *C.P.W.*, VI, p. 88.

between husband and wife.) The Father is omnipresent and invisible: when he wishes to act or to communicate, he does so through the Son. Because identical neither with the Father nor with man, the Son can mediate between them.[1]

'The ultimate object of faith', Milton summed up in the *De Doctrina Christiana*, 'is not Christ the Mediator but God the Father.' 'Solus pater est verus Deus': Milton slipped this anti-Trinitarian statement into *The Art of Logic*. Between the impersonal Father and the Son who is capable of humanity, there is a wide gap. The Holy Ghost Milton hardly discusses at all. His arguments against the Trinity are ultimately logical and common-sensical: why create mystifications which are not to be found in the Bible?[2] We should think a good deal more deeply about Milton's failure to emphasize the Incarnation and the Crucifixion, his abandonment of traditional ideas of Christ's atonement; his virtual silence on the subject of the Ascension and on the descent of the Holy Ghost at Pentecost. Milton plays down all the miraculous elements in the Gospel story. Paradise is regained by human resistance to temptation, not by the sacrifice of a God. A desire to exalt the dignity of man is traditional in the popular anti-Trinitarian heresy of Familists and Socinians.

The name Christ does not occur in any of the three great poems. In the whole of his poetical works Milton uses it only in the title of *The Nativity Ode* and in the sonnet protesting against forcing consciences 'that Christ set free'.[3] Freedom here seems more important than Christ. Milton is, however, careful to speak of Christ throughout the chapters of the *De Doctrina* which deal with regeneration. For Milton the Son, unlike the Father, is capable of change. In *Paradise Lost* he moves closer and closer to the Father. In *Paradise Regained* the Son slowly learns what his destiny is. The *De Doctrina* emphasizes that the human Jesus has emptied himself of divine understanding and will: *Paradise Regained* shows him uncertain and in some respects ignorant until his moment of self-realiza-tion. Similarly all angels and men can ultimately attain oneness with God through Christ if they love and trust the Father as perfectly as the Son does. This eventual unity of all creation under the Son will lead to the final abdication of Christ's kingly power when God shall be all in all.[4]

---

[1] Servetus, pp. 105, 205; Owen, XII, pp. 220, 265, 271; MacCallum, pp. 90, 103; Hunter (1960), pp. 362–3; *C.P.W.*, VI, pp. 730–5. Cf. Vane (1662), p. 6.

[2] *C.P.W.*, VI, Book I, chapters V, XV. Cf. pp. 295–6 below.

[3] Cf. *C.P.W.*, IV, pp. 374–9: although Christ 'assumed the form of a slave' he never failed to preserve the heart of a liberator; cf. IV, p. 534. See also Miner (1974), p. 277.

[4] Revard, pp. 47–58; see pp. 303–5 below. For Anti-Trinitarianism in *Paradise Lost*, cautiously expressed, see *C.P.W.*, VI, p. 110 and n.

Wherever Milton got his anti-Trinitarianism from, there was plenty of it about in the England of the sixteen-forties – and indeed in the two preceding generations. Christopher Marlowe taught that Christ was only a human being; other Kentishmen seem to have held anti-Trinitarian views.[1] Milton's doctrine of the Trinity has affinities with the Hermetic tradition. This taught that the supreme God, the Father, manifests all things but is himself not manifested; the Logos, the Son of God, was the first of all created things. The Son was the Creator, the demiurge. Sometimes the Son was the sun, or light; sometimes the immortal cosmos made by the Father in his own image. He was never a saviour.[2] Only the Father is good, because he is not subject to perturbation; the second God, the material God, the cosmos, was not good because subject to movement; but not evil because immortal. These doctrines fuse the Platonic demiurge with the immanent God of the Stoics, leaving the transcendent Platonic God as the supreme Father.[3] Some early Christian heretics had also distinguished between the creator God and the supreme, unmoved God. Others identified the Hermetic Logos or Son of God with Christ. These Hermetic ideas were reproduced in seventeenth-century England by Robert Fludd.[4]

Milton's version of anti-Trinitarianism also has affinities with the doctrines of Bernardino Ochino, who from 1547 to 1553 was pastor to the Italian church in London. At the accession of Mary, Ochino withdrew to the Continent, arriving at Geneva in time to denounce the burning of Servetus for anti-Trinitarianism. Ochino and Milton both questioned the doctrine of predestination and believed in religious toleration. Both advocated divorce and defended polygamy, on which the *De Doctrina* appears to repeat many of Ochino's arguments.[5] Some have heard echoes of Ochino's *A Tragoedie or Dialogue* (translated into English by John Ponet in 1549) in *Paradise Lost*. Both Ochino and Milton stress the mathematical unity of the godhead. Both thought that the Son was created in time, but that he received and participated in the divine essence. Both tended to pantheism in their accounts of the creation. Milton's anti-Trinitarianism is much closer to Ochino than to the radical Polish Socinianism, which stressed the humanity of Christ. Despite the probability of Ochino's influence on Milton, the latter rather curiously fails to

---

[1] P. Clark, chapter 3.
[2] W. Scott, I, pp. 12–13, 116–17, 156–9, 174–5, 188–9, 300–1, 389; II, pp. 308–9.
[3] *Ibid.*, I, pp. 168–9, 194–7, 348–9, 549; II, pp. 6–7, 25, 32.
[4] Hutin (1971), *passim*. See also p. 110 above and pp. 324–8 below. The Arian Sir Isaac Newton still valued Hermes Trismegistus highly (Manuel, 1974, pp. 44–5; *C. and C.*, p. 256).
[5] *C.P.W.*, VI, pp. 357–60, 576–7; see pp. 137–8 above.

mention him in his published writings. But he refers to him in his Commonplace Book, in relation to polygamy, an entry probably made at the time he was hunting for support among the early reformers for his own views on divorce.[1] Milton may have felt that Ochino's notorious radicalism made it imprudent to acknowledge indebtedness to him.[2]

At Servetus's trial in 1553 the prosecution had strongly emphasized the socially subversive consequences of his heresy. Pacifism and rejection of oaths tended to be associated with the same group of heresies. A ballad about John Lewis, burnt in 1583 for anti-Trinitarianism, adds the interesting detail that he 'did thou each wight', i.e. he employed the outward symbol of insistence on human equality which was later to be adopted by the Quakers.[3] An Oxford don in 1636 thought that Socinians maintained points 'which are repugnant to our state and government'.[4] Socinus was a mortalist: Samuel Gorton, who emigrated to New England in the same year 1636, became an anti-Trinitarian, a mortalist and an antinomian. The more radical doctrines of the Socinians, stressing the humanity of Christ, spread to England from Poland via the Netherlands in the early seventeenth century, linking up here with the indigenous radical tradition.

After 1612 burnings ceased in England because they were found to be ineffective as a deterrent:[5] anti-Trinitarianism did not disappear. There are traces of congregations in 1613 and in the sixteen-twenties, but they covered their tracks too carefully. We have to judge from the violence of the reaction of the orthodox. In 1639 Archbishop Neile wrote to Laud, reminding him that the burning of Legate and Wightman 'did a great deal of good in this church'. He feared that 'the present times do require like exemplary punishment'.[6] Laud himself 'was very careful to suppress this growing damnable heresy in the Dutch churches, as fearing from hence it might creep over to us in England'.[7] Grotius, whom Milton 'ardently desired' to meet in Paris in 1638, was suspected of Socinianism.

---

[1] L. A. Wood, pp. 27, 32, 44–86, and *passim*. Wood's case would have been strengthened if he had known of Milton's reference to Ochino in the Commonplace Book (*C.P.W.*, I, p. 412). Cf. G. H. Williams, pp. 538–41. A possible allusion to Ochino in *Paradise Lost* is suggested by McNair, p. 361.

[2] Hanford (1921), pp. 121–2.

[3] Rollins, pp. 54–61; cf. Emmison, pp. 126, 207, for similar examples of 'thouing' from Essex in the fifteen-eighties and -nineties. For Lewis see also Fuller (1842), III, p. 67.

[4] Crosfield, pp. 85–6.

[5] Fuller (1842), III, p. 256. See p. 73 above.

[6] *C.S.P. Domestic, 1639*, pp. 455–6. I owe this reference to the kindness of Andrew Foster, whose Oxford D. Phil. thesis *A Biography of Archbishop Richard Neile (1562–1640)* is still in preparation. It was a Kentish anti-Trinitarian whom Neile wanted to burn.

[7] Raymond, p. 32.

The Canons of 1640 fulminated against 'the damnable and cursed heresy of Socinianism', especially prevalent among 'the younger or unsettled sort of people', like undergraduates. There had been Transylvanian students at Cambridge in Milton's time: it is unlikely that none of them were Socinians.[1] 'Fear of Socinianism', wrote Sir John Suckling in 1641, 'renders every man that offers to give an account of religion by reason suspected to have none at all.'[2] Was the elder Gil so suspected, one wonders?

In the liberty of the forties Socinian congregations appeared from underground. In 1641 George Walker published a confutation of the heresy, and a sub-committee of the House of Lords was discussing it.[3] By 1643 Francis Cheynell thought it necessary to launch a full-scale attack on *The Rise, Growth and Danger of Socinianisme*. He had at first believed the heresy should be answered only in Latin; but enough unorthodox books had appeared for him to feel that they should be refuted in the vernacular.

John Goodwin, 'the great red dragon of Coleman St.', was often accused of anti-Trinitarianism. Under the auspices of Hartlib and Dury Goodwin published and possibly translated in 1648 the first four books of Acontius's very influential *Satanae Stratagemata*. Acontius, one of the Edwardian radical immigrants and a disciple of Ochino, had not been a Unitarian, but he regarded the Trinity and the divinity of Christ as non-essential doctrines. In 1644, Thomas Webbe, later to be a Ranter, was preaching anti-Trinitarianism in London. Early in 1645 the divinity of Christ was being denied in crowded churches in Bell Alley and Coleman St., in 1646 in Red Cross St. The Trinity was decried as 'a popish tradition'. There were similar groups in Bath and Bristol, and in the army.[4] The London Baptist minister Samuel Richardson, a defender of toleration, was thought by Baillie to be unsound on the Trinity: Daniel Featley extended the accusation to the whole Baptist sect. Most of the Baptists in Kent and Sussex, we are told at a slightly later date, denied the Trinity, were mortalists and believed that God existed in the shape of a man. This reminds us of Elizabethan anti-Trinitarianism in Kent; and the combination of the three tenets suggests that some of these Baptists were associated with what later became the Kentish group of Muggletonians.[5]

---

[1] *C.P.W.*, IV, p. 615; Wilbur, p. 148.
[2] Suckling, II, p. 237; cf. pp. 250–2. For Socinianism in the Great Tew circle, see Aubrey, II, pp. 150–1.
[3] G. Walker, *passim*; Fuller (1842), III, p. 416.
[4] Gustafsson, pp. 102–12; Wilbur, pp. 174–5; T. Edwards, I, pp. 21, 26, 81–2, 106–7, 113; II, p. 7; III, p. 93. Cf. *A Catalogue of the severall Sects and Opinions in England and other Nations* (1647).
[5] See pp. 65–75 above. Featley, p. 2; C. E. Whiting, pp. 89–90; cf. White, *Records*, p. 183.

In February 1645 Paul Best was called before Parliament because of a Socinian treatise which he had written for private circulation in manuscript. A committee proposed that he should be hanged. He defiantly published from prison *Mysteries Discovered* (1647) – which Parliament burnt even though they could not burn the author. Some think that Milton owned and annotated this book.[1] Best survived because the radicals rallied to his defence – Selden in the Commons, Walwyn and Goodwin (probably) outside; the sectaries generally, Edwards tells us, spoke bitterly against the House on this issue.[2] Fast Sermons, on the other hand, denounced anti-Trinitarianism to Parliament.[3] In 1646 Thomas Lushington published an openly anti-Trinitarian work.[4]

Best – a gentleman with theological interests – was a lightweight by comparison with John Bidle, the father of English Unitarianism. Bidle, like Milton, was a schoolmaster, a poet and a serious Biblical scholar, who (again like Milton) studied the Bible 'for sundry years together' in order 'to reduce our religion to its first principles'.[5] For him this meant stressing the humanity of Christ. By 1644 heresy-hunters in Gloucestershire were after him, and in 1646 he too was imprisoned by Parliament. Like Best, he published a heretical tract from prison – *Twelve Arguments drawn out of Scripture* (September 1647), refuting the divinity of the Holy Spirit. There is no such thing as original sin, he announced flatly. Parliament foolishly advertised this book too by ordering it to be burnt: it sold well, and other writings followed. The apparent rashness of Best and Bidle in publishing despite their imprisonment can only be explained by the strength of the popular movement outside Parliament at this time, especially in the army, in full revolt in 1647; even in the House of Commons Vane spoke up for Bidle. In 1648 he was released on bail, but was soon re-arrested, until the Act of Oblivion of February 1652 set him free. He remained at liberty until persecution returned with an elected Parliament in December 1654.

In 1649 the Rump of the Long Parliament had been horrified to find an anti-Trinitarian in its midst. This was John Fry, a Dorset gentleman, elected M.P. in 1640 but disqualified. He served on the Wiltshire county committee, and after Pride's Purge was called to take up his seat. This may well have been because he was willing to be nominated one of the King's

---

[1] T. Edwards, I, p. 38; McLachlan (1951), pp. 152–62.
[2] T. Burton, I, p. 65; T. Edwards, II, pp. 13, 22, 149, 178; III, pp. 46, 135–6, 235–6.
[3] Newcomen, O. Sedgwick.
[4] *The Expiation of a Sinne in a Commentary upon the Epistle to the Hebrews.*
[5] Bidle (1654), pp. xxv–xxvi. Bidle published verse translations of Virgil's *Bucolics* and of the first two satires of Juvenal (*Life of Bidle*, in Bidle, 1691, p. 4. First published 1653).

judges. He sat once, and would probably have been a regicide if he had not been suspended because of his theological views, which emerged when he tried to help the imprisoned Bidle. Fry explained, and was restored to the House in February 1649, perhaps as a concession to Leveller pressure for toleration; but like Best and Bidle before him Fry published a defence of his views, *The Accuser Sham'd*. In this he attacked priests and lawyers generally, as well as those who had profited financially by the Civil War.[1] This book called forth another massive tome from the indefatigable Francis Cheynell, *The Divine Trinunity* (1650). Fry retorted with *The Clergy in their Colours*, a fierce counter-attack against the Presbyterian clergy, with strong Miltonic emphases. 'Many thousands in England' were 'protestants upon no other account but because it is the religion their parents own, and the profession of the country'. In this they are 'no wiser than parrots'. It was contrary to Protestantism 'to walk by an implicit faith'. Men should 'reflect upon those things which are taught, not believing anything because their teachers say so but because what is taught is rational and grounded upon the Scriptures'. 'Till men understand what they do, and from solid principles act those things which are truly Christian, how easy is it for men of parts and craft to lead them they know not whither? . . . For till *from a principle within* a man can say that he hath the makings out of the love of God to him, he can have but a conceited peace.'[2] Fry was expelled from Parliament, and his books condemned to be burnt. His enemies said that he associated with 'the deified atheists of the Family of Love'. Fry himself complained that he was 'accused by blackcoats of being a main-tainer of licentiousness', and he jeered at the 'tricks' of the Presbyterian clergy in a way that anticipates John Phillips.[3]

Fry was not the only anti-Trinitarian in high places. Scoutmaster-General Watson, an intimate of Oliver Cromwell and Ireton, with alchemical interests, was described in February 1649 as publicly disputing against the Trinity.[4] Tom May, fellow-translator with Milton for the Council of State, spoke 'slightingly of the Holy Trinity', and kept 'beastly and atheistical company', such as Thomas Chaloner, Henry Marten and possibly Marchamont Nedham.[5] D.P., author of *The True Primitive State of Civill and Ecclesiasticall Government* (1649), was a middle-of-the-road man, who criticized Levellers no less than Presbyterians. Nevertheless he

---

[1] Fry (1649), pp. 6–8, 13–14; Worden, p. 241.
[2] Fry (1650), pp. 16, 64.
[3] *Ibid.*, pp. 40–8, 58–9; cf. *Mercurius Politicus*, No. 38, 20–27 February 1651, pp. 616–18. For Phillips see Appendix 2 below.
[4] Carte, I, pp. 220–2. I owe this reference to the kindness of Professor Clive Holmes.
[5] Aubrey, II, p. 55; A. Wood, II, p. 295; III, p. 531.

seems to have regarded 'all doubtful points about the Trinity' as open for discussion, lest error be *retained*.[1] Even the blamelessly conservative Ralph Josselin was reading Socinian books in 1648.[2]

Another army anti-Trinitarian was John Knowles (c. 1625–77), son of a Gloucestershire merchant. He too echoes Milton in his refusal 'to pin my faith on another's sleeve, nor believe as the church believes, being not desirous to try truths by wholesale but to receive it as God discovers it'.[3]

Meanwhile the Socinian Racovian Catechism, stressing Christ's humanity, had been published in England – in Latin in 1650, in English two years later, despite the burning of the Latin text. The 1650 edition was almost certainly licensed by Milton. When questioned by Parliament, he is said to have admitted the fact, and referred them to *Areopagitica* for his reasons.[4] The English translation was in its turn condemned to the flames, but Socinian books remained on sale in London. There was a *Life of Socinus* in English translation. John Owen's schemes for re-establishing a persecuting state church with a carefully defined theology – proposals which outraged Milton – may have originated in horror at the publication of the Racovian Catechism.[5]

In 1654 the strength of anti-Trinitarianism was such that the Council of State called upon Owen, now Vice-Chancellor of Oxford University, to refute it. This he did in 750 pages and with considerable alarm. The tendency of Bidle's writing, Owen said, was 'to increase infidelity and sin in the world'. The majority of men must be 'overpowered by the terror of the Lord' and of eternal punishment in hell if mankind was to be preserved from 'the outrageousness and unmeasurableness of iniquity and wickedness, which would utterly ruin all human society' if we 'cast down and demolish the banks and bounds given to the bottomless lust and corruption of natural men'. By contrast, Owen put forward a very old-fashioned defence of Christ's propitiatory human sacrifice which would have outraged Professor Empson, and which Milton perhaps did not like very much. 'There is not a city,' Owen added, 'a town, scarce a village in England, wherein some of this poison is not poured forth'; and he spoke of 'the flames of Socinianism kindling upon us on every side'.[6] There is much evidence to confirm this. The poet Joseph Beaumont was worried

---

[1] *Op. cit.*, p. 21.
[2] Josselin, p. 62.
[3] In Eaton, pp. 233–5; cf. Knowles (1648), Preface; (1650), p. 6.
[4] Parker, pp. 395, 994. Among those examined by Parliament on this occasion was Francis Gouldman, one of Milton's contemporaries at Christ's.
[5] Masson, IV, pp. 438–43.
[6] Owen, XII, pp. 52, 47, 586–7, 433. For similar anxiety about Socinianism and libertinism in the same year see Fawne, pp. 1–9.

about anti-Trinitarianism. Francis Osborn thought the Socinians were the most rational part 'of our many divisions', and that their doctrine seemed 'in reason to plead for approbation'. The objections were social rather than intellectual.[1]

Thomas Edwards had observed that anti-Trinitarianism was often combined with other heresies, such as mortalism, denial that the Scriptures were the word of God and of the existence of hell. In March 1647 a preacher told the House of Commons that 'every ... vagrant itinerant huckster' denied the Trinity, the authority of the Bible, the historicity of Jesus Christ. Walwyn, in addition to being a Leveller, spoke slightingly of the Trinity.[2] The Leveller authors of *Englands New Chaines Discovered* spoke up for Bidle and Fry in March 1649. Winstanley in effect denied the Trinity by allegorizing away the Son and the Holy Ghost. The Ranter Jacob Bauthumley denied that Christ was any more divine than other men.[3] In 1651 the Behmenist John Pordage was charged with anti-Trinitarianism and with expressing a hope that the saints would take over the property of the wicked. Captain Robert Everard was spreading Socinianism and Arianism in Newcastle-upon-Tyne in 1652.[4] Socinians try to pass themselves off as Familists, declared Cheynell in 1650. None but Ranters deny the Trinity, said Culpeper in 1654; but the northern Quakers were accused of it in 1655.[5]

In 1655 *The Faithfull Scout*, a moderately radical newspaper edited by the former scrivener Daniel Border, was sympathetic to a man who had denied the divinity of Christ. *The Faithfull Scout* was also favourable to Levellers and Fifth Monarchists, and moderate in reporting on the Diggers. It supported toleration, and was suppressed in 1655.[6] James Nayler the Quaker agreed with Milton that 'the Lord God Almighty, to whom belongs all the kingdoms in heaven and earth, does nothing therein but by his Son. ... By him he creates and governs, by him he saves and condemns, judges and justifies.'[7] Among anti-Trinitarians, or those accused of the heresy, we may include John Reeve and Lodowick Muggleton,[8] William Erbery,[9]

---

[1] Beaumont (1880), II, pp. 116–17; (1914), pp. 56–9, 200; Osborne, I, p. 91.
[2] T. Edwards, I, pp. 86, 106–7, 113–16; II, p. 28; III, pp. 93, 120; Hodges, p. 55.
[3] Wolfe (1944), p. 402; McLachlan (1951), pp. 120, 134, 220–4; C. E. Whiting, pp. 89–90; Sabine, pp. 131, 134; cf. pp. 96, 112, 114, 120; Cohn, pp. 337–8.
[4] J. Pordage (1655), *passim*; *W.T.U.D.*, p. 286.
[5] Cheynell (1650), Sig. Bv.; Culpeper (1654), Sig. A 3v.; Hall, pp. 229–30.
[6] Frank (1961), pp. 358, 248, 227, 214, 91, 176.
[7] Barbour and Roberts, p. 105.
[8] Muggleton (1764), pp. 76–7.
[9] Erbery, pp. 264, 278–9; T. Edwards, II, p. 21; III, pp. 89–92, 250; Cheynell (1646), pp. 42–6. Erbery claimed not to have read Socinian writings, but knew a 'Polonian expression' when he heard one. This is rather my point: Socinianism was in the air.

Clement Writer,[1] Jock of Broad Scotland,[2] Paul Hobson, Benjamin Worsley, John Graunt (for a time),[3] Ralph Cudworth and various Quakers from Nayler to William Penn. Penn, who found himself in the Tower in 1668 on this account until he recanted, seems to have queried the Trinity on numerical-logical grounds similar to those of Fludd and Milton.[4] Milton's friends included Andrew Marvell and Sir Robert Howard (and probably Peter Sterry), all of whom were accused of Socinianism, as well as Nathan Paget, whose library contained a fair collection of Socinian books.[5] Milton's early biographer, John Toland, was thought to be a Socinian, and Milton was accused of anti-Trinitarian heresies by Charles Leslie in 1698, by Dennis in 1704.[6] Defoe, who was a great reader of Milton, had no doubt that in *Paradise Lost* the poet was 'not orthodox' on the Trinity, but 'lays an avowed foundation for the corrupt doctrine of Arius, which says there was a time when Christ was not the Son of God'. Milton was good on God and the devil, 'but he has made a mere *je ne scai quoi* of Jesus Christ'.[7]

In *Pax Terris* (published 1647) Joseph Hall thought that toleration was permissible for all save Arians and Socinians. The Blasphemy Ordinance of 1648 was in no small part inspired by fear and hatred of anti-Trinitarianism. It was rarely enforced in its full rigour; but Bidle spent most of his life in prison; his, Best's and Fry's books were burnt, together with the entire edition of the Racovian Catechism. Bidle was not exactly a Socinian, though he was probably the translator of the Racovian Catechism.[8] Like Milton, Bidle worked out his own theological position from the Bible.[9] We may speculate that if Milton had not been called to serve the cause of God and the Commonwealth in defending regicide, he too might have felt obliged to testify publicly to his beliefs about the nature of God.

After 1660 anti-Trinitarianism was perforce less vocal – the London Baptists felt it necessary to denounce it[10] – but it was certainly not extinct. 'To argue from a man's silence', as McLachlan observes, 'that he did *not* hold an opinion for which he might be ruined and imprisoned or, up to

---

[1] T. Edwards, I, pp. 113–16; II, p. 149.
[2] *W.T.U.D.*, p. 209.
[3] *C.P.W.*, VI, p. 67; Aubrey, I, p. 272; *C. and C.*, pp. 262–3.
[4] Bunyan, I, p. 614; II, p. 292; McLachlan (1951), pp. 225–6, 303–7; Sewel, pp. 114, 478–9; *C.P.W.*, VI, p. 213; cf. *Mercurius Politicus*, No. 341, 24 December 1656, p. 7469.
[5] Legouis, p. 222; Oliver, pp. 285–6, 289. Baxter accused Sterry of a mixture of Platonism, Origenism and Arianism (Pinto, 1934, p. 87).
[6] Shawcross, pp. 22, 118, 130.
[7] Defoe (1840), pp. 63–8.
[8] McLachlan (1951), p. 193.
[9] Kinloch, p. 129; MacCallum, p. 95.
[10] *C. and C.*, p. 268.

1699, even hanged, seems rather absurd.' Mrs. Aphra Behn was perhaps no less discreet when she recorded without comment that the noble savage who is the hero of *Oroonoko* could accept all of Christianity but the Trinity.'[1] 'The Socinians multiply upon us', complained Henry Stubbe in 1670. John Locke and Isaac Newton, with Milton the three greatest names of the period, could not find Trinitarianism in the Bible. Newton seems to have shared Milton's view that the Son was the divine agent in the Creation, and that the Father was a *deus absconditus*.[2]

Milton's account of the relationship of the Son to the Father is close to that of Arius, but it is best to label him merely anti-Trinitarian.[3] In 1641 Milton was 'orthodox' in his views on the Trinity, as on predestination. In 1649 he described Arianism as a heresy. It may well be that Milton, like Servetus before him and Newton after him, simply regarded rejection of the Trinity as the logical consequence of Protestantism.[4] In view of the overwhelming evidence of widespread anti-Trinitarianism in England during the forties and fifties we do not need to go back to Origen or Lactantius for Milton's views. He knew and quoted the Fathers when he agreed with them, as Bidle quoted Lactantius;[5] but everything we know about Milton and his attitude to authority in general (and that of the Fathers in particular) suggests that he would not regard patristic backing as any reason for accepting an opinion. He got his ideas from the Bible, though the questions which he asked of the Bible came from the world in which he lived and discussed, the world of Best and Bidle and Fry and Nathan Paget. (Whether or not the annotated copy of Paul Best's book is Milton's, it is unlikely that he had not read it). Milton's fierce handling of La Place in the *De Doctrina* implies taking up a position on the side of the Socinians.[6]

Part of Milton's hostility to the orthodox doctrine of the Trinity is logical. Three persons in one seemed to him a contradiction in terms. A similar point was made in the Racovian Catechism. Milton's belief that creation was *ex deo* rather than *ex nihilo* has analogies with Socinus's position, but was not derived from that source alone.[7] Milton accepted

---

[1] Her intimate friend Charles Blount was apparently a mortalist (Pinto, 1962, p. 191).
[2] Stubbe (1670), p. 3; McLachlan (1951), pp. 225–6, 303–7, 327–31, 338; *C. and C.*, pp. 261, 268, 273–4. See chapter 26 below.
[3] Cf. Manuel (1974), p. 58, on Newton.
[4] *C.P.W.*, I, p. 498, 533–5, 553, 966; III, p. 507; *C. and C.*, p. 267. In 1611 Howson alleged that the notes to the Geneva Bible leant towards Arianism (Fuller, 1842, III, p. 248). Fuller denied the charge (1840, p. 542).
[5] McLachlan (1951), p. 177.
[6] Pittion, p. 143.
[7] *C.P.W.*, VI, pp. 212–13, 216, 262–4; cf. p. 240 above, and chapter 25 below.

the view of the Racovian Catechism that 'soul and body are so conjoined as that a man is neither soul nor body.'[1] His views on baptism have been described as 'Socinian-Anabaptist immersionism'.[2] The Socinian rationalist approach to theology must in general have appealed to him. John Owen's main complaint against Socinians was that they reduced all to right reason.[3] If Milton encountered the view expressed in 1637 by the Socinian Crell, that truth will always prevail in fair argument, it may have contributed to *Areopagitica*. Like Bidle, Milton had not much use for mysticism: he was 'much closer in his views to the Socinianism of Bidle than to the Platonism of [Henry] More'.[4]

The Familist tradition of spiritualizing and allegorizing the Bible lent itself to a type of rationalism; and it fused early with the Hermetic tradition which identified the demiurge with the Logos. Boehme's Wisdom nearly became a member of the Trinity. Bidle regarded the Wisdom of God as a created being which he equated with the Spirit of God.[5] We recall Wisdom playing 'in presence of the Almighty Father' in *Paradise Lost* (VII. 10–12).[6]

Milton differentiated himself sharply from the Socinians' most radical tenet, the mere humanity of Christ. He agreed that the Son was not equal to the Father, but he believed, as Socinians did not, that the Son existed before Jesus was born, that he was the Father's agent in creating the world and will ultimately (with the saints) be its judge. Milton retained the legalistic idea that Christ's death was a necessary form of 'satisfaction' for Adam's sin: 'Die he or justice must.'[7] Unlike Socinians, Milton did not deny the existence of the Holy Spirit, only his status as a member of the Trinity. The Son for Milton was man, but more than man. At this point ambiguity takes over.

II Sons of God

Milton's theology was as masculine as Crashawe's was feminine. He thought of God as 'a most indulgent Father governing his church as a family of sons' – 'no servants but all sons'. This had been true of Protest-

---

[1] Kelley (1935), pp. 223–34; cf. *The Racovian Catechism* (1652), pp. 28–9.

[2] *C.P.W.*, VI, p. 544n.

[3] Owen, VII, p. 6.

[4] MacCallum, pp. 92–5.

[5] McLachlan (1951), p. 193. Bidle interpolated a passage to this effect in the Racovian Catechism (pp. 35–6).

[6] Cf. *C.P.W.*, II, pp. 596–7, and p. 58 above.

[7] *C.P.W.*, II, p. 604; VI, pp. 63, 218, 265, 419–24, 444.

ants generally since the Virgin and female saints had been rejected as
mediators. In contrast to Erikson's aphorism 'father religions have
mother churches',[1] Milton mocked at bishops who spoke of 'your Mother
the Church of England' – 'an idolatrous mother'.[2] Now that we have
thrown off the authority of 'our pretended Father the Pope', Milton saw
the church not under 'the awful notion of a Mother' to whom implicit
obedience was owed, but as a young bride under strict control, 'strait
tuition'.[3] Yet for Milton the Father does not really seem to have been
'most indulgent'. He reminds us at least as much of that ruthless and
grasping scrivener, the elder John Milton.[4] Milton's anti-Trinitarianism,
his aspiration to union with the Son, seems to have as its aim the elevation
of humanity – at least of the male half of the species. In a passage otherwise quoted *verbatim* from Wollebius Milton changed 'we revere the
Word and majesty of God' to 'we revere God as the supreme Father and
judge of all.' Milton's concept of sonship rejected Calvin's God, who
'elects those whom he chooses for sons . . . according to the good pleasure
of his will, without any regard to merit'; the Son in *Paradise Lost* was 'by
merit more than birthright Son of God'.[5]

Milton stressed the literal meaning of Genesis 1:26: God created man
in his own image. Milton came close to the Muggletonian 'six-foot God'
when he wrote: 'If God attributes to himself again and again a human
shape and form, why should we be afraid of assigning to him something he
assigns to himself?'[6] That man was created in the image of God is the
greatest argument for human dignity. Comus's rout had lost 'their human
countenance, / The express resemblance of the gods'; they 'roll with
pleasure in a sensual sty' (68–77). They were at the opposite pole to
regenerate believers, all of whom are properly called Sons of God. Comus
appeared to make the distinction when he referred to the temperate who
'live like Nature's bastards, not her sons' (726). For Milton the process of
regeneration 'restores man's natural faculties of faultless understanding
and of pure will'. We are 'freed from the slavery of sin and restored to the
divine image'; we 'have already begun to be blessed' whilst still on earth.
Perseverance depends on our own volition. God adopts the regenerate
as his sons, and 'the first result of adoption is liberty'. We are 'ingrafted in
Christ', and thereby freed 'from the slavery of sin and thus from the rule

[1] Erikson, p. 257; cf. pp. 54, 163.
[2] *C.P.W.*, I, pp. 727–8, 837, 848, 940–1; cf. VI, p. 592.
[3] *Ibid.*, I, pp. 728, 755.
[4] See pp. 22–3 above.
[5] *C.P.W.*, I, p. 547; VI, pp. 19, 441; Calvin, II, p. 234.
[6] *C.P.W.*, VI, p. 136.

of the Law and of man'. Full perfection is not to be hoped for in this life, but we can strive towards it. So long as an adopted son is not wanting in himself, so long as he does not extinguish the spirit, he is already beginning to be blessed.[1] 'The saints ... are said to have been begotten by God', Milton wrote, though in a much less exalted sense than Christ. The point was made in the Racovian Catechism.[2]

At the end of the *Epitaphium Damonis* Milton saw Diodati 'among the gods' (lines 197–205). Angels are Sons of God in the *De Doctrina* and *Paradise Lost*. At the conclusion of *Of Reformation* Milton foresaw the awarding of angelic titles to those believers 'that by their labours, counsels and prayers have been earnest for the common good of religion and their country'. This verged on very radical doctrine. 'Men that are wholly taken up into God are called angels', Winstanley told his readers. He gave as examples Jesus Christ and men who have been made perfect. The Ranter Abiezer Coppe had been acquainted with angels 'in the shapes and forms of men'. William Franklin's disciples were known as angels.[3]

In *The Reason of Church Government* Milton argued that God governed the church as the father of sons, all of whom are priests. ('The slave does not stay in the house for ever, but the son stays for ever': Milton quoted John 8:35 in the *De Doctrina*. Cf. Walter Cradock: 'It is base to tie a son as much as a servant.'[4]) Sons of God in this sense, Milton argued in 1659, must not be persecuted by the magistrate: if they are reduced to servility towards him, the gospel is abolished. Without Christian liberty, no possibility of perfection.[5] In *Paradise Lost* 'that sober race of men, whose lives / Religious titled them the Sons of God' is Milton's gloss on Genesis 6:1–2 (*P.L.* XI. 621–2).

Believers who lived before Christ, and Jews or pagans who believe in God alone, can all be Sons of God.[6] In *Paradise Lost* the Son, addressing the Father, calls man 'thy youngest son'; in *Paradise Regained* 'sons of God both angels are and men'. The Son's *manhood* is exalted to the throne of God: he is 'destined man himself to judge man fallen' (*P.L.* III. 313–14, X. 61–2). Jesus is 'this perfect man, by merit called my Son' (*P.L.* II. 5–6), as Satan was 'by merit raised' to rule in hell. Satan claims to have been and

---

[1] *Ibid.,* VI, pp. 135–6, 547, 461–4, 478–83, 502–6, 511–13, 516, 495–7, 536–7; *C.M.,* VI, pp. 31–2.

[2] *C.P.W.,* VI, pp. 207–8 and n.

[3] *Ibid.,* VI, p. 233; I, p. 616; Winstanley (?1648), pp. 64–8; Sabine, 95–6, 215; Coppe (1649–50), p. 12.

[4] *C.P.W.,* VI, p. 506; Nuttall (1946), p. 107.

[5] *C.M.,* VI, pp. 30–2.

[6] *C.P.W.,* VI, pp. 197, 207–13, 475, 547.

therefore still to be the Son of God. Sir Isaac Newton in his commonplace book, no less than Satan in *Paradise Regained*, was worrying about the precise meaning of the phrase 'Son of God'.[1]

The doctrine of the sonship of all believers is of course Biblical. 'As many as are led by the Spirit of God, they are the Sons of God', St. Paul said (Romans 8:14). It is therefore accepted by all Protestants, and is mentioned in the Westminster Confession of Faith of 1647.[2] But the emphasis I have been citing was especially characteristic of the radicals. In the early seventeenth century the covenant of John Smyth's General Baptist church declared 'We shall be his sons, calling him Father by the spirit whereby we are sealed.' The church believed that 'Christ's redemption stretcheth to all men.'[3] This version of the doctrine, as Milton very well knew, trembled on the edge of antinomianism. 'What have we, Sons of God, to do with Law?' Many of his contemporaries were pushing it over the edge, as Thomas Münzer had done a century earlier when he said 'We must all become gods.'[4]

Edwards quoted sectaries who said 'Every creature is God. . . . A man baptized with the Holy Ghost knows all things even as God knows all things.'[5] Winstanley in 1648 believed that 'God now appears in the flesh of the saints.' Jesus Christ and his saints make one perfect man. He soon extended this from the saints to all mankind. 'Every creature . . . is a Son to the Father.' The same spirit that filled Christ 'should in these last days be sent into whole mankind'. 'Christ . . . is now beginning to fill every man and woman with himself.' This Christ in everyone, 'that perfect man, shall be no other but God manifest in the flesh'. 'He will spread himself in sons and daughters . . . till this vine hath filled the earth.' 'Everyone that is subject to reason's law', Winstanley declared, 'shall enjoy the benefit of sonship' – which for him meant participation in communal ownership and cultivation.[6]

George Fox criticized Ranters who claimed to be equal with God, but he himself was accused of affirming 'that he had the divinity essentially in him', 'that he was equal with God, . . . that he was as upright as Christ'.[7] Ranters and Quakers blended Familist and Hermeticist traditions in a

---

[1] Manuel (1974), p. 41. Cf. p. 422 below.
[2] See a letter from Mr. Paul Helm in *The Times Literary Supplement*, 13 December 1974.
[3] White (1973), pp. 135, 139. Smyth, we recall, was a Christ's man.
[4] Kaplow, p. 325.
[5] T. Edwards, I, pp. 21–2.
[6] Winstanley, *The Mysterie* (1648), pp. 40, 48; *The Breaking* (1648), pp. 15, 35, 73; (?1648), pp. 63, 85–6, 118–25, 132; Sabine, pp. 114, 131–2, 166–8, 198, 225; cf. pp. 161–71, 176, 207, 229–30, 448, 453–4; *W.T.U.D.*, pp. 113, 119, 316–18. Erbery echoed this: see p. 300 below.
[7] Mortimer, pp. 16–17.

very democratic mixture. The Hermetic texts described how man could discover the divine within himself, and through knowledge become like God. 'A man on earth is a mortal God; ... a God in heaven is an immortal man.'[1] In *Paradise Lost* the Father himself seems to recall some such idea when he tells the angels ironically

> O Sons, like one of us man is become
> To know both good and evil, since his taste
> Of that defended fruit.
>   (XI. 84–6)

The Hermeticist doctrine had been taken over by the Familists, who believed that every member of the Family of Love by obedience of love became a Son of God. Or, as Croll put it, man 'riseth to such perfection that he is made the Son of God, transformed into the same image which is God and made one with him'.[2] Robert Fludd taught that heaven was attainable on earth. 'The Rosicrucians call one another brethren because they are Sons of God' in this sense. Christ dwells in man 'and each man is a living stone of that spiritual rock'. Of these stones the true Temple will be constructed, of which the temples of Moses and of Solomon were only types. 'When the Temple is consecrated, its dead stones will live ... and man will recover his primitive state of innocence and perfection.'[3] This may perhaps enrich our sense of the scene in *Paradise Regained* when the Son of God miraculously stands on the pinnacle of the Temple. 'The Son and the saints make one perfect man', declared William Erbery; 'the fullness of the godhead dwells in both in the same measure, though not in the same manifestation. ... The fullness of the godhead shall be manifested in the flesh of the saints as in the flesh of the Son' – i.e. on earth.[4]

Servetus drew extensively on the Hermetic literature as well as on the pre-Nicene Fathers. He shared the Hermeticist view that the supreme God is invisible, incomprehensible, inaudible, transcending all things. He could be known only through the Logos, first of created things, through whom the world was made and animated. God is the essence of all created things: 'all things are a part and portion of God', Servetus thought. 'God fills all things, even hell itself.' For Servetus, Christ was not a hypostasis but a human being. But the Logos existed as the Son of God before taking flesh as a man. Since his life on earth all men are

---

[1] W. Scott, I, pp. 204–5; cf. pp. 128–9, 294–5; IV, p. 357.
[2] P. J. French, pp. 69–71, 74–5; Jessop, pp. 88–90; Rutherford (1647), p. 10; (1648), I, p. 59; Croll, p. 65.
[3] Hutin (1971), pp. 87, 90, 160–1; K. V. Thomas (1971), p. 225; cf. Dell, p. 74.
[4] Erbery, pp. 3–11, 15, 23, 40, 93, 103; cf. p. 282 above, pp. 419–20 below.

capable of becoming Sons of God by adoption, through faith in Christ; of participating in the divine nature. 'We are in heaven when we believe that Christ is the Son of God.'[1]

We do not know whether Milton got his conception of the sonship of all Christians from the Hermetic, the Familist or the anti-Trinitarian tradition, or direct from the Bible. But he cannot have been ignorant of any of these traditions. In 1641–2 Milton attacked the distinction between clergy and laity because it obscured 'the glorious titles of saints and sons'. A Christian's self-respect derived from consciousness of 'the dignity of God's image upon him, . . . enobled to a new friendship and filial relation with God'.[2]

Bidle agreed that 'there are many Sons of God', men who become such through faith. The Socinian John Knowles said: 'A son is of a father: angels and men are called the Sons of God.'[3] Again these views were capable of antinomian interpretation. Captain Francis Freeman had Christ in him, John Robins and William Franklin were deified by their disciples; Thomas Tany was God's high priest, Jacob Bauthumley and many other Ranters thought that God dwelt in the flesh of all men. Clarkson wrote of 'the perfect liberty of Sons of God', in the sense that they were exempt from the moral law.[4] For Peter Sterry the Father was 'the Manifester', the Son 'the Manifested'. Sterry thought that the Second Coming was already in progress. Christ the eternal Son 'goes out into the spirits of men', and forms 'a new sort of immortality' spreading through the world: legality and traditional morality must give way. Sterry took pains to differentiate himself from the Ranters, but Clarkson claims to have preached 'at Bow in Mr. Sterry's place' around 1647.[5]

Some of the radicals extended the masculine theology to include women more specifically. Gerrard Winstanley envisaged Christ rising in sons *and daughters*, on earth, now. The Quaker William Deusbury quoted Romans with the same addition when he said 'As many as are led by the spirit of God are the Sons and Daughters of God.'[6] Winstanley, especially in his early tracts, made much of the anointing of believers, by which they

---

[1] D. P. Walker (1972), pp. 40–1, 117–18; Bainton, pp. 46–53, 132–3, 138–9, 186, 195–6; Servetus, pp. 4, 70, and *passim*. Cf. Bidle (1647) and *The Racovian Catechism, passim*. On the parallels between Servetus and Milton see Larson, *passim*. Both were strict Scripturalists, their theories of creation were similar, both differentiated between the Logos, the Son and Jesus Christ. They agreed on baptism, faith, predestination, the relationship of law and gospel, nature, the possibility and efficiency of good works; that Christ is light.

[2] *C.P.W.*, I, pp. 547, 842; cf. p. 837. Cf. Walter Cradock, quoted by Nuttall (1967), p. 126.

[3] Bidle (1647), p. 15; Knowles (1650), pp. 16–17.

[4] K. V. Thomas (1971), pp. 136–7; Cohn, pp. 337–8, 332–3; Clarkson (1660), p. 27.

[5] Pinto (1934), pp. 20–1, 77–8, 92, 99–100, 108–9; Clarkson (1660), p. 23. For Sterry see pp. 42, 228 above. I have benefited by discussing him with Dr. J. P. Laydon.

[6] Sewel, p. 120; Barbour and Roberts, pp. 156, 254.

became Christs. Milton too referred to Christ's people (and not the monarch), as 'the Lord's anointed'.[1] Emphasis on sonship, on the family of God, recalls the Family of Love: those who stress it most are in that tradition – Erbery, Quakers, Socinians, Winstanley, Sterry, the Behmenist Samuel Pordage – and Milton. We should add Thomas Traherne, who carried on many interregnum heresies in quietist form. He wrote that Christ 'was the Son of God as you are'. Everyone is 'the Son of God in greatness and glory'.[2] Milton was one of the first to associate equality and fraternity (*P.L.* XII. 26; cf. VII. 487). This is not an aspect of his thinking on which he lays great stress; he says at least as much about the inequality of man as about equality. And yet if all men are – or can become – Sons of God, fraternity is a fact rather than a virtue.

Antinomianism, Socinianism, the theology of Ranters, Diggers and early Quakers, all stress the perfectibility of man on earth, the possibility of all men becoming Sons of God. Milton never emphasized Christ's humanity at the cost of denying his divinity – far from it; but he did stress the possibility of the unity of believers with Christ in sonship. It seems almost in a deliberate attempt to differentiate himself from the radicals that Milton, like Servetus, stresses Christ's role as creator and judge of the universe. The Father is remote, impersonal. The Son is created, exists in time. He mediates between the faceless Father and humanity: he it is who in the Old Testament appears to and speaks to men. In the New Testament the Father speaks only as a disembodied voice to declare his pleasure in the Son. The Father is justice, the Son is mercy. It is the Son to whom humanity can approximate, the Son whose *manhood* is exalted to God's throne (*P.L.* III. 315–16).[3] The Son creates alone: he judges together with his saints.

We can therefore look upon the Son as perfect man rather than as incarnate deity – Milton was never very interested in the Incarnation as such. Christ is not the only mediator: he was preceded by Moses (*P.L.* XII. 239–41), looking forward to the 'one greater man' who shall restore mankind to Paradise (*P.L.* I. 4–5). Even Christ when on earth 'does not know absolutely everything, for there are some secrets which the Father has kept to himself alone'. Christ was 'a supreme prophet'.[4] 'Sion's songs' in the Bible praise 'godlike men' equally with God (*P.R.* IV. 347–8). Milton's hints of perfectibility on earth look to a unity of sons in the Son. His Arminianism means that salvation is potentially open to all, and is attained by good works.

[1] *C.P.W.*, IV, pp. 403, 499.
[2] Traherne, pp. 191, 206; cf. pp. 213, 314, 328–9.
[3] Cf. Vane (1662), p. 6; Bouchard, pp. 64, 97–101.
[4] *C.P.W.*, VI, p. 265; Ricks (Sphere), p. 270; Owen, XII, p. 412.

'Everyone born of God cannot sin', Milton wrote in the *De Doctrina*, 'because God's seed remains in him' – so long as he does not himself extinguish it. Such a man, 'ingrafted in Christ', is 'raised to a far more excellent state of grace and glory than that from which he had fallen'.[1] All men and angels can thus attain to oneness with God through oneness with the Son, 'united as one individual soul / For ever happy . . . under his great vicegerent reign' (*P.L.* V. 609–11; cf. 829–31). The saints who rule and judge the earth in the last days are perhaps not to be distinguished from Christ, in whom they are incorporated.[2] This human perfectibility led Empson to discover the doctrine of the ultimate abdication of God in *Paradise Lost* (III. 332–41). After the Last Judgment, after the thousand-year 'reign of Christ and his saints on this earth', the end of time will come. 'Hell her numbers full . . . shall be for ever shut' and the world destroyed; the just shall inherit the new heaven and the new earth. Christ's rule will end.

> Then thou thy regal sceptre shalt lay by,
> For regal sceptre then no more shall need,
> God shall be all in all
>
> (*P.L.* III. 339–41)

– a God who exists within each regenerate being, angel or man or woman. The Son agrees that

> in the end
> Thou shalt be all in all, and I in thee
> For ever, and in me all whom thou lovest.
>
> (*P.L.* VI. 731–3)

> All my redeemed . . .
> Made one with thee as I with thee am one.
>
> (*P.L.* XI. 43–4)

The end of Christ's kingdom 'will not be one of dissolution but of perfection and consummation'.[3] Again the source of these passages is Biblical (1 Corinthians 15: 28; John 17: 21–3). But the emphasis, the emotional content, recalls Servetus: 'All reason for ruling will then end, all power and authority shall be abolished, every ministry of the Holy Spirit shall cease, since we shall no longer need an advocate or mediator because God will be all in all.'[4]

---

[1] *C.P.W.*, VI, pp. 461–4, 477, 506, 511–13. Emphasis on the two seeds was popular with the radicals, from Dell and Saltmarsh to Winstanley, the Quakers and Muggletonians.
[2] *C.P.W.*, VI, p. 499; cf. pp. 392–3, 475 below.
[3] *Ibid.*, VI, pp. 623–7; cf. pp. 357–8, 419–21 below.
[4] Bainton, p. 5.

For the radicals this emphasis involves an ultimate withering away of the church (Christ's kingdom) as well as of the state, a perfect democratic anarchy in a classless society, since the unregenerate are no longer with us.[1] This point seems to be emphasized by the vigorous transition in the passage I have just quoted. Addressing the angels, the Father continues 'God shall be all in all. But all ye gods . . .'. It is the only time he calls them by the name which makes them equal with him, though Satan addresses the rebel angels as 'ye gods' (X. 502).[2] Here perhaps we have a solution to the paradox that Milton the great republican appeared to favour monarchy in heaven. The ultimate ideal state is no longer monarchical, because the concepts of power and obedience have no meaning when we are all gods. In the Seventh Prolusion, probably written in the early sixteen-thirties, Milton in a Baconian passage had envisaged man's control over nature being virtually complete – 'as if indeed some god had abdicated the throne of the world and entrusted its rights, laws and administration to him as governor'.[3]

It has to be admitted that the full doctrine that Empson divined in *Paradise Lost* is not to be found in the *De Doctrina*, which is as cautious in discussing this subject as Marx when discussing the classless society, whose ultimate advent he nevertheless confidently expected.[4] Empson was, however, probably not aware of the analogies in Servetus and among Milton's radical contemporaries when he urged that the poet intended the ultimate abdication of God; so it may be worth citing one or two more examples. For Peter Sterry 'God is the heavenly Jerusalem where all things are fellow-citizens.'[5] Erbery and Winstanley had a similar vision, though they expected the abdication to take place on earth, in this life. For Erbery the Second Coming is 'God appearing in the saints', not Christ descending from the clouds.[6] For Winstanley this Second Coming/abdication had socio-economic consequences. 'Upon the rising up of Christ in sons and daughters, which is his second coming, the ministration of Christ in one single person is to be silent and draw back, and set the spreading power of righteousness and wisdom in the chair, of whose kingdom there shall be no end. . . . And now the Son delivers up the

---

[1] Ross, pp. 109–10.
[2] Revard, p. 58; Maxwell ('Gods', 1948), p. 235. Gilbert thinks this is a late addition to the epic (1947, pp. 137–8). See also pp. 392–3, 420–1 below, where this point is elaborated.
[3] *C.P.W.*, I, p. 296.
[4] *Ibid.*, VI, pp. 626–70. But cf. p. 282 above, where the saints sit in judgment on all worldly powers. Similar views were held by William Aspinwall, John Brayne and Mary Cary.
[5] Empson (1961), pp. 130–46; Pinto (1934), p. 101.
[6] Erbery, p. 40: God and the saints 'shall punish kings of the earth upon the earth'. '

kingdom unto the Father; and he that is the spreading power, not one single person, becomes all in all in every person; that is, the one King of righteousness in everyone.' 'And this God or almighty ruler becomes all in all, the alone King in that living soul or earth, or the five living senses.' There will be no more buying and selling, but 'the earth shall be common to all, for now . . . the Lord is all in all.'[1] Similarly Robert Coster gave

> A hint of that freedom which shall come
> When the Father shall reign alone in his Son.[2]

As so often, Blake inherited this tradition when he wrote: 'Everything has as much right to continual life as God, who is the servant of man. His judgment shall be forgiveness, that he may be consumed on his own throne.'[3] From a very different angle, Professor Bouchard arrives at conclusions similar to Empson's. 'God's purpose . . . is his own eradication before man's freedom. . . . One is almost tempted to say . . . that only through a radical Christian position verging on heresy, if not atheism, can one begin to value the real import of the epic: God is dead that man may live.' 'No privileged status any longer for the Father; no one beyond the law, but a community of Sons responsive to an internalized word.'[4]

When a modern theologian writes 'it would no longer seem appropriate to speak of a God existing apart from man, or a human self existing apart from God',[5] we may dismiss this as an attempt to adapt Christianity to an alien modern world, to preserve a God who is in fact dead. But we should not let our scepticism about trendy modern theologians reflect back upon the fantastic daring of the seventeenth-century thinkers who expressed their hard-won belief in the importance of human beings through the medium of theology. For them it was not a trick, not a last hope of drawing a congregation; it was a tremendous and tremendously new concept, won through spiritual torment and exaltation. Milton does not go as far as Winstanley in expecting the abdication of Christ to occur on earth in this life; but he may hint that the ultimate abdication of the Son, when all believers have attained to Sonship through him, would mean in effect the abdication of the Father too, since God will then be all in all. 'Thou art a man, God is no more', wrote Milton's admirer Blake.[6]

---

[1] Sabine, pp. 162–3, 184, 486.
[2] *Ibid.*, p. 673; cf. Bauthumley, pp. 45–57.
[3] W. Blake, p. 1030.
[4] Bouchard, pp. 64, 97–101.
[5] Review in the *Observer*, 14 July 1974, of J. S. Dunne, *The City of the Gods*.
[6] *C.P.W.*, VI, pp. 521–41; W. Blake, p. 138 (*The Everlasting Gospel*).

Chapter 24

Approaches to Antinomianism

> Whosoever is born of God doth not commit sin; for his seed remain-
> eth in him: and he cannot sin, because he is born of God.
>
> 1 John 3:9
>
> 'Tis not the place but the state which makes heaven and happiness.
>
> Sir Isaac Newton

I The religion of the heart

Milton's Arminianism, his acceptance of adult baptism, his political
libertinism and his perilous path on the fringes of antinomianism, all
derive from the Protestant emphasis on the religion of the heart. In
sacraments it is the attitude of the recipient that matters, not the ceremony.
'The matter is not great which way we turn our faces', Ralegh wrote, 'so
the heart stand right.'[1] Sir Thomas More had long ago shrewdly pointed
out how easily the Protestant emphasis on the motive of the heart could
slide over into antinomianism.[2] In the *De Doctrina* Milton quotes 1 Samuel
16:7: 'Jehovah looks on the heart' at a crucial point in his discussion of
freedom of the will.[3]

> To prayer, repentance and obedience due,
> Though but endeavoured with sincere intent,
> Mine ear shall not be slow, mine eye not shut

the Father says in *Paradise Lost* (III. 191–3).

A man may be a heretic in the truth, if he takes over at second hand a
doctrine which he has not made his own: conversely, a man cannot be a
heretic if he follows his conscience sincerely – even 'though against any
point of doctrine by the whole church received'. The heretic is 'he who

---

[1] Ralegh, I, p. 78.
[2] T. More (1974), pp. 163–8.
[3] *C.P.W.*, VI, p. 187.

follows the church against his conscience and persuasion grounded on the Scripture'. This is the basis for Milton's theory of toleration: no Protestant 'of what sect soever, following Scripture only, . . . ought, by the common doctrine of protestants, to be forced or molested for religion'. 'No man in religion is properly a heretic at this day but he who maintains traditions or opinions not probable by Scripture (who, for aught I know, is the papist only')[1] (cf. Luther: 'Neither pope nor bishop nor anyone else has the right to impose so much as a single syllable of obligation upon a Christian man without his own consent.')[2] 'Chiefly for this cause do all true protestants account the Pope Antichrist', Milton continued; 'for that he asssumes to himself this infallibility over both the conscience and the Scripture.'[3] Hence the arguments for complete toleration for all Protestants do not apply to papists.

A great many conclusions follow from this absolute emphasis on conscience, on sincerity. The efficacy of any sacrament depends on the proper attitude of the recipient, and therefore 'Infants are not fit for baptism', since 'they cannot believe or undertake an obligation.' Attendance at church is not necessary: 'the worship of the heart is accepted by God even where external forms are not in all respects observed.'[4] But *Samson Agonistes* suggests that Milton agreed with Muggleton that we should abstain from attending the worship of the restored Church of England.[5]

The same emphasis gives a standard by which to judge of obscenity. No words or actions are in themselves obscene: it is only when they are used with filthy intent that they offend.[6] The difference between the pure inter-course of Adam and Eve before the Fall, and their lustful intercourse after it, lay entirely in their mental attitudes, in the 'shame' which now accompanied their nakedness. Milton had anticipated this conclusion in *Tetrachordon*, where he argued that loveless copulation in marriage is 'at best but an animal excretion'. Divorce is justified if the husband puts away his wife 'with the full suffrage and applause of his conscience, not relying on the written bill of law'. A white lie, or concealment of the truth, may be justified if it proceeds from a charitable motive.[7] In *Paradise Regained* Christ's rejection of the banquet and the kingdoms which Satan offers

---

[1] *C.M.*, VI, pp. 12–14.
[2] Luther, I, p. 268.
[3] *C.M.*, VI, p. 8.
[4] *C.P.W.*, VI, pp. 544–5.
[5] See pp. 438, 485 below; Reeve and Muggleton, pp. 23–4.
[6] *C.P.W.*, VI, p. 170. See p. 453 below.
[7] *C.P.W.*, II, pp. 608–9, 670; VI, pp. 762–4.

him turns on the motives of the giver. But by this date Milton seems to put less exclusive emphasis on sincerity of motive. Christ refuses to use evil political means even to attain good ends. In *The Ready and Easy Way* Milton stressed that 'Good intentions do not make good deeds, and cannot prevent the consequence of bad deeds from being bad.' 'Who had not rather follow Iscariot or Simon the magician, though to covetous ends, preaching, than Saul, though in the uprightness of his heart persecuting the gospel.'[1] So Milton could reject the 'sincerity' argument for intolerance; this line of thought proved useful against antinomianism.

Milton could have found some of his arguments in Bodin's *Heptaplomeres*, where it is suggested that before God honest intention, even if erroneous, is all that matters.[2] The same idea was carried to its extreme by Ranters, and especially Clarkson. But however difficult it is to draw the line, and however much Milton ultimately came to feel that the drawing of lines was necessary, the starting point of the doctrine is pure Protestantism. 'To steal, rob and murder', Tyndale had said, 'are holy when God commandeth them.'[3] During the revolutionary decades some antinomians persuaded themselves that God commanded all these and more.

II Internalizing heaven and hell

Elizabethan Familists had been accused of reducing Christ and the devil, heaven and hell, to allegories.[4] Marlowe's Mephistopheles said that hell was where he was, and this idea was repeated by the Spenserians. William Browne wrote that hell was where the devil is; Phineas Fletcher anticipated Milton's 'better to reign in hell than serve in heaven'.[5] Such doctrines (reinforced by the influence of Jacob Boehme) were proclaimed publicly by radicals during the Revolution, and extended to denial of the existence of a geographical hell. Mrs. Attaway thought that hell existed only in the consciences of men and women. Edwards reports a social egalitarian from Northamptonshire who 'holds there is no hell'. By 1647 it was common form to denounce radicals who did not believe in the immortality of the

---

[1] *C.M.*, VI, p. 114.

[2] Bodin, pp. 47–9.

[3] Tyndale, p. 407.

[4] Perkins, III, p. 392. Cf. Tanner MS. 70, ff. 181–181v for Familists in London in 1638 who believed heaven and hell were in this life and denied the existence of the devil or of sin. I owe this reference to the kindness of David Zaret.

[5] W. Browne, II, p. 402; P. Fletcher, 'O let him serve in hell, who scorns in heaven to reign'; 'To be in heaven the second he disdains/So now the first in hell.' 'In heaven they scorned to serve, so now in hell they reign.' 'Serve then in hell, who scorn with him in heaven to reign' (I, pp. 133–4; II, pp. 88, 329). The idea had been expressed by Justice in the interlude *Respublica* (1553), line 15.

soul and who held that 'all the heaven there is is here on earth'.[1] Walwyn
was said to think it 'silly to believe there was any hell except a bad conscience'; men would not be 'tormented for ever without end for a little time
of sinning in this world'.[2] George Wither, Richard Overton, Thomas
Collier, John Bidle, Peter Sterry, Sir Henry Vane, John Reeve and Lodowick Muggleton, Samuel Pordage and many Quakers believed that hell
was an internal state. William Erbery, Gerrard Winstanley, Joseph
Salmon, Jacob Bauthumley, Richard Coppin, Laurence Clarkson and
other Ranters held the Familist view that the Fall, the Second Coming, the
Last Judgment and the end of the world were all events which take place
on earth within the individual conscience. 'Whether there were such
outward things or no,' Winstanley observed, 'it matters not much.'[3]

Many radicals spoke in Joachite terms of three advents of Christ – first
in the flesh in Palestine, finally in the Last Judgment, but in between
there will be a 'middle advent' when Christ rises in believers. Or there are
three resurrections of the dead – the first of Jesus in A.D. 33, the last at the
general resurrection: in between comes the rule of the saints in the new
dispensation. For Winstanley Christ's resurrection is not in one single
person. 'Mankind is the earth that contains him buried, and out of this
earth he is to rise', within us. 'The rising up of Christ in sons and
daughters . . . is his second coming.' Every saint is a true heaven, because
God dwells in him and he in God, and the communion of saints is a true
heaven. For Ranters too Christ's coming meant 'his coming into men by
his spirit'.[4] Fludd had believed that man could attain to heaven on earth.[5]
Seekers, Saltmarsh, Dell, Quakers and Muggletonians held similar views.
Erbery, whose views are close to those of Milton on many points, believed
that the Second Coming meant 'the appearing of that great God and
Saviour in the saints. . . . The saints shall judge the world, that is first
destroy but afterwards save and govern the world.'[6]

Such beliefs, as all conservatives knew, undermined an essential pillar
of the social order. Milton could have learnt from Lactantius that it is
folly to be virtuous on earth if there are no rewards in the after life.

[1] T. Edwards, I, pp. 27, 35, 112; II, pp. 150–1; Petegorsky, p. 86; *W.T.U.D.*, pp. 175–6, 187–8.
[2] Haller and Davies, pp. 296–7.
[3] Hensley, pp. 140–2; Erbery, pp. 40–1; Sabine, pp. 39, 44, 107–8, 114, 176, 215, 462, 480–1;
    Reeve (*Joyfull News*, 1706); Reeve (?1682), p. 9; Reeve and Muggleton, pp. 7–10, 233;
    Petegorsky, pp. 128, 132; Cohn, pp. 324, 338, 348; K. V. Thomas (1971), p. 571; *W.T.U.D.*,
    pp. 113, 116, 141–2, 166–77, 183, 191.
[4] Reeves, pp. 112–13; Winstanley (*The Mysterie*, 1648), pp. 62–3; (?1648), pp. 72–3, 82–4;
    Sabine, pp. 95, 161–2, 229–35; *W.T.U.D.*, pp. 232–3.
[5] Hutin (1971), p. 90.
[6] Erbery, pp. 23, 40.

Thirty-five years after the poet's death the Rev. Henry Sacheverell, preaching before the Lord Mayor of London, called 'the eternity of hell torments' 'the great sanction of the gospel'.[1] But by that time, thanks to the radicals of the English Revolution, the decline of hell of which D. P. Walker writes had gone far. Milton accepted the existence of a geographical hell. But at Cambridge he had argued that uprightness led men to enjoy a 'kingdom in themselves far more glorious than any earthly dominion.'[2] In *Comus* the Elder Brother anticipated Satan in the words 'He that hides a dark soul ... / Himself is his own dungeon' (lines 382–4). Milton's Satan alludes to an old tradition, of which Milton had long been conscious, when he says 'Myself am hell' (cf. 'Never more in hell than when in heaven' – *P.R.* I. 420). Milton hinted that heaven is more like earth than men think, apropos the war in heaven: we recall Winstanley's 'this living soul is the heaven in which the battle is fought between the curse and the blessing, Michael and the Dragon.' The conclusion of *Paradise Lost*, that the Paradise within is happier far than the external Paradise which Adam and Eve had lost, was shared by Richard Coppin and many radicals.[3]

In Marlowe's case putting words into the mouth of Mephistopheles may have been the only safe way to express on the stage the view that hell is an internal state rather than a geographical location – a view which we know was current in the circle of Ralegh–Hariot–Marlowe. Milton may have pursued a similar tactic in *Paradise Regained* when he put his own views on baptism into Satan's mouth (I. 72–5).[4] There is no 'relish of damnation' either in the *De Doctrina* or in *Paradise Lost*, no gloating over the tortures of the damned such as Dante or Cowley prepared in hell for their political enemies, such as Milton himself had envisaged for bishops in *Of Reformation*.[5] Hell is accepted, as it must be; but enjoying watching the torments of the damned is no part of heavenly bliss, as it so often had been in the Christian tradition. By Milton's time, even more than in Marlowe's, emphasis on an internal hell was bound to recall the more radical doctrine of Familists and those whom Boehme influenced – denial of the local existence of hell altogether.[6]

Like Coppin, Winstanley believed that our future righteousness on earth

[1] Viner, p. 72; Sacheverell, p. 13.
[2] *C.P.W.*, I, p. 297.
[3] Sabine, p. 476; cf. pp. 120, 149, 226; *W.T.U.D.*, p. 398; Coppin, p. 1.
[4] Wittreich (1975), p. 133, quoting W. MacKellar.
[5] *C.P.W.*, I, p. 617; Cowley (1973), pp. 100–3; Empson (1961), pp. 269–73; Frye (1966), p. 86; Gardner, p. 46. *P.L.* II. 596–614 is curiously impersonal.
[6] *C.P.W.*, VI, pp. 628–30; Bailey, p. 158; cf. *W.T.U.D.*, pp. 170–82, and D. P. Walker (1964), *passim*.

could exceed that of Adam and Eve before the Fall. Winstanley said that we need not go to heaven to find God.[1] Milton too insisted that 'the liberty we have in Christ' restores us 'in some competent measure to a right in every good thing, both of this life and the other'.[2] No special sanctity is attached to Paradise: as hell is where Satan is, so each believer can create his own happier Paradise within (*P.L.* III. 477, XI. 836-8, XII. 585-7). Milton thought that even in this life men might be 'filled with a certain awareness . . . of present grace and dignity, . . . so that we have already begun to be blessed', and man can reach 'a far more excellent state of grace and glory than that from which he fell'. He had seen the condemnation of Charles I by good men in 1649 as a foretaste of the Last Judgment, when the elect would join Jesus Christ in pronouncing sentence.[3]

Milton's answer to the charge that this verged on antinomianism would be the same as Dell's: that good men have wholly internalized the moral law. Book II of the *De Doctrina* spells out how they will behave 'when the spirit of God works within us'. Labouring 'as ever in my great Task-master's eye', discipline for Milton became custom, a habit taken for granted.[4] But this was not the case with the majority of the population, as the poet was to discover. Milton then skirted very near to the radical doctrine which saw heaven and hell *merely* as internal states, but he never denied their geographical existence, for which the Bible was his authority. Similarly he emphasized the spirit within the godly without ever emancipating it from the Word of God which that spirit interpreted.

III   Antinomianism

The dictionary definition of antinomian is 'opposed to the obligatoriness of the moral law'. An antinomian is one who maintains that the moral law is not binding upon Christians under the law of grace. Antinomianism can be a Calvinist heresy – the elect carrying to excess the consciousness of liberation from the Law which Christ's imputed righteousness gives them. Or it can be a lower-class rejection of upper-class moral standards. Richard Sibbes wrote of 'some of the meaner ignorant sort of people', whose 'wicked, sensual conceit' was that 'they can commit no sin offensive to God'.[5] In 1632 three men were accused in Star Chamber of saying that

---

[1] *W.T.U.D.*, p. 145.
[2] *C.P.W.*, II, p. 601; cf. *P.R.* II. 379-82.
[3] *C.P.W.*, VI, pp. 502, 415. Cf. Cook, quoted on p. 282 above, and Erbery on pp. 300, 304, 309.
[4] *C.P.W.*, VI, esp. p. 638; cf. *W.T.U.D.*, pp. 327, 400.
[5] Sibbes, II, p. 316.

'to the believer all things are pure', and that David pleased God as much when he committed adultery as when he danced before the ark. The accused denied the charge, but admitted holding that 'God's love was not less to David for his sins of adultery and murder; for God's love is unchangeable.'[1] Wyclif had been accused of holding the same doctrine 250 years earlier.[2] Similar ideas were attributed to Mrs. Anne Hutchinson and her followers in New England in the sixteen-thirties.[3]

With the breakdown of the censorship in the forties antinomianism could be freely preached. The House of Commons was concerned about it in September 1643; Robert Baillie reported that antinomianism was growing even faster than Independency and Anabaptism. He kept his Scottish correspondents regularly informed of its expansion, especially in the army.[4] In 1643 Francis Quarles was attacking antinomians who 'will have no repentance',[5] and John Sedgwick published *Antinomianisme Anatomized*. He was followed by John Arrowsmith and Obadiah Sedgwick in Fast Sermons.[6] Walwyn was one of the few who did not reject the name: the Independent John Cook, more cautiously, was prepared to accept antinomian theory if not the practice of all antinomians; so was John Saltmarsh.[7]

Elizabethan Familists and Jacob Boehme had believed that 'God must become man, man must become God; ... the earth must be turned to heaven.'[8] Many radicals in the interregnum taught that God or Christ was in all the saints – William Sedgwick, Thomas Collier, Gerrard Winstanley, Jacob Bauthumley, Richard Coppin, William Erbery, John Pordage, Thomas Tany. Some Ranters believed that Christ was in all men: so did the early Quakers, according to their adversaries.[9] When Nayler was being condemned for this belief, Colonel Sydenham suggested that it was near to a glorious truth.[10] The Grindletonians, Mrs. Attaway and William Jenny, William Dell, George Fox and Edward Burrough all proclaimed the possibility of attaining to perfection in this life. So did

---

[1] Gardiner, pp. 313–14.
[2] Fuller (1842), I, p. 444.
[3] Hull, pp. 202, 302, 358.
[4] *Commons Journals*, III, pp. 237, 252; Baillie (1775), I, pp. 408, 437, 449; II, pp. 4, 12, 19, 28, 46–7, 55, and *passim*.
[5] Quarles (1880), I, p. 143.
[6] Arrowsmith, p. 25; O. Sedgwick, pp. 31–3.
[7] Haller and Davies, p. 361; Cook (1647), p. 8; Saltmarsh (1646), p. 116.
[8] Boehme (Everyman), p. 121; cf. pp. 115–16, 132; (1960), pp. 596, 634.
[9] *W.T.U.D.*, pp. 190–3, 205–7, 219–26, 236–7; W. Sedgwick, *Some Flashes* (1648), pp. 88, 110; Winstanley (?1648), pp. 89–90.
[10] T. Burton, I, pp. 69, 86.

countless nameless sectaries.[1] The maids of Aldgate, whom Milton defended in 1645, claimed to be 'godded with God' and to be incapable of sin.[2] Bidle denounced original sin, and Levellers defended him. Roger Crab, Coppin, Laurence Clarkson, thought that sin had been invented by the ruling class to keep the poor in order. But now, said the Ranters, we are freed from the curse. We are freed from the law and sin, said Saltmarsh and Dell. We can get back to the state of righteousness in which Adam lived before the Fall, said Coppin, Winstanley and Fox.[3]

Edwards had denounced the heresy that 'Christians are freed from the mandatory power of the Law', and listed heretics who taught that there was no sin in murder or drunkenness if committed by someone in a state of grace. Clarkson, Coppe and other Ranters soon confirmed this: since sin existed only in the imagination, adultery, drunkenness and swearing, if acted with sufficient conviction, could be as holy and virtuous as prayer.[4] Clarkson carried the doctrine that to the pure all things are pure to the extent of advocating (and practising) adultery in the interests of moral purity. 'The title Sin, it is only a name without substance' he said: it 'hath no being in God nor in the creature, but only by imagination'.[5]

One of Empson's more brilliant guesses concerns Eve at the Fall. At the moment of writing Milton 'believed that Eve would have been justified if she had eaten the apple with sufficient faith that God wanted her to do it in spite of God's repeated instructions to the contrary'.[6] Clarkson himself drew the line at murder, though he admitted to having broken most of the other commandments. But it was difficult to see why, on antinomian principles, murder was any worse than theft or adultery. John Cook worried about this.[7] Andrew Smith of Forfar stabbed Quarter-Master Farley during divine service on the Sabbath because 'Jesus Christ commanded him so to do.'[8] Thomas Tany acted upon a similar divine instruction when he 'laid about him with a drawn sword at the Parliament House' in 1654.[9] If Clarkson stopped short at murder, Milton's Samson did not. God may dispense with his own law, the chorus tells us (*S.A.*

---

[1] *W.T.U.D.*, pp. 83, 166–7, 188, 208, 229, 251–2.
[2] *C.P.W.*, II, p. 750.
[3] *W.T.U.D.*, pp. 166–7, 206–7, 214–22; cf. pp. 236–8; Dell, pp. 316–18, 325–8; Saltmarsh (1702), p. 111; cf. p. 126 (a possible reference to the Family of Love).
[4] T. Edwards, I, p. 25; Cohn, pp. 319–24. Cf. Baxter (1649), p. 330.
[5] Clarkson (1650), pp. 8–12, 16. Familists in 1623 had said that Sin was Antichrist come to life after Adam sinned (C. Hill, 1971, p. 143).
[6] Empson (1961), p. 180; *W.T.U.D.*, pp. 401–3. Cf. p. 397 below.
[7] Cook (1652), pp. 10–11; cf. (1647), p. 8.
[8] Firth (1899), pp. 381–2.
[9] C. Hill (Panther, 1969), p. 305.

309–14). Samson believed he was divinely prompted both to marry Dalila and to be present in Dagon's temple 'at idolatrous rites' (1377–9). He presumably believed that the 'rousing motions' which led him to destroy the Philistines (1382) also came from God. Milton seems much more concerned about the possibility that Samson was guilty of suicide than about the death of the Philistines. It might help to think of the Ranters when reading *Samson Agonistes*.[1]

On the dictionary definition it is difficult to say that Milton was not an antinomian. Like the Ranters he believed that 'the entire Mosaic Law is abolished' – not just the ceremonial law but 'the whole positive law of Moses'. Milton indeed wore his antinomianism with a difference, for he thought that 'the law is now inscribed on believers' hearts by the spirit'; but many whom we call antinomians would have said the same, and for Milton when the spirit is at variance with the letter 'faith not law is our rule'.[2]

'The practice of the saints interprets the commandments', he wrote as his considered opinion. 'We are released from the decalogue.' 'Christ our liberator frees us from the slavery of sin and thus from the rule of the law and of men.' 'Attention to the requirements of charity is given precedence over any written law.'[3] His remark in *Of Civil Power* that we ought 'to believe what in our conscience we apprehend the Scripture to say, though the visible church with all her doctors gainsay', is only one remove from Clarkson's 'no matter what ... saints or churches say, if that within thee do not condemn thee, thou shalt not be condemned.'[4] The remove is quite considerable, since the word which I omitted from my quotation from Clarkson is 'Scripture': he was prepared to back conscience against the Bible, Milton to back conscience in interpreting Scripture. But Edwards might have thought this a distinction without a difference. In the *De Doctrina* Milton recognized that 'precise compliance with the commandments, ... when my faith prompts me to do otherwise, ... will be counted as sin. ... The faithful may ... sometimes deviate from the letter even of the Gospel precepts ... in pursuance of their over-riding motive, which is charity.' 'I am not one of those who consider the decalogue a faultless code.'[5] Milton drew very different

---

[1] See p. 447 below.
[2] *C.P.W.*, VI, pp. 525–32.
[3] *Ibid.*, VI, pp. 368, 521, 526, 537–41; cf. pp. 558, 652; *P.L.* X. 300–6, 523–4.
[4] *W.T.U.D.*, p. 215.
[5] *C.P.W.*, VI, pp. 639–40, 711. It would be interesting to know which of the commandments Milton thought faulty. Apart from the overriding supremacy of charity, and his own special definition of adultery, I suspect that the fourth commandment would seem to him the least relevant. Cf. p. 409 below for scepticism about the commandments.

conclusions from Laurence Clarkson, who justified adultery if 'in purity it be acted as no sin'.[1] But the similarities in their theoretical starting-point are clear, and horrifying to the orthodox.

Milton believed that 'those things alone are great which either render this life of ours happy, or lead us to the other, happier, life'. And he suggested that 'the greatest burden in the world is superstition . . . of imaginary and scarecrow sins', which 'enslave the dignity of man, . . . a vain and shadowy menacing of faults that are not'.[2] 'The ways of God' never 'cross the just and reasonable desires of men, nor involve this our portion of mortal life into a necessity of sadness and malcontent'. It is 'the tyranny of usurped opinions' that hales us into 'a multitude of sorrows which God never meant us'. Jonathan Richardson denied that 'these notions savour of libertinism, of licentiousness'. But he knew that Milton's contemporaries thought they did.[3] The Milton with whom Blake conversed grew out of this milieu. 'Happy is the man that condemns not himself in those things he alloweth of', wrote Clarkson, who like Milton believed that matter was good and eternal.[4] A Ranter like Jacob Bauthumley only pushed a little further positions which Milton held, for instance that hell and the devil are within us; that it is sinful to perform an action authorized by the Bible if 'the commanding power which is God in me' forbids it.[5] If we controlled our prejudice against the anti-feminism of 'He for God only, she for God in him', we might notice that Milton is stating that God is in at least 50 per cent of humanity – a semi-antinomian position, so to speak.

However careful Milton was to distinguish his position from that of 'spiritual Levellers, men that would level God, . . . to make God like them', as Henry Lawrence described them,[6] Edwards and his like would have had no hesitation in classifying Milton with the antinomians if they had read the De Doctrina. Erbery and Sterry also had difficulty in differentiating themselves from Ranters, and the early Quakers were only marginally distinguishable. In 1650 George Fox was imprisoned at Derby for saying that he was sanctified. Seven years later Edward Burrough declared that 'They that are reconciled to God . . . are not under the law,

---

[1] W.T.U.D., pp. 215–16.
[2] C.P.W., IV, p. 601; II, p. 228; cf. p. 221. Cf. Bunyan's warnings against excessive scrupulosity in Grace Abounding (I, pp. 17–38); also Richard Norwood's Journal, p. 45; cf. pp. 7, 12; Thomas Case, quoted by Richardson, p. 35. Cf. pp. 125, 247 above.
[3] Darbishire, pp. 241–3.
[4] Clarkson (1650), p. 11.
[5] Bauthumley, pp. 14, 28–31, 42–54, 76–7.
[6] Lawrence, Sig. A 2v; cf. Parker, p. 485.

nor the law hath no power over them.'[1] Tobias Crisp in 1643, Abiezer
Coppe in 1648, accepted the name of Libertine: it was applied to the
Story–Wilkinson Quaker separation by William Penn after the Restora-
tion.[2] It was also applied to Milton.

These considerations bring into sharper relief Milton's Biblicism.
I suggested earlier[3] that his insistence on the authority of the Bible was
necessary to protect the institutions of society against the anarchy of
individual consciences; though his equal insistence on the right of
properly qualified Christians to interpret the Bible for themselves allowed
at least men like Milton to follow their own consciences. He never arrived
at satisfactory definitions which would provide the sort of liberty which he
demanded for himself without allowing the 'licence' which some radicals
claimed for themselves, on similar principles. 'Not I, but sin that dwelleth
in me', explained a delinquent servant.[4] This was dangerous doctrine for
the lower orders. Milton abhorred the social consequences of antinomianism; yet his theological safeguards against it are in the last resort
internal and subjective. He may not have thought about it as deeply as he
should have done, since his two convictions of the necessity of liberty for
himself and discipline for others were sub-intellectual. But it seems to me
helpful to see his ideas in the light of the contemporary antinomianism
which both attracted and repelled him – attracted him subjectively,
repelled him by its potential social consequences.

---

[1] *W.T.U.D.*, pp. 192–8; Pinto (1934), pp. 108–9; Barbour and Roberts, pp. 247, 364.
[2] *W.T.U.D.*, pp. 186, 210–11, 255. Cf. p. 109 above.
[3] See pp. 248–51 above.
[4] Trapp, p. 501.

Chapter 25

Mortalism

> Our sphere of action is life's happiness,
> And he who thinks beyond, thinks like an ass.
>
> The Earl of Rochester

N. T. Burns insists on Milton's indebtedness to verbal traditions of mortalism existing long before 1640.[1] There were three variants of the heresy: that the soul sleeps from death until the general resurrection; that it dies with the body but is resurrected at the Last Judgment; or annihilationism, the belief that at death the soul totally ceases to exist and the body returns to the elements from which it was composed. Richard Overton and Milton held that 'the whole man dies', body, spirit and soul. Some Familists, Seekers and Ranters denied or allegorized away the resurrection. Milton described the ultimate resurrection of the dead as a necessary vindication of God's providence and justice; but his references to it are brief: he gives more space to proving that the soul dies with the body, which seems to interest him more. The intervening two hundred pages of the *De Doctrina* discuss the regeneration of believers on earth, the really important subject for Milton.[2]

We do not know when Milton became a mortalist. We should not attach too much importance to the fact that the dead Edward King was described in *Lycidas* as sleeping. The *Epitaphium Damonis* (line 123), the dedication to Parliament of *The Judgment of Martin Bucer* and the sonnet which Milton wrote to the memory of Mrs. Thomason in 1646 seem to express non-mortalist sentiments; but Milton published the poems in 1673, when his mortalism is hardly in doubt. Once we have the clue we can find mortalism in *Paradise Lost* (III. 245–9; X. 789–92; XI. 61–5; XII. 434).

---

[1] Burns, chapters 1 and 2, *passim*, and pp. 73–5, 147, 166–9, 174, 182, 199. See also pp. 73–4 above.

[2] *C.P.W.*, VI, pp. 400–14, 619–21; cf. pp. 92–4, and pp. 303–5 above. R.O. is similarly unemphatic about the resurrection in *Mans Mortalitie*.

Mortalism was not invented by R.O. in 1643, nor was he an isolated figure. Without going back to Origen, we can find mortalism among fifteenth-century Lollards; Luther, Tyndale and Frith believed in the sleep of the soul. Mortalism was one of the few beliefs penalized in More's Utopia.[1] Servetus was charged with this heresy. *Mans Mortalitie* was only expressing ideas which were 'a commonplace of Socinian and Baptist theology' (and of Familist theology).[2] They had long circulated in the radical underground – for example in Elizabethan Kent, Essex and Suffolk.[3] They had the intellectual backing of those libertines who read Pomponazzi or Bodin's *Heptaplomeres*. In Ralegh's circle, Thomas Hariot was said to deny the Resurrection and eternal life; Nicholas Hill seems to have been a mortalist.[4] Sylvester's translation of Du Bartas depicted the soul as inseparable from the body.[5] For Henoch Clapham in 1608, and for many later commentators, mortalism went with – was a justification for – libertinism.[6] Mrs. Hutchinson in New England was a mortalist: John Cotton and John Davenport argued that Familists and other libertines used mortalist doctrines to justify community of women.[7] Sir Thomas Browne's flirtation with mortalism seems to date to some time before 1635. In 1646 he rejected mortalism with the same fervour as he rejected the scepticism about the existence of witches with which he associated it: both were of Satanic origin.[8]

There were mortalists, including two scriveners, in St. Giles's parish, London, in 1638.[9] In the forties mortalism appeared above the surface. By 1644 it was alarming the House of Commons. Edwards and others attributed the heresy to Clement Writer the Biblical critic, who was suspected of being the author of *Mans Mortalitie*. Mortalism was discussed by Lamb's Baptist church at the Spittle, and in Red Cross St. It was accepted by Mrs. Attaway and William Jenny, by 'one Crab of Southwark', a feltmaker, and by at least one member of William Kiffin's church. It was proclaimed in Kent, Sussex, Lancashire and Cheshire.[10] It was preached by a lieutenant in Bristol in 1645, and in London by Thomas Webbe, soon to

---

[1] Burns, chapters 1 and 3, *passim*; T. Moore (Everyman), pp. 102–3.
[2] Henry, p. 249.
[3] P. Clark, chapter 2; Emmison, pp. 110, 295.
[4] Harvey; Nicholas Hill; Shirley, pp. 24, 27, 112–13; Kyd, pp. lxx–lxxiii, cxiii–cxvi. Cf. Marlowe, quoted on p. 308 above.
[5] G. C. Taylor, pp. 16, 22.
[6] Clapham, *passim*.
[7] Hull, pp. 300–1, 354–60; *Publications of the Prince Society*, XXI (1894), p. 292.
[8] Sir T. Browne, II, pp. 329–30; I, p. 84.
[9] Tanner MS. 70, f. 181–2. I owe this reference to the kindness of David Zaret.
[10] T. Edwards, I, pp. 26–7, 113–16, 217–19; II, pp. 17–18; III, pp. 36–7, 66–7, 93, 110, 167; Underhill, p. 44n.; C. E. Whiting, p. 90; Burns, p. 73.

be a Ranter. The Ranters had the reputation of being mortalists, and Laurence Clarkson certainly was, though Samuel Rutherford attributed the heresy generally to 'the Anabaptists', and in particular to Giles Randall the Familist/Seeker. Burns thinks mortalism was common among General Baptists until after the Restoration, which is of interest to us in view of Milton's possible links with that sect, of which his third wife was certainly a member.[1] Edwards accused John Goodwin of being a mortalist. Daniel Featley attributed mortalism to Anabaptists, Ephraim Pagitt to Familists, Baillie to antinomians and 'Familistic Anabaptists'. Jeremy Taylor identified the Socinians as soul-sleepers but not annihilationists. Bunyan called the Quakers mortalists.[2] Nomenclature varies, but the radical tendency of the heresy, whose best-known spokesman was a Leveller leader, is clear.

In 1645 Thomas Blake associated anti-Trinitarianism, soul-sleeping and opposition to religious persecution as Anabaptist doctrines: they were also Milton's. In January 1645 mortalism was denounced by John Whincop in a Fast Sermon preached before the Commons, in May by Jeremiah Whitaker before the Lords. The Westminster Assembly condemned it.[3] Next year Matthew Newcomen and Obadiah Sedgwick joined the chorus.[4] As usual this publicity may have helped the sale of the books attacked: Henry Oxinden was specially ordering a book on the mortality of the soul to be sent to him in Kent in April 1645.[5] In 1647 *A Discovery of the Most Dangerous and Damnable Tenets that have been spread within these few yeares* included the ideas that the immortality of the soul is a fiction, and that 'all the heaven there is is here on earth'. Mortalism was enthusiastically proclaimed by the Muggletonians, combined with anti-Trinitarianism and materialism. John Reeve's book on the mortality of the soul

---

[1] See p. 296 above. Milton was probably an adherent of no sect, but he shared many of the views of the General Baptists. 'Mr. Smith, chemist, ... who had been servant to Mr. R. Boyles' told the master of the Ranelagh School (now Bracknell) that Milton was probably 'an antipaedobaptist of the Independent persuasion'. This information dates from the middle of the eighteenth century, when the writer was about seventy years old; but gossip about Milton coming from the Boyle family is worth something. (I owe this information to the kindness of Edward Thompson, who took it from Memorandum Book I, p. 170, of the Rev. Will Waterson, Vicar of Winkfield, Berks., and master of the Ranelagh School.) Isaac Newton was an anti-Trinitarian who was 'hearty for the Baptists' (*C. and C.*, p. 261).

[2] Underdown (1973), p. 146; T. Edwards, I, p. 86; III, p. 117; Rutherford (1648), I, p. 9; II, pp. 179–80; Featley, p. 153; Pagitt, Sig. B 3v, pp. 85, 139–41; Baillie (1775), II, p. 3; Henry, p. 243; Bray, III, p. 98; *Racovian Catechism* (1652), pp. 28–9; Bunyan, I, p. 21; II, pp. 182–3. Taylor was not a mortalist, as is sometimes asserted (Burns, p. 103).

[3] T. Blake, To the Impartiall Reader; Whincop, p. 10; Whitaker, pp. 32–40; Mitchell and Struthers, p. 275.

[4] See p. 312 above.

[5] *Oxinden and Peyton Letters*, pp. 76–7; cf. Bastwick, Sig. G 4v – H.

was called *Joyfull News* (1658). For Muggleton this doctrine 'yielded me much peace of mind', since he had previously dreaded the thought of eternal damnation. Belief in the mortality of the soul was one of the six principles 'upon which dependeth the eternal happiness of men'.[1] Satan in *Paradise Lost* similarly tried, not very successfully, to console himself with the hope of annihilation (II. 92–159).

John Bidle translated a mortalist tract. Other mortalists were Milton's friend Sir Henry Vane, Agricola Carpenter, Samuel Gott (author of *Nova Solyma*, a work once attributed to Milton), John Brayne and Thomas Hobbes.[2] A respectable landowner like Sir Peter Leicester regarded mortalism as an open question in 1653.[3] Henry More published a poem against the heresy in 1647, emulating Sir John Davies, whose *Nosce Teipsum* was republished in 1653, followed by a prose paraphrase in 1658. At this heady time even John Evelyn thought that the soul was mortal, though he later was very ashamed of this socially undesirable belief.[4] Walter Charleton dedicated a whole treatise to *The Immortality of the Human Soul* (1657). Final proof of the wickedness of the mortalist heresy was given when it was attributed to Miles Sindercomb, the former Leveller who committed suicide in prison after an unsuccessful attempt to assassinate Oliver Cromwell. Sindercomb even sank so low as to hope that all mankind might be saved.[5]

The doctrine that 'the whole man dies', and that at death the body returns to the elements from which it was composed, goes back to the Hermetic writings, and to the Lollards.[6] For R.O. as for Clarkson, soul and body are so closely intertwined that the soul can be said to eat, drink, defecate and copulate. Mortalism is thus linked with materialism.[7] The Racovian Catechism insisted that soul and body were so conjoined that a man was neither soul nor body. In the *De Doctrina* Milton, like Overton, argued that body and soul are jointly generated, the soul being contained potentially in the semen.[8]

---

[1] Petegorsky, p. 86; Reeve (1711), pp. 19–20, 71–6; Muggleton (1764), pp. 25–8, 76–9, 102, 122–3; Reeve and Muggleton, pp. 12, 38.

[2] Burns, p. 142; Jacob, p. 18, quoting Boyle's account of a sermon by Vane; Carpenter, pp. 11–12, 21 (p. 24 may echo *Areopagitica* – 'an America of knowledge yet unfound out, discoverable by the efforts of some wiser Columbus'); Gott, I, pp. 353–4; Brayne, *passim*; Hobbes (Penguin), chapter 44. Boyle was very worried about mortalism at this period (Jacob, *passim*).

[3] Leicester, pp. xxiii–xxiv.

[4] H. More (1878), pp. 101–3, 123–4; Sharp, p. 336.

[5] Lutaud, p. 92.

[6] R.O., pp. 7–8, 86.

[7] See pp. 326–31 below.

[8] *The Racovian Catechism*, pp. 28–9; R.O., p. 41; *C.P.W.*, VI, pp. 321–2. R.O. got this last point from Wither's translation of Nemesius.

The doctrine that the soul is the blood was held by some mortalists, including Servetus, Fludd and Hobbes; it was attacked by Henry More. William Harvey taught that the soul is in the blood. There is no evidence that he was a mortalist like his friends Fludd and Hobbes, despite the fact that (like Sir Thomas Browne) he studied medicine at Padua, notorious for the heresy. But awareness of heretical possibilities may account for the great caution which Harvey showed in publishing his theory of the circulation of the blood. Interestingly enough, one of the rival claimants to the discovery, Servetus, was a mortalist; and the other, Walter Warner, moved in the mortalist circles of Hariot and Nicholas Hill.[1]

In 1648 two Royalist newspapers declared that the mortalist heresy had been partly responsible for the revolutionary nature of the Civil War.[2] In 1672 Lord North said that lack of belief in life after death was to be found 'especially among the vulgar'.[3] In 1679–80 Rochester and Charles Blount thought it necessary to be very cautious in discussing mortalism.[4] Mortalism could seem a logical conclusion of Protestantism. It made belief in the existence of Purgatory finally impossible. But, as Sir Thomas Browne and Henry More noted, denial of a soul apart from the body also discouraged belief in the existence of ghosts. 'No spirit, no God', declared More.[5] Joseph Glanville and other early Fellows of the Royal Society devoted much time and energy to proving the existence of both spirits and God. Mortalism emphasized the importance of this life. Seeing man as part of nature, as an animal, mortalists like Overton, Reeve and Milton were in this respect more scientific and rational than many of the scientists.[6] Their doctrine may have contributed significantly to that decline of belief in the supernatural which Aubrey attributed to the 'liberty of conscience and liberty of inquisition' of the revolutionary decades.[7] The republican M.P. Henry Marten referred to 'my ghostless dust'.[8] Together with the Puritan contempt for ceremonies, mortalism led Milton and some sectaries to deny that burial need be a religious ceremony at all.[9]

---

[1] H. More (1878), p. 127; Hill (1974), esp. pp. 169–72, 193–4; cf. p. 208 and a counter-argument by Gweneth Whitteridge on pp. 182–8. See also Shirley, pp. 112, 125.

[2] Frank (1955), p. 299.

[3] K. V. Thomas (1971), p. 172. For possible mortalism in Cambridgeshire in 1681 see Spufford, p. 343.

[4] Pinto (1962), pp. 189–92. Cf. Rochester's translation of the chorus from Seneca's *Troas* (1968, pp. 150–1) and the epigraph to this chapter.

[5] H. More (1653), p. 164.

[6] R.O., pp. 28–9, 55, 64, 86; C.M., XI, pp. 244–7; Reeve (1711), p. 72.

[7] Aubrey, II, p. 318; K. V. Thomas (1971), pp. 590–3; cf. Muggleton (1669), *passim*: there can be no spirit without a body.

[8] A. Wood, III, pp. 1242–3.

[9] *C.P.W.*, VI, pp. 744–5; K. V. Thomas (1971), p. 604.

We must end by emphasizing the distinction between annihilationism and other variants of mortalism. In *Paradise Lost* the more radical doctrine is suggested by Moloch (II. 92–8). For Winstanley, Christ rising in sons and daughters was all the heaven he expected: it was in this world only, as it was for Clarkson, Bauthumley and other Ranters. 'To reach God beyond the creation, or to know what he will be to a man after the man is dead, if any otherwise than to scatter him into his essences of fire, water, earth and air of which he is compounded, is a knowledge beyond the line or capacity of man to attain to while he lives in his compounded body.'[1] Marlowe's Faustus, in his last despairing speech, prayed that his soul might 'be changed into small water-drops, / And fall into the ocean, ne'er be found'. This was an old Familist image, repeated by Clarkson: 'Even as a stream from the ocean was distinct in itself while it was a stream, but when returned to the ocean was therein swallowed and became one with the ocean: so the spirit of man whilst in the body was distinct from God, but when death came it returned to God, and so became one with God, yea God itself.' Clarkson expected to 'know nothing after this my being was dissolved'.[2] The Diggers demanded 'Glory here!': not in heaven but on earth, not after death but now. Whether there was any life after death seemed to Winstanley a matter on which it was unprofitable to speculate. His body would rejoin the elements.[3] Shelley's consolation for the death of Adonais, 'He is made one with nature', is a later example of this English radical tradition of thought, a tradition whose significance for the formation of Shelley's ideas has perhaps been insufficiently emphasized.

As early as *Tetrachordon* Milton claimed that 'the liberty we have in Christ' should 'restore us in some competent measure to a right in every good thing both of this life and the other'.[4] Soul-sleepers were not so totally this-worldly as annihilationists: full union with Christ was to be expected after the resurrection. Milton did not believe in perfectibility on earth even to the extent that the Quakers did. Yet, for all that, a part of the consolation of mortalism – for Muggleton and as a temptation for the young Bunyan – was that it removed the fear of eternal damnation.[5] It was easy for a mortalist to slip into the idea that at the Last Judgment hell would be shut up, the damned would be either annihilated, as Bidle believed,[6] or punished by exclusion from bliss rather than by physical

---

[1] Sabine, p. 565; cf. pp. 114, 117; *W.T.U.D.*, pp. 179, 207; Burns, pp. 83–4.
[2] Sabine, p. 600.
[3] Empson (1961), p. 142; Clarkson (1660), pp. 28, 33; cf. pp. 32, 61.
[4] *C.P.W.*, II, p. 601.
[5] *W.T.U.D.*, pp. 173–4. Blake associates Milton with 'Eternal Annihilation' (pp. 528–30).
[6] D. P. Walker (1964), p. 93.

torments. Mortalism was a less ferocious as well as a more this-worldly doctrine than orthodox Christianity. In his 'most precious and dearest possession' Milton devoted very little space to 'the other', that immortal life which should be the crown of Christian hopes. Nor did he ever have much to say about the torments of hell. The sonnet 'Avenge O Lord', unlike *Lycidas*, finds no consolation in immortality: its hope is that the suffering of the Vaudois will help to bring other Italians to abandon Catholicism on earth.[1] 'Methought I saw' looks forward to Milton's reunion with his wife in heaven, but this brings little consolation: the sonnet is about the pain of her absence in this world. Even in *Lycidas* the hope of immortality is neither central to the poem nor the note on which it ends. 'To-morrow to fresh woods and pastures new' brings us back to face the everyday life still going on. So do the marvellous conclusions of the three great poems. For all his obeisance to traditional theological concepts, Milton's emotional interests were as profoundly this-worldly as those of the more extreme radicals.

The orthodox in the seventeenth century believed – or pretended to believe – that mortalists became libertines. But so, it was argued, did antinomians; and antinomianism, as we have seen, could derive from heavy emphasis on the sonship of all believers, which was one possible variant of anti-Trinitarianism. Both mortalism and rejection of the Trinity thus seemed to produce antinomian justification of sexual promiscuity. So there was a logic in the sermon which John Whincop preached to the House of Commons in January 1645, when he attacked in one breath mortalism, antinomianism and advocacy of divorce.[2] Whether or not Whincop had Milton in mind, all three heresies could be attributed to him, and contemporaries therefore assumed that he was a libertine. They were wrong, but he had given them some reason for their mistake.

---

[1] Grossman, p. 289.
[2] See p. 245 above for Whincop, and pp. 74–5 for the highly traditional link between mortalism and sexual licence. For Milton's reputation as a libertine see also pp. 451–2 below.

Chapter 26

Materialism and Creation

I am ... hesitant about adopting [the] suggestion that what contemporary authorities regarded as the religious 'ignorance' or
'scepticism' of the lower classes was really a coherent alternative
system of religious symbolism. The popular utterances ... seem too
heterogeneous to be easily fitted into any coherent alternative (or
alternatives) to orthodox theology, though they do suggest a widespread tradition of materialism.

Keith Thomas (1975)

Milton, like Wyclif, did not believe that God created the universe
ex nihilo. To create something out of nothing seemed to Milton both
logically meaningless and an impossible translation of the relevant Hebrew,
Greek and Latin texts of the Bible. He believed in creation *ex deo*: 'the
world was made out of some sort of matter', which must 'either have
always existed, independently of God', which is inconceivable, 'or else
originated from God at some point in time'. 'All things came from God',
which is the reason why 'no created thing can be utterly annihilated'
(another doctrine which Wyclif held, or was alleged to have held). The
original matter, Milton thought, 'was good, and it contained the seeds of
all subsequent good'.[1]

These are not original ideas. Many of them can be traced back to
classical antiquity, but they had been revived by fifteenth-century neo-
Platonists and by publication of the Hermetic writings, which taught that
matter was eternal. Nothing in the cosmos is destroyed. The Hermetic
account of Creation recalls that of Genesis: 'there was darkness in the deep,
and water without form: and there was a subtle breath which permeated
the things in chaos with divine power.'[2] Fludd made this doctrine of the

---

[1] *C.P.W.*, VI, pp. 305–10; Fuller (1842), III, p. 445; Leff (1967), II, p. 510; Saurat, pp. 96, 166,
182.
[2] W. Scott, I, pp. 146–7, 176–7; cf. pp. 114–21, 188–9.

Creation his own. God 'produced and created all things out of himself'. 'Before the creation of the waters there was a certain matter in the highest mystery, that is to say in the divine puissance, or dark and unformed abyss.' Chaos was not merely negative but '*in potentia ad actum*. . . . Hermes terms it *potentia divina*.'[1] God is in consequence in all things, as their root and the source of their being. Matter, body, substance, are manifestations of God's working.[2] The divine principle is fecundity. God said 'increase and multiply'. Human procreation is an imitation, a manifestation, of the creative energy of God. Sex, like matter, is inherently good.[3]

In the Hermeticist sexual myth of creation, which Boehme echoes, light – the Son of God – was the masculine element; the feminine was first chaos, then the earth.[4] Fludd accounted for creation and all the goings-on of the universe by the sexual activity of the two principles, light and darkness, the *voluntas* and *noluntas* of God, matter and form, Apollo and Dionysus.[5] Similar doctrines appear systematically and elaborately in *Mans Mortalitie*. The sun is the dwelling-place of Jesus Christ, the veil between us and his glory: when Christ comes unveiled to judgment the creation will be consumed by fire. 'If God were not light, the world could never have been.' Overton's paean to light has been suggested as one of the sources of the invocation at the beginning of Book III of *Paradise Lost*.[6] In the epic the sun and the moon were

> male and female light
> Which two great sexes animate the world.
>
> (VIII. 150–1)

The sun figures frequently as the source of life in the sexual sense (II. 1035–8; III. 582–6, 606–12; V. 300–2; VIII. 94–9; XI. 720–2). It is therefore of some significance that in the lines of *Paradise Lost* which Edward Phillips recalled as among the earliest written, Satan declared his hatred of the light.

These ideas can be found in *Heptaplomeres*, Bruno and Du Bartas/ Sylvester.[7] Ralegh's friends Hariot and Warner denied creation *ex nihilo*, and believed in the indestructibility of matter.[8] Creation *ex deo* can be

---

[1] Fludd, pp. 42–4; W. Scott, I, p. 425.
[2] *Ibid.*, I, pp. 154–5, 162–3, 236–7; cf. *C.P.W.*, VI, p. 322.
[3] W. Scott, I, pp. 124–5, 216–17, 332–5; II, p. 109; cf. III, p. 138.
[4] *Ibid.*, I, pp. 114–21, 124–7; II, pp. 20, 430.
[5] Fludd, pp. 66, 188; Hutin (1971), pp. 24, 79, 89, 113, 123–5, 141, 144–5, 148–50; cf. p. 52.
[6] R.O., pp. 49–54, 93–4; cf. Saurat, pp. 270–2.
[7] Empson (1961), p. 171; Reesing (1957), pp. 160, 168; Hirst, pp. 90–1; Hutin (1971), pp. 78–81 and *passim*; Sylvester, I, pp. 57–9.
[8] Aubrey, I, p. 286; Shirley, pp. 6, 108, 120.

found in the Racovian theology, and in a modified form in Henry More.[1]
The doctrine was associated by Edwards with anti-Trinitarianism and
mortalism: the heretics whom he reported believed that God subsisted in
the creatures, and that ultimately the whole creation would be annihilated
and 'reduced into the divine essence again'. Samuel Rutherford denounced
Familists who said that God is 'the being of things'. Robert Norwood
thought the human soul was part of the divine essence. Van Helmont and
John Reeve denied that God created *ex nihilo*.[2] 'In the beginning', Reeve
wrote, 'out of an eternal chaos of confused matter, God created all
things.' Like Milton, he asserted that matter was everlasting, and thought
that at the last day the earth would return into eternal dark chaos.[3] Milton
gives the theory idiosyncratic twists, but he is not original.

Milton envisaged a material God, who derived a prime matter from his
own substance.[4] (This is the eternal, uncreated Night of *Paradise Lost*,
which is also to be found in Grotius's *Adamus Exul*.) The prime matter
forms Chaos, from which everything can be made, but which is nothing
in itself. 'Seeds of all things from the womb / Of pregnant Chaos spring.'[5]
Chaos is in a permanent state of internal warfare, because it is divorced
from Providence, its metaphysical opposite. The creation of the universe
is the assertion of Providence over Chaos, the imposition of form on
inchoate matter, the replacement of the discords of Chaos by the music
of the spheres (*P.L.* III. 708–15; V. 469–76; VII. 168–71, 233–41,
271–3).[6] Chaos continues to exist after the creation of the world, as
one possible mode of existence to which matter may revert – 'the womb
of nature and perhaps her grave'; we recall Othello's 'Chaos is come
again'.

The goodness of matter and the freedom of man's will are linked
concepts for Milton. A return to chaos occurs when God's goodness is
withdrawn, or not put forward: it means an end to human freedom.
Adam and Eve are 'in a troubled sea of passion tossed' (*P.L.* X. 718) after
the Fall as Chaos appears to invade Eden, just as the people of England
lost their freedom when understanding ceased to rule them in the late

---

[1] Woodhouse (1945), pp. 217–33; H. More (1878), p. 97.
[2] T. Edwards, I, p. 219; Rutherford (1647), p. 358; Staudenbaur, p. 168; C. Webster (1975),
pp. 330–1; G. E. Aylmer, p. 295; Reeve (?1682), p. 2.
[3] Reeve (*Joyfull News*, 1706), p. 22; (?1682), p. 2; cf. *C.P.W.*, VI, p. 310.
[4] For the following paragraphs I have relied heavily on A. B. Chambers; W. B. Hunter (1946),
pp. 68–76, 327–36, and (1952), pp. 551–62; Woodhouse (1945), pp. 216–34.
[5] Fanshawe, p. 20. In the preceding stanza Fanshawe had invoked Spenser. Cf. Grotius, in
Kirkconnell, pp. 106 ('timeless Night'), 122–4, and H. More (1878), p. 114 ('Old Night').
[6] This may come via the Hermetic tradition: Milton is, however, unusual in locating hell in
Chaos (McColley, p. 33).

fifties, and 'sensual appetite ... from beneath / Usurping over sovereign reason claimed / Superior sway' (*P.L.*, IX. 1121–31).

Recognition of Milton's dependence on the Hermetic tradition may help us to place his materialism and his attitude towards science. The idea that God gives form to matter by putting forth his goodness (*P.L.* VII. 167–72) need not come from Jewish sources, as Saurat ingeniously suggested; it can also be found in the Hermetic tradition. So can Milton's doctrine that 'bodies may at last turn all to spirit' (*P.L.* V. 497–500). It is much more likely to be from this source, direct or via Fludd, that Milton got his view that 'spirit is a flowering of matter'. The words are J. B. S. Haldane's.[1] Milton's reference to a 'divorcing command' by which 'the world first rose out of chaos' reproduces a Paracelsan doctrine which was developed by Fludd and was strongly contested by the orthodox, including Mersenne.[2]

In describing the processes of creation Milton again seems to echo Hermes Trismegistus – as Spenser had done. The demiurge first impregnates the earth: living creatures are ready to emerge when God calls them forth.[3] Creative energy is then placed in the sun, which is the source for the replenishment of life throughout the whole universe (*P.L.* III. 606–12; VIII. 94–9). Light preceded the separation of the elements (*P.L.* III. 8–12). Planets, moon and stars drink from the sun and distribute light to the earth,

> Lest total darkness should by night regain
> Her old possession, and extinguish life
> In nature and in all things.
> (*P.L.* IV. 66–73; cf. VII. 352–66; and *Comus*, 330–4)[4]

The sun as the source of physical and spiritual energy helps to explain Milton's acceptance of the climatic theory: his belief (based on sound evidence at that date) that 'the sun ... ripens wits as well as fruits', that genius flourished in the Mediterranean area rather than further north.[5]

Spenser, who no doubt got it from Hermes Trismegistus, perhaps via Ficino, believed that there was a physical circuit of energy in the universe.[6] So did Milton. The sun receives its life-giving power directly from God.

---

[1] Haldane, p. 220; W. Scott, I, pp. 128–9.

[2] *C.P.W.*, II, p. 273; Debus (1974), pp. 237, 240, 246, 249, 253–4. For the importance of chaos in the thinking of 'An Hermetic Philosopher', see Samuel Butler, p. 98.

[3] W. Scott, I, pp. 114–23.

[4] Cf. Spenser's *Second Hymne*. But Milton could equally well have found the idea in Grotius's *Adamus Exul* (Kirkconnell, pp. 124–130), or in Sir Francis Kynaston's *Leoline and Sydanis* (1642): 'But wanting of their heavenly light/They turn to Chaos's endless night' (Saintsbury, II, p. 159).

[5] *C.P.W.*, I, p. 814; II, p. 490; V, p. 451; *P.L.* IX. 44–6. Cf. pp. 6–7 above.

[6] Spenser, *Second Hymne*, lines 99–117; *The Faerie Queene*, Book III, Canto vi, stanzas 9, 37–8; W. Scott, I, pp. 266–7; IV, p. 391.

This energy – light – dwells for a time in all living creatures; when they die and dissolve into their elements it returns to its place of origin.[1] But Milton, unlike Spenser, includes the human soul itself among the material objects which return to the sun after dissolution. All matter is indestructible because originally part of God's substance.[2]

'All entity is good.' Evil does not come from God; it is the consequence of the fall of Lucifer and the rebel angels, and of Adam's free choice of evil for which all his posterity is punished. Milton rejects any form of dualism. Though he distinguishes between soul and body, he does not conceive of their separate existence. 'The human soul is generated by the parents in the course of nature, not created daily by the immediate act of God'; otherwise how can we explain the transmission of Adam's original sin to all his descendants?[3] We may not think this a very good explanation of the origin of evil: Milton was no more successful than other theologians in preserving both man's freedom and God's omnipotence. His theory also runs the risk of appearing to equate God and matter. But none of Milton's contemporaries could find better arguments; it would have been very difficult in the seventeenth century to account for the existence of the universe except by postulating a Creator.[4]

Familism drew on the Hermeticist tradition. John Everard (1575– c. 1650) was a Familist-influenced clergyman who by preference preached to tinkers and cobblers, disliked the Protestant ethic, and believed that heaven and perfectibility could be won on earth.[5] He translated Hermes Trismegistus, and possessed a copy of the manuscripts of Nicholas Hill (of Ralegh's and Hariot's circle), who himself was deeply influenced by Hermeticism. John Webster, the reformer of the universities, valued the Hermetic philosophy highly, and wanted to see the ideas of Bacon, Harvey and Fludd taught at Oxford and Cambridge.[6] Henry Pinnell, translator of Paracelsus, praised Hermes, and several other early Quakers were interested in Hermeticism, astrology and alchemy.[7]

Samuel Butler's 'Hermetic Philosopher' read Jacob Boehme, and Hudibras's Rapho was both a sectary and a Behmenist.[8] Boehme was

---

[1] *C.P.W.*, VI, pp. 399–414; *P.L.* V. 171, 404–26; cf. III. 608–11; IV. 665–73; VIII. 140–57. Cf. p. 410 below on the link between Milton's theory of inspiration and this Hermetic cycle of energy within the universe.

[2] Debus (1975), p. 41.

[3] *C.P.W.*, VI, pp. 310, 317–23, 390–8; cf. W. Scott, I, pp. 314–15, and p. 320 above.

[4] Cf. p. 249 above.

[5] I have learnt about John Everard from an unpublished paper by Brenda Szittya.

[6] See *C. and C.*, p. 172; cf. pp. 329, 332 below.

[7] *W.T.U.D.*, p. 291. For Boyle's use of Hermeticism, see Jacob, pp. 14–15.

[8] Butler, p. 105.

another who denied creation *ex nihilo*. For him God was in everything, nature was the body of God. Heaven and hell were within men. Boehme preferred the inner light to the letter of the Bible. For him as for Milton, the creation of the world was the consequence of the fall of Lucifer; in God's new plan man took the place of Lucifer and his angels. Lucifer fell freely, and his fall brought evil into the universe: like Milton, Boehme rejected predestination to damnation and built liberty into his universe from the start.[1]

Translations of Hermes, Paracelsus and Boehme abounded in the sixteen-forties and -fifties. In 1646 Charles Hotham, who had been an undergraduate at Christ's College slightly after Milton, defended Boehme's doctrines at Cambridge, rejecting creation *ex nihilo* in favour of creation from the matter of the abyss: this led him on to discuss the origins of evil. Hotham, who was also an admirer of Hermes, wrote an introduction (in which he praised Milton) to his brother Durant's translation of Boehme's *The Teutonic Philosophie* (1650). Durant Hotham, a journalist, also published a life of Boehme (1654), in which he asserted that 'man . . . shall have a Paradise, a land, . . . but all this is in himself, the land is himself.'[2] Charles Hotham was intruded as a Fellow of Peterhouse by the Parliamentary Commissioners, was ejected in 1662, and emigrated to Bermuda. 'Much addicted to chemistry', mathematics and astrology, he was a correspondent of Milton's friend Henry Oldenburg, and became a Fellow of the Royal Society in 1668.[3]

Boehme's writings were influential among radicals – Rosicrucians, Ranters like Tany and Bauthumley, the millenarian Mary Cary, Quakers and Muggletonians. Boehme's 'philosophical light was above all men's that doth profess religion', said Lodowick Muggleton in 1661, until it was superseded by Muggletonianism. Like Richard Baxter, Muggleton thought Boehme had especially influenced the Quakers.[4] Boehme also appealed to John Webster; another would-be reformer of the universities, Samuel Hering, wanted Parliament to set aside two colleges for teaching Behmenism.[5] 'The astrologers' . . . religion is the same with Jacob Behmen the German conjuror', wrote a pamphleteer in 1652, 'as appears by Master Lilly's recommending his works so highly for Gospel light in

[1] J. Pordage (1776), pp. 50, 71–2; K. V. Thomas (1971), pp. 227, 271, 375–7; *W.T.U.D.*, pp. 185, 288–90; Shirley, pp. 125–6, 110, 113; Koyré, pp. 33, 113, 157, 181, 216, 378, 405, 417, 428, 442 and *passim*; Woodhouse (1945), p. 234; Stoudt, pp. 243–57. See also pp. 275–6 above
[2] D. Hotham, p. 4.
[3] Oldenburg, VI, pp. 535–6; C. Webster (1975), p. 135.
[4] Reeve and Muggleton, pp. 45–6; Muggleton (1668), p. 5.
[5] *W.T.U.D.*, pp. 176, 293.

one of his almanacs'.[1] Other admirers of Boehme include William Erbery, Peter Sterry, John and Samuel Pordage. John Pordage believed that he was summarizing Boehme when he argued, with Milton, that God created the universe out of himself, drawing on the prime matter of Chaos; and therefore that matter was good. His son Samuel published in 1661 *Mundorum Explicatio*, a long poem whose theme (if little else) has affinities with *Paradise Lost* and with *Pilgrim's Progress*. It opens with an *Encomium* on Boehme and his English translator, the law reformer John Sparrow.[2] The suggestion that Milton was significantly influenced by Boehme is probably unfounded: Boehme was only one component in the Familist/ Hermeticist lore on which Milton drew. But his friend Nathan Paget had an impressive collection of Boehme's works, both printed and manuscript, in his library;[3] and Milton's nephew, Edward Phillips, became an expert in 'the Teutonick Philosophy'.[4] So Boehme would hardly be unknown to Milton.

Creation *ex deo* could lead to pantheism, of which Ochino had been accused.[5] Mortalism too is often associated with materialistic pantheism, or something approaching it – from Servetus to Winstanley and the Ranters. God is in all matter, Servetus taught; 'Christ fills all things'. 'This bench and this sideboard, and everything you could show me, is the substance of God.'[6] Ranters carried Servetus's argument about the ubiquity of God to a point at which he virtually ceased to exist. God was in everything – dog, cat, chair, stool, toad, table, tobacco pipe. Jacob Bauthumley saw God in 'man and beast, fish and fowl, and every green thing, from the highest cedar to the ivy on the wall'. 'He does not exist outside the creatures.' Even a relative conservative like Lord President Lawrence believed that God was in 'every stone, in every creature'.[7] 'The whole creation', proclaimed Winstanley, 'is the clothing of God. . . . He is in all things, and by him all things consist.'[8] This line of thought led Bauthumley and Clarkson to argue that there is no God but all comes by nature – an idea that had been attributed to English Familists as early as 1561, and was expressed by an Essex husbandman long before the Civil

---

[1] [William Rowland], To the Christian Reader; Lilly, *Predictions* (1652), p. 25; (1655), Sig. A 4v. Lilly also cited Hermes Trismegistus approvingly (*Annus Tenebrosus*, 1652, p. 31).

[2] Erbery, p. 333; Hirst, pp. 277–8; *W.T.U.D.*, pp. 224–6; J. Pordage (1776), pp. 8–19, 52–3; S. Pordage, Sig. a 4–5.

[3] Bailey, *passim*. For Paget see Appendix 3 below.

[4] See Appendix 2 below.

[5] L. A. Wood, p. 84. See p. 287 above.

[6] Bainton, pp. 132–6, 195–6; D. P. Walker (1972), pp. 119–20.

[7] *W.T.U.D.*, p. 206; T. Burton, I, p. 62.

[8] Sabine, p. 451. Cf. W. Blake: 'If all but God is not infinite, they shall come to an end, which God forbid' (p. 936).

War.[1] Edwards in 1646 reported from Somerset the view that matter came from God, who 'doth subsist in the creatures; and hereafter the whole creation shall be annihilated and reduced into the divine essence again'. These heretics were also mortalists. That report – which impresses us with Edwards's accuracy – looks forward to Winstanley and the Ranters.[2] The idea that all comes by nature was familiar to Lodowick Muggleton and attracted George Fox. A passage in *Paradise Lost* (V. 850–61) and several pages in the *De Doctrina* attack this Ranter idea. It was defended by Satan (*P.L.* IX. 718–22).[3] John Reeve in the early fifties was combating the theory, held by Clarkson, that the world is eternal, that all comes by nature and that God is in all things.[4]

Milton thus differentiated himself sharply from the pantheist materialism which verged on atheism. Yet his own materialism, no less than that of the Hermeticists, Winstanley and the Ranters, was associated with rejection of asceticism, especially celibacy. 'The body is for the Lord and the Lord for the body.' 'Our maker bids increase; who bids abstain / But our destroyer?' (*P.L.* IV. 748–9). Hence Milton's insistence, contrary to orthodox tradition, that Adam and Eve made love in Paradise before the Fall: the body, like all matter, is good until man falls, and can be good thereafter. Since all matter derives from God, the differences between angels and men, soul and body, spirit and matter, are of degree, not of kind. This enables Milton to suggest in *Paradise Lost* that heaven may be more like earth than we assume, and so opens up a world of allegory.[5]

One consequence of belief in the goodness of matter, and of Milton's rejection of dualism, was his insistence on the corporeality of angels, which upsets some readers of *Paradise Lost*. Not only do they 'shed tears such as angels weep'; they also bleed, eat, digest, excrete, blush and interpenetrate sexually, though in a suitably angelic manner. (We recall R.O.'s pleasantries about 'an evacuating soul' in *Mans Mortalitie*, his object being the same as Milton's – to deny the separation of soul and body. Clarkson and Muggleton made the same point: the soul eats and drinks.)[6]

---

[1] *W.T.U.D.*, pp. 173–9, 184, 205–6; K. V. Thomas (1971), pp. 170–1; Cohn, p. 333; Burns, p. 63.

[2] T. Edwards, I, p. 219; A. Williams, p. 49. See p. 397 below.

[3] Cf. *C.P.W.*, VI, pp. 130–1, where Bishop Sumner thought Milton was attacking the Stoics. We may suspect that his target was nearer home. Cf. p. 244 above.

[4] Reeve (1711), p. 73; Clarkson (1660), p. 32. Cf. Butler, p. 113, where the belief that nature is the first cause is attributed to 'an atheist'.

[5] The closest analogy known to me is in Samuel Pordage's *Mundorum Explicatio,* where Adam and Eve 'like angels . . . /Enjoy the pleasures of eternal love' (p. 125). Hell and heaven are expressly likened to earth (p. 113). Cf. *P.L.* V. 469–90.

[6] Clarkson (1660), p. 61; Muggleton (1764), p. 102. Swedenborg was later vividly to describe angels copulating (*Chaste Delights of Conjugal Love,* a reference which I owe to the kindness of Edward Thompson).

Milton's heresies about angels eating and digesting (not 'in mist, the common gloss / Of theologians' – *P.L.* V. 434–8) seem only to be fully paralleled in Fludd, though there are suggestions in Sylvester/Du Bartas and Boehme; the radical John Webster later proclaimed, in opposition to Henry More, that angels had bodies.[1] The doctrine is ancient, but by the seventeenth century it was associated with the magical, Hermeticist/ Paracelsan tradition: it was accepted by the Baptist Henry Lawrence, Robert Gell, Hobbes, Hale and Gilbert Burnet.[2] Conservatives like Donne and Sir William Davenant specifically denied sex to angels.[3]

Milton wanted to relate his angels closely to men and women, and to proclaim the dignity of sex. These particular heresies, interestingly enough, are not developed in the *De Doctrina*. It looks as though the poet attached emotional rather than intellectual significance to them; or else that their main point was to establish the goodness of matter.[4] Angelic mingling in sex might come from Hermes Trismegistus, who contemplates the possibility of 'the deity manifested in either sex through the mingling of male and female' being 'put to the blush'.[5] Or perhaps from Paracelsus.[6] Or did Milton take a hint from Cartwright's poem, 'Ariadne deserted by Theseus', to which he refers in his sonnet to Henry Lawes? Cartwright wrote:

> Till my eyes drank up his
>   And his drank mine
> I ne'er thought souls might kiss
>   And spirits join.[7]

For the Ranters and to a lesser extent for Winstanley materialism led to a glorification of the senses which Milton would have rejected; but Edwards would certainly have classed them together. Milton's own particular heresy, that it was 'lawful for a man to put away his wife upon indisposition, unfitness or contrariety of mind arising from a cause in nature unchangeable',[8] was just what conservatives expected from one

---

[1] Angels eat in Sylvester's Du Bartas, but they temporarily assume a body for the purpose (Sylvester, I, pp. 17, 173); Boehme (1960), pp. 125–6; J. Webster, chapter X. Broadbent sensibly points out that Milton could have found a lot of materialism in the Apocrypha (1960, pp. 130, 280).

[2] Woodhouse (1945), p. 233; Patrides, pp. 47–8; Hobbes (1928), p. 43; Burnet, *Hale,* pp. 121–2; cf. Lewis (1942), p. 107.

[3] Donne, 'The Relique'; Davenant (1972), p. 22.

[4] As suggested by West (1953, pp. 39, 52).

[5] W. Scott, I, pp. 334–5.

[6] West (1955), pp. 170–2. For Milton and Paracelsus see also Waddington, pp. 278–82, and Empson (1961), pp. 89, 170–1.

[7] Cartwright, pp. 59–63.

[8] T. Edwards, I, p. 34.

who on principle rejected asceticism. Antinomians, Ranters and Quakers held doctrines of human perfectibility on earth: here too Milton would have drawn distinctions which Edwards would have thought sophistical.

To be and to act are the same, Nicholas Hill thought. God is power infinitely manifested in action.[1] 'Every action is intrinsically good', said Milton. Justice ('all strength and activity') is therefore superior to Truth ('properly no more than contemplation'), just because the former 'hath a sword put into her hand, to use against all violence and oppression on the earth'. 'Faith is an action'; faith necessarily leads to the works by which the regenerate will reform society.[2] Hence Jesus's rejection of contemplative knowledge in *Paradise Regained*. This picks up another radical emphasis. 'Action is the life of all,' cried Winstanley, 'and if thou dost not act, thou dost nothing.' Clarkson and Bunyan echoed him.[3] Traherne held that 'philosophers are not those that speak but do great things', Rochester that 'where action ceases, thought's impertinent.'[4] So much was this attitude believed to be characteristic of the radicals that the separatist in John Wilson's *The Cheats* (1663) says 'We must be a doing people as well as a saying people.'[5] 'God only acts and is', Blake wrote in *The Marriage of Heaven and Hell*, 'in existing beings or men.'[6]

I see Milton, then, as both emotionally and intellectually very close to the enthusiastic activists of the Revolution. He shared their materialism, though not their pantheism or rejection of any God outside themselves. He remained in dialogue with them.

---

[1] Shirley, p. 110; cf. W. Scott, I, pp. 234–5, 396–7.
[2] *C.P.W.*, III, p. 582; VI, p. 391; cf. I, p. 319.
[3] Sabine, p. 315; *W.T.U.D.*, pp. 216, 386, 407.
[4] Traherne, p. 316; Rochester (1968), p. 98.
[5] Wilson, p. 187.
[6] W. Blake, p. 198.

Chapter 27

Society and Heresy: between Two Cultures

> The sacred Milton was, let it ever be remembered, a republican and a
> bold inquirer into morals and religion.
>
> Shelley, Preface to *Prometheus Unbound* (1820)

I suggested earlier that there might be social reasons for Milton's
reluctance to abandon the Bible.[1] Perhaps we can extend this idea to some
of Milton's heresies. His insistence on freedom for the elect, deriving
from his profound, almost sub-rational individualism, drove him to the
verge of antinomianism. The elect, like Milton, can internalize discipline.
But Milton never abandoned the distinction between the elect and the
reprobate, for which he had indeed good Biblical authority: he never
supposed, as some radicals did, that all men would be saved.[2] As he grew
older and more discouraged he probably thought of the elect as a smaller
proportion of humanity than he had done in the early forties. But always
he saw the necessity for controls: the masses of the population cannot be
free. Hence in *Areopagitica* profanity, popery and licentiousness are to
be punished.[3] Hence the transitional dictatorship of *The Ready and Easy
Way*.

Free for what? one must ask. Freedom for the elect is necessary for
their self-realization. Such men must be free to choose evil for themselves;
but the unregenerate must not be free to impose evil on the regenerate,
which is what democracy would mean in the seventeenth-century English
context, no less than the personal government of Charles I. Hence the
church must be separated from the state. Similarly the rights of women to
divorce and remarriage must be subordinated to the rights of male householders. Freedom is for the élite, not for the masses. Milton faced in its

---

[1] See pp. 246–50 above.
[2] Cf. 272 above.
[3] See pp. 157, 256 above.

purest, least self-conscious form the bourgeois dilemma which was to recur in subsequent revolutions.

The tension between discipline and liberty, the individual and society, predestination and free will, is expressed theologically by the tension between the supreme God whose will is fate and the human Jesus: Milton is on the libertarian, anti-Trinitarian side. For him the anti-Trinitarian heresy was a continuation of the logic of the Reformation revolt against priestly or heavenly mediators, who mirrored the earthly hierarchy of feudal society. It was an assertion of monotheism, of law. The distinction between the supreme God and the demiurge helped to contribute to the idea of scientific law. The Father, remote, unmoved, is on the way to becoming the Supreme Being of eighteenth-century deism.[1] Anti-Trinitarianism is one of many streams contributing to the rise of modern science.

From the time when Milton abandoned his early poem on the Passion, he placed relatively little emphasis on the atonement – Christ's sacrificial and propitiatory role. Instead he depicted the Son of God as an exemplar of strenuous effort in good conduct, and stressed internal struggle rather than vicarious satisfaction and ransom.[2] Perhaps this is a further example of a bourgeois emphasis: but here we are dealing with something common to most Protestants from Calvin onwards, though carried to its extreme by Familists and other radicals. It is not peculiar to Milton.

Some versions of anti-Trinitarianism were very radical, emphasizing the humanity to the exclusion of the divinity of Christ. Milton did not accept this democratic doctrine: he clung on to the formulations of the Bible. Stress on the letter of Scripture as against the spirit in believers, or on the need for careful scholarship in interpreting the Bible, both in the last resort carry social implications, aim (however unconsciously) at preserving the institutions which protected the privileged position of intellectuals. Milton did not want to reject usury and oaths: such consequences of the Fall were necessary for bourgeois man and society. The deism and unitarianism which prevailed in the eighteenth century had been tamed of the 'excesses' of radical Socinianism, had absorbed aristocratic post-Restoration Hobbism, combining social and political conservatism with abstract intellectual radicalism.

Mortalism was a logical extension of the Protestant rejection of Purgatory: intense emphasis on this world (denial of the existence of heaven and

---

[1] Cf. Caudwell, p. 69.
[2] Cf. *C.P.W.*, VI, pp. 620, 430–7, where the emphasis is on the transformation in human nature which Christ brings about.

hell) led on to a morality based not on rewards and punishments but on
the consciences of men. Mortalism had its more and less radical variants,
turning on whether the ultimate resurrection was asserted or denied: the
half-way house, Milton's, was to assert and then virtually ignore it. He
held back from Ranter antinomianism, though his advocacy of divorce
for incompatibility went much further than orthodox Puritans liked, and
seemed to them indistinguishable from libertinism. He is a materialist but
not a pantheist; he believes in creation *ex deo*, not in the eternity of matter
independent of God. In all these respects – Arminianism, attitudes
towards the Bible, anti-Trinitarianism, antinomianism, mortalism,
materialism, there seems to be a common factor in Milton's position
between the second and third cultures. The parallel with the Muggletonians may be recalled again. Milton works at a vastly higher level of
intellectual sophistication: but many of his reactions against Ranter
versions of radical ideas are similar to those which appealed to the craftsmen among whom Muggletonianism flourished.[1]

If we extend our view to Milton's politics, we find that he agreed with
the Levellers in many of their criticisms, but rejected their platform as
unrealistic. He remained in some undefined position between Cromwell
and the Independent Grandees on the one hand, and Levellers on the
other; but since Milton accepted office under the republican government
he had to accept its responsibilities and constraints.[2] On the subject of
toleration, tithes and a state church he remained with the radicals to the
last, but in his educational theories he was at least as interested in training
an élite as in mass education.

Similarly, though he shared the widely held millenarian hopes of the
sixteen-forties, he rejected the plebeian Fifth Monarchism of the fifties,
which advocated revolt to expedite the Second Coming. Yet after the
Restoration, in his disillusion with the politics of the Parliamentarian
revolutionaries, he came to believe that a convergence of the human
with the divine would be necessary before a good society could be built.
This seems to be implied in *Paradise Regained* and *Samson Agonistes*. The
problem of liberty turned out to be insoluble in the sort of revolution in
which Milton was caught up. Similar dilemmas were to confront others
in later revolutions.[3]

Milton, then, is the great eclectic, taking ideas from wherever he found
them. He took more from the radical tradition than most orthodox

[1] See pp. 111–12 above.
[2] See pp. 156–7 above.
[3] Cf. p. 237 above, pp. 303, 392–3, 475 below.

'Puritans', and evolved other ideas of his own in dialogue with the third culture. But something more mysterious appears to be going on. Milton is not merely rationally discussing and choosing between two sets of ideas – though he is doing that – but in his poetry he reveals a personality which is also in some deeper way internally torn – between Adam's love for Eve and his orthodox theology, in Milton's attitudes towards Comus, Satan, Samson, towards pagan myth and classical learning. We shall have to look at these points when we consider the great poems. Here I suggest only that Milton's rational political dialogue and his deeply divided personality both relate to his position between the two cultures. We may perhaps return to the passage from Hopkins which I quoted on p. 96 above, 'Horrible to say, in a manner I am a communist.' Hopkins was dismayed and disturbed that social evils made him accept ideas of which one part of him strongly disapproved. His uneasiness is more explicit than Milton's, and the gap between his conservative political outlook and communism is far wider than that between Milton and the radicals; but Hopkins's awareness of a dialectical relationship to communism is analogous to Milton's deep personal divisions.[1]

This uncertainty at the heart of Milton's personality must be borne in mind when we come to consider the poetic tasks which he set himself in *Paradise Lost* – to assert eternal providence and to justify the ways of God to men. Such tasks have perplexed middle-of-the-road radicals since history began – how to reconcile providence and free will, how to have liberty and discipline, justice and inequality, liberty and property, how to bridge the gap between the God whose will is fate and men whose will is free. To the great poems we now turn.

---

[1] I owe this point and much help with this aspect of Milton to the generosity of Christopher Ricks.

PART VI

THE GREAT POEMS

The Enlightened Soul said: '... Paradise must thus spring up again in thee, through the wrath of God, and hell be changed into heaven in thee. Therefore be not dismayed, ... and whatsoever shall befall thee, take it all from his hands, as intended by him for thy highest good. ...'

The Distressed Soul ... entered into hope.

> Boehme, *A Discourse between A Soul Hungry and Thirsty,*
> *... and A Soul Enlightened*

[*Paradise Lost*] contains within itself a philosophical refutation of that system of which, by a strange and natural antithesis, it has been a chief popular support.

> Shelley, *A Defence of Poetry*

Chapter 28

The Fall of Man

> Is it a mere coincidence that the Fall of Man became less and less
> necessary as a vehicle of moral and religious truth once this astonish-
> ing poet had devoted his great, and greatly subversive, energies to it?
> Blake was right. . . .
> C. Ricks, reviewing Parker in *The Sunday Times*, 1 September 1968

I History, myth and allegory

To understand Milton's attitude towards myth and allegory it may be
useful to begin by looking at his view of history. In the *History of Britain*
he regards as self-evident the analogy which he draws between Britain
after the withdrawal of the Romans and England after Parliament's victory
in the seventeenth-century Civil War. The common factor is the chance of
establishing a free commonwealth, which was lost in each instance owing
to the moral inadequacy of the inhabitants of the country.[1] This seems to-
day a very implausible and unhistorical approach, but was common in the
seventeenth century. It was shared by the censor who read Milton's
criticisms of the Anglo-Saxon clergy as applying to post-Restoration
England.[2] It is part of the mental attitude which treated the Biblical
narrative simultaneously as historically true and as an allegory for later
times. Arise Evans, whom I quoted above, believed that Revelation 8 to 11
– chapters on which Milton drew in *Paradise Lost* for his account of the war
in heaven – and Amos 8 to 9 gave an account of English history in the
sixteen-forties.[3] This attitude was prevalent among London radicals during
the Revolution. It led some to reject the historical truth of the Gospel
story altogether, to treat it merely as an allegory of the soul's quest.
Milton, occupying a middle position as usual, accepted the Bible as the

---

[1] See Professor Fogle's Introduction to the *History of Britain* in *C.P.W.*, V.
[2] Cf. pp. 218 above, 405 below.
[3] Evans (1652), *passim*; see p. 246 above.

Word of God, and the literal truth of its narrative; but he also believed that it contained fundamental truths about humanity. The moral defects shown by Adam and Eve, even more than the moral defects of the ancient Britons, illuminated the failure of the English people in the sixteen-fifties.

It was generally assumed in the seventeenth century that classical myths were often – in Ralegh's words – 'crooked images of some one true history', echoes or distorted recollections of the Biblical narrative. The myth of Deucalion related to Noah's Flood, and so on.[1] It was thus easy to read allegorical truths into the myths of classical antiquity, even whilst drawing attention (as Milton frequently did) to their historical untruth. Bacon had set a rather fanciful example of this procedure. Milton fused Biblical stories with legends of classical Greece and Rome. The myth of Orpheus seems to have made a greater emotional impression on him than the story of the Crucifixion, if we can judge by the frequency of its occurrence in his writings. In *Areopagitica* and elsewhere the Fall is mixed with the legends of Psyche and Osiris; in *Paradise Lost* the descriptions of heavenly bliss combine pagan with Christian elements. The Paradise of Fools in Book III is a poetic invention.[2] If we were to take it seriously it would make a nonsense of Milton's mortalism: there is no Paradise of Fools in the *De Doctrina*. Raphael makes it clear that the six days of creation are not to be taken literally. On minor points Milton allowed himself even to modify the Bible. In Judges and in *Paradise Lost* Dalila is Samson's harlot; it suits the plot of *Samson Agonistes* better that she should be his wife. Milton likewise gave different explanations in *Paradise Lost* and *Paradise Regained* of the story of Genesis 6:2 that 'Sons of God' coupled with 'daughters of men'.[3] Descriptions of God in the Bible, Milton says in the *De Doctrina,* are adapted to the capacity of human beings to understand. This very ancient line of thought, popularized by Calvin, proved useful to astronomers in reconciling the Copernican theory with the letter of the Bible.

We must distinguish between allegory, in which characters have a single and consistent significance, and the method of allusion.[4] When in describing Eve Milton mentions Venus as well as the Virgin Mary (*P.L.* V. 379–87), he is neither treating the goddess of love as a historical character in the same sense as Mary, nor allegorizing.[5] He is drawing on the cultural heritage which had collected round the story of Venus to enrich his

---

[1] MacCaffrey, pp. 12–14.
[2] Not necessarily Milton's invention: there is something very similar in S. Pordage, pp. 95–6.
[3] C. and F., pp. 581, 589–90, 785; *P.L.* IX. 1060–1; XI. 581–92; *P.R.*, II. 178–81.
[4] Hough, pp. 129–37.
[5] Kermode, p. 89; cf. McKeon, pp. 82–9.

portrait of Eve. He clearly is not identifying Eve and Venus. 'Who would claim that things which are analogous must correspond to each other in every respect?'[1] Similar allusions abound. Given Milton's political pre-dilections, it is natural that, as Addison put it, Milton 'has related the fall of those angels who are his professed enemies'.[2] They have many Royalist characteristics. (Lucifer had been 'the first prelate angel' in *The Reason of Church Government*.) But Satan is also the battle-ground for Milton's quarrel with himself:[3] he alludes to some of the worst characteristics of the revolutionaries – to the avarice and ambition of the generals who betrayed the republic, and to the irreligious speculations of Ranters and others which had diverted and divided the supporters of the Good Old Cause.

Satan then is not a flat allegorical figure, to be equated either with Royalists, Ranters or major-generals. Milton saw the Satanic in all three: recall his warning that greedy Parliamentarians were in danger of becoming Royalists themselves.[4] Though Satan comes to represent evil, he was once an angel of light. Evil may be found in those who think they are serving God. In conceiving Satan Milton may have recollected some of the passions and 'vain reasonings' which had led him too astray: in *Paradise Regained* Satan tempts the Son of God with aims and objectives which had formerly appeared tempting to Milton.[5] The allusions are often complex. Satan giving birth to Sin from his head alludes to Zeus, the rebel God who gave birth to Athene. Sin's immaculate conception exonerates God from responsibility for evil.[6] But it also parallels the creation of Eve from Adam's rib. And Athene was the goddess of learning: the allusion may prefigure Jesus's attack on learning in *Paradise Regained*.

The allusive method gave full rein to Milton's ambiguity. In *Paradise Regained* he appears to put his own beliefs about baptism into Satan's mouth: it was one way of getting past the censor. Commentators have often noted the conflict between the poet's republicanism and the Royalist imagery which he used to describe the Father. The paradox is, however,

---

[1] *C.P.W.*, VI, p. 547; Miner (1974), pp. 114–16, 227–9, 244, 258–65, 332–4.
[2] Shawcross, p. 149.
[3] See pp. 366–7 below.
[4] Cf. p. 435 below, where I make a similar suggestion about Harapha.
[5] See pp. 416–17 below.
[6] Does it also suggest that Sin is ultimately a figment of Satan's imagination? (Broadbent, 1960, p. 130; G. D. Hamilton, p. 93). Clarkson had suggested this (see above). Sin is 'not ... really an action' but 'a deficiency' (*C.P.W.*, VI, p. 391; but cf. p. 382). Shelley thought that 'evil is not inherent in the system of the creation, but an accident that might be expelled' (Mrs. Shelley's note on *Prometheus Unbound*).

no greater than in describing Eve in terms of the pagan goddess of love. God in *Paradise Lost* is at once different from the kings of the earth and precisely like them: in the end he will cease to be a king at all. In *Paradise Regained* these ambiguities begin to be cleared up. The Son of God is dissociated from the symbolic royalism of *Paradise Lost,* which is restricted to the corrupt kings of the earth. In *Samson Agonistes* God is never referred to as king, and Samson is neither king nor ruler but an outcast. The disappearance of Royalist symbolism in its traditional connotation may be related to the fact that Charles II and not King Jesus ultimately succeeded Charles I. To that extent it is a social as well as a literary phenomenon. But it might reflect a growing conviction that no authority will be needed when God is all in all.[1]

The Fall of Man then was a historical event for Milton. But it also had symbolic significance, as an allegory of man's inability to live up to his own standards. Winstanley thought 'it matters not much' whether the Biblical stories were true or not.[2] Milton would not have been so light-hearted about the history; but for him too the Fall was a mystery, metaphor as well as truth. The War in Heaven and the Fall of Man were not different in kind from the historical events recorded in Books XI and XII. Events which occur in time – those revealed or related by Michael, classical legends or modern English history – are examples of the archetypal happenings in heaven and hell before history began.[3] England in 1659–60 re-enacted as macabre farce the tragedy of the Fall.

We must see Milton in the precise historical situation of the post-Restoration decade, and understand his attitude towards his subject-matter. Otherwise we shall be in danger either of dismissing the theology of the great poems as useless lumber, or of reading into it twentieth-century preconceptions, whether they are those of C. S. Lewis, William Empson or Irene Samuel. *Paradise Lost* tells an epic story which (in Milton's view) is also a true story; but the story sums up the whole of human experience, including the valuable experience recorded in the myths of classical antiquity. It is truth and myth at the same time, and on both counts it has something to say to God's servants who had been defeated in the English Revolution.

Such an approach, it seems to me, enables us to respond to the design of *Paradise Lost* as a whole rather than as a collection of episodes: the epic has a tough intellectual structure. It also disposes of some of the accusations

---

[1] Ross, pp. 111, 119, 126, 134, 139, and *passim*. See pp. 303–5 above.
[2] See p. 309 above.
[3] I owe this point and much in the following paragraphs to Margot Heinemann.

brought against Milton – for instance that hell is imperfectly and in-consistently visualised.[1] Sometimes it is a place of eternal torment, whose heat is blazingly intolerable; at others it permits of athletic exercises and meandering philosophical discussion. God's omnipotence could of course be called on to explain this; but if we see hell as a metaphor, an internal state as well as a place, divine intervention is not necessary. Hell is where Satan is: it is a state in which we may all find ourselves. Fire and brimstone would have added nothing to the torments of the deprived Satan as he watched Adam and Eve from outside Paradise.

This approach may also illuminate some complexities. Eve is not only the beloved sexual partner, the perfect wife who takes her astronomy at second hand from her husband; she becomes, under temptation, intel-lectually arrogant and over-confident, setting freedom above dedicated acceptance of God's will. If there is something of the Ranter in Satan,[2] at this stage he infects Eve with the same heresy. Finally this approach may help us to understand Milton's failure to make God a sympathetic charac-ter. God is history, is the world as it really is, not as we would romantically like it to be.[3] Milton is no more able than any other theologian to explain how beneficent omnipotence has been unable to make a better job of running the universe. God, as M. M. Ross put it, 'sometimes talks as if he had mercy, and sometimes acts as if he had not'.[4]

I am not putting forward a new interpretation of *Paradise Lost,* nor of *Paradise Regained* or *Samson Agonistes.* I have started from the hypothesis that in all three poems Milton is grappling with problems set by the failure of God's cause in England, and I have tried to re-read the poems in the light of this not very original hypothesis. Awareness of the world in which Milton wrote, and of the audience for whom he wrote, ought to help us to understand not only what his conscious self thought he was doing, but what other more hidden intentions he may have had, which myth and allegory helped him both to realize and to disguise from himself.

II   Restoration politics and the Fall

The doctrine of the Fall of Man was central to seventeenth-century explanations of the origin of private property, social inequality, the state

---

[1] Waldock, pp. 93–5; Leavis (1976), p. 20. For a convincing refutation of the allegation that Milton's visual imagination was inadequate, see R. M. Frye, 'Milton's *Paradise Lost* and the Visual Arts', *Proceedings of the American Philosophical Soc.,* Vol. 120 (1976), pp. 233–44.

[2] See pp. 396–8 below.

[3] Cf. *C.P.W.,* V, p. xxvii, and pp. 359–60 below.

[4] Ross, p. 216. See pp. 473–5 below.

and the monogamous family. If Adam had not fallen, men would have been equal, property would have been held in common; a coercive state has become necessary to protect inequalities in property, which are the consequences of post-lapsarian greed and pride. Without it fallen men would destroy one another, society would be impossible. The doctrine of the Fall summed up the sadness of oppressed humanity throughout the ages. There had been a golden age, now lost: in heaven we shall receive our compensation. Meanwhile our inherited sinfulness, for which it is difficult to understand why *we* are to blame, nevertheless explains and justifies the social inequality, class oppression, unfreedom which we see around us.[1]

Any revolutionary theory, therefore, had to take account of mid-seventeenth-century discussions of the Fall. Most radical of all was Gerrard Winstanley, who stood traditional orthodoxy on its head. So far from property, inequality and the state being necessary consequences of the sinfulness of man since the Fall, Winstanley argued that the introduction of private property *was* the Fall, that from it followed covetousness, social inequality and the state which protects the property of the rich. If we abolish private property and wage labour we shall be back in the pre-lapsarian state of innocence and bliss. Ranters, Quakers and others, without rising to a theory with the sweep of Winstanley's, also rejected the concept of original sin. Milton wished to preserve private property and inequality, and so could not accept Winstanley's analysis. But he would have agreed the doctrine of the Fall had social implications. It explained why there were rich and poor, why some ruled and others obeyed, why divorce was necessary.[2] The hope of getting back behind the Fall on earth was shared by alchemists, by Paracelsans, by Bacon, by Hakewill and by George Wither as well as by Familists, Winstanley and Fox.[3] It links up with the Protestant desire to return to the pure state of the early Christian church before it became contaminated with politics, and with the primitivism of Levellers and others who wanted to get back to an imagined Anglo-Saxon freedom. In all three cases the backward look became a programme for future action. As demands for equality, for human rights, became more insistent, so Diggers, Ranters, Arminians and Quakers kept up a continuous discussion about the Fall, about sin, a discussion which interwove the social and the individual. *Areopagitica* stresses the doctrine – old as St. Ambrose, but often associated with radicals and heretics – that the Fall had in certain respects been fortunate. Wyclif, Langland, Sylvester/Du Bartas

---

[1] See *W.T.U.D.*, chapter 8 *passim*.
[2] See p. 127 above.
[3] See pp. 309–11 above; cf. C. Hill (1965), pp. 89–90, 200.

and Giles Fletcher were among those who accepted this doctrine.[1] Knowledge of good and evil came from the rind of one apple tasted, knowledge of good through knowledge of evil. Loss was gain and gain was loss. This approach introduced a dialectical element into the thinking of men like Milton, saved them from seeing history as a cycle, or as a linear process of continuing decay – or continuing improvement.

This historical perspective stood Milton in good stead, when from the late fifties the Fall came more and more to the foreground of his thinking to explain the failure of God's cause in his chosen nation. (The only other general theory of explanation that Milton toyed with from time to time was the climatic theory, the deficiencies of the North.[2]) Milton had to explain the degeneration of the Revolution to which he and so many others had devoted their energies for many years, and to which Milton had sacrificed his eyesight. Milton's fame had rung through Europe, but in less than a dozen years *Eikon Basilike* had triumphed over *Eikonoklastes,* magic over reason. Long before 1660 Milton had to face the fact that God's kingdom was not to be established in England yet. The disunity of the radicals, the ambitions of the generals, the self-interested a-politicism of the mass of middle-class Englishmen, had defeated the hopes of Milton and his kind for creating a good society in England. Clarendon's view that God had intervened miraculously to restore Charles II seemed more plausible than the view that the routed Parliamentarians had been the interpreters of God's will.

Paradise Lost accepts the fact of defeat. 'The Lord had . . . spit in their faces and witnessed against their perfidiousness', declared Major-General Fleetwood[3] – the general in Cromwell's entourage whose political outlook must have been least uncongenial to Milton, and whom the poet certainly knew personally. What had happened to God's cause? Fleetwood referred to the events of the winter 1659–60. But for Milton things had gone wrong long before then – with the 'ambition and avarice' of men like Fleetwood in great part to blame. Those who had proclaimed God's cause had won power, and had failed, failed utterly.[4] This failure must have been manifest to Milton by 1658, when he probably began writing *Paradise Lost;* the restoration of Charles II in 1660 was only the last and greatest of the many disasters which had befallen the Cause. Who was to blame?

---

[1] Lovejoy, pp. 164–79.
[2] Fink, pp. 94, 191–2. See p. 6 above.
[3] *Clarke Papers,* IV, p. 220.
[4] For Milton's denunciation of the 'illegal and scandalous, I fear me barbarous' behaviour of the generals in 1659 see *C.M.,* VI, p. 102.

Fleetwood blamed God. Satan in *Paradise Lost* attacked God's arbitrary and incomprehensible ways. So did the unregenerate Samson. There must have been moments when Milton, like Adam, had his doubts (cf. *P.L.* X. 720–844; XI. 417–514). But there was nothing predestinate about what had happened. The English people, or their leaders, had had their chance, and had failed to take it. They had fallen freely. Like the rebel angels, 'firm they might have stood/ Yet fell' (*P.L.* VI. 911–12).

Milton had dedicated his life to becoming the English national poet, and since 1640 he had been the steadfast propagandist of the English Revolution, which he had hoped would open up new possibilities for poets to become acknowledged legislators. Now both the Revolution and his own poetic role had been called in question. Milton being Milton, it would have been astonishing if the three last great poems had *not* been about politics. Their lesson is not resignation, but a different type of political action from those which have failed so lamentably. Milton no longer has the high hopes for the English nation that he held in the forties, nor the belief that a few good men can act on behalf of the nation, which he held (or tried to persuade himself that he held) in the fifties. He is still searching for an audience which will appreciate him, 'fit though few', as Oliver Cromwell throughout the sixteen-fifties was seeking an electorate which would support him.[1] In *Of Education* and *Areopagitica* Milton had thought in terms of the regeneration of society; in *Paradise Lost* and the *De Doctrina* the reconstruction of individual leaders seems to come first. It is the Old Testament doctrine of the remnant, the few just men who save the city. But still the emphasis is on change and on this world. Poets and Christians must change this world, not merely explain it, as philosophers did;[2] nor offer the consolations of another world, as traditional theology had done.

Milton had an overwhelming sense of guilt: not personal, but collective, on behalf of the English people. God had spat in their face, but not before they had denied their Saviour. Adam expresses Milton's viewpoint:

> Him after all disputes
> Forced I absolve: all my evasions vain
> And reasonings, though through mazes, lead me still
> But to my own conviction: first and last
> On me, me only, as the source and spring
> Of all corruption, all the blame lights due.
>
> (*P.L.* X. 828–33)

---

[1] Radzinowicz, p. 457; Miner (1974), p. 244.
[2] Rivers, pp. 95–100; Frye (1966), p. 61.

The problem most in need of solution in the sixties was how good men fail, how people with the right ideas come to make the wrong choices. A poem about the Fall would among other things provide explanations of the failure of the godly in the English Revolution. Adam had been free to fall, and to fall he chose: the English people had taken a captain back for Egypt. To turn God's Englishmen to God again, God's ways must be justified to them. In theory at least Milton accepted the justice of England's punishment, however much one part of his free spirit raged against its consequences, as Samson was to rage against his fate. In the first instance Milton blamed the leaders of the Parliamentary cause. It was probably in 1648 that he wrote 'They who but of late were extolled as great deliverers[1] and had a people wholly at their devotion' so discharged their trust that they 'did not only weaken and unfit themselves to be dispensers of what liberty they pretended, but unfitted also the people, now grown worse and more disordinate, to receive or to digest any liberty at all'. 'For liberty hath a sharp and double edge, fit only to be handled by just and virtuous men; to bad and dissolute it becomes a mischief unwieldy in their own hands.'[2] Milton henceforth was continually nagging at the problem of liberty. When he published *The History of Britain* in 1670, he concluded from Anglo-Saxon experience that 'when God hath decreed servitude on a sinful nation, fitted by their own vices for no condition but servile, all estates of government are alike unable to avoid it.'[3]

Sin then is social. Not merely individuals fall but whole nations. But only chosen peoples can fall – the people of Israel and the people of England: 'that people victor once, now vile and base,/ Deservedly made vassal' (*P.R.* IV. 132–3). Milton explained in 1673 that if a nation failed to respond to the chastisements of 'pestilence, fire, sword or famine' (the first three at least of which had visited England in the sixties), God might proceed to inflict 'his severest punishments', hardness of heart and idolatry.[4] The chosen nation had been made vassal, because none can love freedom heartily save good men, and when the test came not enough were good – i.e. disinterested. So Milton was pushed back into a greater emphasis on sin, on the reconstruction of individuals as a necessary preliminary to the transformation of institutions.

Spenser, who like Milton identified public and private morality, stated

---

[1] Supporters of an early date for *Samson Agonistes* should make more use of this passage. Cf. pp. 431–2 below.

[2] *C.P.W.*, V, p. 449.

[3] *Ibid.*, V, p. 259. This may have been written in the mid-fifties or even in the sixties (*ibid.*, pp. xxxix–xliii). Cf. *P.L.* XII. 90–101, and *C.P.W.*, IV, p. 684, quoted on p. 236 above.

[4] *C.M.*, VI, p. 179.

the aim of *The Faerie Queene* as 'to fashion a gentleman or noble person in virtuous and gentle discipline'.[1] Milton hoped to fashion perfect men – with less reservation of class than Spenser, though he was no democrat. Freedom is self-reliance, is internalized virtue, but it is also co-operation with God's purposes, knowledge of necessity, disciplined preparation without impatience. In rather the same way in the fifteen-nineties, after the defeat of Presbyterianism, the Puritans had retreated from political organization and action to the cultivation of strong moral personalities. They built up an army of dedicated servants of the Lord, so successfully that the retreat was followed by the great leap forward of the sixteen-forties. Milton, consciously or not, was advocating a similar move away from political solutions to inner change, in preparation for the next signal from God.[2] The time-scale had changed, the early optimism had proved unfounded. But the conclusion is not despair: it is that the foundations must be dug deeper, into the hearts of individual believers, in order to build more securely.

The English Revolution had gone wrong because the revolutionaries had failed to allow for the resilience and adaptability of the English gentry, their powers of adjustment. The radicals had tried to take political short cuts, had relied on individuals who turned out to be avaricious and ambitious, or hypocrites. The desire for reformation did not sink deeply enough into the consciences of supporters of the Revolution, did not transform their lives. They had passively handed politics over to their leaders, as to some factor.[3] The leaders had betrayed the cause, had accepted cowardly compromises, had sacrificed principles to what they thought was economic expediency. Milton was not rejecting the commitment of 1641–5 and 1649–51: he was asking himself why the aims which he had then proclaimed had not been realized. Blame for failure lies not in the aims – which were God's, and remain right – but in the English people, Milton included. Political failure was ultimately moral failure. 'Whose fault' was the Fall, God asked. 'Whose but his own' – Adam's.

> They themselves decreed
> Their own revolt. . . .
> I formed them free, and free they must remain
> Till they enthrall themselves . . .
> They themselves ordained their fall.
>
> (*P.L.* III. 96–128)

---

[1] See p. 66 above.
[2] Mohl, pp. 69–70, 84; cf. *S. and P.*, pp. 485–90.
[3] See p. 158 above.

The Fall had been the consequence of the wrong sort of solution, of Eve's attempted short cut towards a godlike power, instead of achieving this by self-knowledge and self-discipline, which would give true control. As early as *The Doctrine and Discipline of Divorce* Milton had warned the man who 'finds the fits and workings of a high impatience frequently upon him', in consequence of matrimonial misfortune, not to 'open his lips against the providence of heaven or tax the ways of God and his divine truth; for they are equal, easy, and not burdensome, nor do they ever cross the just and reasonable desires of men'.[1] He now had to try out this advice in respect of a disaster even greater than that which had befallen his first marriage. 'Even the saints', he observed in the *De Doctrina*, 'are sometimes tempted to commit' the sin of 'impatience towards God'.[2] 'Inexplicable / Thy justice seems', cried Adam in *Paradise Lost* (X. 754–5). So the theme of the Fall of Man, which had always fascinated Milton, acquired a more directly political relevance in the late fifties and early sixties.

God was becoming a problem for many mid-seventeenth-century Englishmen. Protestants emphasized the Bible as an infallible guide to conduct; they could hardly fail to observe contrasts between the morality which sufficed for a tribal society in the eastern Mediterranean and the rather different standards of seventeenth-century England.[3] The difficulty of reconciling God's justice with his mercy, legalism with love, was age-old. But the unique freedom of the forties and fifties allowed such problems to be discussed, verbally and in print. *Paradise Lost* assumes the whole interregnum discussion on the Fall, in which Diggers, Ranters, Socinians, Quakers as well as others more conservative had participated.[4] The 'outcry against God's justice', the feeling that there was something that needed justification, was common to Isaac Pennington, John Reeve, William Sedgwick, Bunyan, Dryden, Rochester and many others.[5] Samuel Pordage's *Mundorum Explicatio* (1661), another poem about the Fall, starts from the triumph of evil in the world, the scoffing of atheists: its theme is the assertion of human freedom and the recovery of Paradise on earth.[6]

It was a turning-point in human thought. Just as after 30 January 1649 kings never forgot that they had a joint in their necks, so God was never quite the same after he had been called to the bar of judgment in popular

---

[1] *C.P.W.*, II, p. 342.
[2] *Ibid.*, VI, p. 663.
[3] See p. 277 above.
[4] *W.T.U.D.*, pp. 397–9.
[5] See pp. 358–60 below. Cf. G. D. Hamilton, pp. 87–100.
[6] S. Pordage, pp. 1–2, and *passim*.

discussion.[1] The processes which led to the decline of hell, of belief in a God who predestined the mass of mankind to eternal damnation, the replacement of a morality based on rewards and punishments, were expedited. Milton was wrestling to retain the God of Jacob at an unpropitious time. Adam, after calling God's justice inexplicable, continued 'Yet to say truth, too late/ I thus contest' (X. 755–6).

Milton, so far as I know, is the first to turn to the story of the Fall to explain the failure of a revolution. Many before him, including Spenser,[2] had used human sinfulness as a reason for rejecting demands for equality. 'A natural and complete freedom from all sorrows and troubles was fit for man only before he had sinned, not since', Walwyn was told in 1649. 'Let them look for their portion in this life that know no better, and their kingdom in this world that believe no other.'[3] Godfrey Goodman, Hakewill's opponent, had used this argument against the radicals: 'if Paradise were to be replanted on earth, God had never expelled man [from] Paradise.'[4] That is why Milton's Fall had to be Arminian: the elect are not predestined, any of us are capable of the efforts necessary to achieve salvation. Redemption is for all men, not just for a pre-selected elect – however pessimistic Milton may have become about the numbers of those who heeded the call by the time he came to write the De Doctrina.[5] All merely human political aspirations are likely to fail, because of the Fall. But this is something we can learn to understand and correct, by putting right the inner man. Men can be regenerate on earth: that is the theme of Paradise Regained. Then God will show ways in which political problems, which now seem insoluble, can solve themselves: that is the theme of Samson Agonistes.

For Milton human sinfulness explains how things have gone wrong this time. But that is not the end: the Fall remains fortunate.[6] It exonerates God from responsibility for the existence of evil in the world. And Milton's version of the story also preserves human freedom.[7] We must accept what the omnipotent God wills, for what he wills is fate. But we must still keep our powder dry, and be ready to do better next time.

The reason which Milton gave in the De Doctrina for belief in the existence of God is worth pondering. He appeals to 'many visible proofs,

---

[1] Cf. C.P.W., II, p. 292, quoted on p. 387 below.
[2] The Faerie Queene, Book V, canto ii.
[3] Haller and Davies, p. 312; cf. W.T.U.D., p. 168: a similar answer given to the Diggers.
[4] Goodman, p. 90.
[5] Barker (1969), pp. 71–4. Cf. pp. 275–7 above.
[6] See pp. 346–7 above, 386–7 below.
[7] Cf. C.P.W, VI, pp. 397–8.

the fulfilment of many prophecies', which 'have driven every nation to the belief that either God or some supreme evil power . . . presides over the affairs of men'. But it is 'intolerable and incredible that evil should be stronger than good, and should prove the true supreme power. Therefore God exists. Further evidence for the existence of God is provided by the phenomenon of conscience or right reason. This cannot be altogether asleep, even in the most evil men. If there were no God, there would be no dividing line between right and wrong.'[1] Milton found it equally difficult to find convincing arguments against the view that God is the author of sin. 'If I should attempt to refute them, it would be like inventing a long argument to prove that God is not the devil.'[2]

As early as 1634 Milton had written

> Evil on itself shall back recoil,
> And mix no more with goodness, when at last
> Gathered like scum, and settled to itself
> It shall be in eternal restless change
> Self-fed, and self-consumed; if this fail,
> The pillared firmament is rottenness,
> And earth's base built on stubble.
>
> (*Comus*, 592–8)

He never produced evidence for believing that good would prevail: his certainty was intuitive. Life otherwise is a meaningless jungle. Since Darwin we have learnt to live in the jungle; but Milton here anticipates, even if only to brush them aside, the agonies of nineteenth-century agnosticism. He did not say that if God did not exist it would be necessary to invent him: God must exist if any meaning was to be left in the lives of Milton and the revolutionaries who had sacrificed so much and in whose faces God had spat.

---

[1] *Ibid.*, VI, pp. 131–2.
[2] *Ibid.*, VI, p. 166. Contrast, among others, Perkins, II, p. 614.

Chapter 29

Paradise Lost

> The same kind of labour may be *productive* or *unproductive*. For example Milton, who wrote *Paradise Lost* for £5, was an *unproductive labourer*. On the other hand, the writer who turns out stuff for his publisher in factory style, is a *productive labourer*. Milton produced *Paradise Lost* for the same reason that a silk worm produces silk. It was an activity of *his* nature.
>
> Karl Marx, *Theories of Surplus Value*, Part I
>
> It is a new barbarism to suppose that an appreciator of an artwork is professionally unconscious of its social background.
>
> William Empson, *Milton's God*

1 The historical context

Paradise Lost is a poem, not a historical document. The surface meaning is not necessarily to be taken at its face value, as though it were a series of statements in prose. (Nor, for that matter, should historians take most prose statements at their face value without careful critical examination of the context, the author's probable intentions, and so on and so forth.) But *Paradise Lost* should not be taken out of history. It is possible simply by 'reading the poem' to find in it meanings which seem unlikely to have been consciously intended by Milton, as Empson has found hatred of the Christian God, and A. D. Ferry has differentiated between Milton and 'the narrator' in *Paradise Lost*.

Our problem is to decide whether Milton *had* intentions other than his professed aim of justifying the ways of God to men. Waldock and Empson produce enough evidence of apparent resentment towards God in the epic to convict Milton either of great carelessness or of more complex intentions than those of which his conscious self was aware. The emotion with which Adam chose death with Eve rather than Paradise without her is contradicted shortly afterwards by the narrator's moralizing comment. It is

354

gratuitous to assume here that Milton intended the narrator to look foolish, that the latter's views are different from the poet's. But the poetry warns us that the narrator protests too much. The contradictions in Milton are fascinating historical evidence: we must not arbitrarily resolve them one way or another.

The poem is there for any reader to interpret. We may think of Milton as a forward-looking genius who somehow leapt out of his own time and believed in the supremacy of romantic love, or in the wickedness of the Christian God, or whatever suits contemporary fashions. This may help some twentieth-century readers. But in so far as we are trying as biographers and critics to find out what Milton's conscious beliefs were and what he was up to, then certain historical canons must be observed. According to Aubrey, the composition of *Paradise Lost* dates from about 1658 to about 1663, and this has been generally accepted, though earlier passages were no doubt incorporated from the abortive drama on the Fall of Man. *Paradise Lost* was thus probably written after Milton had defined most of his heresies in the *De Doctrina Christiana*.

Defenders of Milton's 'orthodoxy' emphasize the apparent differences between the epic and the theological treatise, the latter far more outspokenly heretical than the former. It is theoretically possible that the experience of writing *Paradise Lost* caused Milton to abandon views which he had previously elaborated in the *De Doctrina*. But there is no need to postulate any such change of heart. Quite apart from the difficulty of precisely dating the two works, any defender of this opinion must explain why Milton did not alter the *De Doctrina* to bring it into line with *Paradise Lost*, since he went on working on it till the end of his life, carefully prepared it for the press and apparently tried to arrange for its posthumous publication.[1]

The *De Doctrina* could not be published, not even anonymously and overseas. So it is less likely than the great poems to contain compromises between what Milton thought and what he felt it expedient (or possible) to say in print. Milton desperately wanted *Paradise Lost* to be published – partly because he knew it was a great poem, partly because it contained some at least of his hard-won message for God's people in Restoration England. It was not a treatise on dogmatic theology: its publication did not sacrifice truth to expediency. Publication was reasonably purchased at the price of playing down the heresies. Christopher Ricks has indeed argued that the style of *Paradise Lost* is at its best when Milton could not

---

[1] See chapter 18 above.

write with total directness.[1] So the necessity to write obliquely may have turned to Milton's advantage. After Addison had given it his blessing, the epic was accepted as 'orthodox'. But some of Milton's more intelligent readers, even without knowing of the existence of the *De Doctrina*, suspected anti-Trinitarianism in *Paradise Lost*: so did some of its eighteenth-century editors.

Between February 1659 and April 1660 Milton moved from the revived optimism of *Civil Power* to the despair of the second edition of *The Ready and Easy Way*. Later in 1660 he was in prison, in danger of his life. When released he had to live in obscurity and fear of assassination. These are the years in which he was writing *Paradise Lost*. Even if Milton had been a much less political character, it is unlikely that such events would have left him unaffected. The calm and distanced effect of *Paradise Lost* is astonishing, remarkable testimony to Milton's art and sense of decorum; but it is also deceptive. Not to grasp the magnitude of the disaster which had overwhelmed the poet would be a serious failure of imagination.

By mid-1660 Milton must have realized that the possibilities of political pamphleteering were exhausted, even if the censorship had not made it impossible for him to continue. The end of *The Ready and Easy Way* clearly recognizes defeat: in Professor Stavely's words, it is not a pamphlet but a poem.[2] Milton had thought of his pamphleteering prose as war carried on by other means. Now prose wearied; it had performed what prose could do, and had failed (cf. *P.L.* VI. 694–5). Milton returned to the greater power of poetry. If Abdiel was Milton the prose pamphleteer, fighting on uselessly rather than surrender, ideally poetry should gain the miraculous and instantaneous victory of Messiah. Hence Milton's high bardic claims. Some of the former Parliamentarians, in defeat, persuaded themselves that all their problems would be solved by a Fifth Monarchy. John Reeve and Lodowick Muggleton believed that they had been directly commissioned by God to reveal his will. Diggers and Ranters thought that Christ's Second Coming would be his rising in sons and daughters. Milton was directly inspired by Urania, the Spirit of God.

This was no new claim. As early as 1643–4 Milton seems to have believed that it was under divine inspiration that he had recovered the true Christian doctrine of divorce.[3] In the *Second Defence of the English People* he stated his belief that 'I and my interests are . . . under the protection of God.' In a postscript added to the 1658 edition of the *Defence* he claimed that 'a deed

---

[1] Ricks (1963), pp. 148–50.
[2] Stavely, p. 65.
[3] *C.P.W.*, II, pp. 340, 433, 436–8.

so lofty and noble' as the English Revolution 'was not successfully undertaken and completed without divine inspiration'. 'The same assistance and
guidance led to its being recorded' in Milton's treatise.[1] The poet's blindness brought home to him the apostolic reference to those who won
strength out of weakness. This is part of a wider concept of the blind
bard, the seer whose blindness brings him closer to the gods and their
mysteries.[2] But Milton's claim to inspiration is not merely traditional: it
relates to the specific political situation. Milton was no ordinary poet. He
saw himself as one of a line of prophets, of whom Christ was the greatest.
He seems to have believed that he was inspired in writing *Paradise Lost*: in
the night the Muse brought him the lines which he dictated to his amanu-
ensis next morning. Similarly *Paradise Regained* was 'my prompted song'
(P.R. I. 12). In his priestlike role the poet is a potential Messiah, a Son of
God. Church-outed by the prelates, state-outed by the restored monarchy,
poetry was the only medium through which Milton could communicate
after 1660.[3] The cool medium of prose being no longer open, there
remained the fire and fury of Messiah's overwhelming chariot. In his
Abdiel role, using his left hand, Milton had done his best. Now circumstances – i.e. God's will – commanded him to use his right hand if
he was to fight at all. Milton, in Marvell's phrase, made his destiny his
choice.

The circumstances in which Milton wrote may help to explain the
aloofness, the defensiveness of the Father in *Paradise Lost*. Quite apart from
the intrinsic difficulty of making abstract omnipotence interesting, and the
fact that there is Biblical authority for most of what the Father says,
Milton felt out of tune with him. The Father mocks men in a way that
offends modern taste. But so did the God of the Old Testament:[4] so did
the God whom Milton and the Parliamentary revolutionaries had served.
His irony at their expense was brutal and callous. In the *De Doctrina* too
the least strongly-felt passages are those in which the Father-God of
absolute will dominates. In *Paradise Lost* the Father was kicked upstairs –
formally accepted, but not felt. In the later books of the poem he recedes,
and is replaced by the Creator-Son.[5] It is the Son who is goodness and
mercy, who manifests divine love in the plenitude of creation. And the
Son becomes man, believers become Sons. So we move on to the final

---

[1] *Ibid.*, IV, pp. 550, 557-8, 536.
[2] *Ibid.*, pp. 589-90. See pp. 210-11 above.
[3] Riggs, pp. 35, 44, 51, 154, 179-82.
[4] See pp. 235-6, 242-3 above.
[5] Sewell, pp. 175, 112, 116, 156-7.

stage in which the abstract God of will dissolves and is replaced by the composite body of Christ – the community of Sons.[1]

I see Milton bitterly – because he must – accepting the Father whose will is Fate, but aspiring more and more to the position of Sonship, to union with the perfect man who becomes God's Son by merit. The possibility of regeneration salvages something of man's dignity, freedom and responsibility from the wreckage of 1660. Milton's mood must have been like that in which his friend Isaac Penington reluctantly recognized God's absolute sovereignty. Writing in 1650, in what may have been his Ranter period, he said:

'He that bringeth both the perfect and the wicked upon the stage may turn either of them off from the stage when he will. There is no more to hinder him from destroying the perfect than there is to hinder him from destroying the wicked. They are both equally his. They are both at his dispose. They are one and the same under several representations, and he has appointed them both to one and the same end, which is destruction. . . . Ye think to secure yourselves by his faithfulness, his word, his promises, to which he must be faithful; and will ye not have him faithful to his sovereignty? He is Lord of all, and has the dispose of all, and let him make never so many deeds of gifts, . . . still he has the power of life and death in his own hands. . . . All dispensations are but for a season, they are not everlasting. Therefore eternity delights to swallow them up. Perfect and wicked are both of the same lump, only differently clothed to act their several parts, which when they have done, their clothes must be taken off, and they turned back into the lump again. There is nothing durable but *the eternal state of things*. Now therefore hath God treasured up destructions for all dispensations, because it is suitable for all dispensations.'[2] Penington was grappling with Milton's problem. 'Just or unjust', sang the chorus in *Samson Agonistes*,

> alike seem miserable,
> For oft alike both come to evil end.
>
> (703–4)

Similarly Lodowick Muggleton thought that 'God did seem to be more cruel than man', but accepted that 'a prerogative power and will of God is not to be contended with.'[3]

---

[1] See pp. 303–5 above.
[2] I. Penington, *Light or Darknesse* (1650), in Barbour and Roberts, pp. 228–9.
[3] Muggleton (1764), pp. 25, 27–31.

One of the revealing things about *Paradise Lost* is God's defensiveness about his responsibility for evil (the Fall, the Restoration). Just as Adam (ultimately, and ill-advisedly) left Eve free to fall, so God

> Hindered not Satan to attempt the mind
> Of man, with strength entire and free will armed,
> Complete to have discovered and repulsed
> Whatever wiles of foe or seeming friend.
>
> (X. 8–11)

God's (and Milton's) continual harping on human freedom shows uneasiness about this part of the argument. Why did God let Satan out of hell to tempt Adam and Eve? Satan himself mockingly asked the question, and Gabriel seemed surprised at his emergence, referring (rather unflatteringly to God's omniscience) to 'the facile gates of hell too slightly barred' (IV. 897–9, 967). Satan, Sin and Death, says the Father,

> imputed
> Folly to me . . . that with so much ease
> I suffer them to enter and possess
> A place so heavenly, and conniving seem . . .
> as if transported with some fit
> Of passion I to them had quitted all
> At random yielded up to their misrule.

God on the contrary claimed to have called Sin and Death

> to lick up all the draff and filth
> Which man's polluting sin with taint hath shed
> On what was pure.
>
> (X. 620–32)

These words apply better to Milton's vision of what was happening in England in 1660 than to a world of which Adam and Eve were the sole inhabitants.[1]

As we saw, Milton was not alone in his awareness that God was on trial.[2] George Rust in 1661 was one of many who complained that men emphasized 'the justice of God' to the exclusion of his mercy.[3] Lines formerly attributed to Rochester asked the gods, 'were you as good in will' as in power, 'How could you ever have produced such ill?'

---

[1] Cf. Fowler's uneasy note on 'perhaps the most appalling of all God's decrees', which Milton explicitly approves (X. 644n.).

[2] See pp. 274–7, 351–2 above.

[3] Patrides, pp. 141–2. See p. 228 above.

'Tis therefore less impiety to say,
Evil with you has coeternity
Than blindly taking it the other way,
That merciful and of election free
You did create the mischiefs you foresee.[1]

We may compare a recent view of the theology of Milton's junior contemporary and fellow-worker in Oliver Cromwell's government, John
Dryden. 'What is at issue ... is the inhumanity of history, or, to put it
another way, the wickedness of God.' Dryden, W. Myers tells us, rejected
the absolutist concept of God for the godlike quality of mercy. But 'to be
divine like Christ is to be of no account like Christ': this leads Dryden to
renunciation of politics and to a resigned emphasis on the after life. '''Tis
hope of futurity alone', he wrote, 'that makes this life tolerable, in expecta-
tion of a better.' Myers sums up: 'there is an outrageousness, by human
standards, at the centre of things, in history and the human mind, which
only humility can accommodate.' Dryden admired those who show 'fortitude in the face of a Providence which, from a human point of view,
operates without visible regard for justice'. 'Forgive the gods the rest',
Dryden concludes.[2]

Milton never learnt humility. But he had to face the same historical
problems, the same Providence which operated without visible regard for
justice: he felt called upon to justify the outrageousness at the centre of
things. Unlike Dryden, he did not restrict himself to fortitude, in expecta-
tion of a better life hereafter, nor to forgiving the gods; nor did he turn to
passivity, as the Quakers did. Milton still hoped on – in *Paradise Lost* for
the happier Paradise within, in *Paradise Regained* to become a Son of God,
in *Samson Agonistes* still to serve God actively on earth when the divine
moment comes. But the analogy between his position and Dryden's is
interesting.

II 'Some British theme, some old/Romantic tale' (Wordsworth, *The Prelude*, I, lines 168-9)

Milton's earliest epic plans were for an Arthuriad or other historical poem
glorifying the English people. This would have fitted the mood in which
Areopagitica was written. Arthur was traditionally the sleeping hero who
will one day reappear to lead his people to victory, or to lead the saints

---

[1] Rochester, *Poems* (ed. V. de Sola Pinto, 1953, p. 72: not in Vieth's edition). Cf. G. D. Hamilton,
   p. 92.
[2] Myers, pp. 176, 108, 132, 156; cf. pp. 92–3; Miner (1974), p. 310.

against Antichrist. Under the Tudors Arthur had become something of a monarchical symbol; after they had completed the unification of England, and their successors had forfeited the confidence of many of their subjects, the name of Arthur lost some of its glamour.[1] Milton had been brought up at St. Paul's in a linguistic patriotism, and for a time the Anglo-Saxons may have replaced Arthur. In the forties he had contemplated poems and dramas about English history as well as on Biblical subjects, poems which would have glorified God's Englishmen. But he soon lost his buoyant confidence that a newly united nation would take the place of the monarchy.

His historical studies disillusioned him with early English history (and its historians), at about the same time as he was losing confidence in the English people of his own day. In 1641 he wrote proudly of 'our progenitors that wrested their liberty out of the Norman gripe with their dearest blood and highest prowess'.[2] But seven years later he had come to think that, like the Anglo-Saxons, the English people were valiant in battle but injudicious and unwise in peace. They had a special genius for liberty, but could not discipline themselves sufficiently to make proper use of it. Their history had little of interest to teach, and in any case the legends of Geoffrey of Monmouth and his like were 'too palpably untrue to be worth rehearsing in the midst of truth'. More and more the Bible came to seem to Milton the best and surest source.[3] The elect nation yielded place to an emphasis on the salvation of individuals.

Milton's original plan had been to deal with the Fall in a tragedy. Only gradually, as the Arthuriad faded into the background, was the tragedy transformed into an epic. This may in some part account for Milton's delay in starting to write. When he did start, he no longer wished to glorify God's Englishmen. As the Good Old Cause degenerated into an anarchy of individualisms, so the patriotic epic of Milton's earlier intention changed into an epic about man. In the same way the Levellers shifted their emphasis from a defence of the historical rights of Englishmen to a demand for the natural rights of man. The Fall is a more democratic subject than the unwritten Arthuriad: the hero of *Paradise Lost* is Everyman, not a king or a knight.

None of the three great poems published after 1660 is about England. *Samson Agonistes* comes nearest, since the chosen people on whose behalf Samson struggles bear a strong resemblance to the English people after

---

[1] Brinkley, chapter 1.
[2] *C.P.W.*, I, p. 592.
[3] *Ibid.*, V, pp. 67, 450.

1660; but it is a poem about the people of God in defeat anywhere. All three poems are deeply political, wrestling with the problem of the failed revolution, the millennium that did not come. They ask how good men should live in a world dominated by the powers of evil. The English people, victor once, have in the long run done no better than the corrupt rulers of Caroline England: and so at this day they serve, and justly.[1]

So by the time he came to write his epic, the theme of 'some king or knight before the Conquest', as 'the pattern of a Christian hero', no longer seemed to Milton the ideal subject. He rejected the military virtues. Michael virtually quoted Ralegh's *History of the World*: those whom men call 'great conquerors,/Patrons of mankind, gods and sons of gods', Michael thought, are more rightly seen as 'destroyers . . . and plagues of men' (*P.L.* XI. 695-697). The War in Heaven, specifically compared to war on earth, threatened to 'let loose the reins . . . to disordered rage' until the Son intervened (*P.L.* V. 574-6). The debate among the devils in Pandaemonium – thought to be a late addition to the poem[2] – takes off and rebukes the fine posturing speeches of which Milton must have heard so many. Coleridge saw Satan as the archetypal military leader. His feudal-military attitudes and postures are suddenly but completely overthrown by the intervention of the Son. Cervantes said that the devil invented artillery, and by Milton's day the Satanic invention of gunpowder had become a cliché. But the poet's description of the horrors consequent on the use of cannon contains deep personal feeling – its imagery taken from the 'drawing' of the bowels of a traitor, the fate which Milton may have been anticipating for himself at the time he wrote.[3]

The experience of civil war and its aftermath had made Milton suspicious of force as a means of settling earthly disputes. The sonnet to the Parliamentarian general Fairfax, written in August 1648, asks:

> For what can war but endless war still breed
> Till truth and right from violence be freed?

The civil war in heaven reduced both sides to a common denominator of blind violence, in which the rights and wrongs of the quarrel were becoming irrelevant, until the decisive intervention of the Son. We should, however, not see this intervention as merely metaphorical: the Son revealing himself and so judging the rebel angels who were self-defeated, 'exhausted, spiritless, afflicted, fallen' (VI. 852).[4] This might be more

---

[1] Cf. Rivers, pp. 93-4.
[2] *C.P.W.*, I, pp. 813-14; Gilbert (1947), pp. 159, 101-5.
[3] Dobbins, pp. 42-3; Gardner, p. 60; Broadbent (1973), p. 139.
[4] Bouchard, pp. 129-33.

acceptable to the sensitivity of modern liberal Christians, but it is not what Milton wrote. The Son assured the Father that

> whom thou hatest I hate, and can put on
> Thy terrors.
> (VI. 734–5)

He did not spare the Father's 'dreadful thunder' as he drove 'o'er the necks . . . / Of warring angels disarrayed . . . / To execute fierce vengeance on his foes' (III. 393–9).

Milton differentiates sharply between divine vengeance (the Son's, Samson's, the regicides') and that of men who lack divine authority, who subject 'truth and right' to violence. He had called Fairfax to the 'nobler task' of subduing 'avarice and rapine', just as four years later he was to tell Cromwell that 'peace hath her victories/ No less renowned than war', the enemy now being the hireling clergy.[1] The Fairfax sonnet is recalled by the Son of God's renunciation of mere militarism in *Paradise Regained*:

> What do these worthies,
> But rob and spoil, burn, slaughter and enslave
> Peaceable nations, neighbouring or remote,
> Made captive, yet deserving freedom more
> Than those their conquerors?
> (III. 74–8)

Paradise Lost rejects the epic tradition of classical fables or of chivalrous romances.

> Not sedulous by nature to indite
> Wars, hitherto the only argument
> Heroic deemed, . . . chief mastery to dissect
> With long and tedious havoc, fabled knights
> In battles feigned; the better fortitude
> Of patience and heroic martyrdom
> Unsung.
> (IX. 27–33)

'The wit of the fables and religions of the ancient world is well-nigh consumed', Thomas Sprat said in the year *Paradise Lost* was published. 'They have already served the poets long enough.'[2] The heroic dramas of the sixteen-sixties and -seventies in England, of the Earl of Orrery, Cromwell's faithful counsellor, and many others, illustrate what Milton and Sprat were very sensibly rejecting: they were sentimentalized, unrealistic and

---

[1] Cf. pp. 194–5, 209–10 above, pp. 442–5 below.
[2] Sprat, p. 414; cf. Bateson, pp. 157–8.

written in rhymed couplets. Dryden was drawing this contrast when he summarized the plot of *Paradise Lost* as the Giant driving the Hero 'out of his stronghold to wander through the world with his lady errant'.[1]

Michael warned Adam that he must not think of the conflict between Messiah and Satan 'as of a duel'. The problem is not

> destroying Satan, but his works
> In thee and in thy seed.
>
> (*P.L.* XII. 387–95)

The true fight is fought first in the hearts of men. When that is won, no external enemies will remain to overcome. War therefore, so far from being glorious, defeats its own ends because it produces the wrong virtues. True glory comes from renunciation of glory – a conclusion to which Milton returned in *Paradise Regained,* whose truly heroic theme is 'one man's firm obedience fully tried', and in *Samson Agonistes,* where Samson achieves true heroism when he stops wanting to be a hero.[2]

Paradise Lost was not the glorification of the chosen nation that Milton had at one time envisaged, but it was still 'doctrinal and exemplary to a nation'. By helping to discover where God's cause had been misinterpreted, it might lead to a recovery of hope and the prospect of more effective action in the future. The most dreadful thing Milton said about hell in *Paradise Lost* was that there

> hope never comes
> That comes to all.
>
> (I. 66–7)[3]

Milton, and no doubt many others, in the years after 1658 desperately needed to recover hope. One thing that prevents us seeing Milton in Satan is the latter's despair and desperation.

What is astonishing about the last three poems is that they were written at all, and that they were written without hysteria, without self-pity, with complete decorum. The anguish which Milton had suffered made them greater poems than the Arthuriad he might once have written: but the anguish is recollected in tranquillity, a tranquillity derived not from illusions, for Milton now has none, but from confidence in the eternal justice of continuing to do what he believed to be right. The historian

---

[1] Dryden, II, p. 165.
[2] See p. 441 below.
[3] Cf. Samson:

> Nor am I in the list of them that hope;
> Hopeless are all my evils, all remediless.
>
> (*S.A.* 647–8)

T. M. Lindsay used to preach a sermon on the text 'But if not', from Daniel 3. Shadrach, Meshach and Abed-Nego hoped that when they were cast into the burning fiery furnace God would miraculously preserve them; but if not, they still would not bow down and worship what they knew to be evil.[1] Milton would have appreciated that. In the last resort he was not so much justifying the ways of God to men as asserting the ineluctable rightness of just men acting justly, in accordance with their own consciences, regardless of consequences. God may or may not come to their help, as he came to the help of the Lady in *Comus*, of Samson in the temple, and of the Son of God on the pinnacle. But if not, there they stood, they could no other.[2]

III 'I sing ... unchanged' (*P.L.* VII. 24): political analogies

Seen in this light, and remembering always the strict censorship under which Milton had to work, the political allusions in *Paradise Lost*, veiled though they had to be, are not indecipherable. The poem was no doubt planned as a whole before the Restoration of May 1660. Nevertheless there must have been a break in 1660, when Milton was in danger of his life and had to go into hiding; and a further interruption when he was in prison. It would have been dangerous for friends to visit his hiding-place for the sole purpose of taking down from his dictation, and impossible when he was imprisoned. The invocation to Book VII suggests a fresh start, under more difficult circumstances; the conjecture that Books I to VI were written (at least in first draft) before the Restoration, Books VII to XII after it, appears to be borne out by the evidence of style, which links the last six books with *Paradise Regained* and *Samson Agonistes* more closely than with the first six books.[3] But 'I sing ... unchanged' may also be intended to recall to the fitter audience for whom *Paradise Lost* was written the John Milton whom they knew as the defender of divorce, regicide and the republic.[4]

There is a shift of emphasis in the last six books of the epic. Until April 1660 the revolutionaries still held power, however insecurely. The Royalists had been defeated, although they were desperately scheming revenge. In Books I and II Satan is wrong but grandly wrong. His attempt 'against the omnipotent to rise in arms' (VI. 136) seemed as absurd as a

---

[1] D. Scott, p. 261.
[2] See pp. 47–8 above, chapters 30 and 31 below.
[3] Oras, pp. 128–95.
[4] See p. 238 above.

Royalist attempt to reverse the verdict of history.[1] But after May 1660 Satan was not trying vainly to recover power in England: he had won it. His degradation in the second half of the epic is the greater because of Milton's disgusted realization of the power and influence of evil. It is paralleled by the stepping forward of the Creator-Son and the withdrawal of the impersonal Father. We should not then see Satan just as the apotheosis of rebellion. One subject of *Paradise Lost* is indeed rebellion, but Milton had himself been a rebel; he wanted now to know where he and his fellows had been mistaken, what kind of rebellion was justified and what not.

Satan, no less than Christ, is a king. His approach to Eve is a parody of the rituals of courtly love at Henrietta Maria's court.[2] Satan was 'by merit raised' to kingship in hell, as the Son had been in heaven. The analogy with the Son is stressed throughout. Sin, Death and Satan are the infernal Trinity: I see no reason why Milton should not parody this concept, in which he himself did not believe.[3] In the early books Satan's 'grandeur' and 'ruined splendour' predominate.[4] But Satan is also an Asiatic tyrant, associated with Turkish despotism (X. 457) – as Charles I had been in *Eikonoklastes*. Since 1649 another group of men had been called Turkish bashaws – Cromwell's Major-Generals. It is not unlikely that there is something of them in the fallen angels. The latter are not mere personifications of evil. They were angels of light who have rejected the light. As Northrop Frye says, 'into Satan Milton has put all the horror and distress with which he contemplated the egocentric revolutionaries of his time', whose romantic rhetoric had got them – and those who trusted them – nowhere.[5]

If, among other things, the character of Satan alludes to some of the ways in which the Good Old Cause had gone wrong, it is to be expected that he will contain a good deal of Milton, who recognized that he too was not without responsibility for its failure. Milton's intellect now told him that he must accept God's will, if only because the Father is omnipotent: but his submission to the events of 1655–60 was highly reluctant. Satan, the battleground for Milton's quarrel with himself, saw God as arbitrary power and nothing else. Against this he revolted: the Christian, Milton knew, must accept it. Yet how could a free and rational individual accept

---

[1] Cf. Stavely, p. 127.

[2] Cf. pp. 178–9 above.

[3] Wolfe (*Milton in the P.R.*, 1941), p. 344; Kelley (1962), pp. 99–100; Empson (1935), p. 165; Miner (1974), p. 236. Cf. *C. and F.*, 485n., though I think Fowler exaggerates when he tries to give Satan twelve disciples.

[4] Coleridge, quoted by Gilbert (1947), pp. 55–6.

[5] *C.P.W.*, III, pp. 453, 574–5; cf. p. 313; Hughes (1964), pp. 128–9; Frye (1966), p. 28.

what God had done to his servants in England? On this reading, Milton expressed through Satan (of whom he disapproved) the dissatisfaction which he felt with the Father (whom intellectually he accepted).

Milton does not *identify* with Satan and the rebel angels, who embody and criticize the defects of the military leaders of the Revolution, as well as – more obviously – of the Royalists.[1] The essence of Satan is his selfish ambition. Jealousy of the exaltation of the Son caused his rebellion. As Defoe observed, Milton gave no real explanation of Satan's fall;[2] it is taken as given from the start of the poem. The exaltation of the Son is one of Milton's inventions, and it appears to be a late insertion in the epic: it is not in the Bible, the commentaries or – still more significant – in the *De Doctrina*. Milton seems to have invented it in order to have an unexplained divine decree leading to the fall of the angels analogous to that which led to the Fall of Man, so as to reinforce the parallel between earth and heaven.[3] Angels, like men, elect their own salvation. This is Arminian doctrine. Milton endowed Satan with conscience (IV. 23) and appears to envisage the possibility of his repenting (IV. 71–104). This too must be intended to stress the analogies between him and mankind.[4]

Satan has freedom without self-discipline, dynamic energy and driving individualism with no recognition of limits. 'Satan has more to say about liberty than any other character in *Paradise Lost*. Milton had heard the name of liberty bandied about a good deal by either side during the civil war.'[5] Satan's kind of liberty, like the Ranters' kind, became licence – and so ceased to be truly free.[6] Satan also has much to say about equality (*P.L.* I. 248–9).

This approach enables us to admit a great deal of Milton in Satan without reviving the view of Blake, Shelley, Belinsky – all romantic radicals, we note – that Satan is the hero of *Paradise Lost,* or that he is the first Whig. Satan *is* heroic: as heroic as Milton still thinks the English Revolution had been. But the Revolution had utterly failed. It had failed because the men were not great enough for the Cause. Satan had always been a rebel for the wrong reasons – self-interest, jealousy, ambition. Like Muggleton's Satan, Milton's personified selfish Reason.[7] As early as 1641 Milton had been

---

[1] Sewell, pp. 109–13.
[2] Defoe (1840), pp. 65–6.
[3] Gilbert (1947), pp. 118, 126; Gardner, pp. 52–4; Rajan (1969), pp. 122–3; Kelley (1962), p. 105. But cf. Dobbins, pp. 8–16, 133, and see p. 373–4 below.
[4] *C.P.W.,* VI, p. 343; Martz (1971), pp. 81–2. But cf. *P.L.* III. 131–2.
[5] Mahood, p. 212.
[6] See p. 398 below.
[7] Muggleton (1764), pp. 11, 37–8.

arguing that the selfishness and greed which were mixed up with the motives of the original reformers did not destroy the value of the Protestant Reformation. Now perhaps he saw deeper. We must, however, not take Milton's condemnation of Satan as condemnation of rebellion, any more than we should take his acceptance of a hierarchy of being from man up to God as acceptance of a traditional social hierarchy of 'degree'. Milton's is a hierarchy of virtue, of merit. In *Paradise Lost* Adam increases in virtue as Satan decreases; in *Paradise Regained* Christ grows in merit. Only God's virtue is by definition absolute: that is why he must be obeyed.

Nevertheless the magnificent Satan of the early books of the epic does convey some of the defiance which Milton himself must have felt tempted to hurl in the face of omnipotence as the republic crashed about his ears. The rebellious energy ebbs in the later books, after the restoration of Charles II has brought Milton to recognize the full magnitude of the rethinking that is required. Perhaps Milton felt that he and his peers had been too tolerant of the Satanic fellow-travellers of the Revolution. God, after all, is not only King of the English Commonwealth, he is also the historical process: what he wills is fate. So Satan is a rebel against history itself, not someone Milton can identify with. In the *De Doctrina* Milton began his list of the sins involved in the Fall of Man with credulity in Satan and lack of confidence in God; it ends with deceit, aspiration to divinity, pride and arrogance.[1] Presumptuous aspiration, use of the wrong means, pride and arrogance: they are the vices against which Milton and other radicals had warned Oliver Cromwell and his generals.[2] Deceit: like Dalila quoting

> that grounded maxim
> So rife and celebrated in the mouths
> Of wisest men, that to the public good
> Private respects must yield;
>
> (*S.A.* 865–8)

or like Cromwell pleading 'public reason just, / Honour and empire', to justify an aggressive foreign policy. (Milton underlined the point for contemporaries by referring to Satan's use of 'necessity, /The tyrant's plea' in the following lines. The phrase recalled accusations that Cromwell made necessities in order to plead them – e.g. by Joseph Beaumont in *Psyche* (1648), and by George Cony, an old Parliamentarian stalwart, when refusing to pay taxes to Cromwell: Cony himself was echoing Hampden's lawyer

---

[1] *C.P.W.*, VI, pp. 383–4.
[2] See pp. 193–6 above.

in the Ship Money Case, and Hampden was Cromwell's cousin.)[1] In Book
V Satan plans to recover power 'by violence, no, for that shall be with-
stood,/ But by deceit and lies' (V. 242–4).

The Satanic Parliament gave Milton the chance to stress what was most
lacking in 1658–60 – unity among the defenders of the Good Old Cause:

> O shame to men! Devil with devil damned
> Firm concord holds, men only disagree
> Of creatures rational, though under hope
> Of heavenly grace: and God proclaiming peace
> Yet live in hatred, enmity and strife
> Among themselves, and levy cruel wars,
> Wasting the earth, each other to destroy:
> As if (which might induce us to accord)
> Man had not hellish foes enow besides
> That day and night for his destruction wait.
>
> > (II. 496–505)

(Cf. the hints of a return to chaos in II. 907–16, unless God decides
otherwise.)

'O for that warning voice', Milton cried in the invocation to Book IV,
that

> when the dragon, put to second rout,
> Came furious down to be revenged on men,
> > ... that now
> While time was, our first parents had been warned
> The coming of their secret foe, and scaped.
>
> > (IV. 1–8)

It was still possible for Adam and Eve to withstand temptation (570–1).

Satan's hope was clear: 'to try once more ... for possession ... here in
hope to find/ Better abode' (IV. 937–41) – like Charles II in exile,

> plotting how he may seduce
> Thee also from obedience, that with him
> Bereaved of happiness thou mayst partake
> His punishment, eternal misery.
>
> > (VI. 901–4)

Gabriel's retort to Satan

> Thou sly hypocrite, who now wouldst seem
> Patron of liberty, who cringed more than thou
> Once fawned and cringed and servilely adored
> Heaven's awful monarch?

---

[1] Ludlow, I, p. 413; cf. Joseph Beaumont (1880), I, p. 214.

makes a good point about Royalist and neo-Presbyterian advocates of 'a free Parliament' in 1659–60, though again at the cost perhaps of some reflection on 'Heaven's awful monarch, . . . the acknowledged power supreme' (IV. 956–60 – cf. VI. 164–82). The reference in the next book to 'the tedious pomp that waits/ On princes' reveals Milton's attitude to monarchy in 1659–60:

> their rich retinue long
> Of horses led, and grooms besmeared with gold
> Dazzles the crowd, and sets them all agape.
>   (V. 354–7)[1]

In Book VI the Abdiel incident gets us close to the political theme, and to Milton's own personal feelings. (A. H. Gilbert thought this episode was a late insertion. It was probably written at or after the Restoration.) What the poet has to say about Abdiel could have been said of Milton's own courage in publishing the second edition of *The Ready and Easy Way* just before the return of Charles II:

> Among the faithless, faithful only he;
> Among innumerable false, unmoved,
> Unshaken, unseduced, unterrified
> His loyalty he kept, his love, his zeal;
> Nor number, nor example with him wrought
> To swerve from truth, or change his constant mind
> Though single.
>   (V. 897–903)

Milton may well have written those lines in hiding, daily expecting to be condemned to the horrible death of a traitor.

> From amidst them forth he passed
> Long way through hostile scorn, which he sustained
> Superior, nor of violence feared aught;
> And with retorted scorn his back he turned
> On those proud towers to swift destruction doomed.
>   (V. 903–7)

The reference to *The Ready and Easy Way* is almost explicit in the divine praise of Abdiel in the next book:

> Servant of God, well done, well hast thou fought
> The better fight, who single hast maintained
> Against revolted multitudes the cause
> Of truth, in word mightier than they in arms;

---

[1] Cf. pp. 264–5 above.

And for the testimony of truth hast borne
Universal reproach, far worse to bear
Than violence: for this was all thy care
To stand approved in sight of God, though worlds
Judged thee perverse.
(VI. 29-37)

'Few sometimes may know, when thousands err', Abdiel himself claimed (VI. 148). Enoch too was saved by God from popular violence when ('the only righteous in a world perverse') he dared

single to be just,
And utter odious truth, that God would come
To judge them with his saints.
(XI. 701-6)

Raphael's account of the War in Heaven offers many analogies with the English Civil War.

What if earth
Be but the shadow of heaven, and things therein
Each to other like, more than on earth is thought?
(V. 574-6)

Both the heavenly choir ('this new-made world, another heaven' – VII. 617) and Satan confirm ('O earth, how like to heaven' – IX. 99). It was an analogy which Milton had drawn as early as 1641.[1] (Raphael's question, it will be noted, is addressed to the seventeenth-century reader rather than to his ostensible audience.)[2]

Milton's wide knowledge of the Bible allowed him to press many covert parallels. Satan, like Charles I, raised his standard in the north (V. 685-93). 'Those that come out of the North are the greatest pests of the nation', declared Samuel Highland in 1656. He was thinking of Diggers and 'the northern Quakers', but he was drawing on a popular saying. Milton had spoken of 'the false North' in his sonnet to Fairfax. Invading Scottish armies came thence in 1648 and again in 1651, when Sterry gave Parliament a sermon of thanksgiving for *Englands Deliverance from the Northern Presbytery*.[3] In 1659-60 Monck too had come from 'the false North' treacherously to restore Charles II.[4] Even more significant, the Scotland ruled over by Lauderdale in the sixties was a by-word for torture and

---

[1] *C.P.W.*, I, pp. 752-3.
[2] Miner (1974), p. 244.
[3] *W.T.U.D.*, p. 80; Broadbent (1960), p. 162. Cf. Vane (1662), p. 55. A pamphlet of 1647 had referred to 'that old Scot the Devil' (Carruthers, p. 20).
[4] Cf. Daniel 11: 13-43; Isaiah 14:12-15; Zechariah 6:1-8; Revelation 7:1-4. For prophecies about kings from the north, see Trout, pp. 81-3, 89, 126, 222-3, 272. See also Dobbins, p. 28.

tyranny, a country from which absolutism might be brought to England.[1]
Satan came out of the north and west for the final temptation in *Paradise
Regained* (IV. 448–9).[2] About one-third of the angelic host supported Satan
– higher than the traditional one-tenth, but roughly the proportion of
M.P.s who adhered to Charles I; though Satanic propaganda, like Royalist
propaganda, was apt to exaggerate the number.[3] The revolted angels, like
the Royalists, expected

> That self-same day by fight, or by surprise
> To win. . . . But their thoughts proved fond and vain.

To the good angels

> strange . . . it seemed
> At first, that angel should with angel war,
> . . . who wont to meet
> So oft in festivals of joy and love
> Unanimous.
>   (VI. 86–95)

> Brutish that contest foul,
> When reason hath to deal with force.
>   (VI. 124–5)

Many supporters of Parliament had similar feelings at the beginning of the
English Civil War.

The first battle in heaven was as inconclusive as Edgehill. The rebels,
after inventing fire-arms, offered truce negotiations with as little sincerity
as – Parliamentarians said – the Royalists did in 1643. The angelic retort of
hurling mountains at their adversaries may covertly refer to the *levée en
masse* in London in 1643 which produced the army of train-band men
which relieved Gloucester and fought the first Battle of Newbury on their
way back. Stalemate then resulted, and the possibility of social breakdown.

> War wearied hath performed what war can do,
> And to disordered rage let loose the reins,
> With mountains as with weapons armed, which makes
> Wild work in heaven, and dangerous to the main.
>   (VI. 695–8)

Two days having passed (1642–4?), the third (1644–5?) was God's. The
Son intervened with the same devastating effect as Fairfax's New Model
Army of the godly, sweeping all before it, with an effect comparable to that

---

[1] I owe this point to Professor J. R. Jones.
[2] Cf. *P.L.* I. 351–3 – northern barbarians; J. F. Forrest, *Notes and Queries*, 222 (1977).
[3] Cf. *C.P.W.*, I, pp. 717–18, echoing Revelation 8:7–12; cf. 12:4; Muggleton (1665), pp. 78–9,
85–9.

of Samson's divinely inspired action at the end of *Samson Agonistes,* or the judicial condemnation of Charles I in 1649.[1]

Milton's picture of the War in Heaven as a long-drawn-out and indecisive struggle until the Son's intervention was unusual. Most Biblical commentators speak of an abrupt fall of Satan, without a struggle. In the *De Doctrina* too Milton says that the combatants in the War in Heaven 'separated after a fairly even fight'. The proof-text which he cites, Revelation 12: 7–8, does not justify this.[2] Why did he attach such importance to this innovation? He was no doubt thinking both of the contest between good and evil in the individual soul, and of the political contest between Christ and Antichrist as well as of its earthly enactment in the English Civil War. The advantage of Milton's method is that the same narrative can refer to more than one series of historical events. Perhaps the two days were two decades; after 1660, with Satanic forces temporarily in the ascendant, 'doubtful conflict' reigned. The pattern of success/ counter-success/ stalemate/ triumphant intervention was no doubt common epic form. In Cowley's *The Civil War* an initial Royalist advance was checked by hastily erected earthworks outside London and then by the advance of the London train-bands across England to relieve Gloucester. Cowley had intended to complete the pattern by final Royalist victory.[3] But the God of Battles decided otherwise, at Newbury and elsewhere. Milton had more confidence in the ultimate outcome of his unfinished war. Our knowledge that the restored monarchy had come to stay was concealed from Milton and his contemporaries, however conscious they were of the magnitude of their defeat.

The Son's victory in the War in Heaven incorporates many features from Revelation which refer to the Second Coming, to the end of history. And so Book VI looks forward to ultimate liberation from Satanic thraldom by the Son's intervention.[4] The fall of the rebel angels leads straight to the

---

[1] Cf. p. 311 above, and chapter 31 below.

[2] *C.P.W.,* VI, p. 347; Daniels, pp. 430–2; Fish (1967), p. 150. It might one day be worth someone's while to check through Milton's use of proof-texts: interesting results might emerge.

[3] Cowley (1973), *passim.*

[4] 'The theology underlying this use of an apocalyptic vision to portray the earliest events of redemptive history', Fowler's note rightly says, 'has still to be worked out' (VI. 749–59n.). Professor Hunter attempted to work it out, arguing that the three-day War in Heaven is intended to allude to the Crucifixion as well as to the defeat of Satan in Revelation. He concludes that 'the depiction of man's salvation through the sacrifice of the Son is an overwhelming concern of *Paradise Lost*' (1969, pp. 215–31). If so orthodox a conclusion had been Milton's 'overwhelming concern', it is difficult to understand why it should have been so indirectly and obscurely expressed. Professor Dobbins seems to me more plausible in deriving the three-day war from Revelation (chapter 2 *passim*). My suggestion is that Milton's impulse to fuse the two myths is political even more than theological. See p. 393 below.

plenitude of creation. We are, I think, expected to retain in our minds this fusion of the creation with the Second Coming throughout Book VII. The angelic choir celebrates the Son's return by singing

> to create
> Is greater than created to destroy. . . .
>   Easily the proud attempt
> Of spirits apostate and their counsels vain
> Thou hast repelled, while impiously they thought
> Thee to diminish, and from thee withdraw
> The number of thy worshippers. Who seeks
> To lessen thee, against his purpose serves
> To manifest the more thy might: his evil
> Thou usest, and from thence createst more good
> Witness this new-made world, another heaven.
>   (VII. 606–17)

In a sense *Paradise Lost* was Milton's answer to the brutal question which Roger L'Estrange addressed to him in *No Blinde Guides,* published in April 1660, the same month as the second edition of *The Ready and Easy Way*: 'Do you then really expect to see Christ reigning upon earth?'[1] There was a time when Milton could have answered that question with a straightforward 'Yes!'; but not in 1660. This was part of the rethinking that he and so many others had to do. The words of the angelic choir would be consoling to the defeated of the sixteen-sixties. But jumping too easily to Fifth-Monarchist conclusions about the Second Coming, Milton suggests in the invocation to Book VII, may lead to catastrophe similar to that of Bellerophon when he tried to ride Pegasus to heaven and was thrown, blinded, into the field of error. 'Erroneous there to wander and forlorn' (VII. 17–20: see pp. 394–5 below for 'forlorn'). We must keep a firm grasp on brutal reality, Milton implies; and he proceeds with the desolate but determined invocation:

> More safe I sing with mortal voice, unchanged
> To hoarse or mute, though fallen on evil days,
> On evil days though fallen, and evil tongues;
> In darkness, and with dangers compassed round,
> And solitude; yet not alone, while thou
> Visit'st my slumbers nightly.
>   (VII. 24–9)

In the invocation to Book III Milton had referred poignantly to his blindness, but not as here to the evil times on which he had fallen. He probably wrote these lines, himself in hiding, amidst the rejoicings, the

---

[1] *Op. cit.,* p. 8: in Parker (1940).

drunkenness and Rump-burnings which heralded the return of our most religious King:

> But drive far off the barbarous dissonance
> Of Bacchus and his revellers,

hostile to poets (VII. 32–8).

It is no accident that Raphael began his account of the creation of the world by attributing to God the harsh words

> necessity and chance
> Approach not me, and what I will is fate.
>
> (VII. 172–3)

There is no easy way of exonerating God from the terrible thing that has happened in England. Nevertheless, the angelic choir reminds us of the rout of the rebel angels: God has

> driven out the ungodly from his sight
> And the habitations of the just.

His wisdom has 'ordained/ Good out of evil to create' (VII. 185–91). The Son steps forward as the divine agent to subdue Chaos,

> the vast immeasurable abyss
> Outrageous as a sea, dark, wasteful, wild,
> Up from the bottom turned by furious winds
> . . . to assault
> Heaven's height.
>
> (VII. 211–15)[1]

With the brief command 'Silence, . . . your discord end', the Son rode 'far into chaos and the world unknown'. And 'Chaos heard his voice' (216–21). It is the beginning of Creation, the image of the new world which the remainder of the poem moves towards.

IV Adam and Eve

So we come to Adam and Eve in Paradise. 'This turn hath made amends' cries Adam when he sees the newly created Eve (VIII. 491): he too seems to have thought God's ways in need of justification. In discussing our first parents we must recall what no one in the seventeenth century would ever forget, the analogy between marriage and the state. Countless political treatises and guides to godliness had instilled the lesson that the family was a little church, a little state; that the fifth commandment was concerned

---

[1] 'Up from the bottom' has politico-social suggestions. Cf. p. 376 below.

with political obligation as well as with filial obedience; that the subordination of the wife to the husband figured Christ's rule over his church,
and the lawful sovereign's rule over the state. Milton specifically compared the marriage contract to the political contract between king and
people.[1]

> My author and disposer, what thou bidst
> Unargued I obey,

said unfallen Eve, adding for good measure 'so God ordains' (IV. 635–6).
The relationship between Adam and Eve is not just a marriage: it can also
at any time be an analogy for the political relationship, or the relationship
of Christ to his church.

Male superiority in marriage can signify by analogy the control of the
reasoning few over the passionate majority. 'Was she thy God?' the Son
asks Adam,

> that her thou didst obey
> Before his voice, or was she made thy guide
> Superior, or but equal, that to her
> Thou didst resign thy manhood? ... Her gifts
> Were such as under government well seemed,
> Unseemly to bear rule, which was thy part
> And person, hadst thou known thyself aright.
>   (X. 145–56)

I do not think it is only my distaste for the sentiment as applied to the
relation of the sexes that makes me wish to emphasize the political echoes
in that passage – 'obey', 'equal', 'government', 'rule'. But both in marriage
and in politics God must come first. Adam and Eve surrendered to

> sensual appetite, who *from beneath*
> Usurping over sovereign reason claimed
> Superior sway.
>   (IX. 1128–31. My italics: cf. p. 375 note)

Milton's attitude to Eve is as full of paradoxes as his attitude towards
women in general, and the political analogy complicates our understanding
of them. In *Paradise Lost* romantic love gets some of the finest lines ever
written to celebrate it.[2] We may compare the sense of loss in the nearly
contemporaneous sonnet, 'Methought I saw my late espoused saint', probably written after the death of Milton's second wife.[3] To remind ourselves

---

[1] Haller (1955), p. 99; cf. *C.P.W.*, II, pp. 152–3, and W. Sedgwick, *Leaves* (1648), pp. 3–4.
[2] See pp. 128–9 above.
[3] I see here another reason for rejecting Parker's odd fancy that the sonnet was written about
Mary Powell.

how banal the relationship of Adam and Eve in Paradise could be in the poetry of the period, we have only to glance at Sylvester's Du Bartas, Joseph Beaumont's *Psyche* or Davenant's *Gondibert*.[1]

Some have said that on Milton's own logic Adam should have 'divorced' Eve when she fell: Milton, like many of the sectaries, accepted that marriages with obstinate unbelievers were invalid.[2] This is all very well in theology, but it makes no sort of sense against the poetry. Here again it may be helpful to suppose that Milton is thinking of political allegiance as well as of matrimonial ethics. If we take Adam as personifying the regenerate among the Parliamentarian leaders in the sixteen-fifties, the latter should certainly not have been influenced by 'the link of nature' to follow mere majority opinion (IX. 914–16).[3] Adam's fallacious reasoning before joining Eve in eating the apple might have been addressed to a Fleetwood bewildered by the rapid political transformations of 1659–60. He imagines Satan saying:

> fickle their state whom God
> Most favours, who can please him long? Me first
> He ruined, now mankind; whom will he next?
>
> (IX. 948–50)

Adam and Eve spent 'fruitless hours . . . in mutual accusation', but neither admitted error, and so 'of their vain contest appeared no end' (IX. 1187–9). That was the lowest ebb in Paradise: it could recall the hopeless recriminations of the revolutionaries in 1659–60.

The opening to Book IX emphasizes the *political* aspects of the Fall:

> foul distrust, and breach
> Disloyal on the part of man, revolt
> And disobedience: on the part of heaven
> Now alienated, distance and distaste,
> Anger and just rebuke, and judgment given.
>
> (IX. 6–10)

The words describe the events of 1660 no less than those of 4004 B.C. Hence too the powerful, incessant emphasis on the freedom of angels and men to fall or not to fall, the absolute necessity of liberty for any moral decision. 'Go', Adam told Eve, 'for thy stay, not free, absents thee more'

---

[1] Sylvester, I, pp. 110–11; Beaumont (1880), I, pp. 117–18; Davenant, *Gondibert*, Book II, Canto vi.

[2] *C.P.W.*, VI, p. 369. Cf. White, *Records*, pp. 140–1.

[3] Cf. Fowler's note on IX. 482–8: 'It is quite possible that [Milton] intended the tragedy of Eve's fall to typify (among other things) the tragedy of a people betrayed by its intellectuals and leaders.' See also his notes on IX. 703–9, 1127–31; X. 307–11.

(IX. 372). She went, and fell, as Adam had foreseen she might. Eve afterwards reasonably complained,

> Being as I am, why didst not thou the head
> Command me absolutely not to go,
> Going into such danger as thou saidst?
> Too facile then thou didst not much gainsay,
> Nay didst permit, approve, and fair dismiss.
> Hadst thou been firm and fixed in thy dissent,
> Neither had I transgressed, nor thou with me.
>
> (IX. 1155–61: cf.

> Dalila's argument, which Samson accepted: 'To what I did thou
> show'dst me first the way' – S.A. 778–824)

By the same logic, God could be held responsible for the Fall since he had
the power to prevent it. And he could likewise be held responsible for
the failure of the English Revolution.

The crux of the poem, and Milton's greatest difficulties, come with the
temptation and the Fall. How does 'innocent frail man' (IV. 11) fall freely
without being able to blame God for it? Satan tempts Eve with arguments
drawn from *Areopagitica,* arguments which she had previously used to
Adam:

> What is faith, love and virtue unassayed
> Alone, without exterior help sustained
>
> (IX. 335–6)

> If what is evil
> Be real, why not known, since easier shunned?

Satan asked Eve (IX. 698–700). She meditated:

> What forbids he [God] but to know,
> Forbids us good, forbids us to be wise?
>
> (IX. 758–9)

Milton had covered himself in advance by making it clear, even in 1644,
that the virtue and knowledge recommended in *Areopagitica* were those
appropriate to *fallen* man. Just as there was a different astronomy before
the Fall, before the earth's axis was shifted, so there was a different
morality. The angels' knowledge is intuitive, as Agricola Carpenter said
Adam's was, rather than discursive; reason, memory, logic, the syllogism,
are consequences of the Fall.[1] Intuitive understanding of God's purposes,
and consequent obedience to them, were expected of Adam and Eve. One

---

[1] Carpenter, p. 17. For astronomy before the Fall see p. 399 below.

of Milton's problems, which he did not solve, was to differentiate between unfallen innocence and ignorance. In his conversation with Raphael Adam's mental processes are not different from those in his post-lapsarian discussion with Michael. In each he is enquiring, anxious to be informed, very human. Yet he was expected to accept the prohibition on the tree of knowledge without rational explanation, as Satan had been expected to accept the exaltation of the Son. In the *De Doctrina* Milton made the unusual point that the sin of our first parents 'was only a sin of ignorance', since they were unaware of its consequences.[1] This ignorance was, however, no excuse, nor did it help posterity.

It is at such points that the analogy with the English Revolution may help.[2] Blame for its failure, in Milton's eyes, rested with its leaders. They ought to have abstained from certain temptations – from avarice and ambition – and they and their followers ought to have known that God so wished. If they ought to have had this intuitive knowledge, so *a fortiori* ought unfallen Adam. Milton probably failed to argue this point because it was so obvious to him. But without the analogy of the English Revolution it is more difficult to see *why* it was so obvious. A part of Milton's *proof* of the existence of God in the *De Doctrina* is man's innate consciousness of the distinction between good and evil.

For Eve the tree works magic· it transforms men and women into gods (IX. 790, 877). Milton is cautious here (since his sources were ambiguous); but he had no use for magic, least of all for magic that works by sacramental eating or drinking, and in his post-1660 mood no use for political short cuts to the millennium. He knew that neither virtue nor victory was attained at a single stroke, that they did not come from outside, in response to magic. They had to be won, slowly and painfully. To look to magic rather than to human effort was both sinful and useless. The tree once tasted turned to dust and ashes in the rebel angels' mouths, to lust and post-coital sadness in the mouths of Adam and Eve. Knowledge of good and evil is won by humanity in the course of long and bitter experience, not from the rind of one apple tasted. What God prohibited was not knowledge of good and evil (the knowledge of the gods) but the attempt to attain it by magic, by short cuts. In the end humanity would win it the hard way, and to that extent the Fall was fortunate. Adam's idolatry of Eve, Eve's idolatry of the tree of knowledge, recall the Laudian church which worshipped ceremonies and buildings rather than Christ: they

[1] *C.P.W.*, VI, p. 390.
[2] Cf. chapter 27 above.

reinforce the rejection of sacramental magic; both recall the idolatry of monarchy (IX. 795–838).[1]

Sin tells Satan that his

> virtue hath won
> What thy hands builded not, thy wisdom gained
> With odds what war hath lost, . . . and all this world . . .
> Here thou shalt monarch reign,

dividing sovereignty with God (X. 372–9). The words are equally applicable to Charles II. Yet at the moment of Satan's greatest triumph he sinks to his deepest degradation. When he addresses the rebel angels as 'ye gods', their reply is 'a dismal universal hiss'. They have all been transformed into serpents (X. 502 seq.)[2] Evil cannot, must not, prevail for long.

V Education by history

The education of Adam is completed by a vision of human history. The history lesson is given by the Archangel under whose leadership the War in Heaven had not been won. The unsuccessful leader of one campaign explains how ultimate victory will be gained in the war on earth.[3] If Michael (or Milton) chose the episodes in Books XI and XII with the situation in post-1660 England in mind, he could hardly have selected better. (In what follows I suggest parallels which might have been in Milton's mind. Though of course I cannot demonstrate this, their effect seems to me cumulative.) The contrast with Milton's patriotic vision of English history in the thirties and forties is striking: both chosen nations have proved inadequate. In a succession of incidents Michael shows national failure contrasted with, and sometimes temporarily redeemed by, the efforts and example of just men. At first man's inhumanity to man fills Adam with the naive horror felt by many of the English revolutionaries when they had to face the apparent injustice of the Restoration. 'Is piety thus and pure devotion paid?' Adam cries when he is shown Cain murdering Abel (XI. 452). Even seemingly just men succumb through 'effeminate slackness' to the temptations of a corrupt commercial civilization (XI. 556–687). Enoch, who spoke 'of right and wrong/ Of justice, of religion's truth and peace', warning 'that God would come/ To judge them *with his*

---

[1] Cf. Mahood, pp. 241–5; Rivers, p. 96; Bouchard, pp. 58–9, 82, 100; see pp. 178–80 above.
[2] Cowley's Satan in *The Civil War* similarly addresses the devils as 'my friends and fellow gods' (p. 103). Cf. *P.L.* I. 116, 629; II. 352, 391; VI. 156, 452.
[3] I owe this point to Florence Sandler of the University of Puget Sound.

saints',[1] was in danger of being lynched because he was 'the only righteous in a world perverse'; he had to be rescued by God (XI. 664–706).

Before the Flood, as in the England of the early sixties,

> The brazen throat of war had ceased to roar,
> All now was turned to jollity and game,
> To luxury and riot, feast and dance,
> Marrying or prostituting, as befell.
> (XI. 713–16)

'I had hope', Adam protests,

> When violence was ceased, and war on earth,
> All would have then gone well, peace would have crowned
> With length of happy days the race of man.
> But . . . now I see
> Peace to corrupt no less than war to waste.
> (XI. 779–84)

Michael's correction sounds like an up-dating of Milton's earlier warnings to the Parliamentarian military leaders. Adam's vision is of men

> First seen in acts of prowess eminent
> And great exploits, but of true virtue void,

who by military success achieve 'fame in the world, high titles, and rich prey', until wantonness and pride undo them (XI. 789–96). And what of their subjects?

> The conquered also, and enslaved by war
> Shall with their freedom lost all virtue lose
> And fear of God, from whom their piety feigned
> In sharp contest of battle found no aid
> Against invaders; therefore cooled in zeal
> Thenceforth shall practise how to live secure,
> Worldly or dissolute, on what their lords
> Shall leave them to enjoy . . . .
> So all shall turn degenerate, all depraved,
> Justice and temperance, truth and faith forgot.
> (XI. 797–807)[2]

So in England Milton had seen his fellows prostituting truth and faith to 'the vain and groundless apprehension that nothing but kingship can restore trade'.[3]

---

[1] My italics.
[2] 'One of the few passages in the poem which editors are probably justified in regarding as direct topical allusion,' says Fowler in his note. It is odd that he did not add the passage which I am just about to quote.
[3] See p. 200 above.

Noah – the one just man alive – saves humanity in the Ark (XI. 818, 874–8, 890–6): he recalls Abdiel among the angels. But evil returns. Monarchy succeeds the republic of the patriarchs.

> One shall rise
> Of proud ambitious heart, who not content
> With fair equality, fraternal state,
> Will arrogate dominion undeserved
> Over his brethren, and quite dispossess
> Concord and law of nature from the earth, . . .
> From heaven claiming second sovereignty;
> And from rebellion shall derive his name,
> Though of rebellion others he accuse.
>
> (XII. 24–37)[1]

This unnamed rebel is Nimrod, cited with approval by Charles I and Salmasius. He is joined by other ambitious spirits anxious to tyrannize under him. Adam is learning fast, and gets the point at once. 'Man over man' God

> made not lord; such title to himself
> Reserving, human left from human free.

Monarchy is usurpation (XII. 64–72). *Paradise Lost,* like Milton in 1641,[2] looks forward to the end of all earthly tyrannies. Michael drives home the moral that the real blame for this attempt 'to subdue/ Rational liberty' lies with its victims:

> Since thy original lapse, true liberty
> Is lost, which always with right reason dwells
> Twinned, and from her hath no dividual being:
> Reason in man obscured, or not obeyed,
> Immediately inordinate desires
> And upstart passions catch the government
> From reason, and to servitude reduce
> Man till then free. Therefore since he permits
> Within himself unworthy powers to reign
> Over free reason, God in judgment just
> Subjects him from without to violent lords;
> Who oft as undeservedly enthral
> His outward freedom: tyranny must be,
> Though to the tyrant thereby no excuse.
> Yet sometimes nations will descend so low

---

[1] Fowler's note cites parallels with *The Tenure of Kings and Magistrates.* Even more telling is the parallel with the passage from *Eikonoklastes* cited on p. 178 above.
[2] *C.P.W.,* I, p. 616.

> From virtue, which is reason, that no wrong,
> But justice, and some fatal curse annexed
> Deprives them of their outward liberty,
> Their inward lost.
>
> (XII. 83–101)

After that summary explanation of the Restoration the story continues. God decides to concentrate on 'one peculiar nation', sprung from 'one faithful man', Abraham (XII. 113–29). But this nation was soon enslaved in Egypt, and Moses and Aaron, 'sent from God to claim / His people from enthralment', had first to overcome 'the lawless tyrant, who denies/ To know their God'. He had to be 'compelled by signs and judgments dire' to release the Israelites (XII. 169–75). In *Eikonoklastes* Milton had compared Charles I to Pharaoh.[1] The judgments on the Egyptians included plague and fire, the portents in most Englishmen's minds when Milton published. In *Annus Mirabilis* Dryden had attempted to counter widespread belief that the Plague of 1665 and the Fire of London of 1666 were signs of God's wrath. Sprat in his *History of the Royal Society* also attacked the wrong sort of belief in portents – evidence that it existed and had considerable effect.[2]

The journey of the chosen people through the wilderness gave them the opportunity to set up representative government 'to rule by laws ordained' (219–26, 239–46).

> The rest
> Were long to tell, how many battles fought,
> How many kings destroyed.
>
> (XII. 261–3)

The kings who succeeded David were 'part good, part bad, of bad the longer scroll', guilty notably of idolatry (335–42).

Return from the Babylonian captivity leads to the reflection that wealth produces faction:

> But first among the priests dissension springs,
> Men who attend the altar and should most
> Endeavour peace.

They seize power, and then lose it to a stranger (as the Presbyterians had done in 1660),

> that the true
> Anointed king Messiah might be born
> Barred of his right
>
> (XII. 353–60)

---

[1] *Ibid.*, III, p. 516.
[2] Cf. pp. 405–6 below.

as he would be if he returned to post-Restoration England. (Milton's reference to the duty to promote peace of 'men who attend the altar' is a delicious example of the double-talk and covert irony he had to employ. He did not think that ministers should 'attend the altar' at all, or have anything to do with politics).[1]

Even the establishment of Christianity apparently made no lasting difference. Priestly wolves succeeded the apostles, and they followed the lure of 'lucre and ambition, and the truth/ With superstitions and traditions taint'. Grabbing 'places and titles, . . . secular power' they forced 'spiritual laws by carnal power . . . on every conscience,'

> Whence heavy persecution shall arise
> On all who in the worship persevere
> Of spirit and truth, the rest, far greater part
> Will deem in outward rites and specious forms
> Religion satisfied.
>   (XII. 507–35)

The reference to Restoration England could hardly be more explicit.[2]

'Finisher/ Of utmost hope' cried Adam after Michael had told him about the Incarnation – picking up the reference to hope at the beginning of the poem (XII. 375–6; I. 66–7; cf. p. 364 above). But again he is admonished. The contest between the Son and Satan is not 'a duel', and is not won vicariously on man's behalf. Satan must be destroyed not by outward violence but inwardly, 'his works/ In thee and in thy seed' (XII. 386–95; cf. p. 364 above). This is the point of the Son's life and death. Evil is overcome neither by violent war, nor by finding scapegoats – as Adam and Eve had mutually accused each other of responsibility for the Fall. In Paradise the Son helped them to recognize their own responsibility, and so to live at peace with each other even under divine judgment. On earth Jesus's constancy under temptation and even to death will show how Adam's sin can be overcome.[3]

The moral then has been slowly built up as we proceed through the epic. 'To be weak is miserable', Satan declared (P.L. I. 157). 'All wickedness is weakness', Samson confirmed (S.A. 834). But strength is of divers kinds, as Samson learnt and Satan did not. In the invocation to Book IX of Paradise Lost Milton contrasted with the feigned virtues of chivalry

---

[1] Cf. C.P.W., III, p. 241.
[2] Cf. the reference to the Satanic conclave in Paradise Regained as 'a gloomy consistory' (I. 42).
[3] Cf. Bouchard, pp. 97–101, 132–3.

> the better fortitude
> Of patience and heroic martyrdom
> Unsung.
>
>   (IX. 31–3)

'Unsung': Milton had no doubt himself contemplated such an end to his career in 1660, his epic uncompleted as well as himself uncommemorated. He returns more than once to the theme of courage 'though to the death', in face of persecution and torture.

> Suffering for truth's sake
> Is fortitude to highest victory,
> And to the faithful death the gate of life.
>
>   (XII. 492–7, 569–71)

'Matchless fortitude' was what Milton had praised in Oliver Cromwell in 1652. We may compare the passage in *Samson Agonistes*:

> But patience is more oft the exercise
> Of saints, the trial of their fortitude.
>
>   (*S.A.* 1287–8)

After the Fall Adam's first instinct had been to escape, to hide in rural solitude, like many who withdrew from politics after 1660.[1] But this was a panic reaction. Self-analysis, self-knowledge and consequent repentance were what he, like the English revolutionaries, like Samson, needed. Against such an approach God has not closed his ears by any absolute decree. He is present 'in valley and in plain' just as much as on the heights of Paradise (XI. 335–54). The preview of history in the last two books brings home to Adam the full sense of his own responsibility, of the consequences of his sin of ignorance.

Adam thus gained the experience which Milton had already undergone – first in his matrimonial tragedy, which led him to rethink the social consequences of the Fall; then in his blindness, and perhaps in the death of his son and his second wife; finally in the Restoration.[2] *Paradise Lost* is about the education of Adam. The lessons of history are discouraging. God's goodness had been shown in the Creation, but something had gone desperately wrong with humanity's use of what God had given them. In *Of Reformation* Milton had hoped that the Revolution would free England from the institutions which had frustrated previous attempts at reform.[3] But this optimism had not survived the betrayals of the fifties. In *The Ready and Easy Way* Milton the politician could suggest only a dictatorship of

---

[1] Røstvig, esp. pp. 430–42.
[2] *C.P.W.*, II, pp. 661–2, 666–7.
[3] *Ibid.*, I, pp. 614–15; Fixler (1964), pp. 89–90.

those who had remained true to the Cause. What else was realistic? It looked as though the cycle of false dawn leading to corruption had taken over again and would continue till the Second Coming.

But the last two books of *Paradise Lost* open up a different perspective. They depict Adam – i.e. humanity – learning how to prepare for Christ and for his kingdom on earth. They represent Milton's attempt to be utterly realistic in facing the worst without despair. It seemed to be true that there was a cyclical return of evil after every good start; true that the faithful were a small remnant. God's people in England after 1660 must learn to escape from history as circular treadmill, must become free to choose the good, as the English people had failed to choose it during the Revolution. Patient, courageous, stubborn work on limited objectives is the way to prepare for the new heaven and the new earth. There will be no miraculous intervention by an external Saviour merely because we impatiently expect it. It is Satan who offers short cuts.[1]

Milton's emphasis on the tragedy of history comes not from Augustine, or only incidentally; it comes from the sixteen-fifties. The fact that it had a lot of traditional wisdom behind it made it all the sadder, but Milton was not one to be taken with merely traditional wisdom not confirmed by his own experience. He offset his sense of the tragedy of history by his continuing hope, the survival of the forties, that Christ's kingdom was coming. *Paradise Regained* tells us to prepare for it: *Samson Agonistes* shows how, when the time comes, an individual can co-operate to bring it about. In *Samson Agonistes* history has ceased to be cyclical. Here I profoundly disagree with Parker, who sees the play only as desperately tragic and pessimistic, because he relates it too literally to the story of Samson in the Old Testament, the outcome of which was indeed a resumption of the cycle. But if we see it as Milton's vision of the future of the English Revolution it looks different.[2]

Adam ultimately came to see that the Fall itself may be fortunate.

> Full of doubt I stand,
> Whether I should repent me now of sin
> By me done and occasioned, or rejoice
> Much more, that much more good thereof shall spring.
>
> (XII. 473–6)

In terms of abstract theology the Fall may be fortunate only for the elect, and only at the end of time. But for the morale of the Miltonic warfaring,

---

[1] Bouchard, pp. 118–19, 165–71. Cf. p. 389 below.
[2] See chapter 31 below.

wayfaring Christian, Adam's outburst was valid, even though Michael greeted it with an ambiguous theological silence.[1] Milton, like Bacon, like Winstanley and the radicals of the English Revolution, saw a hope for humanity on earth in the future, attainable by human effort and self-discipline. 'The world was all before them.' Like Bunyan Milton transmutes the popular myth in retelling it. Paradise within is won only after the external visible Paradise has been lost, just as Milton's blindness enhanced his inner vision.[2]

But the conclusion that the Fall had after all been fortunate was not reached easily. It was won after the anguish of the self-betrayal of Adam and Eve, their re-education and ultimate recognition of God's purposes. The anguish, the consciousness of self-betrayal, the re-education, were Milton's as well as Adam's. In the second edition of *The Doctrine and Discipline of Divorce* he had said that God 'gives himself to be understood by men, judges and is judged, measures and is commensurate to right reason'.[3] 'Judges and is judged' was a bold phrase in 1643: it looks straight forward to the opening of *Paradise Lost*.

Michael's bitter words,

> So shall the world go on,
> To good malignant, to bad men benign,
> Under her own weight groaning[4]

come just after Adam's 'O goodness infinite, goodness immense', and are intended to help the reader to face the worst, to learn that no form of secular government has yet brought salvation to man; that 'the sum/ Of wisdom' lies in recognizing this fact and yet continuing to fight on in God's cause

> till the day
> Appear of respiration to the just,
> And vengeance to the wicked, at return
> Of him so lately promised.
>   (XII. 537–42)[5]

Adam concludes with complete confidence in God. We must not attempt to anticipate his purposes by trying to hasten his kingdom, but it will come if we co-operate,

---

[1] Miner (1968), pp. 43–53. Cf. pp. 346–7, 352 above.

[2] Ferry, p. 38, and *passim*.

[3] *C.P.W.*, II, p. 292.

[4] Everybody in the seventeenth century would recognize a reference to the name 'Malignants' given to Royalists during the Civil War.

[5] Cf. *S.A.* 11: 'leave me to respire'. The *Oxford English Dictionary* gives as one meaning of 'respire' – 'to breathe again after trouble, recover hope, courage or strength'.

> by small
> Accomplishing great things, by things deemed weak
> Subverting worldly strong, and worldly wise
> By simply meek.
>   (XII. 566–9)

It was the lesson that John Foxe had taught in his *Book of Martyrs* – not a
passivist book; the lesson that led Bacon and the early experimental
scientists to emphasize the meticulous study of 'small and mean things' as
the key to make 'mighty things from small beginnings grow'.[1] Cromwell
echoed the idea in his assurance before the Battle of Naseby that 'God
would, by things that are not, bring to nought things that are'.[2] Milton
stressed again and again that Christ chose 'the mean things of this world,
that he might put under the high'; that God included 'few wise or learned
men, few who are powerful or noble' to 'carry out his decrees against the
most powerful monarchs of this world'.[3] It is the Old Testament doctrine
of the remnant,[4] though now given a class content. The ultimate object for
Milton is still subversion, but it must be done in God's way, in God's time.

In his speech to the rebel angels Mammon had anticipated part of
Adam's conclusion:

> Our greatness will appear
> Then most conspicuous, when great things of small, . . .
> We can create, and in what place so e'er
> Thrive under evil, and work ease out of pain
> Through labour and endurance.
>   (II. 257–62)

Abdiel told Satan that God

> Out of smallest things could without end
> Have raised incessant armies to defeat
> Thy folly.
>   (VI. 137–9)

It almost sounds like a reference to the New Model Army. In *Paradise
Regained* the Son of God advances 'step by step', 'thought following
thought'. His 'weakness shall o'ercome Satanic strength/ And all the
world' (I. 192, 161). He expected to be tried by

---

[1] C. Webster (1975), pp. 421, 506; McKeon, pp. 170–1, quoting Dryden.
[2] Cromwell, I, p. 365. Cf. W. Blake, who thought that 'He who would do good to another must
do it in Minute Particulars;/General good is the plea of the scoundrel, hypocrite and flatterer'
(p. 655).
[3] *C.P.W.*, I, pp. 525, 825–33, 849–51; IV, p. 338; cf. VI, p. 436, and *C.M.*, VI, p. 24.
[4] See pp. 210, 348 above, pp. 441–2, 446 below.

> things adverse
> By tribulations, injuries, insults,
> Contempts and scorns, and snares, and violence,
> Suffering, abstaining, quietly expecting
> Without distrust or doubt.
> (III. 189-93)

Lest we should think of Milton's lines too passively, compare them with Lenin's slogan in a similar post-revolutionary period after 1905: 'smaller but better'. 'The unresistable might of weakness' had been a favourite Miltonic theme since his first pamphlet.[1] Its classic expression is in *Of Civil Power*, where Milton stresses the ability of 'conscious and conscientious men, who in this world are counted weakest' to overcome 'the force of this world'. 'It is the ... set purpose of God ... by spiritual means which are counted weak to overcome all power which resists him.' Milton's lack of confidence in immediate political force by no means meant that he had abandoned ultimate political objectives.[2]

Why, we might ask, should Adam, lord of the world, undisputed head of his community of two, want to subvert worldly great and worldly wise? Once we ask the question, the answer is clear. The lesson is not intended for Adam about to leave Paradise but for Englishmen facing the problems of the sixteen-sixties. For men who felt like Milton, if not for Adam, the time was ripe for God to subvert worldly great and worldly wise.

True heroism is 'by small accomplishing great things': struggling on, in blindness and poverty, when listeners are few and the atmosphere hostile. For, despite everything, God 'all this good of evil shall produce'. This is 'the sum of wisdom'. No scientific knowledge, no worldly wealth or power can compare with it. But wisdom must lead to action. Michael's sole correction, this time, of Adam's formulation is

> only add
> Deeds to thy knowledge answerable,

the active virtues; Adam will then 'possess/A Paradise within thee, happier far' (XII. 575-87).[3]

This process of internalizing God's will, and externalizing the Satanic, is an important part of what Milton is trying to convey in *Paradise Lost*. It does not necessarily go with disillusionment or abandonment of political struggle. Adam advances from external obedience (or disobedience) to God's command to obedience to his own enlightened conscience. The law

---

[1] *C.P.W.*, I, p. 525.
[2] *C.M.*, VI, pp. 20-4. Cf. pp. 418, 445 below.
[3] Fish (1967), p. 204. Cf. pp. 475-6 below.

is internalized, as in the *De Doctrina* Milton said the Mosaic law should be. Paradise within balances Satan's 'Myself am hell'. External obedience, of the sort that C. S. Lewis admired, is appropriate only for children. In *The Tenure* Milton spoke of 'the falsified names of loyalty and obedience'. Blind submission – Satan's idea of what obedience means – is as bad as implicit faith. In the New Testament faith replaced the obedience of the Old Testament.[1] Michael does not include obedience among the virtues which are essential to the Paradise within. Adam could not obey with internal conviction in Paradise since he did not know why God had prohibited the forbidden fruit. So at the end of the poem he is freer than in Paradise: that is why his Paradise within is 'happier far'. Adam has grown up. Milton perhaps thought it better to live in a fallen world, because he most admired virtues like stubborn courage and self-discipline in adversity. But Milton also wanted men to achieve a state in which they could enjoy the creation without sin.[2]

So what are we to take as the 'theme' of *Paradise Lost*? Adam is a representative person, is all of us. He fell, though he was as free to stand as Jesus was on the pinnacle of the temple. Salvation is, however, not vicarious, not a gift made to mankind by Christ's death on the cross. It comes from man's own effort, and his own understanding. This was to be the theme of *Paradise Regained*. The true Paradise is to be found within, on earth, as the radical tradition had taught. Meanwhile, the struggle must go on, but it is longer, soberer, less exhilarating, than in the heady days of *Areopagitica* or the *Defensio*. It had been bitter for Milton to come down from the heights of 1644 and 1649–50 to the trivialities and dissensions of 1659–60. It was a story to be repeated after every great revolution. Milton gritted his teeth to face the worst. Short of a miracle, Christ's kingdom was postponed to kingdom come. Meanwhile, great things are achieved by small: the tiny ripple rather than the big splash, the tortoise not the hare. Abdiel's supreme virtue was that he retained his faith in God's purposes; his heroism was the greater because apparently unsuccessful. They also serve who only stand and wait.[3]

VI Some problems

I have no wish to suggest that my interpretation exhausts the content of *Paradise Lost*, any more than the political allegory is all that matters in *The*

---

[1] *C.P.W.*, II, p. 527; III, p. 19; VI, p. 177. Cf. p. 267 above.
[2] Frye (1966), pp. 116–19; Empson (1961), esp. p. 192; Rajan, pp. 110–11; cf. Hughes (1971), p. 7.
[3] Bouchard, pp. 83–4; Fish, pp. 188–9.

Faerie Queene or *Pilgrim's Progress* or *Gulliver's Travels*. But the structure I have suggested makes sense in the light of Milton's known preoccupations at the time of writing. It may be retorted that Milton did not invent his story: it is Biblical, and therefore cannot relate to England in 1660. This argument, however, applies to a great deal of comment on *Paradise Lost*. We must ask not only why Milton chose the theme of the Fall – a theme already enriched by centuries of commentary – but also why he emphasized certain elements in the traditional story and not others. 'Hirelings' is a Biblical phrase, but not all commentators applied it to clergymen of the Church of England as Milton did in his pamphlet of 1659 and as he appears to do in *Paradise Lost* IV. 193, comparing them to Satan entering Paradise. There is nothing in the Bible, but much in post-Restoration England, to justify the pun on 'pontifical' as an adjective to describe the causeway constructed by Sin and Death between hell and earth: 'bridge-building' and 'episcopal' – 'this *new* wondrous pontifice' (X. 312–13, 348 – my italics). Thanks to these pontifical activities, Sin tells Satan, 'thine now is all the world' (X. 371–2 – cf. the priests who plot against Samson in *Samson Agonistes* but not in the Bible). When Abdiel proudly said to Satan 'My sect thou seest' (VI. 147–8), he used the word which post-1660 authorities in England, secular or ecclesiastical, applied to those whom Milton regarded as Christians.

Milton's 'good friend', Theodore Haak, coadjutor of Hartlib, a link between the group of London scientists in the sixteen-forties and the Royal Society of which he was a Fellow, translated the first three books of *Paradise Lost* into German. In 1686–7 he read this translation to the Hanoverian pastor, H. L. Benthem. From this reading and from talking to Haak, Benthem gathered the impression that Milton's poem was really about politics in Restoration England. When Milton's friends were told the title of the poem, they feared that it would be a lament for the loss of England's happiness with the downfall of the revolutionary régime. But when they read it they saw that the prudent Milton had dealt only with the fall of Adam; reassured, they withdrew their objections to publication. But ('so far as I understand from what Haak told me and what I read for myself'), although at first sight the epic's subject was indeed the fall of our first parents, in fact 'this very wily politician ("dieser sehr schlau Politicus") concealed under this disguise exactly the sort of lament that his friends had originally suspected.'[1] Some have thought that this story shows how silly Benthem (or Haak) was; but by now we may think otherwise. Haak was

---

[1] Benthem, p. 58; Barnett, pp. 156, 162–3. Benthem had also read another German translation.

as likely to know what Milton was up to as anyone. We might bear in mind Benthem's story about the initial political anxieties of Milton's friends when we read Marvell's 'On *Paradise Lost*': 'The argument/ Held me awhile misdoubting his intent.'

With Benthem (or Haak) we may compare, for instance, Richard Baxter's account of what the Restoration meant for Puritans. 'England had been like in a quarter of an age to become a land of saints and a pattern of holiness to all the world, and the unmatchable paradise of the earth. Never were such fair opportunities to sanctify a nation lost and trodden underfoot as have been in this land of late.'[1] For Milton the English Revolution began to decline earlier than it did for Baxter, and the outlook of the two men was very different; but the sense of lost opportunities is the same in both.

A perplexing passage is given to the Son in Book III. After the Crucifixion and Resurrection, he tells the Father, when he has ruined all his foes, 'Death last',

> Then with the multitude of my redeemed
> Shall enter heaven long absent.
>   (III. 260–1)

'Long absent'? What was Christ doing between the Resurrection and the Last Judgment, here apparently conflated? Had he not ascended to heaven? Surely his soul did not sleep like those of his elect? (*P.L.* XII. 456–65 gives the more orthodox sequence of events.)

The Father provides a clue in his reply. The Son must become man:

> Their nature also to thy nature join
> And be thyself man among men on earth.

The regenerate shall

> Live in thee transplanted, and from thee
> Receive new life.
>   (III. 282–93)

The Son is man, the 'one perfect man', 'one greater man'. One object of Book XII is to give a sense of the way in which divinely guided men have decisively intervened in history, time and again, to rescue their fellows when all seemed lost – Noah, Moses the Mediator, Joshua, Samson, Christ the supreme prophet. All look forward to the Second Coming. The name

---

[1] Baxter (Everyman), p. 84, quoted with relevant comments by Rivers, pp. 85–6.

Christ means also Moses, the prophets and the Apostles, Milton tells us in the *De Doctrina*. Solomon was 'another Christ'. And there were others, 'chosen of peculiar grace/ Elect above the rest' (III. 183–4) – Abraham, Enoch, Job, perhaps even Deborah.[1] The Christ who returns to heaven after long absence will have subsumed all these and the subsequent regenerate – 'godlike men', they are called in *P.R.* IV. 348 – into his own person. The Son agreed when Adam suggested that he could 'raise thy creature to what height thou wilt/ Of union or communion, deified' (*P.L.* VIII. 430–1). The Son of God's

> humiliation shall exalt
> With thee thy manhood also to this throne,
> Here shalt thou sit incarnate, here shalt reign
> Both God and man.
> (III. 313–16)

In the same way, before their fall the angels were all 'under one head more near/ United', with God concerned 'to exalt our happy state', the Son reigning 'equal over equals' (V. 829–32). The frontispiece to Hobbes's *Leviathan* shows the sovereign incorporating all his subjects; so Christ embodies all the elect. After ruling on earth for a thousand years with his saints, this composite Christ will re-enter heaven 'long absent' in order to 'lay by' his 'regal sceptre'.[2]

If this is a correct interpretation, many points become clearer. Milton's insistence that the Last Judgment is carried out by Christ *and his saints* makes better sense if Christ incorporates all the elect into his own person; so does the idea that the condemnation of Charles I, and perhaps Samson's destruction of the Philistines, were anticipations of the Judgment. In the War in Heaven which incorporates features of the Last Judgment, 'the inviolable saints' struggled on unsuccessfully until they were 'under their head embodied, all in one' (VI. 398, 779).[3] Raphael deliberately emphasized the parallels between earth and heaven in this war.[4] This interpretation would also suggest that the 'one greater man' of whom the opening of *Paradise Lost* speaks is not only Christ but what mankind can – must – become: this is the theme of *Paradise Regained*. The Golden Age lies not in the past, but in the future of men and women who understand their destiny. *Paradise Lost* is a poem about the education of humanity.

---

[1] *C.P.W.*, VI, pp. 126, 178. For Deborah see p. 120 above, and for 'peculiar grace', p. 276.
[2] Cf. pp. 303–5 above, p. 475 below.
[3] I owe this point to Gary Hamilton.
[4] See also pp. 282, 371–4 above, pp. 419–21 below.

The ultimate conclusion then is that salvation does not come from without, either by the magic of eating forbidden fruit (or popish sacraments), or by a duel between Christ and Satan (as the Calvinist theory of imputed righteousness seemed to suggest). It does not come by a vicarious atonement at all. Christ works through his regenerate: salvation comes when the regenerate attain to unity with Christ. That is the Paradise within. In Comenius's phrase, we have moved from 'the labyrinth of the world' to 'the Paradise of the heart'.[1] When Paradise is within all the regenerate, then Christ's kingdom will have come and will have become superfluous: for God will then be all in all.

'The earth is all before me', sings Wordsworth at the beginning of *The Prelude*, 'free as a bird to settle where I will'. The words echo the conclusion of *Paradise Lost*, but the significance of that youthful light-heartedness is poles apart from the tough acceptance of Milton's epic. The end of *Paradise Lost* is like the end of a Chaplin film, but without any shadow of sentimentality. Instead of the little fellow shambling off alone to meet his destiny, Adam and Eve are now hand in hand again, purged of all illusions. At our first view of them in Paradise 'hand in hand they passed' (IV. 321); 'handed they went . . . into their inmost bower' to make love (IV. 738–9). When Eve finally got her own way and left Adam to work separately from him (and so exposed herself to Satan's temptation),

> from her husband's hand her hand
> Soft she withdrew.
>   (IX. 385–6)

After the Fall Adam 'seized' Eve's hand, in a new and lustful gesture (IX. 1037). Only in the penultimate line of the poem are they reunited to pursue 'their solitary way' out of Paradise. At such a moment of the poem a good Latinist like Milton would not accidentally commit the paradox of using 'solitary' – from *solus* – for more than one person. It may refer back to the time when God teases Adam for not wanting to be 'solitary' in Paradise (VIII. 402). Adam got perhaps more than he bargained for in Eve. Yet by the end Adam and Eve are united again – one flesh, one family, one community – acknowledging God's providence, prepared for whatever history may bring, as they take their solitary way together.

Similar echoes can be heard in Milton's use of the word 'forlorn': the very word is like a knell. Forlorn and wild are first used by Satan to describe the landscape of hell (I. 180); then by anticipation of the fate of

---

[1] The title of Comenius's allegory was *The Labyrinth of the World and the Paradise of the Heart* (1623).

Adam and Eve (IV. 374).[1] Milton applies it hypothetically to himself in the invocation to Book VII, when he supposes that without divine assistance he might come such a cropper as Bellerophon, who was thrown from Pegasus on to

> the Alean field . . .
> Erroneous there to wander and forlorn.
>
> (VII. 17–20)

Finally Adam sees himself living 'again in these wild woods forlorn' – Paradise without Eve – if he does not join her in transgression (IX. 910).[2]

The spirit in which Adam and Eve set out into the unknown future is thus far indeed from the Utopian enthusiasm with which Milton had greeted the Revolution in the early sixteen-forties. But it is neither despairing nor passivist. Like everyone except hell's inmates, Adam and Eve hope. They 'found . . . new hope to spring/ Out of despair' (XI. 137–9). And the better future for which they hope is to be lived on earth.[3]

The state of innocence was not just a honeymoon or a boring holiday. In his attitude towards labour in Paradise, Milton was more radical than the Geneva Bible, which he seems to have used by preference so long as he retained his sight; his readers seem to have preferred the Authorized Version.[4] The Geneva Bible's note on Genesis 2:15 said 'God would not have man idle, though as yet there was no need to labour.' The theme of divinely ordained labour in Paradise was familiar to lower-class radicals – those who worked themselves. Jack Cade's followers in Shakespeare's *Henry VI* emphasized that 'Adam was a gardener.' Winstanley assumed that Adam and Eve worked before the Fall.[5] Labour before the Fall had been interpreted – in Ralegh's *History of the World*, for instance – as an allegory of reason controlling the passions. But there was a real job for Adam and Eve to do in Milton's Paradise, however pleasurable it was to keep the luxuriant garden under control. Their innocence was not effortless, their virtues neither fugitive nor cloistered. The plants in the garden had to be *taught* how to grow. Constant vigilance was needed to preserve

---

[1] Cf. Kermode (1960), p. 114.

[2] In his Seventh Prolusion Milton had described primitive man wandering wild in the woods, in something like a Hobbist state of nature (*C.P.W.*, I, p. 299). Cf. Grotius's Eve: 'Ergone vacuos vidua, deserta et vaga/ Curram per agros, mistaque errabo feris?' (Kirkconnell, p. 204).

[3] Cf. C. Hill (Penguin, 1969), pp. 202–4, and p. 322 above.

[4] H. F. Fletcher, pp. 93–4; Sims, p. 4. In *Of True Religion* Milton appears obliquely to recommend the Geneva Bible, of which his widow owned a copy. Apparently he used the Geneva Bible for *Samson Agonistes*. This need not be an argument for an early date for that poem, since he might be relying on his memory (Low, p. 181).

[5] Sabine, pp. 289, 423; cf. K. V. Thomas (1964) for the long mediaeval tradition of labour before the Fall.

the balance of forces on which the perfection of the garden depended. 'These forces, being natural, are always trying to grow, so they must be controlled.'[1] Goodness is fecundity, but discipline is still required against licence. Even unfallen nature can be 'overgrown' and 'wanton'. Eve's hair 'in wanton ringlets waved/ As the vine curls her tendrils'. The garden work of Adam and Eve 'led the vine/ To wed her elm'. Marriage, like gardening, imposes order on the plenitude of nature.

Years earlier Milton had said that God 'pours out before us even to a profusion all desirable things, and gives us minds that can wander beyond all limit and satiety', at the same time that he commands temperance, justice, continence. We recall Marvell's vision of Mary Fairfax:

> 'Tis she that to these gardens gave
> That wondrous beauty which they have;
> She straightness on the woods bestows . . .[2]

The happiness of unfallen man was contingent on nature's tendency to over-abundance and wanton growth being curbed. 'Hunger, thirst, curiosity and sexual desire become evil only when they are not properly disciplined.' This is 'the real originality of Milton's account of man's pre-lapsarian life', and it is based on the equally original concept that 'without this tendency to over-abundance and wanton growth Man's original condition would have been neither free nor happy'. 'The difference between unfallen and fallen Man is simply the difference between a well- and a badly tended garden. It is a difference of degree, not of kind. That is why Paradise can be regained.'[3] The relevance of this to an analysis of post-revolutionary politics is apparent. The teeming creative plenitude glorified in *Areopagitica* had disintegrated into wrangles between Leveller democratic politics, Digger communism, Ranter immoralism, Nayler and his Quaker ladies, the avarice and ambition of the generals. What all lacked was discipline, control, good gardening. Even after the Fall, Adam coolly observed that 'idleness had been worse' than the curse of labour which had just been announced to him (*P.L.* X. 1055).

I suggested that Satan and the fallen angels incorporate some of the attitudes of the radicals whose irresponsibility Milton felt to be in large part to blame for the catastrophe of the Revolution: Coleridge said some-

---

[1] J. M. Evans, chapter X. I have drawn heavily on this illuminating study. Broadbent hints that gardening is an emblem of moral or even political activity: cf. Shakespeare's *Richard II* (Broadbent, 1960, pp. 177–85).

[2] *C.P.W.*, II, p. 528. Cf. pp. 128, 259–61 above.

[3] J. M. Evans, pp. 268–71. Whether Milton would have been entirely happy gardening to all eternity is another question.

thing similar.[1] Satan's philosophy appears to be that of some Ranters, with its emphasis on fate, chance and necessity, its denial of the divine providence which Milton is asserting. God no doubt had the Ranters as well as Satan in mind when he bleakly declared 'What I will is fate.' Necessity and chance cannot touch God (VII. 172–3; cf. p. 375 above). Like some Hermeticists and Ranters, Satan believes (or affects to believe) that all comes by nature.[2] 'Space may produce new worlds' (I. 650). The rebel angels were not created but

> Self-begot, self-raised
> By our own quickening power, when fatal course
> Had circled his full orb, the birth mature
> Of this our native heaven, ethereal sons.
> Our puissance is our own.
>   (V. 860–4 – cf. IX. 146–7)[3]

Ironically, the only character in *Paradise Lost* who was neither produced by natural generation nor directly created by God was Sin.[4] To Eve Satan denies that 'the gods' created anything,

> for this fair earth I see,
> Warmed by the sun, producing every kind,
> Them nothing.
>   (IX. 720–2)

Satan's mockery of the Fall turning on so trivial a matter as the eating of an apple recalls the flippancy of the Ranters (X. 485–93). His speech tempting Eve abounds with Ranter echoes. Empson grasped this point, without perhaps fully appreciating it, when he attributed to Eve the Ranter view that she was justified in eating the apple as long as she was firmly convinced that this was what God wanted her to do.[5] Eve's sin was that of the Ranters and of many other radicals recorded by Edwards, 'affecting godhead' (III. 206). We may compare Satan's praise in *Paradise Regained* of tragedians who 'treat/ Of fate and chance and change in human life' (IV. 264–5), and the Son of God's retort

> Much of the soul they talk, but all awry,
> And in themselves seek virtue, and to themselves
> All glory arrogate.

---

[1] Wittreich (1970), pp. 207–8.
[2] Cf. pp. 330–1 above.
[3] The Phoenix in *Samson Agonistes* was 'self-begotten' (line 1699). Cf. p. 445 below.
[4] See p. 343 above.
[5] Empson (1961), p. 180. See p. 313 above.

They accuse God under the name of fortune or fate of being 'regardless quite/ Of mortal things' (IV. 313–17).[1]

Ranters and others like them held what Milton regarded as an ultra-libertarian position, ignoring the self-discipline, the subordination to wider purposes, which must accompany true liberty. 'Licence they mean when they cry liberty.' Satan expresses a Ranter viewpoint in Book VI:

> At first I thought that liberty and heaven
> To heavenly souls had been all one; but now
> I see that most through sloth had rather serve.

Satan depicted his revolt as a contention of freedom versus servility. Abdiel replied, in Miltonic terms, that servitude is

> To serve the unwise, or him who hath rebelled
> Against his worthier, as thine now serve thee,
> Thyself not free, but to thyself enthralled.

In this respect 'God and nature bid the same' (VI. 164–81).

Paradise Lost is not a *roman à clef* in which Satan = Lambert (or Clarkson), Beelzebub = Fleetwood (or Coppe). I am suggesting only that one possible source for Milton's conception of the rebel angels is the people he had encountered, whose activities had done (in his view) harm to the cause he believed in, although their ideas started from premises alarmingly close to his. My hypothesis is not intended to be exclusive: but the way in which good men fall is likely to have been one of the problems which most concerned him at the time of writing the epic.

We may even hear echoes of disputes with Ranters and others in the astronomical discussions in *Paradise Lost*. Milton was dashingly modern in using words like 'prospective glass', 'telescope' and 'microscope' in his poems (*At a Vacation Exercise*, line 71; *P.R.* IV. 42, 57).[2] He knew that the moon was 'spotty' (*P.L.* I. 291): the celestial bodies were not more excellent than terrestial matter. In this sense he rejected the great chain of being. As early as *Comus* he conveyed a sense of the smallness of 'this dim spot, which men call earth, . . . this pinfold here' (lines 5–7). Many others were disturbed by the inconceivable vastness of space, newly revealed. Boehme stressed the isolation of man in his tiny corner of the universe, with God apparently uninterested in his fate: we must look for God in our own hearts.[3] Milton had not felt Pascal's terror of infinite space, but he

---

[1] Cf. Reeve and Muggleton, p. 186.
[2] Cf. S. Pordage, p. 313: 'the perspective we look through'.
[3] Koyré, pp. 21–2, 29.

appreciated other consequences of the Copernican astronomy – the possibility of a plurality of worlds, of life on other planets, with all the disturbing implications for the Christian scheme of salvation (*P.L.* III. 459, 565–71, 667–70; V. 261–3; VII. 620–2; VIII. 15–38, 140–76). C. S. Lewis called Milton 'our first poet of space', and suggested that he may owe to Bruno his idea that the heavens are not only wide but also pathless. Satan's journey through space seems to have been Milton's invention.[1]

In *Paradise Lost* Milton did far more than hedge between the astronomical models of Ptolemy, Copernicus and Tycho Brahe – though this would have been a very sensible thing to do in the state of the evidence at the time. In the year of Milton's death the Secretary of the Royal Society still knew that the Copernican hypothesis was unproven.[2] Milton constructed his own model of an unfallen astronomy before the axis of the earth was tilted (or the plane of the sun's orbit was shifted, in Ptolemaic terms).[3] Here Milton is correcting Joseph Mede, who restricted the consequences of the Fall to 'the sublunary heavens only'. In the upper heavens order always reigned, undisturbed by the goings-on of humanity. This, Madame Labrousse suggests, may have reflected an unconscious desire to proclaim the untouchability of the social and political order, so precarious in the mid-seventeenth century. Milton would have none of that.[4] We can never be too carefully on the look-out for evidence of his radicalism even in the most apparently neutral places.

Milton, who had read his Wilkins, was fascinated by contemporary discussions on the possibility of a plurality of worlds and yet aware of the relativity of planetary motion (VIII. 70–1, 114–40, 159–80). He consequently wanted to stress that this is not the crucial issue either for the Christian or for the revolutionary politician. He had no doubt heard much idle speculation in intellectual circles; Raphael's astronomy lecture refutes thought which by definition cannot lead to action. Accepting the immensity of the universe he emphasizes not its meaninglessness, but the dignity of man's place in it. He goes out of his way to tell Adam that there is nothing wrong with scientific enquiry. But – and Adam agrees –

> Apt the mind or fancy is to rove
> Unchecked, and of her roving is no end.

---

[1] Lewis (1960), p. 251; MacCaffrey, p. 193. Lewis's reference is to *Il Penseroso*.
[2] Oldenburg, X, pp. 555, 561. Cf. Flamsteed, p. 322.
[3] Fowler gives a vigorous exposition and defence of Milton's astronomy, and shows him to have been far more sophisticated than his critics have appreciated. See especially C. and F., pp. 447–9, and notes on pp. 644, 684, 689–90, 778, 817–20, 959–61.
[4] Mede, pp. 614–15; Labrousse, pp. 74–6.

The point is

> Not to know at large of things remote
> From use, obscure and subtle,

but of 'that which before us lies in daily life', lest we become 'in things that most concern/ Unpractised, unprepared, and still to seek' (VIII. 188–97).[1] It was Belial who treasured 'those thoughts that wander through eternity' (II. 147). Temperance in knowledge is no less necessary than temperance in eating and drinking (VII. 126–30).

Satan told Eve that after eating the forbidden fruit he turned his thoughts 'to speculations high or deep', and 'considered all things visible in heaven/ Or earth, or middle' – though his account of these high speculations wandered off into exaggerated praise of Eve's beauty (IX. 602–4), a bathetic conclusion to which Ranters were alleged to be prone. We recall the reasoning high of the fallen angels,

> Of providence, foreknowledge, will and fate,
> Fixed fate, free will, foreknowledge absolute,
> And found no end, in wandering mazes lost.
>
> (II. 559–61)

Raphael suggested that Adam should accept that the Biblical narrative conveys enough for the practical purposes of life. Idle speculation, random philosophizing, tied the fallen angels up in knots. The science of astronomy is all very well in its proper place as a specialist study, but in the last resort it does not matter to the Christian whether Ptolemy or Copernicus or Tycho Brahe is right. (Blake thought that Milton's role was 'to cast off the idiot Questioner who is always questioning/ But never capable of answering'.)[2] Milton had disliked Cambridge scholastic disputations, because they were not to edification, did not lead to action. He was already copying out quotations on the vanity of speculation in the earliest pages of his Commonplace Book.[3] He might have found the theme in the Hermetic writings. Like Winstanley and Erbery, he had observed for himself how abstract discussions of this sort diverted and split the radicals.[4]

Milton – like Fludd in this too – felt a need to hold on to the Bible as the source of knowledge of the physical world. Copernican astronomy, whatever the professions of the astronomers, was eroding belief in the Biblical

---

[1] Fowler's note quotes Bacon to a similar sceptical effect about 'astronomers, which did feign eccentrics and epicycles and such engines of orbs, to save the phenomena; though they knew there were no such things'. Milton is not being obscurantist: he is in good scientific company.
[2] W. Blake, p. 546; cf. Schultz (1955), pp. 182–3.
[3] *C.P.W.*, I, pp. 380–1.
[4] *W.T.U.D.*, p. 377 and references there given.

account of Creation.[1] Gossipy disputations about astronomy were un-settling ordinary people's belief in a divinely ordered universe, and in the Biblical accounts of it. Wisdom, the intuitive wisdom of the Christian, was greater than the knowledge of the Schools, and even of astronomers.[2] Anticipating Newton, Christ in *Paradise Regained* spoke of the collection of such knowledge as 'children gathering pebbles on the shore' (IV. 330).[3]

Milton's enduring reputation for orthodoxy in England has something to do with his apparent defence of the Bible against astronomy: this was to be a sticking point for many good Protestants during the next two and a half centuries. But Milton's attempt to brush under the carpet the challenge of astronomy fits in with his general purposes. Seventeenth-century science was splitting up the unity of the cosmos. Over the centuries the Galenic physiology, the Ptolemaic astronomy, the macro/microcosm parallel, the argument from analogy, the humanization of nature in the mediaeval bestiaries – all this had formed a cultural unity. Those who in the seventeenth century were still trying to hold the universe together were the Hermeticists, Fludd, the Comenians and Winstanley. Milton's encyclo-paedic learning, his emphasis on the oneness of truth, his desire to synthe-size all knowledge, associate him with those who wanted to preserve a unified concept of culture against the growing specialization and frag-mentation of the age, just as his insistence on creation *ex deo* links him with the mystical tradition of some of the sects, in conscious opposition to a mechanical universe.[4] Samuel Barrow, the doctor who contributed a Latin poem to the second edition of *Paradise Lost,* spotted the all-embracing universalism of the epic, the eternal conflict of chaos and order, the mediating role of Christ:

> Res cunctas et cunctarum primordia rerum
> Et fata et fines, contenit iste liber. . . .
> Et sine fine Chaos, et sine fine Deus
> Et sine fine magis (siquis magis est sine fine)
> In Christo erga homines conciliatus amor.

Barrow also noted that Satan was 'hardly less grand than Michael himself'.[5]

---

[1] Allen (1963), pp. 37–9, 154.

[2] Hoopes, pp. 193–6, 199; cf. *C.P.W.,* I, p. 246 – Third Prolusion.

[3] Milton may have been quoting Donne's sermons or the Hermeticist John Everard (see *C. and C.,* pp. 353–4).

[4] I have argued this at greater length in *W.T.U.D.,* chapter 14, esp. p. 304; cf. Svendsen (1956) *passim*; Adamson, pp. 770–8. But the one truth may have many shapes (cf. p. 449 below).

[5] Parker was wrong to translate Barrow's opening line as 'You who read *Paradise Lost,* . . . why do you read it except complete?' Barrow's meaning is rather 'in reading *Paradise Lost* you read about everything' (Parker, pp. 635–6).

Paradise Lost held popular imagination in the eighteenth and nineteenth centuries as *the* Christian poem in the English language, ranking with *Pilgrim's Progress,* because it subsumed popular concepts of what the world was like. It was the culmination of an attitude towards the Bible which in the age of Clement Writer, Samuel Fisher, Spinoza and Richard Simon was to succumb to new critical methods.[1] Milton's *Art of Logic* similarly sums up and concludes a century-long tradition of right reason, based on Christianity.[2] Traditional popular Christianity was beginning to be killed, together with magic, by the advance of the mechanical philosophy. Darwin only gave the *coup de grâce.* Milton places Adam in the old cosmos, whose unity modern science was to disrupt. We no longer believe that human sin *could* affect nature. What had been the strength of *Paradise Lost*'s appeal became a weakness when it appeared to be tied to a Biblical astronomy which was no longer acceptable.

VII 1667 and after

'Let the King come in', Harrington had said, 'and call a Parliament of the greatest Cavaliers in England, so they be men of estates, and let them sit but seven years, and they will all turn Commonwealth's men.'[3] Punctually seven years after the Restoration, the Cavalier Parliament drove into exile the Earl of Clarendon, the minister who thought that God had miraculously intervened to restore Charles II.[4] *Paradise Lost* appeared just when Clarendon's fall demonstrated the possible instability of the Restoration settlement. The moment was ripe for Milton's justification of an anti-monarchical God.

Paradise Lost also appeared in the same year as Sprat's *History of the Royal Society.* Like Milton's epic, Sprat's *History* had been thought over for a long time. It too was trying to find solutions to problems posed by the English Revolution and the Restoration. Sprat is the true quietist that some have seen in Milton. For Sprat enthusiasm and political concern are bad things in themselves. A main social contribution of science and the Royal Society was to expose prophecies and prodigies. Sprat's praise of 'the present genius of this nation', 'the present inquiring temper of this age', picks up some of the themes of *Areopagitica.* 'The absolute perfection of the true philosophy is not now far off ... for methinks there is an

---

[1] A. Williams, pp. 258, 265; cf. *W.T.U.D.,* chapter 11.
[2] Svendsen (1956), *passim;* Hoopes, pp. 199–200.
[3] Aubrey, I, p. 291.
[4] See p. 347 above.

agreement between the growth of learning and civil government.'[1] Rejection of Milton's politics seemed to Sprat (who had been unfortunate enough to praise Cromwell at the wrong time) to guarantee the victory of experimental science. But it was a science separated from what Milton thought so much more important – from setting up Christ's kingdom of freedom on earth.

Milton disagreed with Henry Oldenburg's suggestion that his pamphleteering had been a waste of time; he stated at length the benefits it had brought to his country.[2] Milton perhaps gained as an artist from what is sometimes treated as an unfortunate interruption in his creative life. *Paradise Lost* subsumes Milton's experience in the forties and fifties, and because of this is a richer poem than the Arthuriad he might have written if there had been no Revolution. The discipline of writing English prose aided the transformation from *Comus* to *Paradise Lost*. Stylistic experiments like the 'hymns in prose' in *Of Reformation* and *Animadversions* may have contributed more than anything Milton learnt from Greek or Latin or Italian epics.

Did Milton think of poetry as something very different from prose? He followed the English school of Ramists in believing that poets and orators were both employing rhetoric; only the words were organized in a different way.[3] Perhaps our sharp distinction between the two is something that dates from the seventeenth century, from Bacon, the Levellers and the utilitarian pamphleteers of the revolutionary decades. In Hooker, the Bible, Donne, Sir Thomas Browne, the distinction is less clear cut. Only in his later pamphlets does Milton adapt himself to the popular pamphleteering style which had become necessary if large numbers of people were to be reached and convinced. The plain sinewy prose of the Levellers, which looks forward to Bunyan and Defoe, never appealed to Milton, though he seems to have been aware of Martin Marprelate, a model for Overton at least.[4] It is the poetic nature of Milton's prose rather than the influence of Latin that makes it seem old-fashioned. Milton's vocabulary is less latinate than that of Hooker, Browne or Jeremy Taylor. 'Three-quarters of its words are "pure Anglo-Saxon." ' The latinity of his sentence structure has been exaggerated too.[5]

Milton's verse differs from that of the Elizabethan dramatists and Donne

---

[1] Sprat, pp. 78, 372, 29; cf. pp. 3, 114.
[2] See p. 183 above.
[3] *C.P.W.*, II, p. 403; K. G. Hamilton, pp. 90–3.
[4] Le Comte, p. 51; cf. *C.P.W.*, III, p. 138.
[5] Neumann, pp. 102–20; Boone, pp. 125–7; see C. and F., pp. 431–3 for a judicious summing up – also Stavely, *passim*.

in the same way as his prose differs from that of Overton and Winstanley. It is deliberately removed from spoken, conversational English. He was writing neither for a popular audience nor for a closed circle of chosen friends. Like the *Defence of the People of England,* Milton's great poems were public utterances, designed for 'fit audience . . . though few': the grand style of *Paradise Lost* was deliberately adopted for the purpose. It seems perhaps more remote to-day than it did in the seventeenth century, when the Biblical stories and Biblical language were familiar to all literate people; but it was never intended to be popular in the sense that Bunyan intended *The Pilgrim's Progress* to be popular.

'The greatest master in our language of freedom within form', Eliot called Milton.[1] Stylistically he achieved the combination of liberty with discipline which eluded him in politics. Milton himself thought that by rejecting 'the troublesome and modern bondage of rhyming' he recovered 'ancient liberty to heroic poem'.[2] The daring, breathtaking confidence in his freedom justified the form. It is typical that Milton thought of himself as preserving the heart of a liberator to the last – in blank verse no less than in republicanism.[3] The long paragraphs of *Paradise Lost,* free from the straitjacket of the couplet, and the irregular versification of *Samson Agonistes,* were seen as liberating by Blake and by G. M. Hopkins. That they were not so seen in the century and a half after the publication of *Paradise Lost* was due to the complex social circumstances which followed the defeat of the English Revolution. Regularity, the rules, rejection of the word inspiration,[4] were political and social as well as literary imperatives: they transformed the nature of Milton's influence. The great liberator became a pernicious model for unliberated poetasters. Milton's style is an ultimate: R. M. Adams compares Crashawe, Hopkins, Joyce.[5] Even in his own lifetime Milton was becoming isolated. His poetic diction is as far removed from the artificialities of Restoration heroic drama as is his prose from the cut and thrust of Restoration comedy, which had learnt so much from the pamphleteers of the Revolution.

Working under a censorship, Milton had to express himself with great care. I suggested above possible overtones in an apparently innocuous passage like 'I sing . . . unchanged'.[6] The lines occur immediately before Milton appeals to 'fit audience . . . though few' (*P.L.* VII. 24–31), as

---

[1] Eliot, p. 19.
[2] C. and F., p. 457; cf. appendix 1 below.
[3] Cf. p. 417 below.
[4] See p. 410 below.
[5] Adams, p. 199.
[6] See pp. 238, 365 above, p. 477 below.

though to alert his more discerning readers. Milton knew all about censorship – not only from attacking it in *Areopagitica,* but possibly from exercising it himself under the Commonwealth; certainly from seeing it in opera-
tion and taking part in discussions about it.[1] Not being able to say certain
things directly Milton would expect his readers – at least the fit readers,
however few – to be alert to hints, to allusions for which we have to strain
our ears to-day, to analogies, to perhapses.[2] It is possible that I have
imagined interpretations which were not in Milton's mind at all. Suggestions of this kind can hardly be proven, any more than hypotheses about
numerological or structural patterns in *Paradise Lost.* But my argument
stands or falls as a whole, and the evidence seems to me to be cumulative.
It could do no harm if readers of the epic were alert to the dangerous
world in which Milton lived and had to write.

Critics have made fun of the censor who was worried by the reference in
Paradise Lost to an eclipse which 'with fear of change /Perplexes monarchs'
(I. 594–9). They are right in that this was the least of reasons for wishing to
censor the epic; but they are wrong if they forget that contemporary
opinion was with the censor. The younger Alexander Gil suggested in
1632 that eclipses 'may portend events upon earth'.[3] Chamberlayne's
Angliae Notitia in 1669 pointed out that the eclipse of 29 May 1630,
Charles II's birthday, had been a 'sad presage' that his power 'should for
some time be eclipsed'.[4] This idea followed naturally from the doctrine of
Hermeticists and others: if the sun was the source of life and energy, its
eclipse naturally boded ill.[5]

The eclipses of 1652 and 1654 gave rise to much speculation and alarm.
'Many did fear/ That Doomsday it was nigh.'[6] *The Glorious Rising of the 5
Monarch* was 'deduced from the eclipse of the sun' by one pamphleteer of
1652. Culpeper believed that it foretold the downfall of monarchy everywhere: 'Your sceptre's gone, democracy takes place.'[7] Comets similarly
had for centuries been regarded as portents prognosticating woe. In 1643
a preacher was still telling the House of Commons that the Christian
world was being influenced by the comet of 1618, the year in which the
Thirty Years War began. Rushworth quotes suggestions that the comet of

---

[1] See pp. 64–6, 217–19 above.
[2] See pp. 408–9 below.
[3] Gil (1632), p. 21.
[4] Chamberlayne, p. 175.
[5] W. Scott, I, pp. 417–19; Labrousse, p. 40; cf. pp. 325–8 above.
[6] (Anon.), *The Late Eclipse unclasped* (1652); cf. K. V. Thomas (1971), pp. 299–300. See Labrousse,
passim, for the alarm all over Europe.
[7] Culpeper (1652), p. 20; Lilly, *Annus* (1652), pp. 27, 33, 41–2; (1653), Sig. B 3–3v.

1618 boded especially ill for England.[1] The comets of 1664 and 1665 raised renewed apprehensions.[2] John Wilson's *The Cheats* of 1663, Dryden's *Annus Mirabilis* of 1665 and Sprat's *History of the Royal Society* in 1667 were concerned to refute just such popular beliefs as the censor thought might be hinted at in Milton's lines.

Milton himself had written in 1641: 'Let the astrologer be dismayed at the portentous blaze of comets and impressions on the air, as foretelling troubles and changes to states.'[3] The bark in *Lycidas,* plausibly identified with the Laudian church, had been 'built in th'eclipse, and rigged with curses dark'.[4] In *The History of Britain* he lists comets among other natural events which foreboded the Norman Conquest.[5] Keats got the point of the lines that worried the censor: 'How noble and collected an indignation against kings!' They 'should have had power to pull that feeble animal Charles from his bloody throne'.[6]

Richard Baxter was told by a licencer that censorship was exercised against an author's reputation as well as against a specific book.[7] That is no doubt why the first edition of *Paradise Lost* was not registered over Milton's full name; at least one early title-page attributes the poem merely to 'J.M.' His references to England, his analysis of the failure of the Revolution, could not be direct. But to imagine, as some scholars do, that there is something demeaning in the suggestion that *Paradise Lost, Paradise Regained* and *Samson Agonistes* are related to Milton's personal problems or to the problems of the English Revolution, is totally to misconceive both Milton and the situation in England after 1660. It is the sort of mistake which could be made only by readers who have never experienced political commitment or attempted to produce creative writing under a hostile censorship, and who have too little imagination to make good this lack. They might consider the difference in tone and content between the official letters which Andrew Marvell wrote as Member of Parliament to his Hull constituents, and the letters to his nephew William Popple which deal in a more relaxed way with the same events. Once we have a clue to Marvell's attitude from the Popple correspondence, nuances of meaning reveal themselves in the bland text of his official reports. Marvell's political

---

[1] Rushworth, I, pp. 8–10.

[2] Greenhill, p. 13; Burnet (1897), I, pp. 389–90; cf. *C. and C.*, p. 272; Hayden, pp. 120, 140. For a refreshing reappraisal of the whole subject see McKeon, chapters 5, 7 and 8, pp. 158, 226, 231.

[3] *C.P.W.*, I, p. 585.

[4] See pp. 51–2 above, and Berkeley, pp. 63, 146–8. Was this the eclipse of 1630?

[5] *C.P.W.*, V, p. 394.

[6] Wittreich (1970), p. 556.

[7] Baxter (1696), p. 123.

poems of the Restoration period circulated in manuscript: he took considerable pains to preserve his anonymity when he published *The Rehearsal Transpros'd* and *An Account of the Growth of Popery and Arbitrary Government in England.*[1]

Nearer our own day, such critics might read the letters of Chekhov, in which we see this great writer, much less politically committed than Milton, writhing and wriggling in his attempts to say as much as he possibly can of what he must communicate if he is to be true to himself and his art. Sometimes he made concessions, of the same sort as when Milton decided to omit the anti-Trinitarian heresies from *Paradise Lost.* Sometimes Chekhov haggled with the censor, as Milton did about eclipses. Some works could not be published at all. In Milton's case the *De Doctrina,* the sonnets to Fairfax, Cromwell, Vane, and one of those to Cyriack Skinner had to be excluded from the 1673 volume of poems. In 1670 *The History of Britain* had to appear without 'some passages' which the censor thought 'too sharp against the clergy'. This must have added to the pleasure with which Milton published in the following year, in *Samson Agonistes,* unkind remarks about the Philistine priests, for which there is no Biblical warrant.[2] Four years later government censorship prevented Milton publishing his state letters with *Epistolae Familiares.*[3] We might indeed ask ourselves why *Paradise Lost* did not appear until 1667, though Aubrey suggests that it was finished by 1663. The Plague and the Fire of London may be invoked as explanations; but why was it not published in 1664 or early 1665? It is only a guess, but it seems to me not an implausible guess, that in 1663–5 greater vigilance was exercised against former revolutionaries than in the year of Clarendon's fall and the rise of the Cabal. Milton could only hint at anti-Trinitarianism, mortalism and polygamy in *Paradise Lost.*[4]

Always the possibility of censorship was there: as Professor Ricks suggests, the indirection which it forced on Milton may paradoxically have stimulated his vast imaginative resourcefulness, so that he wrung a peculiar strength from this apparent weakness.[5] His allusions are never explicit, but for the alert reader they do not need to be. Take for instance the phrase 'Sons of Belial'. It was frequently used during the Civil War to describe Cavaliers – by Stephen Marshall, John Goodwin and many others.[6] It had

---

[1] For similar difficulties on the opposite political wing, cf. Cowley (1973), p. 189.
[2] *C.P.W.,* V, p. 412. See p. 438 below.
[3] *C.P.W.,* V, p. 471.
[4] A reference to 'wide-ranging pestilence' was added in the second edition (XI. 485–7). Rudrum is good on the discretion which had to be exercised (pp. 19–23).
[5] Cf. pp. 355–6, 404–5 above, and p. 462 below.
[6] G. W. Whiting, pp. 223 seq.; Manning, p. 252. Cf. *C.P.W.,* III, p. 394.

a considerable history as a pejorative epithet – preferably for somebody roisterous and boisterous. William Ames, for instance, said that the enemies of the Puritans included 'lewd persons and all sons of Belial'. Joseph Mede had spoken of the Senior Fellow of Christ's College as 'a son of Belial'.[1] Milton used the phrase in 1642 for a drunkard or a swearer, and in 1643 to describe 'the draffe of men, for whom no liberty is pleasing but unbridled and vagabond lust without pale or partition'.[2] Everyone would understand his reference to Belial reigning 'in courts and palaces', and 'in temples and at altars, when the priest/ Turns atheist'; as well as to 'the sons/ Of Belial, flown with insolence and wine' – the neo-Cavalier bullies who came out 'when night/ Darkens the streets', to commit 'riot, . . . injury and outrage' (I. 494–502). On the other side Matthew Griffith argued that in 1 Samuel 10:27 those who despised the King were called 'Sons of Belial', and that the Prayer Book described the regicides as 'cruel men, sons of Belial'.[3]

One of Milton's ways of drawing attention to a remark upon which he wished the fit reader to ponder was by using words like 'perhaps', 'what if', 'some say'. Chaos is 'the womb of nature and perhaps her grave' – for Chaos may return again if Satan, Sin and Death prevail (P.L. II. 911).

> What if the earth
> Be but the shadow of heaven, and things therein
> Each to other like, more than on earth is thought?

Raphael asked. He must surely have known the answer to his question, though he covered himself by saying that 'perhaps' it was 'not lawful to reveal . . . the secrets of another world' (V. 569–76). Adam in his turn told Raphael that the origin of the universe 'may no less perhaps avail us known' (VII. 85–97). 'The parsimonious emmet' was a 'pattern of just equality perhaps' in a republic (VII. 487). Milton had been able to make the point more directly in The Ready and Easy Way.[4] 'Every star perhaps a world/ Of destined habitation', sang the heavenly host, hedging their astronomical bets (VII. 621), as Raphael did with 'what if' and 'perhaps' in the next book (VIII. 122–52; cf. III. 588–90), and as the poet himself did with 'some say' (twice) to introduce the changes in the solar system consequent on the Fall (X. 668–70). God himself, Raphael told Adam,

---

[1] Sprunger, p. 97; Peile, p. 183.
[2] C.P.W., I, p. 893; II, p. 225; cf. C.M., VI, p. 68.
[3] M. Griffith, p. 105.
[4] C.M., VI, p. 122. Cf. Milton's sarcasms at Salmasius's refuge behind 'perhaps' (C.P.W., IV, p. 408).

> the fabric of his heavens
> Hath left to their disputes, perhaps to move
> His laughter at their quaint opinions wide
>
> (VIII. 75-7)

– one of the passages often cited to suggest that Milton cannot possibly expect us to respect the God he depicts. The trumpet which was blown in heaven before God announced the expulsion of Adam and Eve from Paradise was 'heard in Oreb since perhaps', when God descended to deliver the ten commandments to Moses, 'and perhaps once more/ To sound at general doom' (XI. 74-6, cf. IX. 139). One of Milton's most intriguing fusions of classical with Biblical myth suggests that Eurynome was 'the wide-/ Encroaching Eve perhaps' (X. 581-2). In *Samson Agonistes*, after the scathing denunciation of 'unjust tribunals under change of times/ And condemnation of the ungrateful multitude', the chorus continues

> If these they escape, perhaps in poverty
> With sickness and disease thou bowest them down.
>
> (695-8)

Finally, the Son of God in *Paradise Regained* found himself led into the wilderness 'to what intent / I learn not yet, perhaps I need not know' (I. 292-3). Readers who pondered over that surprising 'perhaps' would be given an advance idea of what the brief epic was about.[1]

One piece of (I suspect) fairly deliberate mystification in *Paradise Lost* concerns Milton's invocations of the Muse, of Urania. On the surface it sounds as though the poet is invoking the Holy Ghost, and this is no doubt what he intended unwary readers of the poem to think. But in the *De Doctrina* he specifically rejects invocation of the Holy Ghost, to whom he denies divinity, so he is hardly likely to have invoked him himself in *Paradise Lost*. His Muse is the Father, says Kelley. No, Urania is the third Sephira, the intelligence of the Kaballah, says Saurat; the Logos, the Son before he is begotten, says Robins.[2] The only importance of this little academic bicker is to show how successfully Milton concealed what he was up to, by deliberately leaving several meanings open. Urania occurs in Spenser, and for Du Bartas was the Muse of Christian poetry (VII. 1-7n.). 'My Muse ... is Urania and her song's divine', sang Samuel Pordage six years before *Paradise Lost* was published.[3]

---

[1] See p. 314 above, 424 below. Does the Oreb 'perhaps' hint doubt about the decalogue?

[2] Kelley (1935), pp. 231-4; Saurat, p. 240; Robins, pp. 159-73.

[3] S. Pordage, Sig. b.8. Urania appears with Melpomene, Erato and Clio in Marshall's unfortunate engraving of Milton in the 1645 *Poems*. Cf. Drummond, 'Urania, or Spirituall Poems' in 1619 and Samuel Austin's *Urania or the Heavenly Muse : being a true story of mans fall and redemption* (1629). Cf. p. 133 above.

Perhaps Fludd can help us to identify the 'holy light' which Milton invokes. In prophecy, Fludd thought, an inward illumination may be produced that is comparable to the concentration of formerly diffuse light into the centre of the sun, which took place on the fourth day of Creation. When the rays of the soul are collected in his way, the nature of the inward man is reduced to simplicity. There will be little distance between him and the divine.[1]

> So much the rather thou, celestial light,
> Shine inward, and the mind through all her powers
> Irradiate, there plant eyes. All mist from thence
> Purge and disperse, that I may see and tell
> Of things invisible to mortal sight.
>   (*P.L.* III. 51-5)

Milton's theory of inspiration is thus linked with his theory of the cycle of energy within the created universe.[2]

'Inspiration – a dangerous word', the Royalist Sir William Davenant called it, 'which many have of late successfully used.' Hobbes, in his answer to Davenant, joined in condemning those who claim 'to speak by inspiration, like a bagpipe'.[3] Such critics were not thinking only of poetic inspiration. They were thinking also of the claims to inspiration of uneducated sectarian preachers, those who held – with Milton – that a craftsman endowed with the grace of God could preach better than a university-trained scholar lacking grace. The Son of God in *Paradise Regained* brings the two together, as Milton brought them together. Sectaries claiming that God spoke to them direct were regarded as subversive revolutionaries in post-Restoration England: Thomas Sprat, future bishop, thought that it was no mean part of the Royal Society's task to expose their claims to inspiration. Davenant's 'dangerous word' fell out of favour in the neo-classical world of the Augustans. Inspiration as the essence of poetry had to be picked up again by the Romantics in the next great upheaval of the French Revolution. Then we get Blake confident that 'to prove that there is no such thing as inspiration' will be 'particularly interesting to blockheads', and praising Milton because he 'cast aside from poetry all that is not inspiration'.[4] The young Wordsworth acclaimed Milton's politics, and saw himself as a dedicated poet: 'by our own spirits are we deified'.

The romantic in Milton is fascinating because he did not entirely

---

[1] Josten (1964), p. 330.
[2] See p. 328 above. Samuel Pordage no doubt drew on the same tradition when he wrote 'Thou Eternal Everlasting Day!/ Illuminate my darker soul, I pray' (p. 310; cf. pp. 123-5).
[3] Davenant (1971), pp. 22, 49.
[4] W. Blake, pp. 986, 546. ' "Mere Enthusiasm" is the all in all' (p. 985).

succumb to it – rather less so than some of the minor Spenserians.[1] We are meant to disapprove of Adam's great cry to Eve in Book IX, leading up to his choice of death with her rather than Paradise without her. Yet the poetry speaks for the genuineness of Milton's emotion, and must always have given the lie to the poet's repudiation of Adam's action. One part of him applauds Adam's decision whilst another part reprimands him. It is easy for us, looking through the rose-tinted spectacles of romanticism, to assume that to lose all for love is right, to quote E. M. Forster's hope that he would have the courage to betray his country rather than his friend. But to Milton it appeared rather more serious than that. A better analogy would be a man in the French resistance movement during World War II (or in South Africa to-day) who had to choose between his wife and his cause. Milton did not feel about his cause as Forster felt (or pretended to feel) about his country. Paradise alone, or the world with Eve: what a choice to be faced with! What a God to face Adam with it! Can such a God be justified to men? (It is rather like J. J. Rousseau undertaking to justify the chains in which civilization had bound men.) God can surely be justified only if the ultimate object is to obliterate the distinction, to have both Eve and Paradise, when men become Sons of God in the new heaven and earth, when God becomes all in all.

Satan can express a similar romantic heroism which appealed to the generation of Blake and Byron and Shelley more perhaps than to Milton's contemporaries, more than Milton wished it to appeal to himself. It is an open question whether we are meant to admire Tennyson's Ulysses when he says:

> Though much is taken, much abides; and though
> We are not now that strength which in old days
> Moved earth and heaven; that which we are, we are;
> One equal temper of heroic hearts,
> Made weak by time and fate, but strong in will
> To strive, to seek, to find, and not to yield.

We are certainly not meant to admire Satan when, in similar circumstances, he asked:

> What though the field be lost:
> All is not lost; the unconquerable will,
> And study of revenge, immortal hate,
> And courage never to submit or yield:
> And what is else not to be overcome? . . .
>
> The mind is its own place and in itself
> Can make a heaven of hell, a hell of heaven. . . .
> Better to reign in hell than serve in heaven.

---

[1] Grundy, p. 48.

Milton had seen too much revolutionary romanticism, in Parliamentarian generals or in Ranter and Fifth Monarchist anarchists. He was more impressed by Abdiel's obstinacy in resistance, by Michael's insistence on 'deeds to thy knowledge answerable, add faith/ Add virtue, patience, temperance and love.' This was not the romantic self-realization of the Byronic generation. It was the courage of constancy in defeat, un-flamboyant, day-to-day, unheroic, but steadfast to eternity. Milton's revolution had been defeated, and he could see no forces in society capable of reviving it. But that was not a reason for giving up the fight in this world, for postponing hope until the after-life.

Here freedom and necessity intersect again. A man can write great poetry only if he is divinely inspired. Milton could not will the Muse's visits: he could only pray for them.[1] Yet it remained his duty, as it always had been, to work hard in preparing himself to be the Muse's mouthpiece. The long years of self-education in the thirties were no more wasted than the left-handed prose writings of the forties and fifties.

In *Paradise Lost* Milton appears to envisage the possibility that mankind is entering into a new dark age, in which all that God's servants can do is, like the Waldensians, to keep the truth pure and hand it on. 'They also serve who only stand and wait.' But we must always be alert and ready to seize opportunities of serving more actively if they should arise. In *Paradise Regained* the perfect man, in *Samson Agonistes* a more ordinary sinful man, held on until their opportunity came.

---

[1] Summers, *passim*.

Chapter 30

Paradise Regained

'All men are Sons of God.'
   Milton, *Paradise Regained*, IV. 520. The words are Satan's.

Thomas Ellwood claimed that he was responsible for giving Milton the idea of writing *Paradise Regained*. 'Thou hast said much here of Paradise Lost, but what hast thou to say of Paradise Found?' Milton 'made me no answer, but sate some time in a muse'. Next time they met (apparently) Milton showed Ellwood *Paradise Regained,* and said, 'This is owing to you, for you put it into my head by the question you put to me at Chalfont, which before I had not thought of.'[1] Milton I fear was being ironical at Ellwood's expense. Whether or not his question set Milton on writing the brief epic, Ellwood clearly had failed to grasp the point of *Paradise Lost,* or to appreciate what Milton intended by 'a Paradise within thee, happier far'. Adam had a profound sense of responsibility for the tragedy of human history, just as Milton felt responsible for the failure of the English Revolution. For Ellwood, perfectibility was attainable on earth by abstention from political action, by contracting out of history. To Milton this must have seemed shallow, almost frivolous. He was totally involved in history; the good man must play a full part in the world. By 1660 Milton would have criticized most proponents of the third culture, whether Ranters or Quakers, on these grounds: they ignored the world as it really is, in all its brutality: they were fundamentally unserious, as self-regarding as a modern hippie.

Paradise Regained, no less than *Paradise Lost,* is about how men should live in the real world, not ignoring or flying from the unpleasantness of

---

[1] Ellwood, pp. 199–200. If anybody wanted to support Parker's idea that *Paradise Regained* was written before the Restoration, the speed with which Milton appears to have produced it might be used as an argument. But it is not clear how long the interval between the two meetings was.

413

post-Restoration England. By contrast with the cosmic grandeur of *Paradise Lost,* the brief epic is bleakly simple. Jesus, after being baptized by John the Baptist and hearing God's voice acclaim him as his beloved Son, goes into the wilderness to meditate on his future course of action. Here he is subjected to a series of temptations. These take the form of Satan offering short cuts, instant political solutions to Israel's problems, trying to lure him to call for divine intervention to overcome all obstacles. Jesus's refusal, his rejection of the miraculous, stresses his humanity: where Adam and Eve fell by aspiring to be gods, the Son of God triumphs by staying human. The 'perfect man' remains man.[1]

Jesus is subject to human passions and anxieties. He dreams of food when he is hungry (II. 264-5). Satan found him 'Firm/ To the utmost of mere man, both wise and good,/ Not more': his achievements are not superhuman (IV. 534-7). ('Mere' in the seventeenth century could mean 'essential': Jesus sums up the human qualities, as perhaps the Son of God subsumes all the elect.[2]) The temptation in the wilderness, Boehme said, was 'the combat which Adam should have undergone in Paradise'. Or, as Milton put it, what was lost 'by one man's disobedience' was recovered 'by one *man's* firm obedience, fully tried' (I. 2-4: my italics). Jesus 'avenged/ Supplanted Adam, and . . . regained lost Paradise'. 'The incarnation could not have done it alone', wrote Boehme; for Milton the Son's successful resistance to temptation is more important than the incarnation, and the crucifixion is merely the last example of his heroic fortitude.[3] His success where Adam failed was the triumph of reason over passion. This may in itself throw some light on Milton's choice of subject. Neither the incarnation nor the passion could be seen as reason's triumph. Moral integrity, the overcoming of temptation, are more important than vicarious sacrifice, than sacramentalism.

The wilderness in which the action of *Paradise Regained* takes place recalls that which Adam and Eve entered at the end of *Paradise Lost*. The lost garden is rediscovered in the wilderness.[4] Milton's friend Sir Henry Vane represented the kingdom of Christ by the figure of Jesus in the wilderness, and Milton himself many times depicted the chosen people in the desert, torn between Egypt and Canaan. On at least one occasion he used the Israelites' forty years in the wilderness as an image of the English

---

[1] Bouchard, pp. 165-6; cf. Weber, pp. 82-5.
[2] I owe this point to John Andrews of the Folger Library. Cf. pp. 303-5 above.
[3] Boehme added the passion to the temptation in the wilderness (Everyman, pp. 114, 132; cf. p. 147); J. M. Evans, pp. 92, 102-4.
[4] Miner (1974), pp. 50, 270-2.

Civil War.[1] For Erbery and Vane England was a desert in which God's people were 'be-wildernessed'.[2] As in *Paradise Lost* the Israelites learnt constitutional government in the wilderness (XII. 224–7), so in *Paradise Regained* the Son of God made use of the wilderness as a place for re-thinking, for casting the balance, from which he emerged ready for action. Eden, the Paradise within, had been 'raised in the waste wilderness' (*P.R.* I. 7).

Paradise Regained, like *Comus,* is a poetic exercise in dialectic, reminiscent of Cambridge disputations. But what exactly is the question in dispute? One view is that the temptations set before Jesus are concerned with the way in which the kingdom which is the church should be governed.[3] This links *Paradise Regained* with the pamphlets of 1659 against force and hire in church affairs, rather than with *The Ready and Easy Way* of 1660, which is about politics. Yet this does not narrow the poem's scope as much as might appear. For the orthodox in seventeenth-century England, the church was co-extensive with the state. For most sectaries, the church was limited to the elect, but this made it imperative to set it free from political control. Separation of church and state is a continuing theme of Milton's later writings. 'External force should never be used in Christ's kingdom', he wrote in the *De Doctrina.* 'The weapons of those who fight under Christ are only spiritual weapons.' Christ rules 'by those things which, in the opinion of the world, are the weakest of all'.[4] Winstanley had said 'man's recovery will be to reject outward objects and to close with the spirit of truth, life and peace within, preferring this kingdom within before the outward kingdom. . . . It was said of Jesus Christ that when the Tempter came to him he found nothing in him, that is, Jesus Christ had not an imaginary covetous power in him to seek a kingdom or happiness without himself in those objects of pleasure, riches and honours of the world, but preferred the kingdom within him before that without him.'[5]

For Milton as for many of the radicals, the most important question about the kingdom of God was when it would appear. Milton's attitude towards this question changed. The 'shortly expected king' of 1641 had turned by 1649 into a 'kingdom which we pray incessantly may come soon', to the destruction of all tyrants. By 1651 this coming is something which we must, more vaguely, 'look for'.[6] By 1659 Milton was emphasizing

---

[1] Vane (1662), p. 2; *C.P.W.,* III, p. 580; cf. Fixler, p. 222. See pp. 206–7 above.
[2] *W.T.U.D.,* pp. 193, 195.
[3] Schultz (1955), p. 223 and *passim*; cf. *C.P.W.,* III, p. 509.
[4] *Ibid.,* VI, p. 436; cf. the conclusion of *Paradise Lost.*
[5] Sabine, p. 494.
[6] *C.P.W.,* III, p. 256; IV, p. 428.

that Christ's 'spiritual kingdom' is 'able, without worldly force, to subdue all the powers and kingdoms of this world, which are upheld by outward force only'.[1] In the *De Doctrina* Milton is cautious and vague about dating: the time of Christ's coming cannot be foreknown, but it will be followed by the reign of the saints.[2] In *The Ready and Easy Way* Milton held out the possibility that the balanced constitution which he there sketched might last 'even to the coming of our true and rightful and only to be expected King'. It is difficult to suppose that even he believed that his ramshackle makeshift constitution would last very long.[3]

After 1660 the kingdom of Christ was not quite so confidently expected in the near future: Milton like other millenarians had to rethink and re-date. Hence the rejection in *Paradise Regained* of premature political solutions: they were Satanic temptations. The poem, it has been suggested, contains among other things a rebuke to Fifth Monarchist activists for their impatience.[4] Milton's pragmatic approach to politics, his Oliverian refusal to be wedded and glued to forms of government, derive from the fluid conception of Christ's kingdom. This was not an Utopian model constitution: it was rather a state of mind, not fixed once for all: 'those unwritten or at least unconstraining laws of virtuous education, religious and civil nurture, ... the bonds and ligaments of the Commonwealth'. Hence 'Christ's kingdom could not be set up without pulling down' that of Charles I, once the latter had resorted to violence 'to uphold an antichristian hierarchy'.[5]

Yet *Paradise Regained* is also an example of Milton's dialectical approach. Satan is not the rhetorical deceiver of *Paradise Lost*, but one half of the poet talking to the other half. His arguments are nearly always rational, and he defends many views which Milton had at one time held. It was Satan who was convinced that the Son of God aimed at an earthly kingdom, just as Muggleton thought that 'it was the reason of man that took Christ . . . up into an exceeding high mountain and showed him all the kingdoms of the world.'[6]

Jesus is an intellectual, a potential leader facing political decisions. Military action had attracted him at one time:

---

[1] *C.M.*, VI, p. 20; cf. pp. 281–2 above.
[2] *C.P.W.*, VI, pp. 614–27.
[3] *C.M.*, VI, p. 133.
[4] Fixler, pp. 96–7, 120, 156–7, 161, 171, 206, 214; Tuve, pp. 63–5, 69; Schultz (1955), p. 231; cf. Weber, pp. 81, 108, Vane, quoted on p. 428 below, and p. 284 above.
[5] *C.P.W.*, II, p. 526; III, p. 536; Fixler, *passim*.
[6] Muggleton (1764), p. 37. For Muggleton reason was the devil.

> victorious deeds
> Flamed in my heart, heroic acts, one while
> To rescue Israel from the Roman yoke,
> Thence to subdue and quell o'er all the earth
> Brute violence and proud tyrannic power,
> Till truth were freed, and equity restored.
>
> (P.R. I. 215–20)

'Now, now, for sure, deliverance is at hand', the disciples told one another after Jesus's baptism (II. 35). These were the dreams of the English revolutionaries in the forties and early fifties, that the overthrow of the Norman Yoke in England would lead to international revolution. As late as 1651 Milton had said that Christ 'made all the more possible . . . our worthy struggle for freedom'. He 'never failed to preserve the heart of a liberator'.[1] Satan even tried to meet the Son of God's rejection of political ambition by arguing

> If kingdoms move thee not, let move thee zeal
> And duty, . . . duty to free
> Thy country from her heathen servitude.
>
> (III. 171–6)

The Son of God rejected the kingdoms of the earth when Satan offered them: he did not repudiate the possibility of an earthly kingdom. He rejected Satan's proffered banquet for the same reason, but did not refuse food when provided by good angels.[2] Similarly the temptation to turn stones into bread was made by a poor old man in terms that would have appealed to the ideals of the reformers of the forties: 'us relieve/ With food, whereof we wretched seldom taste' (I. 344–5).

Satan's argument that the prophecies could not be realized 'without means used' (III. 356) – i.e. without conventional political action – would also in the forties and early fifties have seemed acceptable to Milton. The discussion on 'the use of means' was familiar to Puritans.[3] Satan tried to lure the Son of God into premature or ill-conceived political action – for instance by allying with Parthia to overthrow Rome – as Cromwell allied with France against Spain. ('By him thou shalt regain, without him not' – as any of Oliver's councillors might have said – III. 371.) Satan rightly recognized that this was a stronger temptation than Belial's more directly sensual lures. Third world countries face similar problems to-day.

Milton had learnt a good deal about foreign policy in the sixteen-fifties:

---

[1] *C.P.W.*, IV, pp. 374–5. On all this see Rivers, pp. 98–100.
[2] See p. 425 below.
[3] Cf. Hill (Penguin, 1972), pp. 219–32.

compare his reference to embassies which were

> But tedious waste of time to sit and hear
> So many hollow compliments and lies,
> Outlandish flatteries.
> (P.R. IV. 123–5)

('Outlandish' – foreign – is more appropriately spoken by the Commonwealth's Latin Secretary than by the Son of God.) One reason for the
failure of the English Revolution was the unfavourable international
situation in the fifties: the shortcomings of the English people were com-
plemented by the survival of international Antichrist. For both reasons
Milton had lost confidence in the use of state power to achieve international
revolutionary ends. *Paradise Regained* suggests that he now thought pre-
occupation with foreign alliances had been a temptation to which Cromwell's government had succumbed – unlike Samuel Pepys and those in his
circle who, at about the time Milton was writing, admired the brave things
Oliver did 'and made all the neighbour princes fear him'.[1]

'Liberty', Milton had said in 1654, 'is best achieved not by the sword,
but by a life rightly undertaken and rightly conducted.' In 1656 he rejected
the 'force and strength' of 'mutton-heads' who 'can powerfully butt down
cities and towns'.[2] Michael contemptuously dismissed 'great conquerors'
(*P.L.* XI. 689–99; cf. XII. 386–95). In *Paradise Regained* the Son of God
declared 'that cumbersome luggage of war' to be 'argument/ Of human
weakness rather than of strength' (III. 400–2). Battles and leagues were
'plausible to the world, to me worth naught' (III. 392–3). It was premature
to attempt a war of liberation. 'As for those captive tribes, themselves were
they/ Who wrought their own captivity.' They – like the people of Catholic
Europe – must repent and turn to God before he will bring them back to
freedom. (The reference to Catholic Europe is almost explicit: ' a race . . .
distinguishable scarce/ From Gentiles but by circumcision vain' (i.e. by
baptism); 'and God with idols in their worship joined' – III. 423–6.)
Meanwhile the Son of God decided that it was both more human and more
heavenly to 'make persuasion do the work of fear': only the stubborn were
to be subdued (I. 221–2). No more Protestant crusades! God's people
were beleaguered even in England: they could no longer think of using
state power to fulfil their international obligations.

Milton's interpolations in the Biblical story include the banqueting
scene, the storm scene, use of the temptation of the pinnacle as an

---

[1] Pepys, *Diary*, 12 July 1667; cf. 19 February 1664, 12 April 1665, 8 September 1667.
[2] *C.P.W.*, IV, pp. 553, 624; *C.M.*, XII, pp. 80–1. Cf. pp. 194–5, 210, 362–3 above.

identity-test for the Son of God (IV. 538–40), and Satan's fall. But his failure to mention the crucifixion more than incidentally is also a startling departure from orthodoxy in a poem about the recovery of Paradise for all mankind (I. 3). In the temptation of the pinnacle Satan employed the violence which Jesus had abjured. It was preceded by the thunder and lightning of the storm – another of Milton's inventions – which may recall the persecutions and Royalist propaganda attacks of the Restoration decade. The final scene is so abrupt, so elliptic, that many interpretations of it are possible. Here is how Boehme used it:

'The human property in body and soul in the person of Christ had ... cast itself into the resignation out of its selfhood into God's mercy, and stood still in the resignation, viz. in the divine will, and would not cast himself down or do anything but what God alone did by it, and said to the devil, "It is written, Thou shalt not tempt the Lord thy God", which is as much as if he had said ... the creature ... must be God's instrument, with which he works and does only what he pleases.'[1]

Milton's version of the scene recalls *Paradise Lost*: the Son of God, like Adam and Eve, was 'sufficient to have stood though free to fall'. The miracle came to Messiah after self-discipline and self-abnegation had been attained. His passivity in this temptation – indeed in all the temptations – can be related to Milton's 'They also serve who only stand and wait.' It recalls the Lady in *Comus*, and Abdiel in *Paradise Lost*, just as the rejection of false glory recalls *Lycidas* and the sonnets to Fairfax and Cromwell as well as *Samson Agonistes*. In the *De Doctrina* Milton quotes 1. Corinthians 2: 'since he himself [Christ] suffered with patience when he was tempted, he is able to come to the help of those who are tempted.'[2] The Son of God resisted those temptations to which politicians are especially exposed: he is the model for those of the elect who will form the composite Son, who will ultimately come to judge the earth and to rule on earth. The miracle of the pinnacle looks forward to Christ's headship of the church: he sustains and will be sustained by the community of sons. Milton believed that the Spirit of God preferred 'before all temples th'upright heart and pure' (*P.L.* I. 17–18). In *Areopagitica* he had spoken of believers as stones from which the true temple will be built when 'all the Lord's people are become prophets'.[3] Then the Son will stand securely on the pinnacle, uplifted by

---

[1] Boehme (Everyman), pp. 115–16.

[2] *C.P.W.*, VI, p. 426.

[3] *Ibid.*, II, pp. 555–6; cf. VI, pp. 499–500. This was something of a radical Puritan commonplace, accepted for example in 1637 by the colonists of Dedham, Massachusetts (Lockridge, p. 28). Lord Brooke had attributed the view to Brownists in 1641 (quoted in *C.P.W.*, I, p. 148; cf. p. 300 above).

angels 'lest at any time /Thou chance to dash thy foot against a stone' (IV. 557–9).

Satan's fall is a remarkable invention, recalling that in Book I of *Paradise Lost*. But it also stresses the parallel between the Son's temptation and Adam's. In *Paradise Regained* Milton immediately compares Satan's fall to the Sphinx's self-destruction 'for grief and spite' once her riddle was solved. The answer to the Sphinx's riddle was: 'Man.' Is Milton telling us that Satan despaired because he discovered the same answer: 'mere man' could withstand his force as well as his fraud?[1]

As in *Paradise Lost* the Restoration ambience is clear if we remain alert. Satan is a 'dictator' – a single person like Cromwell no less than like Charles II (I. 113). Satan assumes that 'democraty' is likely to appeal to Jesus (IV. 267–71). The disciples are bewildered by the disappearance of the promised Messiah ('shortly expected King'). 'Whither is he gone?' The kings of the earth 'oppress/ Thy chosen', who long to be freed 'from their yoke' (II. 39–48). Mary refers to 'the murderous king', Herod, and she seems almost to personify the English people looking backwards after 1660: 'I to wait with patience am inured', 'recalling what remarkably had passed' (II. 76–107). Clerical tyranny is hinted at, as in *Paradise Lost,* here by reference to the Satanic conclave as a 'consistory' (I. 42 – see pp. 384, 407 above). The rulers have violated the Temple and the Law (III. 161). Satan urged that it was Messiah's 'duty to free/ Thy country from her heathen servitude' (III. 76). The Son did not deny the servitude or the duty, but 'all things are best fulfilled in their own time' (III. 182). He expected 'tribulations, injuries, insults,/ Contempts, and scorns, and snares, and violence' (III. 190–1). But 'who best/ Can suffer, best can do'. Why anyway should Satan be so anxious to overthrow his own kingdom? (III. 194–202). 'That people victor once' was 'now vile and base,/ Deservedly made vassal'.

> What wise and valiant man would seek to free
> These thus degenerate, by themselves enslaved,
> Or could of inward slaves make outward free?

Before the time comes for the Son of God 'to sit on David's throne', regeneration must spread and overshadow all the earth, 'like a tree',[2] or like the Biblical stone which grew until it 'became a great mountain and filled the whole earth', after smashing the kingdoms.[3] When all the elect are truly kings (II. 466–80), 'godlike men,/ The Holiest of Holies, and his

---

[1] I owe this point to Stanley Fish.
[2] Cf. the passages from Winstanley quoted on pp. 299, 304–5 above.
[3] Daniel 2:31–5; 4:10–11.

saints' (IV. 348–9), when the sons are all incorporated in the Son, then 'all monarchies . . . throughout the world' shall be overthrown (IV. 132–50). That is still Milton's aim. Victory comes when the Son of God overcomes Satanic violence by his moral strength. 'A fairer Paradise is founded now.' But the conclusion is not passivity. 'On thy glorious work/ Now enter and begin to save mankind' (IV. 634–5) is a call to action. The beginning of Jesus's preaching ministry is the climax of the poem, as the expulsion of Adam and Eve from Eden had been the climax of its predecessor.

These considerations may help to account for what some readers find the excessively negative attitude of Jesus in *Paradise Regained*. Milton's concept of liberty was itself rather negative.[1] But here the Son of God is rejecting, one by one, temptations which had led the English revolutionaries astray – avarice and ambition, the false politics of compromise with evil, clerical pride or ivory-tower escapism, the urge for instant solutions. In the case of the church, the all-important thing is that it should be left alone. This explains, twice over, the Son of God's dismissal of political solutions. He is rejecting antichristian tyranny over the church, whether by the Pope or by Laudian bishops or by Presbyterian consistories. Christ's kingdom is not of this world. But Milton had also learnt by the sixteen-sixties that Parliaments cannot be trusted to legislate for the church either, and this too is contained within the Son of God's rejection of politics.[2] 'The spirit of faith hath no government', Muggleton observed. 'Hence the devil could offer Christ all the kingdoms of the world.'[3] Milton's battles for liberty were in the last resort for *Christian* liberty, and he now has come to realize that his objectives are in the first resort internal, until Christ himself comes. But this is not a quietist doctrine. The kingdom of Christ is a kingdom of preaching, and its ultimate object is 'to conquer and crush his enemies'.[4] 'Who best/ Can suffer, best can do'.

Where I would differ from Schultz – on whom I have drawn a good deal in what precedes – is in his statement that in *Paradise Regained* Milton 'meant the head of the Christian church to set a pattern not primarily for the Christian layman, but for the church and its ministers'. Milton attached little significance to the distinction between clergy and laity: 'we are all equally priests in Christ.'[5] As in the pamphlets of 1659, Milton is concerned in *Paradise Regained* to ward off the self-styled ministers of any state

---

[1] See chapter 20 above.
[2] Schultz (1952), pp. 804–6; cf. Frye (1966), pp. 138–41.
[3] Muggleton (1751–3), p. 18.
[4] *C.P.W.*, VI, pp. 435–7; cf. Rivers, pp. 98–100.
[5] Schultz (1955), pp. 223, 231; *C.P.W.*, VI, p. 594; cf. II, p. 109. See also pp. 103–5 above.

church from arrogating a position of authority over other Christians. In particular he is rejecting any temporal payment for the clergy, and any ecclesiastical jurisdiction. His aim is to set a pattern for all members of Christ's kingdom, of the church.[1]

In *Paradise Regained* it is Satan who wants to know exactly who Jesus is; the Son of God himself does not ask speculative questions. He acts, or refrains from acting, and trusts in God to act through him.[2] Throughout the brief epic Satan is trying to find out in what sense Jesus is the Son of God. The phrase, he observes,

> bears no single sense;
> The Son of God I also am, or was,
> And if I was, I am; relation stands;
> All men are Sons of God.
>   (IV. 517–20)[3]

In the miracle of the pinnacle Jesus arrives at full understanding of his own nature:[4] regaining, as Milton expressed it in the *De Doctrina,* the divine understanding which he had previously possessed by means of the Father's teaching but of which he had emptied himself on taking up human nature. He was acclaimed after his baptism as 'this perfect man *by merit* called my Son' (I. 166 – my italics). The Most High tells Gabriel that Jesus is 'far abler to resist' temptation than even a good man like Job (I. 151). But until the very end of the poem his consciousness of himself is that of any potential Son of God exposed to temptation, any 'godlike man' (IV. 348).[5] Paradise was recovered 'to all mankind/ By *one man's* firm obedience' (I. 3–4 – my italics again). Christ was 'a supreme prophet', Milton tells us in the *De Doctrina.*[6] 'The mind of Christ is in . . . every believer', Milton had written;[7] 'in every wise and virtuous man' he now repeated (*P.R.* II. 468). So the conclusion of *Paradise Regained* – that Satan

> never more henceforth will dare set foot
> In Paradise to tempt –

must mean that Sons of God can rise superior to temptation.

---

[1] Lewalski, pp. 283, 410. See pp. 198–9 above.
[2] Miner (1974), pp. 272–85.
[3] In Job 1:6 Satan is numbered among the Sons of God.
[4] Fletcher compares the Lady's self-recognition in the act of recognizing Comus (lines 755–98) (A. Fletcher, p. 214).
[5] Except perhaps in II. 383–6, where Jesus appears to claim ability to perform miracles. I owe this point to Edward Weissmiller.
[6] *C.P.W.,* VI, p. 265. Cf. Martz (1964), pp. 180–3, 191; Lewalski, p. 163; Empson (1961), pp. 38, 45, 61, 83. See also *P.L.* III. 308, 313–14, and pp. 392–3 above.
[7] *C.P.W.,* I, p. 166; VI, p. 583.

> For though that seat of earthly bliss be failed,
> A fairer Paradise is founded now
> For Adam and his chosen sons. . . .
> Where they shall dwell secure, when time shall be
> Of tempter and temptation without fear.
>
> (IV. 610–17)

If men follow Jesus's example, the Fall can be reversed, as was promised at the end of *Paradise Lost*: they can on earth recover the lost internal Paradise and themselves become Sons of God. Then they will no longer need the learning of the Schools:

> God . . . sends his spirit of truth henceforth to dwell
> In pious hearts, an inward oracle
> To all truth requisite for men to know.
>
> (I. 462–4)

'Perfect man is the Son of the Father', Winstanley had said.[1] It is perhaps because this doctrine moves so close to antinomianism that Milton introduced the banqueting temptation which has perplexed critics because it is neither in Scripture nor in the commentaries (II. 337–65 and n.). Milton's object may have been to make the Son of God reject Clarkson's Ranter version of the doctrine that to the pure all things are pure.[2] The Son acknowledges his right to eat anything; but he refuses the food and drink which Satan offers. When at the end of the epic good angels provide food, Jesus eats heartily of 'fruits fetched from the tree of life' (IV. 589).[3] As in *Comus*, 'none/ But such as are good men can give good things' (701–2).

Such an approach to the poem places in proper perspective the Son of God's rejection of Athens and learning – always a worrying subject for commentators. There is no temptation of learning in the Bible. Milton, who may have noticed something like it in Quarles's *Job Militant,* went out of his way to put it into *Paradise Regained.* Learning was one of the glories of the world whose seductions Milton himself had known. The man whom his radical admirers called 'learned Mr. Milton' must have been more tempted to make an idol of learning than of anything else.[4] In *Of Education* he had hoped that learning would counteract the Fall. In *The Likeliest Means,* he spoke not 'in contempt of learning or the ministry . . . but hating the common cheats of both'.[5] Rejection of human learning was to be found in

---

[1] Sabine, pp. 114, 131–3.
[2] See pp. 313–15 above.
[3] Samuel Pordage's Pilgrim enjoyed a 'heavenly banquet' of fruits from the same tree (p. 265).
[4] Pope, p. 67; Rajan (1967), p. 63; cf. pp. 226–7 above.
[5] *C.M.,* VI, p. 96.

the Familist tradition and in Boehme; it was shared by William Dell, Anna Trapnel, John Reeve, Andrew Marvell, Henry Stubbe, John and Samuel Pordage among many others.[1] Milton had in mind contemporary controversies about mechanic preaching and the universities. The learning of Oxford and Cambridge was irrelevant to the church: on this all the radicals insisted. 'Human learning hath its place among human things', declared William Dell. But it 'hath no place in Christ's kingdom'. This was a specific attack on those university divines who argued that human learning is necessary for the guardians of orthodoxy. Almost every defender of learning soon found himself defending tithes, since Oxford and Cambridge colleges depended financially on impropriations. Milton, in company with all educational reformers, indignantly insisted that learning did not depend on a university-trained priesthood, nor on tithes; he certainly had no wish to see a clerical caste maintained by tithes to defend orthodoxy against heretics like himself. Although in the *De Doctrina* and *The Likeliest Means* Milton envisaged ministers of sorts, this does not mean that logic and rhetoric are necessary to preaching.[2]

But *Paradise Regained* is about something far more fundamental than controversies about university teaching. The learned and cultivated Parliamentarians had won all the intellectual battles, but in 1660 they had lost the war. Milton had routed Salmasius, and in *Eikonoklastes* he had exposed monarchy; but kingship came back in 1660, opposed (in print) almost single-handed by Milton/Abdiel. Rational arguments were not enough. Moral commitment was in the last resort more important. This is the context in which we must set the Son of God's hostility to learning, his emphasis on faith rather than knowledge. *All* men can have faith: the learning of the educated is nothing worth unless it is used to further God's cause. Abstract political speculation had merely divided the radicals during the Revolution. The Son, like Samson, follows 'strong motions' wherever they lead, without questioning: 'perhaps I need not know' (I. 290–2).

Paradise Regained's attitude to learning is really very conventional.[3] Bacon for instance had argued that knowledge is 'to be accepted of with caution and distinction', 'to be limited by religion and to be referred to use and action'.[4] Classical learning is not essential to salvation. If it were,

---

[1] Rutherford (1648), pp. 45–7; Stoudt, p. 156; Reeve (*Sacred Remains*, 1706), p. 69; Marvell (1927), I, p. 11; Stubbe (1659), pp. 87–106; J. Pordage (1776), p. v; S. Pordage, pp. 210–11, 236. Cf. C. Webster (1975), pp. 172–8.
[2] Schultz (1955), pp. 77–80, 91, 194, 218; for Dell see *C. and C.*, p. 138 and chapter 5 *passim*.
[3] Cf., for instance, Henry Vaughan's rejection of profane poetry in the Preface to *Silex Scintillans* (1655) and John Collop's preference for the Bible over the classics (pp. 108–11).
[4] Bacon, III, p. 218.

how will the unlearned get to heaven? Dell and other radicals asked. Those who claim that learning is essential for preaching are wolves more interested in tithes than in true learning. Or they self-indulgently enjoy themselves with classical studies (or astronomy, for that matter),[1] instead of getting on with their proper job: one moral of the temptation of learning is rejection of the merely contemplative for the active life.

Satan offers learning as a source of pleasure, as a way to wealth, rank, fame: almost to positions of emolument and the contempt of the vulgar. In reply the Son of God praises Socrates, who was interested in knowledge for its usefulness, not for its material advantages. This links up with the speeches of Raphael and Michael in *Paradise Lost*: for Christians learning is desirable only as an adjunct to good living, not as an end in itself. It is for action.[2] Academic speculation and disputation are at best self-indulgence, at worst positively harmful. In *Paradise Regained* the restless buzz of Satan is compared to a swarm of flies (IV. 15–21); in *Samson Agonistes* restless thoughts 'like a deadly swarm of hornets' pester the hero (lines 19–20; cf. *P.R.* I. 196–9).[3] This view is not a product of 'post-Restoration disillusion': Milton anticipated it in the Seventh Prolusion, where he had defended learning after telling his audience that his preference would have been to defend ignorance. The learning which he chose to defend, however, was that which is useful. The point recurs in entries in Milton's Commonplace Book from the Horton days, in his early references to the 'unprofitable sin of curiosity' and 'the endless delight of speculation' in the *Letter to a Friend*.[4] He again repudiated 'search after vain curiosities' in his first divorce pamphlet. This attitude was shared by Baconian experimental philosophers of the forties and fifties. 'Unproductive, scholastic disputes', Charles Webster tells us, were judged by them too 'to be subversive to the active Christian life'.[5]

Learning is a real temptation in *Paradise Regained* because it seems to set men free when in fact human reason is as liable to be distorted by 'avarice and ambition' as to be disinterested. Full knowledge, like political liberation, will come in God's good time: there is no point in trying to hurry either process. God's truth is different from human reasoning, overrides and contradicts the calculations of men. The beginning of wisdom is

---

[1] Cf. pp. 398–402 above.
[2] Frye (1966), p. 146; Samuel (1949), pp. 713–23.
[3] Kerrigan, pp. 267–73.
[4] *C.P.W.*, I, pp. 293, 319–20; Hoopes, pp. 193–200; Hanford (1966), p. 121. The Hermetic writings condemned mere academic disputation (W. Scott, I, pp. 192–3).
[5] C. Webster (1975), p. 326. The reference is to the fifties.

awareness of one's own ignorance (*P.R.* IV. 293–4).[1] The temptation of learning in *Paradise Regained* may indeed have been Milton's response to the soubriquet of 'learned'. He wanted to be exemplary not by his human learning but by his sonship.

This emphasis may slightly mitigate the effect of Jesus's ferocious attack on 'the people' as 'a herd confused': 'they praise and they admire they know not what'. Such words fit John Milton in post-revolutionary England better than they fit the Jesus of the gospels. The Son of God's undemocratic remarks are, however, full of Biblical echoes: they are not just an expression of Milton's spleen or disappointment, but a product of his patient gathering of Biblical texts to guide action.[2] The violence of the outburst is also evidence of disillusion – with Parliaments which had failed in the forties, fifties and sixties, especially in respect of religious toleration, and with the electorate which had brought back kings, bishops and intolerance.

The church still needed liberation from secular control. Neither Parliament nor 'people' – who include no doubt a majority of the unregenerate – can claim sovereignty over the church in rivalry to Jesus Christ, any more than Milton now felt they were to be trusted with sovereignty over the state. It is more just, if it come to force, that they should be compelled to be free.[3] But over the church Christ alone is sovereign: 'he rules the mind and conscience of believers', as Milton put it in the *De Doctrina*. It is the Son of God's *duty* to disregard the wishes of those whose standards have been hopelessly vitiated by compliance with the avarice and ambition of this world. Against the undemocratic character of Jesus's diatribe let us not forget that the theme of *Paradise Regained* is the recovery of Paradise '*to all mankind*' (I. 3 – my italics).

The way back to a better Paradise, then, lies through the wilderness, through our own experience of adversity, suffering, temptation. We return not to the cold self-absorbed perfection that Adam might have known if he had dwelt in Paradise alone, without Eve. The end of *Paradise Regained* echoes the last simile in *Paradise Lost*:

---

[1] Bouchard, pp. 169–70.

[2] *C.P.W.*, VI, p. 436; Sims, p. 199. Cf. Newton, quoted in Manuel (1974), p. 108. Cf. pp. 160–3, 185–6 above.

[3] I have said elsewhere of this phrase in *The Ready and Easy Way* that the contortion of the prose reflects the reluctance of the thought (C. Hill, Penguin, 1972, p. 200). Perhaps the self-indulgent, over-emphasizing style of *Paradise Regained* to which Christopher Ricks draws attention, its moral bullying, may express a similar uncertainty at the heart of the poem, resolved only in the simplicity of the pinnacle scene, when the Son of God was at last free to act (Ricks, 1961, pp. 701–4). But Christopher Ricks justly reminds me that he was contrasting the verse of *Paradise Regained* with Milton's usual economy of phrase, whereas contortion occurs in his prose on occasions when there is no reason to suspect reluctant thought.

> As evening mist . . .
> Gathers ground fast at the labourer's heel
> Homeward returning;

and this leads on to Adam and Eve setting out 'hand in hand, with wandering steps and slow', words which the opening lines of *Samson Agonistes* pick up.[1] But whereas at the end of *Paradise Lost* the world lay all before Adam and Eve, a wild and terrifying wilderness, at the end of *Paradise Regained* Jesus, having achieved his supreme moment of triumph by standing and waiting, came quietly back to his task of saving humanity,[2] and 'unobserved/ Home to his mother's house private returned', the second Adam back from the wilderness, reunited in domestic security with the second Eve. In *Samson Agonistes,* more ironically, Samson's body was brought 'with silent obsequy and funeral train/ Home to his father's house' (1732–3). The quiet, assured, consoling close of *Paradise Regained* recalls that of *Lycidas* as well as picking up that of *Paradise Lost*: it anticipates the last choruses of *Samson Agonistes*. This distancing effect is one of Milton's most confident and convincing achievements.[3]

---

[1] See pp. 431–2 below.

[2] Wittreich (1971), pp. 121–3, 132. Wittreich argues that Blake regarded this as Christ's most heroic deed: contemplation leads to action. Christ's work for humanity is greater than his moment of union with the divine.

[3] A 'source' for *Paradise Regained* to which more attention might be paid is William Perkins's *The Combate between Christ and the Devill displayed,* a homily on Matthew 4.1–11. 'As in temptation Christ stood in our room and stead, so is this victory not his alone, but the victory of his church.' 'The drift of Satan in this temptation [that of the pinnacle] was to bring . . . Christ to a vain confidence in his Father's protection.' Satan can quote Scripture: we must try the spirits to check whether the Bible is rightly applied. 'If we forsake our ways, we lose the comfort' of angelic protection, 'and expose ourselves to all God's judgments.' Those who have never undergone temptation are not true members of Christ. Christ's victory was not final: tribulations will return, both for individuals and for the church, 'unless we prepare to meet our God in the practice of speedy and unfeigned repentance'. (Perkins, I, pp. 371–409, esp. pp. 390, 393, 406–8).

Chapter 31

Samson Agonistes: Hope Regained

The heroic Samson . . . thought it not impious but pious to kill those masters who were tyrants over his country.

Milton, *Defence of the People of England* (1651)

You are therefore to know that though the saints who have adventured to oppose the Beast and the kingdom of Antichrist (all along contending in a good cause) have been still crushed and subdued (as is foretold, Revelation XIII. 7), yet the time is coming, yea is even at the door, for God to take the business into his own hands, and to put forth the power of his wrath by heavenly instruments, forasmuch as the earthly ones (as you have seen) have proved ineffectual.

Sir Henry Vane, *Two Treatises* (1662)

The Samson story was familiar to English readers. Samson was a type of Christ – on this people so diverse as Silver-tongued Henry Smith, Bishop Joseph Hall, Thomas Goodwin, George Wither, Francis Quarles, John Bunyan and Edward Taylor all agreed.[1] The myth was used in various ways. The Puritan preacher Thomas Taylor emphasized that Samson was a magistrate, in order to hint at the Calvinist doctrine that revolt might be legitimate if led by subordinate magistrates.[2] George Wither observed that Samson (like Wither himself) could only be 'roused up to execute God's vengeance upon the enemies of his country' after he had suffered personal injury.[3] Quarles, before the *Divine Fancy* of 1632 which compared Samson to Christ, had in 1631 published *The Historie of Samson,* which Milton must almost certainly have known. Only one of its thirty-one sections deals with the action of Milton's play. The other four Samson subjects for tragedies

---

[1] H. Smith, Sig. Dv; Kinloch, p. 66; Goodwin (1861–3), V, p. 149; Quarles (1880), II, pp. 214–15; Bunyan, I, p. 396; E. Taylor, pp. 99–101.
[2] T. Taylor, pp. 378–9.
[3] Wither (1659), p. 27.

which Milton suggested to himself in the early forties concern previous aspects of Samson's career, though *Samson Hubristes* and *Dagonalia* may have overlapped with *Samson Agonistes*. Some of Quarles's emphases may have caught Milton's attention. Thus Quarles's Samson insisted

> Lord, the wrong is thine:
> The punishment is just and only mine:
> I am thy champion, Lord: it is not me
> They strike at: through my sides they thrust at thee.
> Against thy glory 'tis their malice lies. . . .
> Revenge thy wrongs, great God. O let thy hand
> Redeem thy suffering honour and this land.
> Lend me thy power; renew my wasted strength
> That I may fight thy battles.[1]

It is therefore not enough merely to say that Milton had been pondering a Samson subject for a long time. We must ask why he finally chose this one of the five outlined. I find it difficult not to suppose that the choice was influenced by the experience and the defeat of the English Revolution, reinforcing the analogy between Samson's blindness and Milton's own.

Among the revolutionaries, Henry Robinson alluded to the Samson story when in 1645 he warned that the bishops' hair might grow again and with it their strength.[2] More often this part of the myth was used the other way round, as when Lucy Hutchinson said that 'the wicked, with the sharp razors of their malicious tongues' tried 'to shave off the glories' from her husband's head: 'yet his honour, springing from the fast roots of virtue, did but grow the thicker and more beautiful for all their endeavours to cut it off.'[3] Lilburne in 1647 threatened that if he were not released from prison he would by his death do his oppressors '(Samson-like) more mischief than he did them all his life'.[4] Joseph Salmon in 1649 warned the army leaders that if they betrayed God's cause: 'the Lord, our spiritual Samson' will pull down their whole edifice even though 'the Lord will die with it, in it (or rather out of it and from it).'[5] Similarly Arise Evans warned Cromwell in 1655 that his colonels 'dally with you; but in the meantime they cut off your locks in the Army'. The same suggestion was made in 1658, when Oliver was said to be 'like one that have lost his lock of strength and wisdom. . . . Surely he hath not wanted Dalilahs to deprive him of it.'[6] Another radical, Thomas Collier, issued a similar warning to the Baptist

---

[1] Quarles (1880), II, p. 168.
[2] H. Robinson (1645), pp. 15–17.
[3] Hutchinson, p. 12. The Puritan Mrs. Hutchinson much admired her husband's long hair.
[4] Lilburne, p. 1.
[5] Salmon, p. 13.
[6] A. Evans (1655), p. 5; Underdown (1968), p. 107.

churches in 1657. 'While you have been asleep in the lap of this Dalilah [the world] your locks have been cut off and you are but as other men.'[1] Lady Eleanor Davies's *Samsons Fall* appeared in 1642, reprinted in 1649; *Samsons Legacie* in 1643.

An interesting radical treatment of the theme is that in Robert Norwood's *An Additional Discourse* (1653). He uttered the conventional warning to 'take heed of Dalilahs; . . . if thou sufferest thy locks to be shaved off, the Philistines will take thee.' So far 'we have defended and maintained our liberties against kings and Parliaments. . . . Those who have lost their locks, let them grind in the prison-house, if it must be so, until they be grown again; but we wish . . . and pray . . . it may . . . be otherwise.'[2] In 1641 Sir Thomas Aston had criticized those of the nobility and gentry who supported Parliament against the King, fearing lest 'Samson-like in their full strength (but as blind with inconsiderate zeal as he by treachery) any such should lay hold on those pillars of our state that prop up the regulated fabric of this our glorious monarchy, and by cracking them wilfully bring themselves in the rubbish of chaos, which they so pull upon their own heads, seeking to turn our freedom into fetters by cancelling our ancient laws . . . and exposing us . . . to the arbitrary jurisdiction of a new corporation of apron elders, mechanic artisans'.[3] Perhaps the most interesting of all pre-Miltonic uses of the Samson legend was in John Bond's sermon to the House of Commons in March 1644, where he argued that it is better to pull down the pillars of the temple and die together with Antichrist than live only to grind in the mill of slavery.[4] Milton may well have read this sermon. Samuel Pordage was more optimistic. Samson pulled down the 'wall which as a bar did stand/ Between the world and Paradise . . . and then/ A way was made to Paradise again.'[5]

Mid-seventeenth-century readers, then, were accustomed to political applications of the myth, and particularly used to Samson being taken as a figure for the army, or for the revolutionary cause. In Bunyan's *The Holy War* (1682) the captains depended upon the people; they became weak unless the people strengthened and encouraged them. Then they became 'like so many Samsons'.[6]

In *The Reason of Church Government*, Milton compared a sober and temperate king to Samson, with 'his illustrious and sunny locks the laws

---

[1] White, *Records,* p. 94.
[2] Robert Norwood, pp. 21, 57.
[3] T. Aston, Sig. K-K2.
[4] Bond, pp. 59–60.
[5] S. Pordage, p. 233.
[6] Bunyan, III, p. 340.

waving and curling about his godlike shoulders'. So long as he keeps them, 'he may with the jawbone of an ass, that is with the word of his meanest officer', suppress 'any who resist him. . . . But laying down his head among the strumpet flatteries of prelates', the 'prelatical razor' shaves off the tresses of the laws and delivers Samson to 'indirect and violent counsels', which, like the Philistines, put out the 'eyes of his natural discerning and make him grind in the prison-house of their sinister ends and practices upon him'. And even when he recovers his strength, he can only 'thunder . . . ruin upon the heads of those his evil counsellors, . . . not without great affliction to himself'[1] – an understatement for what happened to Samson, but consonant with Milton's desire at this stage not to appear to be threatening the King. Milton returned to Samson in *The Doctrine and Discipline of Divorce* – 'to grind in the mill of an undelighted and servile copulation must be the only forced work of a Christian marriage.' (The metaphor stuck in Milton's mind: in the *De Doctrina* he referred to 'the slavish pounding-mill of an unhappy marriage'.[2]) In *Areopagitica* the poet saw the English nation as a Samson, 'shaking his invincible locks'. And in the *Defence of the People of England* Samson was a rebel who fought against 'those masters who were tyrants over his country' and whom it was his duty to slay even though a majority of his fellow-citizens 'did not balk at slavery'.[3]

In *Paradise Lost,* significantly, the first analogy drawn by Milton after the Fall was between Adam and Eve on the one hand and Samson on the other. Samson

>   waked
> Shorn of his strength, they destitute and bare
> Of all their virtue.
>   (IX. 1059–63)

Both in the case of our first parents and of Samson, repentance consists in a full analysis and admission of failure to comply with God's purposes. Samson too must learn through small things to subvert worldly strength and wisdom.[4] But, unlike Adam, Samson got his chance to strike a decisive blow for God in his own lifetime – or rather by his death. The two poems appear to be linked by the fact that the close of the epic – exit Adam and Eve 'with wandering steps and slow' – is picked up by the opening

---

[1] *C.P.W.*, I, pp. 858–9. In 1660 Matthew Griffith was to use Samson as an image of the King shorn of his power (p. 9).
[2] *C.P.W.*, VI, p. 379. Did Milton recall the pounding paper-mill at Horton? (p. 38 above).
[3] *C.P.W.*, II, pp. 258, 558; cf. III, pp. 461, 545–6; IV, p. 402, cf. p. 1080.
[4] Tillyard (1951), p. 37; cf. Bouchard, p. 149.

lines of *Samson Agonistes* – 'A little further lend thy guiding hand'.[1] At this stage Samson is afflicted with both external and internal blindness. Both poems allude to the predicament of God's servants in England after 1660.

Let us reconsider the poem in this perspective. We first meet Samson, a prisoner, 'blind among enemies' (line 68). But worse than his physical sufferings are his

> Restless thoughts, that like a deadly swarm
> Of hornets armed, no sooner found alone,
> But rush upon me thronging, and present
> Times past, what once I was, and what am now.
>   (19–22)

>   Promise was that I
> Should Israel from Philistian yoke deliver;
> Ask for this great deliverer now, and find him
> Eyeless in Gaza at the mill with slaves,
> Himself in bonds under Philistian yoke.
>   (38–42)[2]

Worst of all is the fact that he alone is to blame for his predicament, for betraying himself and his people. His 'immeasurable strength' had been accompanied by 'wisdom nothing more than mean' (206–7). Hence his 'sense of heaven's desertion' (632). This picture is at least not incompatible with what I believe to have been Milton's feelings about the failure of the English Revolution.

The chorus sees Samson as 'mirror of our fickle state' (164). God had 'solemnly elected' Samson, and he had been

> With gifts and graces eminently adorned
> To some great work, thy glory,
> And people's safety.
>   (678–81)

Yet God had thrown him and his like

>   lower than thou didst exalt them high,
> Unseemly falls in human eye,
> Too grievous for the trespass or omission,
> Oft leav'st them to the hostile sword . . .
> Or to the unjust tribunals, under change of times,
> And condemnation of the ingrateful multitude.
>   (689–96)[3]
>
> Just or unjust, alike seem miserable,
> For oft alike, both come to evil end.
>   (703–4)

---

[1] See p. 427 above.
[2] See p. 349 above for 'great deliverers.'
[3] Cf. Wordsworth's use of 'unjust tribunals' in *The Prelude*, X. 412.

Whoever is to blame, the chorus says, 'Yet Israel serves with all his sons' (240). The catastrophe is national, not merely personal. The two themes of the play henceforth are Samson's recovery and the liberation of his people. The latter depends on the former. Then God's favour and Samson's strength will return, and he will be able to take vengeance on the Philistines, even though at the cost of his own life. (Those who interpret *Samson Agonistes* exclusively as a drama of personal regeneration would do well to recall the order of events in Milton's scheme of salvation. Regeneration comes first, causing repentance, which precedes faith. Punishment can cause repentance in the regenerate. Despair falls on the reprobate alone, but saints are sometimes tempted to impatience towards God.)[1]

Samson – the self-assertive rebel – at first defied God in the way that Satan had done at the beginning of *Paradise Lost*: 'Why am I thus bereaved thy prime decree?' (85). But Samson comes to blame himself exclusively:

> Nothing of all these evils hath befall'n me
> But justly; I myself have brought them on,
> Sole author I, sole cause.
> (374–6)

The echo of Adam's penitent words in *Paradise Lost* is unmistakable:

> On me, me only, as the source and spring
> Of all corruption, all the blame lights due.
> (*P.L.* X. 432–3)

Like Satan, like Eve, like the Ranters, Samson had aspired to godhead – 'swollen with pride', 'like a petty god' (529–32). In marrying Dalila Samson assumed he was right to dispense with God's law (278). Was he mistaken, as the Ranters so often were? If so, we must ask how certain we can be that the destruction of the Philistines at the end of the play was really inspired by God.[2]

'Eyeless in Gaza, at the mill with slaves' looks like a personal allusion to the blind Milton in political defeat. But it is of more general application. The 'great deliverer' was reduced to servitude and sordid poverty because he, like the English revolutionaries, had failed to live up to his high calling. 'At the mill with slaves' looks forward to Blake's 'dark Satanic mills' as a symbol for servile drudgery.[3] Like Adam, like Milton, Samson came to recognize his own responsibility:

---

[1] *C.P.W.*, VI, pp. 446–9, 659, 663.
[2] Samuel (1971), pp. 235–57.
[3] Cf. p. 38 above, and *C. and C.*, chapter 10; see also *C.P.W.*, II, p. 258, and Low, p. 52.

> These rags, this grinding, is not yet so base
> As was my former servitude, ignoble,
> Unmanly, ignominious, infamous,
> True slavery, and that blindness worse than this.
>
> (415–18)

He confirms the chorus's view that his failure has involved the whole nation of Israel.

He has abandoned personal hope:

> the strife
> With me hath end; all the contest is now
> 'Twixt God and Dagon.
>
> (448–65, cf. 240)

But by now he is confident that, despite his personal failure, God will 'arise and his great name assert' (467–73). Yet Samson still doubts his personal role.

> To what can I be useful, wherein serve
> My nation, and the work from heaven imposed,

since he is 'now blind, disheartened, shamed, dishonoured, quelled?' (563–5).

It was believed in the seventeenth century that the name Samson meant 'here the second time'. Samson had his second chance, and took it.[1] So perhaps might the English people. But Samson got his chance only after abandoning his illusions of heroism. There is a double irony in the phrase 'the great deliverer', which in *Paradise Lost* is applied to Christ (XII. 149). Samson failed utterly so long as he relied only on his heroic qualities, his strength: he was made a fool of. Until he recognized that he had been on the wrong tack, his life remained meaningless: no action was possible for him. But gradually he came to reject his aspirations to heroism, to accept the role of God's fool; and by acting the fool he achieved heroism, became a great deliverer in fact, just as in *Paradise Regained* the Son of God achieved divinity by refusing to claim it. (If we accept Parker's view that *Samson Agonistes* is totally pessimistic – as I do not – then we see a triple irony, since Samson's slaughter of the Philistines did not deliver Israel.) Milton weaves the personal and political plots together so successfully that the final irony of Samson's penultimate speech sums up both:

> Masters' commands come with a power resistless
> To such as owe them absolute subjection;
> And for a life who will not change his purpose?
>
> (1404–6)

---

[1] C. and F., p. 340; St. Maur, p. 311.

Samson has been commanded by God as well as by the Philistines, and it is God's command that he finds irresistible. He chooses life when he changes his purpose and goes to pollution and death in the temple of Dagon. Heroic results are achieved – once again – through actions which appear unheroic.[1]

Within this general framework there are many subsidiary political allusions. The imagery of shipwreck, the resentment of fair-weather friends, both suggest the post-Restoration period.[2] So do Manoa and the chorus, continually arguing that Samson has been on the wrong tack, that he has misunderstood God's purposes – a true point falsely made, leading to the utterly wrong conclusion that it is time to compromise with the Philistines.[3]

The idea of Samson as a symbol for the revolutionary cause, and especially for the revolutionary army, would be familiar to seventeenth-century readers.[4] In his first speech Manoa refers to Samson as 'himself an army' (346), and later he speaks of

> those locks
> That of a nation armed the strength contained . . .
> Garrisoned round about him like a camp
> Of faithful soldiery.
>   (1493–8)

Samson picks up the idea in his retort to Harapha, the boastful Philistine who came to jeer at his blind and powerless foe. Harapha, with his 'feudal' notions of honour, could relate to the restored Cavaliers who mocked Milton and his cause, though he may also contain something of the ostentatiously heroic fire-eaters of the New Model Army whom Milton had warned not to turn into Royalists themselves – part of his rejection of romantic revolutionism.[5] When Samson refers to his cause as God's,

---

[1] Stein, pp. 192–202; Summers, *passim*; Bouchard, pp. 151–9; cf. pp. 438–9 below.

[2] Tillyard (1949), pp. 329–54. Carey has an interesting analysis of the 'marine imagery' of *Samson Agonistes,* suggesting a concern with sea power (C. and F., pp. 339–40). Carey rightly says that the famous passage introducing Dalila as a ship 'with all her bravery on and tackle trim,/ Sails filled and streamers waving' is highly traditional. We may add to the examples cited by him (p. 370) John Taylor: 'The Lady-Ship was a very comely ship, set out with most excellent and superfluous cost, and she was richly adorned and beautified with flags, streamers, pennons and waistcloths . . .' ('The Lady-Ship', from *An Armado or Navy of Ships* in *All the Works,* 1630, p. 81). See also Wilson, p. 140.

[3] See Low, pp. 124–5, for a sensible refutation of the once fashionable denigration of Manoa and the chorus.

[4] See pp. 429–30 above.

[5] See pp. 366–7 above. Some suggest that Milton may also have been thinking of Salmasius when he depicted Harapha, remembering the David and Goliath analogy. But this seems to me too narrowly biographical.

Harapha retorts that Samson was a 'murderer, a revolter, and a robber', since his nation was

> subject to our lords.
> Their magistrates confessed it, when they took thee
> As a league-breaker and delivered bound
> Into our hands.
> (1178–85)

('Unjust tribunals under change of times' made exactly the same accusation against the regicides and army leaders after they had been 'delivered bound' into Royalist hands; and 'their carcasses' became 'to dogs and fowls a prey'.)[1] Samson's reply to Harapha is

> I was no private but a person raised
> With strength sufficient and command from heaven
> To free my country.
> (1211–13)

This recalls the insistence in Calvinist political theory that revolt is justified if led by the magistrate. More specifically, it echoes the New Model Army's famous defence of itself in June 1647: 'We were not a mere mercenary army, hired to serve any arbitrary power of a state; but called forth and conjured by the several declarations of Parliament, to the defence of our own and the people's just rights and liberties ... against all particular parties or interests whatsoever.'[2] The New Model, Erbery paraphrased, was 'the Army of God, as public persons, and not for a particular interest'.[3]

Harapha's 'league-breaker' could refer to the Presbyterians' and the Scots' accusation that the army had violated the Solemn League and Covenant by executing Charles I: the Presbyterians' return to power in the spring of 1660 was accompanied by a reaffirmation of the Covenant, rejection of army rule, the arrest and condemnation of many of its leaders. So Samson continues

> If their servile minds
> Me their deliverer sent would not receive,
> But to their masters gave me up for nought,
> The unworthier they; whence to this day they serve.
> (1213–16)

---

[1] There is no need to assume, as Parker makes his straw critics do, that these lines could only refer to the disinterment of Cromwell's, Ireton's and Bradshaw's bodies after the Restoration. The quartered bodies of many other victims were similarly exposed.

[2] Haller and Davies, p. 55; cf. William Sedgwick (*A Second View*, 1649), p. 11.

[3] Erbery, p. 25.

And indeed the Presbyterians after the Restoration found themselves 'the despised and cheated party', as Henry Newcome put it feelingly.[1] (The Presbyterian Scots had not given up Charles I 'for nought': they sold him for £200,000 to Parliament in 1646).

Samson took up Harapha's other point, that 'my nation was subjected to your lords', with a reference to the radical tradition which denounced the 'Norman Yoke' of king and aristocracy as alien conquerors:[2]

> It was the force of conquest; force with force
> Is well ejected when the conquered can.
>
> (1205–7)

And Samson's challenge to Harapha reverberates with the social overtones associated with the Norman Yoke theory:

> Put on all thy gorgeous arms, thy helmet
> And brigandine of brass, thy broad habergeon,
> Vantbrace and greaves, and gauntlet, add thy spear
> A weaver's beam, and seven-times-folded shield.

Samson will meet this caricature of a feudal knight, suddenly made ludicrous by the Biblical 'weaver's beam', himself armed only with 'an oaken staff', the cudgel which was the traditional weapon of the English lower classes – 'clubs and clouted shoon'. 'My heels are fettered, but my fist is free.' Harapha used the social distance between the two as an excuse for not fighting (1119–23, 1164–7, 1235; cf. 1244–5).

Another post-Restoration touch is Samson's view that nations are

> By their vices brought to servitude,
> ... To love bondage more than liberty,
> Bondage with ease than strenuous liberty;
> And to despise, or envy, or suspect
> Whom God hath of his special favour raised
> As their deliverer; if he aught begin,
> How frequent to desert him, and at last
> To heap ingratitude on worthiest deeds?
>
> (269–76)

Milton's additions to and deviations from the story in Judges are all most easily explained if we assume that he is thinking of Samson as in some sense a symbol of the Good Old Cause or its army. Thus Samson's initial weakness of mind – 'O impotence of mind in body strong!' (52) – is not stressed either in the Bible or in the commentaries. Milton's object is surely

---

[1] Newcome, pp. 118–19.
[2] See pp. 100–1 above.

to force the parallel with the English people in the Revolution: 'all wickedness is weakness' (839). Milton's Samson emphasizes that he was not one
of the rulers of Israel (241–6), whereas in Judges he ruled for twenty years.
Manoa's plea to the Philistines for Samson's release similarly has no
precedent in Scripture or the commentaries.

In 1666 Milton had found himself without a country, so to speak. 'One's
country is wherever it is well with one.'[1] So Samson denounced 'thy
country' to Dalila:

> No more thy country, but an impious crew
> Of men conspiring to uphold their state
> By worse than hostile deeds, violating the ends
> For which our country is a name so dear;
> Not therefore to be obeyed.
>
>   (891–5)

Dalila's claim that 'the priest was . . . ever at my ear' urging her to betray
Samson is a gratuitous invention, recalling Milton's hostility to both
Presbyterian and Anglican clergy. So are the special vengefulness and spite
against Samson of those Philistines who 'most reverenced Dagon and his
priests' (875–8, 1462–3). 'The well-feasted priest' is 'soonest fired with
zeal' when in wine. On their holy-days the people were 'impetuous,
insolent, unquenchable' (1418–22). (Saints' days had not been celebrated in
Parliamentarian England between 1642 and 1660 – not officially at least.[2])
In *Of Reformation* Milton had equated prelates with Philistines. The rulers
of the Philistines, like Papists, like Anglicans, like Alexander More,[3] were
struck with 'blindness internal', 'drunk with idolatry' no less than with
wine, just at the moment when Samson

>   though blind of sight,
> Despised and thought extinguished quite

received the inward illumination which roused 'his fiery virtue' to action
'when most unactive deemed' (1670, 1686–91, 1705). Masson realized that
these lines referred to Milton as poet as well as to Samson and the English
Revolution, to be seen as a Phoenix in the next lines.[4] So Samson pulled
down Dagon's temple upon the heads of

> Lords, ladies, captains, counsellors, or priests
> Their choice nobility and flower. . . .
> The vulgar only 'scaped who stood without.
>
>   (1652–9)

---

[1] *C.M.*, XII, pp. 114–15.
[2] Cf. p. 485 below.
[3] *C.P.W.*, I, p. 580; IV, p. 589.
[4] Masson, VI, pp. 677–8; cf. pp. 445–6 below.

The last line is another Miltonic addition for which there is no Scriptural authority. Milton's animosity was directed against the rulers and clergy of post-Restoration England, not its deluded people.

So I reject Parker's view that *Samson Agonistes* is 'intensely, almost unbearably pessimistic', since 'in the perspective of Biblical history Samson dies in vain.'[1] It is true that in the Old Testament the Israelites were not liberated by Samson's achievement. But Milton was not writing history: he was writing for seventeenth-century Englishmen. Whether there was any hope for what had once seemed the chosen nation must be left to God. That was not for Milton to decide. Like Samson, he must do what he could here and now and leave the rest to providence. Milton nowhere mentions the failure of the Israelites to follow up Samson's coup. On the contrary: Manoa in his last speech draws a very different conclusion. Samson has left his enemies 'years of mourning', and

> to Israel
> Honour hath left, and freedom, let but them
> Find courage to lay hold on this occasion.
>
> (1712–16)

It is difficult to pronounce those lines without heavy emphasis on 'them' – the people. Milton was selectively using the Biblical story to suit his own purposes. Pushkin – that very Miltonic poet – indicated in the devastating conclusion of *Boris Godunov* that 'the people are silent' when appealed to. Milton gave no such hint; on the contrary, Samson himself stressed that in the past similar opportunities had been missed (265–7). His death offered his people the chance of liberation. Even if they failed to take it, God had been avenged on his enemies and an example was left which would inflame the breasts of the valiant youth 'to matchless valour and adventures high' (1738–40). History is not always cyclical. An opportunity should not be neglected because the people did not rise to the challenge last time. 'Here the second time'.

'Nothing is here for tears', says Manoa,

> nothing to wail
> Or knock the breast, no weakness, no contempt.
> Dispraise or blame, nothing but well and fair.
>
> (1721–3)

The final chorus agrees:

> All is best, though we oft doubt,
> What the unsearchable dispose

---

[1] Parker, p. 937.

> Of highest wisdom brings about,
> And ever best found in the close.
> Oft he seems to hide his face,
> But unexpectedly returns
> And to his faithful champion hath in place
> Bore witness gloriously.
>
> (1745–52)

Hence not only 'Gaza mourns' but

> all that band them to resist
> His uncontrollable intent.

God's servants are dismissed

> with new acquist
> Of true experience from this great event.
>
> (1752–8)

The ways of God to men have been justified: human freedom has been exonerated, providence again asserted. Like Adam, the chosen people had been taught the lesson of history, which would seem to Milton's public at least as relevant to their England as to the Israel of Samson's time. This lesson is not pessimism, not defeatism. It is the recovery of hope. Samson, like Satan, had felt that he was 'as one past hope'.

> Nor am I in the list of them that hope;
> Hopeless are all my evils, all remediless.
>
> (S.A. 647–8).[1]

But Samson, unlike Satan, came to see that his fall was not final.

Haller seems to me more right than Parker: *Samson Agonistes* is the epic poem of the English people, looking to a glorious future. It is not the celebratory poem that he promised Manso that he would write.[2] *Samson Agonistes* is about re-education, not only of Samson but also of the chosen people whom the chorus represents. *Samson Agonistes* suggests that liberation is still possible; but it will come when God chooses, not when man wants it to come. Meanwhile, we must do what we can in our own sphere. In 1660 a Quaker had written 'We are a people saved by our God from whom we expect our deliverance. And he hath made us willing to wait until he bring it to pass. . . . We do believe that God will overturn, overturn, until he hath brought to pass the thing that he hath decreed, which is to establish righteousness in the earth.'[3] Not a wholly pacifist sentiment!

---

[1] Cf. p. 364 above.
[2] C. and F., pp. 260–7.
[3] Barbour and Roberts, p. 403.

Samson Agonistes is not a historical treatise, and it is not pessimistic. It is in one sense an intellectual and moral analysis of failure and defeat.[1] But the failure is not accepted as final. In the passage quoted as epigraph to this chapter Vane put his hopes in a divine miracle. Milton is more concerned with the human agents through whom God acts. *Samson Agonistes* is a call of hope to the defeated. In *Paradise Regained,* for all his rejection of violence, the Son of God had foretold victory: in the last poem he published Milton shows a rebel avenging his people on their alien overlords. Whether or not he was originally drawn to the Samson theme for political reasons, it fitted post-Restoration England very well.

So Samson got his second chance. God's providence is unpredictable. The very depth of Samson's sufferings, his blindness and his captivity, gave him his opportunity to outwit and destroy his enemies. If there had been no blindness, no captivity, there could have been no victory for God's cause. Samson was rightly punished, together with his people: but the punishment was a means to an end. I cannot see pessimism here. Milton called *Samson Agonistes* a tragedy, it is true: but he also followed Paraeus in calling Revelation a tragedy, the most revolutionary book in the Bible. 'What in all philosophy', Milton had asked himself over thirty years earlier, 'is more important or more sacred or more exalted than a tragedy rightly produced, what more useful for seeing at a single view the events and changes of human life?'[2]

Milton had the springs of political action too deeply embedded in him to have doubts about the duty of action. He was for ever in his Great Taskmaster's eye. His problem was rather to understand the necessity on occasion of inactivity ('They also serve who only stand and wait'); and to grasp the psychology of those who did not feel his compulsion to act. The regenerate have this compulsion: what they do is not sinful. One of Milton's problems after the defeat of the Revolution was to accept the gap between the regenerate and the masses and yet advance to a theory of political action. He is addressing an audience 'fit though few'. In the short run these are the ones who count. The most that one can hope for the vulgar who stand outside the Temple is that they will escape the destruction of the Philistine aristocracy in the day of Babylonian woe, and that they too will learn to take advantage of their second chance. Milton's reflections on defeat are addressed to the potential Samsons, the remnant, even though they are still enslaved at the mill, having been trapped in the

---

[1] As is persuasively argued by Lady Radzinowicz, p. 471.
[2] *C.P.W.*, I, pp. 815, 491 – Commonplace Book.

arms of Dalila. They must understand that both their succumbing to her wiles and their consequent blindness may be part of God's plan for a greater victory over the Philistines. Then they will be ready to act when the time comes. The miracle came to Samson in Dagon's temple, as to the Son of God on the pinnacle of the true Temple: in each case after a prolonged period of standing and waiting, of attainment of self-discipline. Oliver Cromwell arrived at his major political decisions after a similar period of waiting on God.[1] The catharsis of *Samson Agonistes* has a therapeutic effect. Guilt, once understood, is mastered and becomes a yet stronger spring of action. *Paradise Lost* had dealt with the same theme of guilt, though on a cosmic/macrocosmic scale.

About *Samson Agonistes* Empson's 'neo-Christians' are as mealy-mouthed as they are about Milton's defence of polygamy. They emphasize that the poem is about the regeneration of Samson. They do not emphasize that it is also about revenge, about political deceit and murder, and that the two themes are inseparable. At the end Samson may be regenerated, but the Philistines are dead, horribly dead, in large and indiscriminate numbers, even though the lower classes escaped. Their death was less horrible, Milton might have retorted, than the deaths of his old comrades who were shanghaied back from their continental refuge to face the executioner's knife in England; less horrible than the deaths of the misguided London Fifth Monarchists and Scottish Covenanters who revolted prematurely in 1661 and 1666; less horrible than the countless deaths from gaol fever suffered by Quakers and others who refused to pay antichristian tithes to Mammon's son. As horrible, it might be retorted, as the deaths of Cromwell's victims at Drogheda. Milton believed that the war against Antichrist continued, and that it was the duty of God's people to hit back when they could. As for a French patriot in 1943 or a black South African to-day, the question was not whether to resist but when and how to resist most effectively. *Paradise Regained* could be interpreted as a pacifist poem in its rejection of premature political solutions. But *Samson Agonistes,* Milton's last published poem, conforms to what the *De Doctrina* tells us about the religious duty of hating 'the enemies of God or the church', of cursing them in public and private prayer. 'We are not forbidden to take or to wish to take vengeance upon the enemies of the church.' God's enemies may be deceived and robbed.[2] Milton's message seems clear: however difficult the political circumstances, be ready to smite the Philistines when

---

[1] See C. Hill (Penguin, 1972), p. 225.
[2] *C.P.W.*, VI, pp. 675, 743, 755, 762.

God gives the word. 'Few of the literary critics who praise' Samson, Empson observed, 'would be on his side if they met him nowadays'. When Marvell first read *Paradise Lost* he feared lest Milton would ruin his theme:

(So Samson groped the Temple's posts in spite)
The world o'erwhelming to revenge his sight.

But it was his upper-class enemies that Samson overwhelmed, not the world. He acts for 'an underprivileged class or minority group', as Empson puts it. When we read of Samson's 'glorious revenge' (1660), that he died heroically and 'fully revenged', perhaps we should add Jacobean revenge tragedies to the list of possible influences as well as Aeschylus and Sophocles.[1]

Such an approach may help us to escape from seeing Dalila as an outlet for Milton's misogyny. Once he had decided to use the Samson myth, how could he have avoided the hostility towards Dalila shown by his sources? He hardly chose the story for this reason, even if it did not displease him. As with Comus and Satan, Milton gave Dalila the best arguments he possibly could, in the old Cambridge manner. He made her Samson's wife – a status the Bible did not give her, nor Milton himself in *Paradise Lost* – as surely he would have done if *Samson Agonistes* had been written first?[2] It seems clearer that Samson should have divorced Dalila than that Adam should have divorced Eve when she ate the apple.[3] If Milton thought in terms of allegorical symbolism at all, he may have seen Dalila as the Presbyterians who pretended to ally with the revolutionaries – indeed covenanted with them – and then betrayed them, proclaiming their continued allegiance to the alien rulers. Dalila could also spring (among other things) from a reflection on the harm done to the cause of religious toleration by Martha Simmonds's usurpation of leadership from a Nayler who seemed to be clay in her hands.[4] (I do not stress the contribution to Dalila of memories of Mary Powell, since this is a commonplace. Milton accepted Mary's proffered reconciliation in 1645; Samson's confident rejection of Dalila's similar offer may represent what Milton with hindsight thought would have been a more correct course of action.)

Irene Samuel argues that Milton did not think of Samson as a model to be followed, that Dalila voices a caricature of Samson's aspirations to be a national hero, and that there is little to choose between Harapha and

---

[1] Empson (1961), p. 213; cf. p. 484 below.
[2] See appendix 1 below.
[3] Empson (1961), p. 220; Frye ('The Revelation', 1969), pp. 44–5.
[4] See pp. 135–6 above.

Samson.[1] I find this unconvincing. Milton often seems deliberately to blur the external distinctions between good and evil in order to emphasize the all-importance of the internal spirit. Thus in *Paradise Regained* Christ refuses Satan's banquet, accepts the angels'. Unfallen and fallen sex in *Paradise Lost* are each to other like, more than on earth is sometimes thought. Satan quotes *Areopagitica* to Eve. Dalila hoped that 'in my country where I most desire', she would

> be named among the famousest
> Of women, sung at solemn festivals,
> Living and dead recorded . . .
>   my tomb
> With odours visited and annual flowers.
>
>   (980–7)

Manoa appears to echo this when he proposes to build a monument to the dead Samson:

> The virgins also shall on feastful days
> Visit his tomb with flowers.
>
>   (1734–41)

The point surely is that Dalila's self-conscious aspiration to heroism is corrupt, serves the wrong God. Samson recognizes his failure in the analogous role of 'great deliverer'; by doing his duty in small things he achieves the greatness which is no longer his objective. Milton indeed emphasizes the difficulty of distinguishing between a true motion of the spirit and what may be genuinely but wrongly believed to be such. Samson's first marriage to a Philistine was 'motioned . . . of God'; his second was not, though Samson 'thought it lawful from my former act' (222, 231). Nor can it be argued that Harapha is Samson's counterpart, just as the War in Heaven reduces loyal and rebel angels to a common impotence of violence. Samson's challenge 'by combat to decide whose God is God' is no doubt exactly how Michael told Adam he should not think of the contest between good and evil (*S.A.* 1176; *P.L.* XII. 386–7). But Samson, no private person, never forgets his public capacity, never sinks to mere braggadocio. Anthony Low is nearer the mark when he says that Harapha represents what Samson would have become without divine help.[2]

In arguing that we are intended to disapprove of Samson to the end, I suspect that Irene Samuel attributes to Milton a modern liberal Christianity which he did not share. Samson slays the Philistine aristocracy and

---

[1] Samuel (1971), *passim*.
[2] Low, p. 163. Cf. pp. 436–7 above.

priests, and it is right to ask whether Milton thought this action really was inspired by God. But in *Paradise Lost* Adam did not so much lament 'for one whole world of wicked sons destroyed' as he rejoiced that God vouchsafed 'to raise another world' from Noah (XI. 874–8). We have noticed other occasions in *Paradise Lost* where the use of violence on behalf of God's cause was applauded. For Milton the Philistines, like the government of Restoration England, were enemies of God who could not be removed except by violence.[1] The passage from the *Defence of the People of England* cited as epigraph to this chapter is decisive evidence that Milton did not disapprove of Samson at the date at which Parker thinks he was putting the finishing touches to the drama. There is nothing to suggest that Milton changed his views on this matter. He did not become an absolute pacifist, as the Quakers did after 1660. The Civil War had shown that fighting *by itself* solved nothing; the War in Heaven suggests the right combination of force and justice. But Milton never wholly repudiated the military leaders of the Revolution: he rebuked their avarice and ambition. Samson failed as a leader, as the generals had done; but this need not exclude the possibility of leadership. Why should Milton have invented 'the vulgar only scaped who stood without' if not to stress that God master-minded Samson's exploit? It may be regrettable that Milton could view with relative equanimity the slaughter of the Philistine aristocracy and clergy; but as early as 1633 he thought that 'all mortals . . . aspire to offend their enemies', and in the *De Doctrina* he described hating God's enemies as a religious duty.[2] Milton was not a modern liberal Christian. He lived in a world as savage and brutal as that of Europe between 1939 and 1945, when many liberal Christians thought that resistance to tyranny justified killing those who were only indirectly responsible.

A word about the Phoenix in *Samson Agonistes*. Its use as a symbol for Christ goes back at least to Origen and Milton's favourite Lactantius. In the Hermetic literature the Phoenix symbolized alchemical resurrection; Paracelsus used it to represent the philosopher's stone as well as Christ.[3] Milton's Phoenix is 'self-begotten', as Satan in *Paradise Lost* suggested the rebel angels were.[4] The Phoenix could be an emblem of the sun and renewal of life. On the cups[5] which Manso gave to Milton and to which the latter referred in *Epitaphium Damonis* the Phoenix watches the sun rise

---

[1] See pp. 362–3, 442–3 above.
[2] *C.P.W.*, I, p. 319; VI, pp. 675, 743.
[3] Robins, pp. 177–80; Waddington, pp. 280–2; Yates (1972), p. 88.
[4] See p. 397 above.
[5] Or were they books? See Carey's note to lines 181–97.

over the Red Sea (lines 185–9). Raphael was likened to a Phoenix in *P.L.*
V. 271–4. The bird had been put to political uses as recently as 1661 in
The Phoenix of the Solemn League and Covenant, an unlicensed pamphlet which
reminded its readers that Charles II had taken the Covenant and that the
Presbyterian Edmund Calamy had threatened the direst fate for oath-
breakers. The pamphlet thus ingeniously attacked both King and Presbyterians with a single stone, just as I believe *Samson Agonistes* did much less
directly.[1]

My conclusion is that Empson is right to say that *Samson Agonistes* 'was
calculated to strike the first readers as about Milton himself and *a fortiori*
about current politics'.[2] Milton had lost confidence in the people, and in
the middling sort whom he had previously regarded as natural leaders. He
now put his hope in the efforts of regenerate individuals – rather like
Narodnaya Volya in similar discouraging circumstances in the eighteen-
seventies and -eighties. Salvation when it comes will seem as prodigious as
the Son standing on the pinnacle of the Temple, as Samson destroying the
Philistines.[3] Yet the miracles had been prepared as carefully as Oliver
Cromwell's victories. Dagon's temple yielded to the faith of the strong man
because it was made with hands; on the pinnacle of the true temple the Son
was supported by the elect, each stone in its place, ready.

We can trace a progression in the three great poems. *Paradise Lost* deals
with Adam succumbing to temptation, with humanity, with Everyman. In
Paradise Regained the hero is a perfect man, withstanding temptation and
saving humanity by his example. In *Samson Agonistes* there is no mention
of Christ, of whom in the orthodox tradition Samson was normally
regarded as a type. Samson performs Christ-like actions, bringing salvation
to his people by his own death. But – even more than Jesus in *Paradise
Regained* – Samson is a man, a man acting, not merely suffering. His
individuality is not unique: he is what any fallen sinner can become when
he recovers and co-operates with Providence. Like Jesus in *Paradise
Regained,* Samson does not fully understand himself or his historic role
until the end, when he, like the Son of God, has abandoned all self-interest,
surrendered himself as a willing instrument of God's purposes as and when
God shall instruct him.[4] Samson shows how the remnant, the conscious
minority, should behave. He is also, we note from the text, a man who

---

[1] *C.S.P. Domestic, 1661–2,* pp. 23, 50; J. Walker, p. 232. For *Samson Agonistes* and the Presbyterians, see pp. 436–7 above.
[2] Empson (1961), p. 217.
[3] Sewell, p. 201; C. Hill (1972), p. 240.
[4] Low, pp. 71, 86–9.

thinks exclusively in this-worldly terms. There is no hint of an after life in *Samson Agonistes*. Milton must have known that Samson's last words would have been more correctly translated 'Let my soul die with the Philistines' than in the emasculated versions of the Geneva Bible and the Authorized Version. They were words appropriate to a mortalist.[1]

Even if, *per impossibile,* it could be shown that Milton wrote *Samson Agonistes* before *Paradise Lost* and *Paradise Regained,* he was right to print it last.[2] If we see one aspect of *Paradise Lost* as Milton settling accounts with generals and Ranters, and *Paradise Regained* as (among many other things) a rejection of Fifth Monarchism,[3] *Samson Agonistes* seems to be picking up something of what had been rejected. Samson was as entirely dependent on the motions of the spirit as Quakers, Ranters and other extreme radicals. Clarkson, who felt that he was exempt from the moral law unless his conscience told him otherwise, drew the line at murder: Samson did not. But then Samson was at war with the Philistines: Milton would have criticized the Ranters for not being political enough. He may be trying to link the anarchy of individual consciences to some sort of social purpose, to solve in a new way his old problem of reconciling discipline and liberty.[4] The Ranters, in Milton's view, extended liberty too widely, did not relate it to the service of God's purposes. But discipline, to be effective, must be internal, in the individual's conscience. And then how do you exclude Ranter individualism? The Fifth Monarchists have discipline, but how to get them to apply it in accordance with human reason? The questions are not easily answered. Perhaps they are unanswerable: discipline cannot be internalized in any agreed form except by long-term processes, such as the pressures of the capitalist market. But if it had been possible to get agreement on what God's purposes were (as the *De Doctrina* tried to do) then this could have been as successful as if the premises of Hobbes's *Leviathan* had been accepted.

Milton's next move after publishing *Samson Agonistes* was to write an anti-Catholic tract. It was the nearest he could get to political pamphleteering: he was using his opportunities as Samson had used his. Nor was that the end. Milton's prose writings contributed to the revolutionary tradition of 1688 and after, in England, America, France.[5] Milton/Samson

---

[1] But Milton does not quote Judges 16:30 in the chapter of the *De Doctrina* which discusses mortalism (*C.P.W.*, VI, pp. 399–415).

[2] See appendix 1 below.

[3] Fixler, chapter VI, *passim.*

[4] See chapter 20 above.

[5] See pp. 468–9 below. Thomas Holles saw William III as a Miltonic Samson, 'a deliverer' who 'rescued us from the Philistine oppressors' (Wittreich, 1975, p. 61).

achieved immortality – for his left hand as well as his right. Blake picked up the image of Samson as 'a gigantic national hero, who fights against foreign tyrants'. He saw him as a sun-figure, and – picking up *Areopagitica*'s image – as Albion rising 'from where he laboured at the mill with slaves', like a strong man after sleep shaking his invincible locks.[1]

---

[1] Frye (*Fearful Symmetry*, 1969), pp. 362–3.

PART VII

TOWARDS A CONCLUSION

You will consider that these were only minutes and tumultuary hints relating to ampler pieces, inform and unfit to be put into the building, but prepared to work on. It is not imaginable to such as have not tried, what labour an historian (that would be exact) is condemned to. He must read all, good and bad, and remove a world of rubbish before he can lay the foundation. So far I had gone, and it was well for me I went no further; and better for the reader on many accounts, as I am sure to find by what I have already been so weak as to show you, and yet I cannot forbear. . . . You know how difficult a thing it is to play an after-game when men's minds are perverted and their judgments prepossessed.

> John Evelyn to Samuel Pepys, 28 April 1682

[It is] not impossible that [Truth] may have more shapes than one.

> John Milton, *Areopagitica*

Chapter 32

Milton's Milton versus Milton

> A reader of Milton must be always upon duty.
> Jonathan Richardson

I suggested earlier that Milton's autobiographical remarks were an obstacle in the way of the biographer.[1] He made many public statements about himself, each of which must be evaluated in the light of the circumstances which gave rise to it. Milton tells us that he cut short his journey through Italy in 1639 in order to hurry home to take part in the struggle for liberty: the cold light of scholarship reveals that he hurried very slowly. This was what he wanted to think rather than what actually happened. When Milton claims to have written successively about civil liberty, domestic liberty and liberty of the press, as though in execution of a preconceived plan, this too appears to be an *ex-post-facto* rationalization. If we examine other remarks about himself equally carefully they may tell us things rather different from what Milton intended.

In 1642, countering the attacks of Bishop Hall (or his son), Milton felt that he was defending the anti-episcopal cause, 'whereof I was persuaded and whereof I had declared openly to be a partaker'. So he must not allow 'the least spot or blemish in good name' to remain. This is the reason for the long autobiographical passage in *An Apology*, in which Milton rejected the charge of 'levity' no less than the accusation that he had misspent his years at Cambridge in riot, and had since haunted theatres and brothels. He therefore emphasized 'a certain niceness of nature, and honest haughtiness'.[2] It is interesting that the charge of licentiousness was made *before* he wrote the divorce tracts. Once they had been published it was natural to denounce him as a libertine, an accusation which clearly rattled Milton. When he published his Cambridge elegies in the *Poems* of 1645 Milton

---

[1] See p. 9 above.
[2] *C.P.W.*, I, pp. 871, 890.

carefully apologized for 'these vain trophies of my profligacy'. Everything
he wrote about himself around this time and later must be related to his
desire to differentiate himself from those who meant licence when they
cried liberty.[1]

In the fifties, as spokesman for the Commonwealth, Milton was even
more self-consciously a public person. Since he mocked Salmasius for his
matrimonial misadventures, and accused Alexander More of sexual mis-
conduct, it was important to clear himself of the old charges of undergraduate debauchery and libertinism. In the autobiographical passage in
the *Second Defence* Milton named six Italian friends, of whom he was
presumably proud. If we compare this list with those to whom he sent
greetings via Carlo Dati in 1647, we find that one name mentioned in the
private letter is missing from the public tract. It is that of the lewd and
libertine Malatesti. In the same work Milton argued that the ideas which
his enemy denounced as Anabaptist were in fact to be found in Cicero.[2] In
1660 he carefully quoted Aristotle against monarchy, 'lest this doctrine be
thought sectarian, as the royalist would have it thought'.[3] After the
Restoration Milton wished to appear as 'orthodox' as possible without
actually denying what he believed. Otherwise he might never have been
able to publish *Paradise Lost*.[4]

Milton's statements about himself should therefore always be checked
carefully against other evidence. This is especially necessary because the
image which Milton created of himself seems to coincide with the stereotype of a 'Puritan'. Until the publication of the *De Doctrina* there was little
reason to suppose that Milton was not a 'Puritan', and after its publication
there has remained an understandable reluctance to recognize how great a
revaluation of the poet its heresies made necessary.

I have argued against the myth of Milton the aloof austere scholar.
Some points may be added here.[5] Hartlib's early description of him as a
great traveller and projector hardly fits this image. Nor does Milton's
readiness to challenge clerical critics of his views on divorce to a public
disputation.[6] Milton was apparently quite at ease with Italian academicians,
including the libertines among them. The astonishing conclusion to the
Epitaphium Damonis does not suggest prudery, nor do his light-hearted
references to 'casual adultery', in which 'nothing is given from the

---

[1] Cf. *ibid.*, II, p. 233, and Sonnet XII.
[2] *C.P.W.*, II, p. 765; IV, pp. 616–17, 643.
[3] *C.M.*, VI, p. 136.
[4] See pp. 212, 234–5 above.
[5] See pp. 57–9 above.
[6] *C.P.W.*, II, p. 579.

husband which he misses': it is easily forgotten and forgiven;[1] nor does Book VII of *Paradise Lost*. Milton's possession of a manuscript of Bodin's *Heptaplomeres* makes sense if we think of the poet as being at home in English libertine circles. He noted in his Commonplace Book that Bodin was in favour of divorce, though he chose to quote 'the famous French writer' in public only in favour of discipline.[2] Milton's attempt to help Jean Labadie, an ex-priest whose doctrines had much of the Ranter in them, and who had a shaky sexual reputation,[3] points in the same direction. So does his friendship with Sir Peter Wentworth, denounced by Oliver Cromwell as a whore-master, 'living in open contempt of God's commandments', together with his crony Henry Marten. Wentworth remembered Milton in his will.

It used to be thought that Isaac Newton took to theology at the age of fifty, after a nervous breakdown; but historians have informed themselves better. It is equally unplausible to suggest that the easy conviviality of Milton's later sonnets was something that developed only as he matured with his triumphs in the early fifties. In *Of Education* he says that those 'of a more delicious and airy spirit' who 'retire themselves (knowing no better) to the enjoyments of ease and luxury, living out their days in feast and jollity', follow a wiser and safer course than those products of the universities who are shallow controversialists or mercenary careerists.[4] In *Areopagitica* he pointed out that the Athenians did not censor Epicureans, Cynics 'or that libertine school of Cyrene'. Plato commended to his royal scholar Dionysius 'the reading of Aristophanes, the loosest of . . . all' the comedians.[5] In 1659 Milton argued eloquently against the use of political power to enforce morality: 'to compel the licentious in his licentiousness' is as bad as compelling the conscientious against his conscience.[6] 'Strictly speaking', he sensibly observed in the *De Doctrina*, 'no word or thing is obscene'. The obscenity is 'in the dirty mind of the man who perverts words or things out of prurience or to get a laugh'. The Bible uses many 'dirty' words.[7] Richard Leigh, referring to passages in *An Apology* and *Areopagitica* of which 'religion and morality forbid a repetition', concluded that 'the more modest Aretine, were he alive in this

---

[1] *Ibid.*, II, pp. 331–3, 591, 674; VI, p. 381. See pp. 31, 57–8, 129–30 above.

[2] *C.P.W.*, I, pp. 409, 834.

[3] Masson, V, p. 595; Kolakowski, pp. 719–85, esp. pp. 771–2. Masson pointed out that Milton must have known all about Labadie by 1674, when he authorized publication of the friendly letter which he wrote to him in April 1659.

[4] *C.P.W.*, II, p. 376.

[5] *Ibid.*, II, p. 495.

[6] *C.M.*, VI, pp. 35–6, 38–9.

[7] *C.P.W.*, VI, p. 770. See p. 307 above.

age, might be set to school again, to learn his own art of the blind school-master'. I cite this not as accurate comment, but as the opinion of a contemporary, very prejudiced but who had read Milton carefully.[1]

The view that Milton had no sense of humour dies hard. Let us look at some of his jokes, many based on word-play, most of them sarcastic. For instance his jeering reference to the eccentricities of the liturgy – 'those thanks in the woman's churching for her delivery from sunburning and moonblasting, as if she had been travelling not in bed but in the deserts of Arabia'. Here the joke turns on the pun travailing/travelling, spelt inter-changeably in the seventeenth century. In *Animadversions* Milton depicts 'a learned hypocrite . . . with much toil and difficulty wading to his auditors up to the eyebrows in deep shallows that wet not the instep'. He answers the argument that bishoprics and deaneries must be preserved so that the gentry will think it worth while to 'put their sons to learning': 'they may as well sue for nunneries, that they may have some convenient stowage for their withered daughters, because they cannot give them portions answerable to the pride and vanity they have bred them in.'[2] There is the vignette in *Areopagitica* of the man who entrusts his religion to his minister. 'His religion comes home at night, prays, is liberally supped and sumptuously laid to sleep, rises, is saluted, and after the malmsey or some well-spiced brewage . . . his religion walks abroad at eight, and leaves his kind entertainer in the shop trading all day without his religion.'[3]

Milton specializes in throwaway lines, like 'the dissolute rabble of . . . courtiers, . . . both hes and shes – if there were any males among them'. Or on set forms of prayer: 'as if it were constancy in the cuckoo, to be always in the same liturgy'.[4] Milton noted that Salmasius claimed to have deferred his attack on the papacy until he had finished with Milton. 'Thus have I brought deliverance to the papal supremacy, which was on the verge of destruction. . . . Certainly more than a cardinal's hat will be due to me for this debt. I fear that the Roman pontiff, transferring to me the ancient title of our kings [whom Milton has abolished] will dub me Defender of the Faith', Fid. Def. Having to sit listening for a lifetime to a parson whom one had not chosen Milton grimly likened to 'the sheep in their pews at Smithfield'.[5] In 1673 Milton said that the name Roman Catholic contained a self-contradiction. It was 'one of the Pope's bulls, as

[1] Leigh (1673), pp. 136–7. Leigh refers to passages reprinted in *C.P.W.*, I, pp. 902–4; II, pp. 518–21.
[2] *C.P.W.*, I, pp. 939, 720, 718.
[3] *Ibid.*, II, pp. 244–5.
[4] *Ibid.*, III, pp. 455, 507.
[5] *Ibid.*, IV, pp. 566, 581–2.

if he should say "universal particular"'.[1] Milton anticipated Cromwell's remark that preventing lay preaching for fear of heresy was like keeping all wine out of the country lest men should be drunk.[2]

If we had recognized Milton as a humorist we might have been spared a lot of speculation about whether his sonnet 'Captain or colonel or knight at arms' was actually stuck on his door when the attack was intended on the City, and whether it reveals a regrettably timorous attitude in the great revolutionary poet.[3] (Milton could hardly have made the point clearer: the Royalist troops were as little likely to be commanded by mediaeval knights at arms as they were to be armed with spears.) It is a jest at the enemy's expense, presumably written for friends after the attack had failed to materialize; it breathes confidence rather than timidity.[4] Some of Milton's jokes have a secularist flavour, as when he says that Zanchius is as cocksure in his exposition of the virgin birth 'as if he had been present in Mary's womb and witnessed the mystery himself'.[5] In *Animadversions* (1641) Milton described anger and laughter as the 'two most rational faculties of human intellect'. He exercised both faculties a good deal himself. But we should not take too seriously his claim that his laughter is only 'grim . . . in an austere visage'.[6]

Although Milton was a man of firm and indeed fierce principle, this does not seem to have affected his personal relationships. He distinguished sharply between individuals as symbols, as arguments, and individuals as people. To the former he could be brutal and merciless if they were symbols which he rejected, arguments which he had to overthrow. 'As good almost kill a man as kill a good book', he had declared in *Areopagitica*.[7] So in their turn Joseph Hall, Salmasius and Alexander More were denounced as monsters of iniquity, and even the Marian martyr bishops were not spared when it had to be shown that their sufferings did nothing to justify episcopacy. But Milton's anti-Catholicism did not prevent him establishing cordial relations with many Italian intellectuals, including a cardinal; nor did it stop him later befriending Edmund Spenser's papist grandson at about the time when he was calling on God to avenge the

---

[1] *C.M.*, VI, p. 167. Cf. pp. 220 above and 472 below for what may be one of Milton's best jokes.
[2] *C.P.W.*, II, pp. 525–6, 634–5. The joke was not original: it had been made by Robert Burton, and no doubt by others (cf. C. Hill, Penguin, 1972, pp. 122, 277).
[3] See for instance *C.P.W.*, II, p. 764, note 9.
[4] Parker supports this reading of the sonnet (I, p. 232); it seems to me difficult to make sense of any other.
[5] *C.P.W.*, VI, p. 422.
[6] *Ibid.*, I, pp. 663–4.
[7] *Ibid.*, II, p. 492.

slaughtered Vaudois. Despite his Parliamentarianism Milton retained the friendship of Royalists like Henry Lawes, Sir William Davenant and Sir Robert Howard; and of Nedham, who changed allegiance at least four times. Milton's Puritanism did not stop him helping the Laudian Brian Walton, sometime curate to Stock at All Hallows, to win official support for his Polyglot Bible in the sixteen-fifties; nor being 'intimately acquainted' with the papist William Joyner after the Restoration.

In the fifties Milton may have come to see that too much could be sacrificed to public duty: the quiet enjoyment of human friendship which was the ultimate aim of the work tended to be neglected for the work. This is the point of 'And when God sends a cheerful hour, refrains'. When the work failed, or proved to have been misguided, only human society and ultimate confidence in God's providence remained. The strenuous athleticism should perhaps first be applied to one's own perfecting, only after that to saving others.

The traditional austere, aloof Milton has to be preserved by circular arguments and unprovable assumptions. Malatesti is rebuked for foolishly dedicating La Tina to him, though Milton happily accepted the dedication. Milton's use of 'foul language, words naked and unchaste', jests 'taken from the stews and the tavern', 'the pleasantries of dissolute prodigals',[1] has to be shrugged off, though the poet obviously very much enjoyed the riot of untranslatable puns on mulberries (=morus) and figs in the high-spirited Second Defence, where he described how More demonstrated to his girl friend methods of grafting mulberries on figs to produce a grove of sycamores.[2] Biographers have perhaps also been too hasty in assuming that Milton had nothing to do with his nephew John Phillips's A Satyr against Hypocrites of 1655. Hypocrisy, 'the only evil that walks/ Invisible, except to God alone' (P.L. III. 682–5), was one of the vices towards which Milton, like Winstanley,[3] was most consistently severe. Satan 'was the first/ That practised falsehood under saintly show' (P.L. IV. 121–2 – cf. IV. 744–7, quoted on p. 130 above). It was through hypocrisy that enemies of God's cause had attached themselves to the Revolution, only to betray it in the hour of need. Hypocrisy seemed to Milton the character-istic vice of the Presbyterians and especially of the clergy of the Crom-wellian state church. So there is no reason to suppose that John Phillips's savage lampooning of the established clergy would have upset his uncle. The serious parts of the Satyr against Hypocrites might have been written

---

[1] Ibid., IV, pp. 743, 771. The words are Alexander More's.
[2] Ibid., IV, p. 566 etc.
[3] E.g. Sabine, pp. 446–8.

by Milton so far as sentiment goes.[1] There is nothing in the poem that would have shocked Milton except possibly occasional lapses in taste – and of these he was guilty himself from time to time. To speak of 'turning the Lord's Supper into a cannibal feast', and evacuating 'Christ's holy body ... into the latrine' would fall short by some standards.[2] In 1662 Milton was reported as lamenting that 'he is no longer allowed to write satire'.[3] It would be interesting to know which of his works he regarded as satires.

An alternative Milton is possible once we look at the evidence without prepossessions. I came to my version of Milton through a long period in the company of Seekers, Ranters, early Quakers and other 'new notionists' of the late sixteen-forties and early -fifties. Milton seems to me to relate to this background in the same way as do George Fox, John Bunyan, Lodowick Muggleton. None of them were Ranters, all were influenced by this intellectual milieu. Most of them, Milton included, attacked its ideas at many points; all of them were involved in it.

One of the most striking characteristics of Milton's this-worldly emphasis, a characteristic which he shared with the radicals,[4] is his rejection of the age-old view that this world is a vale of tears: that we must seek our happiness elsewhere. On the contrary: there was 'enormous bliss' in Paradise, where Adam was 'happier than I know' (P.L. VIII. 282). Yet the earthly Paradise within will be 'happier far'. In the remarkable exchange between God and Adam the Creator asks his creation

> What thinkest thou then of me. . . .
> Seem I to thee sufficiently possessed
> Of happiness, or not? Who am alone
> From all eternity.
>
> (VIII. 403–6)

This may be intended to stress the difference between even unfallen man and God, because the question is unanswerable. It may have been a joke at Adam's expense, who had asked for a helpmeet: 'What happiness can I enjoy alone?' (VIII. 365). The granting of this request was to have an ironical outcome. God needs no companion, conversing only with

> the creatures which I made, and those
> To me inferior, infinite descents
> Beneath what other creatures are to thee.
>
> (VIII. 409–11)

---

[1] See appendix 2 below. Four of the 'Advice to a Painter' poems, in similar vein, were attributed to Milton in 1697 (Marvell, 1927, I, p. 269).

[2] C.P.W., VI, pp. 554, 560; cf. pp. 826–7. Milton took especial pains with the passage quoted, rewriting it several times. See p. 74 above for Lollard antecedents.

[3] Parker, p. 579.

[4] See pp. 310–11, 323–5 above.

Or we may be intended to infer a similarity within difference between man and God: otherwise why should God have asked the question?

Milton was with the great liberators Luther and Blake in his attempt to break the bonds of guilt, to relieve mankind from the superstition of scarecrow sins. 'He alone is to be called great who either performs or teaches or worthily records great things.' 'Those things alone are great which either render this life happy . . . or lead to the other, happier life.'[1] Happiness was not a place, it was a state of mind, a search. Milton, who erewhile the happy garden sang, envisaged a Paradise 'happier far' built in the wilderness of this world. Bunyan's *Pilgrim's Progress* is about getting to heaven, where we seek our reward; all Milton's great poems are about living on earth. When the Founding Fathers of the American republic spoke of 'life, liberty and the pursuit of happiness',[2] we think at least of the last as a post-enlightenment demand. But it was a demand which Milton would have understood. Here too he had parted from traditional Puritanism and was in the modern world. 'The happier Eden' was Adam and Eve 'emparadised in one another's arms' (*P.L.* IV. 506–7).[3]

---

[1] *C.P.W.*, IV, p. 601.

[2] When they described as 'self-evident truths' what many thought not at all self-evident, we recall Milton's 'no man who knows aught can be so stupid to deny that all men naturally were born free' (*C.P.W.*, III, p. 198).

[3] Leo Miller ingeniously suggests that Marshall's engraving for the 1645 *Poems*, which Milton so disliked, was the result of malice, not of incompetence. 'This engraver of Anglican bishops saw Milton, the heretic divorcer', whether he 'drew Milton from life or from a circa 1629 original' (Miller, 'Milton's Portraits', *Milton Quarterly*, special issue, 1976).

Chapter 33

The Relevance of Milton

> Counter-culture radicalism *is* in some respects more personal and introspective than past radicalisms normally have been. . . . This . . . reflects the perception that the revolutionary theory and practice of the past have placed too much faith in economic and institutional changes, and have neglected the need to change people's way of thought and modes of personal behaviour.
>
> Anthony Arblaster, *Times Literary Supplement*, 6 June 1975

I Milton Agonistes

Mr. Arblaster might have excepted Milton from the charge against 'past radicalisms'. Milton's political experience led him to attach more importance to changes in people's modes of thought and conduct, less to political manipulation and institutional change. This would seem to give him a certain modern relevance.

But we have to work a little to grasp Milton's relevance. We cannot just 'let the poetry speak for itself'.[1] Some of it will, most of the ideas will not; and Milton is nothing if not a poet of ideas. To understand his relevance we must see him as a man of total political commitment. Like Wordsworth, he started out with extravagantly high hopes: unlike Wordsworth, he strove to cling on to them. Like Yeats, Milton wrote his greatest poetry when he was over the age of fifty. Like Blake, unlike Wordsworth and Auden, Milton did not renegue on the political convictions which had inspired him in his younger days. When Milton's revolution had turned sour, he did not seek the facile way out of saying that his God had failed. He knew that any human beings who thought God had failed them must have idolatrously set up as an object of worship their own desires and fancies. Believers were included in the failure: self-

---

[1] See p. 4 above.

respect prevented Milton from looking for a divine scapegoat. Defeat of his cause left him not bewailing and lamenting but probing deeper into his own nature and that of others, in order to find out what was needed for the good cause to succeed. Milton wrestled with God for the blessing which had so signally been withheld, convinced that it was not unattainable. His most mature writings were aimed at the politically dedicated minority, fit though few, who could with him face defeat without whining, without self-exculpation.

But Milton's relevance can hardly be grasped without some understanding of his theology, through which his initial radicalism and his final synthesis were expressed. If we regard the theology as merely out-of-date lumber – which on the surface it is – or, worse still, if we regard it as something we have to believe if we are to appreciate the poetry, then Milton is mostly dead for us. We must see, for instance, the Fall of Man as a myth or metaphor through which Milton (and not only Milton) expresses determination to change *this* world: only so can we grasp the relevance of his poetry to men and women living in a world which still needs transforming but which is not going to be transformed except by human effort. Above all Milton *fought*: this determination not to surrender what he believes to be right, however complete the apparent defeat of his cause, makes Milton every age's contemporary. Properly understood, he will be outdated only when the millennium arrives. And that, he would have grimly agreed, is long enough.

I have spoken of Milton as an individualist. But the this-worldliness of his thought makes him far less concerned with his own soul or with the after life than many of his contemporaries. There is no evidence that Milton ever underwent the conversion that was almost *de rigueur* among certain Puritan groups. There is in him none of the fevered search for personal salvation that we find in Vaughan on the one hand, in Bunyan on the other. Milton is concerned with Christ's kingdom, the good society, rather than with personal consolations or rewards. Even in *Lycidas*, where it would have been most appropriate, the reference to personal immortality is perfunctory: the real consolation is the two-handed engine, ready like Samson to smite the enemies of the church, of Christ's kingdom. Milton's virtual abandonment of the idea of sacrificial atonement, his failure to emphasize the miracles of the New Testament, including the incarnation, the resurrection, the ascension and pentecost, all make his approach verge on the secular.

The dominant characters in Milton's last three great poems are not merely individuals: they are public persons, representatives. This role is traditional for Adam and Jesus Christ in the Christian scheme of salvation. ('Adam, the parent and head of all men, either stood or fell as a representative of the whole human race.'[1]) The Son of God is the second Adam throughout *Paradise Regained*, though at the very end 'he unobserved/ Home to his mother's house private returned' (IV. 638–9), divesting himself of his public persona as he had earlier divested himself of his divinity. Milton also emphasizes that Samson was 'no private' but a public person, that the fate of Israel is totally linked with his fate. The role of 'perfect men' throughout history is to save their people by their example – Moses, Enoch, Noah, Abraham, Job, Samson, Jesus – or Abdiel on a different plane. It is a shallow view which sees Milton as the hero of *Paradise Lost*. Milton is included in Adam, the informed conscience of humanity. Samson of course recalls Milton, who had hoped to liberate his people and who had suffered defeat and blindness; but we must not allow this to obscure the representative character which Samson shares with Adam, and with the Son in *Paradise Regained*. The seventeenth century invented the new science of 'political economy': Milton's is almost a political theology.

Milton was not an original thinker, about politics or theology. He synthesized other people's ideas, and he spoke out fearlessly. His attack on Constantine in 1641, his defence of Familism in 1642, his advocacy of divorce, of the accountability of kings to their peoples, his defence of republicanism in 1660, were all acts of great courage. He was a profoundly political character, dedicated to the cause which he believed to be right. But he tried also to be a realist. *Areopagitica* in 1644, *The Ready and Easy Way* in 1660, *Of True Religion, Heresy, Schism, Toleration* in 1673, all show considerable political shrewdness.[2] The Leveller and Digger appeal to a wider democracy is attractive to modern eyes, but Milton was more realistic in his refusal to attack any revolutionary régime that he hoped could be radicalized.

Even Milton's silences were often politically significant. Between 1645 and 1649, as the conflict between Presbyterian City, Independent Grandees and Leveller rank and file shook the unity of the Parliamentarian cause, Milton published nothing. He never attacked Oliver Cromwell so long as the latter lived to unite the Good Old Cause. In 1659–60 Milton tried desperately to popularize his schemes for reunion, and he returned to this

---

[1] *C.P.W.*, VI, p. 384. That this was a conventional view is illustrated by Thomas Tuke: 'As the King, his nobles, knights and burgesses do represent the whole realm in Parliament, even so did Adam represent the persons of his whole posterity' (1609, quoted by Patrides, p. 103).
[2] See pp. 150–3 above.

activity just as soon as the political climate permitted it in the sixteen-seventies.[1] His enemies remained constant – tyranny and superstition, always allied to one another.[2] The defects to which his own side were liable were avarice and ambition, also always twinned.[3]

His heresies were the common currency of radical circles, with their powerful emphasis on this world. Where Milton was unique was in his vast attempt to combine these heresies into a coherent system, and to put it forward in Latin with a view to reuniting the Protestant world. His ambition, his dedication, where what he believed to be God's cause was at stake, knew no bounds. In the *De Doctrina Christiana* and in the last pamphlets we find him still repaying the international obligations which he had incurred in Italy in the thirties. The optimism of the forties, focused on England as the chosen nation, had been succeeded by the beleaguered defensive nationalism of the fifties, the near-despair of the sixties when he felt he had no country. In the seventies hope stirred again.

The failure of Milton's audience[4] was not, as it turned out, unmitigated disaster. Together with the reimposition of the censorship, it enabled and forced him to abandon left-handed prose propaganda and return to poetry. Now he could write for a select audience, no longer worrying about problems of communication, no longer trying ever new styles, none of them totally to his satisfaction. Now he could listen to the Muse and write as she dictated, confident that those would hear who were fit to hear. In poetry he no longer had to pretend that grey was white because it was whiter than black. He could give the devil his due, be as ambiguous and ambivalent as he knew the real world was, without feeling that he was betraying the good cause. Poetry had its own logic and its own rhetoric, and into poetry he could pour all the conflicts, the doubts, the uncertainties that had racked him as he played the propagandist. But in it too he could express the moral certainty, far beyond rational prose argument, of what he knew to be right: Adam's love for Eve, the assurance that worldly strong will be subverted by things deemed weak, that the perfect man will miraculously stand in face of all temptations, that even a failed leader can make good by standing and waiting for the moment in which the Lord delivers the Philistines into his hands, made strong again, as he had delivered the Scots into those of Oliver Cromwell at Dunbar.

---

[1] See pp. 199–204, 218–20 above.
[2] *C.P.W.*, I, p. 107; VI, p. 118; cf. pp. 176–9, 200, 281–2, 382 above.
[3] See *C.P.W.*, VI, p. 598, and pp. 165, chapter 14 *passim*, p. 421 above.
[4] See pp. 403, 407, 441–2 above.

Into the last poems Milton could pour, too, his astonishingly surviving sensuous delight in the plenitude of God's creation, in the overgrown thickets of the earthly Paradise and in the burning brightness of the tigress Dalila, as well as in words, their sonority, their overtones, their ambiguities, their use to conceal as well as to communicate. F. T. Prince illustrates Milton's 'armoury of puns and jingles' in *Paradise Lost*.[1] The sheer vitality of the blind man in his late fifties and sixties is astonishing, the man who had worked so hard and suffered so much, who should have been cynical or self-defensive, and who instead summons God to judgment and finally pronounces him not guilty. I cannot think of Milton as a tragic figure in those last years when, in defeat, he wrote *Paradise Lost*, *Paradise Regained* and *Samson Agonistes*. He was not only affirming the survival of a remnant; he was proclaiming that from these would grow an hundredfold, that victory would still come in the end, however tragic the present, provided we do not lose our heads or our hearts.

Milton's radicalism, I have suggested, had its limits. On occasion it was cut short by social considerations of which he was only partly aware. This relates to the paradox of his passionate and simultaneous belief in both liberty and discipline.[2] Counterposing liberty to licence assumes certain social stabilities as a check on the intellectual iconoclasm which also attracted him. Milton's rejections of conservative views are rational: his rejections to the left are emotional, social. 'For who loves that must first be wise and good' raises questions of definition, which Milton consistently begged. His contemporary Thomas Hobbes had a short way with those who used words like 'justice', 'reason', 'liberty', 'goodness' in Milton's manner. 'Their moral philosophy is but a description of their own passions', Hobbes wrote. 'Whatsoever is the object of any man's appetite or desire, that is it which he for his part calleth good.'[3] Milton's Whiggish use of such words covers a Whiggish double-think about equality.[4]

Part of the difficulty in assessing Milton is that some of his ideas are so advanced that we tend to treat him as though he were our contemporary. Unfortunately, the three areas in which he rightly felt that he was striking blows for freedom are areas in which he now seems old-fashioned. His superb advocacy of religious liberty seems deficient in that it is restricted to Protestants. But this is because international Catholicism no longer

---

[1] Prince, pp. 123–6.
[2] See chapter 20 above.
[3] Hobbes, *Leviathan*, pp. 686, 720.
[4] See p. 467 below.

poses the threat which it did in the seventeenth century. Catholic emancipation now seems to us the acid test of sincerity and consistency in this
respect. But Catholic emancipation is a nineteenth-century phrase. 'The
emancipation of Antichrist' would not have seemed a good slogan to the
English revolutionaries, nor indeed to many Englishmen so long as Louis
XIV's France appeared to threaten national independence. In the sphere of
domestic liberty, Milton's advocacy of divorce for incompatibility now
seems excessively male-orientated. Again we have to put Milton back into
the seventeenth century (and to remember *Jane Eyre* and *Jude the Obscure*)
to see how advanced he was in his day. In the sphere of political liberty
Milton suffers in twentieth-century eyes because he was no democrat. I
have tried to explain the seventeenth-century (and not only seventeenth-
century) problem of republicans faced with an uneducated electorate,
specifically a politically uneducated electorate.[1]

Recognizing Milton's contradictions, and placing them in their social
context, is essential to understanding the poet. 'When a man tells us
unprovoked lies about himself,' Tillyard mildly observed, 'you may
reasonably infer that his emotions are seriously involved.' By saying in
Paradise Lost that he was unskilled in and unstudious of the literary
artifices of the romances, Milton 'betrays the deep feelings which made
him turn against them'.[2] We should look out for all the points at which
Milton is fiercest – in attacking his former allies among the Presbyterian
clergy or the Long Parliament, in denouncing mere humanist culture in
Paradise Regained, in his contemptuous references to the common people
or in his discussion of the relation of the sexes. Here Milton is arguing
with himself, or feels that his ideals or standards have let him down. His
anger springs from disappointment; it may be anger with himself rather
than with those it was ostensibly directed against.

Milton never resolved his tensions – between liberty and discipline,
passion and reason, human love and God's providence, the necessity of
individualism and the necessity of society, radicalism and élitism. They
ultimately perhaps seemed insoluble on earth: the pressures of the everyday world worked against the intensity of Milton's inner vision. But he
tried again and again – in *Areopagitica*, in defending and warning Cromwell,
in his appeal to the virtuous few in *The Ready and Easy Way*. At the end
he was forced into withdrawal from all churches, despite his continuing
belief in the godly remnant. In the great poems he tried to face up to the

---

[1] See pp. 157–8, 168–70 above.
[2] Tillyard (1947), p. 201.

brute facts which he called God. It seemed that only divine intervention could solve the problems of the English Revolution: near hopelessness about effective political action underlies both *Paradise Regained* and *Samson Agonistes*. Yet if no one but God can produce the solutions, what becomes of human freedom? And had God shown himself worthy of this trust? Milton's is a tension between decorum and right reason on the one hand, and on the other the radical revolutionariness of individual consciences through which right reason was expressed. The mediating term was 'the middling sort', among whom he had seen the greatest hope of finding good men who would love freedom. Milton's ideological contradictions must all be related to his social position, and to the nature of the revolution in which he took part. When even the middling sort let him down in 1660, he still wanted to fight on: but he could see no solution beyond concentrating on small things in the hope that great may come of them when God gives the sign. Reformism was forced on him by the failure of the Revolution; he no longer hoped that the masses of the population might bring about the sort of revolution he wanted to see. Moses Wall proved right: centuries of economic development were necessary before solutions were possible on earth without divine intervention.[1]

I tried to suggest, I hope not too schematically, that after the eclipse of the traditional culture of court and bishops, Milton found his allegiance divided between the culture of the Protestant ethic and the lower-class third culture; and that this may underlie many of the tensions revealed in his writings. Newton and Locke, who shared many of Milton's secret heresies and tensions, were of a younger generation, and lived on into the world of triumphant Whiggery. But they still, like Milton, censored themselves before publication. Milton concealed his views so successfully that in the eighteenth and nineteenth centuries he came to be regarded as the orthodox Puritan poet. Newton – secret anti-Trinitarian and millenarian – was seen by Blake as the personification of rational science; Locke – anti-Trinitarian and millenarian, Arminian and mortalist – as the personification of rational philosophy. Against them Blake looked upon Milton as a potential ally. But in fact all three were furtively attracted by many of the ideas of the radical underground which were not to survive the triumph of 'Newtonian' science and 'Lockean' philosophy and politics. There are many ironies here to be incorporated in the history of English popular culture when it comes to be written.

---

[1] See pp. 201–2 above, and cf. Manning, pp. 314–17.

In 1642 Milton used prophetic words which he must have recalled in 1659–60: 'Timorous and ungrateful, the church of God is now again at the foot of her insulting enemies: and thou bewailest. What matters it for thee or thy bewailing? When time was, thou couldst not find a syllable of all that thou hadst read or studied to utter in her behalf. Yet ease and leisure was given thee for thy retired thoughts out of the sweat of other men.'[1] 'Of other men': the reference is not just to his father, but social. Milton was as aware of his responsibilities to society as any guilt-ridden intellectual of to-day.

Milton had passed his own test, had not spared himself. 'If I be not heard nor believed, the event will bear me witness to have spoken truth; and I in the meanwhile have borne witness, not out of season, to the church and to my country.'[2] He early came to see his role as that of the dedicated national poet. In *Of Reformation* he shows himself in the wings, ready to come on stage and celebrate successful revolutionary action. In *Areopagitica* he anticipated a more positive leading role for learned men, and felt a greater confidence in popular creativity. He certainly did not think of himself then as an aloof and austere scholar. Disappointment at the reception of his divorce pamphlets made him want to cut himself off from his too radical admirers; he was more isolated in his self-portraits than in reality. In *Eikonoklastes* and the *Defences of the People of England* he seemed to have attained the position of leader, smashing the idols, defending 'the most heroic and exemplary achievements since the founda-tion of the world',[3] those of the English republican nation. Even in the *De Doctrina Christiana* he still aspired to teach European Protestants in the traditional English manner. *Paradise Regained* renounces some of this. Where is this great deliverer now? But we must not exaggerate the renunciation: the brief epic ends with the Son of God entering on his active mission of preaching. In *Samson Agonistes* the emphasis is again on action after preparatory waiting; perhaps Milton looked forward to publication of the *De Doctrina* as his destruction of the Temple, a secret time-bomb which would ultimately explode in the face of the orthodox. He was not to know how long it would be before it saw the light of day, or how near it came to never being published at all. But he must have smiled with grim irony as men praised *Paradise Lost* who would have recoiled in horror at the heresies of the *De Doctrina*.

The word Agonistes, we are told, means not only wrestler, struggler,

---

[1] *C.P.W.*, I, p. 804. Cf. p. 63 above.
[2] *C.M.*, VI, p. 100.
[3] *C.P.W.*, IV, p. 549. Christ's life on earth was less heroic and exemplary?

but also one who deceives whilst entertaining. Saurat saw Milton Agonistes, 'wrecked in hope, blind and poor, . . . meditating and perfecting the glorious revenge of *Paradise Lost*'. Milton, like Samson, was deceiving his audience whilst entertaining them; he was God's fool at the same time as he was God's wrestler and champion. Job, so influential for the structure and tone of *Samson Agonistes*, was also depicted as a wrestler.[1] Agonistes is a fittingly ambiguous word to describe Milton's relation to his public in the first century and a half after publication of *Paradise Lost*. Now that nearly as long again has elapsed since the appearance of the *De Doctrina*, we might begin to see Milton's point.

II Milton and posterity

I have called Milton a Whig, a revolutionary but no democrat. But though this places him in one respect, it does scant justice to his heretical radicalism. Milton was used by the Whigs in 1688 and after, but not all Whigs applauded regicide. It all depended in whose pocket the King was. Milton's revolutionary principles may have inspired the Calves' Head Club; they had no serious appeal for men of reason and compromise. But if, for instance, the *De Doctrina Christiana* had achieved publication in 1676, what would have been its effect on intellectual history? *Paradise Lost* could never have been built up as the classic of orthodoxy, and the image of Milton would have looked very different. It was exceptionally bad luck for the poet that the accident of historical development made *Paradise Lost* as bad a model for later poets as T. S. Eliot himself has been;[2] and that Milton's dearest and best possession was published too late, when religious heresy was no longer revolutionary. That it should have been translated and edited by a bishop was only the last twist of the knife. The dynamite of the sixteen-sixties became the damp squib of the eighteen-twenties – an embarrassment to Milton's respectable admirers, but one that could be ignored. By this time Milton seemed out of the main stream of republican radicalism. He was no less opposed to clericalism than Voltaire, but since Voltaire those who wished to crush *l'infâme* had different alternatives. Milton's radicalism was still rooted in the Bible, in Christian heresy, in the dialectical thinking of the pre-Newtonian age. Only through Blake was this element communicated to the nineteenth century.

---

[1] Saurat, p. 198; Sellin, pp. 157–62; Lewalski, pp. 22, 105.
[2] See pp. 2, 404 above.

So we must not see Milton only as a precursor of eighteenth-century unitarians and deists, of Priestley and Paine; not only of the radical Whig republicans, the Commonwealthsmen, a man to whom Francis Place and the Chartists looked back with affection and admiration;[1] not only a figure in the international history of revolution, influencing Jefferson and the American revolutionaries, Mirabeau and the French revolutionaries. He also influenced Herzen and the Russian romantic revolutionaries, and this reminds us that Voltaire said that no one before Milton had spoken in favour of romantic love.[2] Even if not strictly true, it was a striking thing for Voltaire to say: and it links *Paradise Lost* with the English romantic poets, with Blake again, with Wordsworth, Keats and Shelley.[3] As against the selfishness, hypocrisy and fear of death taught by priests and churches, Blake saw Milton's role as being

> to teach men to despise death and to go on
> In fearless majesty annihilating self, laughing to scorn
> Thy laws and terrors, shaking down thy synagogues as webs.[4]

Just because Milton participated in the dialogue between the two cultures in seventeenth-century England, he looks forward to Blake as well as to Paine, to romanticism as well as to deistic rationalism. Shelley reunited something of the two revolutionary traditions. Milton was Freud's favourite poet.

The curve of Milton's posthumous reputation is not entirely haphazard. 'Works of inspiration are always being annexed by orthodoxy, which hardens itself against every new incursion of the spirit': Joseph Wicksteed's words are applied to Milton by J. A. Wittreich, who speaks of commentators 'surreptitiously snaring the poet in their own net of orthodoxy'. During the century and more after the defeat and suppression of the third culture Milton became the great Puritan poet. Every decade of the eighteenth century saw on average ten editions of *Paradise Lost* and seven of Milton's complete poems.[5] A change came only with the revival of political activity among the lower and middle classes. Dr. Johnson smelt danger and roundly denounced Milton's ideas. But the radicals picked them up and emphasized unorthodoxies which had been ignored since the revolutionary decades. Blake, who certainly knew about the Ranter past,[6]

---

[1] *The White Hat*, I (1819), pp. 42, 96; *The Chartist Circular*, 13 March 1841; Stevens, pp. 377–88.
[2] Shawcross, p. 250; cf. p. 230 above.
[3] Curran, pp. 133–62.
[4] W. Blake, p. 541.
[5] Wittreich (1975), p. 148; Bate, p. 22. Isabel Rivers tells me that Wesley urged his lay preachers to read *Paradise Lost*; and Methodism contributed to the labour movement as well as to Puritan piety.
[6] Morton, pp. 83–121.

picked Milton out as the historical figure with whom the radicals' argument must be continued. He gave them the last word against Milton by claiming that he was of the devil's party without knowing it;[1] Shelley called Satan the hero of *Paradise Lost*, though in a sense different from Dryden and Dennis. The reforming Major Cartwright associated enthusiasm with love of liberty and hatred of corruption.

The revival of Milton's radical reputation was accompanied by similar revivals of trends which had been suppressed for over a century. Sociological history was picked up by the Scottish school where Harrington had left it, political economy by Adam Smith where Petty had left it. The advance of chemistry, checked since Boyle, was resumed by Priestley and Lavoisier. Political radicals, from Wilkes to the Chartists, looked back to their seventeenth-century precursors, to the Levellers and Milton. After a long struggle, the Reform Bill of 1832 re-enacted something very like the Parliamentary franchise of 1654. Robert Owen and some Chartists rediscovered ideas of communal production, though there is no evidence that they read Winstanley: men did not need to read Milton to reject tithes.[2] English society in the age of the French Revolution had caught up with the teeming freedom of the English Revolution. The publication in 1825 of the *De Doctrina Christiana* ought to have been a match to gunpowder; but by that date political radicalism had left religious heresy behind.

Chartism failed no less than Levellers, Diggers and Fifth Monarchists. Samson's hair was trimmed again. From Macaulay onwards Milton was re-annexed to orthodoxy, this time to English liberalism. In our own day the heirs of the third culture are waving their locks again. The attempt to dislodge Milton having failed, the neo-Christians tried to annex him. In the nineteen-fifties, the decade of the coldest war, which proclaimed the end of ideology, which saw Shakespeare as a Christian humanist and not much else, an effort was made to deny that Milton had really been a heretic at all. History has shown up the superficiality of pretending that ideology can cease to exist in a class-divided society (though, to do them justice, some of the end-of-ideologists imagined that the welfare state had abolished class divisions too – alas!). Shakespeare and Milton have escaped from the little nets which were cast around them. Saurat, Caudwell,

---

[1] Cf. Wittreich (1975), who argues that the Whigs were often called 'the diabolical party' (p. 214).
[2] 'Every man has a right to have what priest he chooses and to pay him what recompense he chooses, but no man or government has a right to force his God down my throat or his priestly hand into my pocket' (*The People's Paper*, 9 July 1853, quoted by Saville, p. 222).

Wolfe, Kelley, Empson, Ricks, have all helped to restore Milton to his proper place in the English tradition.

Milton was *sui generis*, wedded and glued to no forms, the great eclectic. But he was open to the left and closed to the right – intolerant of papists though embracing all varieties of Protestantism, merciless to the Philistine aristocracy and priests but merciful to the excluded vulgar, linking himself with the radicals just as far as his strong sense of the necessity of bourgeois society would permit.

Chapter 34

Keeping the Truth

> I hope ... that all my readers will be sympathetic, and will avoid
> prejudice and malice, even though they see at once that many of the
> views I have published are at odds with certain conventional opinions.
> ... This one thing I beg of my reader: that he will weigh each state-
> ment and evaluate it with a mind innocent of prejudice and eager only
> for the truth.
>
> Milton, *Of Christian Doctrine*

I started by supposing that this would be a fairly easy book to write, after
thinking about Milton off and on over a long period. My brashness was
rewarded by years of wrestling. The moment at which I write 'finis' to the
book will be quite arbitrary: every time I re-read Milton fresh aspects of
his complex personality force themselves upon me. He is elusive, subtle,
devious: he cannot be pinned down by any easy formula – Puritan,
humanist, radical – or at least no one has yet found the formula. Like
Oliver Cromwell, he manifestly held some strong convictions very
pertinaciously; but around them there is a shifting penumbra of – what?
A desire to combine intense ideals with practical realism? A sensitivity to
environment? A divided personality? He is infinitely various.

All Milton's great poems have ambiguities at the centre, and these are
not only the creation of the Milton industry, though that has no doubt
helped. Scholars still argue about the intention of Milton's masque, about
the fact that Comus appears to get the best lines. The great cruces of
Lycidas remain in dispute – who was the pilot of the Galilean lake, what
was the two-handed engine, and many others. The proclaimed theme of
Paradise Lost is itself ambiguous. Is the poet justifying to men God's ways,
or justifying the-ways-of-God-to-men? Or both? From very early days
the central point of the epic has aroused controversy. Was Satan the hero?
Was Milton of the devil's party, unwittingly or consciously? Was the
Fall fortunate? Did Milton really prefer fallen to unfallen life? Should

Adam have rejected fallen Eve? Why is God so boring (if he is)? Who is Urania? The questions are endless. In *Paradise Regained* we do not know what exactly the crucial line means – 'Tempt not the Lord thy God he said, and stood.' Does this mean Do not tempt me, who am your God? Or, Do not tempt God, in whom I trust? Is Christ man or God or both? Or is he safe because he is standing on top of the Temple whose stones are the souls of the faithful? Is *Samson Agonistes* a morality about the triumph of Christian regeneration, or is Samson a tragically flawed hero who remains flawed to the end and is uselessly destroyed in destroying others? Or is it a play bringing hope to the politically defeated?

So many ambiguities cannot be accidental. They are in part explained by the censorship, by Milton's political caution and sense of decorum, as well as by his eclectic political position between the second and third cultures. Milton I suspect *liked* being furtive and evasive. He triumphantly wrote *Paradise Lost*, and got it accepted as a great orthodox poem, whilst secretly holding very subversive views about theology and marriage which, we can now see, are hinted at in the epic. He claimed that the Spirit of God nightly descended to inspire him; and the Spirit of God dictated to him 'No fear lest dinner cool'. Milton had a far greater sense of humour, of fun, than he has been given credit for. He liked teasing. He teased his undergraduate audiences at Cambridge, he teased his (probably) Presbyterian servant, he teased his political allies with his reference to 'a short but scandalous night of interruption'. In *Paradise Lost* and *Samson Agonistes* he teased posterity. His most successful hoax was the *Letters-Patents* of 1674, if indeed it was a hoax. Milton would have enjoyed our uncertainty during three centuries after the event.[1]

But it goes far deeper than teasing. Milton is the great equivocator as well as the great eclectic, and this equivocation is at the heart of his greatest poetry.[2] Empson and Ricks have helped us to appreciate some of these complexities. I hope that this book, written from a very different angle, may suggest other considerations which we should have in mind when reading Milton. I fear that I may have added to the elusiveness rather than removing it. But that might not have displeased Milton Agonistes. It is disconcerting to try to depict a man who has strong moral principles, for which he would die, without being able to state clearly what these principles are, and so being unable to submit them to precise rational analysis. But that too may be part of what Milton has to tell us. L'Allegro and Il Penseroso are the same person, the poet who could

---

[1] See pp. 220, 455 above. Was 'no fear lest dinner cool' teasing Betty?
[2] See pp. 336–7 above.

defend either learning or ignorance, who could wag a solemn finger at
Adam's most moving speech. Heaven is more like earth than we think;
unfallen Eve is as seductive as Venus; classical learning and astronomy
are at once infinitely attractive and totally unnecessary. From the very
beginning Chaos, the source of all matter, was ambiguous, neither good
nor bad in itself until God acted upon it. The knowledge of good and evil
'as two twins cleaving together leapt forth into the world' when the apple
was eaten.[1]

Yet though the border line between right and wrong was narrow and
sometimes appeared arbitrary, it was all-important. The *De Doctrina* was
intended to ascertain border lines, but in *Paradise Lost* they remain blurred.
Perhaps in the last resort it is a greater poem than *Paradise Regained* or
Samson Agonistes just because the acceptance of arbitrary distinctions has
not yet got through to Milton's pulses. In *Paradise Regained* Satan's
arguments are less convincing than Satan's actions in *Paradise Lost*: in
Samson Agonistes Harapha and Dalila are caricatures compared with Satan
and Eve in *Paradise Lost*. Milton was at his best when most divided. What
matters in the last resort is not words but things, not formulations but
conscience, not law but love; and love cannot really be defined. We see
it only as two figures advancing hand in hand together across a vast
wilderness.

But it would be absurd to end with love, as though Milton were
Winstanley.[2] Love has to survive in this world – a world in which mother
with infant is rolled down the rocks, a world 'to good malignant, to bad
men benign' (*P.L.* XII. 537–8), the world of the executioner's knife and
the quartering block. There is justice as well as love.[3] The justice in which
Milton believed was a harsh retributive justice: the Father knew that the
Son must die so that justice might live (*P.L.* XII. 401–4). In *Lycidas* the
'perfidious bark' is sunk; Babylonian woe awaits the persecutors of the
Vaudois. In *Paradise Lost* eternal justice had prepared hell for the rebellious
angels *before* their fall (I. 70–1). Their apparent victory over Adam and Eve
is followed immediately by their transformation into serpents eating soot
and cinders (X. 504–77). In *Paradise Regained* the supreme triumph of the
Son of God is accompanied by the downfall of Satan; in *Samson Agonistes*
the Philistine aristocracy and clergy are slaughtered in an image of the
Last Judgment after which hell shall be shut. It would not be for the good
of humanity that God should 'withdraw his just punishments from us,

---

[1] *C.P.W.*, II, p. 514; cf. MacCaffrey, p. 210.
[2] Waldock, pp. 103, 138; see pp. 266–7 above.
[3] Cf. Miner (1974), p. 257.

and . . . restrain what power either the devil or any earthly enemy hath to work us woe'.[1]

In 1641 and many times later Milton declared that a people whose vices prove them unworthy of freedom would justly be deprived of it. In view of the self-enslavement of 'that people victor once, now vile and base' (*P.R.* IV. 132–45), it would have been *unjust* if the English Revolution had succeeded, just as Adam and Eve 'deserved to fall' (*P.L.* X. 16). The task which Milton set himself was to *justify* the ways of God to men, to demonstrate their justice. The final resurrection, Milton tells us with rather perfunctory orthodoxy, will be the ultimate vindication of God's providence. But he rejected the Calvinist view that predestination demonstrated God's justice. Divine justice can be vindicated only if 'some measure of free will' is 'allowed to men'.[2] And justice is also the retribution that comes on earth. It is 'the sword of God, superior to all mortal things, in whose hand soever by apparent signs his testified will is to put it'. Those who with deliberate understanding and intent execute 'the wrath of God upon evil-doers' act lawfully and are not to be resisted.[3] Samson destroying the Philistines, the regicides sentencing Charles I, all anticipated the Last Judgment.[4] It is God who overthrows 'haughty and unruly kings', who led the way in the English Revolution and who condemned Charles I. Justice – 'all strength and activity' – is superior to merely contemplative truth.[5] 'The instruments of armed Justice in defence of beleaguered Truth' were hammered out in the mansion house of liberty, London, during the Civil War.[6] Cromwell undertook the conquest of Ireland 'in full accordance with the will of God'. 'After your freedom had been won by God's assistance and your own valour', Milton told the English people, for them to return to slavery would be 'to resist your destiny'.[7]

'The bloody fact' of Cain's murder of Abel 'will be avenged' on earth (*P.L.* XII. 457–60). 'Loathesome sickness' is an appropriate punishment for the wicked (*P.L.* XII. 522–5; cf. *C.P.W.*, III, p. 482 for other examples of vengeance from the Old Testament). Hence the reminder to God in the opening of Milton's sonnet 'On the Late Massacre': 'Forget not!'[8] But

---

[1] *C.P.W.*, II, p. 234.
[2] *Ibid.*, I, p. 705; V, pp. 402–3; IV, p. 684; VI, pp. 620, 175, 385–7, 397.
[3] *Ibid.*, III, pp. 193, 198, 564.
[4] See pp. 282, 309 above.
[5] *C.P.W.*, IV, pp. 305, 359, 499; VI, p. 391.
[6] See pp. 94, 333 above.
[7] *C.P.W.*, IV, pp. 458, 532, 536.
[8] See pp. 209–10 above.

the overwhelming catastrophe of 1660 made the impatience of 1655 seem petulantly exaggerated. *Paradise Lost* put God's justice into longer perspective. 'The day . . . of respiration to the just/ And vengeance to the wicked' is deferred till Christ's Second Coming (XII. 539–51). Only so could the justice of God's ways be demonstrated, and eternal providence asserted. (Justice is demonstrated; providence, God's foresight, is *asserted*.)

It is within this framework of justice that the divine mercy operates. Prayer cannot alter the high decrees of heaven (*P.L.* X. 952–3; XI. 307–13).[1] The Father can accept the Son's sacrifice because 'all thy request was my decree', and death is deferred in response to the prayers of Adam and Eve. The Son in pity clothes their nakedness with skins, but they cannot be allowed to remain in Paradise (X. 210–19; XI. 46–52, 146–8, 252–7). I labour this point a little, since modern liberal Christians are reluctant to accept the harsh reality of Milton's God. 'Mercy first and last shall brightest shine' (III. 132–4), but mercy could not be divorced from justice.[2]

At the end of time 'hell shall be shut'. Milton never seems to ask who will be inside hell on that day, or earlier. Perhaps he agreed with Joseph Mede that hell was a place of confinement for the future, not for the past or present.[3] Nor is Milton interested in the agonies of the Crucifixion, in the therapeutic virtues of suffering. Unlike Crashawe, his is not 'a bleeding heart that gasps for blood' from 'those delicious wounds that weep'. He has no poem on 'the bleeding crucifix' or 'the body of our B. Lord, naked and bloody'.[4] He did not think, with Henry Vaughan, that 'sickness is wholesome', nor call for 'crosses here' to prepare him for the after life.[5] Milton's interests were resolutely this-worldly: matter is good, rightly to be enjoyed; justice must come on earth. Even the Second Coming, when the saints rule and judge in Christ, is less a divine fresh start than the culmination of human effort.[6]

Milton's chosen audience was the strenuous few who care, the dedicated, those who cannot know what is right without acting upon it, at whatever cost: those who 'hate the cowardice of doing wrong'.[7] Mede had argued

---

[1] Lodowick Muggleton believed that God does not listen to our prayers, though they may help us (Reeve and Muggleton, p. 186).
[2] Cf. Patrides, pp. 157–9.
[3] Mede, pp. 31, 141–4.
[4] Crashawe, pp. 110–11, 130–5; cf. p. 114.
[5] Vaughan, II, pp. 459, 403.
[6] See pp. 303, 376 above.
[7] *C.P.W.*, II, p. 409; cf. pp. 352–3 above.

that the visibility of God's judgments against sin on earth was one of the strongest proofs of God's existence.[1] Milton postulated the existence of God on an instinctive knowledge of the distinction between right and wrong, knowledge which can be experienced but not analysed. 'If there were no God to reward the good nor punish the evil,' Lodowick Muggleton reflected, 'yet could I do no otherways than I do; for I do well, not because I expect any reward from God, and I refrain from evil, not for fear God should see me; . . . but I do well and refrain from evil to please the law written in my heart, so that I might not be accused in my own conscience'.[2] So Abdiel

> unmoved,
> Unshaken, unseduced, unterrified
> His loyalty he kept, his love, his zeal;
> Nor number, nor example with him wrought
> To swerve from truth, or change his constant mind
> Though single. From amidst them forth he passed,
> Long way through hostile scorn, which he sustained
> Superior, nor of violence feared aught;
> And with retorted scorn his back he turned
> On those proud towers to swift destruction doomed.
>
> (P.L. V. 898–907)

God is the ostensible object of Abdiel's loyalty, love and zeal; but God's existence is established only by such proclamations of will, such determination to cling to one's own standards in the face of a hostile universe. In the last resort it is not God that is justified but man, not eternal providence that is asserted but human steadfastness and courage.

We must end, as Milton's great poems end, by returning to everyday life with a dying fall.[3] The Son of God descends from the pinnacle and 'unobserved/ Home to his mother's house private returned', a public person no longer (P.R. IV. 638–9). Samson is carried 'home to his father's house' from his miraculous triumph, his tomb to be decked with flowers by local girls. Adam and Eve in *Paradise Lost* have to accept total defeat in a malignant universe. 'So shall the world go on . . . / Under her own weight groaning' (XII. 538–9). But they must go on living too, attending to small things while waiting for great things to come of them in God's good time.

---

[1] Mede, p. 148.
[2] Muggleton (1764), p. 140. See Sprunger, pp. 246, 261–2, for Ames and Hugh Peter (perhaps) on the importance of bearing witness for posterity to a good cause.
[3] Cf. p. 427 above.

> For see the morn,
> All unconcerned with our unrest, begins
> Her rosy progress smiling; let us forth, ...
> Where'er our day's work lies.
>
> (XI. 173–7)

> Some natural tears they dropped, but wiped them soon;
> The world was all before them.
>
> (XII. 645–6)

Similarly the blind poet, after descending into hell and ascending to heaven, returned to earth ready to take up his subversive pen just as soon as circumstances permitted. The picture of Milton subsiding into a genial and pacifist old age, in which all conflicts are mental only, is a piece of twentieth-century sentimentalism which the seventeenth-century texts do not justify. But whilst waiting for the day of respiration to come, he sat in the sun outside his house, in a grey coarse cloth coat, chatting cheerfully and listening to Betty preparing a meal for him, frugal but of dishes that he liked. In the last major poem that he published he saw his cause as a Phoenix

> then vigorous most
> When most unactive deemed,
> And though her body die, her fame survives,
> A secular bird ages of lives.
>
> (*S.A.* 1704–7)

The author of *The Doctrine and Discipline of Divorce*, of the *Defences of the People of England* and of *The Ready and Easy Way* wanted discerning readers of *Paradise Lost* to know that he had followed Raphael's last injunction to Adam before the Fall:

> Stand fast: to stand or fall
> Free in thine own arbitrament it lies.
> Perfect within, no outward aid require.
>
> (*P.L.* VIII. 640–2)

Adversity had not led Milton to abandon the beliefs to which he had given his life and his eyes.[1]

> I sing ... unchanged
> ... Though fallen on evil days
> On evil days though fallen and evil tongues.
>
> (*P.L.* VII. 24–6)

He would not want his personal fame to be separated from his Good Old Cause.

---

[1] See pp. 238, 364–5, 404–5 above.

APPENDICES

The Date of *Samson Agonistes*

Most editors assume that in Milton's *Poems* the order of printing is chronological unless there is good reason for thinking otherwise. Until fairly recently commentators took this to apply to the 1671 volume too; so *Samson Agonistes* was Milton's last poem. But Parker has argued for a date considerably earlier than the Restoration for *Samson Agonistes*.[1] Now it may well be that Milton pondered the subject of Samson for a long time: it was clearly very much in his mind when he wrote *The Reason of Church Government* in 1642. Parts of the poem may be of early origin, as Todd conjectured in 1801, and as some lines of *Paradise Lost* are. But I know of no convincing evidence for as early a date as Parker favours – 1646–7, perhaps completed in 1652–3; and there is much circumstantial evidence for the traditional late date.[2]

Parker's starting point is a good one: that a post-Restoration date has been accepted without positive evidence, and that once this date is assumed it is easy to read confirmatory evidence into the text of the drama. So, Parker rightly says, there is a case for looking at it afresh without presuppositions.

Parker attaches great importance to the failure of Edward Phillips and the Anonymous Biographer to put a date to the writing of *Samson Agonistes* whereas the former dated *Paradise Regained* to the years 1667–71, a time at which he was in close contact with Milton. Those who accept this argument (which seems to me to attach excessive weight and precision to words which may not have been intended to be at all precise)[3] still have a wide range of alternative dates for *Samson Agonistes* without accepting Parker's pre-Restoration dating. (The Anonymous Biographer says that both *Paradise Regained* and *Samson Agonistes* were finished after the Restoration.) Woodhouse suggested 1660–2, the only objection to which is that

---

[1] Parker, pp. 903–17; (1971), pp. 163–4.

[2] Sirluck (1961), pp. 773–81; Barker (1964), p. 176. Cf. Oras, pp. 128–97, and Ricks, *Sphere History*, II, p. 309. Parker was not always consistent: at p. 317 he assumes a later date.

[3] Parker himself stresses Phillips's inaccuracy, especially during the period after 1663 (p. 1125).

Milton would then be in the middle of writing *Paradise Lost*. But he spent perhaps four months in hiding in 1660, and at least several weeks in prison, presumably without access to the wide range of sources which must have been drawn on for *Paradise Lost*.[1] Alternatively, we might think of the years 1665–7, when *Paradise Lost* was finished, *Paradise Regained* (apparently) not yet begun. Edward Phillips was at this time in the employment of the Earl of Pembroke and frequently at Wilton, which would prevent his seeing Milton regularly.[2] It is indeed a period in which we know almost nothing of Milton's activities. Milton no doubt saw marks of divine disapproval in the Plague of 1665: he had said in 1660 that plague was always associated with monarchy – correctly. There were big plagues in 1603 and 1625, but no major outbreak between 1635 and 1665.[3] The Fire of 1666 and the disasters of the Second Dutch War would confirm this view. The Pentland Rising of that year may have roused Milton's hopes. Or the blood may just have been returning to his veins after the chilling experiences of the Restoration: pessimism was never in his nature, nor in his theology. God must have an answer. Many in Samuel Pepys's circle at this time looked back to the revolutionary years with renewed favour. A time might after all be approaching when God would raise up a remnant to smite the Philistines.

Another argument of Parker's (to which Carey seems to me to attach undue weight) is that Milton's description of the verse of *Samson Agonistes* in 1671 echoes phrases which he had used in 1647 to describe the verse of his ode to Rous. Others besides Milton have used similar words to describe similar phenomena on different occasions. Even Parker cannot really argue for 1646–7 as more than a beginning date for *Samson Agonistes,* with 1652–3 as the date at which the bulk of it was written. What can be picked up five years later can be picked up fifteen years later.

Another of Parker's arguments concerns the attack on rhyme in the note on the verse added to the 1668 impression of *Paradise Lost*. Could Milton have written *Samson Agonistes* after denouncing rhyme as 'the invention of a barbarous age, to set off wretched matter and lame metre'? But this proves too much. How could Milton *publish*, without explanation or apology, a drama which contained rhymes, only three years after this denunciation? Publish it he did: nor did he seem to think any explanation called for. Why not? He could simply have changed his mind, if we think of 1660–2 or 1665–7 as possible dates for *Samson Agonistes*. But we recall

[1] Woodhouse (1949), pp. 157–75.
[2] Masson, VI, p. 764.
[3] *C.M.,* VI, p. 147.

that in 1644, before Parker's earliest date for *Samson,* Milton had attacked those 'despicable creatures, our common rhymers and playwrights'.[1] The way out is to distinguish more carefully between types of rhymed verse, as Marvell no doubt did when he criticized 'tinkling rhyme' in the rhymed couplets of 'On *Paradise Lost*'. Milton's strictures of 1668 apply to 'heroic verse, in longer works especially'. In his introductory note to *Samson Agonistes* he emphasized that 'our best English tragedies' have rejected rhyme. Milton claimed to have liberated 'heroic poem from the troublesome and modern bondage of rhyming'. He was thinking of the end-stopped couplets of Restoration satire or heroic drama, not of lyrics. The rolling blank verse paragraphs of *Paradise Lost* do in fact approach the liberty of later free verse.[2] So does the verse of *Samson Agonistes,* in which rhyme is totally liberated from the bondage of the couplet. Milton claimed to have followed the ancients and the modern Italians rather than English models, and his 'stanzas framed only for the music' must have seemed to him something quite different from heroic blank verse. He may, as Kermode suggests, have been imitating Hebrew lyrics, pursuing a train of thought initiated by George Wither's *Preparation to the Psalter* (1619). This could be associated with Milton's rejection of the Greek ode in *Paradise Regained,* though I would not want to commit myself to the belief that *Samson Agonistes* was written later than *Paradise Regained*.[3]

It is important to remember the context of the argument, which started in 1664 and reached its height in 1668 with the publication of Dryden's *Essay of Dramatic Poesy*. Milton was intervening, on the side of his friend Sir Robert Howard, in a controversy which began by discussing heroic plays in rhymed couplets of the type written by the Earl of Orrery and by Dryden. There are even political overtones to the argument, since 'King Charles was the first who put my lord [Orrery] upon . . . writing plays in rhyme.' For 'his majesty relished rather the French fashion of plays than the English', and ensured that Orrery's first play was put on by the King's company.[4]

Milton extended the argument to epic. His contribution deals with the monotony and bondage of long stretches of rhymed couplets. In *Samson Agonistes* (apart from one rhymed couplet of Dalila's – 973–4) rhyme occurs only in the lyrics of the chorus and two of Samson's 'stanzas framed only for the music' (80–106, 610–16). This in a closet drama (Milton's

---

[1] *C.P.W.,* II, p. 405.
[2] Goldstein, pp. 133–4. See p. 404 above.
[3] Kermode (1952), pp. 59–63.
[4] Boyle, I, pp. 23–6, 34.

disavowal of any intention of the play being acted comes just after his discussion of the verse) is something very different from the 'troublesome
bondage' which Milton was attacking. Dalila's one couplet is comparable
to the number of rhymes which occur in the blank verse of *Paradise Lost*.[1]

Edward Phillips, quoting his uncle almost *verbatim*, makes exactly this
distinction: rhyme in Pindaric strophes 'would be much more suitable for
tragedy than the continued rhapsody of rhyming couplets', which would
be too stiff and too constraining.[2] Since Parker, in arguing for an early
date for *Samson Agonistes*, builds a lot on Phillips's silence, it is useful to
note that the latter saw no incongruity between Milton's views on verse in
Paradise Lost and *Samson Agonistes*.

Tillyard and Masson detected a number of post-Restoration allusions in
the drama.[3] I think they are right. Parker admits to eight (or nine) possible
political allusions, as well as ten (or thirteen) personal allusions, but claims
to find none of them convincing. His list is by no means complete. Several
others are suggested in Chapter 31 above. Parker fails altogether to notice
the parallel between Israel's servitude and the Norman Yoke theory in
England. Nor does he mention the analogy between Samson and the New
Model Army.[4] It is not easy to convince those whose approach is so
austerely anti-historical. The case is slightly strengthened by noticing the
lines in *Samson Agonistes* which pick up passages in *Paradise Lost* (or vice
versa, if we accept Parker's dating). Thus 'drunk with idolatry, drunk with
wine' (*S.A.* 1670) recalls 'the sons/ Of Belial flown with insolence and
wine' (*P.L.* I. 501–2). 'Unjust tribunals under change of times' (*S.A.* 695),
to me a painfully obvious reference to the Restoration persecution, picks
up 'On evil days though fallen and evil tongues' of *P.L.* VII. 25–6. The
editors of the Longman edition of Milton, who unfortunately accept
Parker's dating of *Samson Agonistes*, recognize that *P.L.* XI. 797–806
alludes to time-servers among the English revolutionaries: practising

> how to live secure
> Worldly or dissolute on what their lords
> Shall leave them to enjoy. . . .
> So all shall turn degenerate, all depraved.

And they add, rightly, that this problem is dealt with more fully in *Samson
Agonistes*. But it is a post-Restoration problem, after the Norman lords
have come back.

---

[1] Diekhoff, pp. 539–43.
[2] E. Phillips, Preface.
[3] Tillyard (1949), pp. 329–54; Masson, VI, pp. 671–7.
[4] See pp. 429–30, 435–6 above.

Similarly Samson seems to refer to the post-Restoration problem of whether attendance at the worship of the Church of England was permissible. Human commands are to be obeyed, so long as they demand nothing 'scandalous or forbidden in our law' (1409). In that case they are to be resisted (1365–74) in the higher cause of duty to God. 'Where the heart joins not, outward acts defile not', the chorus urges. Samson replies 'But who constrains me to the temple of Dagon/ Not dragging?' Only 'for some important cause' could God permit attendance 'at idolatrous rites' (1368–71, 1378–9). There would be no point in raising this question between 1650 and 1660, when church attendance was not compulsory. It is very doubtful indeed whether it was enforced during the sixteen-forties. The heavy emphasis on the idolatry of Dagon's priests would have topical relevance after the restoration of episcopalianism in 1660, none in the forties or fifties.[1]

Another reason for dating the poem late is that the conflict has been completely internalized. *We* can see that the Satan of the opening books of *Paradise Lost* expressed one part of Milton; the poet himself must have appreciated that Samson's rebellion against God was also his own. The external struggles in the epics mirror the internal conflict in the believer. For this reason Saurat suggested that Milton himself was the hero of *Paradise Lost. Paradise Regained* can also be seen as a dialogue between two parts of Milton, or between Milton past and Milton present. But in *Samson Agonistes* there is no devil and no Christ: there is a man, within whose breast the conflicts have to be decided.[2] I do not attach much importance to the fact that Samson's return 'home to his father's house' echoes or is echoed by Jesus's return to his mother's house at the end of *Paradise Regained*.[3] Parker is, however, apparently willing to date the brief epic before the Restoration too, as I think he logically should on the basis of his very precise reading of Edward Phillips's cryptic remarks. No one so far as I know has followed him on to this hobby-horse, and I hope no one will; but anyone who accepts his case for *Samson Agonistes* should at least carefully consider his whole argument. An early date for *Samson* should entail an early date for *Paradise Regained*. Which is absurd but logical, and demonstrates the folly of relying on logic to the exclusion of history.

---

[1] *C.P.W.*, VI, pp. 31, 694; cf. p. 438 above. Low's insistence on 'close compatibility between *Samson Agonistes* and the *Christian Doctrine*' argues strongly against an early date (p. 222; cf. p. 239 above).
[2] Cf. Saurat, pp. 184–5, 198.
[3] See p. 427 above.

It is surely reasonable to ask those who favour an early date to place *Samson Agonistes* in some sort of context. The deep despair which Parker detects in it could perhaps be related to the political circumstances of 1648,[1] though hardly to 1646–7, Parker's preferred date. There is no reason at all for thinking that Milton was politically in despair in 1652–3, when Parker supposes the poem was completed. True, Milton went blind in that year, but to accept this as the sole explanation is to carry biographical subjectivism to even greater lengths than those which Parker purports to deplore. Milton was such a profoundly political animal that the personal is not enough to explain Samson's 'sense of heaven's desertion' (632), his calling God's justice to his people in question. In fact, to judge by the evidence of his personal letters, Milton was optimistic and cheerful in 1652–3. The *Second Defence* of 1654 is still high-spirited and confident in the cause of the English people and their revolution. It contains warnings that things may go wrong; but they are most plausibly attributed to Milton's anxiety about the political tendency of the Protectorate of Oliver Cromwell established in December 1653, *after* the date at which Parker believes *Samson Agonistes* to have been completed. I do not think that Milton at this period shared the gloom of Isaac Penington (quoted on p. 358 above). Penington was committed to the third culture, whether Ranter or Quaker, and this had been hopelessly defeated by 1650. Milton still had hopes of a solution which would achieve some of the aspirations of the proponents of the third as well as the second culture; and he almost certainly retained this hope until the end of 1653 and perhaps even later. On the evidence so far produced, I see no reason to date *Samson Agonistes* before 1660, and many reasons for dating it after the Restoration.

---

[1] See pp. 160–2, 165 above.

John and Edward Phillips

Perhaps there are grounds for reconsidering Milton's relations with his younger nephew, John Phillips. Milton's biographers raise their eyebrows at Phillips's *A Satyr against Hypocrites* (1655) and assume that it must have outraged the 'Puritan' Milton. I am not so sure. The poem was attributed to Milton in 1710, and its conclusion certainly strikes a serious Miltonic note:

> *Oh what will men not dare, if thus they dare*
> *Be impudent to heaven and play with prayer?*
> – Play with that fear, with that religious awe
> Which keeps men free, and that is man's great law.
> What can they but the worst of atheists be
> Who, while they word it 'gainst impurity,
> Affront the throne of God with their false deeds?
> Alas, this wonder in the atheist breeds.
> Are these the men that would the age reform,
> That 'Down with superstition' cry, and swarm
> This painted glass, that sculpture, to deface,
> But worship pride and avarice in their place?
> Religion they bawl out, yet know not what
> Religion is, unless it be to prate.[1]
> Meekness they preach, but study to control;
> Money they'd have, when they cry out 'Your soul!' ...
> Vain foolish people, how are ye deceived,
> How many several sorts have ye received
> Of things called truths, upon your backs laid on
> Like saddles for themselves to ride upon!
> They rid amain, and hell and Satan drove,
> While every priest for his own profit strove. . . .
> They close with God, seem to obey his laws,
> They cry aloud for him and for his cause:

---

[1] Cf. 'They bawl for freedom in their senseless mood'; the next lines recall the rhythm of 'licence they mean when they cry liberty'. Note that 'pride and avarice' are precisely the sins against which Milton was warning at this time (pp. 193–5 above).

But while they do their strict injunctions preach,
Deny in actions what their words do teach.
Oh what will men not dare, if thus they dare
Be impudent to heaven and play with prayer?
Yet if they can no better teach than thus,
Would they would only teach themselves, not us:
So while they still on empty outsides dwell
They may perhaps be choked with husk and shell;
While those who can their follies well refute
By a true knowledge do obtain the fruit.[1]

The main thrust of Phillips's poem is against 'priests', occupants of livings
in the state church – Presbyterians, Independents, tenacious episcopalians
– who force their teaching upon others. Indeed, the 1661 reprint of the
poem gives it the title *The Religion of the Hypocritical Presbyterians*. In *The
Tenure* Milton had attacked the 'formal preachment' and 'belly cheer' of the
Presbyterian clergy, precisely John Phillips's targets.[2] Milton had no use
for a state church, nor for conformists who took their religion from their
minister as from 'some factor'. Phillips also has some back-handed blows at
antinomians – from whom Milton wished to differentiate himself:

Thus they train up their souls with holy words,
Shaving off sin as men shave off their beards
To grow the faster; sins, they cry, are fancies:
The godly live above all ordinances.[3]

But much of the poem is straightforward bawdry. The priests gorge
themselves, and then retire with the admiring wives of their parishioners.
The latter begin

to talk of the several sizes,
Of the long and the short, the little and the great.

John Phillips obviously enjoyed the new permissiveness, freedom to use
four-letter words, to make jokes about parsons copulating with members
of their flock. Before 1640 such ribaldry had been possible only at the
expense of the sects. What *A Satyr against Hypocrites* lacks is taste, decorum.
It may well be that Milton did not think his nephew's pun Habakkuk/have
a cock very funny, though it had already been made by George Chapman.[4]
But the *Satyr's* fierce anti-clericalism would certainly have been to Milton's
taste. We recall the rather disagreeable story of Milton teasing a servant

---

[1] *Op. cit.*, p. 23.
[2] Darbishire, p. xxii; *C.P.W.*, III, p. 241.
[3] *A Satyr*, p. 12.
[4] *Ibid.*, pp. 10–16; Chapman, I, p. 63.

who was 'a constant follower' of 'these pretended divines' so mercilessly that he left the poet's service. From the context this appears to relate to Presbyterians or state-church Independents.[1]

In December 1651 John Phillips had published a Latin *Response* to an anonymous attack on Milton's *Defence of the People of England* – a work with which Milton helped him. He may have been the J.P. who in 1654 summarized a passage from *The Tenure of Kings and Magistrates* in a pamphlet called *Tyrants and Protectors Set Forth in their Colours*.[2] Milton could hardly have taken any responsibility, publicly, for this. But in 1656 John Phillips published *The Tears of the Indians*, a translation from Las Casas, with a signed dedication to the Lord Protector, and a patriotic 'Introduction To all true Englishmen'. This piece of anti-Spanish propaganda must have been entirely to his uncle's liking.

Later in the same year the Council of State ordered Phillips's *Sportive Wit* to be burnt as 'scandalous, lascivious, scurrilous and profane'. It is indeed a very vulgar production, full of sex and four-letter words. But there is no evidence to support the assumption that this incident led to a severance of relations with Milton.[3] Milton's own Hobson poems were reprinted in 1657 and 1658 in *A Banquet of Jests* and *Wit Restored* – less tasteless anthologies, but not totally different from *Sportive Wit*.

John Phillips was a man of small principle. He had a living to make. *Sportive Wit* panders to Royalist bawdy taste. In 1660–2 he produced several almanacs which contain some deplorable jokes about the 'gelding' of the recently executed Hugh Peter. When one recalls how near Milton came to being so gelt, this seems at best insensitive. In the 1673 burlesque of the sixth book of Virgil's *Aeneid* Phillips sneers at the memory of Vane and Bradshaw as well as of Peter, Cromwell and Thomas Scott. He was no staunch devotee of his uncle's Good Old Cause. Perhaps the fact that he was the nephew of regicide's most infamous defender caused him to over-react. It would be nice to think that in 1672 it was he who defended Milton against Eachard as 'a civil grave old gentleman'; but the attribution of *Montelions Predictions* to him is not certain.[4]

But anti-clericalism was something to which John Phillips remained relatively constant. In his *Virgil Travesty* he attacked 'Litigious parsons, still in law/ For a few apples or tithe straw'. In 1681 his *Speculum Crape-*

---

[1] Darbishire, p. 238; contrast Parker, pp. 1168–9.
[2] *Op. cit.*, p. 8; *C.P.W.*, III, pp. 198–205.
[3] Parker, pp. 1047, 657, is very sensible on this.
[4] J. Phillips, *Maronides or Virgil Travesty* (1673), pp. 93–9; Parker, 1147; Nedham in the early sixties similarly attacked his old allies.

Gownorum denounced interference in politics by the clergy, their greed for tithes and their hypocrisy – all good Miltonic themes. This pamphlet reminds us of the *Satyr against Hypocrites* in its bold use of buffoonery and bawdry to support a serious argument. It was the technique of Martin Marprelate, which Milton himself had employed against Salmasius and More. Phillips denounced in Miltonic fashion the smear technique of Roger L'Estrange and the high-flying clergy. ''Tis but calling a dissenter a schismatic, 'tis but calling religion division, and there's an end of the business.' The dissenters are 'men of far more understanding than your-selves'. Part II of the pamphlet goes so far as to refer to the execution of Mary Queen of Scots in arguing for the exclusion of James Duke of York from the succession.[1] Phillips's attack on Marvell's (and Milton's) old enemy, Samuel Parker, Bishop of Oxford – in the safe year 1688 – includes a vigorous defence of toleration in the interests of trade: ' "Trade", cries the Archdeacon, "Trade! No. Let grass grow about the Custom-house rather than abate one tittle of my Ecclesiastical Polity.' "[2] If Wood is right in saying that John Phillips 'early imbibed in most plentiful manner the rankest anti-monarchical principles' from Milton, he did not remain 'principled as his uncle'.[3] But he does seem to have stuck to a dislike of any clerical interference in politics, of which Milton would certainly have approved.

Edward Phillips has had a better press from historians than his brother. He too lacked the sort of higher seriousness that some attribute to his uncle, even if he also lacked John's lusty bawdiness. Edward made a shift to live by his pen – an early example of the temptations of the expanding literary market. He edited Drummond's *Poems* in 1656 – a task which may have been given him by Milton, who may also have had a hand in John Hall's editing of Drummond's *History of Scotland* in the preceding year.[4] In 1658 Edward published *The Mysteries of Love and Eloquence, Or, the Arts of Wooing and Complementing,* whose title accurately describes its frivolous contents. It is at least arguable that Milton would dislike this book – published in the year in which Edward Phillips attended Cromwell's funeral along with his uncle – at least as much as anything John Phillips ever wrote. Edward published a continuation of Baker's *Chronicle,* being supplied with material, Wood tells us, by Sir Thomas Clarges, one of those

---

[1] [John Phillips], *Virgil Travesty,* p. 97; *Speculum Crape-Gownorum: Or, A Looking-Glass for the Young Academicks* (1682), pp. 21–2, 4; Part II, p. 21.

[2] [Phillips], *Samuel Lord Bishop of Oxford, His Celebrated Reasons for Abrogating the Test* (1688), p. 14.

[3] Darbishire, p. 38.

[4] Masson, V, pp. 264–5.

who is believed to have helped Milton to escape at the Restoration.[1] Some
have thought that Milton may have helped his nephew with the *Theatrum
Poetarum* (1675), but there is no evidence for this, and the internal evidence
is against it. In his Preface Phillips refers to Milton, though not by name,
as the author of an English blank verse poem – having first taken very
great care to disavow the heresy of mortalism.

After the Restoration Edward Phillips worked as translator and copyist
for Elias Ashmole. Did Nathan Paget introduce him?[2] Edward was next a
tutor to the son of John Evelyn from 1663 to 1665. Evelyn appreciated the
knowledge of languages which Edward no doubt owed to his uncle, as
well as the fact that he was 'not at all infected' with Milton's principles.
Edward then transferred to the family of Philip, fifth Earl of Pembroke, by
whom he was employed 'to interpret some of the Teutonic philosophy' –
i.e. Boehme.[3] One wonders where Phillips got that interest from. Paget?
So successful was the tutor that at least one volume of translations from
Boehme was brought out under Pembroke's auspices after the Restoration,
and the Earl himself is said to have written a Behmenist tract. He took the
Behmenist John Pordage, father of Samuel, under his protection.[4] But
Edward Phillips did not think Samuel Pordage worthy of inclusion in the
Theatrum Poetarum.

---

[1] Godwin, p. 126.
[2] Hone, p. 163. See p. 493 below.
[3] Evelyn, III, pp. 364–5; Masson, VI, p. 764. Contrast Wood's view of John, p. 490 above.
[4] Hutin (1960), pp. 87–9, 252–3.

Appendix 3

Nathan Paget and His Library

Nathan Paget (1615–1679) was possibly Milton's doctor and certainly his very good friend. He recommended to the poet the lady who became his third wife, Paget's cousin. Paget left her £20 in his will. It was through Paget that Thomas Ellwood got his introduction to Milton. The acquaintance may go back a long time: the house in Petty France to which Milton moved in December 1651 may have been leased from Paget.[1] Paget has been suggested as author of the Anonymous Life of Milton, and there are some arguments in favour of this identification.[2]

Paget, like Locke, Newton and many more doctors and scientists in the late seventeenth century, appears to have led something of a double life. On the surface he was a very respectable character, son and nephew of Puritan divines. His uncle was minister of the Amsterdam Presbyterian church from 1607 to 1637, a friend of Elizabeth of Bohemia; his father was rector of St. Chad's church, Shrewsbury, until his death in 1656.[3] Nathan Paget became a physician, graduating at Edinburgh in 1638 and taking his doctorate at Leiden in 1639. He published his thesis, on the plague, became a licentiate of the College of Physicians in 1640, Fellow in 1646. In 1642 he had incorporated M.D. at Cambridge. He was one of a team of physicians who collaborated with Francis Glisson on a treatise on rickets published in 1650.[4] Milton in 1651 complained about the publication of an unauthorized translation of this work: it seems likely that he was already a friend of Paget's and was protecting his interests.[5] Within six months of Paget's election as Fellow of the College of Physicians he presented the library with Bacon's works in three volumes.[6] He held various official positions in the College, and in 1664 delivered the Harveian Oration. He

---

[1] Parker, p. 999.
[2] Hanford (1945), pp. 92–3.
[3] Parker, p. 1023.
[4] Some of these men were associated with Haak's group of scientists in London in the sixteen-forties, and later joined the Royal Society.
[5] Parker, p. 979.
[6] G. N. Clark, p. 281.

was enough of a supporter of Parliament to accept the office of Physician to the Tower when it was offered to him on 31 December 1649, the year of Charles I's execution. Paget lived in the very radical parish of St. Stephen's, Coleman St., where John Goodwin had his congregation. Paget was a friend of the younger Isaac Penington, whose father had been one of Goodwin's parishioners before he was ejected from the living. Paget remained a bachelor.

The most interesting information about Paget comes from his library, a list of which was printed in 1681 when it was offered for sale after his death.[1] Among over 2,000 titles there are a large number of chemical and alchemical books, including 19 by Paracelsus, 9 by Avicenna, 8 by Glauber, 6 by G. B. Porta, 7 by Nicholas Culpeper, 5 by Boyle, 4 each by Sir Kenelm Digby, Elias Ashmole and Van Helmont, 2 each by Croll and George Starkey, 1 by Bostock. Serious interest in the magical alchemical tradition is shown by the presence of 9 books by Raymond Lull, 4 attributed to Roger Bacon, 3 to George Ripley, 1 to Albertus Magnus and very many other books on magic and alchemy. In 1651 Paget was lending chemical manuscripts to no less an expert than Elias Ashmole.[2]

There are also several books and manuscripts on astrology, by Lilly, Gadbury, Wharton and others. There are very many examples of Hermetic literature, including 6 works attributed to Hermes Trismegistus, the Rosicrucian manifestoes and many books by Thomas Vaughan. Another significant interest is shown by the presence of books by Marsilio Ficino (2), Pomponazzi (2), Giordano Bruno (2), Campanella (3), Fludd (5). There are also works by Ramus (7), Francis Bacon (8), Bodin, Descartes (2), Gassendi, Mersenne, William Harvey (2), Walter Charleton (2), Selden, Oughtred, Wallis, and 2 by Hobbes, including his translations of the *Iliad* and the *Odyssey*. The Comenian group of reformers are represented by Hartlib (6, including *Chemical Addresses*), Dury (3), Gabriel Plattes, Petty's *Advice to Hartlib* and Noah Biggs's *Craft of Physic*.

So far we might think of this as the library of a liberal, reforming, chemically-minded doctor with wide and esoteric interests. But the theological books are even more striking. Some are respectable enough – Calvin (5), Perkins, Gouge, Daniel Rogers, Ames (10), Sibbes (2), Gataker, Stephen Marshall, Anthony Burges, Owen (4), Thomas Goodwin (3), John Wilkins (5), Henry More (9), Richard Baxter (12). Alsted is represented not

---

[1] *Bibliotheca Medica . . . Nathanis Paget, M.D.* (1681). Hanford published a study of 'Dr. Paget's Library' in 1945. Although Hanford drew attention to the presence and significance of the heretical books in this library, nobody seems to have followed up his points.

[2] Josten (1966), II, p. 595. The editor's identification of 'Dr. Paget' as Nathan Paget is almost certainly correct: no other doctor of that name is known at that date. Cf. p. 495 below.

by his apocalyptic writings but by *Cases of Conscience*. Robert Gell, who
probably married Milton to the wife recommended by Paget, is represented
not by his astrological writings but by a volume on the translation of the
Bible. There are also Giovanni Diodati's annotations of the Bible, and
Haak's translation of the Dutch annotations. But there are others much
less orthodox. More books are listed by Fausto Sozzini (21) than by any
other author. There are in addition Castellio's defence of Servetus (and 2
other works) and 2 copies of the *Racovian Catechism*, which Milton got into
trouble for licensing in 1652. There are also 2 pamphlets by John Bidle and
a very large number of other Socinian and Polish works, including 2 of
Lushington's translations of Crell (and other works by him), a book by
John Knowles, 10 works by Grotius, together with anti-Socinian books by
Francis Cheynell and others. Francis Osborn's *Discourse of the Turks* was
notorious for its sympathy both towards anti-Trinitarianism and towards
polygamy.

There are other surprises among the religious books – 2 volumes 'in
Dutch' by Henry Niklaes, founder of the Family of Love, and other books
for and against Familism. These include Stephen Denison's *The White Wolf*
of 1627 – a pamphlet against the Familist box-maker John Hetherington.
There are no less than 16 books and manuscripts by Jacob Boehme, many
in German. Did Paget obtain these during his stay in the Netherlands in the
late thirties? At that time none of Boehme's works were printed in English
translation. I see Paget smuggling in H.N. and Boehme from his first trip
abroad (and Milton perhaps *Heptaplomeres*) rather as my generation
smuggled in *Lady Chatterley's Lover* and *Ulysses*. Paget's library contained 1
work by Joachim of Fiore, and many other prophetical books and manuscripts, from Brightman (3), Alabaster, Nathaniel Homes (7) down to
Christopher Cotter. There is a collection of books dealing with religious
toleration, including Leonard Busher, Lord Brooke on episcopacy, Roger
Williams's *The Bloudy Tenent*, Henry Robinson, *The Ancient Bounds*, Samuel
Richardson's *The Necessity of Toleration* and many others. On the other side
are the 3 parts of Thomas Edwards's *Gangraena* (balanced by William
Walwyn's *A Whisper in the Ear of Mr. Edwards*), Samuel Rutherford's
Survey of the Spirituall Antichrist (and 3 others by him), and 2 books by
Alexander Ross. By Independents are 5 works of Henry Ainsworth, 3 by
John Robinson, 6 each by John Cotton and John Goodwin, the *Apology* of
the Five Dissenting Brethren, 1 by Jeremiah Burroughs. There are 4 works
each by John Tombes and Henry Jessey, and many other Baptist authors,
including Christopher Blackwood (who was alleged to have said that the
doctrines of the Trinity and of the immortality of the soul were anti-

christian),[1] Henry Lawrence (Milton's 'virtuous father'), Thomas Collier, Elizabeth Avery. They are balanced by Daniel Featley's *The Dippers Dipt* and other criticisms of the Baptists. A number of books besides Blackwood's deal with the mortalist heresy.

There are 2 works by Sir Henry Vane, 7 each by George Fox and Isaac Penington (between whom and Milton Paget acted as intermediary when Penington was introducing Ellwood to the poet), 5 by Penn, and several other Quaker and anti-Quaker books. There are writings by William Dell, John Saltmarsh, Samuel Gorton, Henry Stubbe, Israel Tonge, and even by Lodowick Muggleton. Most remarkable of all, there are several books by and about the Ranters, including Abiezer Coppe's *Some Sweet Sips of some Spirituall Wine* and Joseph Salmon's *Divinity Anatomized*. Their presence reminds us of the arch-Ranter Laurence Clarkson's story of the Ranter meeting at which 'Dr. Paget's maid stripped herself naked and skipped'.[2] Paget was clearly a man who in the early fifties might not have been totally unsympathetic to the Ranters himself.

Paget's library also tells us something about his literary tastes. The 14 books by Milton – from the *Apology against a Pamphlet* to *Paradise Regained* – stand out, many of them no doubt presentation copies; but it is interesting to find the 'Puritan' succession of poets strongly represented – by Spenser (2), Sylvester's Du Bartas, Wither and Quarles. There is Harington's translation of *Orlando Furioso* and Sandys's of Ovid's *Metamorphoses* as well as *The Art of Love* and two other Ovids, Ogilby's translation of Virgil, Seneca and Evelyn's translation of Pascal's *Lettres Provinciales*. Other poets represented are Samuel Daniel, Fulke Greville, George Herbert, Denham, Waller, Cowley, Katherine Phillips. There is no Shakespeare, no Ben Jonson; of Donne only *Ignatius his Conclave*; but plays by Beaumont and Fletcher and by Davenant. Marvell's *Rehearsal Transpros'd* is there, together with the anonymous *A Commonplace Book out of the Rehearsal Transpros'd*.

Nathan Paget must have been a man congenial to Milton in many ways. His literary taste seems to have been Spenserian; he was at least strongly interested in anti-Trinitarianism and mortalism; he may have been one of the Socinian Baptists to whom Sewel refers in 1674.[3] His very special interest in Boehme, whom he appears to have read in the original German (he had several German dictionaries), makes it likely that he would have discussed him with the poet. His library, and his friendship with Quakers, suggest that he was interested in exactly the area of radical thought to which Milton belongs.

---

[1] See Thomas Blake, To the Impartiall Reader. Servetus too had thought the Trinity and infant baptism were antichristian doctrines.

[2] Clarkson (1660), p. 28.   [3] Sewel, pp. 525–6.

Bibliography

List of books, articles and theses cited in the notes

The following abbreviations have been used in this list:

C.U.P.	Cambridge University Press
H.L.Q.	*Huntington Library Quarterly*
J.E.G.P.	*Journal of English and German Philology*
J.F.H.S.	*Journal of the Friends' Historical Society*
J.H.I.	*Journal of the History of Ideas*
J.W.C.I.	*Journal of the Warburg and Courtauld Institutes*
M.L.N.	*Modern Language Notes*
N. and Q.	*Notes and Queries*
P. and P.	*Past and Present*
P.Q.	*Philological Quarterly*
P.M.L.A.	*Publications of the Modern Language Association*
S.P.	*Studies in Philology*

Unless otherwise stated, the place of publication for nineteenth- and twentieth-century titles is London.

R. M. Adams, *Ikon: John Milton and the Modern Critics* (Ithaca, 1955).

J. H. Adamson, 'Milton and the Creation', *J.E.G.P.*, LXI (1962).

J. Aiton, *Life and Times of Alexander Henderson* (Edinburgh, 1836).

Gina Alexander, 'Bonner and the Marian Persecutions', *History*, LX (1975).

M. V. C. Alexander, *Charles I's Lord Treasurer: Sir Richard Weston, Earl of Portland* (1975).

D. C. Allen, *The Harmonious Vision* (Baltimore, 1970). First published 1954.

D. C. Allen, *The Legend of Noah* (Urbana, 1963).

E. Arber, ed., *An English Garner* (1895–7, 8 vols.).

John Arrowsmith, *A great Wonder in Heaven* (1647).

J. Arthos, *Milton and the Italian Cities* (1968).

T. Astle, *Life of Abraham Hill*, prefixed to *Familiar Letters . . . between Abraham Hill . . . and several ingenious persons* (1767).

M. Aston, 'Lollardy and Sedition, 1381–1431', *P. and P.*, No. 17 (1960).

Sir T. Aston, *A Remonstrance against Presbytery* (1641).

John Aubrey, *Brief Lives* (ed. A. Clark, O.U.P., 1898, 2 vols.).

G. E. Aylmer, *The State's Servants* (1973).

John Aylmer, *An Harborowe for Faithfull and Trewe Subjectes* (1559).

Francis Bacon, *Works* (ed. J. Spedding, R. L. Ellis and D. D. Heath, 1857–72, 14 vols.).

M. L. Bailey, *Milton and Jakob Boehme* (New York, 1914).

R. Baillie, *A Disswasive from the Errours of the Time* (1645).

R. Baillie, *Letters and Journals* (1775, 2 vols.).

R. H. Bainton, *The Hunted Heretic* (Boston, Mass., 1953).

H. Barbour and A. Roberts, ed., *Early Quaker Writings* (Grand Rapids, Michigan, 1973).

R. Barclay, *An Apology* (1678).

M. Baring, *What I Saw in Russia* (n.d., ?1908).

A. E. Barker, *Milton and the Puritan Dilemma* (Toronto U.P., 1942).

A. E. Barker, 'Milton's Later Poems', in Maclear and Watt (1964).

A. E. Barker, '*Paradise Lost:* The Relevance of Regeneration', in *Paradise Lost: a Tercentenary Tribute* (ed. B. Rajan, Toronto, 1969).

P. R. Barnett, *Theodore Haak (1616–1690)* ('S Gravenhage, 1962).

P. Barwick, *The Life of Dr. John Barwick* (translated by Hilkiah Bedford, abridged and ed. G. F. Barwick, 1903). First published 1721.

J. Bastwick, *The Utter Routing of the whole Army of all Independents and Sectaries* (1646).

W. J. Bate, *The Burden of the Past and the English Poet* (1971).

F. W. Bateson, *English Poetry: A Critical Introduction* (1950).

J. Bauthumley, *The Light and Dark Sides of God* (1650).

R. Baxter, *Aphorismes of Justification* (1649).

R. Baxter, *Reliquiae Baxterianae* (ed. Matthew Sylvester, 1696).

R. Baxter, *Autobiography* (ed. N. H. Keeble, Everyman edn.).

Joseph Beaumont, *Complete Poems* (ed. A. B. Grosart, 1880, 2 vols.).

Joseph Beaumont, *Minor Poems* (ed. E. Robinson, 1914).

H. L. Benthem, *Engeländischer Kirch- und Schulen-Staat* (Lüneberg, 1694).

D. S. Berkeley, *Inwrought with Figures Dim* (The Hague, 1974).

J. Bidle, *Twelve Arguments drawn out of Scripture* (1647).

J. Bidle, *To the Law, and to the Testimonies* (1648).

J. Bidle, *A Twofold Catechism* (1654).

J. Bidle, *The Apostolical and True Opinion concerning the Holy Trinity* (1691).

T. Blake, *Infants Baptism Freed from Antichristianisme* (1645).

William Blake, *Poetry and Prose* (Nonesuch edn.).

J. Bodin, *Colloque des Secrets Cachez* (ed. and trans. P. Chauviré, Paris, 1914).

Jacob Boehme, *The Signature of All Things* (Everyman edn.). First published 1635.

Jacob Boehme, *Aurora* (trans. J. Sparrow, 1960). Written c. 1612, first published 1634, English translation 1656.

John Bond, *Salvation in Mystery* (1644).

L. P. Boone, 'The Language of Book VI, *Paradise Lost*', in Patrick (1953).

J. Boswell, *Life of Dr. Johnson* (Everyman edn., 2 vols.).

D. F. Bouchard, *Milton: A Structural Reading* (1974).

E. Bourcier, ed., *The Diary of Sir Simonds D'Ewes, 1622–1624* (Paris, n.d., ?1974).

Roger Boyle, Earl of Orrery, *Dramatic Works* (ed. W. S. Clark, Harvard U.P., 1937, 2 vols.).

Anne Bradstreet, *Works* (ed. J. Hensley, Harvard U.P., 1967).

H. N. Brailsford, *The Levellers and the English Revolution* (1961).

W. Bray, ed., *Diary and Correspondence of John Evelyn* (1850–2, 4 vols.).

J. Brayne, *A Treatise of the High Rebellion of Man against God* (1653).

Barbara Breasted, '*Comus* and the Castlehaven Scandal', *Milton Studies,* III (1971).

E. Brennecke, *John Milton the Elder and his Music* (New York, 1938).

A. W. Brink, '*Paradise Lost* and James Nayler's Fall', *J.F.H.S.,* 53 (1973).

R. F. Brinkley, *The Arthurian Legend in the Seventeenth Century* (Johns Hopkins U.P., 1932).

E. R. C. Brinkworth, 'The Laudian Church in Buckinghamshire', *University of Birmingham Historical Journal,* V (1955).

J. R. Broadbent, *Some Graver Subject* (1960).

J. R. Broadbent, ed., *John Milton: Introductions* (C.U.P., 1973).

Lord Brooke, *A Discourse opening the Nature of that Episcopacie which is exercised in England* (1641), in Haller (1933).

Sir T. Browne, *Works* (Bohn edn., 1852, 3 vols.).

William Browne, *Poems* (Muses Library, 2 vols.).

Giordano Bruno, *Cause, Principle and Unity* (trans. J. Lindsay, Castle Hedingham, 1962).

J. A. Bryant, 'Milton and the Art of History', *P.Q.,* XXIX (1950).

L. Bryskett, *A Discourse of Civill Life,* in *Works* (ed. J. H. Pafford, 1972).

G. Bullough, 'Polygamy among the Reformers', in *Renaissance and Modern Essays presented to V. de Sola Pinto* (ed. G. R. Hibbard, 1966).

John Bunyan, *Works* (ed. G. Offor, 1860, 3 vols.).

Gilbert Burnet, *Life of the Earl of Rochester* (1774). First published 1680.

Gilbert Burnet, *Life of Sir Matthew Hale* (1774). First published 1682.

Gilbert Burnet, *A History of My Own Time* (ed. O. Airy, O.U.P., 1897, 2 vols.).

N. T. Burns, *Christian Mortalism from Tyndale to Milton* (Harvard U.P., 1972).

C. Burrage, *The Early English Dissenters* (C.U.P., 1912, 2 vols.).

E. Burroughs, *The Memorable Works* (1672).

H. Burton, *A Vindication of the Churches Commonly Called Independent* (1644).

Thomas Burton, *Parliamentary Diary* (ed. J. T. Rutt, 1828, 4 vols.).

Samuel Butler, *Characters and Passages from Note-Books* (ed. A. R. Waller, C.U.P., 1908).

J. Cairncross, *After Polygamy was Made a Sin* (1974).

J. Calvin, *Institutes of the Christian Religion* (trans. H. Beveridge, 1949, 2 vols.).

John Canne, *A Voice From the Temple to the Higher Powers* (1653).

B. S. Capp, *The Fifth Monarchy Men* (1972).

E. Cardwell, ed., *Documentary Annals of the Reformed Church of England* (O.U.P., 1839, 2 vols.).

E. Cardwell, ed., *The Reformation of the Ecclesiastical Laws* (O.U.P., 1850).

Thomas Carew, *Poems*, in *Minor Poets of the Seventeenth Century* (ed. R. G. Howarth, Everyman edn.).

John Carey, *Milton* (1969).

G. Carleton, *Tithes Examined* (1611). First published 1606.

Agricola Carpenter, *Pseuchographia Anthropomagica: Or, A Magicall Description of the Soul* (1652).

K. L. Carroll, *John Perrott* (Friends' Historical Society, 1971).

K. L. Carroll, 'Martha Simmons, a Quaker Enigma', *J.F.H.S.*, 53 (1972).

S. W. Carruthers, 'That great Gorbellied Idol, the Assembly of Divines', *Journal of the Presbyterian Historical Society of England*, 9 (1948–51).

T. Carte, ed., *A Collection of Original Letters and Papers* (1739, 2 vols.).

William Cartwright, *Poems* (ed. R. C. Goffin, C.U.P., 1918).

C. Caudwell, *Further Studies in a Dying Culture* (1949).

F. Chabod, *La Politica di Paolo Sarpi* (Venice, n.d., ?1962).

C. W. Chalklin, *Seventeenth Century Kent* (1965).

E. Chamberlayne, *Angliae Notitia* (1669).

A. B. Chambers, 'Chaos in *Paradise Lost*', *J.H.I.*, XXIV (1968).

C. D. Chandaman, *The English Public Revenue, 1660–1688* (O.U.P., 1975).

George Chapman, *Dramatic Works* (1873, 3 vols.).

(R. Chestlin), *Persecutio Undecima* (1681). First published 1648.

(F. Cheynell), *An Account Given to the Parliament by the Ministers sent by them to Oxford* (1646).

F. Cheynell, *The Divine Trinunity* (1650).

Henoch Clapham, *Errour on the Left Hand* (1608).

Lord Clarendon, *History of the Rebellion* (ed. W. D. Macray, O.U.P., 1888, 6 vols.).

D. L. Clark, 'Milton's Schoolmasters: Alexander Gil and his son Alexander', *H.L.Q.*, IX (1945–6).

G. N. Clark, *A History of the Royal College of Physicians*, I (O.U.P., 1964).

P. Clark, *English Provincial Society from the Reformation to the Revolution: Religion, Politics and Society in Kent, 1500–1640* (1977).

Clarke Papers (ed. C. H. Firth, Camden Soc., 1891–1901, 4 vols.).

Laurence Clarkson, *A Single Eye* (1650).

Laurence Clarkson, *The Lost Sheep found* (1660).

John Cleveland, *Works* (1687).

R. C. Cobb, *Les Armées Révolutionnaires* (Paris, 1961–3).

N. Cohn, *The Pursuit of the Millennium* (1957).

P. Collinson, *The Elizabethan Puritan Movement* (1967).

John Collop, *Poems* (ed. C. Hilberry, Wisconsin U.P., 1962).

J. A. Comenius, *Selections* (ed. J. Kyrášek, Prague, 1964).

G. N. Conklin, *Biblical Criticism and Heresy in Milton* (New York, 1949).

John Cook, *What the Independents Would have* (1647).

John Cook, *King Charls his Case* (1649).

John Cook, *Monarchy No Creature of Gods making* (1652).

B. G. Cooper, 'The Academic Rediscovery of Apocalyptic Ideas in the Seventeenth Century', *Baptist Quarterly*, XVIII (1959–60), XIX (1961–2).

Abiezer Coppe, *Some Sweet Sips of Some Spirituall Wine* (1649).
Abiezer Coppe, *A Second Fiery Flying Roll* (1649–50).
Richard Coppin, *A Man-Child Born* (1654).
H. E. Cory, 'Fletcher and Milton', *University of California Publications in Modern Philology*, II (1912).
John Cosin, *Works* (O.U.P., 1843–55, 5 vols.).
G. G. Coulton, ed., *Social Life in Britain from the Conquest to the Reformation* (C.U.P., 1918).
G. G. Coulton, *Mediaeval Panorama* (C.U.P., 1945). First published 1938.
A. Cowley, *Poems* (ed. A. R. Waller, C.U.P., 1905).
A. Cowley, *The Civil War* (ed. A. Pritchard, Toronto U.P., 1973).
Richard Crashawe, *Poems* (Muses Library).
J. Crell, *Vindiciae pro religionis libertate* (1637).
O. Croll, *Philosophy Reformed and Improved* (trans. H. Pinnell, 1657).
Oliver Cromwell, *Writings and Speeches* (ed. W. C. Abbott, Harvard U.P., 1937–47, 4 vols.).
Thomas Crosfield, *Diary* (ed. F. S. Boas, O.U.P., 1935).
Robert Crowley, *Works* (ed. J. M. Cowper, Early English Text Soc., 1872).
(R. Culmer), *Cathedrall Newes from Canterbury* (1644).
Nicholas Culpeper, *A Physical Directory* (1650).
Nicholas Culpeper, *An Ephemeris for the Year 1652*.
Nicholas Culpeper, *Pharmacopoeia Londinensis* (1654).
B. H. Cunnington, ed., *Extracts from the Quarter Sessions Great Rolls of the Seventeenth Century* (Devizes, 1932).
S. S. Curran, 'The Mental Pinnacle: *Paradise Regained* and the Romantic Four-Book Epic', in Wittreich (1971).

David Daiches, 'The Opening of *Paradise Lost*', in Kermode (1960).
G. Daniel, *Selected Poems* (ed. T. B. Stroup, Kentucky U.P., 1959).
E. F. Daniels, 'Milton's "Doubtful Conflict" and the Seventeenth Century Tradition', *N. and Q.*, CCVI (1961).
Helen Darbishire, *Early Lives of Milton* (1932).
Sir William Davenant, *Gondibert* (ed. D. F. Gladish, O.U.P., 1971).
Sir William Davenant, *Shorter Poems and Songs* (ed. A. M. Gibbs, O.U.P., 1972).
A. G. Debus, 'The Paracelsians and the Chemists', *Clio Medica*, VII (1972).
A. G. Debus, 'The Chemical Philosophers: Chemical Medicine from Paracelsus to Van Helmont', *History of Science*, XII (1974).
A. G. Debus, 'The Chemical Debates of the Seventeenth Century: the Reaction to Robert Fludd and Jean Baptiste van Helmont', in *Reason, Experiment and Mysticism in the Scientific Revolution* (ed. M. L. R. Bonelli and W. R. Shea, New York, 1975).
Daniel Defoe, *Moll Flanders* (Shakespeare Head edn., 2 vols.).
Dainel Defoe, *The Political History of the Devil* (1840). First published 1726.
William Dell, *Several Sermons and Discourses* (1709). First published 1652.
J. G. Demaray, *Milton and the Masque Tradition* (Harvard U.P., 1968).
Sir John Denham, *Poems and Translations* (7th edn., n.d.).

Sir Simonds D'Ewes, *A Complete Journal* (1693).

Sir Simonds D'Ewes, *Journal* (ed. W. Notestein, Yale U.P., 1923).

A. G. Dickens, *Lollards and Protestants in the Diocese of York, 1509–1558* (O.U.P., 1959).

J. S. Diekhoff, 'Rhyme in *Paradise Lost*', *P.M.L.A.*, XLIX (1934).

A. C. Dobbins, *Milton and the Book of Revelation: The Heavenly Cycle* (Alabama U.P., 1975).

J. Dod and R. Clever, *A Plaine and Familiar Exposition of . . . Proverbs* (1611).

J. Dod and R. Clever, *A plaine and familiar Exposition of the Ten Commandments* (19th edn., 1662). First published 1604.

D. C. Dorian, *The English Diodatis* (New Brunswick, 1950).

J. A. van Dorsten, *The Radical Arts: First Decade of an English Renaissance* (Leiden, 1970).

John Dryden, *Essays* (ed. W. P. Ker, O.U.P., 1900, 2 vols.).

John Eachard, *Mr. Hobbs's State of Nature Considered* (1672) (ed. P. Ure, Liverpool U.P., 1958).

S. Eaton, *The Mystery of God Incarnate* (1650).

A. C. Edwards, ed., *English History from Essex Sources* (Chelmsford, 1957).

Thomas Edwards, *Gangraena* (1646, 3 parts).

T. S. Eliot, *Milton* (1947).

T. Ellwood, *The History of the Life* (ed. S. Graveson, 1906). First published 1714.

F. G. Emmison, *Elizabethan Life: Morals and Church Courts* (Chelmsford, 1973).

W. Empson, *Some Versions of Pastoral* (1935).

W. Empson, *Milton's God* (1961).

William Erbery, *The Testimony of William Erbery* (1658).

E. H. Erikson, *Young Man Luther* (1959).

Arise Evans, *A Voice From Heaven to the Common-Wealth of England* (1652).

Arise Evans, *An Eccho to the Voice from Heaven* (1653).

Arise Evans, *The Bloudy Vision of John Farley* (1653).

Arise Evans, *The Voice of the Iron Rod to the Lord Protector* (1655).

J. M. Evans, *Paradise Lost and the Genesis Tradition* (O.U.P., 1968).

R. J. W. Evans, *Rudolf II and his World* (O.U.P., 1973).

John Evelyn, *Diary* (ed. E. S. de Beer, O.U.P., 1955, 6 vols.).

Sir Richard Fanshawe, *Shorter Poems and Translations* (ed. N. W. Bawcutt, Liverpool U.P., 1964).

Luke Fawne and others, *A Second Beacon Fired* (1654).

Daniel Featley, *The Dippers Dipt* (1646).

A. D. Ferry, *Milton's Epic Voice: The Narrator in Paradise Lost* (Harvard U.P., 1963).

Sir Robert Filmer, *Observations on Mr. Milton Against Salmasius* (1652), in *Patriarcha and Other Political Works* (ed. P. Laslett, Oxford, 1949).

Z. S. Fink, *The Classical Republicans* (Northwestern U.P., 1945).

A. P. Fiore, ed., *Th' Upright Heart and Pure* (Pittsburgh, 1967).

C. H. Firth, ed., *Scotland and the Commonwealth* (Scottish History Soc., 1895).

C. H. Firth, ed., *Scotland and the Protectorate* (Scottish History Soc., 1899).

S. Fish, *Surprised by Sin* (1967).

S. Fish, 'Question and Answer in *Samson Agonistes*', *Critical Quarterly*, II (1969).

Samuel Fisher, *The Testimony of Truth Exalted* (1679).

Michael Fixler, *Milton and the Kingdoms of God* (1964).

John Flamsteed, *Gresham Lectures* (ed. E. G. Forbes, 1975).

A. Fletcher, *The Transcendental Masque: An Essay on Milton's Comus* (Cornell U.P., 1971).

Giles and Phineas Fletcher, *Poetical Works* (ed. F. S. Boas, C.U.P., 1908, 2 vols.).

H. F. Fletcher, *The Use of the Bible in Milton's Prose* (Illinois U.P., 1929).

H. F. Fletcher, *The Intellectual Development of John Milton,* II (Illinois U.P., 1961).

Robert Fludd, *Mosaicall Philosophy* (1659). Published in Latin 1638.

George Fox, *Gospel-Truth Demonstrated* (1706).

John Foxe, *Acts and Monuments of the Christian Church* (ed. J. Pratt, n.d., 8 vols.).

J. Frank, *The Levellers* (Harvard U.P., 1955).

J. Frank, *The Beginnings of the English Newspaper, 1620–1660* (Harvard U.P., 1961).

J. M. French, 'Some Notes on Milton's Accedence commenc't Grammar', *J.E.G.P.,* LX (1961).

P. J. French, *John Dee* (1972).

John Fry, *The Accuser Sham'd* (1649).

John Fry, *The Clergy in their Colours* (1650).

Northrop Frye, *Five Essays on Milton's Epics* (1966).

Northrop Frye, *Fearful Symmetry: a Study of William Blake* (Princeton U.P., 1969).

Northrop Frye, 'The Revelation to Eve', in Rajan (1969).

Northrop Frye, *The Stubborn Structure* (1970).

Thomas Fuller, *History of the University of Cambridge* (1840). First published 1655.

Thomas Fuller, *Church History of Britain* (1842, 3 vols.). First published 1655.

S. R. Gardiner, ed., *Reports of Cases in the Courts of Star Chamber and High Commission* (Camden Soc., 1886).

Helen Gardner, *A Reading of Paradise Lost* (O.U.P., 1965).

Elizabeth Gaskell, *The Life of Charlotte Brontë* (World's Classics edn.).

R. Gell, *Noahs Flood Returning* (1655).

Ian Gentles, 'Sales of Crown Lands during the English Revolution', *Economic History Review,* Second Series, XXVI (1973).

L. W. Gibbs, 'William Ames's Technometry', *J.H.I.,* XXXIII (1973).

T. E. Gibson, ed., *A Cavalier's Notebook* (1880).
A. Gil, senior, *Logonomia Anglica* (1619) (ed. B. Danielsson and A. Gabrielson, Stockholm, 1972).
A. Gil, senior, *The Sacred Philosophy of the Holy Scripture* (1635).
A. Gil, junior, *The New Starr of the North* (1632).
A. H. Gilbert, *On the Composition of Paradise Lost* (North Carolina U.P., 1947).
A. H. Gilbert, 'Milton's defence of Bawdy', in Patrick (1953).
Carlo Ginzburg, *Il Nicodemismo* (Turin, 1970).
H. Glapthorne, *Poems* (1639).
H. Glapthorne, *White-Hall* (1643).
W. Godwin, *Lives of Edward and John Philips* (1815).
L. Goldstein, 'The Good Old Cause and Milton's Blank Verse', *Zeitschrift für Anglistik und Amerikanistik,* 23 Jahrgang (1975).
Godfrey Goodman, *The Two Great Mysteries of Christian Religion* (1653).
Thomas Goodwin, *Works* (Edinburgh, 1861–3, 6 vols.).
(Thomas Goodwin), *A Glimpse of Syons Glory,* in Woodhouse (1938).
A. Gordon, *Heads of English Unitarian History* (1895).
S. Gott, *Nova Solyma* (ed. W. Begley, 1902, 2 vols.).
J. Gratton, *A Journal of the Life* (1720).
W. Greenhill, *The Axe at the Root* (1643).
E. Greenlaw, 'A Better Teacher than Aquinas', *S.P.,* XIV (1917).
E. Greenlaw, 'Spenser's Influence on *Paradise Lost*', *S.P.,* XVII (1920).
Fulke Greville, Lord Brooke, *Life of Sir Philip Sidney* (O.U.P., 1907). First published 1652.
Sir H. J. Grierson, *Milton and Wordsworth* (C.U.P., 1937).
A. Griffith, *Strena Vavasoriensis* (1654).
M. Griffith, *The Fear of God and the King* (1660).
A. Grossman, 'Milton's Sonnet, "On the late massacre in Piemont" ', *Triquarterly,* No. 23–4 (1972).
Joan Grundy, *The Spenserian Poets* (1969).
B. Gustafsson, *The Five Dissenting Brethren* (Lund, 1951).
G. W. J. Gyll, *History of the Parish of Wraysbury . . . with the History of Horton and . . . Colnbrook* (1862).

J. Hacket, *Scrinia Reserata* (1693).
J. B. S. Haldane, 'Interaction of Physics, Chemistry and Biology', in *Philosophy for the Future* (ed. R. W. Sellars, V. J. McGill and M. Farber, New York, 1949).
Halifax, George Savile, Marquess of, *Complete Works* (Penguin edn.).
J. Halkett, *Milton and the Idea of Matrimony* (New Haven, 1970).
J. Hall, ed., *Memorials of the Civil War in Cheshire* (Lancashire and Cheshire Record Soc., 1889).
W. Haller, 'Before *Areopagitica*', *P.M.L.A.,* XLII (1927).
W. Haller, *Tracts on Liberty in the Puritan Revolution* (Columbia U.P., 1933, 3 vols.).
W. Haller, *The Rise of Puritanism* (Columbia U.P., 1938).

W. Haller, *Liberty and Reformation in the Puritan Revolution* (Columbia U.P., 1955).

W. and M. Haller, 'The Puritan Art of Love', *H.L.Q.*, V (1941–2).

W. Haller and G. Davies, ed., *The Leveller Tracts, 1647–1653* (Columbia U.P., 1944).

G. D. Hamilton, 'Milton's Defensive God: A Reappraisal', *S.P.*, LXIX (1972).

K. G. Hamilton, *The Two Harmonies* (O.U.P., 1963).

J. H. Hanford, 'Milton and Ochino', *M.L.N.*, XXVI (1921).

J. H. Hanford, 'Dr. Paget's Library', *Bulletin of the Medical Library Association*, XXXVI (1945).

J. H. Hanford, 'Milton in Italy', *Annuale Medievale*, V (1964).

J. H. Hanford, *John Milton: Poet and Humanist* (Western Reserve U.P., 1966).

D. W. Hanson, *From Kingdom to Commonwealth: The Development of Civic Consciousness in English Political Theory* (Harvard U.P., 1970).

Harleian Miscellany (1744–6, 8 vols.).

James Harrington, *The Oceana and Other Works* (1737).

G. L. and M. A. Harriss, *John Benet's Chronicle for the Years 1400 to 1462* (Camden Miscellany, XXIV, 1972).

K. E. Hartwell, *Lactantius and Milton* (Harvard U.P., 1929).

Richard Harvey, *A Theological Discourse of the Lamb of God* (1590).

R. Hayden, ed., *The Records of a Church of Christ in Bristol, 1640–1687* (Bristol Record Soc., XXVII, 1974).

G. W. F. Hegel, *Lectures on the Philosophy of History* (trans. J. Sibree, 1902).

M. Heinemann, 'Middleton's *A Game at Chess*: Parliamentary Puritans and Opposition Drama', *English Literary Renaissance*, 5 (1975).

N. H. Henry, 'Milton and Hobbes', *S.P.*, LXVIII (1951).

C. S. Hensley, *The Later Career of George Wither* (The Hague, 1969).

C. Hill, *Economic Problems of the Church* (O.U.P., 1956).

C. Hill, *Puritanism and Revolution* (Panther edn., 1969). First published 1958.

C. Hill, *The Century of Revolution* (Sphere edn., 1969). First published 1961.

C. Hill, 'William Harvey and the Idea of Monarchy', in *The Intellectual Revolution of the Seventeenth Century* (ed. C. Webster, 1974). First published 1964.

C. Hill, *Intellectual Origins of the English Revolution* (O.U.P., 1965).

C. Hill, *Reformation to Industrial Revolution* (Penguin edn., 1969). First published 1967.

C. Hill, *God's Englishman: Oliver Cromwell and the English Revolution* (Penguin edn. 1972). First published 1970.

C. Hill, *Antichrist in Seventeenth-Century England* (O.U.P., 1971).

Nicholas Hill, *Philosophia Epicurea* (1601).

Desirée Hirst, *Hidden Riches: Traditional Symbols from the Renaissance to Blake* (1968).

Thomas Hobbes, *The Elements of Law* (ed. F. Tönnies, C.U.P., 1928). First published 1650.

Thomas Hobbes, *Leviathan* (Penguin edn.). First published 1651.

T. Hodges, *The Growth and Spreading of Haeresie* (1647).

C. Holmes, *The Eastern Association in the English Civil War* (O.U.P., 1974).

G. Holmes, *The Trial of Dr. Sacheverell* (1973).

R. E. Hone, 'The Period of Edward Phillips's Work for Elias Ashmole', *N. and Q.*, CCI (1956).

Nicholas Hookes, *Amanda* (1653). Reprinted 1923.

R. Hoopes, *Right Reason in the English Renaissance* (Harvard U.P., 1962).

G. M. Hopkins, *Letters to Robert Bridges* (O.U.P., 1935).

I. B. Horst, *The Radical Brethren: Anabaptism and the English Reformation to 1558* (Nieuwkoop, 1972).

D. Hotham, *Life of Jacob Behmen* (1654).

G. Hough, *A Preface to the Faerie Queene* (1962).

L. Howard, ' "The Invention" of Milton's "Great Argument" ', *H.L.Q.*, IX (1945–6).

W. S. Howell, *Logic and Rhetoric in England, 1500–1700* (Princeton U.P., 1956).

M. Y. Hughes, 'The Historic Setting of Milton's *Observations on the Articles of Peace*', *P.M.L.A.*, LXIV (1949).

M. Y. Hughes, 'New Evidence on the charge that Milton forged the Pamela Prayer in *Eikon Basilike*', *Review of English Studies*, N.S., III (1952).

M. Y. Hughes, 'Satan and the Myth of the Tyrant', in Maclear and Watt (1964).

M. Y. Hughes, 'Milton's *Eikon Basilike*', in Wittreich (1971).

D. D. Hull, ed., *The Antinomian Controversy* (Wesleyan U.P., 1968).

W. B. Hunter, 'Milton's Materialistic Life Principle', *J.E.G.P.*, XLV (1946).

W. B. Hunter, 'Milton and Thrice Great Hermes', *J.E.G.P.*, XLV (1946).

W. B. Hunter, 'Milton's Power of Matter', *J.H.I.*, XIII (1952).

W. B. Hunter, 'Milton on the Incarnation: Some More Heresies', *J.H.I.*, XXI (1960).

W. B. Hunter, 'Milton and Richard Cromwell', *English Literature Notes*, III (1965).

W. B. Hunter, 'Milton on the Exaltation of the Son: the War in Heaven in *Paradise Lost*', *English Literary History*, 36 (1969).

Lucy Hutchinson, *Memoirs of the Life of Colonel Hutchinson* (ed. J. Sutherland, O.U.P., 1973). First published 1806.

S. Hutin, *Les Disciples anglais de Jacob Boehme* (Paris, 1960).

S. Hutin, *Robert Fludd (1574–1637): Alchimiste et Philosophe Rosicrucien* (Paris, 1971).

L. W. Hyma, 'Milton's *On the Late Massacre in Piemont*', *English Language Notes*, III (1965).

John Illo, 'The Misreading of Milton', *Columbia University Forum* (1965).

J. R. Jacob, 'The Ideological Origins of Boyle's Natural Philosophy', *Journal of European Studies*, 2 (1971).

L. A. Jacobus, ' "Thaumaturgike" in *Paradise Lost*', *H.L.Q.*, XXXIII (1969–70).

T. James, *A Treatise of the Corruptions of Scripture, 1612* (1843).

H. Jenkins, *Edward Benlowes* (1952).

E. Jessop, *A Discovery of the Errors of the English Anabaptists* (1623).

J. Jewell, *An Apology for the Church of England* (Parker Soc., 1848–50, 4 vols.). First published 1562.

D. Jones, 'Sidney's Erotic Pen: An Interpretation of One of the Arcadia Poems', *J.E.G.P.*, LXXII (1974).

Ben Jonson, *Poems* (ed. G. B. Johnston, 1954).

W. K. Jordan, *The Development of Religious Toleration in England, 1640–1660* (1940).

W. K. Jordan, *Philanthropy in England, 1480–1660* (1959).

R. Josselin, *Diary* (ed. E. Hockliff, Camden Soc., 1908).

C. H. Josten, 'Robert Fludd's Theory of Geomancy', *J.W.C.I.*, XXVII (1964).

C. H. Josten, *Elias Ashmole (1617–1692)* (O.U.P., 1966, 5 vols.).

J. Kaplow, ed., *Western Civilization: Mainstream Readings and Radical Critique,* I (New York, 1973).

M. Kelley, 'Milton and the Third Person of the Trinity', *S.P.*, XXXII (1935).

M. Kelley, *This Great Argument* (Gloucester, Mass., 1962).

F. Kermode, 'Samson Agonistes and Hebrew Prosody', *Durham University Journal,* N.S., XIV (1952).

F. Kermode, ed., *The Living Milton* (1960).

W. Kerrigan, *The Prophetic Milton* (Virginia U.P., 1974).

T. F. Kinloch, *The Life and Works of Joseph Hall* (1951).

W. Kirkconnell, *The Celestial Cycle* (Toronto U.P., 1952).

W. Kirsop, 'The Family of Love in France', *Journal of Religious History* (Sidney), III (1964).

J. L. Klein, 'Some Spenserian Influences on Milton's *Comus*', *Annuale Medievale,* V (1964).

S. Kliger, 'Milton in Italy and the Lost Malatesta MS.', *S.P.*, LI (1954).

J. Knowles, *A modest Plea for Private Mens Preaching* (1648).

J. Knowles, *A friendly Debate . . . Betwixt Mr. Samuel Eaton and Mr. John Knowles* (1650).

L. Kolakowski, *Chrétiens sans Église: La Conscience religieuse et le lieu confessionel en 17e siècle* (Paris, 1965).

A. Koyré, *La Philosophie de Jacob Boehme* (Paris, 1929).

Thomas Kyd, *Works* (ed. F. S. Boas, O.U.P., 1901).

E. Labrousse, *L'Entrée de Saturne au Lion: L'Éclipse de Soleil du 12 Août 1654* (The Hague, 1974).

Lansdowne, Marquis of, ed., *The Petty Papers* (1927, 2 vols.).

M. A. Larson, 'Milton and Servetus', *P.Q.*, XLI (1926).

William Laud, *Works* (O.U.P., 1847–60, 7 vols.).

H. Lawrence, *Some Considerations Tending to the Asserting and Vindicating of the use of the Holy Scriptures and Christian Ordinances* (1649).

F. R. Leavis, *Revaluation* (1967). First published 1936.

F. R. Leavis, *The Common Pursuit* (1976). First published 1952.

E. Le Comte, 'Milton as Satirist and Wit', in Fiore (1967).

G. Leff, 'The Mythology of a Continuous Church', *Papers presented to the P. and P. Conference on Popular Religion* (1966).

G. Leff, *Heresy in the Later Middle Ages* (Manchester U.P., 1967, 2 vols.).

P. Legouis, *Andrew Marvell* (O.U.P., 1965).

Sir Peter Leicester, *Charges to the Grand Jury at Quarter Sessions, 1660–1677* (ed. E. M. Halcrow, Chetham Soc., 1953).

Richard Leigh, *Poems* (Oxford, 1947).

Richard Leigh, *The Transproser Rehears'd* (Oxford U.P., 1673).

B. Lewalski, *Milton's Brief Epic: The Genre, Meaning and Art of Paradise Regained* (1966).

C. S. Lewis, *The Allegory of Love* (1936).

C. S. Lewis, *A Preface to Paradise Lost* (O.U.P., 1942).

C. S. Lewis, *Words* (C.U.P., 1960).

John Ley, *The Fury of Warre, and Folly of Sinne* (1643).

M. Lieb and J. Shawcross, ed., *Achievements of the Left Hand* (Massachusetts U.P., 1974).

J. Lilburne, *The Resolved Mans Resolution* (1647).

W. Lilly, *Annus Tenebrosus; or The Darke Year* (1652).

W. Lilly, *Astrological Predictions* (1652).

W. Lilly, *Of the Comet*, printed with *Astrological Predictions* (1653).

W. Lilly, *Astrological Judgments* (1655).

K. A. Lockridge, *A New England Town: The First Hundred Years* (New York, 1970).

A. O. Lovejoy, 'Milton and the Paradox of the Fortunate Fall', *Journal of English Literary History*, IV (1937).

A. Low, *The Blaze of Noon: A Reading of Samson Agonistes* (Columbia U.P., 1974).

E. Ludlow, *Memoirs* (ed. C. H. Firth, O.U.P., 1894, 2 vols.).

L. Lupton, *History of the Geneva Bible*, V (1973).

T. Lushington, *The Expiation of a Sinne in a Commentary upon the Epistle to the Hebrews* (1646).

O. Lutand, *Des Révolutions d'Angleterre à la Révolution Française* (The Hague, 1973).

Martin Luther, *Reformation Writings* (ed. B. L. Woolf, 1952–6, 2 vols.).

I. G. MacCaffrey, *Paradise Lost as 'Myth'* (1967). First published 1959.

H. MacCallum, 'Most Perfect Hero', in Rajan (1969).

G. McColley, 'The Book of Enoch and *Paradise Lost*', *Harvard Theological Review*, XXXI (1938).

M. McKeon, *Politics and Religion in Restoration England* (Harvard U.P., 1975).

H. J. McLachlan, ed., *Sir Isaac Newton's Theological Manuscripts* (Liverpool U.P., 1950).

H. J. McLachlan, *Socianism in Seventeenth Century England* (O.U.P., 1951).

M. Maclear and F. W. Watt, ed., *Essays . . . Presented to A. S. P. Woodhouse* (Toronto U.P., 1964).

E. MacLysaght, *Irish Life in the Seventeenth Century* (Cork U.P., 1950).

P. McNair, 'Ochino's Apology: Three Gods or three Wives', *History*, 60 (1975).

C. B. Macpherson, *The Political Theory of Possessive Individualism* (O.U.P., 1962).

M. Mahood, *Poetry and Humanism* (1950).

Brian Manning, *The English People and the English Revolution* (1976).

F. Manuel, *A Portrait of Isaac Newton* (Harvard U.P., 1968).

F. Manuel, *The Religion of Isaac Newton* (O.U.P., 1974).

L. Martz, *The Paradise Within* (Yale U.P., 1964).

L. Martz, ed., *Milton: A Collection of Critical Essays* (New York, 1966).

L. Martz, '*Paradise Lost*: The Realms of Light', *English Literary Renaissance*, I (1971).

A. Marvell, *The Rehearsal Transpros'd* (ed. D. I. B. Smith, O.U.P., 1971).

A. Marvell, *Poems* (ed. H. M. Margoliouth, O.U.P., 1927, 2 vols.).

K. Marx, *Grundrisse* (Penguin edn.).

D. Mathew, *The Social Structure of Caroline England* (O.U.P., 1948).

J. C. Maxwell, 'The Pseudo-Problem of "Comus" ', *Cambridge Journal*, I (1948).

J. C. Maxwell, 'Gods in *Paradise Lost*', *N. and Q.*, 193 (1948).

Joseph Mede, *Works* (3rd edn., 1672).

L. Miller, *John Milton among the Polygamophiles* (New York, 1974).

L. Miller, 'Milton's *Areopagitica*: Price 4d.', *N. and Q.*, CCXX (1975).

Perry Miller, *The New England Mind: the Seventeenth Century* (New York, 1939).

Perry Miller, *The New England Mind: from Colony to Province* (Harvard U.P., 1953).

Earl Miner, '*Felix Culpa* in the Redemptive Order of *Paradise Lost*', *S.P.*, XLVIII (1968).

Earl Miner, *The Restoration Mode from Milton to Dryden* (Princeton U.P., 1974).

A. F. Mitchell and J. Struthers, ed., *Minutes of the Sessions of the Westminster Assembly of Divines* (1874).

R. Mohl, *Studies in Spenser, Milton and the Theory of Monarchy* (New York, 1949).

J. W. Montgomery, *Cross and Crucible: J. V. Andreae (1586-1654)* (The Hague, 1973, 2 vols.).

Henry More, *An Antidote against Atheisme* (1653).

Henry More, *The Complete Poems* (ed. A. B. Grosart, 1878).

Sir Thomas More, *Fancies, Sports and Merry Tales* (ed. V. Gabrieli, Bari, 1974).

Sir Thomas More, *Utopia* (Everyman edn.).

R. S. Mortimer, 'Allegations against George Fox by the Ministers in North Lancashire', *J.F.H.S.*, XXXIX (1947).

A. L. Morton, *The Matter of Britain* (1966).
Lodowick Muggleton, *A True Interpretation of the Eleventh Chapter of the Revelation* (1751–3). First published 1662.
Lodowick Muggleton, *A True Interpretation of . . . the whole Book of the Revelation* (1665).
Lodowick Muggleton, *A Looking-Glass for George Fox* (1668).
Lodowick Muggleton, *A True Interpretation Of the Witch of Endor* (1669).
Lodowick Muggleton, *The Acts of the Witnesses of the Spirit* (1764). First published 1699.
W. Myers, *Dryden* (1973).

J. Nalson, *An Impartial Collection* (1683, 2 vols.).
James Nayler, *A Collection of Sundry Books* (1716).
J. H. Neumann, 'Milton's Prose Vocabulary', *P.M.L.A.*, LX (1945).
H. Newcome, *Autobiography* (ed. R. Parkinson, Chetham Soc., 1852).
M. Newcomen, *The All-Seeing unseen eye of God* (1647).
Lady Newton, *The House of Lyme* (1917).
J. Nicholls, *Original Letters and Papers of State* (1743).
Richard Norwood, *Journal* (ed. W. F. Craven and W. B. Hayward, New York, 1945).
Robert Norwood, *An Additional Discourse* (1653).
G. F. Nuttall, *The Holy Spirit in Puritan Faith and Experience* (Oxford, 1946).
G. F. Nuttall, *The Puritan Spirit* (1967).

Henry Oldenburg, *Correspondence* (ed. A. R. and M. B. Hall, Wisconsin U.P., 1965–, 10 vols. so far).
H. J. Oliver, *Sir Robert Howard (1626–1698)* (Duke U.P., 1963).
R. Ollard, *Pepys* (1974).
V. N. Olsen, *The New Testament Logia on Divorce . . . from Erasmus to Milton* (Tübingen, 1971).
Ants Oras, 'Milton's Blank Verse and the Chronology of his Major Poems', in Patrick (1953).
S. Orgel, *The Jonsonian Masque* (Harvard U.P., 1965).
F. Osborn, *Miscellaneous Works* (11th edn., 1722, 2 vols.).
R. O(verton), *Mans Mortalitie* (ed. H. Fisch, Liverpool U.P., 1968). First published 1643.
John Owen, *Works* (1850–3, 6 vols.).
The Oxinden and Peyton Letters, 1642–1670 (ed. D. Gardiner, 1937).

E. Pagitt, *Heresiography* (5th edn., 1654).
H. Parker, *Jus Populi* (1644).
W. R. Parker, *Milton's Debt to Greek Tragedy in Samson Agonistes* (Baltimore, 1937).
W. R. Parker, *Milton's Contemporary Reputation* (Ohio State U.P., 1940).
W. R. Parker, 'The Date of *Samson Agonistes* again', in Wittreich (1971).
R. Parr, *Life of Ussher* (1686).
J. M. Patrick, ed., *SAMLA Studies in Milton* (Florida U.P., 1953).

C. A. Patrides, *Milton and the Christian Tradition* (O.U.P., 1966).

H. Peacham, *The Worth of a Penny* (1676), in Arber, VI. First published 1641.

V. L. Pearl, *London and the Outbreak of the Puritan Revolution* (O.U.P., 1961).

John Peile, *Christ's College* (1900).

John Penry, *Three Treatises Concerning Wales* (ed. D. Williams, Wales U.P., 1960).

William Perkins, *Works* (1609–13, 3 vols.).

D. W. Petegorsky, *Left-Wing Democracy in the English Civil War* (1940).

H. Peters, *Mr. Peters Last Report of the Wars* (1646).

Sir William Petty, *Economic Writings* (ed. C. H. Hull, C.U.P., 1899, 2 vols.).

E. Phillips, *Theatrum Poetarum* (1675).

J. Phillips, *The Reformation of Images: Destruction of Art in England, 1535–1660* (California U.P., 1973).

J. Pilkington, *Works* (Parker Soc., 1842).

H. Pinnell, *Nil Novi* (1655).

V. de Sola Pinto, *Peter Sterry* (C.U.P., 1934).

V. de Sola Pinto, *Enthusiast in Wit: A Portrait of John Wilmot, Earl of Rochester, 1647–1680* (1962).

J.-P. Pittion, 'Milton, La Place and Socinianism', *Review of English Studies*, N.S. XXIII (1972).

J. H. Plumb, *The Death of the Past* (Penguin edn.).

E. M. Pope, *Paradise Regained: the Tradition and the Poem* (Baltimore, 1947).

John Pordage, *Innocence appearing through the dark mists of Pretended Guilt* (1655).

John Pordage, *A Treatise of Eternal Nature* in [Anon.], *A Compendious View of the Grounds of the Teutonick Philosophy*, Part I (1776).

S. P(ordage), *Mundorum Explicatio* (1661).

A. Powell, *John Aubrey and his Friends* (1963).

W. R. Prest, *The Inns of Court under Elizabeth and the Early Stuarts* (1972).

J. Preston, *The New Covenant* (5th edn., 1630).

F. T. Prince, *The Italian Element in Milton's Verse* (1954).

Robert Purnell, *A Word to the World and Two to those that are chosen out of the World* (1649).

Robert Purnell, *Good Tydings for Sinners* (1649).

John Pym, *A most learned and Religious Speech* (1642).

Francis Quarles, *Complete Works* (ed. A. B. Grosart, 1880, 3 vols.).

Francis Quarles, *Hosanna . . . and Threnodes* (ed. J. Horden, Liverpool U.P., 1960).

M. A. N. Radzinowicz, '*Samson Agonistes* and Milton: the Politician in Defeat', *P.Q.*, XLIV (1965).

B. Rajan, ed., *Paradise Lost: a Tercentenary Tribute* (Toronto, 1969).

B. Rajan, 'Jerusalem and Athens: the Temptation of Learning in *Paradise Regained*', in Fiore (1967).

Sir Walter Ralegh, *History of the World* (Edinburgh, 1820, 6 vols.).

T. Raymond, *Autobiography* (ed. G. Davies, Camden Soc., 1917).

J. Reesing, 'The Materiality of God in Milton's *De Doctrina Christiana*', *Harvard Theological Review*, L (1957).

J. Reesing, *Milton's Poetic Art* (Harvard U.P., 1968).

John Reeve, *A Transcendent Spiritual Treatise* (1711). First published 1652.

John Reeve, *Joyfull News from Heaven* (1706). First published 1658.

John Reeve, *A Discourse between John Reeve and Richard Leader* (n.d., ?1682).

John Reeve, *Sacred Remains* (1706).

John Reeve and Lodowick Muggleton, *A Volume of Spiritual Epistles* (ed. A. Delamaine and T. Terry, 1820). First published 1755.

Marjorie Reeves, 'History and Eschatology: Mediaeval and Early Protestant Thought in Some English and Scottish Writings', *Medievalia et Humanistica*, N.S., No. 4 (1973).

B. Rekers, *Benito Arias Montano* (English translation, 1972).

S. P. Revard, 'The Dramatic Function of the Son in *Paradise Lost*', *J.E.G.P.*, LXVI (1967).

R. C. Richardson, *Puritanism in north-west England* (Manchester U.P., 1972).

C. B. Ricks, 'Overemphasis in *Paradise Regained*', *M.L.N.*, LXXVI (1961).

C. B. Ricks, *Milton's Grand Style* (O.U.P., 1963).

C. B. Ricks, ed., *English Poetry and Prose, 1540–1674* (Sphere History of Literature in the English Language, II).

Edgell Rickword, 'Milton: the Revolutionary Intellectual', in *The English Revolution, 1640* (ed. C. Hill, 1940).

W. G. Riggs, *The Christian Poet in Paradise Lost* (Berkeley, 1972).

Johannes Riolanus, Junior, *A Sure Guide: Or, The Best and Nearest Way to Physick and Chyrurgery*, Englished by Nicholas Culpeper and William Rand, 1657.

Isabel Rivers, *The Poetry of Conservatism* (Cambridge, 1973).

F. Robins, *If this be heresy* (Illinois Studies in Language and Literature, LI, 1963).

Henry Robinson, *Liberty of Conscience* (1644).

Henry Robinson, *A Model Answer* (1645).

John Robinson, *Works* (Boston, Mass., 1851, 3 vols.).

Matthew Robinson, *Autobiography* (ed. J. E. B. Mayor, 1856).

Rochester, John Wilmot, Earl of, *The Complete Poems* (ed. D. M. Vieth, Yale U.P., 1968).

Rochester, John Wilmot, Earl of, *Poems* (ed. V. de Sola Pinto, 1953).

T. Rogers, *The Faith, Doctrine and Religion Professed and Protected in the Realm of England* (1681). First published 1607.

H. E. Rollins, ed., *Old English Ballads, 1553–1625* (C.U.P., 1920).

Elliot Rose, *Cases of Conscience: Alternatives Open to Recusants and Puritans under Elizabeth and James I* (C.U.P., 1975).

E. Rosen, 'Hariot's Science, the Intellectual Background', in Shirley (1974).

M. M. Ross, *Milton's Royalism: A Study of the Conflict of Symbol and Idea in the Poems* (Cornell U.P., 1943).

Maren-Sofie Røstvig, *The Happy Man* (Oslo, 1954).

F. J. Routledge, ed., *Calendar of Clarendon State Papers*, V (O.U.P., 1970).

(W. Rowland), *Judiciall Astrologie Judicially Condemned* (1652).
A. Rudrum, 'Polygamy in *Paradise Lost*', *Essays in Criticism*, XX (1970).
John Rushworth, *Historical Collections* (1659–1701, 7 vols.).
Samuel Rutherford, *Lex Rex* (1644).
Samuel Rutherford, *Christ Dying and Drawing Sinners to Himselfe* (1647).
Samuel Rutherford, *A Survey of the Spirituall Antichrist* (1648).
Samuel Rutherford, *A Free Disputation Against pretended Liberty of Con-science* (?1648).

G.S., *The Dignity of Kingship Asserted, 1660* (ed. W. R. Parker, New York, 1942).
G. H. Sabine, ed., *The Works of Gerrard Winstanley* (Cornell U.P., 1941).
H. Sacheverell, *The Perils of False Brethren* (1709).
E. Saillens, 'Une Hypothèse à propos de *Comus*', *Etudes Anglaises*, XII (1959).
E. Saillens, *John Milton – Man – Poet – Polemist* (Oxford, 1964).
Raymond de St. Maur, *The State of Innocence and the Fall of Man* (1745).
G. Saintsbury, ed., *The Caroline Poets* (O.U.P., 1905–21, 3 vols.).
Sallust, *The Conspiracy of Catiline* (Penguin edn.).
J. Salmon, *A rout, a rout* (1649).
J. Saltmarsh, *Free Grace* (10th edn., 1702). First published 1645.
J. Saltmarsh, *An End of One Controversie* (1646).
J. Saltmarsh, *Sparkles of Glory* (1648).
I. Samuel, 'Milton on Learning and Wisdom', *P.M.L.A.*, LXIV (1949).
I. Samuel, '*Samson Agonistes* as Tragedy', in Wittreich (1971).
D. Saurat, *Milton, Man and Thinker* (1944). First published 1925.
John Saville, *Ernest Jones, Chartist* (1952).
R. B. Schlatter, *Richard Baxter and Puritan Politics* (Rutgers U.P., 1957).
H. Schultz, 'Christ and Antichrist in *Paradise Regained*', *P.M.L.A.*, LXVII (1952).
H. Schultz, *Milton and Forbidden Knowledge* (New York, 1955).
Drusilla Scott, *A. D. Lindsay* (O.U.P., 1971).
Ed. W. Scott, *Hermetica* (O.U.P., 1924, 4 vols.).
A.-L. Scoufos, 'The Mysteries in Milton's *Masque*', *Milton Studies*, VI (1974).
O. Sedgwick, *The Nature and Danger of Heresies* (1647).
William Sedgwick, *Zions Deliverance* (1642).
William Sedgwick, *Scripture a Perfect Rule for Church Government* (1643).
William Sedgwick, *Some Flashes of Lightnings of the Sonne of Man* (1648).
William Sedgwick, *Leaves of the Tree of Life* (1648).
William Sedgwick, *Justice upon the Armie Remonstrance* (1649).
William Sedgwick, *A Second View of the Army Remonstrance* (1649).
William Sedgwick, *Animadversions upon a Letter* (1656).
William Sedgwick, *Inquisition for the Blood of our late Soveraign* (1660).
William Sedgwick, *Animadversions Upon a Book Entituled Inquisition for the Blood of our late Soveraign* (1661).
John Selden, *Table Talk* (1847). First published 1689.

P. R. Sellin, 'Milton's Epithet Agonistes', *Studies in English Literature,* IV (1964).

G. A. Sensabaugh, *That Great Whig Milton* (Stanford U.P., 1952).

Michael Servetus, *Two Treatises on the Trinity* (ed. E. M. Wilbur, Harvard Theological Studies, XVI, 1932).

W. Sewel, *The History of the . . . Quakers* (1722).

A. Sewell, *A Study in Milton's Christian Doctrine* (O.U.P., 1939).

L. Sharp, 'Walter Charleton's Early Life, 1620–1659', *Annals of Science,* 30 (1973).

J. T. Shawcross, ed., *Milton: The Critical Heritage* (1970).

M. Shinagal, *Defoe and Middle-Class Gentility* (Harvard U.P., 1968).

J. W. Shirley, ed., *Thomas Harriot, Renaissance Scientist* (O.U.P., 1974).

E. S. Shuckburgh, ed., *Two Biographies of William Bedell* (C.U.P., 1902).

Richard Sibbes, *Works* (Edinburgh, 1862–4, 7 vols.).

Sir Philip Sidney, *A Defence of Poesy* (Boston, Mass., 1890).

F. S. Siebert, *Freedom of the Press in England, 1476–1776* (Illinois U.P., 1952).

J. H. Sims, *The Bible in Milton's Epics* (Gainsville, 1962).

S. W. Singer, 'Dedication to Milton by Antonio Malatesti', *N. and Q.,* VIII (1853).

E. Sirluck, 'Milton Revises "The Faerie Queene" ', *Modern Philology,* XLVIII (1950–1).

E. Sirluck, 'Milton's Idle Right Hand', *J.E.G.P.,* LX (1961).

Smectymnuus, *An Answer to . . . An Humble Remonstrance* (1641).

Henry Smith, *Sermons* (1631).

L. B. Smith, *Henry VIII: the Mask of Royalty* (1973).

L. P. Smith, *Life and Letters of Sir Henry Wotton* (O.U.P., 1907, 2 vols.).

V. F. Snow, *Essex the Rebel* (Nebraska U.P., 1970).

R. Spalding, *The Improbable Puritan: A Life of Bulstrode Whitelocke* (1975).

J. Spittlehouse, *The First Addresses to His Excellencie the Lord General* (1653).

T. Sprat, *History of the Royal Society of London* (1667).

K. L. Sprunger, *The Learned Doctor William Ames* (Illinois U.P., 1972).

M. Spufford, *Two Contrasting Communities* (C.U.P., 1974).

C. A. Staudenbaur, 'Recent Views of the Cambridge Platonists', *J.H.I.,* XXXV (1974).

K. W. Stavely, *The Politics of Milton's Prose Style* (Yale U.P., 1975).

A. Stein, *Heroic Knowledge* (Minnesota U.P., 1957).

Peter Sterry, *Englands Deliverance from the Northern Presbytery* (1651).

A. K. Stevens, 'Milton and Chartism', *P.Q.,* XII (1933).

Richard Stock, *A Commentary upon the Prophecy of Malachi* (Edinburgh, 1865). First published 1641.

J. J. Stoudt, *Sunrise to Eternity: A Study in Jacob Boehme's Life and Thought* (Pennsylvania U.P., 1957).

John Stoughton, *Choice Sermons* (1640).

John Stow, *The Survey of London* (Everyman edn.).

J. Stoye, *English Travellers Abroad (1604–1667)* (1954).

John Strype, *Life . . . of John Whitgift* (O.U.P., 1822, 3 vols.).

(Henry Stubbe), *A Light Shining out of Darknes* (1659).

Henry Stubbe, *A Censure upon Certaine Passages Contained in the History of the Royal Society* (1670).

Sir John Suckling, *Poems, Plays and Other Remains* (ed. W. C. Hazlitt, 1892, 2 vols.).

J. H. Summers, 'Milton and the Cult of Conformity', *Yale Review*, 46 (1956–1957).

W. H. Summers, 'Early Paper Mills in Bucks', *Records of Bucks.*, VII (1892–1897).

Sir John Summerson, *Architecture in Britain, 1530–1840* (1955).

K. Svendsen, *Milton and Science* (Harvard U.P., 1956).

K. Svendsen, 'Milton and Alexander More: New Documents', *J.E.G.P.*, LX (1961).

K. Svendsen, 'Milton and the hundred articles against Alexander More', in Fiore (1967).

J. Sylvester, *The Complete Works* (ed. A. B. Grosart, 1880, 2 vols.).

Edward Taylor, *Poems* (ed. D. E. Stanford, Yale U.P., 1963).

G. C. Taylor, *Milton's Use of Du Bartas* (Harvard U.P., 1934).

John Taylor, *All the Works* (1630, 3 vols.).

Thomas Taylor, *Works* (1653).

K. V. Thomas, 'Work and Leisure in Pre-Industrial Society', *P. and P.*, No. 29 (1964).

K. V. Thomas, *Religion and the Decline of Magic* (1971).

K. V. Thomas, 'An Anthropology of Religion and Magic, II', *Journal of Interdisciplinary History*, VI (1975).

P. W. Thomas, 'Two Cultures? Court and Country under Charles I', in *The Origins of the English Civil War* (ed. C. Russell, 1975).

Edward Thompson, *Sir Walter Ralegh* (1935).

R. Thompson, *Women in Stuart England and America* (1974).

J. A. F. Thomson, *The Later Lollards, 1414–1520* (O.U.P., 1965).

Thurloe State Papers (ed. T. Birch, 1742, 7 vols.).

H. G. Tibbutt, *Colonel John Okey, 1606–1662* (Bedfordshire Historical Record Soc., 1955).

M. P. Tilley, *A Dictionary of Proverbs in England in the Sixteenth and Seventeenth Centuries* (Ann Arbor, 1950).

E. M. W. Tillyard, *Milton* (1949). First published 1930.

E. M. W. Tillyard, *The Miltonic Setting* (1947). First published 1938.

E. M. W. Tillyard, *Studies in Milton* (1951).

Thomas Tomkins, *The Inconveniencies of Toleration* (1667).

Samuel Torshell, *The Hypocrite Discovered* (1644).

Samuel Torshell, *The Womans Glorie* (1645).

Thomas Traherne, *Poems, Centuries and Three Thanksgivings* (ed. A. Ridler, O.U.P., 1966).

J. Trapp, *Commentaries upon the New Testament* (Evansville 1958). First published 1647.

H. R. Trevor-Roper, *Religion, the Reformation and Social Change* (1967).

P. A. Trout, Magic and the Millennium: A Study of the Millenary Motifs in the Occult Milieu of Puritan England, 1640–1660 (University of British Columbia unpublished D. Phil. Thesis, 1974).

A. S. Turberville, *A History of Welbeck Abbey and Its Owners*, I, *1539–1715* (1938).

G. H. Turnbull, *Hartlib, Dury, Comenius* (Liverpool U.P., 1947).

Rosamund Tuve, *Images and Themes in Five Poems by Milton* (Harvard U.P., 1957).

N. Tyacke, 'Puritanism, Arminianism and Counter-Revolution', in *The Origins of the English Civil War* (ed. C. Russell, 1972).

W. Tyndale, *Doctrinal Treatises* (Parker Soc., 1848).

D. E. Underdown, 'Cromwell and the Officers, February 1658', *English Historical Review*, LXXXIII (1968).

D. E. Underdown, *Somerset in the Civil War and Interregnum* (Newton Abbot, 1973).

E. B. Underhill, ed., *Records of the Churches of Christ gathered at Warboys, Fenstanton and Hexham, 1644–1720* (Hanserd Knollys Soc., 1854).

Sir Henry Vane, *A Healing Question*, 1656, in *Somers Tracts*, VI (1809).

Sir Henry Vane, *A Needful Corrective* (1659).

Sir Henry Vane, *Two Treatises* (1662).

F. J. Varley, *Cambridge During the Civil War, 1642–1646* (Cambridge, 1935).

Henry Vaughan, *Works* (O.U.P., 1914, 2 vols.).

Joseph Viner, *The Role of Providence in the Social Order* (Philadelphia, 1972).

Mary Visick, 'John Milton and the Revolution', *The Modern Quarterly*, New Series IV (1949).

R. B. Waddington, 'Melancholy against Melancholy', in Wittreich (1971).

A. J. A. Waldock, *Paradise Lost and its Critics* (C.U.P., 1947).

Clement Walker, *The Compleat History of Independencie* (1661).

D. P. Walker, *Spiritual and Demonic Magic from Ficino to Campanella* (1958).

D. P. Walker, *The Decline of Hell* (Chicago U.P., 1964).

D. P. Walker, *The Ancient Theology* (1972).

G. Walker, *Socinianism in the Fundamental Point of Justification Discovered and Confuted* (1641).

J. Walker, 'The Censorship of the Press during the Reign of Charles II', *History*, XXXV (1950).

William Walwyn, *The Power of Love* (1643).

William Walwyn, *The Compassionate Samaritane* (1644).

Sir Archibald Johnston of Wariston, *Diary* (Scottish History Soc., 1911–40, 3 vols.).

T. Washbourne, *Poems* (ed. A. B. Grosart, 1868).

W. B. C. Watkins, 'Creation', in Martz (1966).

A. L. Wayman, 'Samuel Barrow', *Medical History*, XVIII (1974).

Maria Webb, *The Penns and Peningtons of the Seventeenth Century* (1867).

B. J. Weber, *Wedges and Wings: the Patterning of Paradise Regained* (Southern Illinois U.P., 1975).

Charles Webster, ed., *Samuel Hartlib and the Advancement of Learning* (C.U.P., 1970).
Charles Webster, *The Great Instauration: Science, Medicine and Reform, 1626–1660* (1975).
John Webster, *The Displaying of Supposed Witchcraft* (1677).
C. V. Wedgwood, *Seventeenth Century Literature* (Home University Library, 1950).
J. Weever, *Ancient Funeral Monuments* (1631).
R. J. Z. Werblowsky, 'Milton and the Conjectura Cabbalistica', *J.W.C.I.*, XVIII (1955).
R. H. West, 'The Names of Milton's Angels', *S.P.*, XLVII (1950).
R. H. West, 'The Substance of Milton's Angels', in Patrick (1953).
R. H. West, *Milton and the Angels* (Georgia U.P., 1955).
John Whincop, *Gods Call to Weeping and Mourning* (1645).
M. Whinney and O. Millar, *English Art, 1625–1714* (O.U.P., 1957).
J. Whitaker, *The Christians Hope Triumphing* (1645).
B. R. White, ed., *Association Records of the Particular Baptists of England, Wales and Ireland to 1660* (Baptist Historical Soc., n.d.).
B. R. White, *The Separatist Tradition* (O.U.P., 1973).
Bulstrode Whitelocke, *A Journal of the Swedish Embassy* (1855, 2 vols.).
C. E. Whiting, *Studies in English Puritanism* (1931).
G. W. Whiting, *Milton's Literary Milieu* (North Carolina U.P., 1939).
T. Whythorne, *Autobiography* (ed. J. M. Osborn, O.U.P., 1961).
G. Wickham, *Early English Stages, 1300 to 1660*, II, *1576–1660*, part i (1963).
E. M. Wilbur, *A History of Unitarianism in Transylvania, England and America* (Harvard U.P., 1952).
A. Williams, *The Common Expositor* (North Carolina U.P., 1948).
G. H. Williams, *The Radical Reformation* (Philadelphia, 1962).
Roger Williams, *The Bloudy Tenent of Persecution, 1644* (Hanserd Knollys Soc., 1848).
John Wilson, *The Cheats* (ed. M. C. Nahm, Oxford, 1935).
Gerrard Winstanley, see Sabine, G. H.
Gerrard Winstanley, *The Breaking of the Day of God* (1648).
Gerrard Winstanley, *The Mysterie of God concerning the Whole Creation* (1648).
Gerrard Winstanley, *The Saints Paradice* (?1648).
The Winthrop Papers (Massachusetts Historical Soc. Collections, 4th Series, VI, 1863).
George Wither, *Brittans Remembrancer, 1628* (Spenser Soc. reprint, 1880, 2 vols.).
George Wither, *The Dark Lantern* (1653).
George Wither, *Vaticinium Casuale* (1655), in *Miscellaneous Works*, First Collection, Spenser Soc. Publications, No. 12 (1872).
George Wither, *Epistolium-Vagum-Prosa-Metricum* (1659), in *ibid.*
J. A. Wittreich, ed., *The Romantics on Milton* (Western Reserve U.P., 1970).
J. A. Wittreich, 'William Blake: Illustrator-interpreter of *Paradise Regained*' in *Calm of Mind: Tercentenary Essays on Paradise Regained and Samson Agonistes in Honor of John S. Diekhoff* (Case Western Reserve U.P., 1971).

J. A. Wittreich, *Angel of Apocalypse: Blake's Idea of Milton* (Wisconsin U.P., 1975).
D. M. Wolfe, *Milton in the Puritan Revolution* (New York, 1941).
D. M. Wolfe, 'Lilburne's Note on Milton', *M.L.N.*, LVI (1941).
D. M. Wolfe, ed., *Leveller Manifestoes of the Puritan Revolution* (New York, 1944).
D. M. Wolfe, 'Limits of Milton's Toleration', *J.E.G.P.*, LX (1961).
A. Wood, *Athenae Oxonienses* (ed. P. Bliss, O.U.P., 1813–20, 4 vols.).
L. A. Wood, *The Form and Origin of Milton's Antitrinitarian Conception* (1911).
A. S. P. Woodhouse, ed., *Puritanism and Liberty* (1938).
A. S. P. Woodhouse, 'Notes on Milton's Views on the Creation', *P.Q.*, XXVIII (1945).
A. S. P. Woodhouse, '*Samson Agonistes* and Milton's Experience', *Transactions of the Royal Soc. of Canada*, 3rd Series, XLIII (1949).
A. S. P. Woodhouse and D. Bush, ed., *A Variorum Commentary on the Poems of John Milton*, II, *The Minor Poems* (1972, 3 parts).
A. H. Woolrych, 'Milton and Cromwell: "A Short but Scandalous Night of Interruption" ', in Lieb and Shawcross (1974).
B. Worden, *The Rump Parliament, 1648–1653* (C.U.P., 1974).
Clement Writer, *The Jus Divinum of Presbyterianism* (2nd. edn. enlarged, 1655).

Frances Yates, *Giordano Bruno and the Hermetic Tradition* (1964).
Frances Yates, *The Rosicrucian Enlightenment* (1972).
Frances Yates, *Astraea: The Imperial Theme in the Sixteenth Century* (1975).
Frances Yates, *Shakespeare's Last Plays* (1975).
Thomas Young, *The Lords Day* (English translation 1672). Latin edn., 1639.

Perez Zagorin, *A History of Political Thought in the English Revolution* (1954).
W. G. Zeeveld, *Foundations of Tudor Policy* (Harvard U.P., 1948).
L. Ziff, *The Career of John Cotton* (Princeton U.P., 1962).
L. Ziff, *Puritanism in America: New Culture in the New World* (New York, 1973).

General Index

Abbott, George, Archbishop of Canterbury, 18, 268
Abingdon, 118
Acontius, Jacobus, 289
Adams, Prof. R. M., 404
Addison, Joseph, 343, 356
Ainsworth, Henry, 494
Alabaster, William, 34n., 494
Albertus Magnus, 493
Alchemists, alchemy, 106, 291, 328
Aldgate, the maids of, 109, 313
Ale-houses, 97–8
Alfred, King of England, 100
All Hallows, Bread St., London, church and parish, 24, 33–4, 98, 456
Alsted, John Henry, 34, 65, 493
Alva, Duke of, 13
Ambrose, St., 346
America, 42, 123, 137, 139, 154, 447
American Revolution, the, 230, 458
Ames, William, 32–3, 233, 241, 408, 476n., 493
Amsterdam, 41, 124, 492
Anabaptism, Anabaptists, 70–4, 76, 94–8, 106, 123, 137–9, 158, 160, 219, 250, 273, 296, 312, 319, 452. See also Baptists
Andreae, J. V. (Lutheran theologian), 55
Andrewes, Lancelot, Bishop of Winchester, 42
Andrews, Mr. John, 414n.
Anglesey, Arthur Annesley, Earl of, 208, 215
Anglo-Saxons, the, 100–1, 114, 218, 341, 346, 349, 361

Antichrist, 33, 42, 44–5, 75, 82, 84–5, 90, 105–6, 137–8, 155, 160, 167, 205, 251, chapter 22 *passim*, 307, 361, 373, 418, 428, 442, 464, 495
Anti-clericalism, 51–2, 71, 95, 111, 291, 421–2
Antinomianism, antinomians, 6, 75, 93–5, 98, 106, 297, 302, chapter 24 *passim*, 333, 336, 423
Anti-Trinitarianism, anti-Trinitarians, 27, 72–4, 76, 93, 95–6, 106–7, 110–111, 217–18, 224, 226, 240, 243, 245, 256, 258, chapter 23 *passim*, 319, 323, 326, 335–6, 356, 408, 466, 494–5
Arblaster, Mr. Anthony, 459
Aretine, Pietro, 226, 453
Arians, *see* anti-Trinitarians
Ariosto, Ludovico, 33
Aristotle, 37, 452
Arius, 115, 294–5
Armada, the Spanish, 13, 17, 269
Arminianism, Arminians, 5, 72, 95, 106, 125, 160, 218–19, 224, 254, chapter 21 *passim*, 302, 306, 336, 346, 352, 367, 465
Arminius, Jacobus, 5, 154, 268n., 275
Army, the New Model, 162, 165, 178, 192, 195–6, 215, 372, 388, 429–32, 435–6
Arnold, Christopher (German traveller), 134
Arrowsmith, John (Puritan divine), 312
Arthington, Henry, 70
Arthur, King of Britain, 48, 50, 360–1, 403

Index of References to Milton's Writings